ORDNANC… Y

STREET ATLAS

Buckinghamshire

Contents

IV *Key to maps*

VI *Administrative boundaries*

1 *Street maps*

214 *Index explanation and abbreviations*

215 *Index of towns, villages and rural localities*

216 *Index of street names*

PHILIP'S

First edition published 1990
Third edition published 1994
Reprinted 1996 by

Ordnance Survey® and George Philip Ltd.
Romsey Road
Maybush
Southampton SO16 4GU

George Philip Ltd.
an imprint of Reed Books
Michelin House, 81 Fulham Road, London, SW3 6RB
and Auckland, Melbourne, Singapore and Toronto

ISBN 0-540-05989-7 (hardback)
ISBN 0-540-05990-0 (softback)

To the best of the Publishers' knowledge, the information in this atlas was correct at the time of going to press. No responsibility can be accepted for any errors or their consequences.

The representation in this atlas of a road, track or path is no evidence of the existence of a right of way.

The mapping between pages 1 and 213 (inclusive) in this atlas is derived from Ordnance Survey® Land-Line® data, and Landranger® mapping.

Printed and bound in Great Britain by
Bath Press, Bath

Key to map symbols

- **British Rail station**
- **London transport station**
- **Private railway station**
- **Bus or coach station**
- **Heliport**
- **Police station** (may not be open 24 hours)
- **Hospital with casualty facilities** (may not be open 24 hours)
- **Post office**
- **Place of worship**
- **Important building**
- P **Parking**
- 174 **Adjoining page indicator**
- **No adjoining page**
- **Motorway or dual carriageway**
- A27(T) **Main or through road** (with Department of Transport number)
- **Gate or obstruction to traffic** (restrictions may not apply at all times or to all vehicles)
- **Footpath**
- **Bridleway**
- **Path**
- **Track**

The representation in this atlas of a road, track or path is no evidence of the existence of a right of way

Amb Sta	**Ambulance station**	LC	**Level crossing**
Coll	**College**	Liby	**Library**
FB	**Footbridge**	Mus	**Museum**
F Sta	**Fire station**	Sch	**School**
Hospl	**Hospital**	TH	**Town hall**

0 | ¼ | ½ | ¾ | 1 mile

0 | 250m | 500m | 250m | 1 Kilometre

The scale of the maps is 3½ inches to 1 mile (1:18103)

The small numbers around the edges of the maps identify the 1 kilometre National Grid lines

Key to map pages

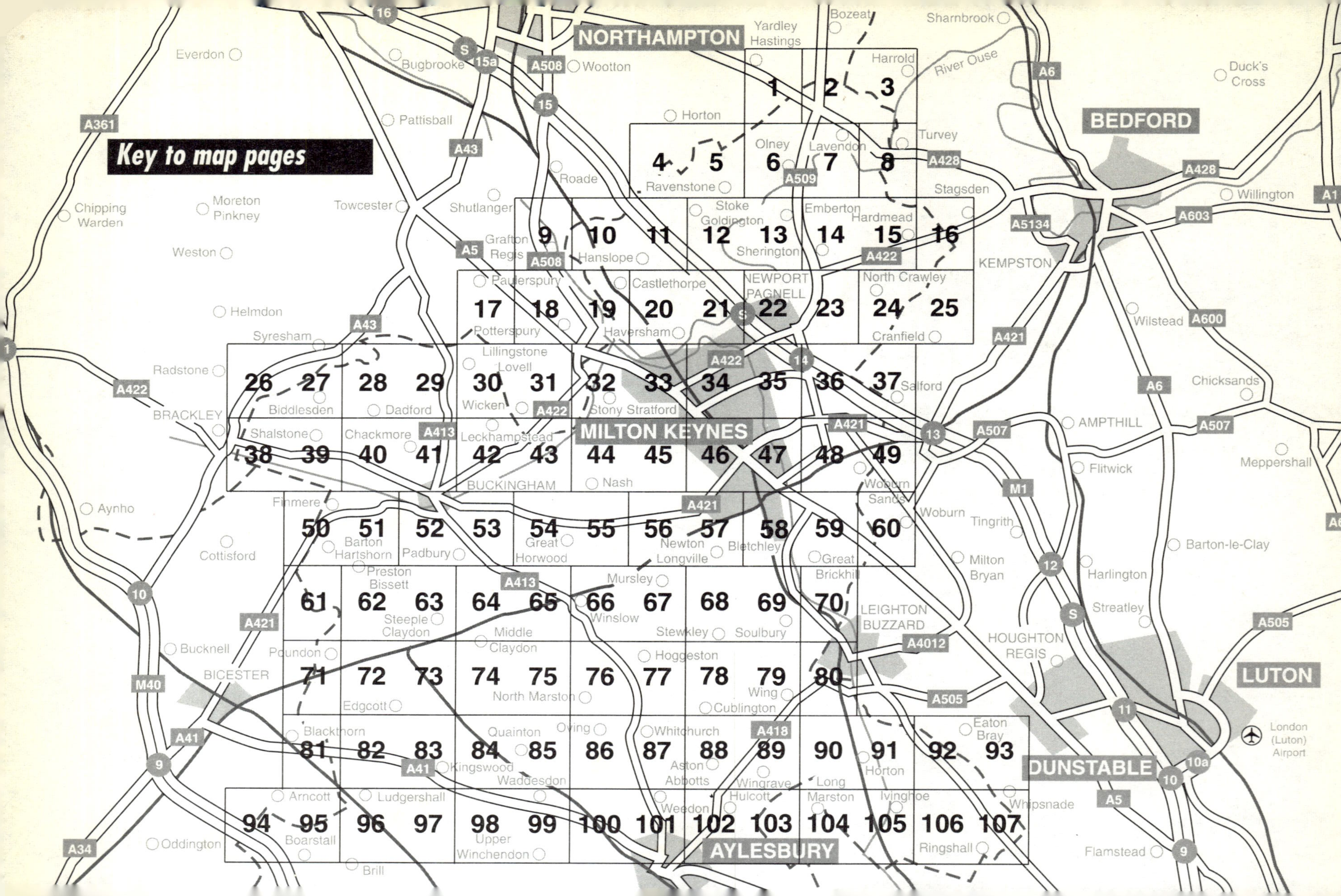

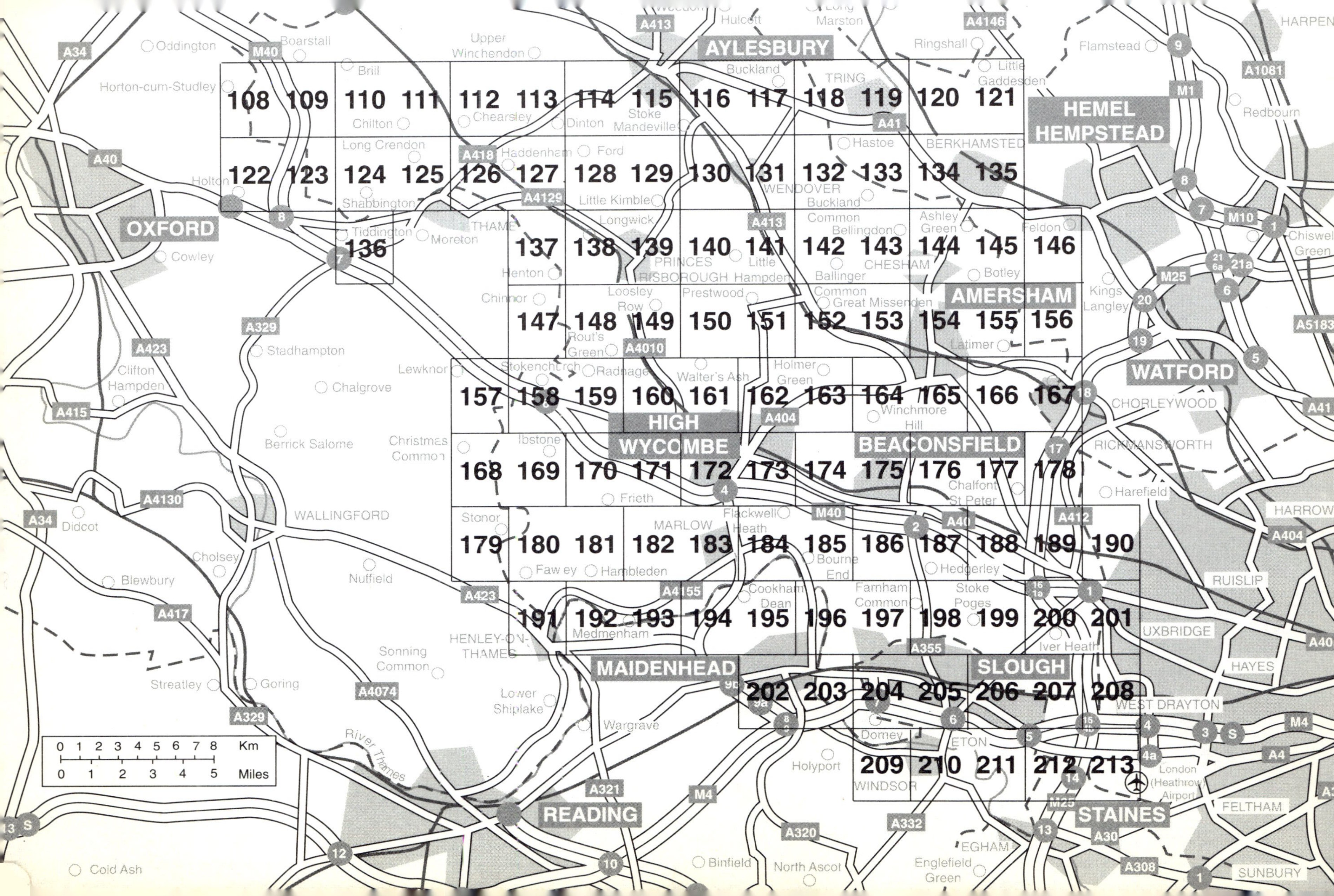
AYLESBURY
HEMEL HEMPSTEAD
OXFORD
AMERSHAM
WATFORD
HIGH WYCOMBE
BEACONSFIELD
MAIDENHEAD
SLOUGH
READING
STAINES
HARPENDEN
RADLETT
CHORLEYWOOD
RICKMANSWORTH
HARROW
RUISLIP
UXBRIDGE
HAYES
EALING
WEST DRAYTON
FELTHAM
SUNBURY
TRING
BERKHAMSTED
WENDOVER
CHESHAM
PRINCES RISBOROUGH
THAME
MARLOW
HENLEY-ON-THAMES
WALLINGFORD
WINDSOR
ETON
EGHAM
Oddington
Boarstall
Horton-cum-Studley
Brill
Chilton
Long Crendon
Shabbington
Tiddington
Moreton
Holton
Cowley
Upper Winchendon
Chearsley
Haddenham
Ford
Dinton
Stoke Mandeville
Little Kimble
Longwick
Henton
Chinnor
Hulcott
Long Marston
Buckland
Ringshall
Little Gaddesden
Flamstead
Redbourn
Chiswell Green
Hastoe
Ashley Green
Feldon
Common Bellingdon
Botley
Ballinger Common
Great Missenden
Little Hampden
Prestwood
Loosley Row
Rout's Green
Latimer
Kings Langley
Stokenchurch
Radnage
Walter's Ash
Holmer Green
Winchmore Hill
Chalfont St Peter
Harefield
Ibstone
Christmas Common
Lewknor
Stadhampton
Chalgrove
Clifton Hampden
Berrick Salome
Frieth
Stonor
Fawley
Hambleden
Flackwell Heath
Bourne End
Hedgerley
Cookham Dean
Farnham Common
Stoke Poges
Iver Heath
Medmenham
Didcot
Blewbury
Cholsey
Nuffield
Streatley
Goring
Sonning Common
Lower Shiplake
Wargrave
River Thames
Dorney
Holyport
London (Heathrow) Airport
Binfield
North Ascot
Englefield Green
Cold Ash
A34
M40
A413
A4146
A1081
M1
A1057
A40
A418
A4129
A41
M10
M25
A5183
A329
A423
A415
A4010
A404
A412
A4130
A417
A4155
A355
A4074
A321
M4
A320
A332
A30
A308
A316
A4
0 1 2 3 4 5 6 7 8 Km
0 1 2 3 4 5 Miles
108 109 110 111 112 113 114 115 116 117 118 119 120 121
122 123 124 125 126 127 128 129 130 131 132 133 134 135
136 137 138 139 140 141 142 143 144 145 146
147 148 149 150 151 152 153 154 155 156
157 158 159 160 161 162 163 164 165 166 167
168 169 170 171 172 173 174 175 176 177 178
179 180 181 182 183 184 185 186 187 188 189 190
191 192 193 194 195 196 197 198 199 200 201
202 203 204 205 206 207 208
209 210 211 212 213

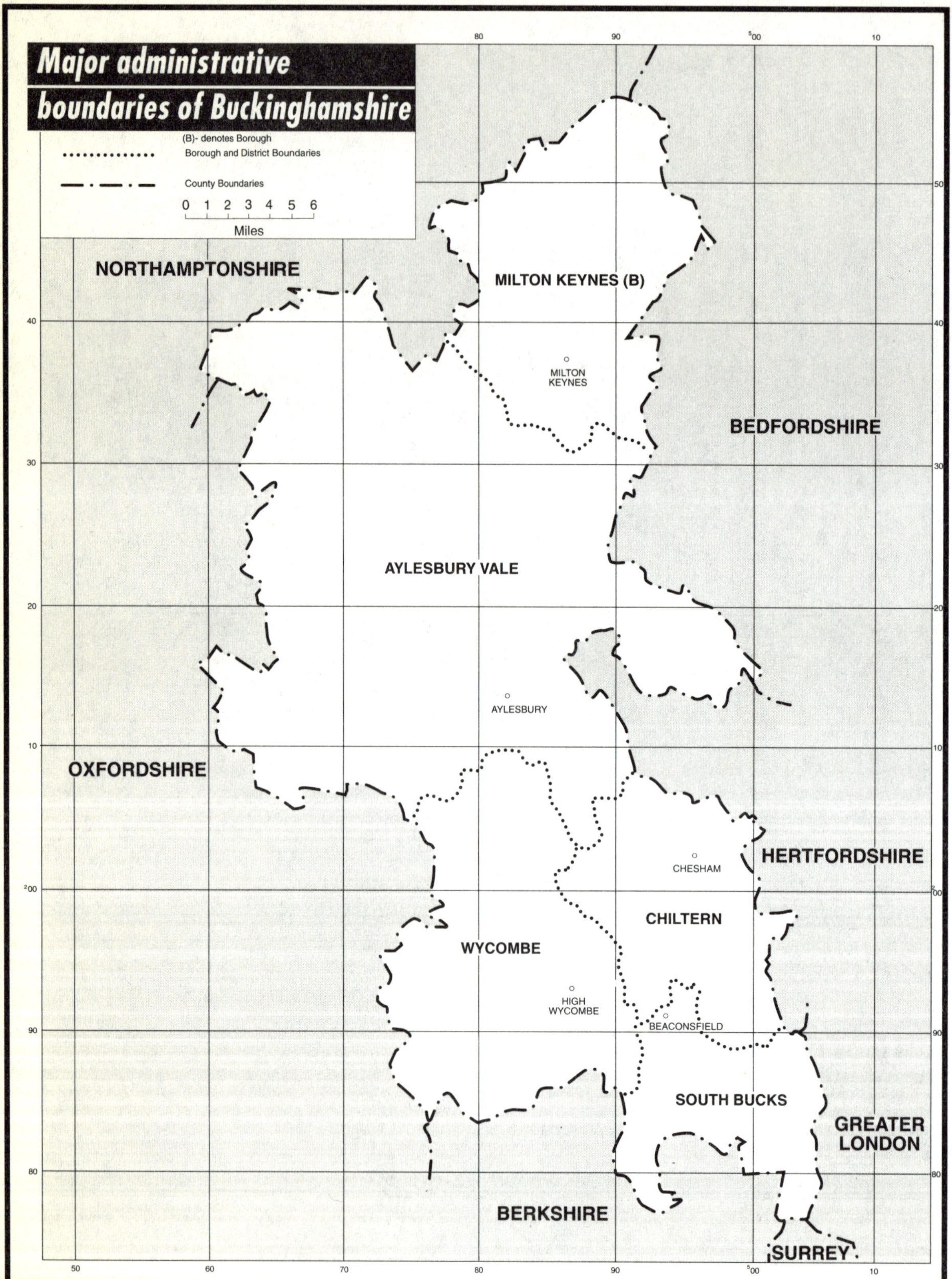
Major administrative boundaries of Buckinghamshire
(B)- denotes Borough
Borough and District Boundaries
County Boundaries
0 1 2 3 4 5 6
Miles
NORTHAMPTONSHIRE
MILTON KEYNES (B)
MILTON KEYNES
BEDFORDSHIRE
AYLESBURY VALE
AYLESBURY
OXFORDSHIRE
HERTFORDSHIRE
CHESHAM
CHILTERN
WYCOMBE
HIGH WYCOMBE
BEACONSFIELD
SOUTH BUCKS
GREATER LONDON
BERKSHIRE
SURREY

A
B
C
4
3
2
1
57
56
55
54
87
88
The Rectory
Island Pond
Sewage Works
Glebe Farm
RECTORY LA
CASTLE ASHBY RD
LITTLE LA
THE GREENYARD
Manor Farm
Church La
Glebe Farm
Sch
THE SQUARE
The Leys
PH
A428(T)
SHOP LA
LITTLE ST
HIGH ST
Church Farm
NORTHAMPTON RD
Yardley Hastings
BEDFORD RD W
Red Lion (PH)
Waterfall Farm
HIGHFIELD WAY
Nursery
CHASE PARK RD
Gee's Farm
SOUTH VALE
Waterfall Farm
B5388
BEDFORD RD E
Cold Oak Copse
Easton Hickel
Long Furlong
Hill's Copse
Roundhay Farm
Old Pastures
Spotley Corner
New Pastures Farm
A 428(T)
Oak Spinney
Warrington Lodge
Yardley Chase
Pig Farm
Old Pond Close
Burnt Quarter
Olney Lane End
Grimpsey Copse
Howbrook Copse
Pastures Farm
B5388

1

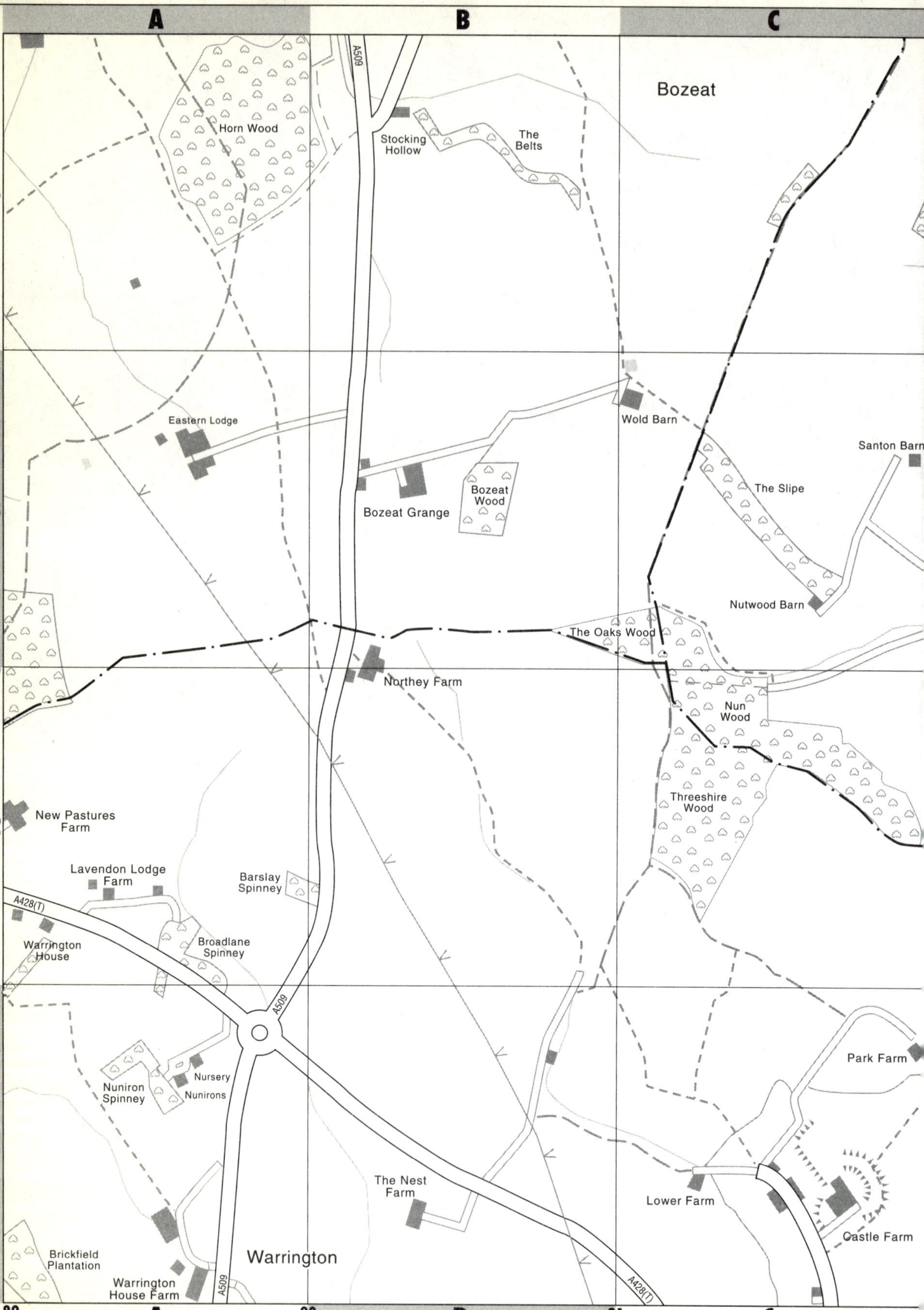
A
B
C
A509
Horn Wood
Stocking Hollow
The Belts
Bozeat
4
57
Eastern Lodge
Wold Barn
Santon Barn
The Slipe
Bozeat Wood
Bozeat Grange
3
Nutwood Barn
The Oaks Wood
56
Northey Farm
Nun Wood
Threeshire Wood
New Pastures Farm
2
Lavendon Lodge Farm
Barslay Spinney
A428(T)
Warrington House
Broadlane Spinney
55
A509
Park Farm
Nuniron Spinney
Nursery
Nunirons
1
The Nest Farm
Lower Farm
Castle Farm
Brickfield Plantation
Warrington
Warrington House Farm
A509
A428(T)
54
89
90
91

1
7

D
E
F
Park Wood
Austin's Spinney
Allot Gdns
Allot Gdns
New Buildings
WOOD RD
ORCHARD LA
BROOK LA
Templegrove Spinney
Manor Farm
The Mansion
57
4
Harrold
MANSION LA
PH
Sch
NEW RD
HIGH ST
MOWHILLS
Priory Farm
Coldharbour Hill
3
Cracknell Hill House
Cracknell Hill
Middle Farm
56
Carlton
River Great Ouse
Millholme Island
Marsh Farm
2
Harrold Lodge Farm
Lavendon Wood
55
Church Farm
Spring Close Farm
TURVEY RD
Valley View Farm
Southfields Farm Cottage
Tollgate House
Snelson Wood
Snelson Cottages
Carlton Hall Farm
Moat
Dovecote
1
Snelson
Carltonhall Wood
Snelson Cobs
HARROLD RD
CARLTON RD
54
92
93
94

8

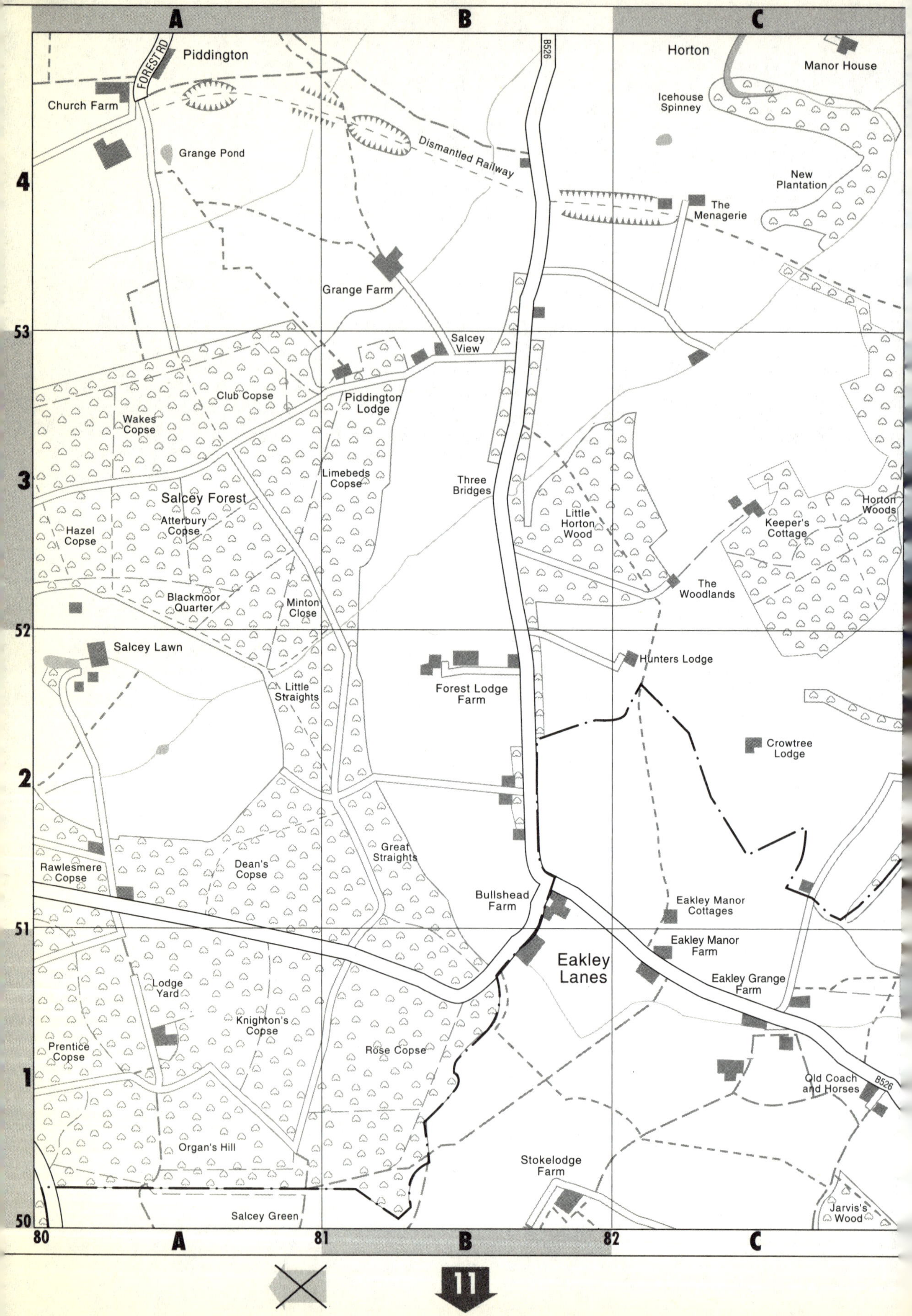
A
B
C
Piddington
FOREST RD
B526
Horton
Manor House
Church Farm
Icehouse Spinney
Grange Pond
Dismantled Railway
New Plantation
The Menagerie
Grange Farm
Salcey View
Club Copse
Piddington Lodge
Wakes Copse
Limebeds Copse
Three Bridges
Salcey Forest
Atterbury Copse
Hazel Copse
Little Horton Wood
Horton Woods
Keeper's Cottage
The Woodlands
Blackmoor Quarter
Minton Close
Salcey Lawn
Hunters Lodge
Little Straights
Forest Lodge Farm
Crowtree Lodge
Rawlesmere Copse
Dean's Copse
Great Straights
Bullshead Farm
Eakley Manor Cottages
Eakley Manor Farm
Eakley Lanes
Eakley Grange Farm
Lodge Yard
Knighton's Copse
Prentice Copse
Rose Copse
Old Coach and Horses
B526
Organ's Hill
Stokelodge Farm
Salcey Green
Jarvis's Wood
4
53
3
52
2
51
1
50
80
81
82
A
B
C
11

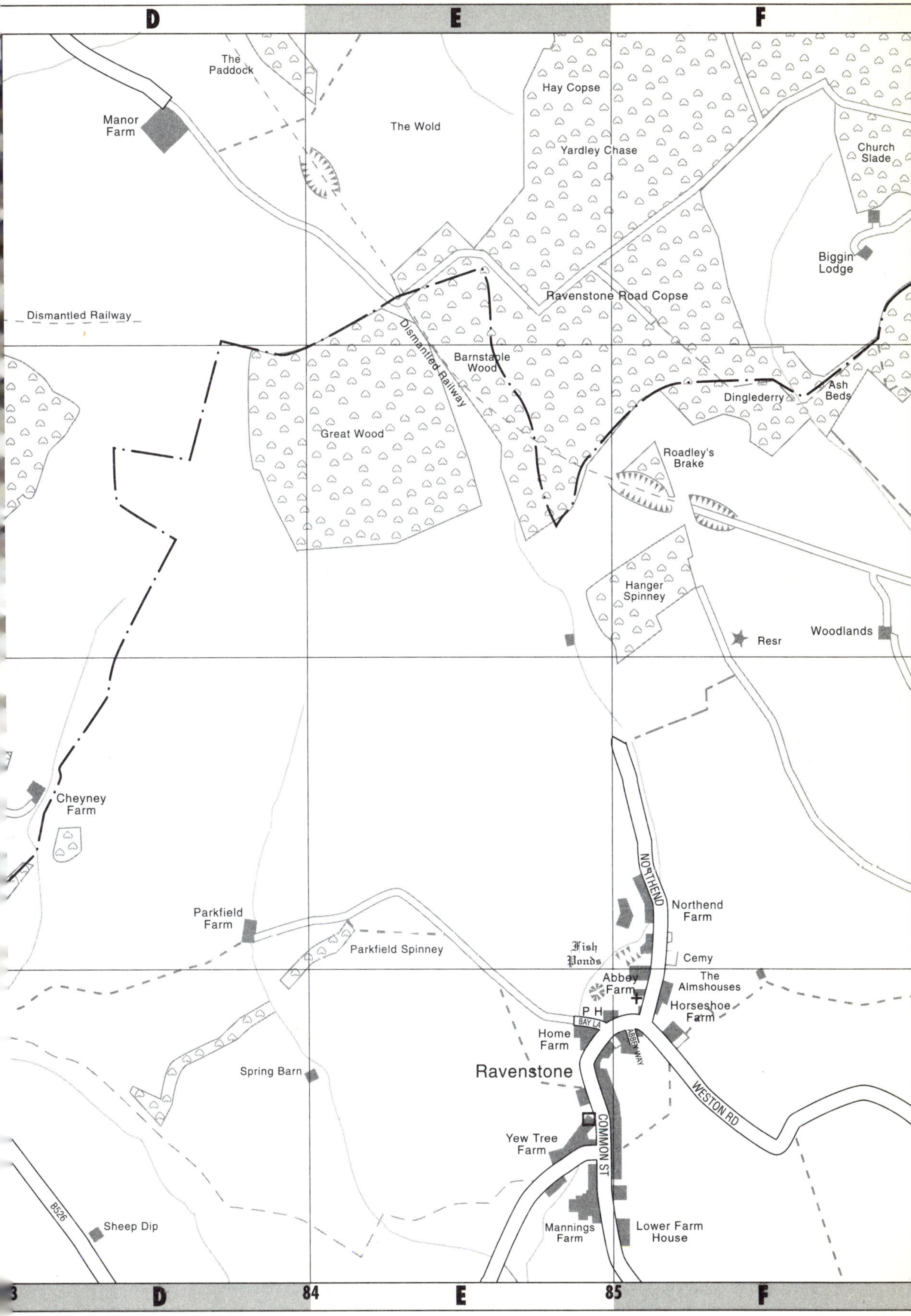
D
E
F
The Paddock
Manor Farm
The Wold
Hay Copse
Yardley Chase
Church Slade
Biggin Lodge
Dismantled Railway
Ravenstone Road Copse
Dismantled Railway
Barnstaple Wood
Great Wood
Dinglederry
Ash Beds
Roadley's Brake
Hanger Spinney
Resr
Woodlands
Cheyney Farm
NORTHEND
Northend Farm
Parkfield Farm
Parkfield Spinney
Fish Ponds
Cemy
Abbey Farm
The Almshouses
P H
Horseshoe Farm
BAY LA
Home Farm
ABBEY WAY
Ravenstone
WESTON RD
Spring Barn
COMMON ST
Yew Tree Farm
B526
Sheep Dip
Mannings Farm
Lower Farm House
4
53
3
52
2
51
1
50
84
85
D
E
F

5
1

A
B
C
Howbrook Copse
Grimpsey Copse
Yardley Chase
Church Slade
Kilwick Wood
B5388
Olney Hyde
Olney Park Farm
Olney Park Cottages
Smith's Farm
Court Farm
Dismantled Railway
YARDLEY RD
Sewage Works
Industrial Estate
STILEBROOK RD
Warrington Road Farm
WELLINGBOROUGH RD
A 509
Hungary Hall
Dickens Spinney
ASPREYS
WHITE HILL
SHORT MASEY 1
CRAB TREE CL 2
Sch
HAWKSWOOD
MOORES HILL
Amb Sta
LONG MASEY
FOXHILL
MAYBUSH WLK
TALBOTS HYDE
GUINEA ORCH
FISHERMANS CL
RIVETTS CL
FLAGGS MEADOW
DARTMOUTH RD
MIDLAND RD
EAST ST
HOLES LA
DINGLEDERRY
Liby
Resr
Long Lane
STOCKEN CL
OXLEYS
WEST SIDE RISE
ST JOSEPHS CL
CHERRY ORCHARD
LONG LA
WEST ST
COBBS GDN
HIGH ST
WHITMEES CL
SPRINGFIELD
ANDING WAY
Pheasants Nest
Sch
ASHLEA
DELLS
ORCHARD RI
ELMLEA DR
THORN LEA CROFT
BACON HILL
SPRING LA
A509
The Alcove
HOLLOW WOOD
Olney
SPINNEY HILL RD
DAGNALL RD
THE PYGHTLE
COWPER CT
STANLEY CT
Mus
MKT PL
BEECH AVE
OAKDOWN CRES
Overbrook Spinney
Weston Park
Zoological Gardens
WESTON RD
OSBORN S CT 1
CHURCH ST 2
LIME ST
HIGH ST
BRIDGE ST
Goosey Bridge
The Wilderness
WOOD LA
Sluice
Laundry Cottage
Otter Pool
Manor House
CROSS LA
HIGH ST
Heron Water
Church Farm
COWPERS ORCHARD
Weston Underwood
River Great Ouse
PEVERS LA
Emberton Park (Country Park)
THE CLOSE
Moat
Grebe Lake
Snipe Pool
The Willows
OLNEY RD
A 509
53
52
51
50
86
87
88
4
3
2
1
A
B
C

5
13

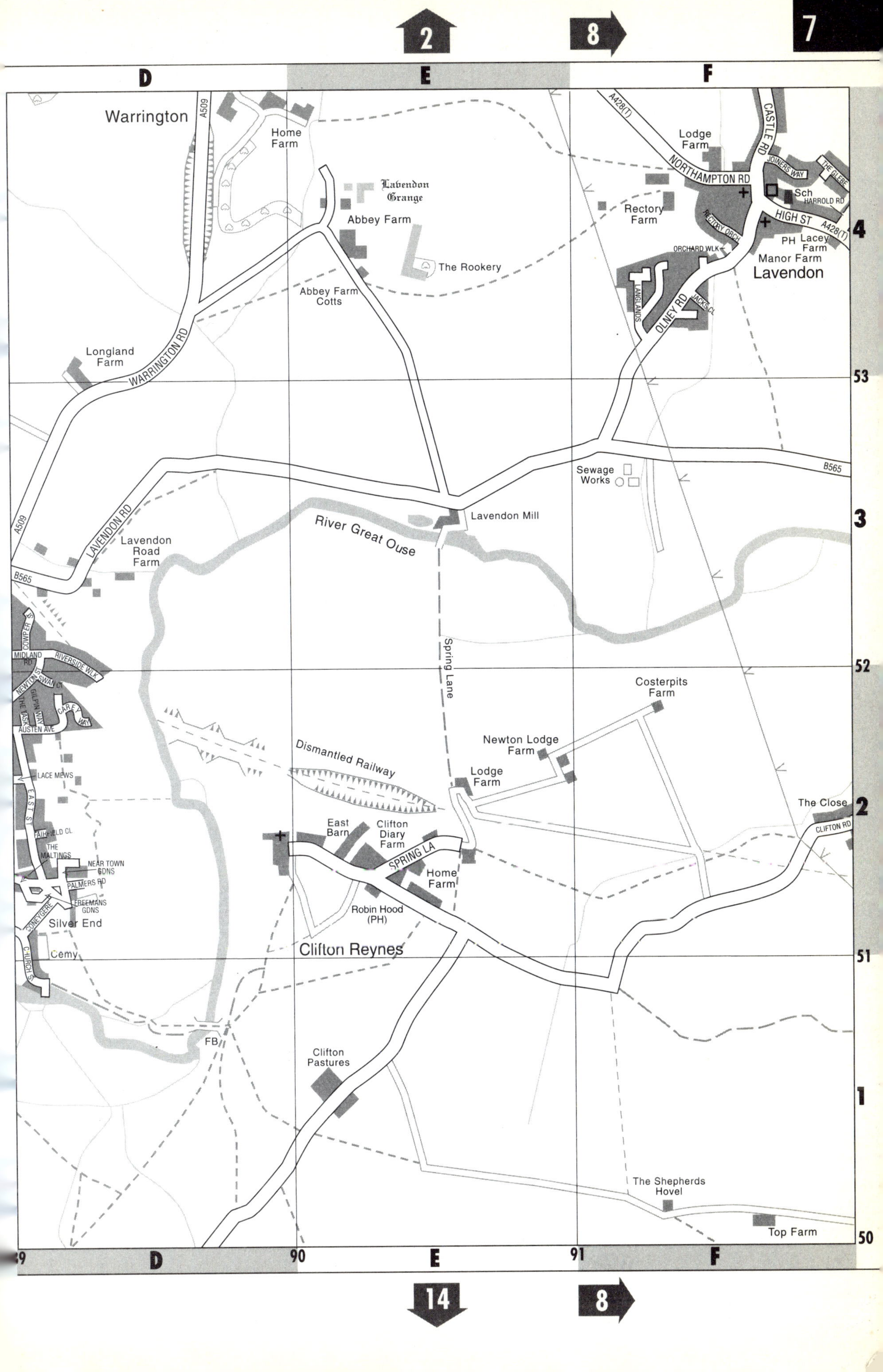

2
8
D
E
F
Warrington
Home Farm
Lavendon Grange
Abbey Farm
The Rookery
Abbey Farm Cotts
Lodge Farm
NORTHAMPTON RD
CASTLE RD
JOINERS WAY
THE GLEBE
Sch
HARROLD RD
HIGH ST
A428(T)
Rectory Farm
RECTORY ORCH
ORCHARD WLK
PH
Lacey Farm
Manor Farm
Lavendon
LANGLANDS
OLNEY RD
JACKS CL
Longland Farm
WARRINGTON RD
A509
53
B565
Sewage Works
Lavendon Mill
River Great Ouse
LAVENDON RD
Lavendon Road Farm
3
COWPER ST
MIDLAND RD
RIVERSIDE WLK
NEWTON ST
SWAN CT
GILPIN WAY
THE TASK
CAREY WAY
AUSTEN AVE
Spring Lane
52
Costerpits Farm
Newton Lodge Farm
Lodge Farm
Dismantled Railway
LACE MEWS
EAST ST
FAIRFIELD CL
THE MALTINGS
NEAR TOWN GDNS
PALMERS RD
FREEMANS GDNS
CONEYGERE
CHURCH ST
Silver End
Cemy
East Barn
Clifton Diary Farm
SPRING LA
Home Farm
Robin Hood (PH)
Clifton Reynes
The Close
CLIFTON RD
2
51
FB
Clifton Pastures
1
The Shepherds Hovel
Top Farm
50
89
90
91
14
8

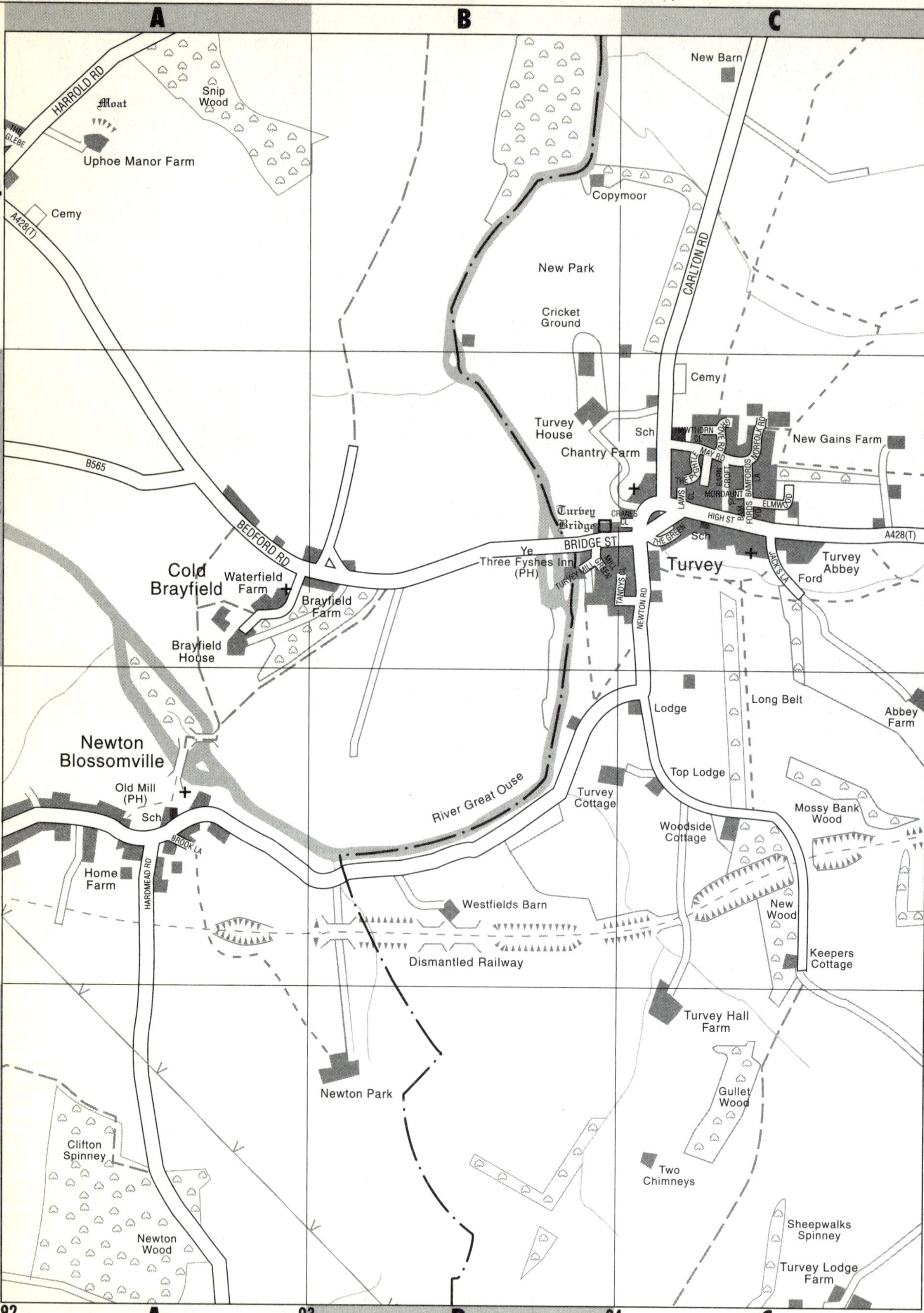
A
B
C
4
53
3
52
2
51
1
50
92
93
94
HARROLD RD
Moat
Snip Wood
THE GLEBE
Uphoe Manor Farm
Cemy
A428(T)
New Barn
Copymoor
New Park
CARLTON RD
Cricket Ground
Cemy
Turvey House
Sch
Chantry Farm
New Gains Farm
HAWTHORN CL
GROVE RD
NORFOLK RD
MAY RD
THE PIGHTLE
LAWS CL
MORDAUNT CL
BAMFORDS LA
ELMWOOD
HIGH ST
CRANES CL
B565
BEDFORD RD
Cold Brayfield
Waterfield Farm
Brayfield Farm
Brayfield House
Turvey Bridge
BRIDGE ST
Ye Three Fyshes Inn (PH)
TURVEY MILL
MILL GREEN
TANDYS CL
NEWTON RD
THE GREEN
Sch
Turvey
JACK'S LA
Ford
Turvey Abbey
A428(T)
Long Belt
Lodge
Abbey Farm
Newton Blossomville
Old Mill (PH)
Sch
BROOK LA
HARDMEAD RD
Home Farm
Top Lodge
Turvey Cottage
River Great Ouse
Mossy Bank Wood
Woodside Cottage
Westfields Barn
New Wood
Dismantled Railway
Keepers Cottage
Turvey Hall Farm
Newton Park
Gullet Wood
Clifton Spinney
Two Chimneys
Sheepwalks Spinney
Newton Wood
Turvey Lodge Farm

10

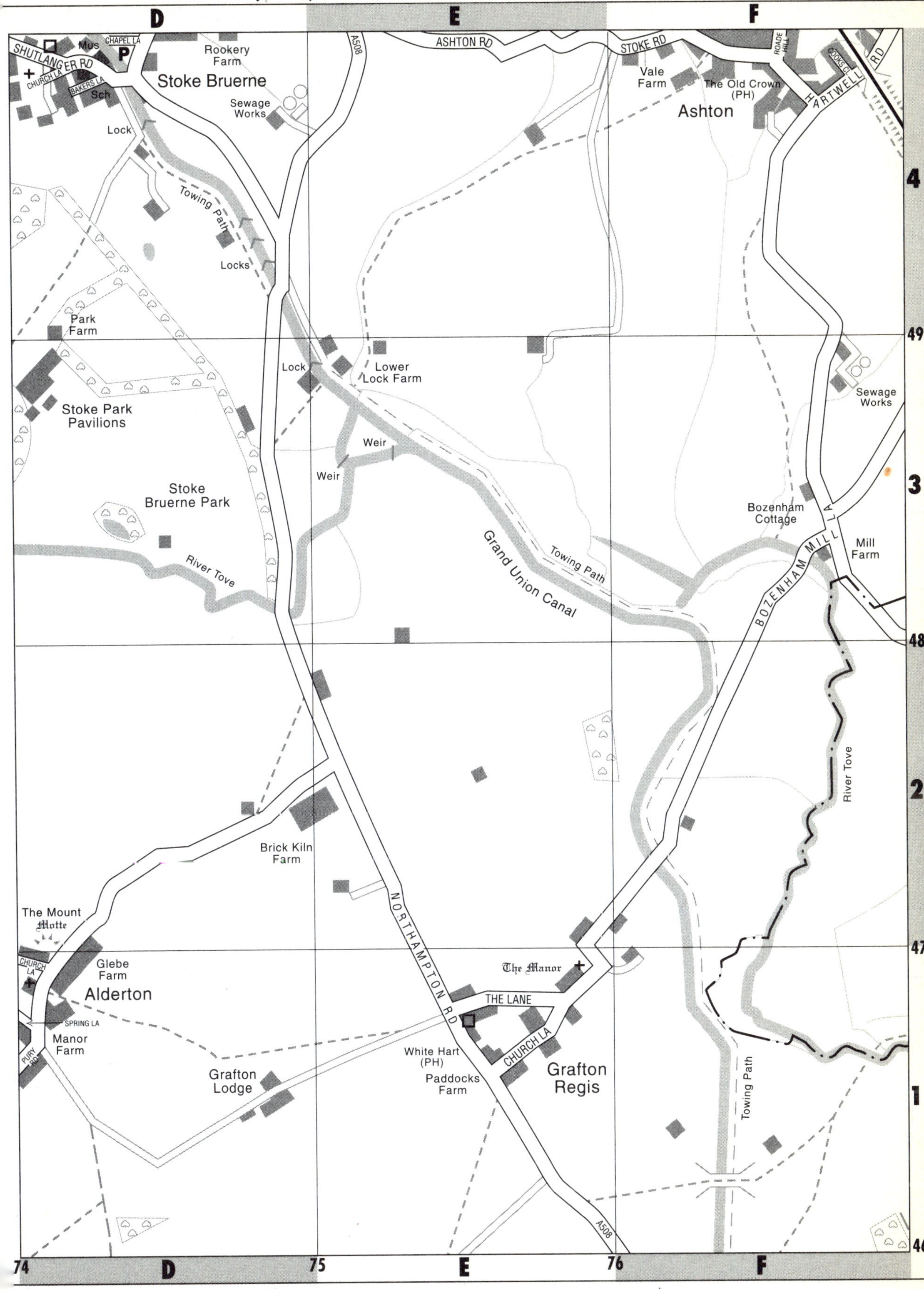
D
E
F
Mus
CHAPEL LA
P
SHUTLANGER RD
CHURCH LA
BAKERS LA
Sch
Rookery Farm
Stoke Bruerne
Sewage Works
Lock
A508
ASHTON RD
STOKE RD
Vale Farm
The Old Crown (PH)
Ashton
ROADE HILL
COOKS CL
HARTWELL RD
Towing Path
Locks
Park Farm
Lock
Lower Lock Farm
Stoke Park Pavilions
Weir
Weir
Stoke Bruerne Park
River Tove
Grand Union Canal
Towing Path
Sewage Works
Bozenham Cottage
Mill Farm
MILL LA
BOZENHAM
River Tove
Brick Kiln Farm
The Mount Motte
CHURCH LA
Glebe Farm
Alderton
SPRING LA
Manor Farm
PURY RD
NORTHAMPTON RD
The Manor
THE LANE
CHURCH LA
White Hart (PH)
Paddocks Farm
Grafton Regis
Grafton Lodge
Towing Path
A508
4
49
3
48
2
47
1
46
74
75
76
D
E
F

18
10

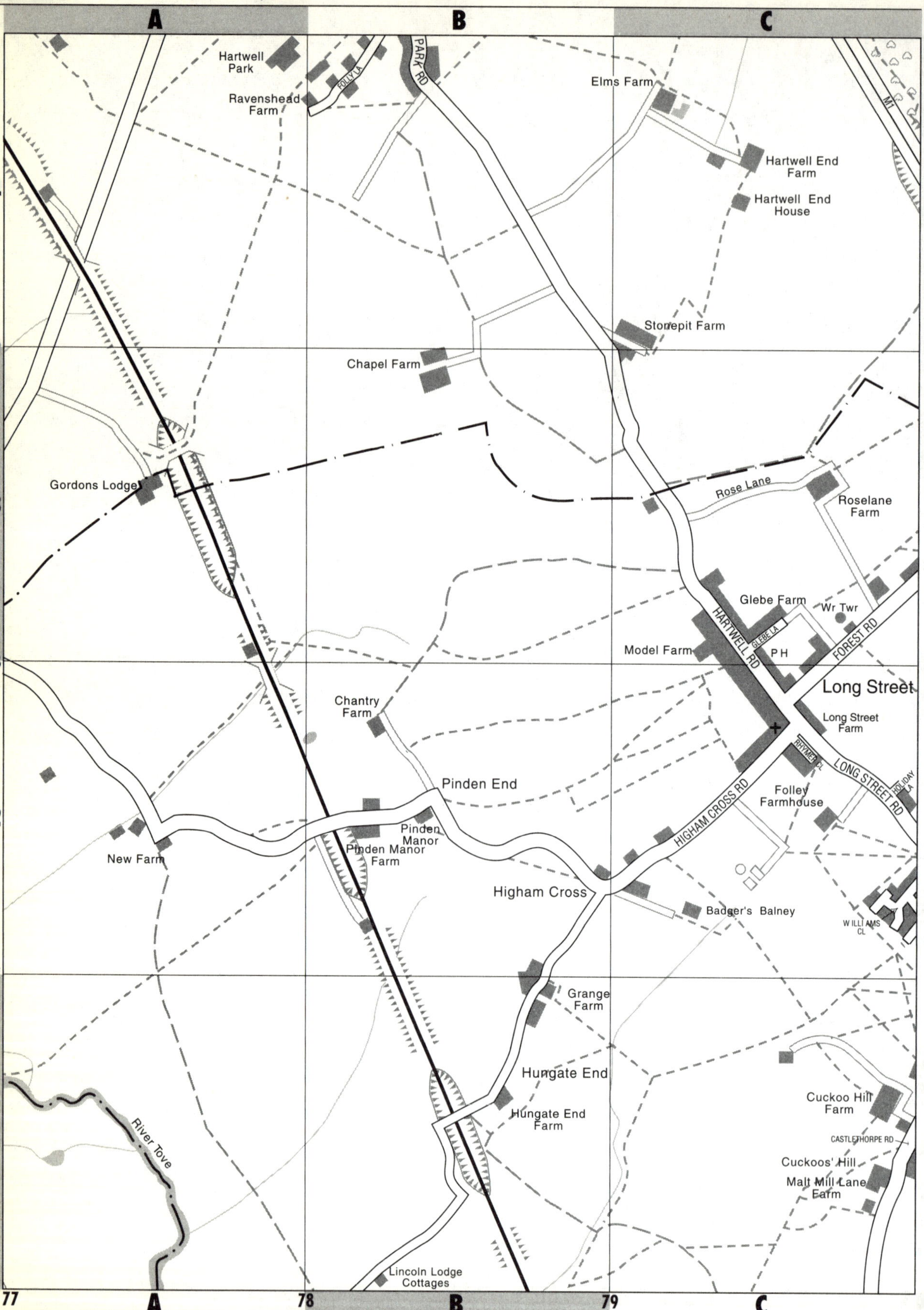
A
B
C
Hartwell Park
Ravenshead Farm
FOLLY LA
PARK RD
Elms Farm
M1
Hartwell End Farm
Hartwell End House
4
Stonepit Farm
49
Chapel Farm
Gordons Lodge
3
Rose Lane
Roselane Farm
Glebe Farm
Wr Twr
HARTWELL RD
GLEBE LA
PH
FOREST RD
Model Farm
48
Long Street
Chantry Farm
Long Street Farm
RHYMER CL
LONG STREET RD
HOLIDAY LA
Pinden End
HIGHAM CROSS RD
Folley Farmhouse
2
Pinden Manor
Pinden Manor Farm
New Farm
Higham Cross
Badger's Balney
WILLIAMS CL
47
Grange Farm
Hungate End
Hungate End Farm
Cuckoo Hill Farm
1
River Tove
CASTLETHORPE RD
Cuckoos' Hill
Malt Mill Lane Farm
Lincoln Lodge Cottages
46
77
78
79
A
B
C

D E F

4
49
3
48
2
47
1
46

0 D 81 E 82 F

11
5

A
B
C
4
49
3
48
2
47
1
46
83
84
85
B526
Church Farm
CHURCH LA
DAG LA
Mount Pleasant
Tel Ex
MOUNT PLEASANT
MALTING CL
HIGH ST
PH
Old Park Farm
Pit (Dis)
Stoke Goldington
LEASIDE
Sch
Ram Alley
Ram Alley
TOWN END CRES
Harley Field Barn
Gothurst House
Longland's Wood
Bunsty Farm
Bunsty Wood
Gayhurst Wood
M1
New Plantation
Digby's Walk
Gayhurst
Gayhurst House
Sir Francis Drake (PH)
Gayhurst Spinney
Bath House
River Great Ouse
Sewage Works
Sand Pit
RAVENSTONE MILL RD
Field Barns
Ravenstone Mill
Park Farm
The Wilderness
Tyringham Hall
BACK DR
Tyringham Bridge

11
21

6
14

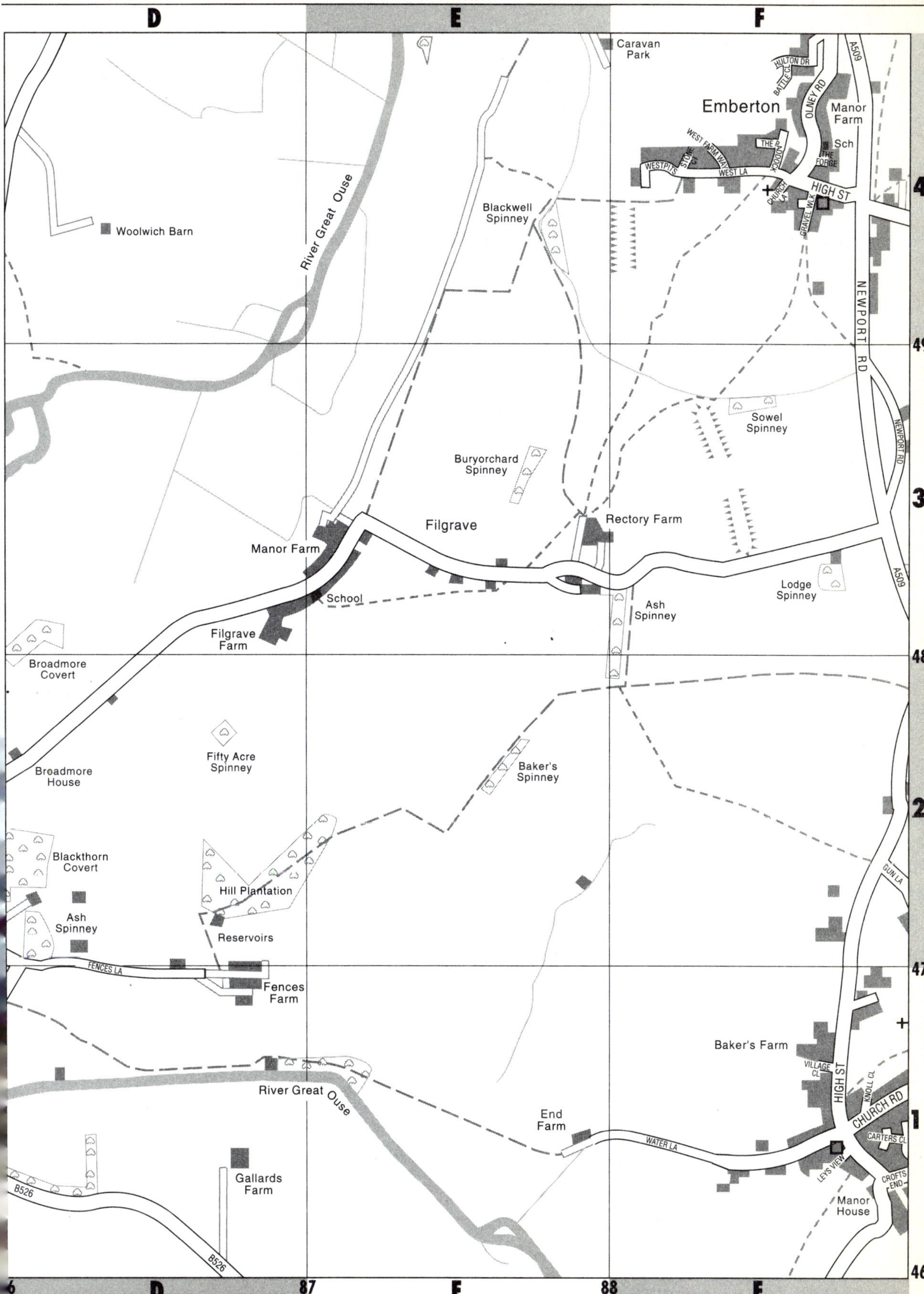
D
E
F
Caravan Park
Emberton
HULTON DR
BATTLE CL
OLNEY RD
Manor Farm
A509
WEST FARM WAY
STONE CL
THE PADDOCK
Sch
THE FORGE
WESTPITS
WEST LA
CHURCH LA
HIGH ST
GRAVEL WLK
4
Woolwich Barn
River Great Ouse
Blackwell Spinney
NEWPORT RD
49
Sowel Spinney
Buryorchard Spinney
3
Rectory Farm
Filgrave
Manor Farm
School
Filgrave Farm
Ash Spinney
Lodge Spinney
Broadmore Covert
48
Fifty Acre Spinney
Broadmore House
Baker's Spinney
2
Blackthorn Covert
Hill Plantation
GUN LA
Ash Spinney
Reservoirs
FENCES LA
Fences Farm
47
Baker's Farm
VILLAGE CL
HIGH ST
KNOLL CL
CHURCH RD
River Great Ouse
End Farm
1
WATER LA
CARTERS CL
LEYS VIEW
CROFTS END
Gallards Farm
B526
Manor House
B526
46
6
D
87
E
88
F

22
14

13
7

A
B
C
4
49
3
48
2
47
1
46
89
90
91
Rectory Farm
Petsoe Manor Farm
Petsoe Manor
Hill Farm
Petsoe End
Clay Farm
Grange Farm
Hollington Wood
Wood Farm
Mulducks
Seven Acre Covert
Parrages Wood
Short Wood
A 509
Oldhouse Farm
Mount Pleasant
Thickthorn Wood
Gowle's Farm
GUN LA
FIELD CL
CHURCH END
PARK RD
CHURCH RD
GRIGGS GDN
SCHOOL LA
Sherington
Sch
Perry La
Grange Farm
Brickyard Cottage
CARTERS CL
CROFTS END
HILLVIEW
BEDFORD RD
Crofts End
CARTERS CL
Moat
Bedlam
BEDLAM LA
Bedlam Spinney
A 422
NEWPORT RD
Chicheley Brook
Brandon's Wood
Moat

13
23

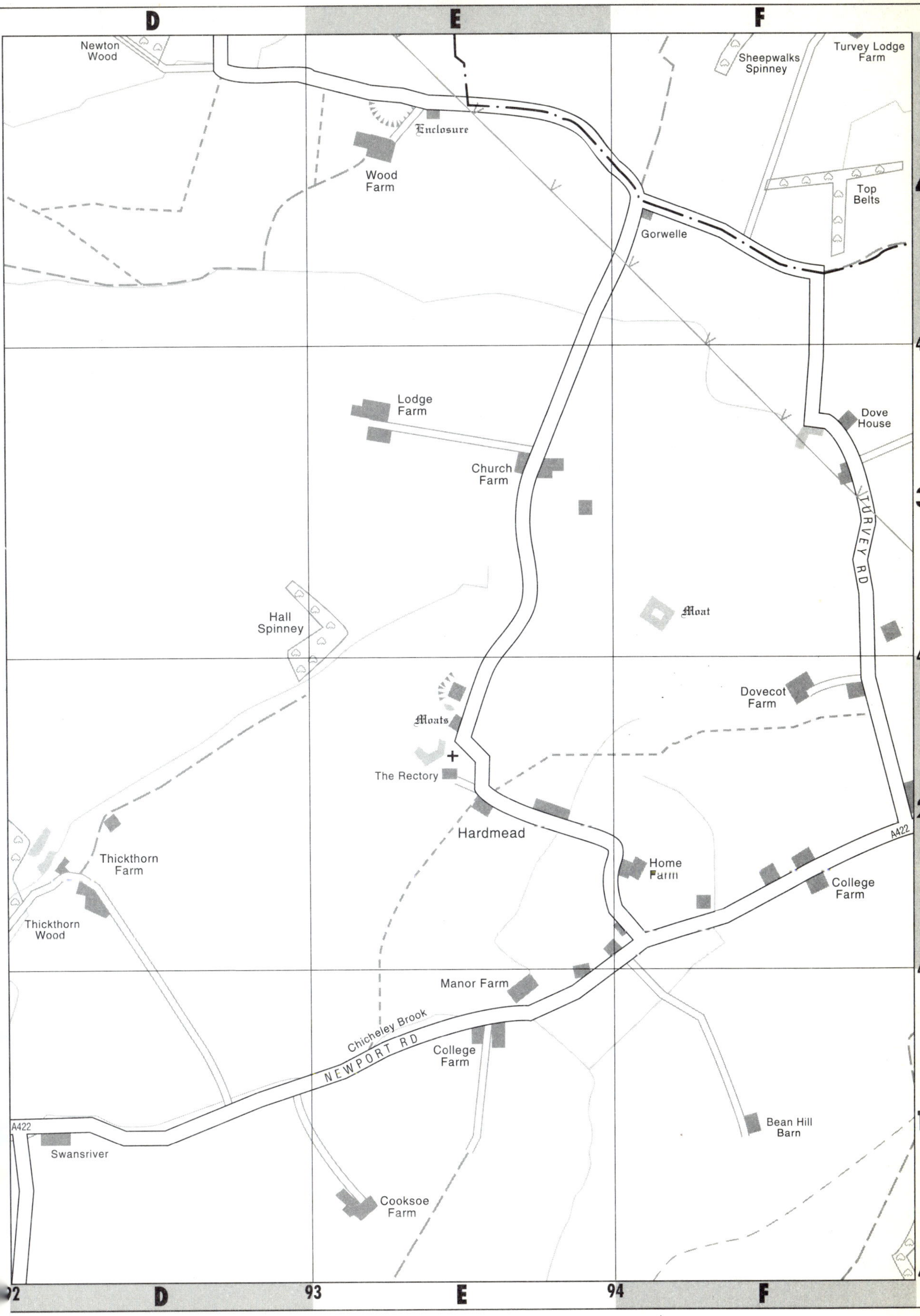
D
E
F
Newton Wood
Enclosure
Wood Farm
Sheepwalks Spinney
Turvey Lodge Farm
Top Belts
Gorwelle
4
49
Lodge Farm
Church Farm
Dove House
3
TURVEY RD
Moat
Hall Spinney
48
Dovecot Farm
Moats
The Rectory
Hardmead
2
A422
Thickthorn Farm
Home Farm
College Farm
Thickthorn Wood
47
Manor Farm
Chicheley Brook
NEWPORT RD
College Farm
A422
Swansriver
Bean Hill Barn
1
Cooksoe Farm
46
92
93
94
D
E
F

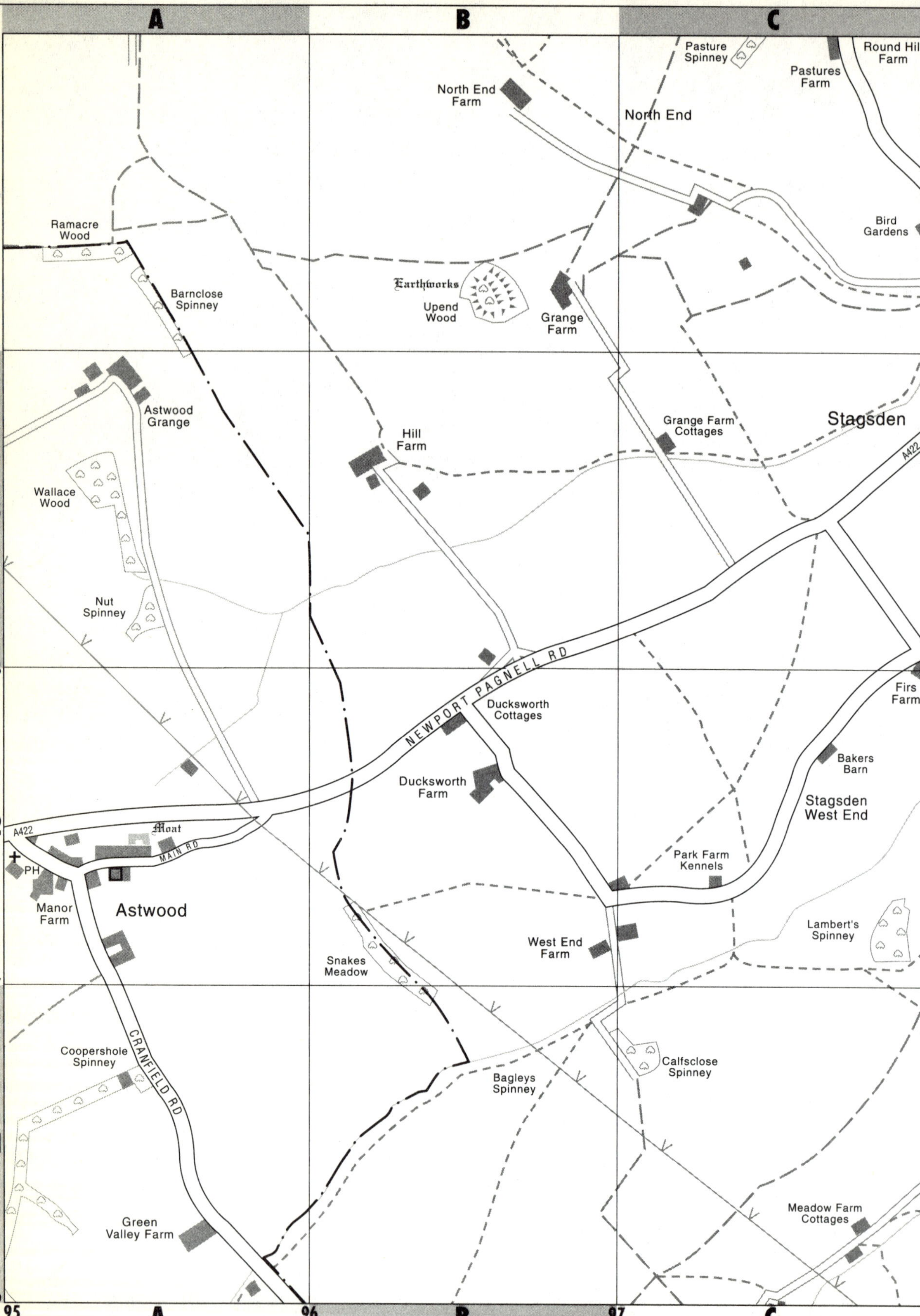
A
B
C
4
3
2
1
49
48
47
46
95
96
97
Pasture Spinney
Round Hill Farm
Pastures Farm
North End Farm
North End
Bird Gardens
Ramacre Wood
Barnclose Spinney
Earthworks
Upend Wood
Grange Farm
Astwood Grange
Hill Farm
Grange Farm Cottages
Stagsden
A422
Wallace Wood
Nut Spinney
NEWPORT PAGNELL RD
Ducksworth Cottages
Firs Farm
Ducksworth Farm
Bakers Barn
Stagsden West End
Moat
MAIN RD
PH
Manor Farm
Astwood
Park Farm Kennels
Lambert's Spinney
West End Farm
Snakes Meadow
Coopershole Spinney
CRANFIELD RD
Bagleys Spinney
Calfsclose Spinney
Meadow Farm Cottages
Green Valley Farm

18
D
E
F
A5(T)
Tew's End
LONGFOOT LA
Works
TEWS END LA
NEWBOLT CL
GRAYS CL
GRAYS LA
Plum Park
Grafton Park
SCRIVENERS LA
Sch
HIGH ST
PLUM PARK LA
4
The Barley Mow (PH)
FAIRFIELD RD
Watling Street
ROMAN ROAD
THE GREEN
LUMBER LA
Kingstons Farm
LOWER ST
PARK LA
Paulerspury
Plumpton End
Plum Park Farm
45
A5(T)
Park Farm
The Gullet
3
Stollage Farm
Grafton Way
Bradlem Pond
King's Copse
44
Lady Copse
Bear's Copse
Say's Copse
Old Tun Copse
Whittlewood Forest
The Kennels
West Waterslade Copse
Kennels Drive
Smalladine Copse
43
Wakefield Lawn
Main Drive
1
Wakefield Lodge
The Pheasantry
Home Farm
Briary Wood
Deanshanger Drive
42
1
D
72
E
73
F
30
18

17
9

A
B
C
4
45
3
44
2
43
1
42
74
75
76
Grafton Cottage Farm
Grafton Fields
A508
NORTHAMPTON RD
Grand Union Canal
GRAFTON RD
Yardley Wharf
Old Wharfe Farm
Queens Oak Farm
Sch
White Rose Farm
Brookfields Farm
Castle (site of)
Castle Barn
Moor End
GRAYS LA
MOOREND RD
HIGHCROFT CL
LIME RD
VICARAGE CL
WOODL CRES
BROWNSFIELD RD
MANOR WAY
SCHOOL LA
HESKETH RD
WARREN RD
MOUNT PLEASANT
HIGH ST
ORCHARD CL
CHESTNUT RD
HORTONSFIELD RD
BUDGE RD
EASTFIELD CRES
MALBOROUGH WAY
Yardley Gobion
Manor Farm
A5(T)
Oakley Spinney
Manor Farm
East Waterslade Copse
YARDLEY RD
Sunnyside Farm
PH
Potterspury
Assart Farm
BLACKWELL END
THE ORCHARD
WATLING ST
ROMAN ROAD
SANDERS LA
MEADOW VIEW
HIGH ST
WOOD LA
CHURCH LA
CHURCH END
BEECH HOUSE DR
Beech House Farm
TOWCESTER DR
Wakefield Gdns
Nursery
Kennels Drive
Greystone Lodge
Wakefield Farm
MAYS WAY
BROWNSWOOD DR
HOMESTEAD WAY
NORTH WAY
FURTHO LA
GRAFTON CL
POUNDFIELD RD
Dairy Quarter
Main Drive Cottages
Main Drive
Potterspury House
Redmoor Copse
Puxley Farm
Cherrytree Lodge
Dairy Farm
A5(T)

17
31

10
20

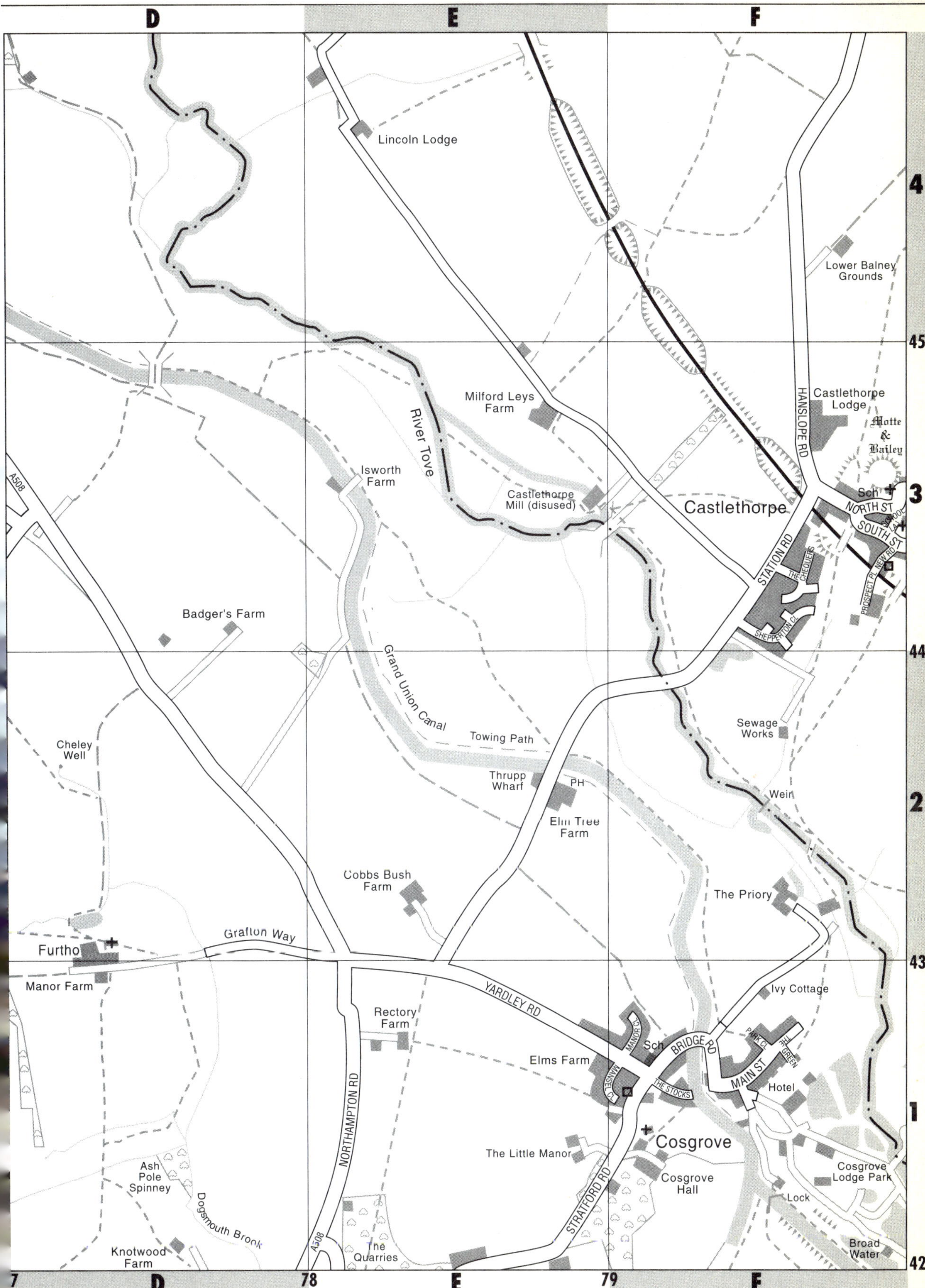
D
E
F
Lincoln Lodge
4
Lower Balney
Grounds
45
Milford Leys
Farm
River Tove
HANSLOPE RD
Castlethorpe
Lodge
Motte
&
Bailey
Isworth
Farm
Castlethorpe
Mill (disused)
Castlethorpe
Sch
NORTH ST
SOUTH ST
SCHOOL LA
NEW RD
STATION RD
THE CHEQUERS
PROSPECT PL
SHEPPERTON CL
3
A508
Badger's Farm
44
Grand Union Canal
Sewage
Works
Towing Path
Cheley
Well
Thrupp
Wharf
PH
Weir
2
Elm Tree
Farm
Cobbs Bush
Farm
The Priory
Grafton Way
Furtho
43
Manor Farm
YARDLEY RD
Ivy Cottage
Rectory
Farm
MANOR CL
Sch
BRIDGE RD
PARK CL
THE GREEN
Elms Farm
MANSEL CL
THE STOCKS
MAIN ST
Hotel
1
NORTHAMPTON RD
Cosgrove
The Little Manor
Cosgrove
Lodge Park
Ash
Pole
Spinney
STRATFORD RD
Cosgrove
Hall
Dogsmouth Brook
Lock
A508
The
Quarries
Broad
Water
Knotwood
Farm
42
7
D
78
E
79
F

32
20

19
11

A
B
C
4
45
3
44
2
43
1
42
80
81
82
Upper Balney Grounds
Manor Farm
PARK RD
Wireless Station
Park House
Masts
Long Plantation
Narrow Leys
Moat
Hanslope Park
Masts
Hanger Quarter
Bullington End
Bullington End
New Buildings
BULLINGTON END RD
THRUPP CL
Castlethorpe
NORTH ST
SOUTH ST
Maltings Farm
Leamington Farm
Pineham Farm
Pikes Farm
Field House Farm
Fox Covert
Otley Farm
Lodge Farm
Haythorn Spinney
Crossroads
Pike's Farm
Haversham
HIGH ST
The Greyhound
Haversham Manor
School
CHALMERS AVE
ROWAN DR
KEPPEL AVE
BROOKFIELD RD
MANOR DR
THE CRESCENT
HAVERSHAM RD
River Great Ouse
Cosgrove Lodge Park
P

19
33

12
22

D
E
F
M1
Dairy Farm
Brownleys Spinney
Quarryhall
Hoo Wood
Mill Farm
Linford Wood
Wd Pp
Wood Farm
Burnt Covert
FLORA THOMPSON DR
The Spinney
Little Linford
Hall Farm
Lakelane Spinney
ELIOT CL
WESTBURY LA
SITWELL
SPARK WAY
KEATES CL
WORDSWORTH AVE
ORWELL CL
LEWIS CL
Portfields Farm
The Serpentine
The Wilderness
Little Linford Park
HEMMINGWAY CL
HUXLEY CL
GOLDSMITH DR
KINGSLEY CL
BURDOCK CT
SORRELL DR
PENNYCRESS WAY
COLERIDGE CL
KIPLING DR
Swan's Way
LITTLE LINFORD LA
Hill Farm
Motel
Service Area
Broadacre
The Walnuts
Works
River Great Ouse
BRICKHILL ST
ROWSHAM DELL
HEDGEMORE CT
BROXBOURNE CL
HARVARD CL
STATION TERRACE
SALISBURY GR
HORTON GATE
Church (remains of)
Study Centre
Swan's Way
THE CRESCENT
SNOWSHILL CT
BROADWAY AVE
Wildfowl Centre
WOLVERTON RD
BOULTERS LOCK
BROMHAM MILL
RUNNYMEAD
Sand and Gravel Pit
Grand Union Canal
The Black Horse (PH)
CAMPION
BEKONSCOT CT
Stantonbury Wharf
Dismtd Rly
MARSH DR
Stantonbury Park
COTTISFORD CRES
HIGH ST
DEERFERN CL
1 BUTLERS GR
2 ANNES GR
PARKLANDS
CHURCH LEES
SANDY CL
ST LEGER DR
LEDBURY
SOLAR CT
WOAD LA
LINFORD PARK
ANDREWES CROFT
Great Linford
4
45
3
44
2
43
1
42
84
85

34
22

21
13

A
B
C
Quarryhall farm
B526
Ash Spinney
CHICHELEY HILL
4
SHERINGTON RD
Bridge House
Sherington Bridge
Inn Farm
Lathbury
CHURCH LA
45
Lathbury Park
River Great Ouse
NORTHAMPTON RD
Kickles Farm
FLORA THOMPSON DR
THOMAS DR
3
Bury Field
Lakes Lane Farm
Woad Farm
NEWPORT PAGNELL
LAKES LA
LEWIS CL
Sch
Liby
F Sta
Tickford Abbey
44
HIGH ST
ST JOHN ST
Tickford End
TICKFORD ST
WOLVERTON RD
LITTLE LINFORD LA
Tickfords Field Farm
2
MARSH END RD
The Green
Schs
Cemy
Caravan Park
NORTH CRAWLEY RD
Hospl
River Ouzel or Lovat
LONDON RD
43
A509
A422
Industrial Estate
Newport Stables
Caldecote Mill
Weirs
Caldecotemill Bridge
Giffard Park
Sch
1
BRICKHILL ST
Tongwell Lake
Blakelands
Caldecote
Caldecote Farm
Grand Union Canal
Industrial Estate
CH
MONKS WAY
M1
42
86
87
88

21
35

D E F

4
45
3
44
2
43
1
42

D 90 E 91 F

A
B
C
4
45
3
44
2
43
1
42
92
93
94
Up End
Horncastle Farm
Little Crawley Farm
Gumbrills Farm
Old Moat Farm
Moat
POUND LA
ORCHARD WAY
HACKETT PL
KILPIN GREEN
BRYANS
YULES
PH
HIGH ST
BROOK END
Sch
CHURCH WLK
CHEQUERS LA
Church Farm
North Crawley
Crawley Grange
Chicheley Brook
Dollars Grove Farm
Dollars Grove
East End Farm
Quaker's Farm
Rookery Farm
Manor Farm
East End
Moat
Broadmead
Ford
Lodge Farm
FOLLEY LA
Ringtail Farm
SHIRE LA
Ring Croft Farm
Murtland's Farm
Rings Wharley Farm
Hurstend Farm
Hurst End
Sewage Works
Wharley Farm
ROYCE RD
WEST RD
PRINCE PHILIP AVE
EAST RD
HENSON CL
REYNOLDS CL
HANDLEY
PAGE CL
DUNCAN RD
MITCHELL RD
STRINGFELLOW CL
MERCHANT LA
THE DRIVE
THE CRESCENT
THE GREEN
COLLEGE RD
LANCHESTER RD
CENTRAL AVE
The Cottage
Wharley End
Cranfield Institute of Technology
Moulsoe Old Wood
Chapelclose Spinney
Wharley End Farm
Cranfield Airfield

D E F

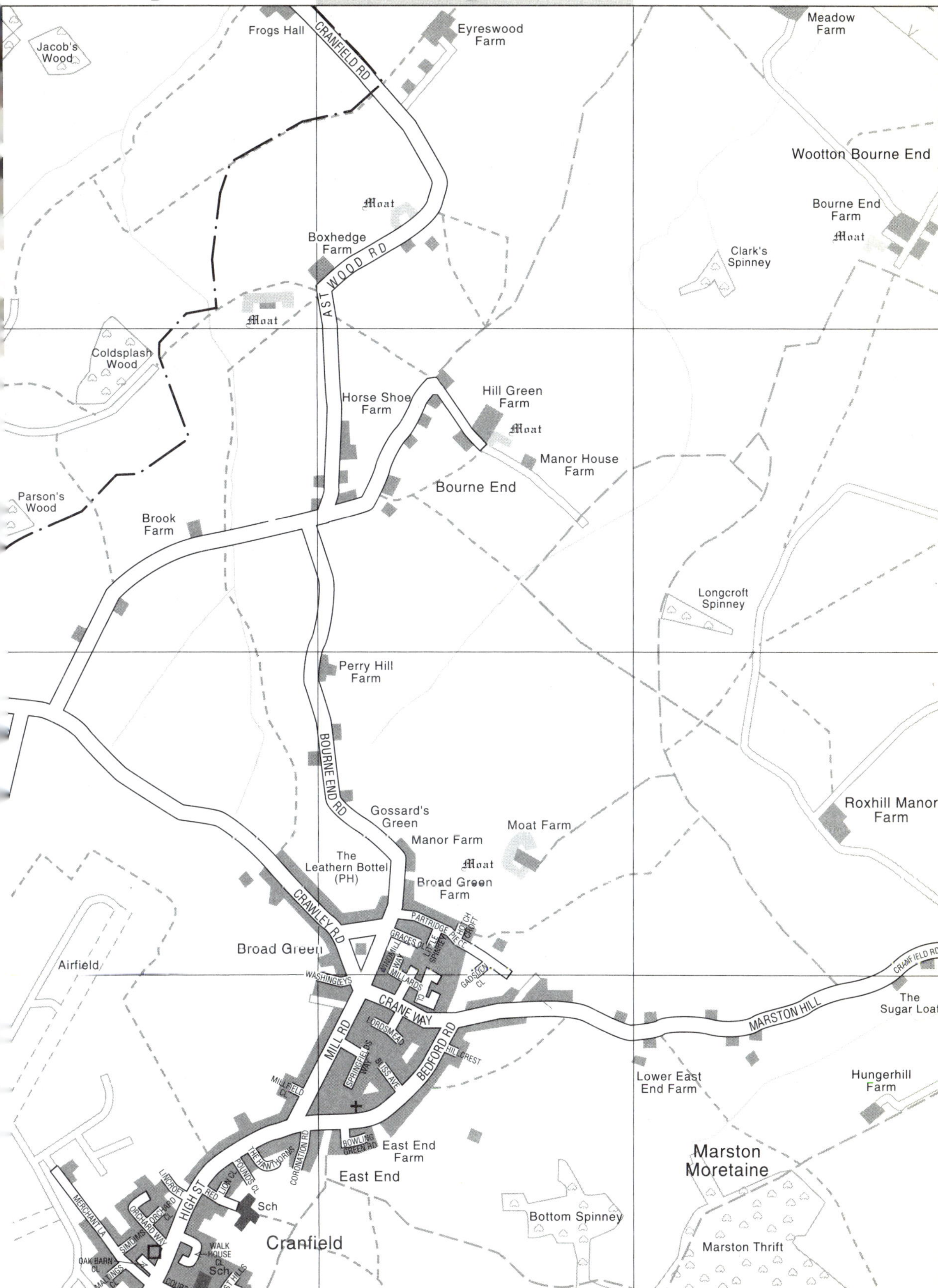
Frogs Hall
Eyreswood Farm
Meadow Farm
Jacob's Wood
CRANFIELD RD
Wootton Bourne End
Moat
Bourne End Farm
Moat
Boxhedge Farm
AST WOOD RD
Clark's Spinney
Moat
Coldsplash Wood
Horse Shoe Farm
Hill Green Farm
Moat
Manor House Farm
Bourne End
Parson's Wood
Brook Farm
Longcroft Spinney
Perry Hill Farm
BOURNE END RD
Gossard's Green
Moat Farm
Roxhill Manor Farm
Manor Farm
The Leathern Bottel (PH)
Moat
Broad Green Farm
CRAWLEY RD
PARTRIDGE PIECE
NOTCH CROFT
GRACES CL
LITTLE SPINNEY
WINDMILL WAY
Broad Green
Airfield
WASHINGLEYS
MILLARDS CL
GADSDEN CL
CRANFIELD RD
CRANE WAY
The Sugar Loaf
MARSTON HILL
LORDSMEAD
MILL RD
BEDFORD RD
HILLCREST
SPRINGFIELDS WAY
BLISS AVE
MILLFIELD CL
Lower East End Farm
Hungerhill Farm
BOWLING GREEN RD
East End Farm
CORONATION RD
THE HAWTHORNS
POUNDS CL
LION CL
East End
Marston Moretaine
LINCROFT
RED
HIGH ST
Sch
Bottom Spinney
MERCHANT LA
ORCHARD CL
ORCHARD WAY
SIMLIMS
Cranfield
Marston Thrift
WALK HOUSE CL
OAK BARN CL
MALTINGS CL
COURT RD
Sch
EAST HILLS
4
45
3
44
2
43
1
42

A
B
C
Helmdon
Falcutt
Hall
Crowfield
Shortgrove
Wood
Staplegrove
Farm
Crowfield
Whistley
Wood
A43(T)
Pimlico
Hoppersford
Farm
Radstone
Coldharbour
Farm
Dismantled Railway
Whitfield House
Farm
THE AVENUE
FARRER CL
CHAPEL LA
Whitfield
Fox
Covert
Manor
Farm
Mill
Bridge
River Great Ouse
Sewage
Works
Ilett's
Farm
Sundale
Bushy End
Wood
A43(T)
Saw
Mill
Versions
Farm
Airfield
(disused)
NORTHAMPTON RD
A43(T)
TURWESTON RD
4
41
3
40
2
39
1
38
59
60
61
A
B
C

D
E
F
Kingshill Farm
Sewage Works
Manor Farm
Syresham
BURNHAM PL
CHURCH END
WAPPENHAM RD
THE HILL
BROAD ST
BELL LA
MAGDALEN CT
MALT LA
THE POUND
HIGH ST
BLENHEIM PL
ABBEY RD
Sch
The King's Head (PH)
King's Hill Bridge
The Green Man Farm
The Green Man Inn
A43(T)
Needles Hall Farm
Brackley Heath
Earl's Wood
MAIN RD
Santhill Plantation
Wood Ground Plantation
Abbey Way House
High Cross
Langley Farm
41
Syresham Fields Farm
River Great Ouse
Magdelen Spring Spinney
Home Wood
3
Briary Wood
Castle Farm
French's Barn
Biddlesden Bridge
Friday's Spinney
Biddlesden
40
Longmoor Spinney
Biddlesden House
Abbey House
Baker's Bridge
2
Biddlesden Park
Dropshort Farm
Whitfield Wood
39
Wood Green
Den Farm
1
Woodgreen Farm
Airfield (disused)
Evershaw Farm
Evershaw Copse
Ten Lands Copse
38
D
63
E
64
F

27

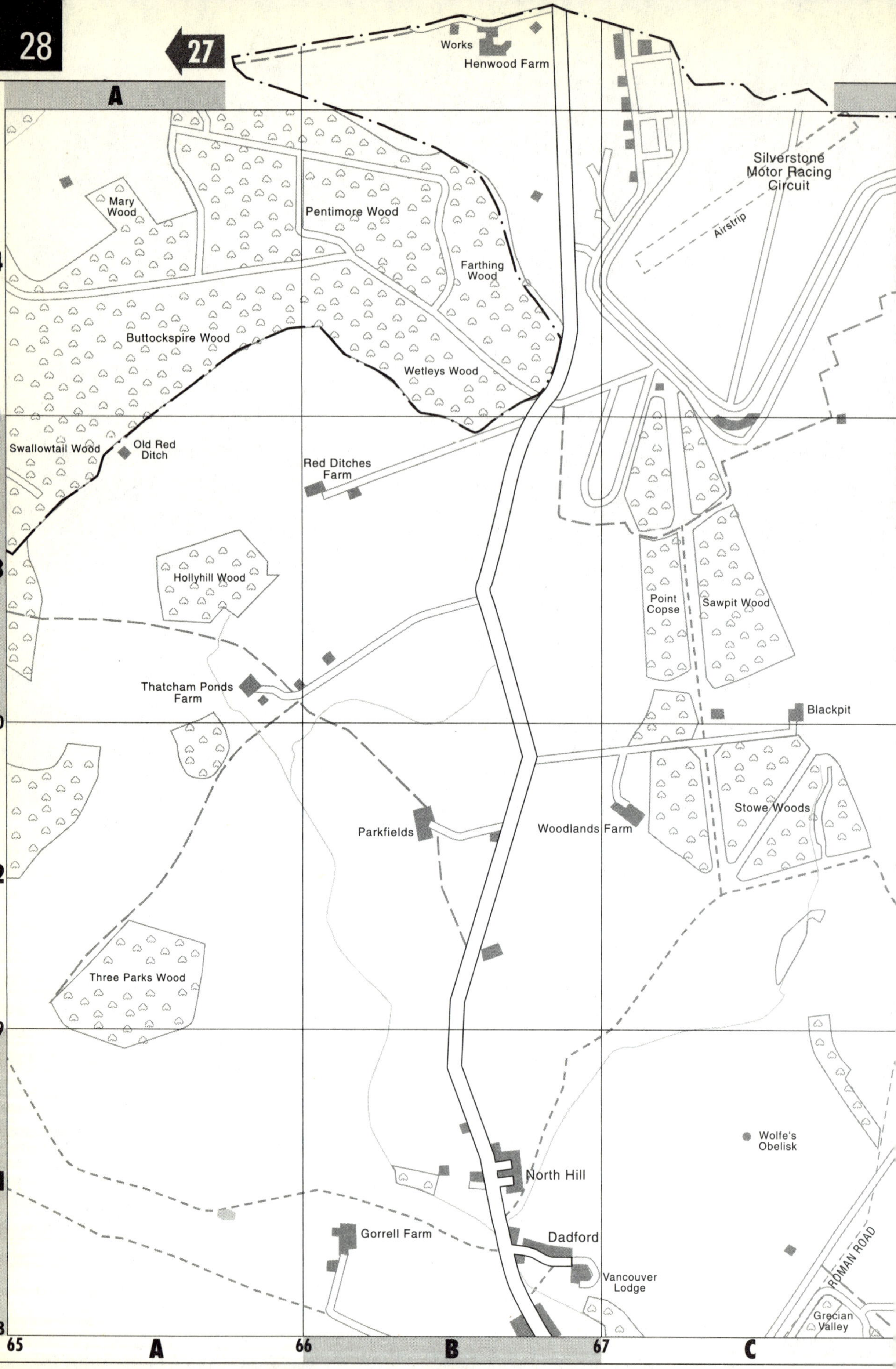

A
Works
Henwood Farm
Silverstone Motor Racing Circuit
Airstrip
Mary Wood
Pentimore Wood
Farthing Wood
Buttockspire Wood
Wetleys Wood
Swallowtail Wood
Old Red Ditch
Red Ditches Farm
Hollyhill Wood
Point Copse
Sawpit Wood
Thatcham Ponds Farm
Blackpit
Parkfields
Woodlands Farm
Stowe Woods
Three Parks Wood
Wolfe's Obelisk
North Hill
Dadford
Gorrell Farm
Vancouver Lodge
ROMAN ROAD
Grecian Valley
4
41
3
40
2
39
1
38
65
A
66
B
67
C

27
40

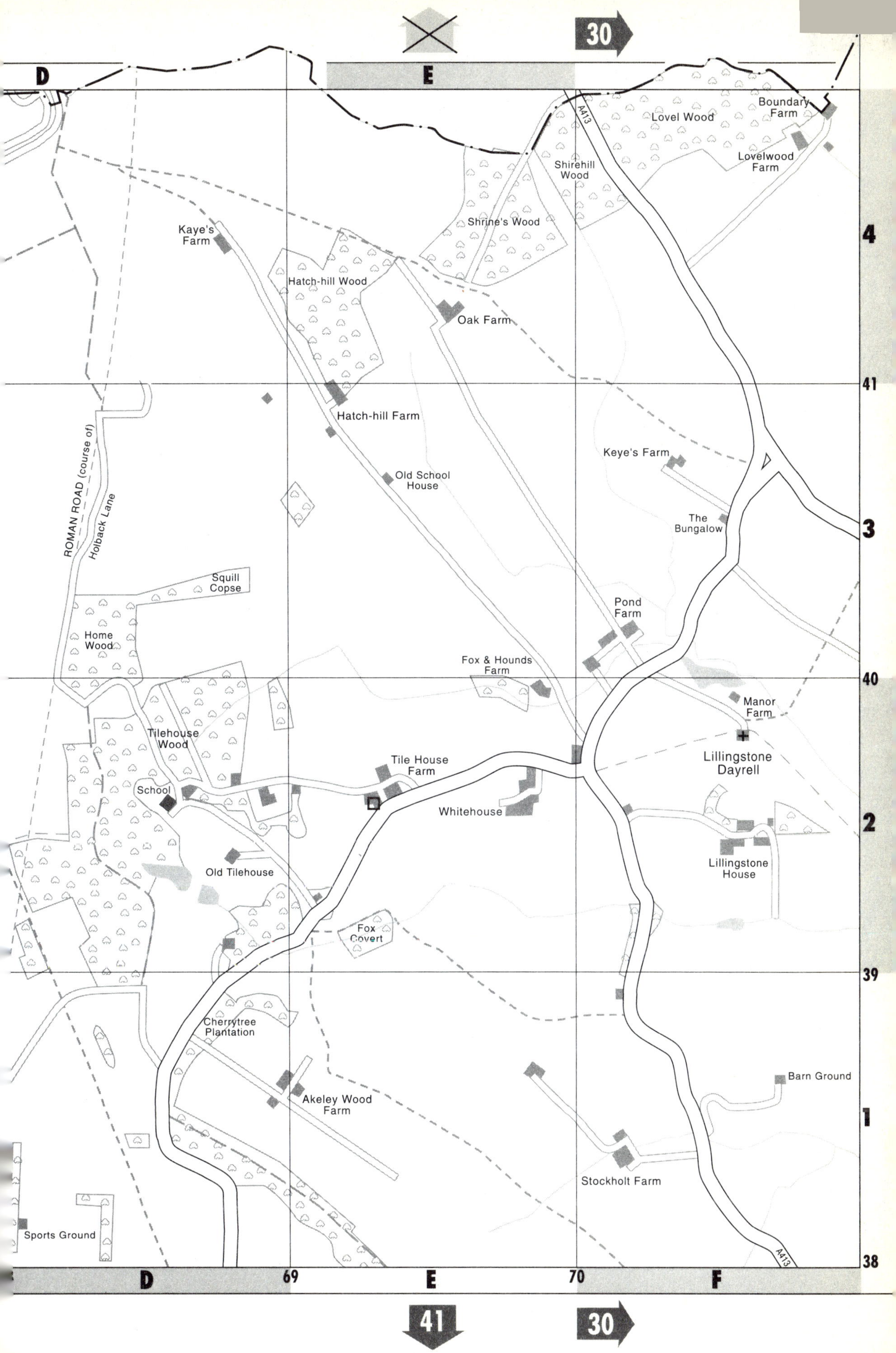

30
D
E
Lovel Wood
Boundary Farm
Lovelwood Farm
A413
Shirehill Wood
Shrine's Wood
Kaye's Farm
Hatch-hill Wood
Oak Farm
Hatch-hill Farm
Old School House
Keye's Farm
The Bungalow
ROMAN ROAD (course of)
Holback Lane
Squill Copse
Home Wood
Pond Farm
Fox & Hounds Farm
Manor Farm
Tilehouse Wood
Tile House Farm
Lillingstone Dayrell
School
Whitehouse
Old Tilehouse
Lillingstone House
Fox Covert
Cherrytree Plantation
Akeley Wood Farm
Barn Ground
Stockholt Farm
Sports Ground
4
41
3
40
2
39
1
38
69
70
F
41
30

29
17

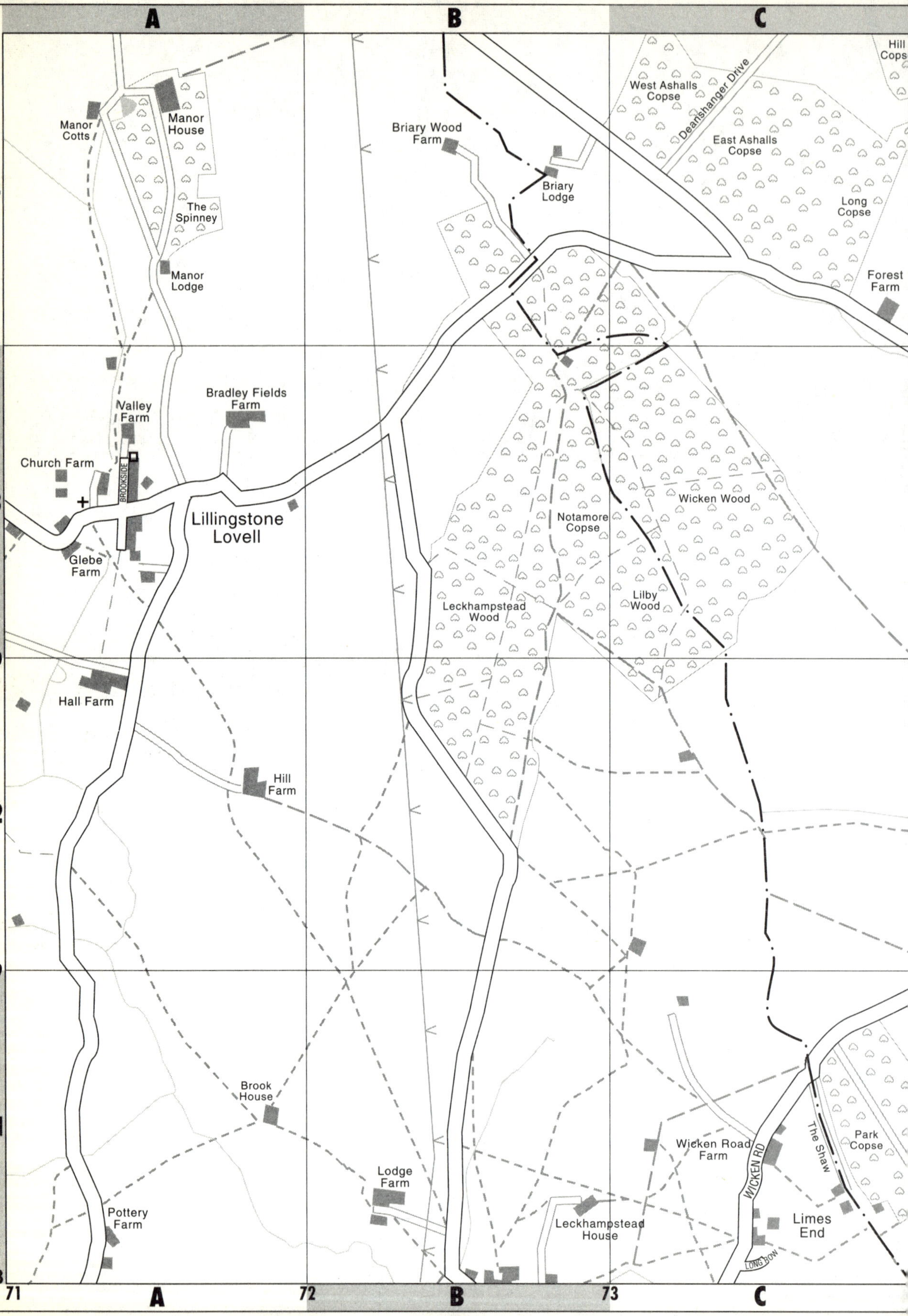
A
B
C
Hill Copse
West Ashalls Copse
Deanshanger Drive
East Ashalls Copse
Long Copse
Forest Farm
Manor Cotts
Manor House
The Spinney
Manor Lodge
Briary Wood Farm
Briary Lodge
Bradley Fields Farm
Valley Farm
Church Farm
BROOKSIDE
Lillingstone Lovell
Glebe Farm
Notamore Copse
Wicken Wood
Leckhampstead Wood
Lilby Wood
Hall Farm
Hill Farm
Brook House
Lodge Farm
Pottery Farm
Leckhampstead House
Wicken Road Farm
WICKEN RD
The Shaw
Park Copse
Limes End
LONG BOW
4
41
3
40
2
39
1
38
71
72
73

29
42

D
E
F
4
41
3
40
2
39
1
38
75
76
A5(T)
Point's Copse
Resr
Green Farm
Puxley
Grange Farm
Shrob Spinney
Old Copse Spinney
Hanger Lodge
Stollage Lodge
Poultry Farm
Folly Fields Farm
Hurst Farm
The Folly
HIGHVIEW
GLEBE RD
PUXLEY RD
RIDGMONT
NORTH WAY
RIDGMONT CL
THE RIDING
WESTFIELD AVE
ELM DR
PORTER'S CL
SPRINGFIELD GDNS
HAYES RD
LITTLE LONDON
BOSWELL LA
Northfields
FOLLY RD
HIGH ST
BROOKWAY
CHURCH LA
STRATFORD RD
A422
Deanshanger
PATRICK'S LA
Sch
THE GREEN
DOVEHOUSE CT
THE BEECHES
Dovehouse Farm
POUND CL
ST JOHN'S LA
Hotel
CHURCH LA
CHURCH CL
CROSS TREE RD
DEANSHANGER RD
Home Farm
White Lion (PH)
WICKEN PARK RD
Wicken
LECKHAMPSTEAD RD
Dagnall Cottages
Dagnall Farm
Grand Union Canal Buckingham Arm
disused
Sparrow Lodge
Pightle Farm
BUCKINGHAM RD
New Barn
Mount Hill Cottages
Wicken Park
Jack's Copse
A422

31
19

Knotwood
Shrobb Lodge Cottages
Shrobb Lodge Farm
Old Stratford
Dogsmouth Bridge
Nature Reserve
The Mill
Wolverton House
Flowers Barn
Stony Stratford
Weir
Manor Farm
Manor House
Passenham
Mill Cottages
River Great Ouse
Calverton Cottage
Shoulder of Mutton (PH)
Almshouses
Lower Weald
Calverton Place
Calverton
Rectory Farm
Middle Weald
Middle Weald Farm
Golf Course
Mill Farm
FB
Sch
Cemy
Liby
Watling Street
ROMAN ROAD
HIGH ST
CHURCH ST
SILVER ST
LONDON RD
WOLVERTON RD
QUEEN ELEANOR ST
STRATFORD RD
TOWCESTER RD
COSGROVE RD
DEANSHANGER RD
CALVERTON RD
WATLING ST
A5(T)
A508
A422
A B C
77 78 79
38 39 40 41 1 2 3 4

31
44

D
E
F
River Great Ouse
Manor Farm
Old Wolverton
COLTS HOLM RD
Works
DICKENS RD
HAVERSHAM RD
GRAFTON ST
Aqueduct
The Galleon (PH)
OLD WOLVERTON RD
BRIDGE TURN AVE
Works
DEAN'S RD
Sports Ground
New Bradwell
NEWPORT RD
Motte & Bailey
Medieval Village of Wolverton (site of)
ARDEN PARK
Grand Union Canal
Wolverton Station
ST MARY ST
ST GILES ST
QUEEN ANNE'S ST
KING EDWARD ST
BOUNTY ST
CALEDONIAN RD
WOOD ST
WALLACE ST
HIGH ST
Sch
Works
Works
Stonebridge
LONGVILLE
TRINITY RD
MANOR
CAXTON RD
SLATED ROW
Wolverton Park
Sch
STRATFORD RD
Lbry
CHURCH ST
CREED ST
GLYN SQ
ST GEORGES WAY
CEDAR LODGE DR
GRAFTON ST
FINGLE DR
41
4
Coll
BUCKINGHAM ST
THE SQUARE
ANSON RD
JERSEY RD
Sch
AYLESBURY ST W
AYLESBURY ST
PEEL RD
CAMBRIDGE ST
OXFORD ST
BEDFORD ST
RADCLIFFE ST
GREEN LA
MOON ST
VICTORIA ST
ETON C
WINDSOR ST
WESTERN RD
OSBOURNE ST
Sch
McCONNELL DR
BLACKWOOD CRES
MORTONS FORK
Warren Farm
Coll
Sch
CULBERTSON LA
VIENNA GR
GARDINER CT
VAN DER BILT CT
BLACKHILL DR
WOBURN AVE
FURZE WAY
Cemy
STACEY AVE
HALTONCHESTERS
Blue Bridge
3
BADMAN GR
AKERMAN CL
BUCKMAN CL
HERDMAN CL
Wolverton
MARINA DR
Mus
GREATCHESTERS
LEATHERSLADE DR
RIDGEWAY
SOKEMAN CL
HARVESTER CL
GLOUCESTER RD
Staceyhill Farm
MILLERS WAY
ILLINGSTON D
CONSTANTINE WAY
MILLS CT
CATCHPOLE CL
Sch
Sch
ARDWELL LA
FIELD LA
HARRARDS
MARRON LA
HOFWERS CROFT
FRANKLINS CROFT
SOUTHERN WAY
JOHNS CRES
WOODLAND VIEW
SPOONLEY WOOD
WILLOWFORD
Bancroft
THRESHER GR
OXMAN LA
BEE
WARD CL
FREEMAN CL
HAYWARDS CROFT
PINDERS CROFT
PLOWMAN CL
TILMAN CL
BARKERS CROFT
CALVARDS CROFT
GREAT MONKS ST
LAMBERTS CFT
SNOWBERRY CL
BRIAR HILL
BURTREE CL
MYRTLE BANK
BUCKTHORN
ALDERMEAD
MAPLE BEAN
WHITE ALDER
Stacey Bushes
1 BENWELL CL
2 CASTLESTEADS
3 RUDCHESTERS
CHESTERS
HADRIANS D
KENCHESTER
OCTAVIAN DR
A5(T)
Greenleys
BOUNDS CROFT
DROVERS CROFT
WAINERS CROFT
GREENLEYS LA
BROOMFIELD
LINGFIELD
40
MOORFOOT
WOOLMANS
Fullers Slade
HODGE LEA LA
REEVES CROFT
STRATHNAVER PL
ROSSAL PL
CULRAIN PL
GLEDFIELD PL
RAVIGILL PL
ALTANDHU PL
DALVINA PL
SKIPPIDAN PL
SKIDDON PL
HOLLIN LA
ERICA RD
HEATHFIELD
MONKS WAY
P
A422
ABBEY RD
SLADE LA
SHEPHERDS
SHEARMANS
MILLERS WAY
GRANGERS CROFT
COLSPIE CROFT
BROOKSIDE
HEATHFIELD
Remains of Priory (Benedictine)
FULLERS SLADE
BELLWETHER
WEAVERS HILL
BURNERS LA
BURNERS LA S
POTTERS LA
ALSTON DR
Bradwell Abbey
2
Kiln Farm Industrial Estate
CARTERS LA
PITFIELD
GUNLEYS
Golf Course
ALSTON DR
MONKS WAY
THE HYTHE
LANGTON DR
HARLOW
GREAT MONKS ST
Hotel
THE APPROACH
CH
GARAMONDE DR
BERLING RD
A5(T)
39
TILERS RD
BRICK CL
ATHERSTONE CT
BADGEMORE CT
KERCROFT
HALDENE
BERCHAM
DENMEAD
DOWNLAND
NORTHINGTON
NORBREY
CLAY HILL
MEDHURST
SANDWELL CT
FAIRWAYS
BELMONT CT
CLARENDON DR
CAVENHAM
Caravan Park
Two Mile Ash
CAMBRON
LEAFIELD RISE
SHORHAM RISE
Wymbush
HARBORNE CT
Two Mile Ash Farm
WESTCLIFFE
THORNCLIFFE
LITTLEMERE
SEDGEMERE
THE HIGH ST
STONE HILL
FENNY MERE
HAITHWAITE
CALDEWELL
THE HIGH ST
THE HIGH ST
Sch
CHURCH HILL
GARSTON
ARINTON
ASTLETHORPE
1
HOGARTHS
Oakhill Lane Farm
CALVERTON LA
WATLING ST
MILESMERE
Sch
TADMERE
BURSWELLE
STONE HILL
CHERLETON
KEPWICK
BERETUN
THORP
CALEWEN
TAVELHURST
DANSTEED WAY
PECKOVER CT
SHELDON
HATCHLANDS
STRATFIELD
LOSELEY CT
GATCOMBE
CHAWTON CRES
CHATSWORTH
ALBURY
KENSINGTON DR
Sch
DORTON CL
FARMERS CT
PETWORTH
PORTCHESTER CT
CORSHAM
BOUGHTON
VYNE CRES
ATTINGHAM HILL
Common Farm
CHARDACRE
PATESWELL
BRADLEBROOK
AVINGTON
38
81
82
D
E
F

A
B
C
4
3
2
1
41
40
39
38
83
84
85
Cemy
WOLVERTON RD
NEWPORT RD
Grand Union Canal
Cycle Track
Stantonbury
Great Linford
ST LEGER DR
MARSH DR
A422
Windmill (dis)
Bradville
BRADWELL RD
MONKS WAY
Trading Estate
Research Centre
MARLBOROUGH ST
Linford Wood
Neath Hill
SAXON ST
Mast
Heelands
Stanton Wood
Conniburrow
A509
Bradwell
GRAFTON ST
DANSTEED WAY
Bradwell Common
PORTWAY
SECKLOW GATE
Offices
Liby
Court
SILBURY BVD
MIDSUMMER BVD
AVEBURY BVD
WITAN GATE
Fishermead
CHILDS WAY
Trading Estate
Rooksley
Racing Circuit
National Badminton Centre
Lodge Lake
Loughton Lodge
GRAFTON GATE
ELDER GATE
Central Milton Keynes
Milton Keynes Central Station
FB
A5(T)
Sch
P

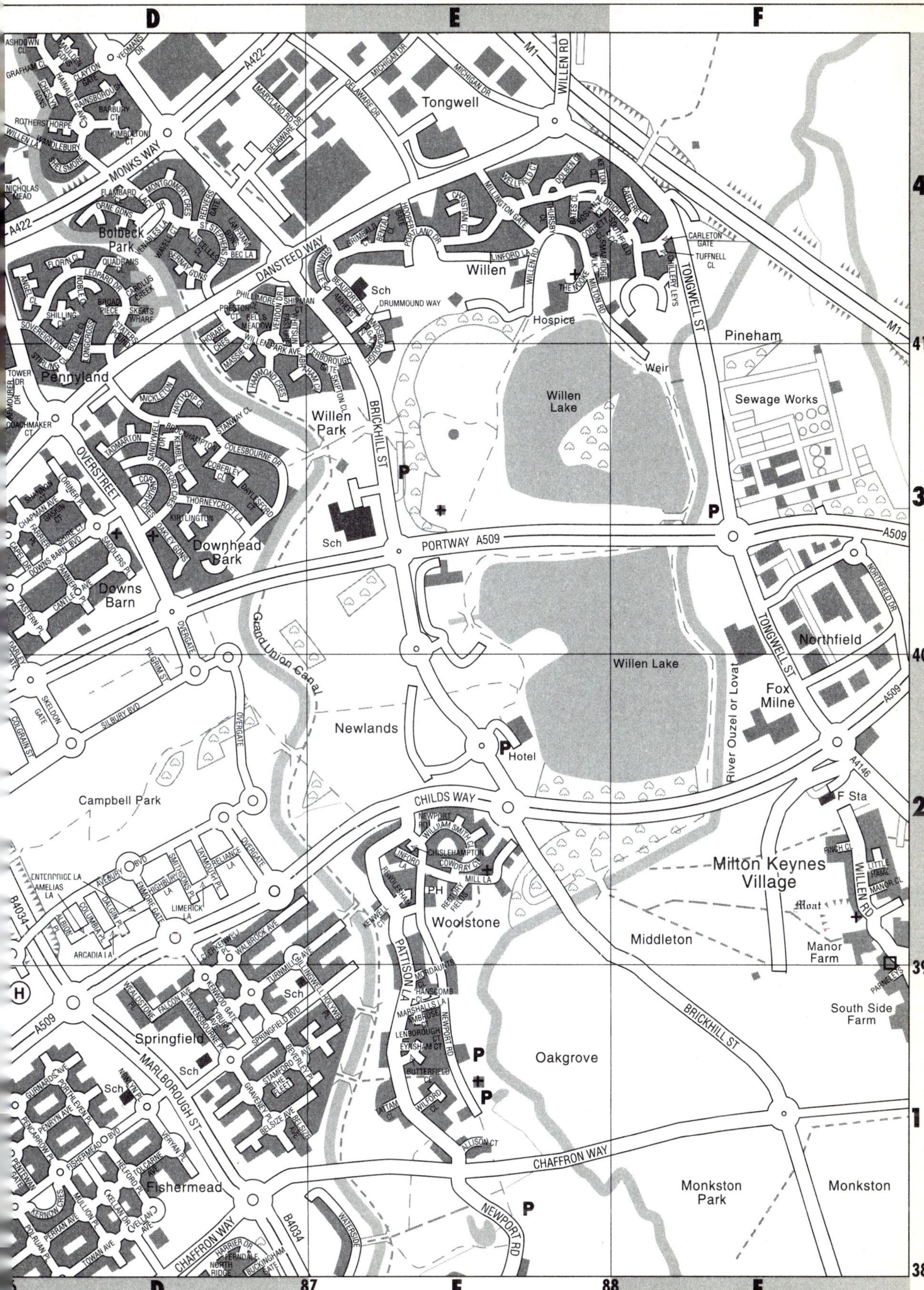
D
E
F
4
41
3
40
2
39
1
38
87
88
Tongwell
M1
WILLEN RD
MICHIGAN DR
DELAWARE DR
MARYLAND RD
A422
MONKS WAY
Bolbeck Park
Pennyland
DANSTEED WAY
Willen
Sch
DRUMMOUND WAY
Hospice
THE NOOKE
LINFORD LA
CARLETON GATE
TUFFNELL CL
HILLERY LEYS
TONGWELL ST
Pineham
Weir
Willen Lake
Sewage Works
Willen Park
BRICKHILL ST
P
Downhead Park
Downs Barn
OVERSTREET
PORTWAY A509
A509
Northfield
Fox Milne
River Ouzel or Lovat
Grand Union Canal
Newlands
Hotel
Campbell Park
CHILDS WAY
A4146
F Sta
Milton Keynes Village
Moat
Manor Farm
South Side Farm
Middleton
Woolstone
PH
PATTISON LA
Springfield
Oakgrove
MARLBOROUGH ST
Fishermead
CHAFFRON WAY
B4034
NEWPORT RD
Monkston Park
Monkston
SILBURY BVD
OVERGATE
AVEBURY BVD
H

35
23

A
B
C
4
3
2
1
41
40
39
38
89
90
91
CRANFIELD RD
Sch
Moulsoe
Glebe Farm
Church Farm
Hotel
A509
NEWPORT RD
Hermitage Farm
M1
Coachway
PORTWAY
CHILDS RD
A509
The Old Rectory
The Manor House
LONDON RD
Brooklands Farm
Broughton Barn
Old Covert
Broughton Barns Cotts
Roundhill Spinney
Atterbury
Business Park
Ravenstone House
Broughton
BROUGHTON RD
A4146
GRIFFITH GATE
MEADOW LA
BROUGHTON RD
HOPKINS CL
CARROCK LA
CLARIDGE DR
DORMANS CL
WALTON RD
TONGWELL ST
CHAFFRON WAY
CHAFFRON WAY
Kingston Bridge
Fen Farm
MANDEVILLE DR
MAIDSTONE RD
Kingston
NEWMARKET CT
Industrial Estate
CHIPPENHAM DR
WHITEHALL AVE
A5130 NEWPORT RD
LASBOROUGH RD
WINCHESTER CIRC
ULVERSCROFT
LANERCOST CRES
LAUNDE
CHETWODE AVE
ST BEES
A4146
STANDING WAY
ETHERIDGE AVE
BRANSWORTH AVE
A421
A421
A421

35
48

D
E
F
Wood End Farm
Lower Wood
Cranfield Airfield
Stilliters Farm
Leys Farm
Conn's Farm
Broughton Grounds
Salford Wood
Holcotmoors Farm
Holcotmoors Lodge
CRANFIELD RD
Whitsundoles Farm
College Farm
Rectory Farm
Mill Farm
BROUGHTON RD
BRITTONS LA
THE COURT
MANOR CL
Salford
MILL LA
Salfordford Bridge
Manor House
Inn
Waterhall
WAVENDON RD
Water Hall Farm
The Islands
Hulcote
Church Farm
Rooktree Farm
Hulcot Manor
Fox Covert
M1
A421
Aspley Hall
Eagle Farm
Wavendon Lodge
LOWER END RD
CRANFIELD RD
4
41
3
40
2
39
1
38
93
94

26

A
B
C
Turweston Manor
Turweston Fields
Burwell Farm
Oatleys Hall
VALLEY CRES
VALLEY RISE
VALLEY CL
VALLEY RD
ST PETER'S RD
EGERTON CL
DALE
MAIN ST
CHAPEL LA
Turweston
OLD TOWN
GLEBE DR
CHURCH
Sch
Old Town
PEBBLE LA
WATER LA
NETHER CL
ST PETERS GATE
MONTABAUR RD
WATERY LA
ROMAN WAY
WESTMINSTER CRES
Brackley
1 CAESERS GATE
2 HADRIANS GATE
3 FLAVIUS GATE
4 REMUS GATE
5 ROMULUS WAY
Oatleys Farm
OCTAVIAN WAY
MILL LA
BUCKINGHAM RD
WESTMINSTER CL
Glebe Farm
Grove Farm
WILLOW RD
FARM RD
A422
BOUNDARY RD
SHIRES RD
COUNTY RD
BOROUGH RD
AVONBURY CT
WARD RD
Hopcrafts Farm
A43(T)
Turweston Hill Farm
A422
BRACKLEY RD
Grovehill Farm
Dismantled Railway
River Great Ouse
Works
MILL LA
Westbury Mill
Dismantled Railway
Ash Beds
South Ground Covert
Evenley Hill Farm
Hill Ground Spinney
Hollow Barn
Mixbury Hall Farm
Mixbury Hall
Mossycorner Spinney
Mossycorner La
Beaumont Castle (remains of)
CHURCH LA
Glebe Farm
4
37
3
36
2
35
1
34
59
60
61

D E F

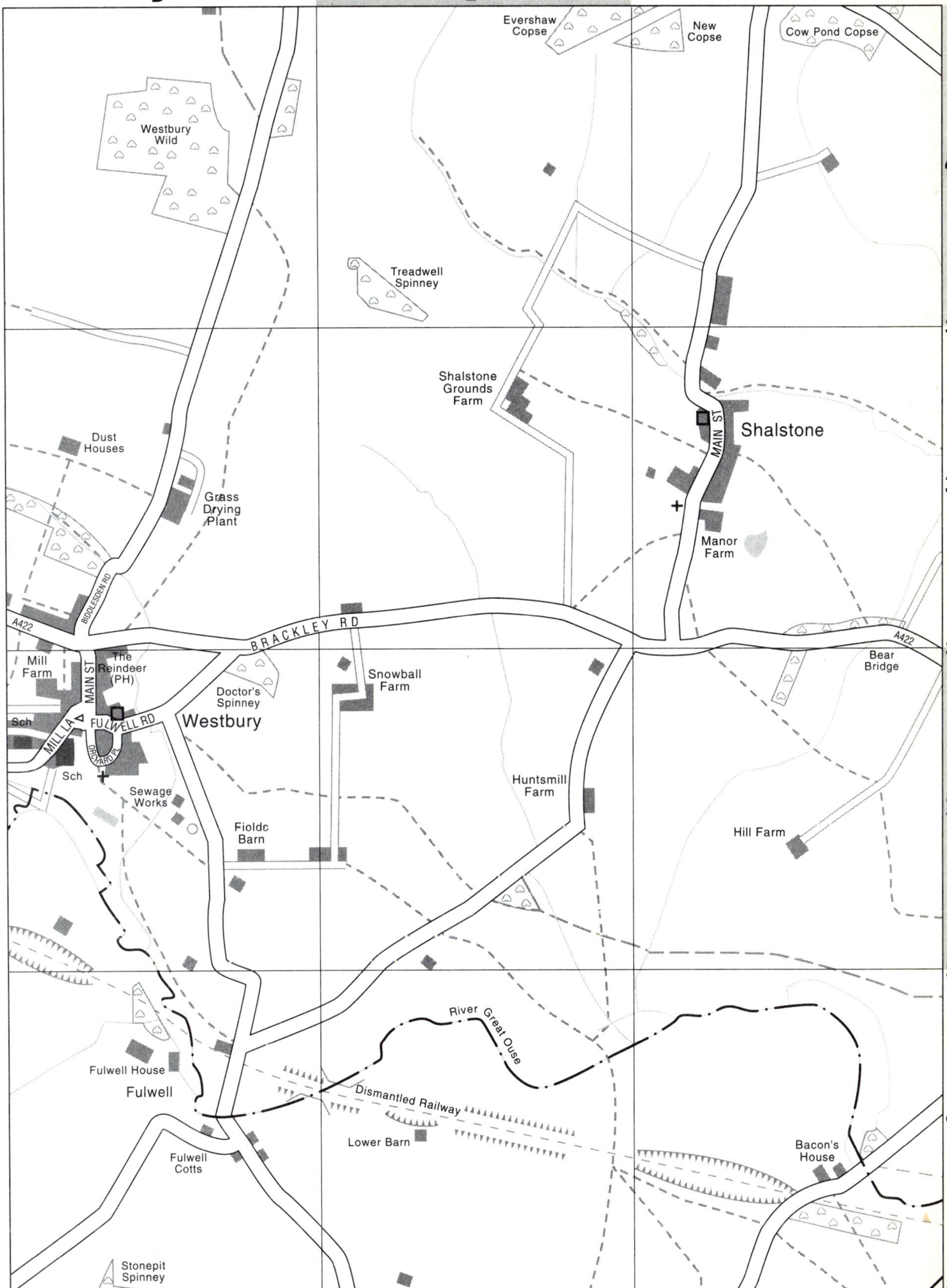
Evershaw Copse
New Copse
Cow Pond Copse
Westbury Wild
Treadwell Spinney
Shalstone Grounds Farm
Shalstone
MAIN ST
Manor Farm
Dust Houses
Grass Drying Plant
BIDDLESDEN RD
A422
BRACKLEY RD
A422
Bear Bridge
Mill Farm
MAIN ST
The Reindeer (PH)
Doctor's Spinney
Snowball Farm
Westbury
Sch
MILL LA
FULWELL RD
ORCHARD PL
Sch
Sewage Works
Fioldc Barn
Huntsmill Farm
Hill Farm
River Great Ouse
Fulwell House
Fulwell
Dismantled Railway
Lower Barn
Bacon's House
Fulwell Cotts
Stonepit Spinney
4
37
3
36
2
35
1
34
62
63
64

D E F

39
28

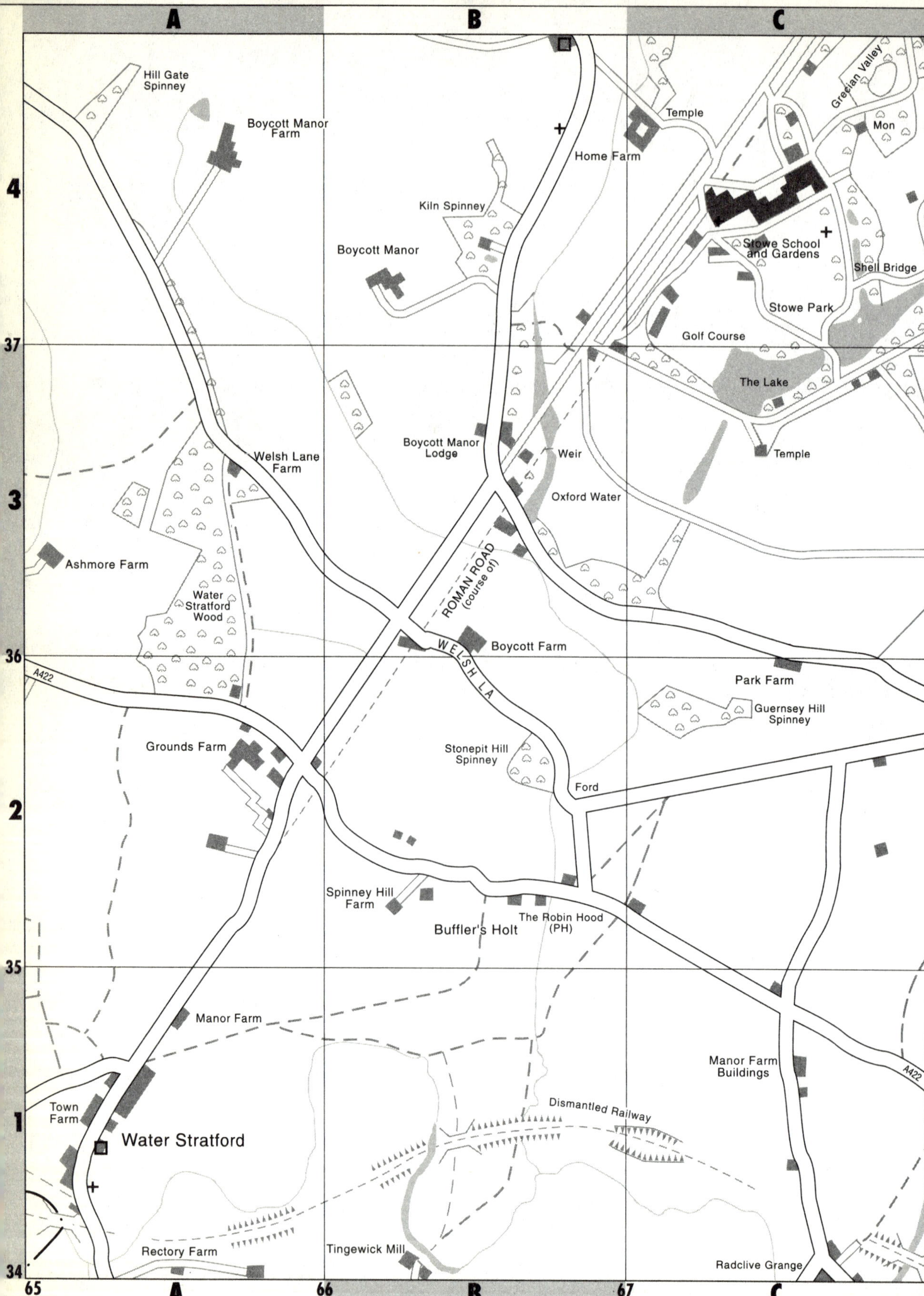
A
B
C
Hill Gate Spinney
Boycott Manor Farm
Temple
Grecian Valley
Mon
Home Farm
Kiln Spinney
Boycott Manor
Stowe School and Gardens
Shell Bridge
Stowe Park
Golf Course
The Lake
Boycott Manor Lodge
Weir
Temple
Welsh Lane Farm
Oxford Water
Ashmore Farm
ROMAN ROAD (course of)
Water Stratford Wood
Boycott Farm
WELSH LA
A422
Park Farm
Guernsey Hill Spinney
Grounds Farm
Stonepit Hill Spinney
Ford
Spinney Hill Farm
The Robin Hood (PH)
Buffler's Holt
Manor Farm
Manor Farm Buildings
A422
Dismantled Railway
Town Farm
Water Stratford
Rectory Farm
Tingewick Mill
Radclive Grange
4
37
3
36
2
35
1
34
65
66
67

39
51

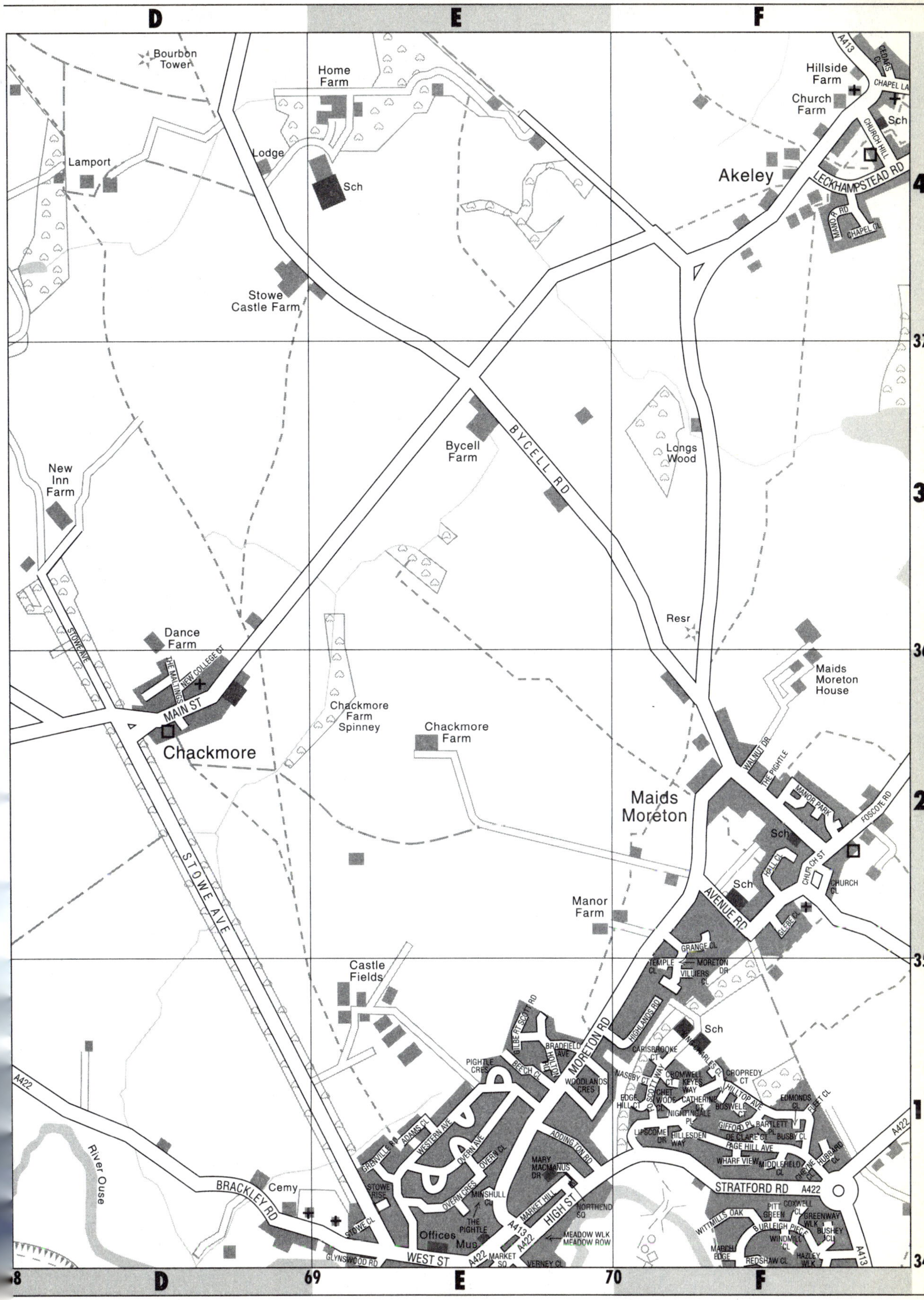
D
E
F
Bourbon Tower
Home Farm
Hillside Farm
Church Farm
CEDARS CL
CHAPEL LA
Sch
CHURCH HILL
A413
Lamport
Lodge
Sch
Akeley
LECKHAMPSTEAD RD
MANOR RD
CHAPEL CL
4
Stowe Castle Farm
37
Bycell Farm
BYCELL RD
Longs Wood
New Inn Farm
3
Resr
Dance Farm
THE MALTINGS
NEW COLLEGE CT
MAIN ST
STOWE AVE
36
Maids Moreton House
Chackmore
Chackmore Farm Spinney
Chackmore Farm
WALNUT DR
THE PIGHTLE
MANOR PARK
FOSCOTE RD
Maids Moreton
2
Sch
HILL CL
CHURCH ST
CHURCH CL
Sch
AVENUE RD
GLEBE CL
Manor Farm
STOWE AVE
35
Castle Fields
GRANGE CL
TEMPLE CL
MORETON DR
VILLIERS CL
HIGHLANDS RD
GILBERT SCOTT RD
BRADFIELD AVE
HOLTON RD
MORETON RD
Sch
CARISBROOKE CT
ST CHARLES CL
PIGHTLE CRES
BEECH CL
WOODLANDS CRES
NASEBY CT
TOSCOTT WAY
CROMWELL CT
KEYES WAY
CROPREDY CT
HILLTOP AVE
EDGE HILL CT
CHETWODE CL
CATHERINE CT
BOSWELL CT
EDMONDS CL
FLEET CL
NIGHTINGALE PL
GIFFORD PL
BARTLETT PL
DE CLARE CT
BUSBY CL
LIPSCOMBE DR
HILLESDEN WAY
PAGE HILL AVE
A422
1
ADAMS CL
WESTERN AVE
GRENVILLE RD
OVERN AVE
OVERN CL
ADDINGTON RD
WHARF VIEW
MIDDLEFIELD CL
CHEYNE CL
HUBBARD CL
River Ouse
MARY MACMANUS DR
STOWE RISE
OVERN CRES
MINSHULL CL
MARKET HILL
NORTHEND SQ
STRATFORD RD
A422
COXWELL CL
PITT GREEN
GREENWAY WLK
BRACKLEY RD
Cemy
THE PIGHTLE
HIGH ST
WITTMILLS OAK
BURLEIGH PIECE
BUSHEY CL
STOWE CL
Offices
Mus
A413
MEADOW WLK
MEADOW ROW
WINDMILL CL
MARCH EDGE
HAZLEY WLK
A413
GLYNSWOOD RD
WEST ST
A422
MARKET SQ
A422
VERNEY CL
REDSHAW CL
34
68
D
69
E
70
F

41
30

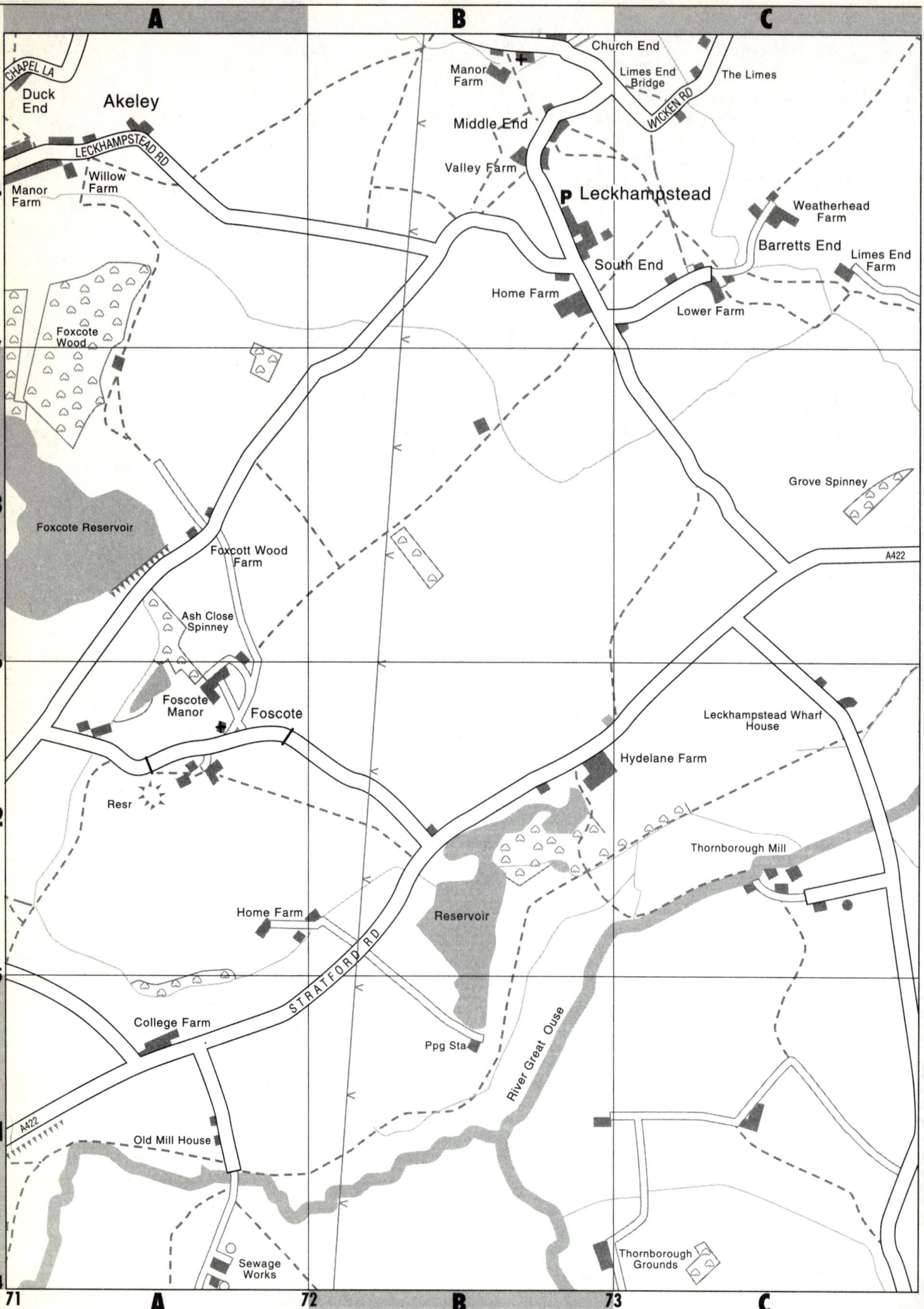
A
B
C
Church End
Manor Farm
Limes End Bridge
The Limes
CHAPEL LA
Duck End
Akeley
Middle End
WICKEN RD
LECKHAMPSTEAD RD
Willow Farm
Valley Farm
Manor Farm
Leckhampstead
Weatherhead Farm
Barretts End
Limes End Farm
South End
Home Farm
Lower Farm
Foxcote Wood
Grove Spinney
Foxcote Reservoir
Foxcott Wood Farm
A422
Ash Close Spinney
Foscote Manor
Foscote
Leckhampstead Wharf House
Hydelane Farm
Resr
Thornborough Mill
Home Farm
Reservoir
STRATFORD RD
River Great Ouse
College Farm
Ppg Sta
A422
Old Mill House
Sewage Works
Thornborough Grounds
4
37
3
36
2
35
1
34
71
72
73
A
B
C

41
53

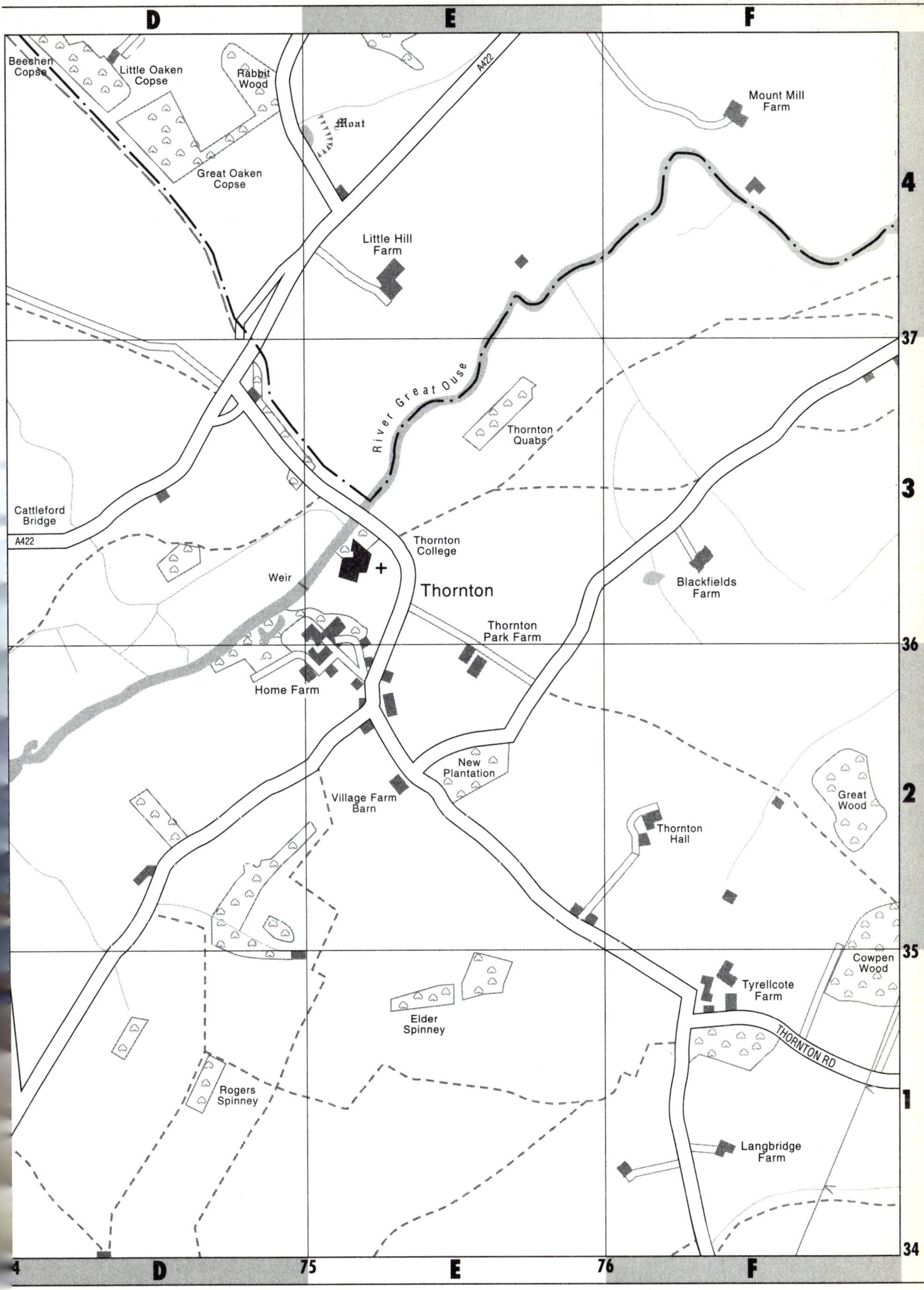
D
E
F
Beechen Copse
Little Oaken Copse
Rabbit Wood
A422
Moat
Great Oaken Copse
Mount Mill Farm
Little Hill Farm
River Great Ouse
Thornton Quabs
Cattleford Bridge
A422
Thornton College
Weir
Thornton
Blackfields Farm
Thornton Park Farm
Home Farm
New Plantation
Village Farm Barn
Great Wood
Thornton Hall
Cowpen Wood
Tyrellcote Farm
Elder Spinney
THORNTON RD
Rogers Spinney
Langbridge Farm
4
37
3
36
2
35
1
34
4
75
76
D
E
F

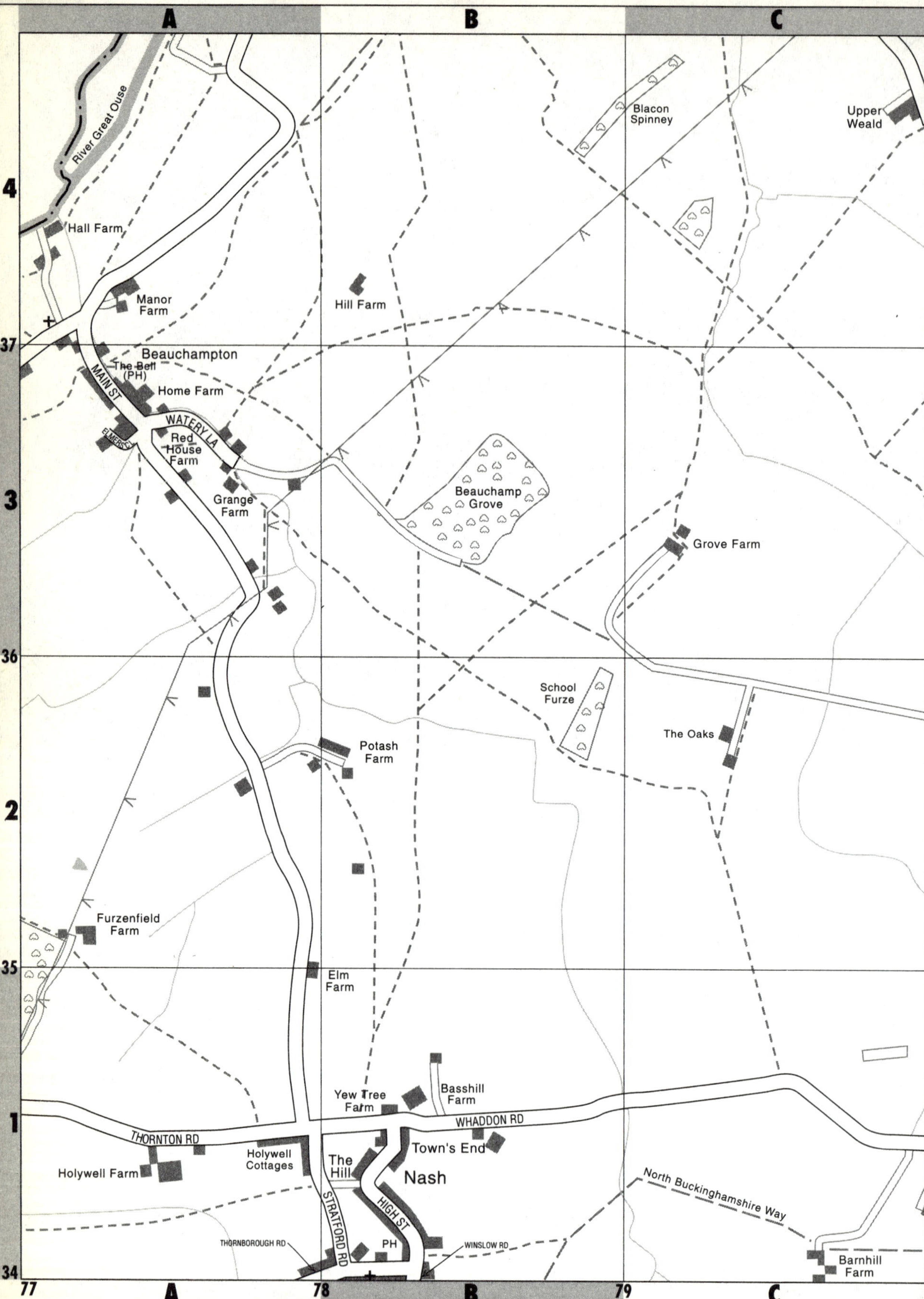
A
B
C
4
37
3
36
2
35
1
34
77
78
79
River Great Ouse
Hall Farm
Manor Farm
Beauchampton
The Bell (PH)
Home Farm
MAIN ST
WATERY LA
ELMERS CL
Red House Farm
Grange Farm
Hill Farm
Blacon Spinney
Upper Weald
Beauchamp Grove
Grove Farm
School Furze
The Oaks
Potash Farm
Furzenfield Farm
Elm Farm
Yew Tree Farm
Basshill Farm
WHADDON RD
THORNTON RD
Town's End
Holywell Farm
Holywell Cottages
The Hill
Nash
STRATFORD RD
HIGH ST
PH
THORNBOROUGH RD
WINSLOW RD
North Buckinghamshire Way
Barnhill Farm

33
46

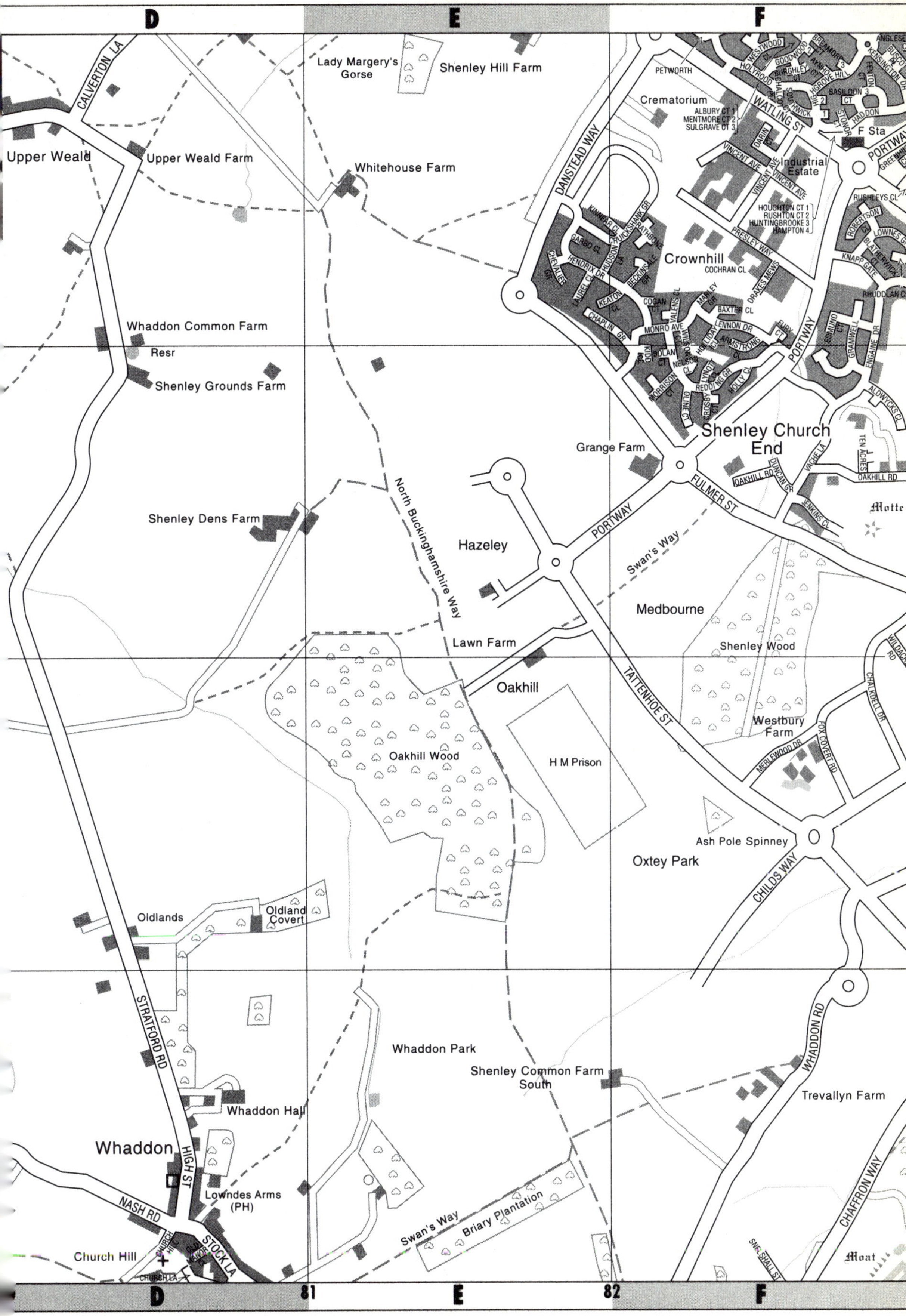
D
E
F
Calverton La
Upper Weald
Upper Weald Farm
Lady Margery's Gorse
Shenley Hill Farm
Whitehouse Farm
Petworth
Crematorium
Watling St
F Sta
Industrial Estate
Portway
Danstead Way
Vincent Ave
Crownhill
Presley Way
Whaddon Common Farm
Resr
Shenley Grounds Farm
Shenley Church End
Grange Farm
Fulmer St
Oakhill Rd
Motte
Shenley Dens Farm
North Buckinghamshire Way
Hazeley
Swan's Way
Medbourne
Lawn Farm
Oakhill
Shenley Wood
Tattenhoe St
Westbury Farm
Oakhill Wood
H M Prison
Ash Pole Spinney
Oxtey Park
Childs Way
Oldlands
Oldland Covert
Stratford Rd
Whaddon Park
Whaddon Rd
Shenley Common Farm South
Trevallyn Farm
Whaddon Hall
Whaddon
High St
Lowndes Arms (PH)
Nash Rd
Swan's Way
Briary Plantation
Chaffron Way
Church Hill
Stock La
Church La
Moat
4
37
3
36
2
35
1
34
81
82

56
46

45
34

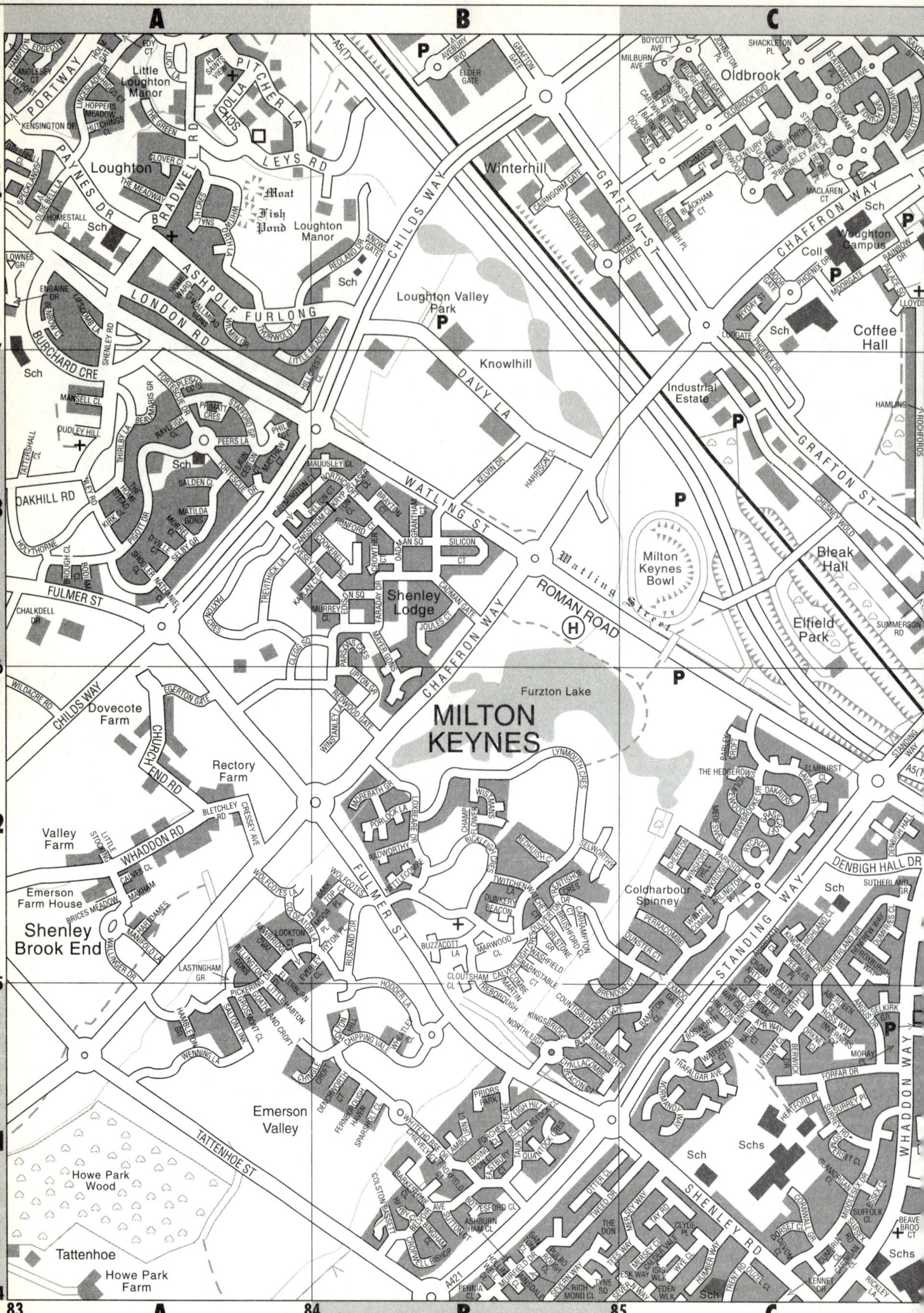
A
B
C
4
37
3
36
2
35
1
34
83
84
85
Little Loughton Manor
Loughton
Moat Fish Pond
Loughton Manor
Oldbrook
Winterhill
Loughton Valley Park
Knowlhill
Coffee Hall
Industrial Estate
Woughton Campus
Shenley Lodge
Milton Keynes Bowl
Bleak Hall
Elfield Park
Furzton Lake
MILTON KEYNES
Dovecote Farm
Rectory Farm
Valley Farm
Emerson Farm House
Shenley Brook End
Coldharbour Spinney
Emerson Valley
Howe Park Wood
Tattenhoe
Howe Park Farm
PORTWAY
PAYNES DR
BRADWELL RD
PITCHER LA
LEYS RD
ASHPOLE FURLONG
LONDON RD
BURCHARD CRES
CHILDS WAY
GRAFTON ST
CHAFFRON WAY
DAVY LA
WATLING ST
Watling Street
ROMAN ROAD
OAKHILL RD
FULMER ST
WHADDON RD
STANDING WAY
DENBIGH HALL DR
WHADDON WAY
SHENLEY RD
TATTENHOE ST
A5(T)
A421

45
57

D
E
F
4
37
3
36
2
35
1
34
87
88
Woughton on the Green
Woughton House Hotel
PH
NEWPORT RD
The Green
The Close
Peartree Bridge
Eaglestone
Leadenhall
Sch
Pear Tree Lane
Cycle Track
Milton Keynes Hospital
Marina
Allot Gdns
Towing Path
STANDING WAY
The Open University
Walton Hall
BRICKHILL ST
A421
MILTON RD
Walton Lake
Woughton Park
The Old Rectory
Netherfield
Tinkers Bridge
MARLBOROUGH ST
Simpson Lodge Farm
Walton Manor
CHAFFRON WAY
TREVONE CT
FULWOODS DR
MARKET HILL
FOREST RISE
MONTAGU DR
MERLIN WLK
HAWKMOOR CL
GOLDEN DR
LANNER WLK
EVERGLADE
KITE HILL
CHADWICK DR
WHITEGATE CROSS
FLEMING DR
LAMPETS CROSS
LLOYDS
VIRGINIA
HAMLINS
ST DUNSTANS
JONATHANS
ELFORDS
GARRAWAYS
DANIELS WELCH
ROBINS HILL
SQUIRES CL
SERLES CL
JAMAICA
CHAPTER
Chapter House
B4034
WATERSIDE
JEEVES CL
WOODLEY HEADLAND
CHADDS LA
VERLEY CL
PINKARD CT
BELLIS GR
LUCAS PL
ROWLES PL
ROGERS CROFT
PASSMORE
CASTLE ROSE
FOXTON
SADDINGTON
BROADWATER
MARSHWORTH
BUCKLAND DR
LANGLAND RD
BEADLEMEAD
FARNBOROUGH
THE HIDE
FARTHING GR
BROADLANDS
BARNFIELD DR
COLNE
HATTON
BLISWORTH
BRENT
ALDENHAM
BASCOTE
CONGREVE
GROVEWAY
OLD GROVEWAY
SIMPSON DR
HAMMER RD
WARREN BANK
Simpson Bridge
Simpson
Fish Ponds
Moats
MOUNT PLEASANT
THE MOUNT
CAPRON
SIMNEL
LAMMAS
CHERVIL
WASTEL
MASLIN DR
TANDRA
DODKIN
WHEATCROFT
DARNEL CL
MARRAM CL
NEAPLAND
MEDALE RD
MELICK RD
WOODRUSH CL
BEANFARE
SUMMERSON RD
GRAFTON ST
DUNSBY RD
WYMBLINGTON RD
MERTON DR
Redmoor
Bean Hill
Ashland
SAXON ST
Stadium
Grand Union Canal
River Ouzel
Weir
Caldecotte Lake
A5(T)
WHADDON WAY
GROVEWAY
CLARKE RD
DAWSON RD
GROVE ASH
AUCKLAND PARK
BOND AVE
Industrial Estate
Mount Farm Industrial Estate
Denbigh Sports Ground
The Beacon (PH)
BRAMLEY RD
MOUNT AVE
WARD RD
SIMPSON RD
A4146
Mount Farm Park
BLETCHAM WAY
WATLING ST
PEVEREL DR
SINCLAIR CT
SPENLOWS RD
DENBIGH RD
LYON RD
GOSLINGTON
BUSHY CL
KERRIA PL
CALLUNA DR
MELROSE AVE
DORCHESTER AVE
GLASTONBURY CL
BUCKFAST AVE
THE LINX
WHALLEY DR
HIGHFIELD CL
ARCHERS WELLS
HOME CL
NEATH CRES
The Leys
TORRE CL
CLEEVE CRES
BOLTON CL
WHITBY CL
SHAFTESBURY CRES
FURNESS CRES
BEAVERBROOK CT
THIRD AVE
SECOND AVE
FIRST AVE
ROMAR CT
Industrial Estates
JAMES WAY
DANE RD
HOLDOM AVE
BILTON RD
HORWOOD CT
THE LAURELS
STAPLE HALL RD
Fenny Stratford Station
Lock
LOCK VIEW LA
LC
Court
BRISTOW CL
DURRANS CT
CHURCH ST
Belvedere Farm
Bletchley Park
SHERWOOD DR
Masts
Schs
Hospl
PARK GDNS
WHALLEY DR
TAVISTOCK ST
DENBIGH WAY
Fenny Stratford
WESTERN RD
PADDOCK WAY
THE CRESCENT
NORTH ST
VISCOUNT WAY
NORTH GATE
DUKES DR
VICTORIA RD
STUART CL
GEORGE ST
AYLESBURY ST
WHARFSIDE
WATLING TERR
P

47
36

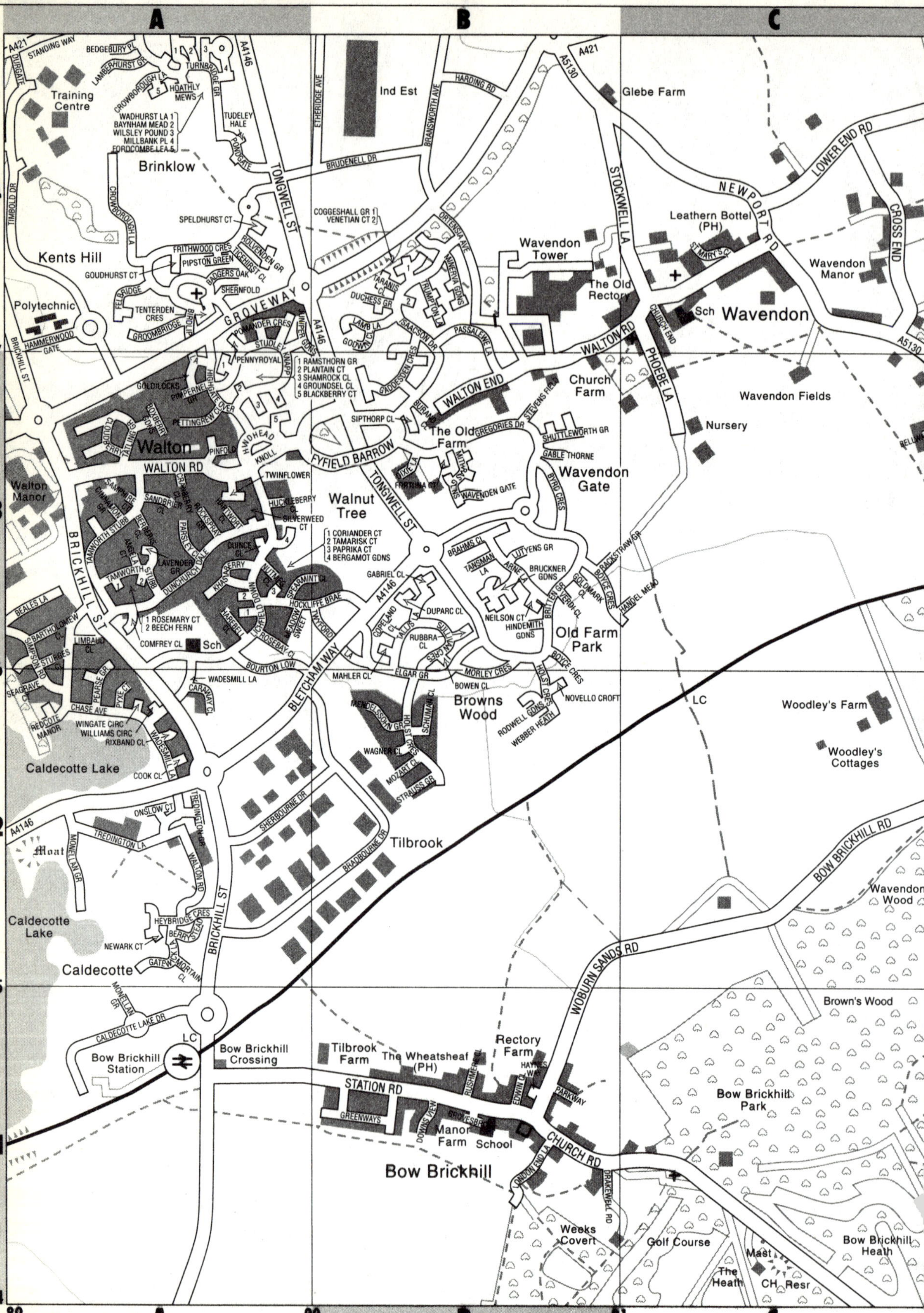
A
B
C
4
37
3
36
2
35
1
34
89
90
91
Training Centre
Brinklow
Kents Hill
Polytechnic
Walton
Walton Manor
Walnut Tree
Caldecotte Lake
Caldecotte
Moat
Bow Brickhill Station
Bow Brickhill Crossing
Tilbrook
Tilbrook Farm
The Wheatsheaf (PH)
Rectory Farm
Manor Farm
School
Bow Brickhill
Weeks Covert
Golf Course
The Heath
Mast
CH
Resr
Bow Brickhill Heath
Bow Brickhill Park
Brown's Wood
Wavendon Wood
Woodley's Farm
Woodley's Cottages
Browns Wood
Old Farm Park
Wavendon Gate
The Old Farm
Church Farm
Wavendon Fields
Nursery
Wavendon
Sch
The Old Rectory
Wavendon Tower
Wavendon Manor
Leathern Bottel (PH)
Glebe Farm
Ind Est
LC
A421
A4146
A5130
GROVEWAY
TONGWELL ST
BRICKHILL ST
WALTON RD
BLETCHAM WAY
FYFIELD BARROW
WALTON END
STOCKWELL LA
PHOEBE LA
NEWPORT RD
LOWER END RD
CROSS END
BOW BRICKHILL RD
WOBURN SANDS RD
STATION RD
CHURCH RD
CALDECOTTE LAKE DR
BRUDENELL DR
BRANSWORTH AVE
HARDING RD
ETHERIDGE AVE
WADHURST LA 1
BAYNHAM MEAD 2
WILSLEY POUND 3
MILLBANK PL 4
FORDCOMBE LEA 5
COGGESHALL GR 1
VENETIAN CT 2
1 RAMSTHORN GR
2 PLANTAIN CT
3 SHAMROCK CL
4 GROUNDSEL CL
5 BLACKBERRY CT
1 CORIANDER CT
2 TAMARISK CT
3 PAPRIKA CT
4 BERGAMOT GDNS
1 ROSEMARY CT
2 BEECH FERN
TWINFLOWER
HUCKLEBERRY CL
SILVERWEED CT
PENNYROYAL
GOLDILOCKS
PETTINGREW CL
PINFOLD
KNOLL
COMFREY CL
WADESMILL LA
CARAWAY CL
BOURTON LOW
ROSEBAY CL
HOCKLIFFE BRAE
SPEARMINT CL
GABRIEL CL
DUPARC CL
RUBBRA CL
MAHLER CL
ELGAR GR
MORLEY CRES
BOWEN CL
NOVELLO CROFT
RODWELL GDNS
WEBBER HEATH
NEILSON CT
HINDEMITH GDNS
BRUCKNER GDNS
LUTYENS GR
BRAHMS CL
HANDEL MEAD
GOLDMARK CL
BOYCE CRES
RACKSTRAW GR
THORNE
GABLE
SHUTTLEWORTH GR
GREGORIES DR
STEVENS FIELD
SIPTHORP CL
WAVENDEN GATE
PASSALEWE LA
ISAACSON DR
DUCHESS GR
LAMB LA
MINERVA GDNS
TRUMPTON LA
GADDESDEN CRES
SPELDHURST CT
FRITHWOOD CRES
PIPSTON GREEN
GOUDHURST CT
BADGERS OAK
SHERNFOLD
TENTERDEN CRES
GROOMBRIDGE
HAMMERWOOD GATE
BRICKHILL ST
TIMBOLD DR
DURGATE
STANDING WAY
BEDGEBURY PL
LAMBERHURST GR
CROWBOROUGH LA
HOATHLY MEWS
TURNBRIDGE GR
TUDELEY HALE
PONDGATE
ROLVENDEN GR
TICEHURST CL
STUDLEY KNAPP
POMANDER CRES
JUNIPER GDNS
HIGHGATE OVER
PIMPERNEL GR
BOXBERRY GDNS
CLOUDBERRY
TATLING GR
HAWDHEAD
SANDBRIER CL
CHILLERY CL
ROCKSPRAY
PARSLEY CL
DUNCHURCH DALE
LAVENDER GR
ANGELICA CL
TAMWORTH STUBB
QUINCE CL
KHASIBERRY
NUTMEG CL
WOODRUFF
HAREBELL CL
BEALES LA
BARTHOLOMEW CL
SIMPSON RD
STURGES CL
LIMBAUD CL
PEARSE GR
SEAGRAVE CT
REDCOTE MANOR
CHASE AVE
WINGATE CIRC
WILLIAMS CIRC
RIXBAND CL
COOK CL
ONSLOW CT
TREDINGTON GR
TREDINGTON LA
MONELLAN GR
WALTON RD
HEYBRIDGE CRES
BERRYSTEAD
NEWARK CT
GATEWAYS
MORTAIN CL
MONELLAN GR
SHERBOURNE DR
BRADBOURNE DR
MENDELSSOHN GR
HOLST CRES
SCHUMANN CL
WAGNER CL
MOZART CL
STRAUSS GR
COPELAND CL
TALLIS LA
SULLIVAN CRES
GREENWAYS
DOWNS VIEW
GROVESBRIDGE
RUSHMERE CL
EDWIN CL
HAYNES WAY
PARKWAY
LONDON END LA
DRAKEWELL RD
BELLWAY

47
59

37

D
E
F
Lower End
LOWER END RD
CROW LA
WAVENDON HOUSE DR
Wavendon House School
Park Farm
Crabtree Farm
SALFORD RD
Glebe Farm
M1
A421
Hayfield Farm
Hunters Moon
Braystone
CRANFIELD RD
Nursery
Deeth Farm
A5130
PARKWAY
BELLWAY
NEWPORT RD
HILLWAY
RIDGWAY
TAVISTOCK CL
DEETHE CL
VANDYKE CL
CHANTRY CL
Crossings Land Farm
Aspley Guise Station
Berrylane Farm
LC
BERRY LA
TRUNK FURLONG ESTATE
BROWNS WAY
Sewage Works (disused)
The Warren
F Sta
Sch
HUTTON WAY
Mill Farm
SADDLERS GREEN
WEATHERCOCK CL
Woburn Sands Station
STATION RD
WEST RD
BURROWS CL
MILL LA
MILL WAY
Common Farm
CHURCH ST
CHURCH RD
Golf Course
SPRING GR
Woburn Sands
BEDFORD RD
WEATHERCOCK LA
THE TERRACE
THE SQUARE
MAPLE GR
ELM GR
THEYDON AVE
BLACKTHORN GR
PINE GR
LIME GR
ASPLANDS CL
RUSSELL ST
P
CH
THE MOUNT
Sch
SPINNEY LA
MOUNT PLEASANT
SAN REMO RD
BOW BRICKHILL RD
THE LEYS
WOOD ST
CHAPEL ST
HIGH ST
VICARAGE ST
ST VINCENTS
WEST HILL
DUKE ST
MENTONE AVE
WOOD LA
GREEN LA
WOBURN LA
TIDBURY CL
HARDWICK PL
Liby
DOWNHAM RD
ASPLEY HILL
HARDWICK RD
WOODLAND WAY
WOODSIDE
PEERS DR
Aspley Guise
Edgewick Farm
HEATH CL
Sch
GYPSY LA
Wavendon Wood
Aspley Wood
NARROW LA
Danesborough
SANDY LA
Aspley Heath
SILVERBIRCHES LA
WOBURN RD
HEATH LA
Sch
ASPLEY LA
Birchmoor Farm
Old Wavendon Heath
New Wavendon Heath
A5130
4
37
3
36
2
35
1
34
92
93
94

60

39

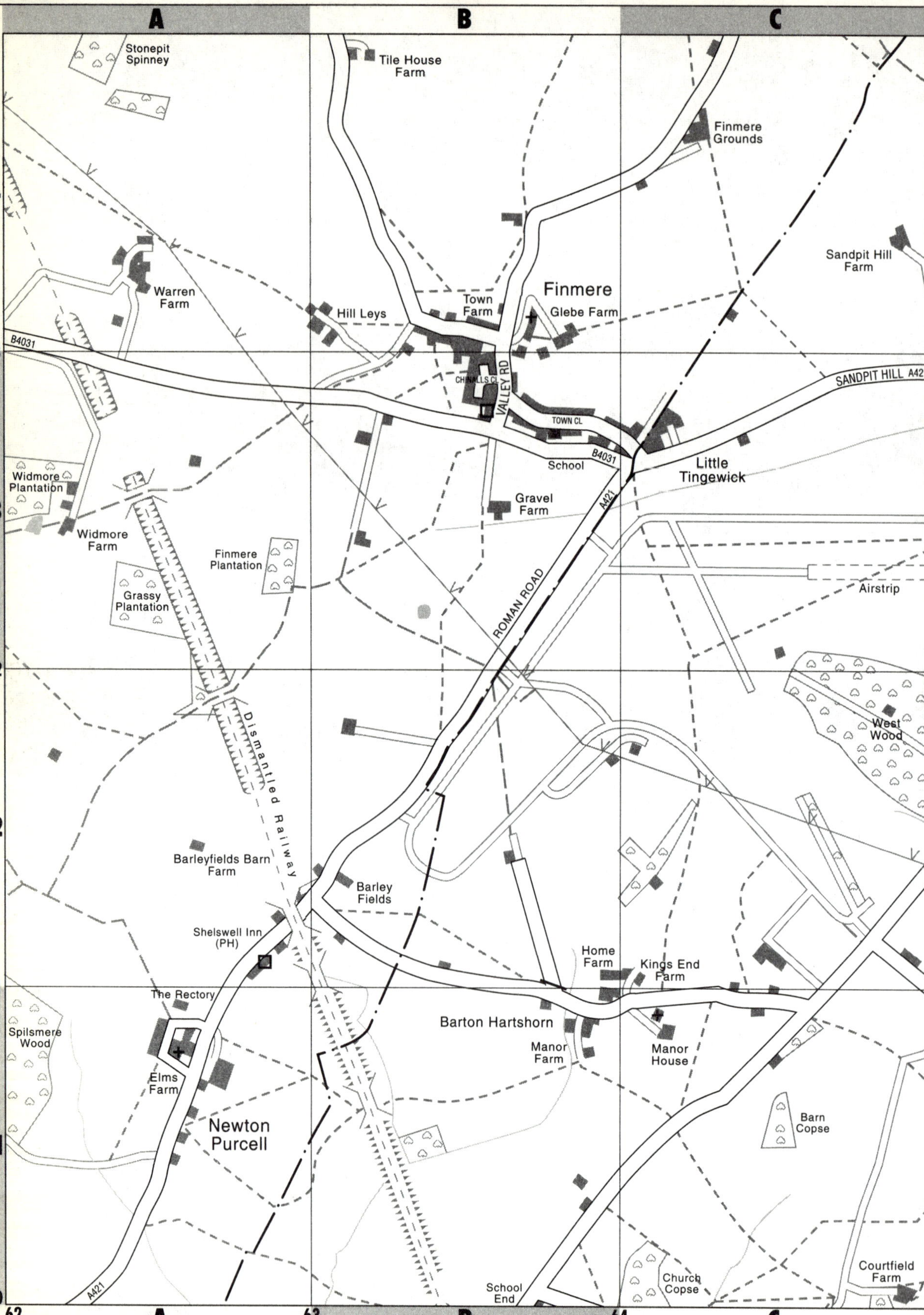
A
B
C
Stonepit Spinney
Tile House Farm
Finmere Grounds
4
Sandpit Hill Farm
Warren Farm
Finmere
Town Farm
Hill Leys
Glebe Farm
B4031
33
CHINALLS CL
VALLEY RD
SANDPIT HILL A421
TOWN CL
B4031
School
Little Tingewick
Widmore Plantation
3
Gravel Farm
A421
Widmore Farm
Finmere Plantation
Airstrip
Grassy Plantation
ROMAN ROAD
32
West Wood
Dismantled Railway
2
Barleyfields Barn Farm
Barley Fields
Shelswell Inn (PH)
Home Farm
Kings End Farm
31
The Rectory
Barton Hartshorn
Spilsmere Wood
Manor Farm
Manor House
Elms Farm
Newton Purcell
1
Barn Copse
Courtfield Farm
School End
Church Copse
A421
30
62
63
64

D
E
F
Radclive
Radclive Manor
River Great Ouse
Grovehill Farm
Golf Course
CH
4
TINGEWICK RD
A421
Rectory Barn
Tingewick
Dudley Bridge
Manor Farm
RADCLIVE RD
Tingewick Hall
Cemy
STOWE VIEW
CHURCH
ST MARYS LA
BUCKINGHAM ST
Sewage Works
33
WEST WELL CL
Sch
A421
A421
SANDPIT HILL
MAIN ST
Durrants Farm
HICKMANS CL
STRANGERS
WEST WELL
OLD FORGE CL
CROSS LA
STOCKLEYS LA
GORRELL CL
The Bungalows
UPPER ST
NEW ST
Woodfield Nursery
The Gables
Parsonage Farm
Gorrell La
WOOD LA
Windbush Farm
Aerodrome Farm
3
Airstrip
Primrose Hill Farm
32
Leyland Farm
HILLSIDE
MAIN ST
Gawcott
NEW INN LA
BACK LA
THE RISE
Tingewick Wood
Eagle's Farm
Sch
CHURCH LA
2
Wood Farm
Lenborough Wood
Round Wood
31
Plough Farm
1
Dairy Farm
Park Spinney
Hillesden
Bushey Lane Farm
BUSHES LA
MAIN ST
The Elms
POUND LA
The Laurels
Lockharbour Farm
Old Park Farm
30
D
66
E
67

A
B
C
Tingewick Road Industrial Park
BUCKINGHAM
Field Farm
TINGEWICK RD
Dismantled Railway
BRISTLE HILL
SCHOOL LA
CASTLE ST
BRIDGE ST
NELSON ST
FISHERS FIELD
RUMBOLDS LA
MANOR ST
BATH LA
HUNTER ST
CHURCH ST
WELL ST
BROOKS CT
ELM ST
FORD ST
Sch
McKENZIE CL
PORTFIELD CL
PORTFIELD WAY
POPLAR RD
BOURTONVILLE
BOURTON RD
F Sta
CHANDOS RD
CHANDOS CL
BROOKFIELD LA
Sch
Schs
Coll
STATION RD
SANDHURST DR
MITRE ST
GAWCOTT RD
Bone Hill
TYRELL CL
MOUNT PLEASANT CL
LENBOROUGH RD
LENBOROUGH CL
Mount Pleasant
A421
High Acre Farm
Radclive Dairy Farm
Gawcott Hill Farm
DUKES PIECE 1
MARE LEYS 2
KROHN CL 3
SANDY CL
VALLEY RD
BURLEIGH PIECE
DOWNER CL
ACKERMAN CL
CAMPBELL CL
SMALL CRES
A413
River Great Ouse
P
Sch
Bourton
Home Farm
THE HOLT
OTTERS BROOK
BEAVER CL
WARREN CL
SQUIRREL WAY
FOX WAY
LARK CL
KINGFISHER RD
ROBIN CL
PARTRIDGE
WILLOW DR
SYCAMORE CL
LIME AVE
DOVE CL
SWALLOW CL
DEERFIELD CL
MARTIN CL
WREN CL
BADGERS WAY
HARE CL
SWAN CL
PLOVER CL
KESTREL WAY
OSPREY WLK
MEADWAY
MEADOW GDNS
A421
LONDON RD
33
4
Gawcott Fields Farm
GAWCOTT RD
Works
Industrial Estate
Benthill Farm
3
RADCLIVE RD
Resr
BUCKINGHAM RD
Wireless Station
Masts
32
OLD BARN CL
MAIN ST
CHURCH ST
PH
Manor Farm
Gawcott Farm
A413
Hill Farm
Lenborough
2
The Keepers
Manor Farm
The Laurels
31
Stocking Wood
1
Stockingwood Farm
Rowley Hill
Lenborough Farm
30
68
A
69
B
70
C

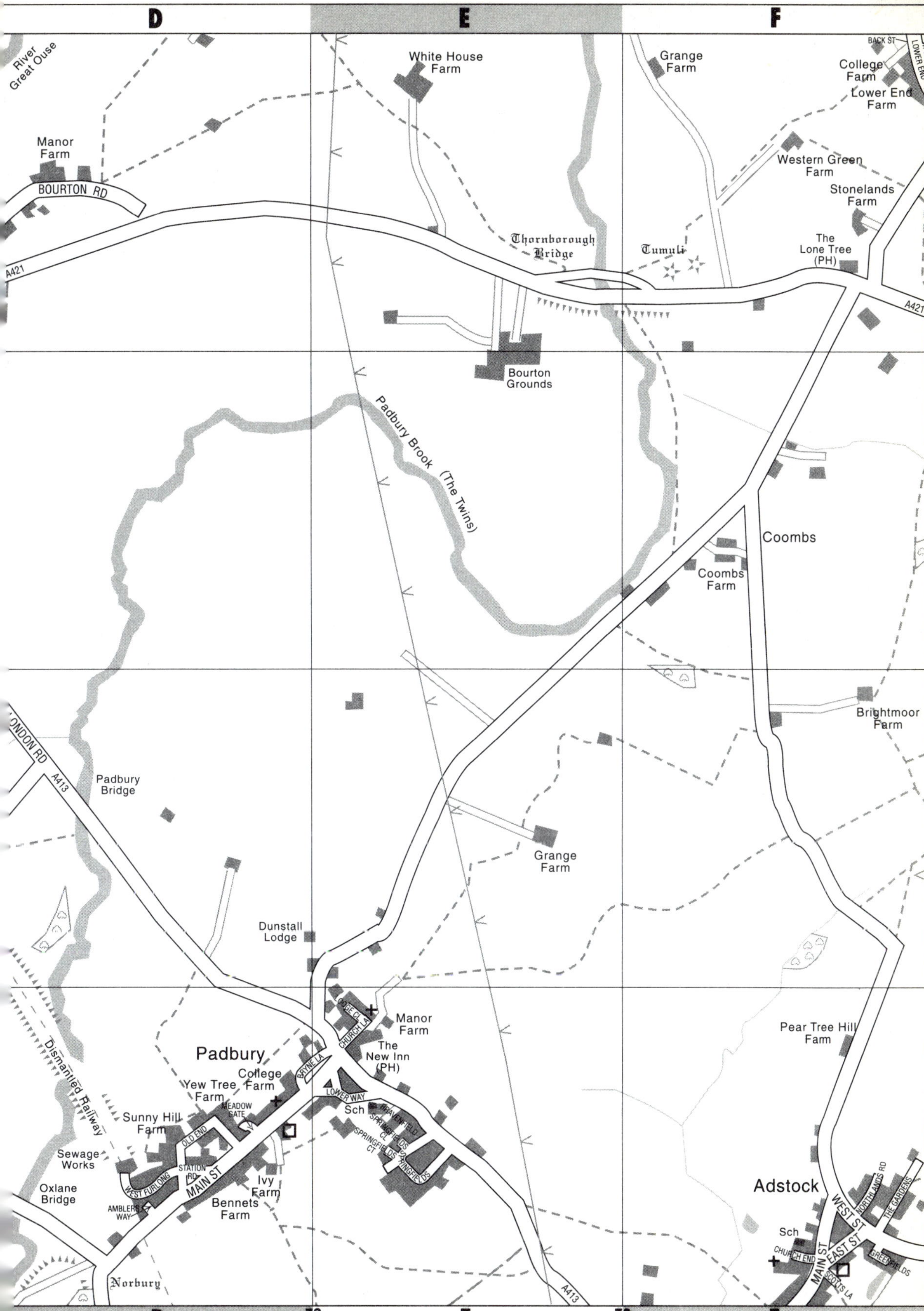
D
E
F
River Great Ouse
White House Farm
Grange Farm
College Farm
Lower End Farm
BACK ST
LOWER END
Manor Farm
BOURTON RD
Western Green Farm
Stonelands Farm
4
Thornborough Bridge
Tumuli
The Lone Tree (PH)
A421
A421
33
Bourton Grounds
Padbury Brook (The Twins)
3
Coombs
Coombs Farm
32
Brightmoor Farm
LONDON RD
A413
Padbury Bridge
2
Grange Farm
Dunstall Lodge
31
Manor Farm
The New Inn (PH)
Pear Tree Hill Farm
Padbury
College Farm
Yew Tree Farm
Dismantled Railway
BRYNE LA
CHURCH LA
LODGE CL
LOWER WAY
MEADOW GATE
Sch
Sunny Hill Farm
OLD END
SPRINGFIELDS CL
SPRINGFIELDS CT
SPRINGFIELDS
GRAVENFIELD
1
Sewage Works
STATION RD
MAIN ST
WEST FURLONG
Ivy Farm
Oxlane Bridge
AMBLERS WAY
Bennets Farm
Adstock
WEST ST
NORTHLANDS RD
THE GARDENS
Sch
CHURCH END
MAIN ST
EAST ST
GREENFIELDS
SCOTTS LA
Norbury
A413
30
D
72
E
73
F

53
43

A
B
C
BACK ST
Ford
PALMERS MOOR
Home Farm
LOWER END
HIGH ST
Sch
CHAPEL LA
THE GREEN
Thornborough
BRIDGE ST
NASH RD
THORNHILL
Nash End Farm
Coates Farm
Bungalow Farm
Willow Farm
Brakes Farm
THORNBOROUGH RD
Dancer's Grave
Nansley's Brake
Middle Shelspit Farm
Lower Shelspit
Upper Shelspit Farm
A421
The Folly
Priory Farm
Maywynn Farm
Mangland Farm
Poultry Farm
Singleborough
Dean Farm
Laurel Farm
Pilch Farm
PILCH LA
Great Furze House
SCHOOL END
Home Farm
B4033
Adstockfields House
Adstockfields Farm
Wigwell Farm
WINSLOW RD
North Buckinghamshire Way
4
33
3
32
2
31
1
30
74
75
76

53
65

44
56

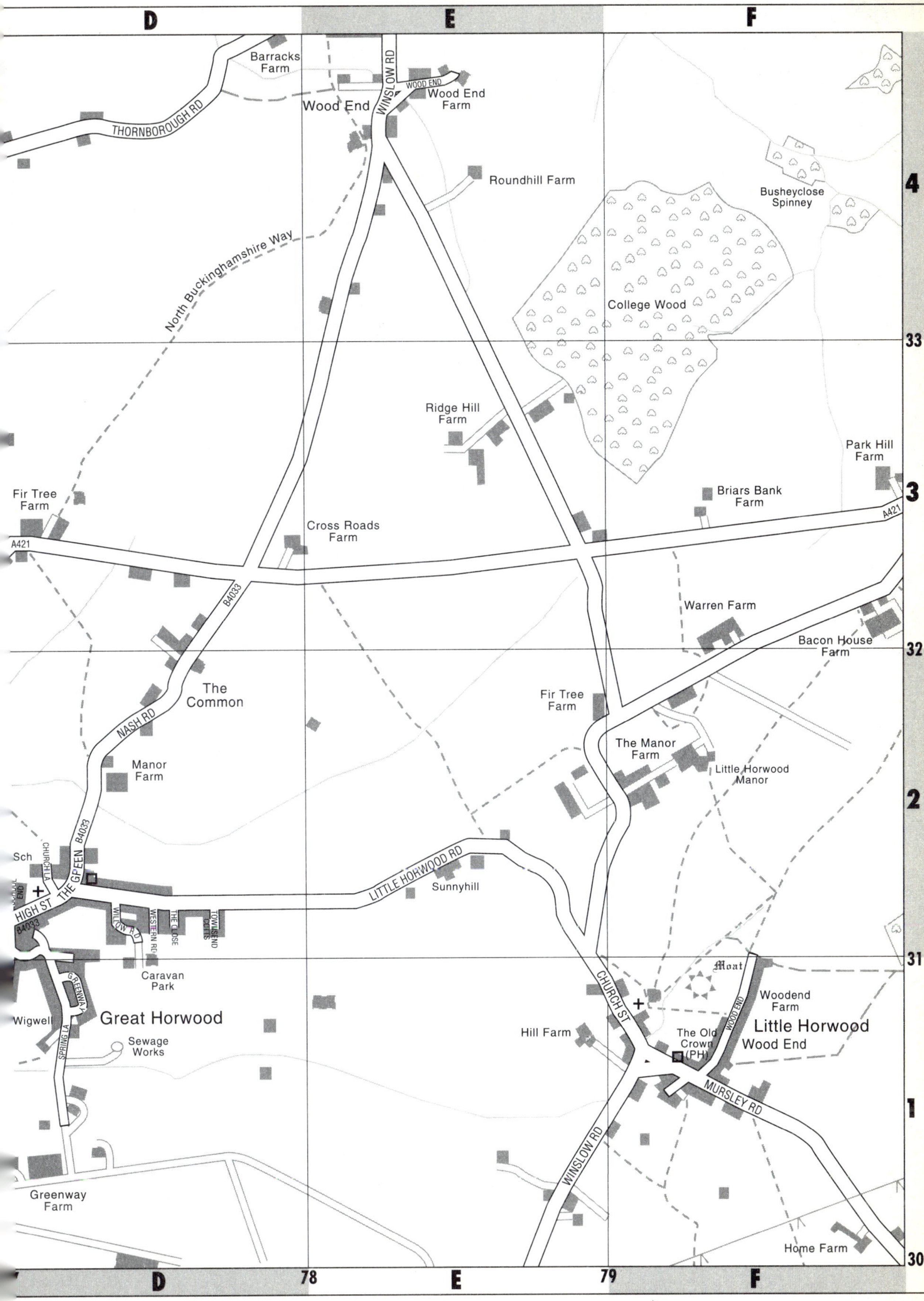
D
E
F
Barracks Farm
Wood End
WINSLOW RD
WOOD END
Wood End Farm
THORNBOROUGH RD
Roundhill Farm
Busheyclose Spinney
North Buckinghamshire Way
College Wood
Ridge Hill Farm
Park Hill Farm
Fir Tree Farm
Briars Bank Farm
A421
Cross Roads Farm
B4033
Warren Farm
Bacon House Farm
The Common
Fir Tree Farm
NASH RD
The Manor Farm
Little Horwood Manor
Manor Farm
Sch
CHURCH LA
THE GREEN
HIGH ST
LITTLE HORWOOD RD
Sunnyhill
WILLOW RD
WESTERN RD
THE CLOSE
TOWNSEND COTTS
Caravan Park
CHURCH ST
Moat
Woodend Farm
Wigwell
GREENWAY
Great Horwood
Sewage Works
SPRING LA
Hill Farm
The Old Crown (PH)
Little Horwood
Wood End
MURSLEY RD
WINSLOW RD
Greenway Farm
Home Farm
4
33
3
32
2
31
1
30
78
79

66
56

55
45

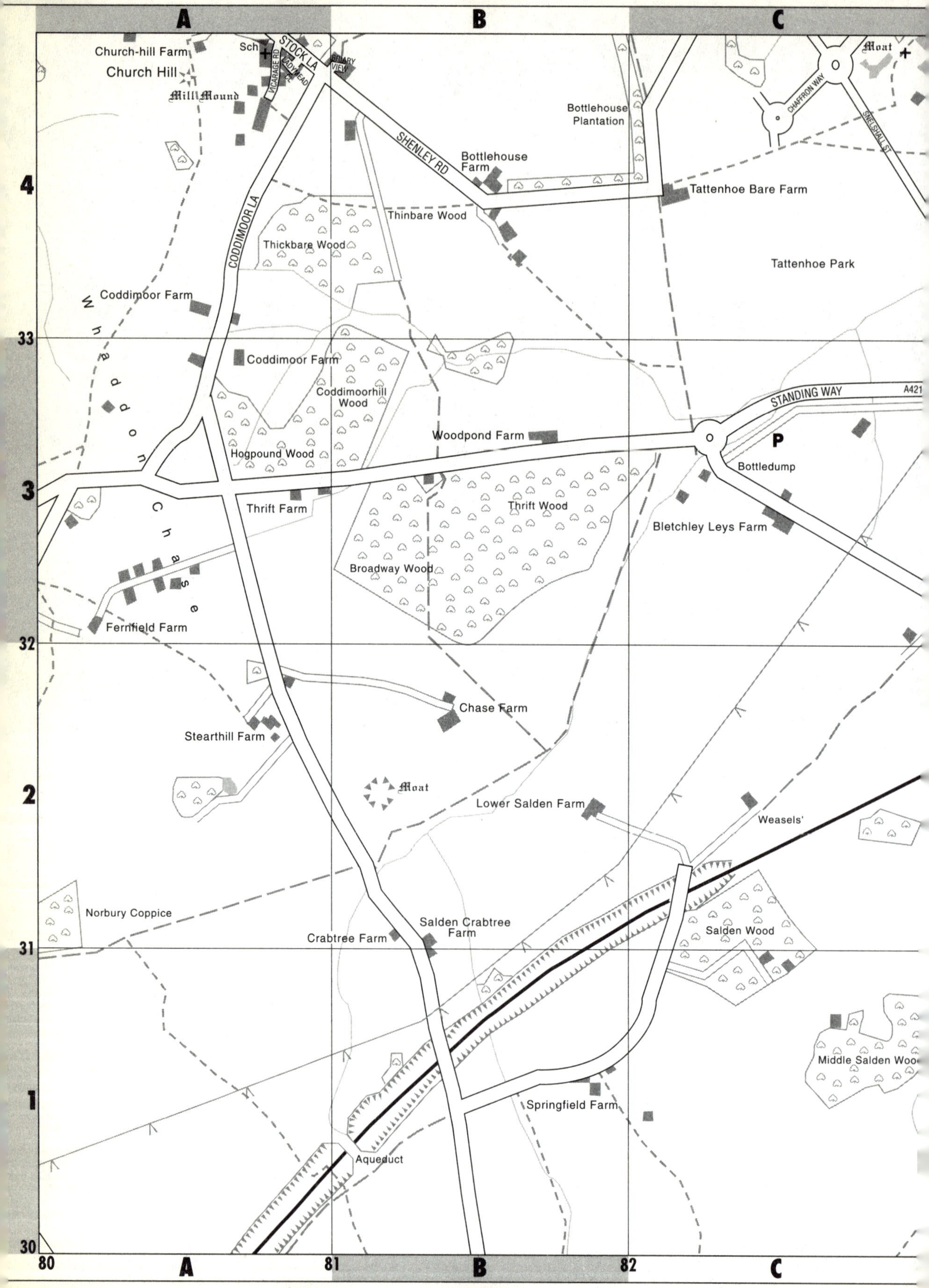
A
B
C
Church-hill Farm
Church Hill
Mill Mound
Sch
STOCK LA
VICARAGE RD
LADYMEAD CL
BRIARY VIEW
SHENLEY RD
Bottlehouse Farm
Bottlehouse Plantation
CHAFFRON WAY
SNELSHALL ST
Moat
Tattenhoe Bare Farm
Thinbare Wood
Thickbare Wood
CODDIMOOR LA
Tattenhoe Park
Coddimoor Farm
Whaddon Chase
Coddimoor Farm
Coddimoorhill Wood
STANDING WAY
A421
Woodpond Farm
Hogpound Wood
P
Bottledump
Thrift Farm
Thrift Wood
Bletchley Leys Farm
Broadway Wood
Fernfield Farm
Chase Farm
Stearthill Farm
Moat
Lower Salden Farm
Weasels'
Norbury Coppice
Salden Crabtree Farm
Crabtree Farm
Salden Wood
Middle Salden Woo
Springfield Farm
Aqueduct
4
33
3
32
2
31
1
30
80
81
82

46
58

D
E
F
Tattenhoe
Tattenhoe Hall Farm
Water Spinney
Golf Course
CH
PORTMARNOCK CL 1
MUIRFIELD DR 2
STANDING WAY
SNELSHALL ST
A421
B4034
WEASEL LA
Weasel Lane
The Leys
BUCKINGHAM RD
WHADDON WAY
TATTENHOE LA
School
Sch
Rickley Park
SHENLEY RD
SHENEY RD
CRAIGMORE AVE
DOVER GATE
CHURCH GREEN RD
CHURCH WLK
TENNYSON GR
KEATS WAY
SHELLEY DR
SELBOURNE AVE
NEWTON RD
ST MATTHEWS CT
WHITELEY CRES
ST GEORGE'S RD
ST CLEMENT'S DR
ST CATHERINE'S AVE
ST JOHN'S RD
ST DAVID'S RD
ST MARY'S AVE
CHELTENHAM GDNS
HIRSK GDNS
WINCANTON HILL
HAYDOCK CL
CARTMEL CL
HAMILTON LA
KEMPTON GDNS
SANDOWN CT
NEWBURY CT
FONTWELL DR
WETHERBY GDNS
WENTWORTH WAY
CARNOUSTIE CL
WINDMILL HILL DR
GLENEAGLES CL
WALTON HEATH
TATTENHOE LA
Brick Works
Clay Pit
BLETCHLEY RD
Recn Gd
Manor Farm
Park Manor Farm
Crooked Billet (PH)
Thick Thorn Farm
WHADDON RD
BERRY WAY
GREEN WAY
BONNARDS RD
BAY TREE CL
APPLECROFT
LONDON END
1 CHURCH END
2 PARADISE
3 THE CHASE
4 RED HOUSE CL
5 EIRE LA
HOME FARM
Litslade Farm
Manor House
MANOR RD
ST FAITH'S CL
COBB HALL
WARNERS RD
LILAC CL
IVY LA
MOORFIELD
BROOKFIELD RD
YEW TREE CL
WESTBROOK END
SCHOOL DR
CROFTS LA
ELM CL
CHESTNUT CL
POND CL
Newton Longville
STOKE RD
DRAYTON RD
Mound
Cowpasture Farm
Borough Farm
4
33
3
32
2
31
1
30
84
85

68
58

57 47

A
B
C
BLETCHLEY
Bletchley Station
College
Sta
Schs
Sch
PRINCES WAY
QUEENSWAY
BUCKINGHAM RD
CHURCH GREEN RD
RICKLEY LA
SHERWOOD DR
SAXON ST
WATER EATON RD
WESTFIELD RD
MANOR RD
EATON AVE
KNOWLES GREEN
CHESTNUT CRES
SAFFRON ST
HUNTER DR
BARTON RD
DRAYTON RD
STOKE RD
WINDERMERE DR
LOMOND DR
MELFORT DR
STRANGFORD DR
DIDDINGTON CL
B4034
A4146
HIGH ST
Watling Street
ROMAN ROAD
MAGIOVINIUM
Roman
Settlement
(site of)
Dropshort
Farm
APPLEBY HEATH
BRAMLEY GRANGE
Eaton Leys
Farm
River Ouzel
Grand Union Canal
Towing Path
Galleylane
Spinney
Clay Pit
Slad Farm
Willowbridge
Old Fox
Covert
Shaw Bridge
Villa
Stoke
House
Chadwell
Farm
Dairy
Farm
Weir
Rectory
Farm
Southlands
Farm
Sewage
Works
Burnell
Farm
4
3
2
1
33
32
31
30
86
87
88

57 69

48 60

D E F

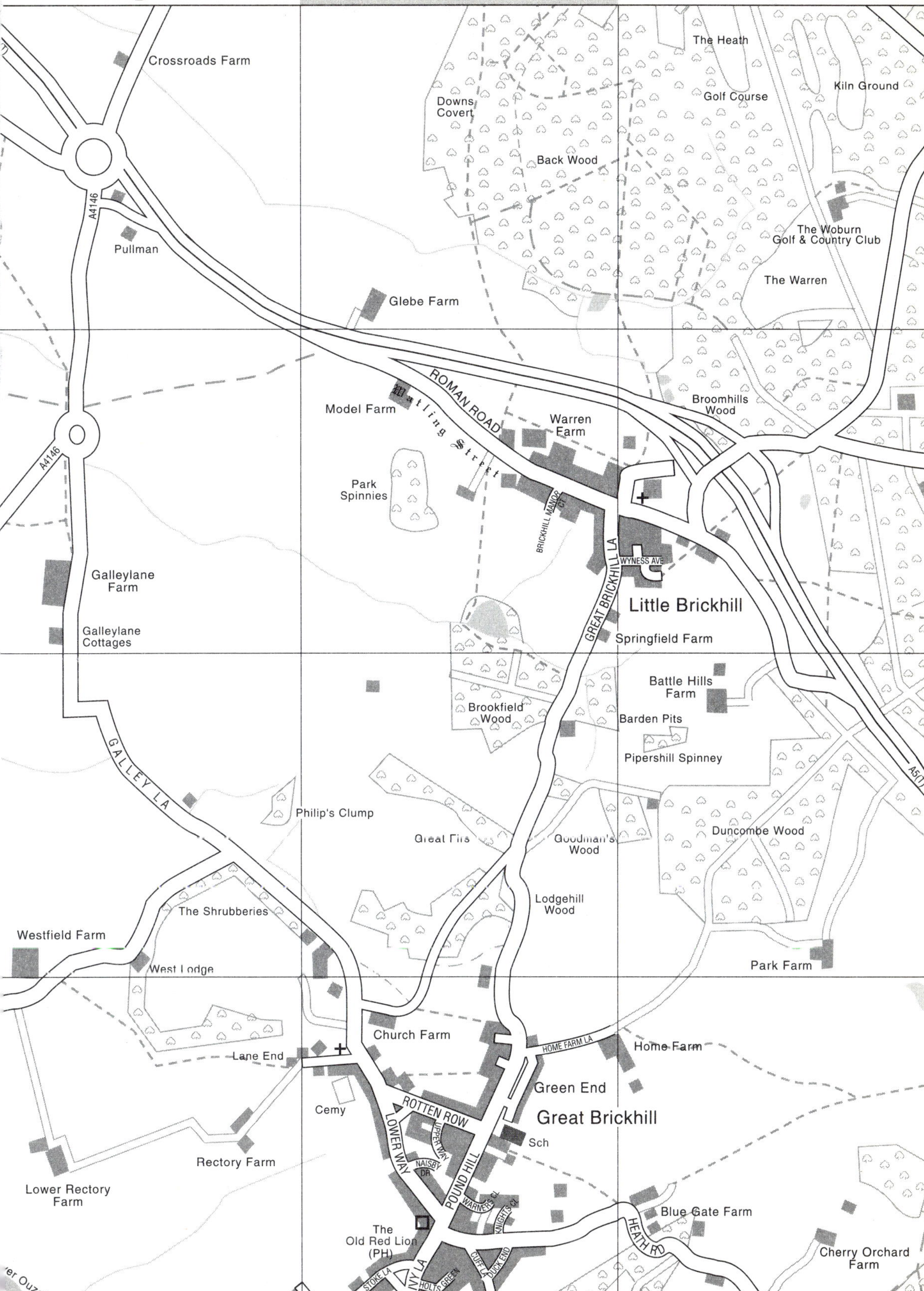

4 33 3 32 2 31 1 30

D 90 E 91 F

70 60

A
B
C
New Wavendon Heath
P
Bells Copse
Tollhouse Grove
Hundreds Farm
Little Brickhill Copse
Charle Wood
Shire Oak
Lowe's Wood
Job's Farm
Greensand Ridge Walk
Buttermilk Farm
Buttermilk Wood
Nun Wood
Apesfield Farm
Sheeplane Belt
Moat
Watling Street
ROMAN ROAD
Rammamere Farm
Bragenham Wood
King's Wood
Rammamere Heath
Heath
WOBURN RD
A418
A5(T)
Sheeplane
The Fox & Hounds (PH)
Bushycommon Wood
Hill Farm
Arnold's Cottages
A5130
WOBURN RD
Birchmoor Green
NEWPORT RD
Birchmoor Arms (PH)
Dolton's Farm
Horsemoor Farm
Woburn
CRAWLEY RD
DRAKELOE
ELEANOR CL
ELEANOR WLK
BEDFORD ST
A4102
CASWELL LA
MARQUIS CT
Church (remains of)
Sch
TH
TIMBER LA
College
LEIGHTON ST
F Sta
BLOOMSBURY CL
LONDON END
Wayn Close
Pinfold Pond
Pinfoldpond
Crowholt Plantation
Utcoate Grange
Circuitt's Covert
4
33
3
32
2
31
1
30
92
93
94

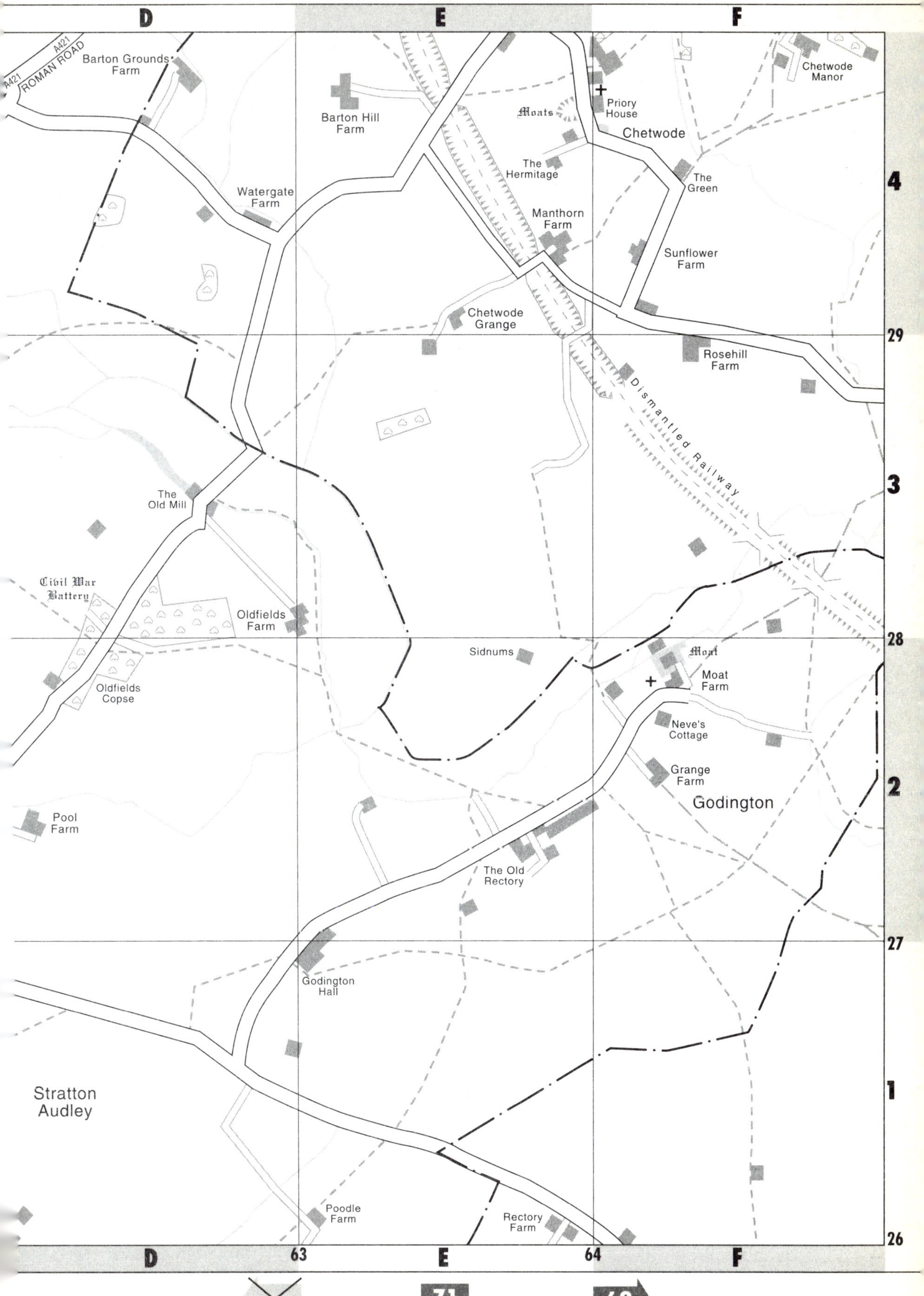
D
E
F
A421
ROMAN ROAD
Barton Grounds Farm
Barton Hill Farm
Moats
Priory House
Chetwode
Chetwode Manor
The Hermitage
The Green
Watergate Farm
Manthorn Farm
Sunflower Farm
Chetwode Grange
Rosehill Farm
Dismantled Railway
The Old Mill
Civil War Battery
Oldfields Farm
Sidnums
Moat
Moat Farm
Oldfields Copse
Neve's Cottage
Grange Farm
Godington
Pool Farm
The Old Rectory
Godington Hall
Stratton Audley
Poodle Farm
Rectory Farm
4
29
3
28
2
27
1
26
63
64

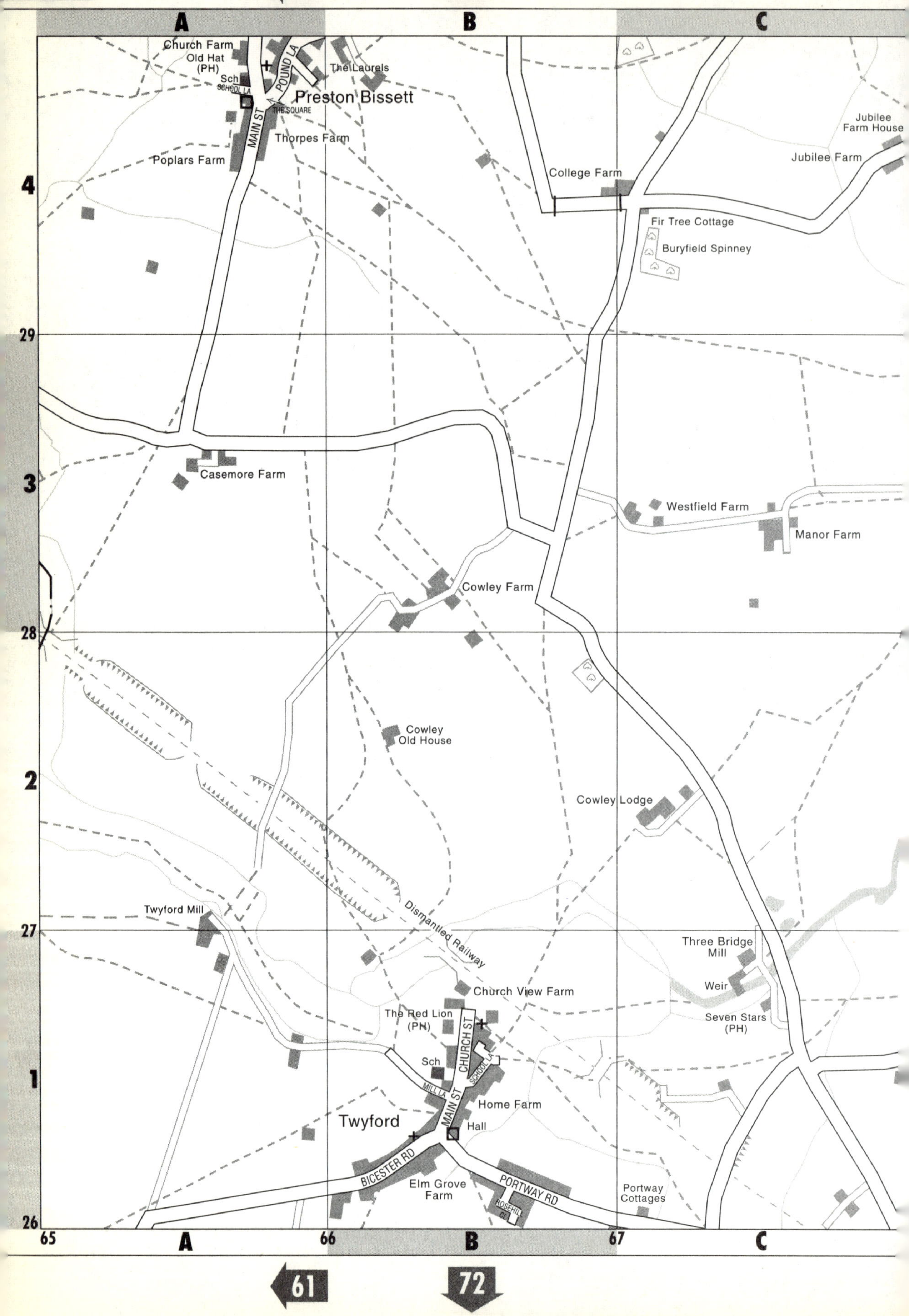
61
51
A
B
C
4
29
3
28
2
27
1
26
65
66
67
Church Farm
Old Hat
(PH)
Sch
SCHOOL LA
POUND LA
The Laurels
Preston Bissett
THE SQUARE
MAIN ST
Thorpes Farm
Poplars Farm
College Farm
Jubilee
Farm House
Jubilee Farm
Fir Tree Cottage
Buryfield Spinney
Casemore Farm
Westfield Farm
Manor Farm
Cowley Farm
Cowley
Old House
Cowley Lodge
Dismantled Railway
Twyford Mill
Three Bridge
Mill
Weir
Church View Farm
The Red Lion
(PH)
Seven Stars
(PH)
Sch
CHURCH ST
SCHOOL LA
MILL LA
MAIN ST
Home Farm
Twyford
Hall
BICESTER RD
Elm Grove
Farm
PORTWAY RD
ROSEHILL CL
Portway
Cottages
61
72

52
64

D
E
F
The Barracks
Brasses Spinney
Padbury Mill
Lower Farm
West Hill Farm
4
Orchard View
The Orchard
Claydon Brook
29
King's Bridge
Home Farm
Lower Kingsbridge Farm
Sch
CHURCH END
Hillesden
Kingsbridge Cottage
Ox House
Kingsbridge Farm
3
Church-hill Farm
Sewage Works
28
Padbury Brook
Northend Farm
Claydon Plank (FB)
2
North End
NORTH END RD
Steeple Claydon
PH
SPORTSMAN CL
OLD SCHOOL YD
Sch
CHESTNUT LEYS
ST MICHAEL'S WAY
BEECH LEYS
BUCKINGHAM RD
ROOKERY WAY
Elm Tree Farm
GREENWOOD PL
SYCAMORE LEYS
MEADOWAY
CHERRY LEYS
MOUNT PLEASANT
27
WEST ST
West End
CHALONERS HILL
VICARAGE CL
VICTORY RD
THE ISLAND
MAPLE LEYS
NIGHTINGALE CL
Liby
CHURCH VIEW
SPINNEY
Briarhill
ADDISON RD
QUEEN CATHERINE RD
Manor Farm
Hog Bridge
VICARAGE LA
Church End
Refuse Tip
Willowvale Farm
COBBETTS MOUNT
CORONATION PL
Camp Close
1
Redland Bridge
Pear Tree House
26
69
70

73
64

63
53

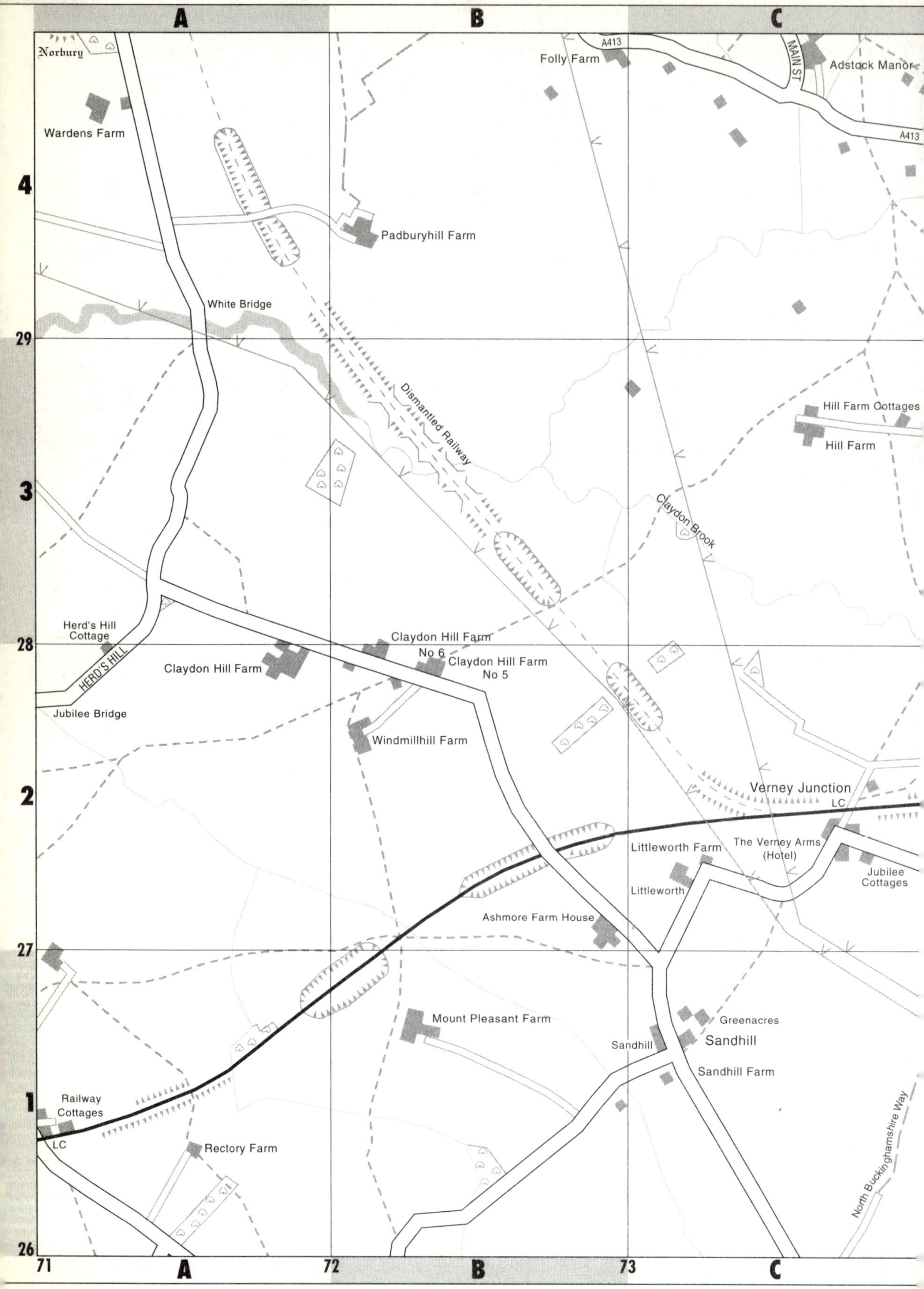
A
B
C
Norbury
Wardens Farm
Folly Farm
A413
MAIN ST
Adstock Manor
A413
4
Padburyhill Farm
White Bridge
29
Dismantled Railway
Hill Farm Cottages
Hill Farm
3
Claydon Brook
Herd's Hill Cottage
28
HERD'S HILL
Claydon Hill Farm
Claydon Hill Farm No 6
Claydon Hill Farm No 5
Jubilee Bridge
Windmillhill Farm
2
Verney Junction
LC
Littleworth Farm
The Verney Arms (Hotel)
Jubilee Cottages
Littleworth
Ashmore Farm House
27
Mount Pleasant Farm
Greenacres
Sandhill
Sandhill
Sandhill Farm
1
Railway Cottages
LC
Rectory Farm
North Buckinghamshire Way
26
71
72
73
A
B
C

63
74

D
E
F
Mill Farm
B4033
WINSLOW RD
Roddimore Stud
4
A413
Fox Covert
North Buckinghamshire Way
Jerico Farm
Roddimore Farm
GREAT HORWOOD RD
Washbrook
North Lake
Hanover Farm
29
Addington
Larch Covert
Keeper's Lodge
Redfield Farm
Seven Gables Lodge
Seven Gables
Five Gables
Brickyard Farm
The Rectory
Addington Manor
3
B4033
BUCKINGHAM RD
Woodwalk Cottages
FURZE LA
Sch
Bridge Farm
28
Bridge Farm Cottages
South Lake
F Sta
Sch
HIGH ST
Furzen Farm
VERNEY RD
VICARAGE RD
Glebe Farm
MISSENDEN RD
BURLEYS RD
HORN ST
Liby
A413
2
WESTERN LA
MARKET SQUARE
Claydon Brook
COURS LA VILLE CL
The Devil in the Boot (PH)
Tinkers End
27
Tuckey Covert
Tuckey Farm
GRANBOROUGH RD
Brook Farm
Sewage Works
1
Tuckey Cottage
Monkomb Farm
Berry Lees
Old Railway House
26
D
75
E
76
F

65
55

A
B
C
Greenway Farm
Mount Pleasant
The Hollows
Horwood House
Fishpond Spinney
Osierbed Spinney
4
29
Roddimore Covert
The White House
Moco Farm
Clare Farm
Canada
Foxhole Farm
TANK HOUSE RD
THE SPINNEY
MAGPIE WAY
RUDDS CL
STATION RD
OLD MILL FURLONG
SCOTT EVANS CT
LOWNDES WAY
LONGLANDS CT
LONGLANDS WLK
KEACH CL
LAMBORNS WAY
MEETING OAK LA
OFFAS LA
BEAMISH WAY
3
Spring Corner
Dodley Hill Farm
Redhall Farm
Abovemead Farm
Sch
28
P
CRICKETERS ROW
OAK WAY
ELMFIELDS GATE
DOVE HOUSE CL
NORTH CR OFF
FAIR MEADOW
GREYHOUND LA
ELMSIDE
COPSE GATE
Hall
Winslow
Ivy Farm
Duck End
A413
SHEEP ST
Shipton Mead Farm
2
HAWKINS LA
DENE CL
Sch
B4032
Rands Farm
Jubilee Cottages
Shipton
B4032
WINSLOW
Shipton Farm
Swanbourne House School
27
Shipton Bridge
Claydon Brook
1
Haybush Farm
Bennett's Hill
North Hill Farm
A413
26
77
78
79
A
B
C

65
76

56
68

D
E
F
Lower Grove Farm
The Wychwood Stud
Salden
Salden House Farm
WHADDON RD
4
Grove Lodge
Station Fields
Station House
Spring Grove Farm
STATION RD
Reservoir
Water Tower
TOWER COTTS
Mast
29
THE LANE
Mursley
The Green Man (PH)
Sch
MAIN ST
Manor Farm
COOKS LA
Church Hill
MARYS CL
THE BEECHAMS
CHURCH LA
3
Church Hill Farm
Moat
Cedars Farm
B4032
Lower Church Farm
Richmond Lodge
28
SWANBOURNE RD
Sharndown
STEWKLEY LA
Ashdean Farm
Nordens Farm
Cold Harbour
STATION RD
2
Sch
Church Farm
WINSLOW RD
Swan Inn (PH)
MURSLEY RD
Deverells Farm
B4032
Ridgeway Cotts
TATHAMS LA
Swanbourne
Nearton End
Nearton End Farm
Cemy
Athawes Farm
Hensmans Farm
Brook Farm
Brises Farm
27
1
Claydon Brook
26
0
D
81
E
82
F

77
68

67
57

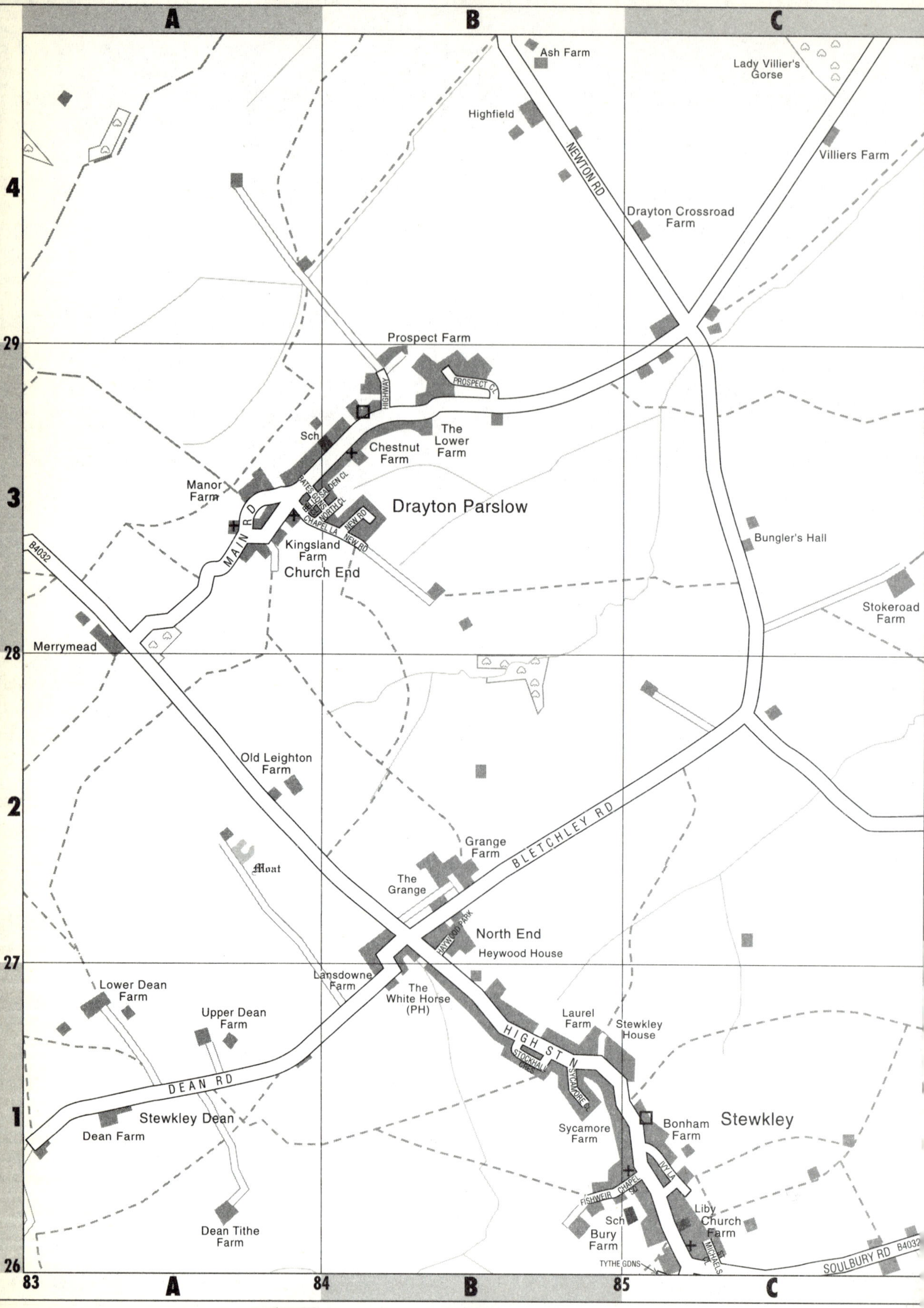
A
B
C
4
3
2
1
29
28
27
26
83
84
85
Ash Farm
Lady Villier's Gorse
Highfield
Villiers Farm
NEWTON RD
Drayton Crossroad Farm
Prospect Farm
HIGHWAY
PROSPECT CL
Sch
Chestnut Farm
The Lower Farm
Manor Farm
BATES GDNS
SELDEN CL
NORTH CL
CHAPEL LA
NEW RD
Drayton Parslow
MAIN RD
Kingsland Farm
Church End
Bungler's Hall
B4032
Stokeroad Farm
Merrymead
Old Leighton Farm
BLETCHLEY RD
Grange Farm
Moat
The Grange
HAYWOOD PARK
North End
Heywood House
Lansdowne Farm
The White Horse (PH)
Lower Dean Farm
Upper Dean Farm
Laurel Farm
Stewkley House
HIGH ST N
STOCKHALL CRES
SYCAMORE CL
DEAN RD
Stewkley Dean
Dean Farm
Sycamore Farm
Bonham Farm
Stewkley
IVY LA
FISHWEIR
CHAPEL SQ
Sch
Bury Farm
Dean Tithe Farm
Liby
Church Farm
TYTHE GDNS
MICHAELS
SOULBURY RD
B4032

67
78

D
E
F
Stoke Hammond Lock
Grove Farm
A4146
SCHOOL LA
TYRELLS RD
TYRELLS GDNS
Swing Bridge
Fairfields
NEWTOWN RD
CHURCH RD
GADSDEN CT
FENNY RD
Stoke Hammond
Tyrells Manor
HILLERSDON CHASE
APPLEACRES
LODGE LA
OLDE BELL CL
Sch
Grand Union Canal
BRAGENHAM SIDE
Oak Farm
LEIGHTON RD
The Dolphin (PH)
Dorcas Farm
Soulbury Ground Farm
Longfield
A4146
Dean Farm
Kings Farm
DEAN FARM LA
Spring Farm
Rislip Farm
Upper Hollingdon Farm
Hollingdon
Wellmead Farm
Hollingdon Farm
Holly Bar Farm
Hill Farm
Grove Farm
ANDREWS CL
B4032
Soulbury
THE MEAD
MOUNT PLEASANT
CHAPEL HILL
HOLLINGDON RD
Red Lion (PH)
CHURCH LA
The Boot (PH)
STEWKLEY RD
HIGH RD
Manor Farm
Larkshill Farm
LEIGHTON RD
B4032
Vicarage Farm
Durrance Farm
Winscott Farm
The Lodge
Llscombe Park
B4032
SOULBURY RD
Soulbury Road Farm
The Plantation
4
29
3
28
2
27
1
26
86
87
88

A
B
C
Sewage Works
Stockgrove Farm
Ivy Lane Farm
River Ouzel
IVY LA
Sch
4
Greensand Ridge Walk
Paper Mill
Partridge Hill
Furze Hill
Oak Wood
Stockgrove Country Park
29
Partridge House
Upper Kiln Farm
Kiln Farm
Red Bridge
Bragenham Farm
Bragenham
BRAGENHAM LA
Shire Oak
Three Locks (PH)
3
A4146
Rushmere Park
Stapleford Mill
Stapleford Farm
Picnic Area
Ludley Cottage
28
LINSLADE RD
Grand Union Canal
River Ouzel
Nares Gadley Farm
Rushmere
Golf Course
2
THE HEATH
HEATH CT
DUKES RIDE
Club House
Chelmscote Manor Farm
Broad Oak
Grange Mill
PLANTATION RD
SANDY LA
REDWOOD GLADE
OLD LINSLADE RD
27
Old Linslade Manor
Old Linslade
TAYLORS RIDE
DINGLE DELL
Corbettshill Farm
1
Dollar Farm
B4032
LEIGHTON RD
STOKE RD
GLOBE LA
Swing Bridge
Linslade Wood
Sewage Works
B4032
A4146
BOSSINGTON LA
THE MARTINS DR
26
89
90
91

61
72

D
E
F
Poodle Gorse
Rectory Farm
Wd Pp
Sow & Pigs (PH)
Hill View Farm
Wireless Station
Lower Farm
Home Farm
Poundon
Manor Farm
Poundon House
Sewage Works
Poundon Hill
Beacon Hill
Hare Leys Farm
Field Farm
Rhonhill Barn
Rhon Hill
Kensington Villas
Westbury Court Farm
STATION RD
The College
MILLFIELD AVE
MILLFIELD CL
Marsh Gibbon
RECTORY CL
Sch
Manor Ho
CASTLE ST
SUFFOLK CT
CHURCH ST
Box Farm
Folly Farm
BICESTER RD
EDGE
The Plough (PH)
Pear Tree Farm
TOMPKINS LA
STILES
WEST EDGE
MOAT LA
CLEMENTS LA
Cemy
Town's End
TOWNSEND
WHALES LA
SPIER'S LA
Towns End Farm
Priory Farm
SCOTTS LA
Sewage Works
The Leverets
4
25
3
24
2
23
1
22
63
64

81
72

71
62

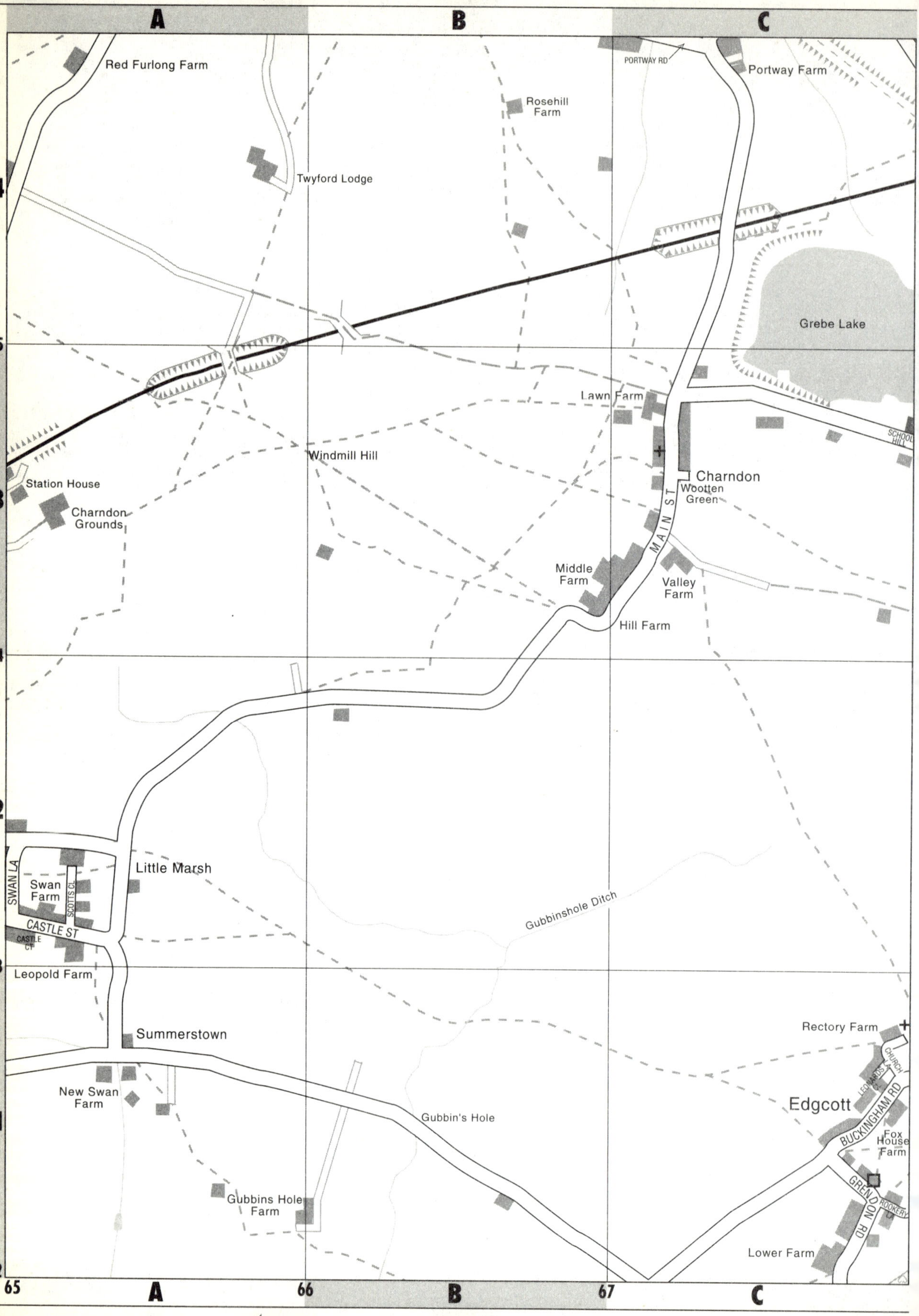
A
B
C
Red Furlong Farm
PORTWAY RD
Portway Farm
Rosehill Farm
Twyford Lodge
4
Grebe Lake
25
Lawn Farm
SCHOOL HILL
Windmill Hill
Station House
Charndon
Wootten Green
3
Charndon Grounds
MAIN ST
Middle Farm
Valley Farm
Hill Farm
24
2
SWAN LA
Swan Farm
SCOTTS CL
Little Marsh
CASTLE ST
CASTLE CT
Gubbinshole Ditch
23
Leopold Farm
Rectory Farm
Summerstown
CHURCH
LEONARDS CT
BUCKINGHAM RD
New Swan Farm
Edgcott
1
Gubbin's Hole
Fox House Farm
GRENDON RD
ROOKERY CT
Gubbins Hole Farm
Lower Farm
22
65
A
66
B
67
C

71
82

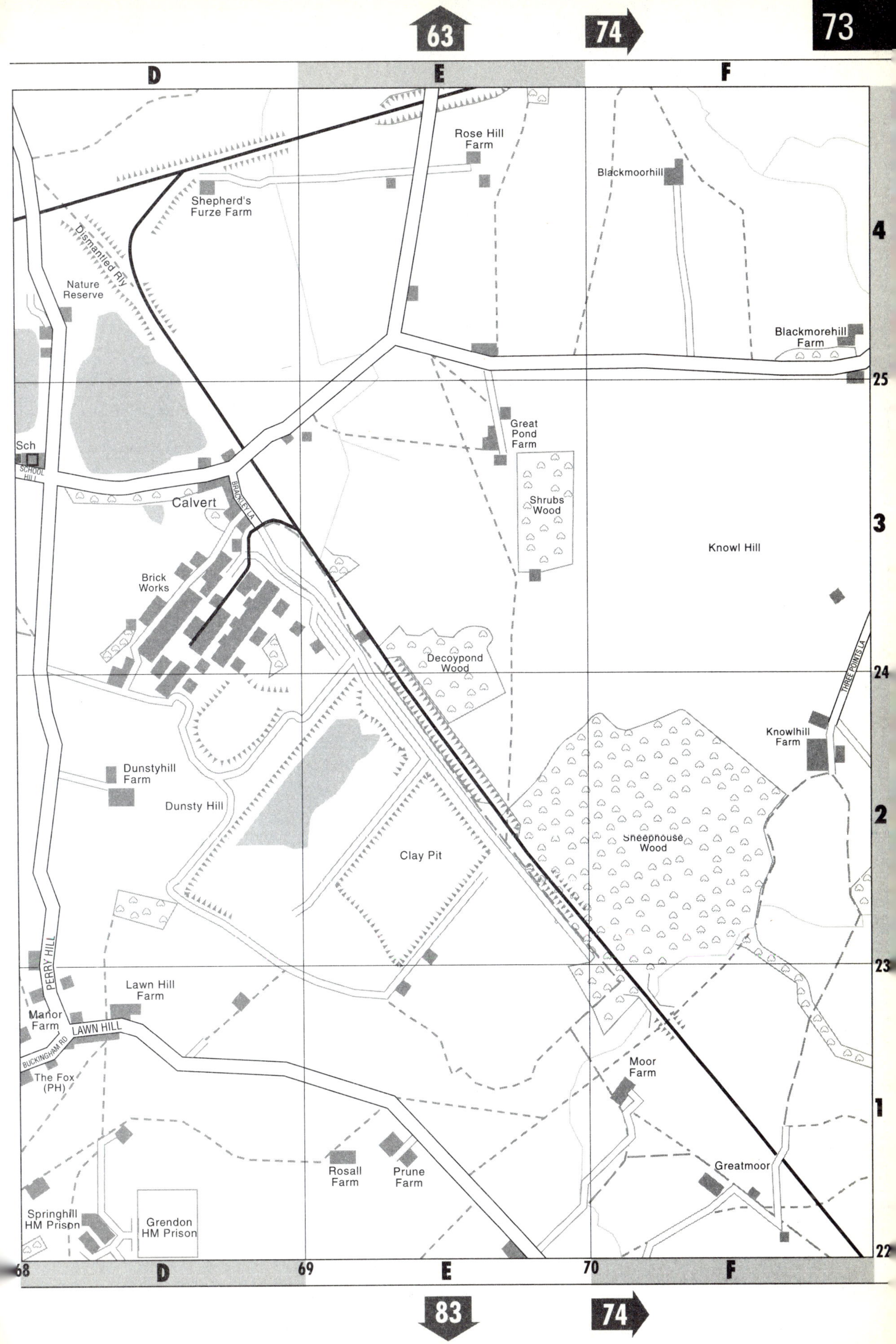
63
74
D
E
F
Rose Hill Farm
Blackmoorhill
Shepherd's Furze Farm
Dismantled Rly
Nature Reserve
Blackmorehill Farm
Great Pond Farm
Sch
SCHOOL HILL
Calvert
BRACKLEY LA
Shrubs Wood
Knowl Hill
Brick Works
Decoypond Wood
THREE POINTS LA
Knowlhill Farm
Dunstyhill Farm
Dunsty Hill
Sheephouse Wood
Clay Pit
PERRY HILL
Lawn Hill Farm
Manor Farm
LAWN HILL
BUCKINGHAM RD
The Fox (PH)
Moor Farm
Greatmoor
Rosall Farm
Prune Farm
Springhill HM Prison
Grendon HM Prison
4
25
3
24
2
23
1
22
68
69
70
83
74

A
B
C
Home Farm
Cemy
Middle Claydon
New Farm
SANDHILL RD
Verney Farm
VERNEY FARM CL
EMERALD CL
CHURCH WAY
ST MARYS CL
CHESTNUT VIEW
East Claydon
Weir
The Old Brick Yard
(disused)
Claydon Park
Claydon House
Catherine Farm
ST MARYS RD
Ivy Nook
Sch
Botolph Farm
South Lodge
Phoenix
Fruit Farm
BOTYL RD
Botolph Farm
Botolph Claydon
ORCHARD WAY
WEIR LA
THREE POINTS LA
Bernwood Farm
Home Wood
Muxwell Farm
Claydon Lawn
Romer Wood
Hogshaw Farm
Runt's Wood
Balmore Wood
Coppice
Lowhill Farm
Three Points La
Hogshaw Farm
Greatsea Wood
Moat
Finemerehill House
Kitehill Farm
4
25
3
24
2
23
1
22
71
72
73

D
E
F
Electricity
Sub-Station
Millknob
Hill
BATES CL
Granborough
WINSLOW RD
HOLLOW HILL END
Rookery
Farm
Ley House
Farm
GREEN END
CHURCH LA
DENHAM VIEW
PARK RD
Sion Hill
Farm
4
25
HOGSHAW RD
MARSTON RD
3
Hogshaw Road
Farm
Wings
Farm
North Buckinghamshire Way
Lower
Farm
24
2
Middlo
Farm
Dismantled Railway
Sewage
Works
23
Brook
Farm
QUAINTON RD
Hill End
Farm
Fulbrook
House
Carters Lane
Farm
Fulbrook
Farm
SWAN'S WAY
CARTERS LA
1
Moat
Quainton Hill
Stonehill
Farm
Hogshaw Hill
Farm
Manor
Farm
22
D
75
E
76
F

75
66

A
B
C
4
3
2
1
25
24
23
22
77
78
79
A413
BENNETT'S HILL
North Hill Farm
Swan's Way
Oakham Farm
Holcombe Cottages
Christmas Gorse
Green End
GREEN END
Lower Green End Farm
Grange Farm
Green End Farm
Buxlow Farm
The Neptune Farm
Lathwells Farm
Maynes Hill Farm
Marstonfields Farm
The Bungalow
Crandon Farm
Buttermilkhall Farm
Guy's Thorns
Stevens Farm
GRANBOROUGH RD
GIBBINGS CL
Church Hill Farm
QUAINTON RD
HILL FARM
The Bell (PH)
School
MARSTONFIELDS RD
SHEPPERDS CL
CARTERS MEADOW
HIGH ST
SCHOOL HILL
Townsend
CHURCH ST
Glebe Farm
Manor Farm
North Marston
NORTON CL
SCHORNE LA
Burnaby Farm
PORTWAY
Ramhill Farm
PULPIT LA
MEADWAY

75
86

D E F

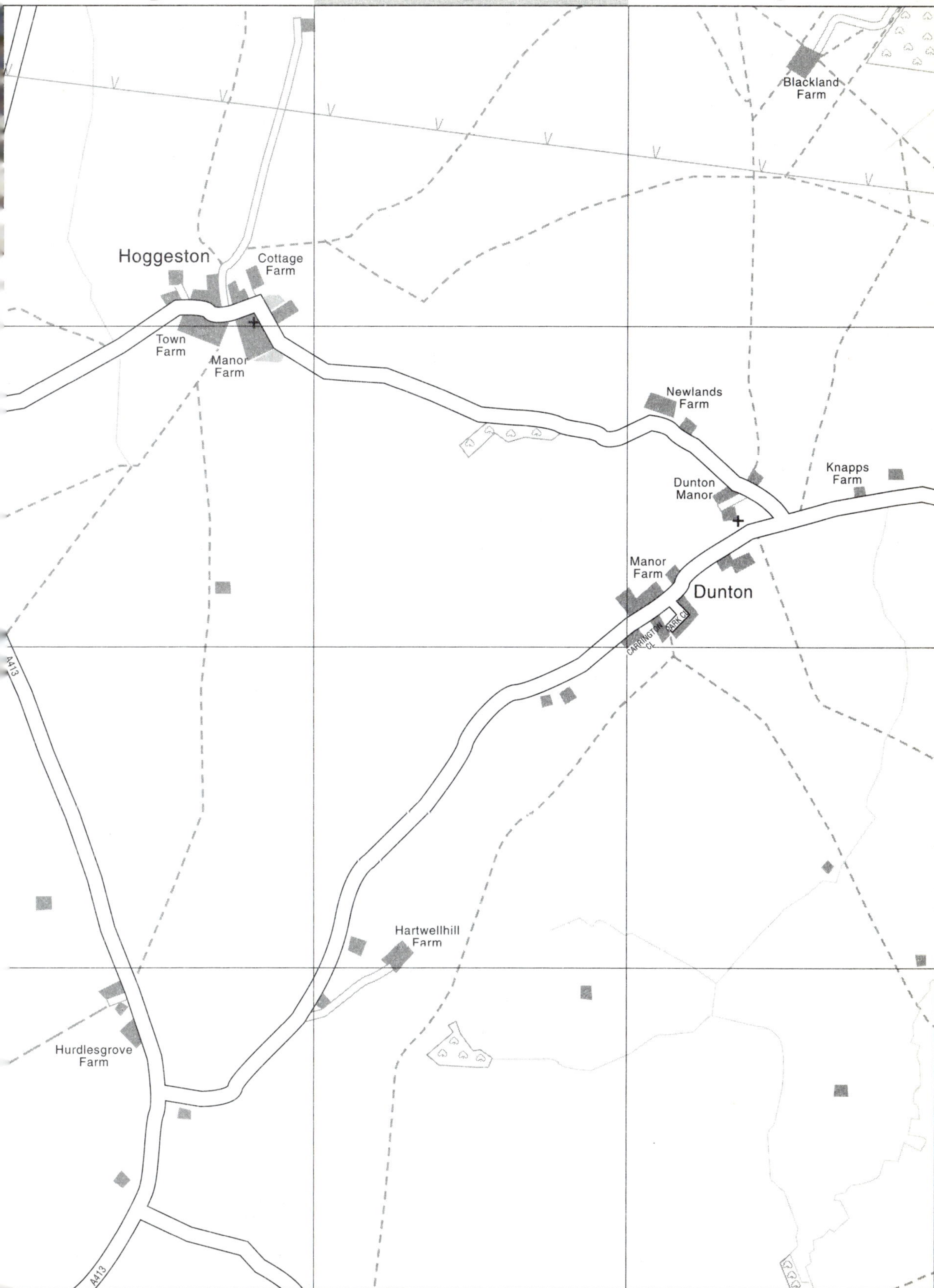
Hoggeston
Cottage Farm
Town Farm
Manor Farm
Blackland Farm
Newlands Farm
Knapps Farm
Dunton Manor
Manor Farm
Dunton
CARRINGTON CL
PARK CL
A413
Hartwellhill Farm
Hurdlesgrove Farm
A413
4
25
3
24
2
23
1
22

D 81 E 82 F

77
68

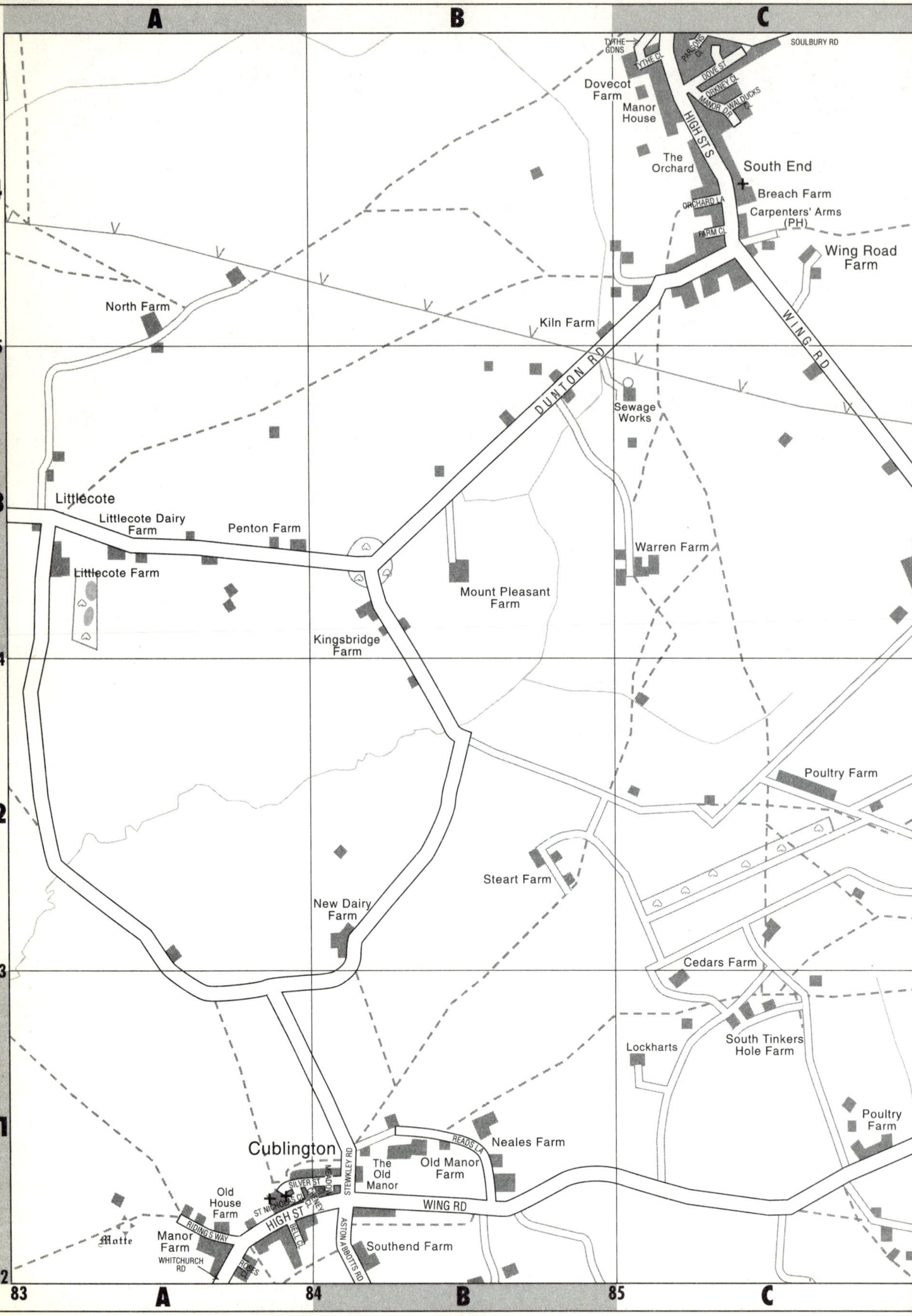
A
B
C
4
25
3
24
2
23
1
22
83
84
85
TYTHE GDNS
TYTHE CL
PARSONS CL
DOVE ST
ORKNEY CL
MANOR DR
WALDUCKS CL
SOULBURY RD
Dovecot Farm
Manor House
HIGH ST S
The Orchard
South End
Breach Farm
ORCHARD LA
Carpenters' Arms (PH)
FARM CL
Wing Road Farm
North Farm
Kiln Farm
WING RD
DUNTON RD
Sewage Works
Littlecote
Littlecote Dairy Farm
Penton Farm
Littlecote Farm
Warren Farm
Mount Pleasant Farm
Kingsbridge Farm
Poultry Farm
Steart Farm
New Dairy Farm
Cedars Farm
Lockharts
South Tinkers Hole Farm
Poultry Farm
Cublington
Neales Farm
READS LA
The Old Manor
Old Manor Farm
STEWKLEY RD
SILVER ST
ST NICHOLAS CL
Old House Farm
HIGH ST
BELL CL
RIDINGS WAY
Manor Farm
WHITCHURCH RD
ROSES CL
Motte
WING RD
ASTON ABBOTTS RD
Southend Farm

77
88

D
E
F
Walducks Farm
Home Farm
Liscombe House
Liscombe Park
4
Blackend Spinney
Ash Farm
Rocklane Farm
25
Burcott Lodge Farm
3
Soulbury Road Farm
Fox Covert
Poultry Farm
Burcott Hall Farm
24
Mount Pleasant Farm
SOULBURY RD
Burcott
HIGH ST
Long Spinney
STEWKLEY RD
Kemsall Wood
2
HAWTHORNE WAY
MEADOW WAY
MOORLANDS
WILLOW WAY
RIDGE WAY
CHESTERFIELD CRES
LITTLEWORTH
MOORHILLS RD
MOORLANDS RD
WILLIAM BANDY CL
COTTESLOE CL
CASTLE CL
DORMER AVE
WANTAGE CRES
WOODMAN CL
COATES WAY
MOORHILLS CRES
WANTAGE CL
Glebe Farm
23
A418
STEWKLEY RD
Liby
LEIGHTON RD
WELL LA
Glebe Close Farm
Castle Hill
Cottesloe
REDWOOD DR
REDWOOD CL
WARWICK
ROTHSCHILD RD
GEORGE ST
HIGH ST
Wing
VICARAGE LA
PROSPECT PL
Old Park
A418
Schs
CHURCH ST
NEWLANDS GDNS
EVELYN CL
1
PARK GATE
Schs
AYLESBURY RD
Lower Ascott
Wing Park Farm
A418
22
D
87
E
88
F

79 70

A
B
C
Hop Gardens
Milebush Farm
B4032
Valley Farm
Linslade
Sch
SOULBURY RD
DERWENT RD
Rock Lane
HIMLEY GREEN
BUNKERS LA
Southcourt Stud Farm
Leighton Buzzard Station
LEIGHTON BUZZARD
Grand Union Canal
STOKE RD
A4146
A418 LEIGHTON RD
Amb Sta
River Ouzel
A505
B488
Waterloo Farm
Ascott Kennels
Grimstone's Furze
Whitefields
Ascott Home Farm
Chelsea Clump
Grove Lock
Sand Pit
Ascott
Round Spinney
Ascott House
WELL LA
Well Lane Dairy
Chucksell's Spinney
Hare & Hounds (PH)
Grove House Stud
4
25
3
24
2
23
1
22
89
90
91

71 82

D
E
F
Marsh Field Farm
Yew Elm Farm
Furze Ground
4
Essex Farm
21
Heet Farm
Grange Farm
3
Blackthorn
A41(T)
Akeman Street
ROMAN ROAD
Heath Bridge
River Ray
Weir Farm
WEIR LA
20
Westbury Farm
A41(T)
Leaches Farm
LOWER RD
STATION RD
Elm Tree Farm
Lower Cow Leys Farm
2
BLACKTHORN CL
Shaw's Farm
THAME RD
Royal Oak (PH)
Piddington Cow Leys
Middle Cow Leys Farm
B4011
19
Blackthorn Bridge
Bridge Farm
Upper Cow Leys Farm
Treadwell's Barn
New Farm
1
B4011
18
D
63
E
64
F

95 82

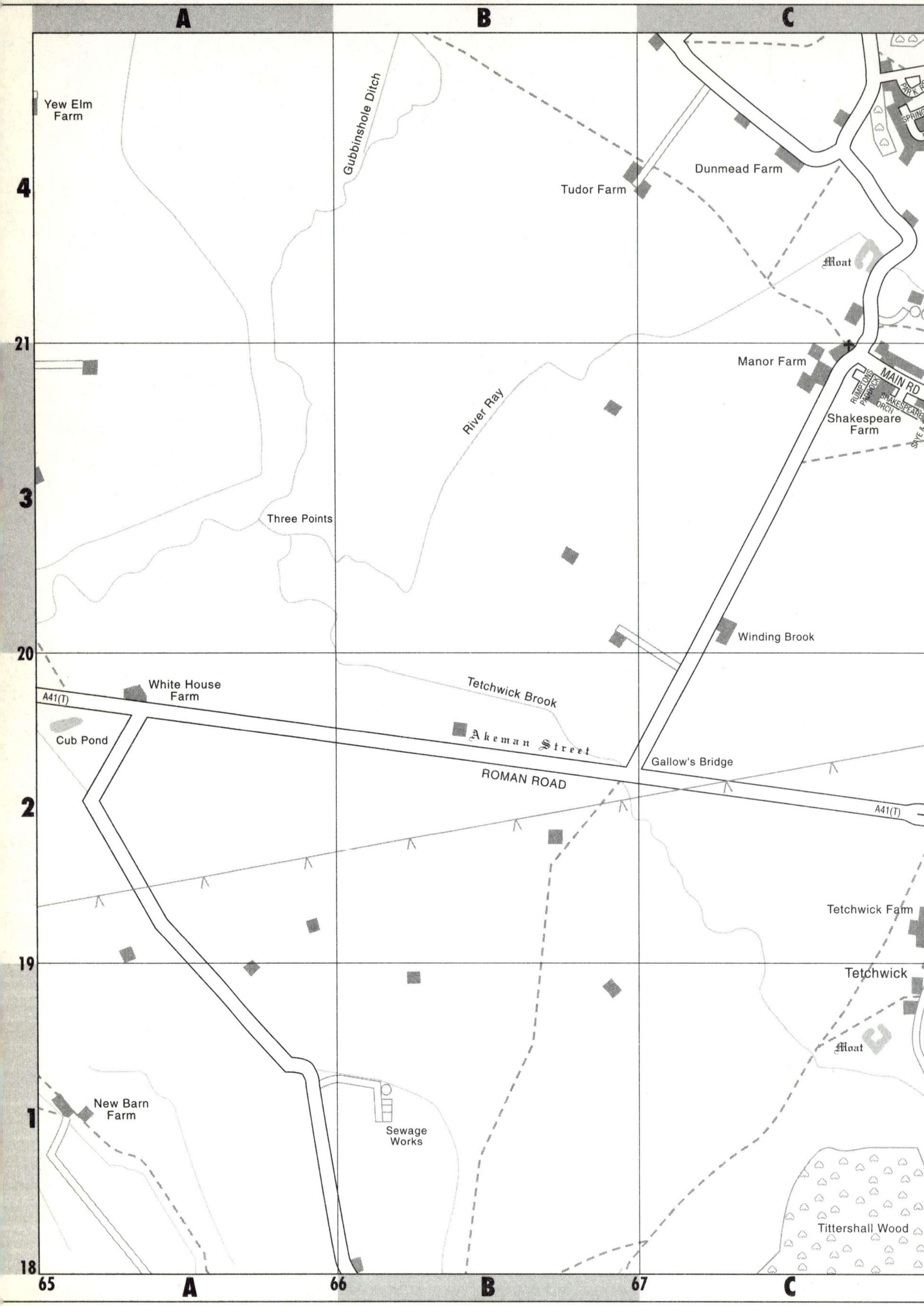
A
B
C
4
21
3
20
2
19
1
18
65
66
67
Yew Elm Farm
Gubbinshole Ditch
Tudor Farm
Dunmead Farm
PARK R
SPRING
Moat
Manor Farm
MAIN RD
RUMPTONS PADDOCK
SHAKESPEARE ORCH
SHAKESPEARE
Shakespeare Farm
River Ray
Three Points
Winding Brook
White House Farm
A41(T)
Cub Pond
Tetchwick Brook
Akeman Street
Gallow's Bridge
ROMAN ROAD
Tetchwick Farm
Tetchwick
Moat
New Barn Farm
Sewage Works
Tittershall Wood

73
84

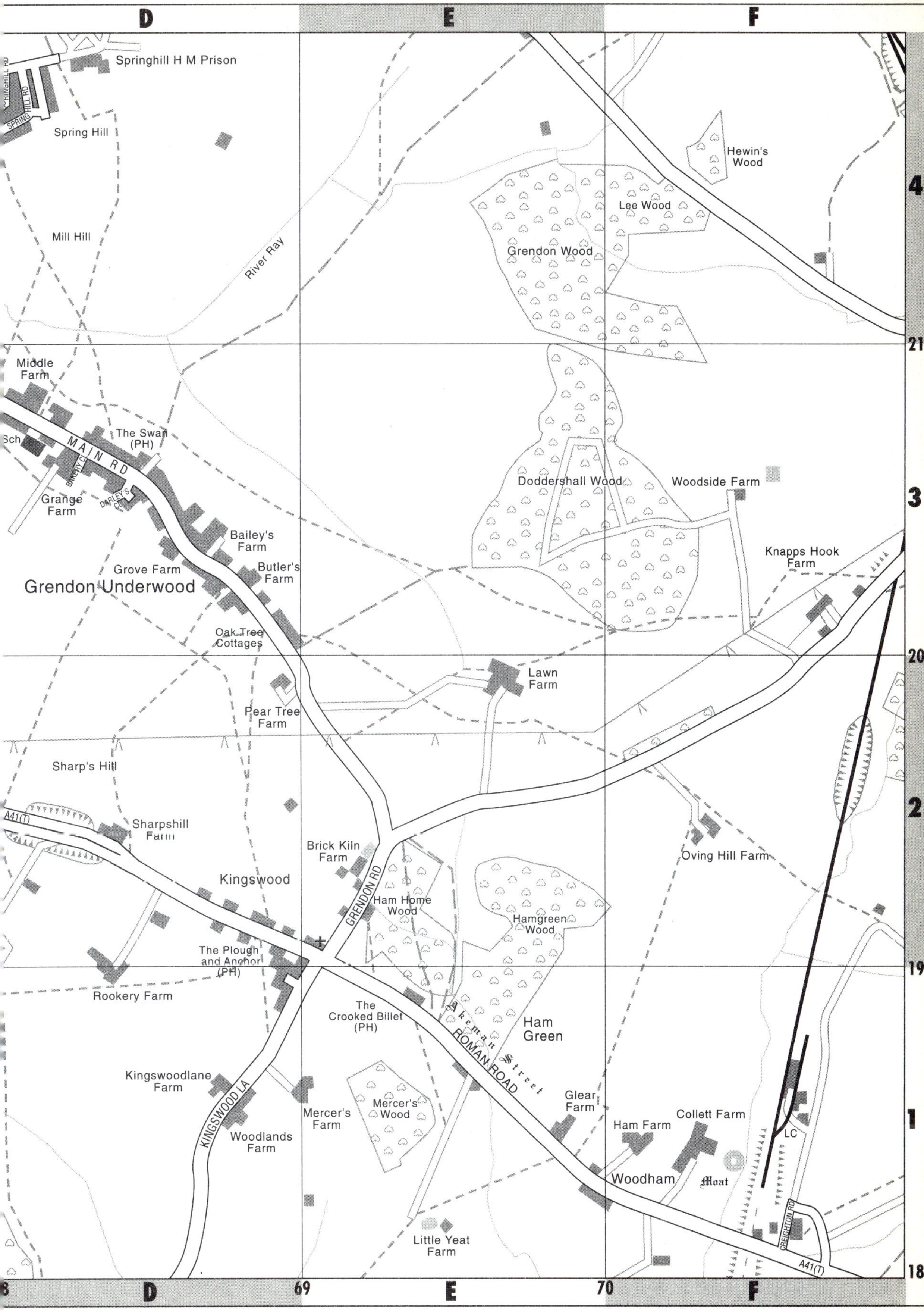
D
E
F
Springhill H M Prison
SPRINGHILL RD
SPRING HILL RD
Spring Hill
Mill Hill
River Ray
Hewin's Wood
Lee Wood
Grendon Wood
4
21
Middle Farm
Sch
MAIN RD
The Swan (PH)
BAKERY CL
Grange Farm
DARLEY'S CL
Bailey's Farm
Butler's Farm
Grove Farm
Grendon Underwood
Oak Tree Cottages
Doddershall Wood
Woodside Farm
3
Knapps Hook Farm
20
Lawn Farm
Pear Tree Farm
Sharp's Hill
A41(T)
Sharpshill Farm
Kingswood
Brick Kiln Farm
GRENDON RD
Ham Home Wood
Hamgreen Wood
Oving Hill Farm
2
The Plough and Anchor (PH)
Rookery Farm
19
The Crooked Billet (PH)
Akeman Street
ROMAN ROAD
Ham Green
Kingswoodlane Farm
KINGSWOOD LA
Woodlands Farm
Mercer's Farm
Mercer's Wood
Glear Farm
Ham Farm
Collett Farm
LC
1
Woodham
Moat
CREIGHTON RD
A41(T)
Little Yeat Farm
18
8
D
69
E
70
F

97
84

83
74

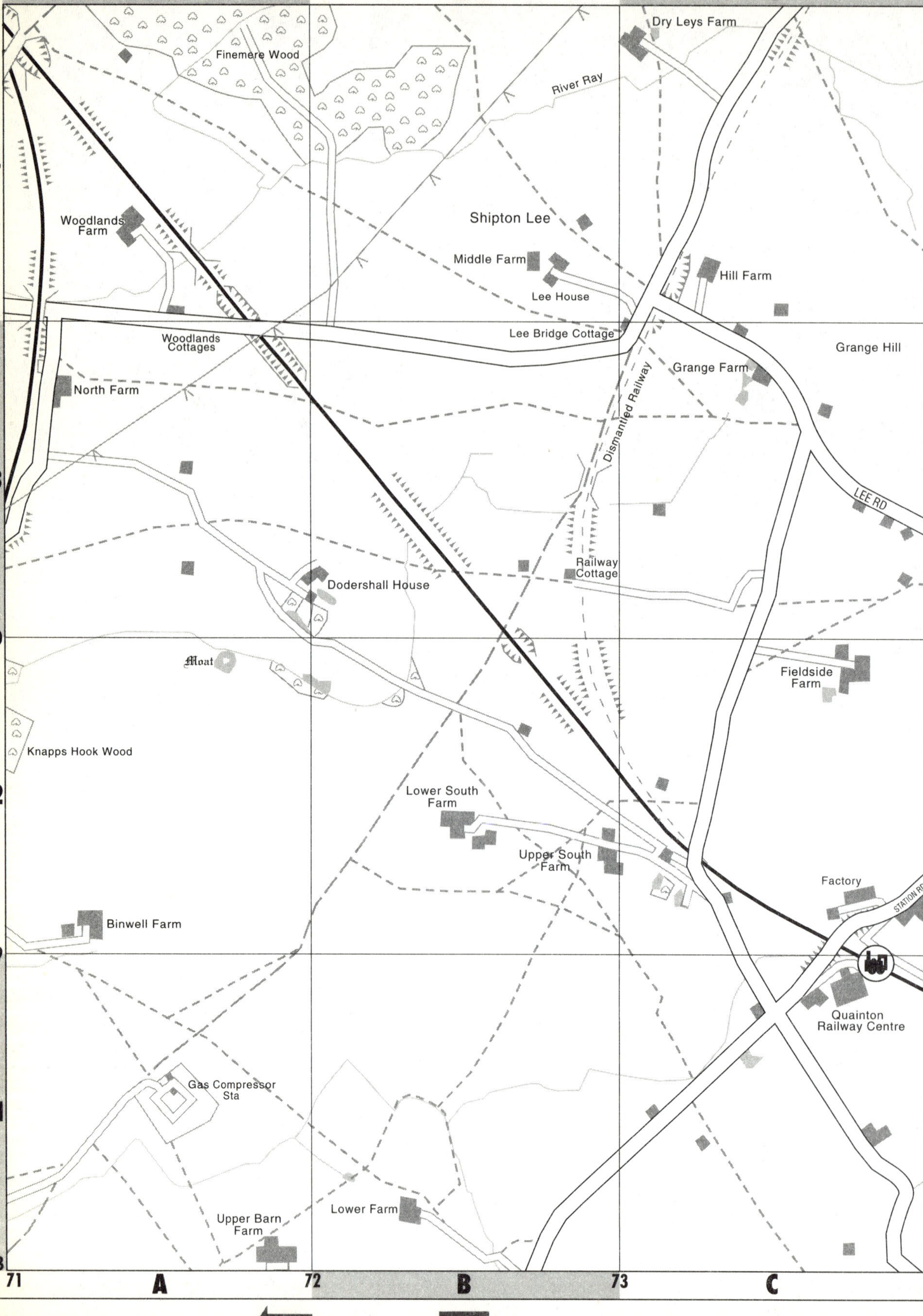
A
B
C
Dry Leys Farm
Finemere Wood
River Ray
4
Shipton Lee
Woodlands Farm
Middle Farm
Hill Farm
Lee House
21
Lee Bridge Cottage
Woodlands Cottages
Grange Hill
Grange Farm
North Farm
Dismantled Railway
3
LEE RD
Railway Cottage
Dodershall House
20
Moat
Fieldside Farm
Knapps Hook Wood
2
Lower South Farm
Upper South Farm
Factory
STATION RD
Binwell Farm
19
Quainton Railway Centre
Gas Compressor Sta
1
Upper Barn Farm
Lower Farm
18
71
72
73
A
B
C

83
98

D
E
F
Conduit Hill
Quainton Hill
Mast
Woad Hill
North Buckinghamshire Way
Denham Farm
Simber Hill
Denham Hill
Denham Leys
Denham Farm Cottage
Moat
Denham Lodge
Denham Hill Farm
Denham
CARTERS LA
Carters Lane Buildings
Lower Farm
Quainton
NORTH END RD
LEE RD
Windmill (dis)
Denham Cottages
Swans Way
UPPER ST
CHURCH ST
PH
PIGOTT ORCH
WINWOOD DR
Sch
THE GREEN
THE PYGHTLES
LOWER ST
CAUTLEY CL
THE STRAND
Ladymead Farm
Allot Gdns
Station Road Farm
The Willows
STATION RD
Sewage Works
North Buckinghamshire Way
Blackgrove Farm House
Lower Denham Farm
Blackgrove Farm
Blackgrove Covert
4
21
3
20
2
19
1
18
75
76

A
B
C
4
21
3
20
2
19
1
18
77
78
79
Bushy Farm
MEADWAY
Home Farm
Crossroads Farm
Oving
BOWLING ALLEY
THE PIGHTLE
Recreation Ground
Black Boy (PH)
Church Farm
CHURCH LA
STONE VIEW
Sch
ASHGROVE GDNS
MANOR RD
DARK LA
Oving House
GREEN ACRES CL
OVING RD
MT PLEASA
PITCHCOTT RD
Bunshill
Barrettstown Estates
MARKET H
Pitchcott Hill
Bolebec Castle (site of)
CASTLE
WEIR LA
Pitchcott Hill Farm
Pitchcott
Holbornhill Farm
Scotshill Farm
Manor Farm
Folly Farm
Upper Blackgrove Farm
Middle Blackgrove Farm
Cow Ground Buildings
Whitesfield Farm
Whitesfield Farm Cottages

77
88

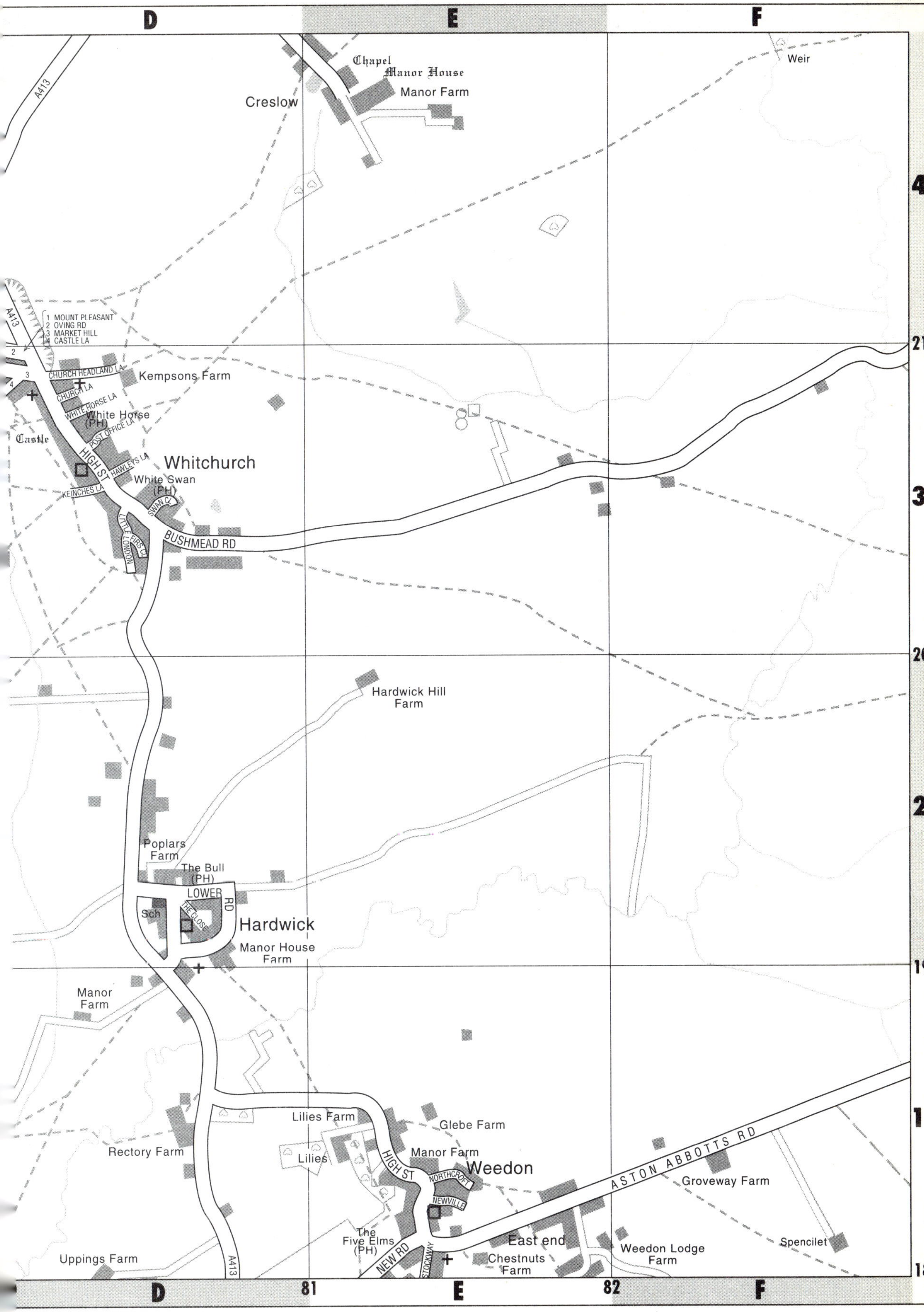
D
E
F
A413
Chapel
Manor House
Manor Farm
Creslow
Weir
4
1 MOUNT PLEASANT
2 OVING RD
3 MARKET HILL
4 CASTLE LA
21
CHURCH HEADLAND LA
Kempsons Farm
CHURCH LA
WHITE HORSE LA
White Horse
(PH)
POST OFFICE LA
Castle
HIGH ST
HAWLEYS LA
Whitchurch
KEINCHES LA
White Swan
(PH)
SWAN CL
LITTLE LONDON
LITTLE FIRS CT
BUSHMEAD RD
3
20
Hardwick Hill
Farm
2
Poplars
Farm
The Bull
(PH)
LOWER
RD
Sch
THE CLOSE
Hardwick
Manor House
Farm
19
Manor
Farm
1
Lilies Farm
Glebe Farm
Rectory Farm
Lilies
Manor Farm
HIGH ST
NORTHCROFT
Weedon
ASTON ABBOTTS RD
Groveway Farm
NEWVILLE
The
Five Elms
(PH)
East end
NEW RD
STOCKWAY
Chestnuts
Farm
Weedon Lodge
Farm
Spencilet
Uppings Farm
A413
18
D
81
E
82
F

101
88

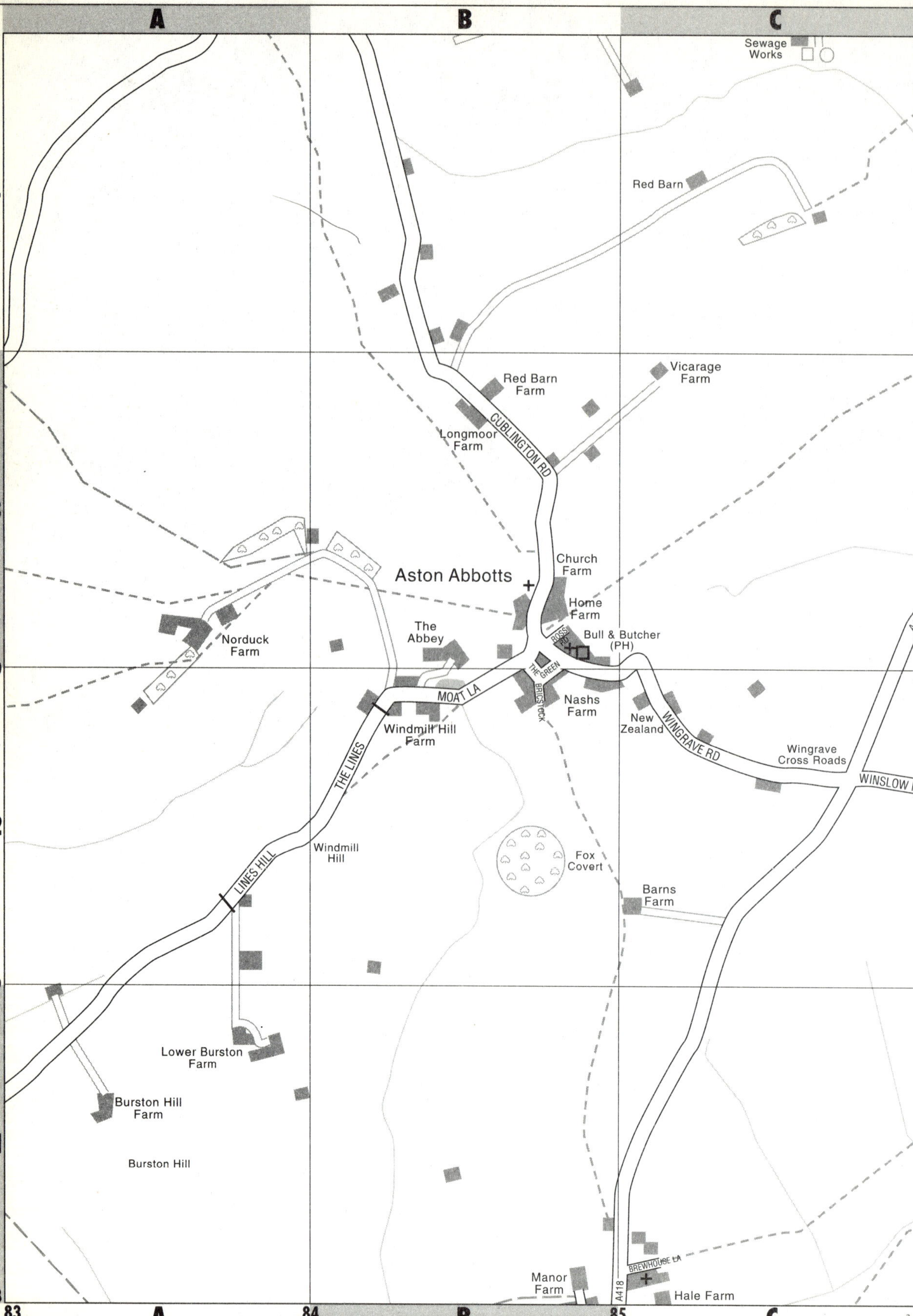
A
B
C
Sewage Works
Red Barn
4
21
Red Barn Farm
Vicarage Farm
Longmoor Farm
CUBLINGTON RD
3
Church Farm
Aston Abbotts
Home Farm
Norduck Farm
The Abbey
ROSS RD
Bull & Butcher (PH)
20
MOAT LA
THE GREEN
BRICSTOCK
Nashs Farm
New Zealand
WINGRAVE RD
Windmill Hill Farm
Wingrave Cross Roads
THE LINES
WINSLOW R
2
Windmill Hill
LINES HILL
Fox Covert
Barns Farm
19
Lower Burston Farm
Burston Hill Farm
1
Burston Hill
BREWHOUSE LA
Manor Farm
A418
Hale Farm
18
83
84
85

D
E
F
A418
The Old Mill
Wingpark
Clump
4
Windmill Hill
Buildings
Ladymead
Lower Wingbury
Farm
21
Westpark
Farm
Oxley's
Farm
Mentmore
Cross Roads
3
Upper Wingbury
Farm
A418
20
Little Chapel
Farm
Crafton
Farm
ABBOTTS WAY
CHILTERN RD
WINSLOW RD
The Boll
(PH)
Nup
End
2
Crafton
LITTLE
MOLLARDS
NAN AIRES
Sch
TWELVE LEYS
BELL LEYS
LEIGHTON RD
BALDWAYS CL
STOOKSLADE
LEADERS CL
Parsonage
Farm
Manor
Farm
Wingrave
NUP END LA
THE DEAN
TATTLERS
HILL
Home Farm
Helsthorpe
Farm
Floyds Farm
19
ORCHARD
CASTLE ST
KNOLLS CL
COBBLERS
WICK
CHURCH ST
MOAT LA
DARK LA
MILL LA
Maltby's Farm
Straws Hadley
Farm
Works
LOWER END
Windmill Hill
Farm
Mitchell Leys
Farm
TRING RD
1
Lower Windmill
Hill Farm
18
D
87
E
88
F
89

A
B
C
Manor Farm
Ledburn
Dennaway Buildings
B488
WELL LA
Ledburn Farm
4
The Lodge
Windmill Hill
Rowden Farm
21
3
Mentmore Stud
The Belt
20
Wing Lodge
Mentmore
The Stag (PH)
Mentmore
Big Wood
Home Farm
Mansom
2
Crafton Stud
Mentmore Park
New Spinney
Crafton Lodge
Model Farm
19
Cheddington Lodge
The Belt
1
18
89
90
91

D
E
F
Billington
A4146
Home Farm
4
Whaddon Farm
River Ouzel
Slaptonbury Mill
MILL RD
LEIGHTON RD
21
A4146
Hall Farm
Bury Farm
CHURCH RD
RECTORY CL
Church Farm
Carpenter's Arms (PH)
HORTON RD
SLAPTON LA
3
Orchard Cottages
Slapton
Slapton Lock
Horton Hill Farm
Whistlebrook Farm
Bridge Farm
Hill Farm
20
Grand Union Canal
Towing Path
Whistle Brook
Lock
Horton Wharf
2
Moat
Horton Hall
Horton Wharf Farm
Horton
BROCAS WAY
19
HORTON RD
Willow Farm
1
Ivinghoe Locks
STATION RD
Foxons Farm
Glebe House
B488
Grove Farm
18
D
93
E
94
F

91

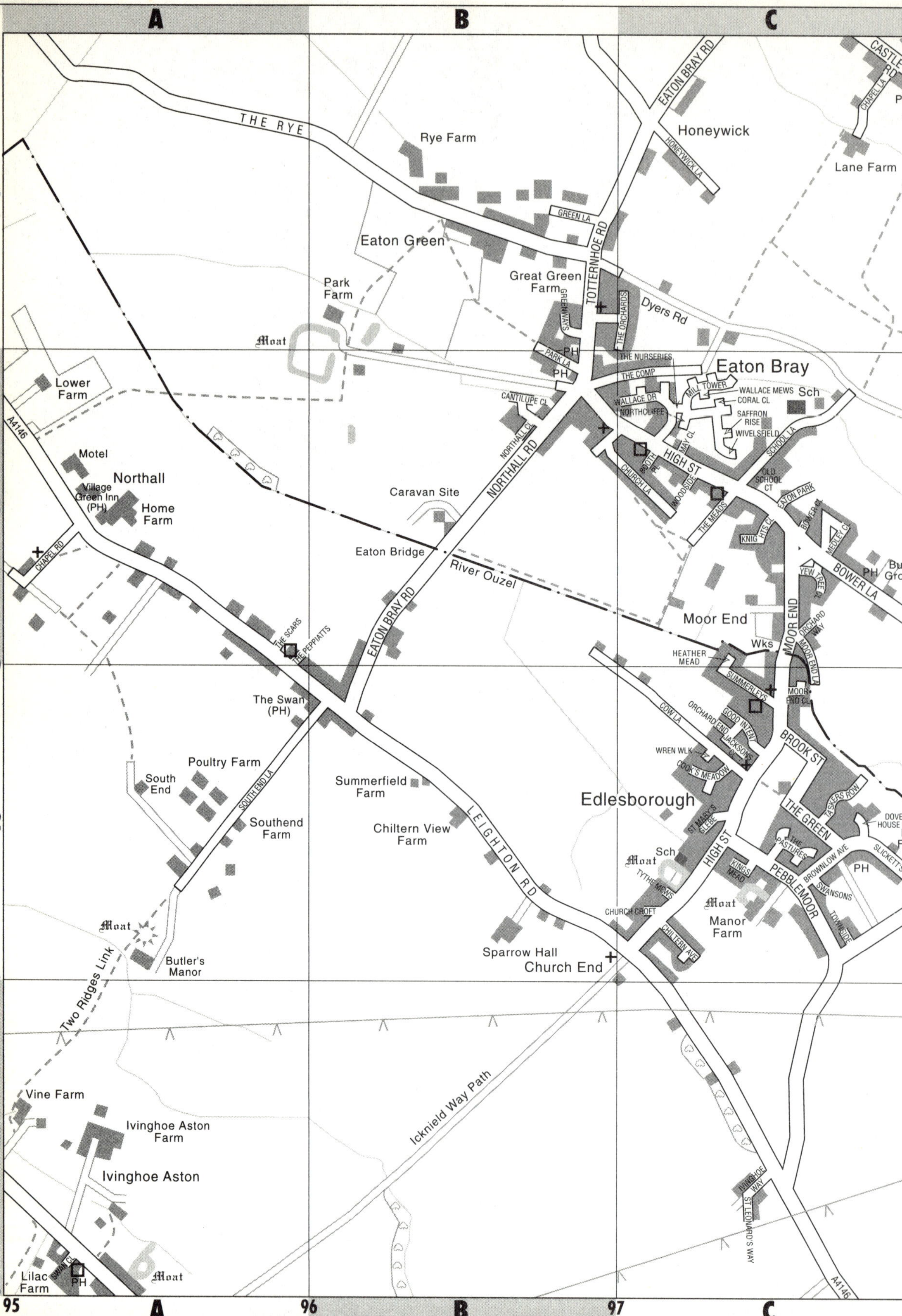

A
B
C
THE RYE
Rye Farm
EATON BRAY RD
Honeywick
HONEYWICK LA
CASTLE RD
CHAPEL LA
Lane Farm
GREEN LA
TOTTERNHOE RD
Eaton Green
Park Farm
Great Green Farm
GREENWAYS
THE ORCHARDS
Dyers Rd
Moat
PH
PARK LA
THE NURSERIES
THE COMP
Eaton Bray
MILL TOWER
WALLACE MEWS
Sch
WALLACE DR
CORAL CL
NORTHCLIFFE
SAFFRON RISE
WIVELSFIELD
CANTILUPE CL
NORTHALL CL
NORTHALL RD
MAY CL
BOOTH PL
HIGH ST
SCHOOL LA
CHURCH LA
WOODSIDE
OLD SCHOOL CT
EATON PARK
THE MEADS
KNIG
HTS CL
BOWER CL
MEDLEY CL
Lower Farm
A4146
Motel
Northall
Village Green Inn (PH)
Home Farm
Caravan Site
CHAPEL RD
Eaton Bridge
River Ouzel
YEW TREE CL
BOWER LA
PH
Moor End
ORCHARD WAY
MOOR END
MOOR END LA
Wks
HEATHER MEAD
THE SCARS
THE PEPPIATTS
EATON BRAY RD
SUMMERLEYS
MOOR END CL
COW LA
The Swan (PH)
ORCHARD END
GOOD INTENT
JACKSONS CT
WREN WLK
COOK'S MEADOW
BROOK ST
Poultry Farm
South End
SOUTH END LA
Summerfield Farm
Edlesborough
TASKERS ROW
Southend Farm
Chiltern View Farm
LEIGHTON RD
ST MARY'S GLEBE
THE GREEN
DOVE HOUSE
THE PASTURES
Sch
HIGH ST
KINGS MEAD
BROWNLOW AVE
SLICKETT'S
TYTHE MEWS
PEBBLEMOOR
PH
SWANSONS
Moat
CHURCH CROFT
Manor Farm
TOWNSIDE
CHILTERN AVE
Butler's Manor
Sparrow Hall
Church End
Two Ridges Link
Icknield Way Path
Vine Farm
Ivinghoe Aston Farm
Ivinghoe Aston
IVINGHOE WAY
ST LEONARD'S WAY
Lilac Farm
SWAN CL
PH
A4146
4
21
3
20
2
19
1
18
95
96
97

D
E
F
4
3
2
1
21
20
19
18
99
00
Middle End
Picnic Site
Poplar Farm
CASTLE HILL RD
BROWNLOW RISE
CASTLE CL
PARK AVE
LANCOTBURY CL
Totternhoe
Recn Gd
DUNSTABLE RD
CHURCH GREEN
FURLONG LA
Church End
Sch
Allot Gdns
PH
Vic
THE RIDE
CHURCH RD
ELLESMERE CL
BRIGHTWELL AVE
Church Farm
WELL HEAD RD
Well Head
Ware Hill Cottage
Doolittle Mill (disused)
DUNSTABLE RD
Common Farm
Rosebury Farm
Bellows Mill
Poultry Farm
Wellhead Farm
Norfolk House Farm
HARLING RD
Patrick's Cottage
Harling House
Ford
Edlesborough Mills (disused)
Edlesborough Hill
Plough Inn (PH)
ICKNIELD WAY
Shepherds Farm
Icknield Way Farm
B4506
River Ouzel
B4540
DAGNALL RD
Valence-end Farm
Willow Farm
B489
Sch
SAXON CL
BEDFIELD CL
NORMAN WAY
WEATHERBY
COOKFIELD CL
BUNHILL CL
WESTFIELD RD
DROVERS WAY
LORING RD
Beecroft
BEECROFT WAY
CROFT GREEN
HAMBLING PL
PASCOMB RD
BEECROFT
Green La
SPINNEY CRES
WORTHINGTON RD
FRANKLIN RD
BENNING AVE
Sch
LANCOT DR
LANCOT AVE
OAKWELL CL
BEECHWOOD CT
WEST ST B489
MEADWAY
TOTTERNHOE RD
HARVEY RD
MARINA DR
GARDNER'S CL
BEACON AVE
COOMBE DR
TRING RD
THE AVENUE
B4541
PIPERS CROFT
ROYCE CL
SPOONDELL
Tumuli
Five Knolls
WHIPSNADE RD
Icknield Way
California
London Gliding Club
Dunstable Downs
CH
Golf Course
Picnic Area
P
Robertson Corner
B4541
Mast
Swallowspring Wood
Chute Farm
Tree Cathedral
Whipsnade
P
B4540
B4506
D
E
F

107

A
B
C
Astley Bridge Farm
River Ray
PH
PALMER AVE
Offices
LC
PATRICK HAUGH RD
Upper Arncott
BUCHANAN RD
Depot
CH
Arncott Hill
MURCOTT RD
Arncott Hill Farm
Arncott Wood
Depot
ARNCOTT WOOD RD
M40
FIELD RD
Boarstall Lane
New Park Farm
Red House Farm
Murcott
Marlake House
Latchmeads
Four Winds Farm
Oldhouse Spinney
Whitecross Green
Panshill Farms
Pans Hill
Manor Farm
Upper Panshill Farm
Whitecross Green Wood
Nature Reserve
Upper Wood
Oriel Wood
4
17
3
16
2
15
1
14
59
60
61

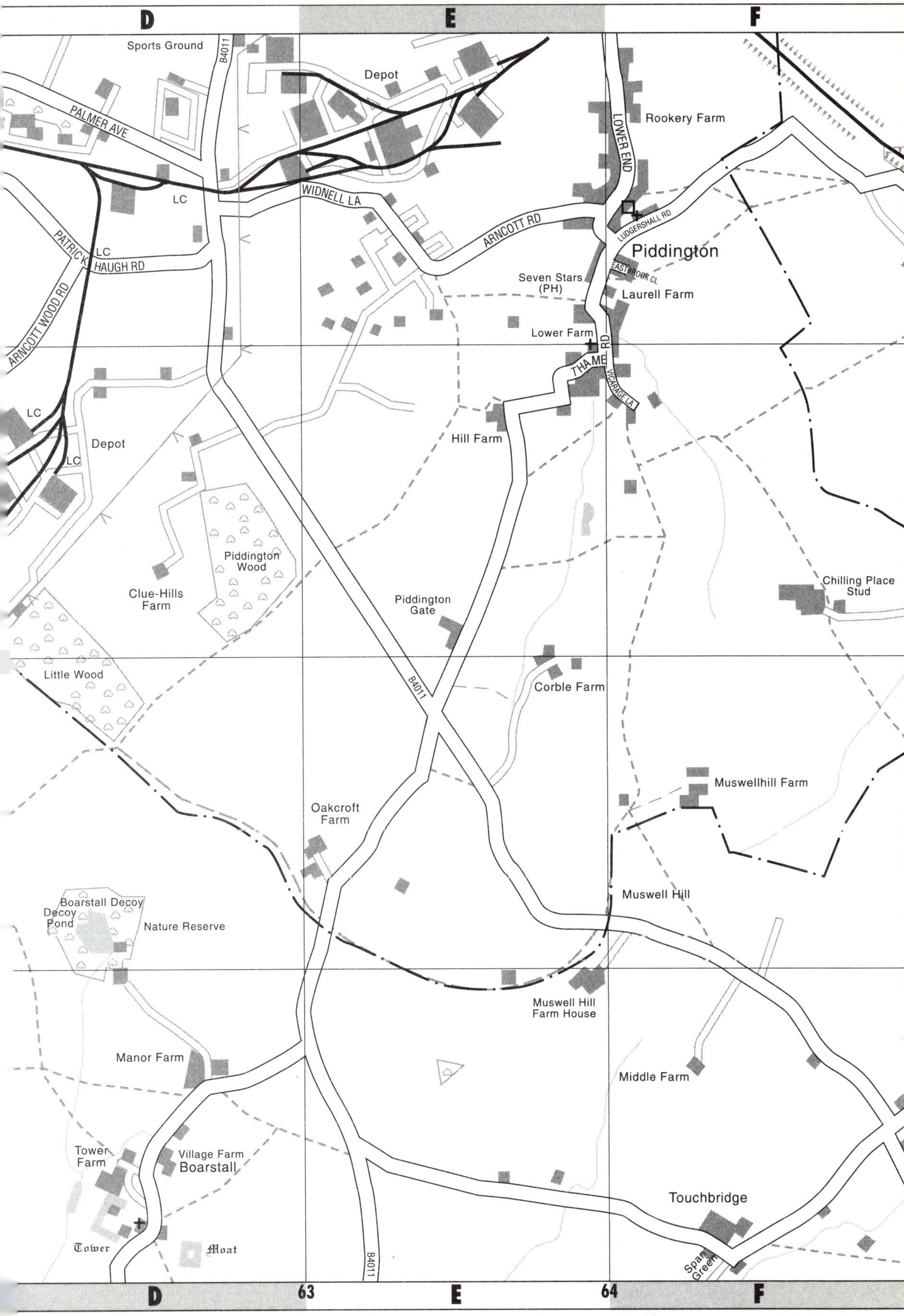
D
E
F
Sports Ground
B4011
Depot
Rookery Farm
LOWER END
PALMER AVE
LC
WIDNELL LA
ARNCOTT RD
LUDGERSHALL RD
Piddington
PATRICK HAUGH RD
LC
ARNCOTT WOOD RD
Seven Stars
(PH)
EASTBROOK CL
Laurell Farm
Lower Farm
THAME RD
VICARAGE LA
LC
Depot
LC
Hill Farm
Piddington
Wood
Clue-Hills
Farm
Piddington
Gate
Chilling Place
Stud
Little Wood
B4011
Corble Farm
Muswellhill Farm
Oakcroft
Farm
Muswell Hill
Boarstall Decoy
Decoy
Pond
Nature Reserve
Muswell Hill
Farm House
Manor Farm
Middle Farm
Tower
Farm
Village Farm
Boarstall
Touchbridge
Tower
Moat
B4011
Span
Green
4
17
3
16
2
15
1
14
D
63
E
64
F

A
B
C
Nursery
Kings Farm
PIDDINGTON RD
D'Oyley's Farm
BICESTER RD
Rookery Farm
The Green
DUCK LA
Tittershall Wood
Bridge Farm
Bull & Butcher (PH)
SALTERS LA
SOLTERS CL
Ludgershall
Manor Farm
BROOK CL
WHITE HART
HIGH ST
4
Ludgershall Farm
CHURCH LA
Glebe Farm
BRILL RD
Sch
WOTTON END
Moat
17
KINGSWOOD LA
The Lake
Clearfields Farm
3
Long Wood
Poletrees Farm
Lapland Farm
The Warrell
16
Fivearch Bridge
Fivearch Wood
Rushbeds Wood (Nature Reserve)
Grenville's Wood
2
Lawn Farm
Tramway Farm
Sawmill
Rid's Hill
15
Brillbury Hall Farm
Coldharbour Farm
TRAMHILL
1
Dorton Park Farm
Brill Common
North Hill
Chinkwell Wood
Brill
Dorton
THE LAWNS
WINDMILL ST
TEMPLE ST
Windmill
HIGH LAND CL
Brook Farm
PH
F Sta
Sch
BRAE HILL
Magistrates Court
14
65
A
66
B
67
C

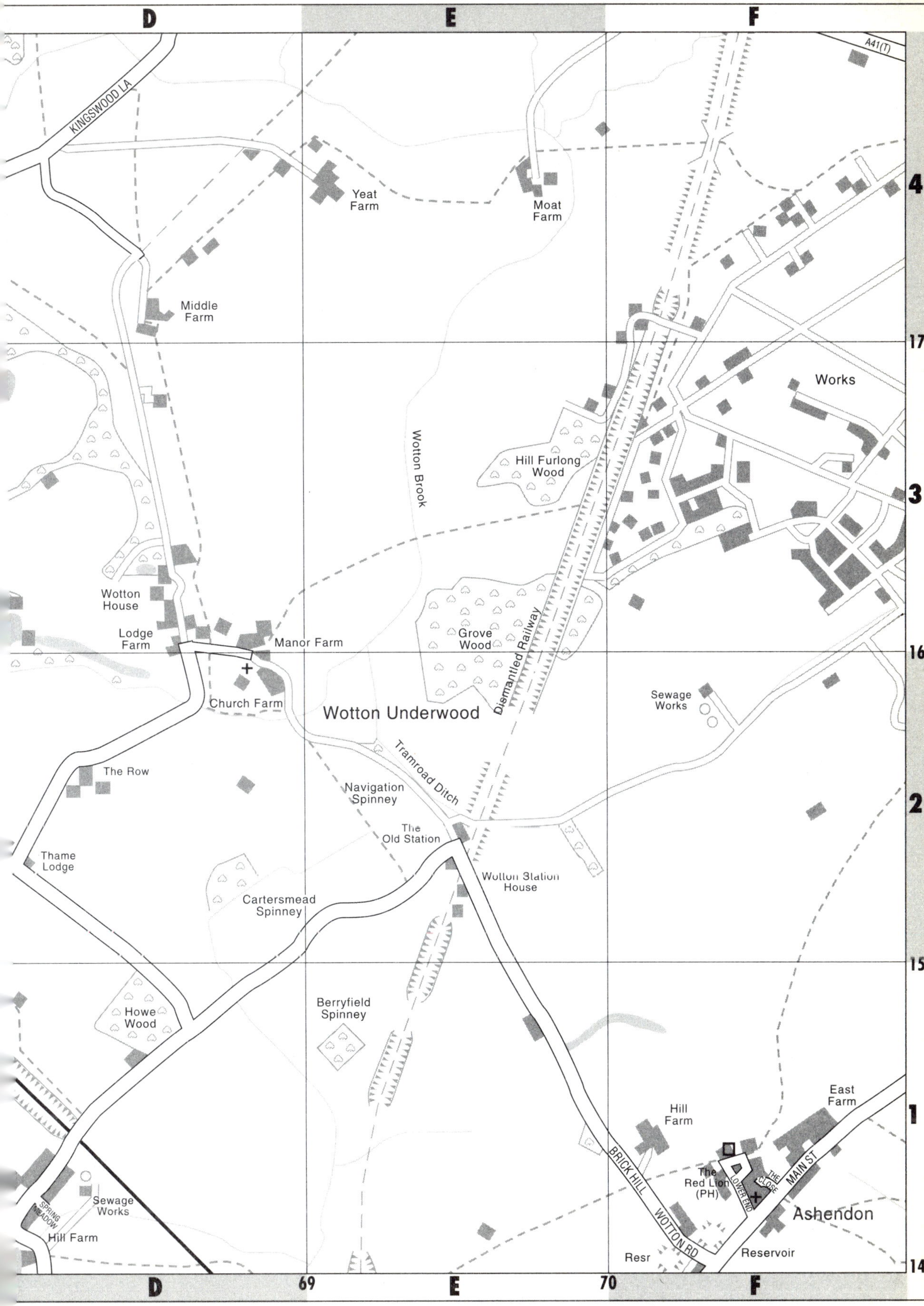
D
E
F
A41(T)
KINGSWOOD LA
Yeat Farm
Moat Farm
4
Middle Farm
17
Works
Wotton Brook
Hill Furlong Wood
3
Wotton House
Lodge Farm
Manor Farm
Grove Wood
Dismantled Railway
16
Church Farm
Wotton Underwood
Sewage Works
The Row
Tramroad Ditch
Navigation Spinney
2
The Old Station
Thame Lodge
Wotton Station House
Cartersmead Spinney
15
Howe Wood
Berryfield Spinney
East Farm
Hill Farm
1
The Red Lion (PH)
LOWER END
THE CLOSE
MAIN ST
BRICK HILL
WOTTON RD
Ashendon
Sewage Works
SPRING MEADOW
Hill Farm
Resr
Reservoir
14
D
69
E
70
F

97
84

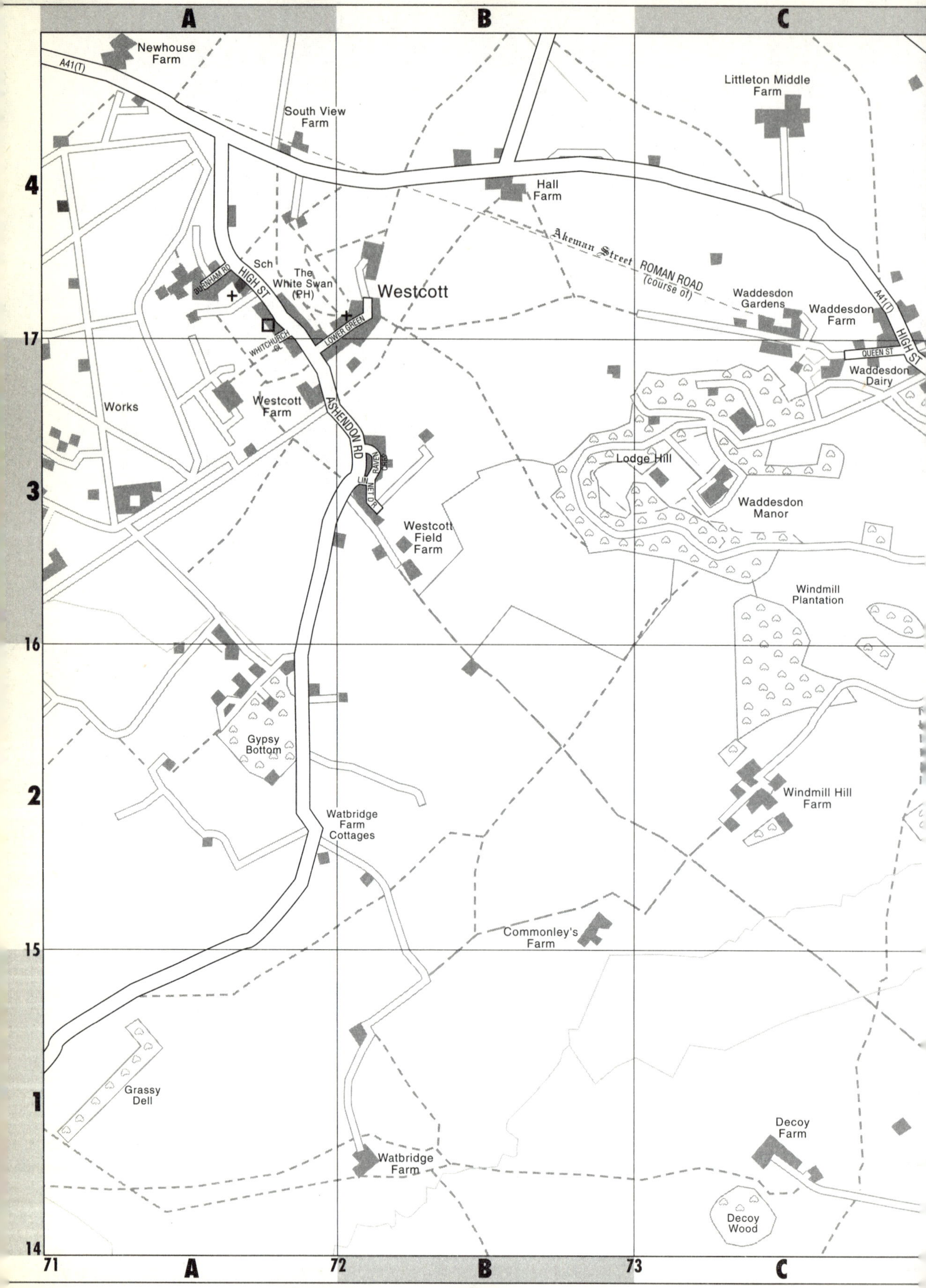
A
B
C
Newhouse Farm
A41(T)
South View Farm
Littleton Middle Farm
4
Hall Farm
Akeman Street ROMAN ROAD (course of)
Sch
The White Swan (PH)
Westcott
BURNHAM RD
HIGH ST
LOWER GREEN
WHITCHURCH CL
Waddesdon Gardens
Waddesdon Farm
A41(T)
HIGH ST
QUEEN ST
Waddesdon Dairy
17
Works
Westcott Farm
ASHENDON RD
RAVEN CRES
LINNET DR
Lodge Hill
3
Westcott Field Farm
Waddesdon Manor
Windmill Plantation
16
Gypsy Bottom
2
Watbridge Farm Cottages
Windmill Hill Farm
Commonley's Farm
15
Grassy Dell
1
Decoy Farm
Watbridge Farm
Decoy Wood
14
71
72
73
A
B
C

97
112

D
E
F
Blackgrove Covert
Lapstone House
Little Manor Holding
Glebe Farm
Lower Blackgrove Farm
Waddesdon
Briar Hill Farm
FREDERICK ST
ORCHARD CL
QUAINTON RD
NEW ST
WOOD ST
LITTLE BRITAIN
ANSTEY CL
RECTORY DR
HIGH ST
A41(T)
F Sta
PH
CHESTNUT CL
THE GROVE
BAKER ST
GROVE WAY
SILK ST
SCHOOL LA
GOSS AVE
SHARP'S CL
WARMSTONE CL
WARMSTONE LA
Sch
Little Blackgrove Farm Cottages
The Lodge
Akeman Street
ROMAN ROAD (course of)
Wormstone Farm
Wormstone
Cranwell Farm
North Buckinghamshire Way
The Bungalow
Waddesdon Stud
Lower Cranwell
WADDESDON HILL
Waddesdonhill Farm
Upper Cranwell Farm
Coneyhill Farm
North Lodge
Sheepcothill Wood
The Wilderness
Fox Covert
Swan's Way
Manor House
Eythrope Park Farm
Upper Winchendon
SCHOOL LA
MAIN RD
Eythrope Park
Model Farm
4
17
3
16
2
15
1
14
4
75
76

99
86

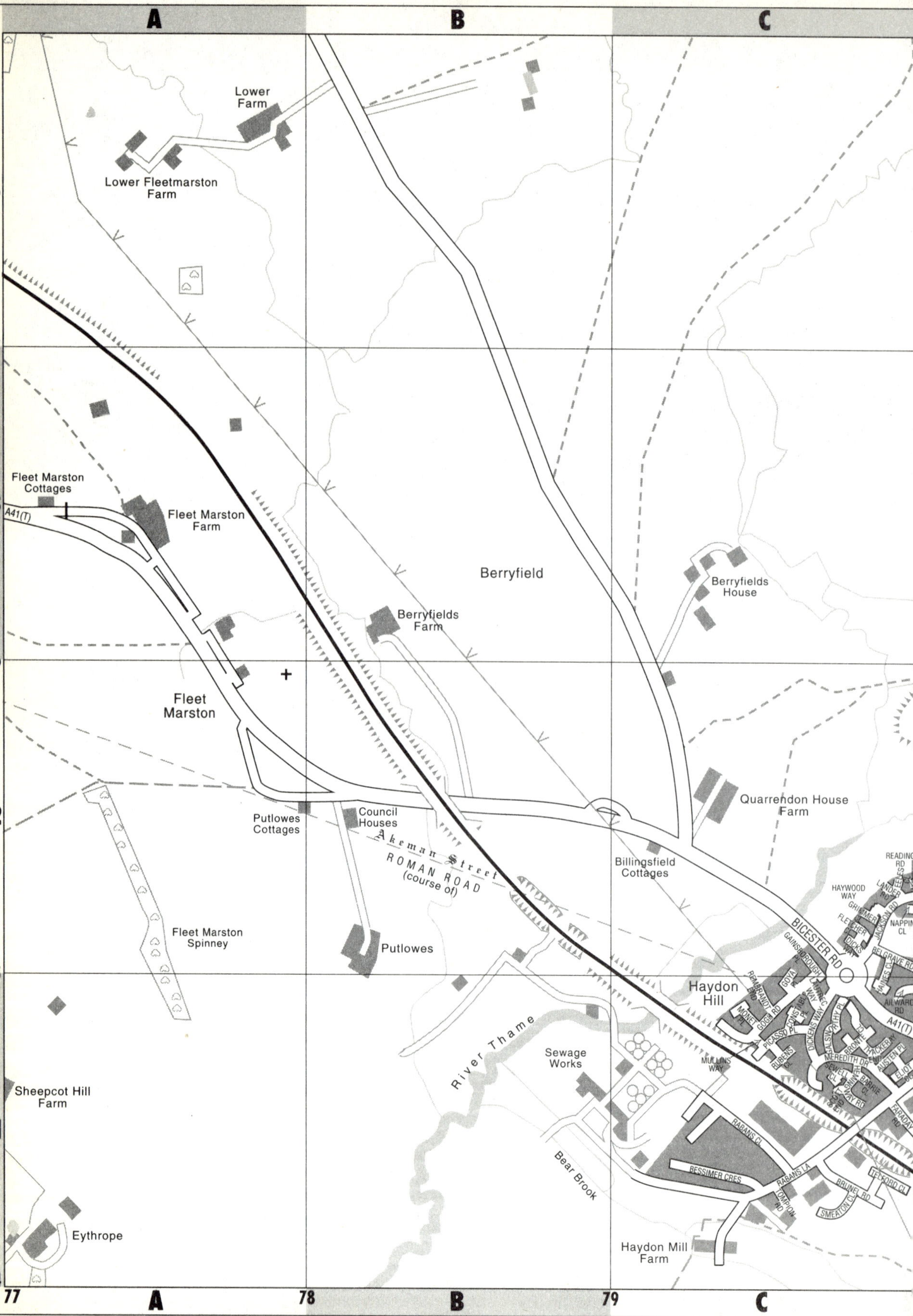
A
B
C
4
17
3
16
2
15
1
14
77
78
79
Lower Farm
Lower Fleetmarston Farm
Fleet Marston Cottages
A41(T)
Fleet Marston Farm
Berryfield
Berryfields House
Berryfields Farm
Fleet Marston
Quarrendon House Farm
Putlowes Cottages
Council Houses
Akeman Street
ROMAN ROAD (course of)
Billingsfield Cottages
BICESTER RD
Fleet Marston Spinney
Putlowes
Haydon Hill
River Thame
Sewage Works
MULLINS WAY
Sheepcot Hill Farm
Bear Brook
RABANS CL
BESSIMER CRES
RABANS LA
TOMPION RD
BRUNEL RD
SMEATON CL
TELFORD CL
HAYWOOD WAY
READING RD
JACKSON RD
BELGRAVE RD
AILWARD RD
A41(T)
Eythrope
Haydon Mill Farm

99
114

87
102

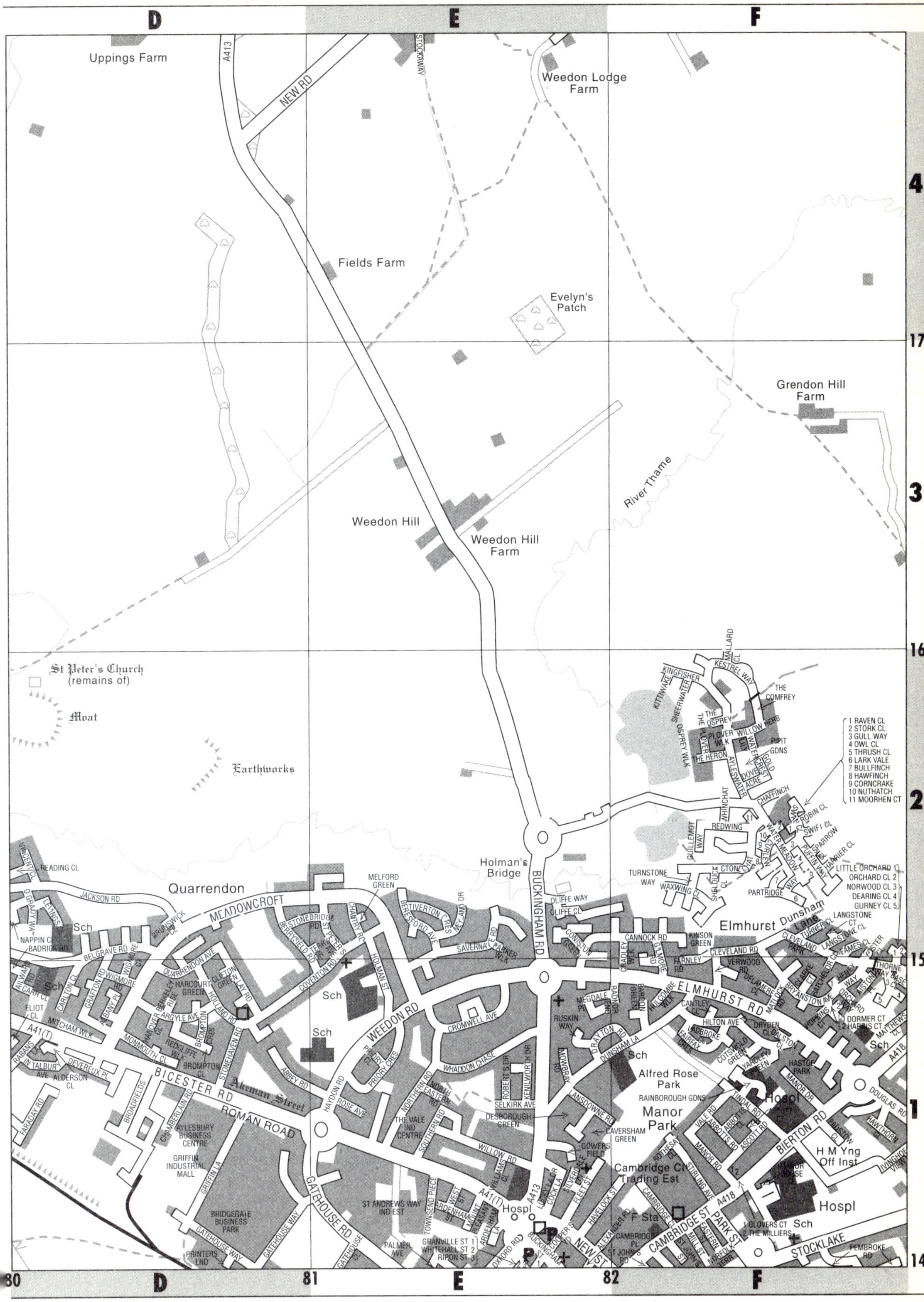

115
102

101
88

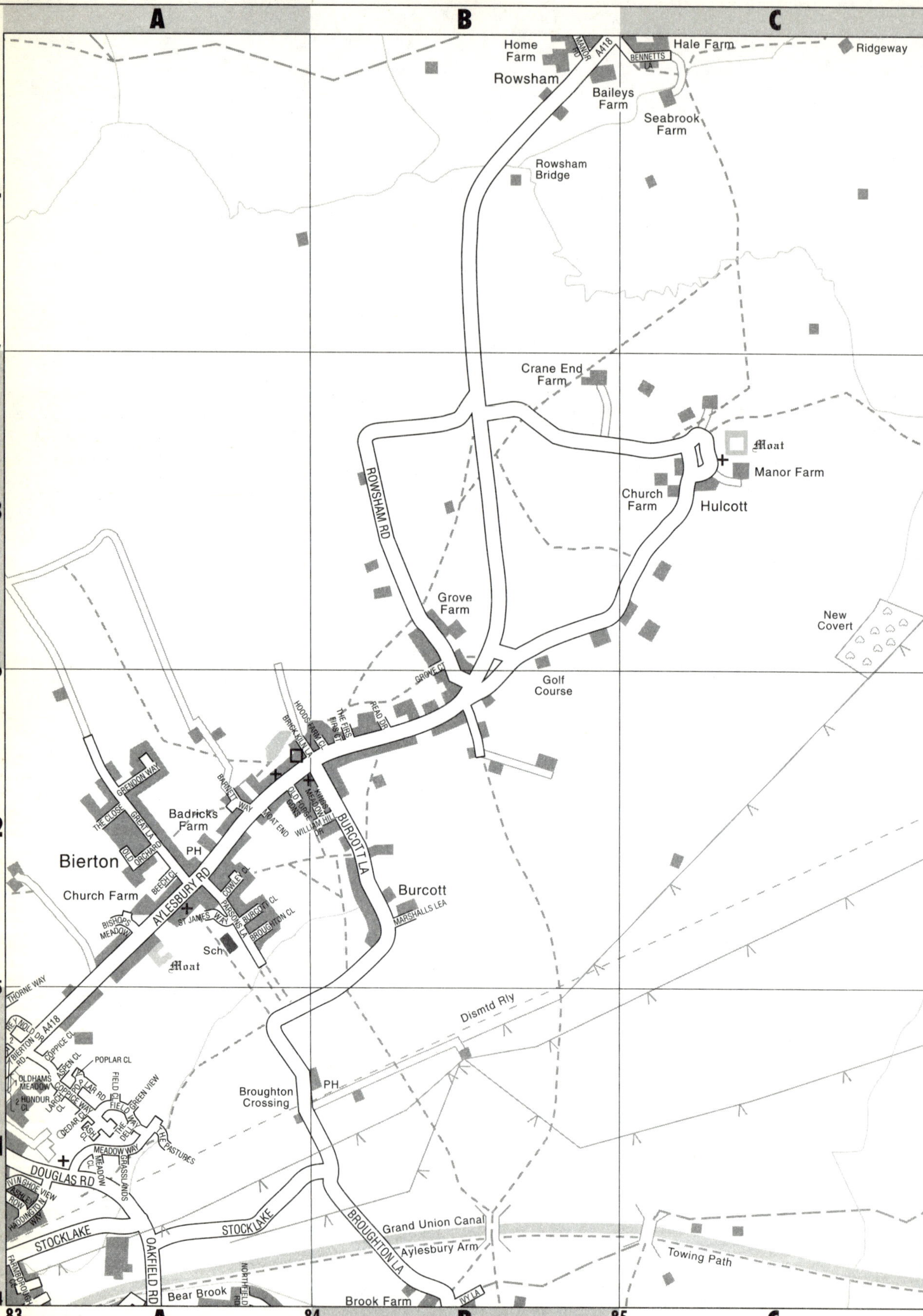

101
116

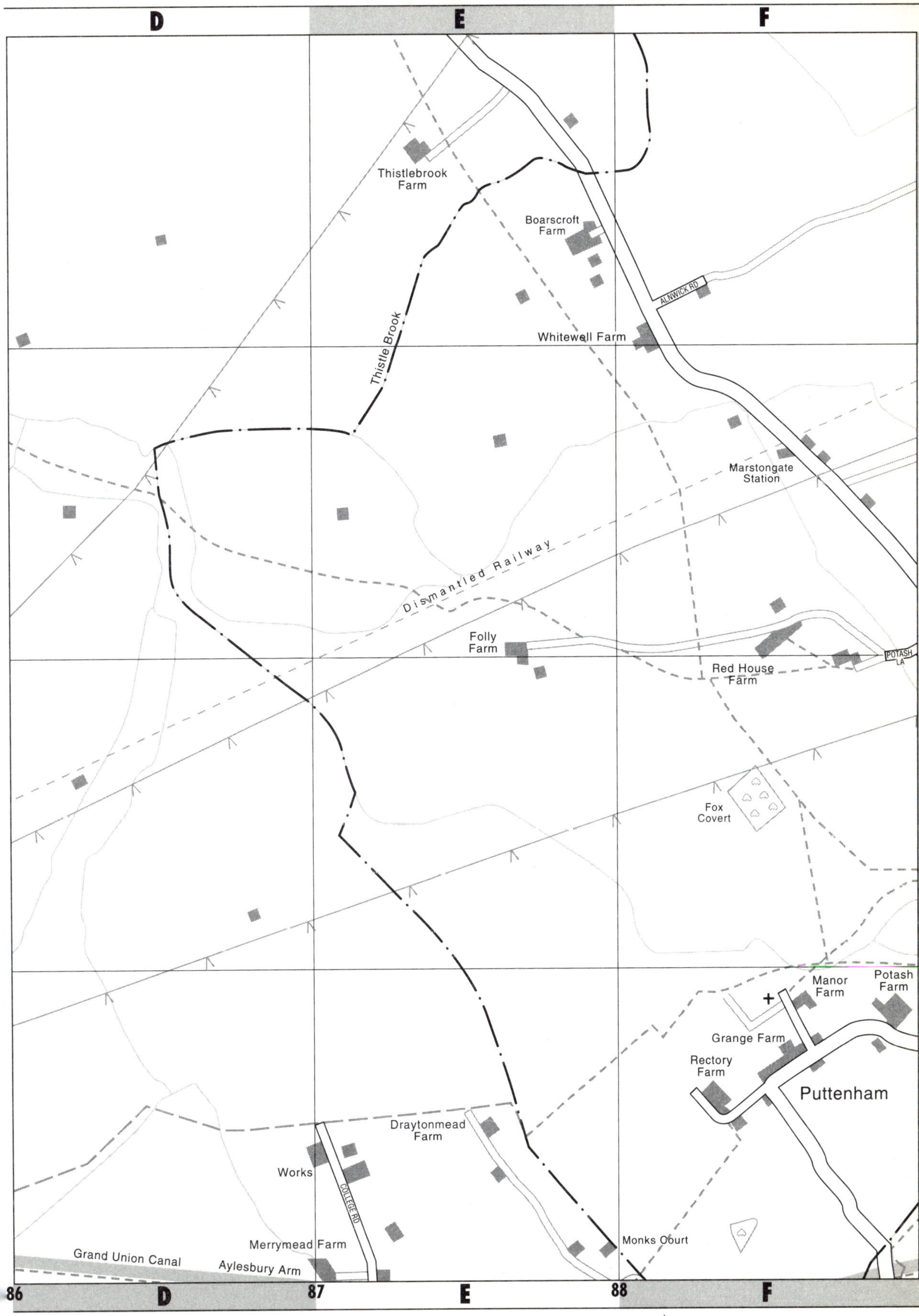
D
E
F
Thistlebrook Farm
Boarscroft Farm
ALNWICK RD
Whitewell Farm
Thistle Brook
Marstongate Station
Dismantled Railway
Folly Farm
POTASH LA
Red House Farm
Fox Covert
Manor Farm
Potash Farm
Grange Farm
Rectory Farm
Puttenham
Draytonmead Farm
Works
COLLEGE RD
Merrymead Farm
Grand Union Canal
Aylesbury Arm
Monks Court
4
17
3
16
2
15
1
14
86
87
88
D
E
F

103
90

103
118

91
106

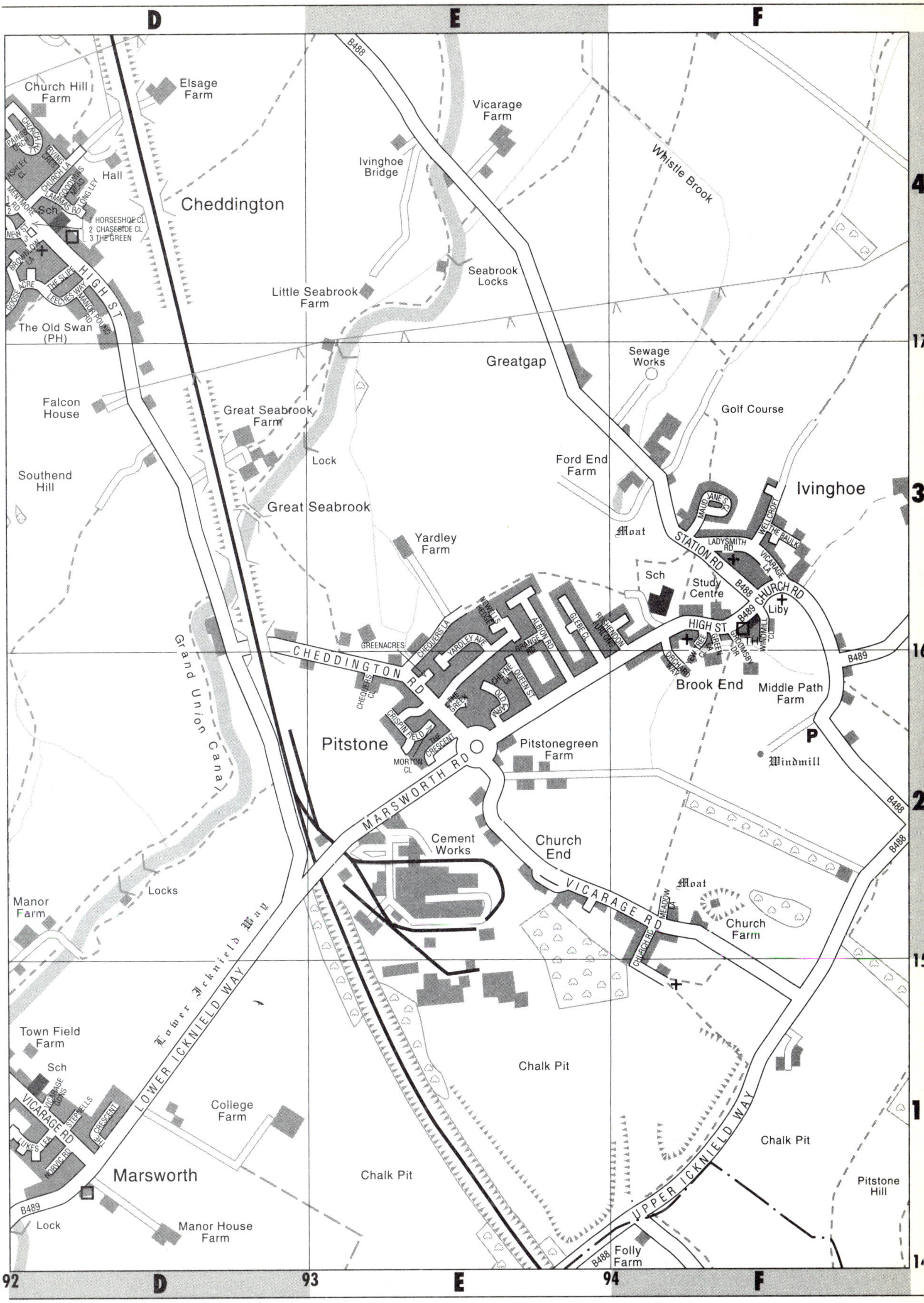

119
106

105
92

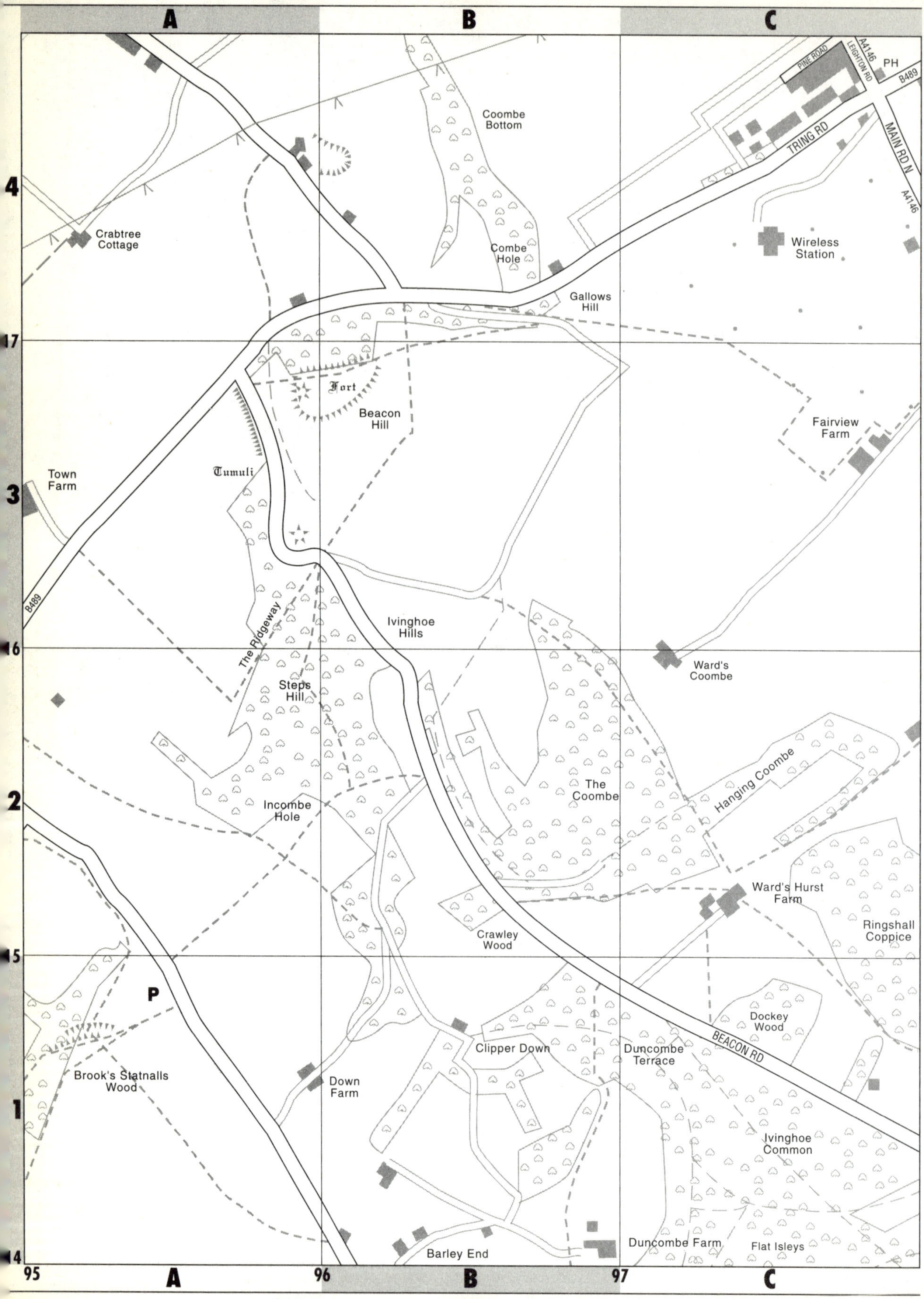

105
120

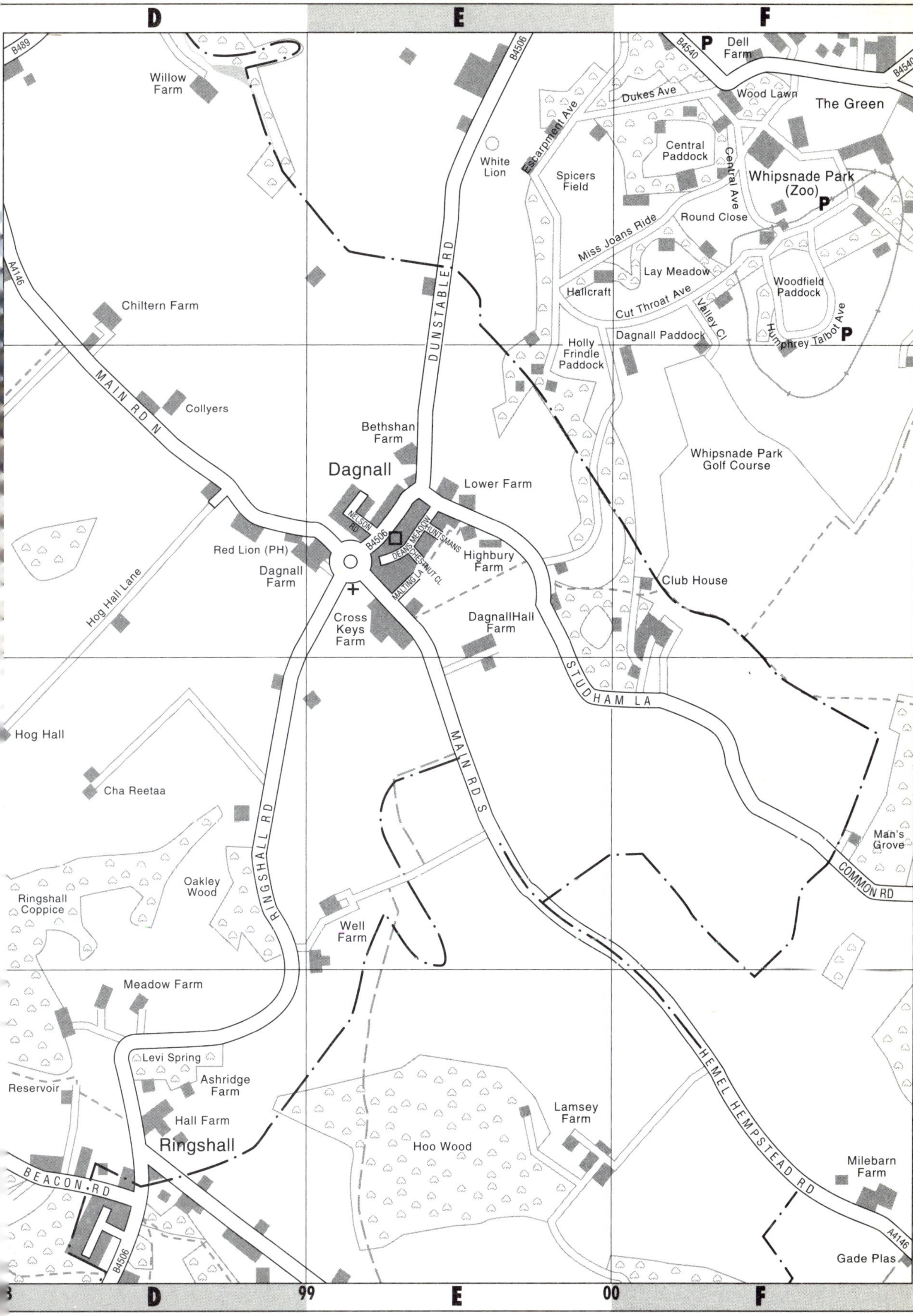
D
E
F
B489
Willow Farm
B4506
B4540
P
Dell Farm
Dukes Ave
Wood Lawn
The Green
Escarpment Ave
Central Paddock
Central Ave
White Lion
Spicers Field
Whipsnade Park (Zoo)
Round Close
Miss Joans Ride
Lay Meadow
Woodfield Paddock
Hallcraft
Cut Throat Ave
Valley Cl
Humphrey Talbot Ave
Dagnall Paddock
Holly Frindle Paddock
A4146
Chiltern Farm
DUNSTABLE RD
MAIN RD N
Collyers
Bethshan Farm
Whipsnade Park Golf Course
Dagnall
Lower Farm
NELSON RD
DEANS MEADOW
HUNTSMANS
CHESTNUT CL
MALTING LA
Highbury Farm
Red Lion (PH)
Dagnall Farm
Hog Hall Lane
Club House
Cross Keys Farm
DagnallHall Farm
STUDHAM LA
Hog Hall
MAIN RD S
Cha Reetaa
RINGSHALL RD
Man's Grove
Oakley Wood
Ringshall Coppice
COMMON RD
Well Farm
Meadow Farm
Levi Spring
Ashridge Farm
Reservoir
HEMEL HEMPSTEAD RD
Lamsey Farm
Hall Farm
Ringshall
Hoo Wood
Milebarn Farm
BEACON RD
Gade Plas
4
17
3
16
2
15
1
14
99
00

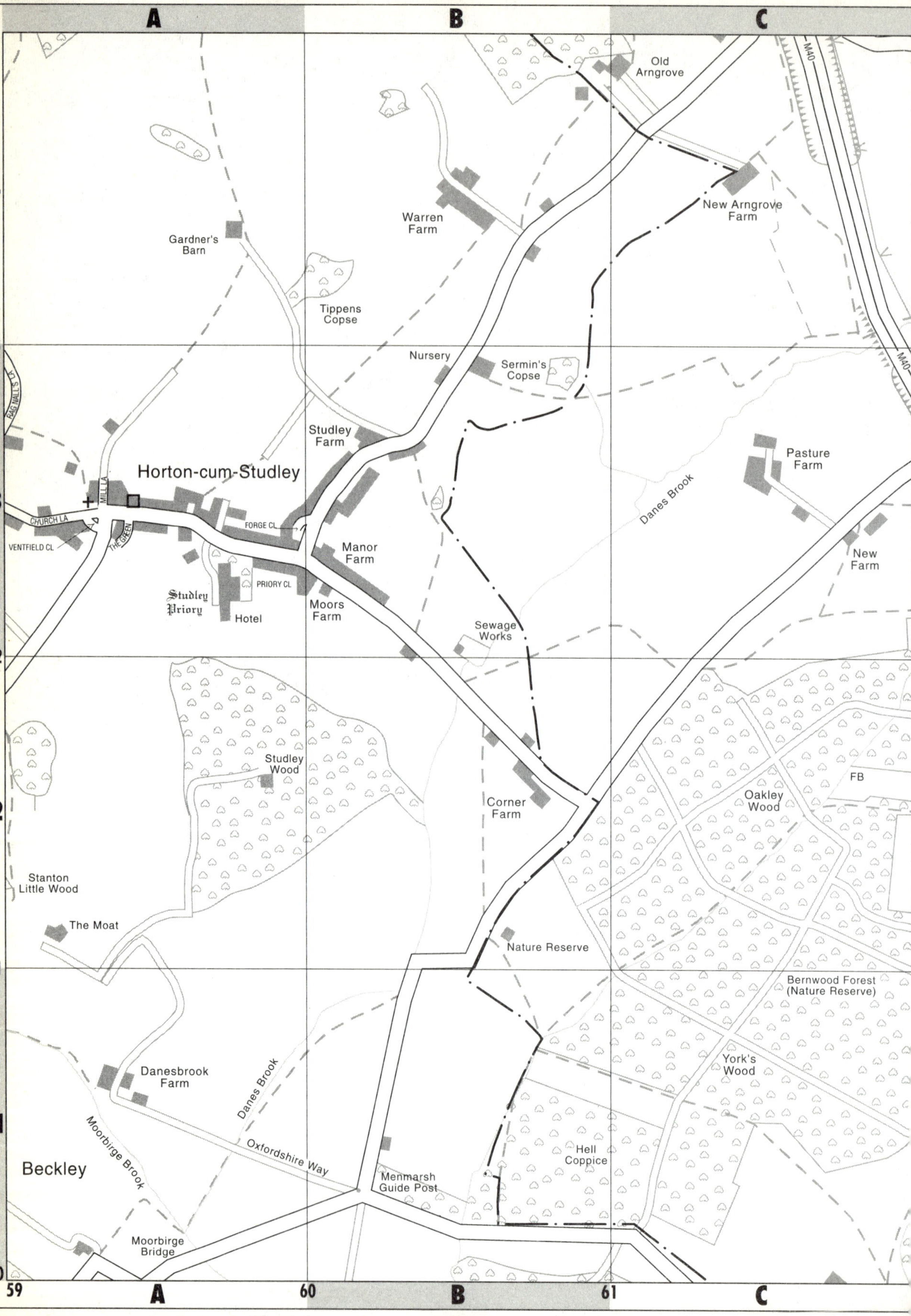
A
B
C
4
13
3
12
2
11
1
10
59
60
61
Old Arngrove
New Arngrove Farm
M40
Warren Farm
Gardner's Barn
Tippens Copse
Nursery
Sermin's Copse
Studley Farm
Horton-cum-Studley
RAG WALLS LA
MILL LA
CHURCH LA
VENTFIELD CL
THE GREEN
FORGE CL
PRIORY CL
Manor Farm
Moors Farm
Studley Priory
Hotel
Pasture Farm
Danes Brook
New Farm
Sewage Works
Studley Wood
Corner Farm
FB
Oakley Wood
Stanton Little Wood
The Moat
Nature Reserve
Bernwood Forest (Nature Reserve)
York's Wood
Danesbrook Farm
Danes Brook
Moorbirge Brook
Beckley
Oxfordshire Way
Menmarsh Guide Post
Hell Coppice
Moorbirge Bridge

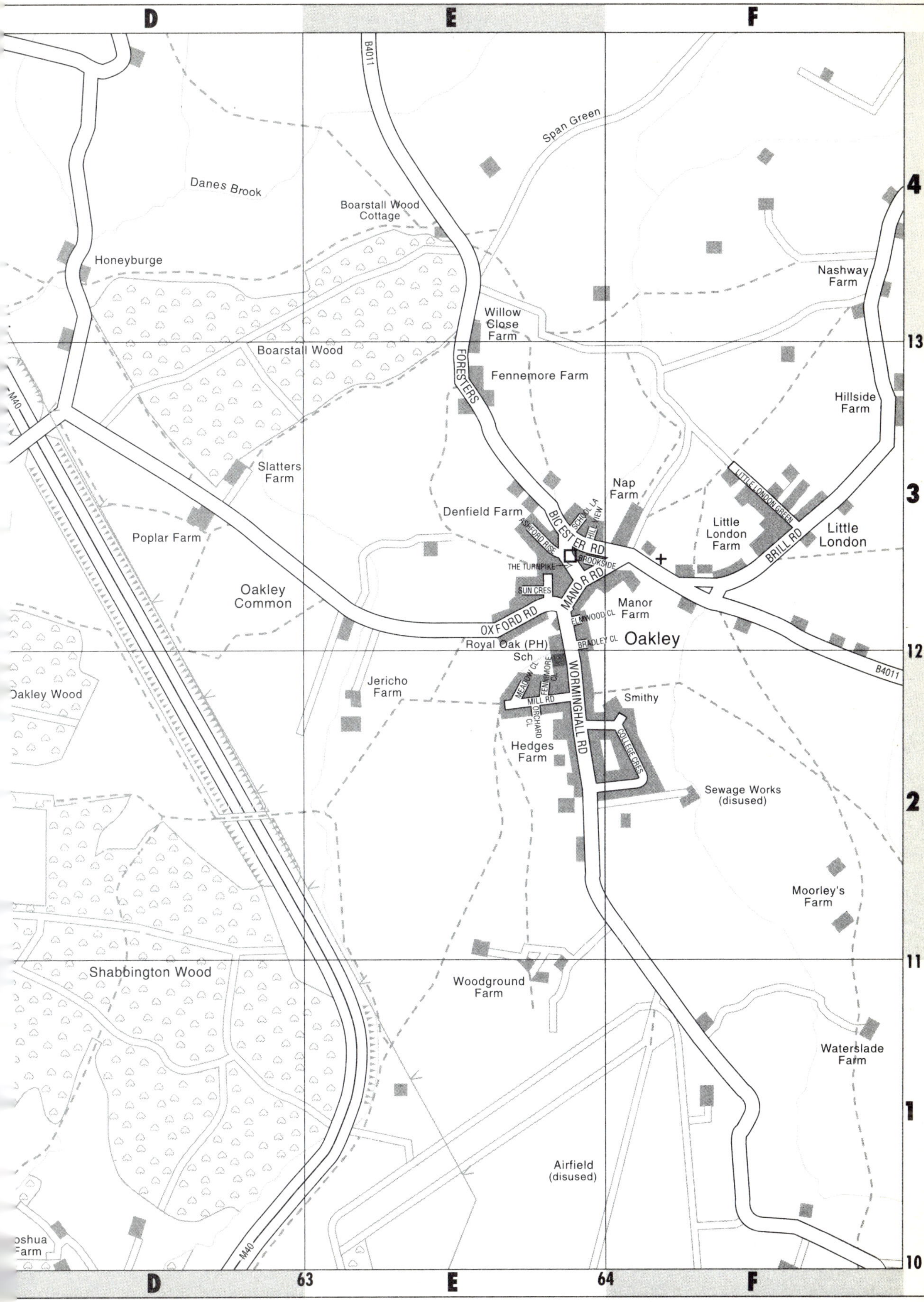
D
E
F
B4011
Span Green
Danes Brook
Boarstall Wood Cottage
Honeyburge
Nashway Farm
Willow Close Farm
Boarstall Wood
FORESTERS
Fennemore Farm
Hillside Farm
M40
Slatters Farm
Nap Farm
LITTLE LONDON GREEN
Denfield Farm
BICESTER RD
SCHOOL LA
HILL VIEW
ASHFORD RISE
Little London Farm
Little London
BRILL RD
Poplar Farm
THE TURNPIKE
BROOKSIDE
MANOR RD
Oakley Common
SUN CRES
Manor Farm
OXFORD RD
ELMWOOD CL
Oakley
Royal Oak (PH)
BRADLEY CL
B4011
Sch
Oakley Wood
Jericho Farm
MEADOW CL
FENNIMORE CL
WORMINGHALL RD
Smithy
MILL RD
ORCHARD CL
COLLEGE CRES
Hedges Farm
Sewage Works (disused)
Moorley's Farm
Shabbington Wood
Woodground Farm
Waterslade Farm
Airfield (disused)
oshua Farm
M40
4
13
3
12
2
11
1
10
D
63
E
64
F

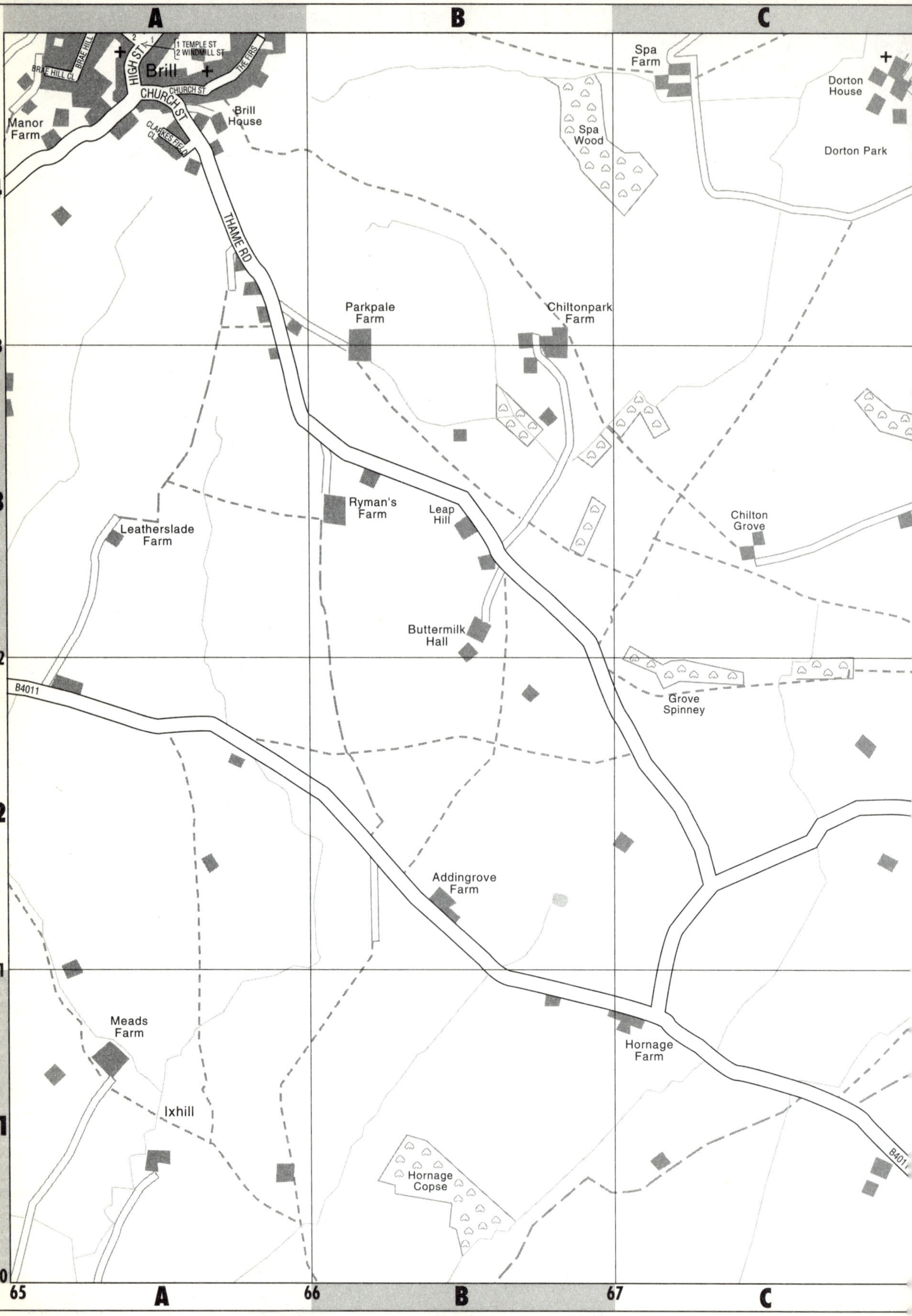
A
B
C
1 TEMPLE ST
2 WINDMILL ST
BRAE HILL CL
BRAE HILL
HIGH ST
Brill
CHURCH ST
THE FIRS
Manor Farm
Brill House
CLARKES FIELD CL
THAME RD
Spa Farm
Spa Wood
Dorton House
Dorton Park
Parkpale Farm
Chiltonpark Farm
Ryman's Farm
Leap Hill
Leatherslade Farm
Chilton Grove
Buttermilk Hall
B4011
Grove Spinney
Addingrove Farm
Meads Farm
Hornage Farm
Ixhill
Hornage Copse
4
13
3
12
2
11
1
10
65
66
67

D
E
F
Dorton Park
Upper Pollicott
Valley Farm
Upper Pollicott Farm
Dismantled Railway
4
Arrow Cotts
Lower Pollicott
13
Manor Farm
3
Dorton Hill
Camp Farm
12
Home Farm
Townhill Farm
CHURCH RD
Chilton House
Chilton
BRILL RD
2
Wurtemburg Farm
CHAPEL LA
Chilton Grounds
Sewage Works
Canoncourt Farm
THAME RD
PRINCES CL
Crawley Farm
11
Wombwell's Farm
Ashtree Tree Cotts
1
Easington
EASINGTON LA
Lower Easington Farm
The Rising Sun (PH)
B4011
Mount Pleasant
10
D
69
E
70
F

111
98

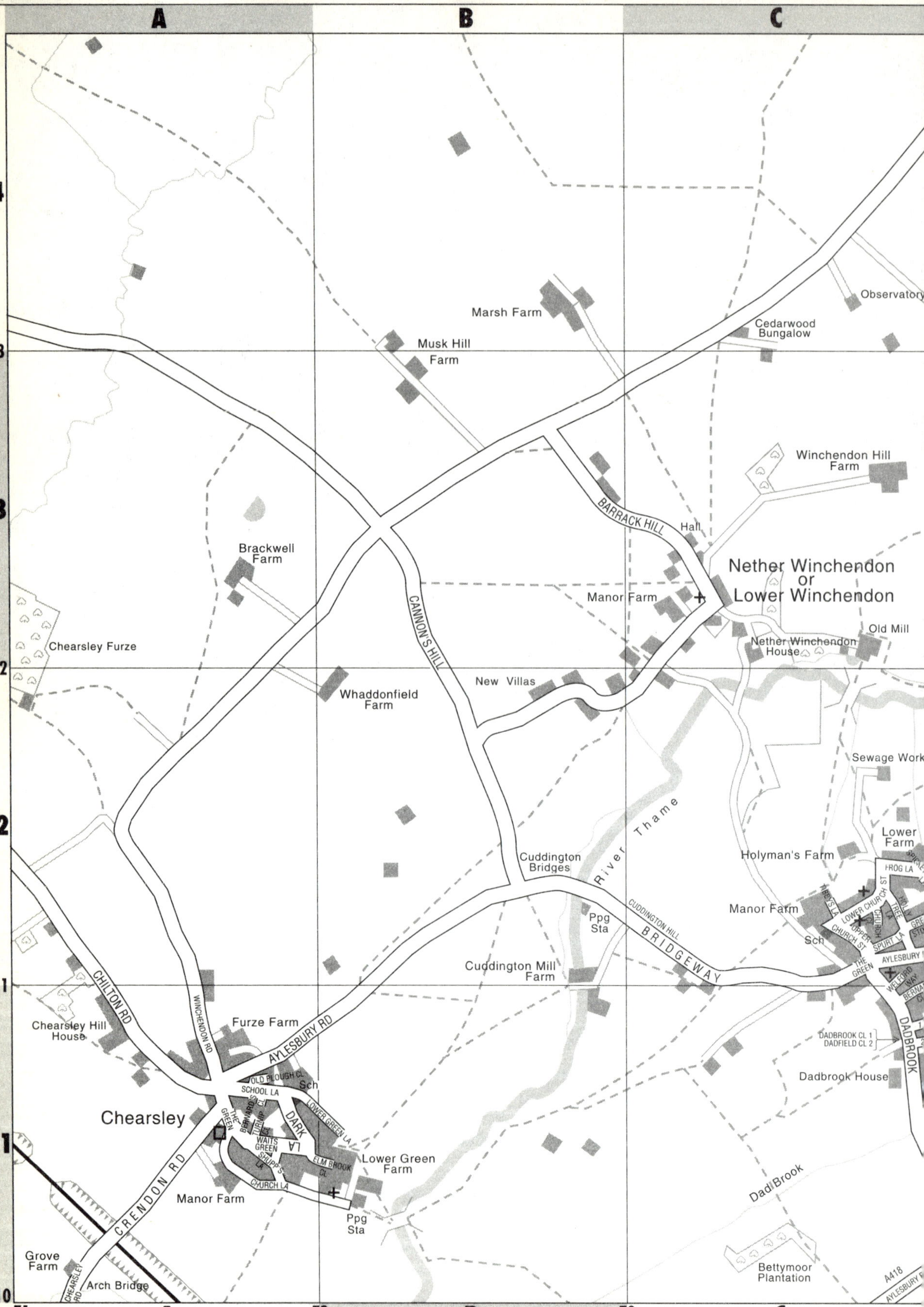
A
B
C
4
13
3
12
2
11
1
10
71
72
73
Marsh Farm
Observatory
Cedarwood Bungalow
Musk Hill Farm
Winchendon Hill Farm
BARRACK HILL
Hall
Nether Winchendon or Lower Winchendon
Brackwell Farm
Manor Farm
CANNON'S HILL
Old Mill
Nether Winchendon House
Chearsley Furze
New Villas
Whaddonfield Farm
Sewage Work
River Thame
Lower Farm
Holyman's Farm
Cuddington Bridges
FROG LA
Manor Farm
LOWER CHURCH ST
UPPER CHURCH ST
Ppg Sta
CUDDINGTON HILL
BRIDGEWAY
Sch
SPURT LA
AYLESBURY
THE GREEN
Cuddington Mill Farm
CHILTON RD
WINCHENDON RD
DADBROOK CL 1
DADFIELD CL 2
DADBROOK
Furze Farm
AYLESBURY RD
Chearsley Hill House
OLD PLOUGH CL
Dadbrook House
SCHOOL LA
Sch
THE GREEN
DARK LA
LOWER GREEN LA
Chearsley
TURNIP CL
WAITS GREEN
SHUPP'S LA
ELM BROOK CL
Lower Green Farm
Dad Brook
CHURCH LA
CRENDON RD
Manor Farm
Ppg Sta
Grove Farm
Bettymoor Plantation
CHEARSLEY RD
Arch Bridge
A418
AYLESBURY RD

99
114

127
114

113
100

A
B
C
4
13
3
12
2
11
1
10
77
78
79
Bear Brook
Coldharbour Farm
Eythrope Park
River Thame
Weir Lodge
Weir
North Buckinghamshire Way
Littleworth Farm
Whaddon Hill Farm
Tumulus
Arthur's Gorse
Burn Hill
Lower Hartwell
Lower Hartwell Farm
The Nursery
Botts Furlong Farm
Upper Hartwell
Barnet's Close
Hartwell House
Park Hill
Cemy
EYETHROPE RD
BELLE VUE
COTTAGE GROUNDS
CROMHAMSTONE
THE SPIERT
OXFORD RD
DARWILL RD
LONG FURLONG
THE GLEBE
CHURCH WAY
STONE CROFT
MANOR FARM CL
Sch
ROUND HILL
LEE CRES
CHILTERN CL
CHILTERN AVE
Beech Walk
A418
MEADOWAY
MAYFLOWER CL
WILLOWMEAD
Stone
BISHOPSTONE RD
PH
Colley Farm
Hospital
Stone House
BITTENHAM CL
PORTWAY
Peveral Court
SEDRUP LA
Upton
UPTON RD
HOMESTEAD FARM
Lower Farm
LOWER FARM GATE
Sedrup
Alwyn Lawn
BISHOPSTONE
Wallace Farm
Sewage Works
Meadow Cottages
Pasture Farm
Chilboro Hill Farm

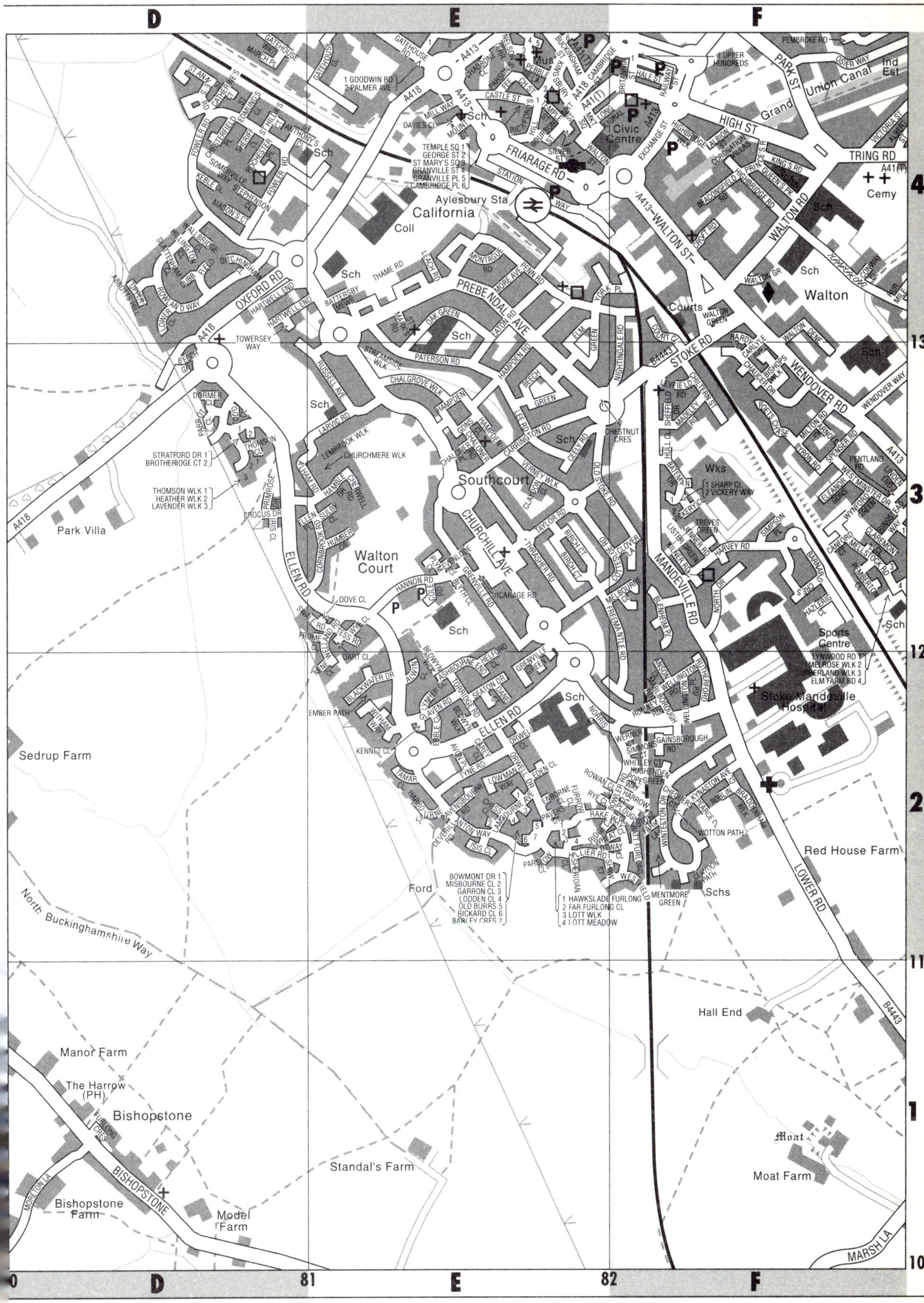
D
E
F
Aylesbury Sta
California
Coll
Sch
Civic Centre
FRIARAGE RD
HIGH ST
Grand Union Canal
Ind Est
TRING RD
Cemy
WALTON ST
WALTON RD
Walton
Courts
STOKE RD
WENDOVER RD
OXFORD RD
A418
TOWERSEY WAY
PREBENDAL AVE
Southcourt
CHURCHILL AVE
Walton Court
ELLEN RD
MANDEVILLE RD
Sports Centre
Stoke Mandeville Hospital
Wks
Park Villa
Sedrup Farm
Red House Farm
LOWER RD
B4443
North Buckinghamshire Way
Ford
Schs
Hall End
Manor Farm
The Harrow (PH)
Bishopstone
Bishopstone Farm
Model Farm
Standal's Farm
Moat
Moat Farm
MARSH LA
4
13
3
12
2
11
1
10
81
82
BOWMONT DR 1
MISBOURNE CL 2
GARRON CL 3
LODDEN CL 4
OLD BURRS 5
BICKARD CL 6
BARLEY CRES 7
1 HAWKSLADE FURLONG
2 FAR FURLONG CL
3 LOTT WLK
4 LOTT MEADOW
STRATFORD DR 1
BROTHERIDGE CT 2
THOMSON WLK 1
HEATHER WLK 2
LAVENDER WLK 3
LYNWOOD RD 1
MELROSE WLK 2
SUTHERLAND WLK 3
ELM FARM RD 4
1 SHARP CL
2 VICKERY WAY
TEMPLE SQ 1
GEORGE ST 2
ST MARY'S SQ 3
GRANVILLE ST 4
GRANVILLE PL 5
CAMBRIDGE PL 6
1 GOODWIN RD
2 PALMER AVE

115
102

115
130

D
E
F
Grand Union Canal (Aylesbury Arm)
College Farm
4
Works
COLLEGE RD
Dropshort Farm
Cherry Farm
13
Sewage Works
ASTON CLINTON RD
Moat
A41(T)
Lower Farm
Model Row
Sunny Brook Farm
Buckland
Moat
Vatche's Farm
NORMILL TERR
Akeman Street ROMAN ROAD
AYLESBURY RD
Aston Clinton
Church Farm
Moat Farm
3
Brook Farm
BROOK ST
LONG PLOUGH
Manor Farm
Nield's Farm
PUTNAMS DR
GREEN END ST
Sch
B4544
WESTON CT
WESTON RD
LONDON RD.
LOWER ICKNIELD WAY
B489
CHESTNUT CL
ROSEBERY RD
BEACONSFIELD RD
12
Park Farm
CHURCH LA
BROOKFIELD FARM
Rookery Farm House
Bridgeway Farm
A41(T)
Aston Clinton Park
Old Rectory Farm
B489
2
Splash Covert
Green Park
STABLEBRIDGE RD
Wellonhead Bridge
Bye Green
Airfield
B4544
BROOK END
ANSTEY BROOK
Brook End
B439
11
A4011
Brook Farm
MILL LA
Sewage Works
Mill Farm
CHILTERN WAY
Rosemead Covert
Harelane Bridge
UPPER ICKNIELD WAY
1
Halton Camp
Grand Union Canal
(Wendover Arm) (disused)
Marl Copse
CH
Wendover Woods
Lower Farm
OLD SCHOOL CL
Halton
MCEWEN RIDE
Church Farm
BROOKSIDE
CHURCH VIEW
ST MICHAEL'S CL
Halton House
ROSEMEAD
A4011
Aston Hill
MANSION HILL
10
86
87
88

117
104

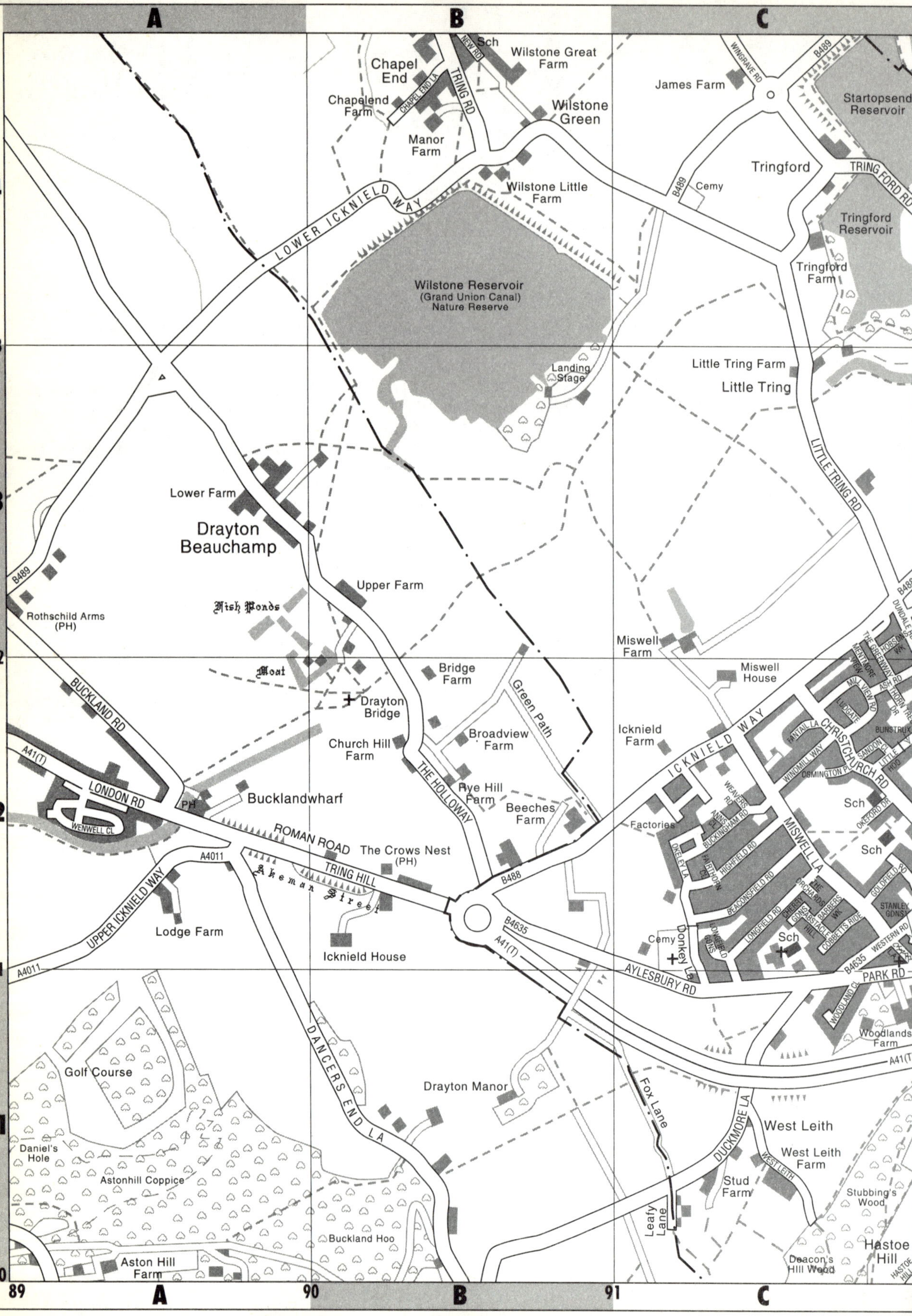

117
132

105
120

133
120

119
106

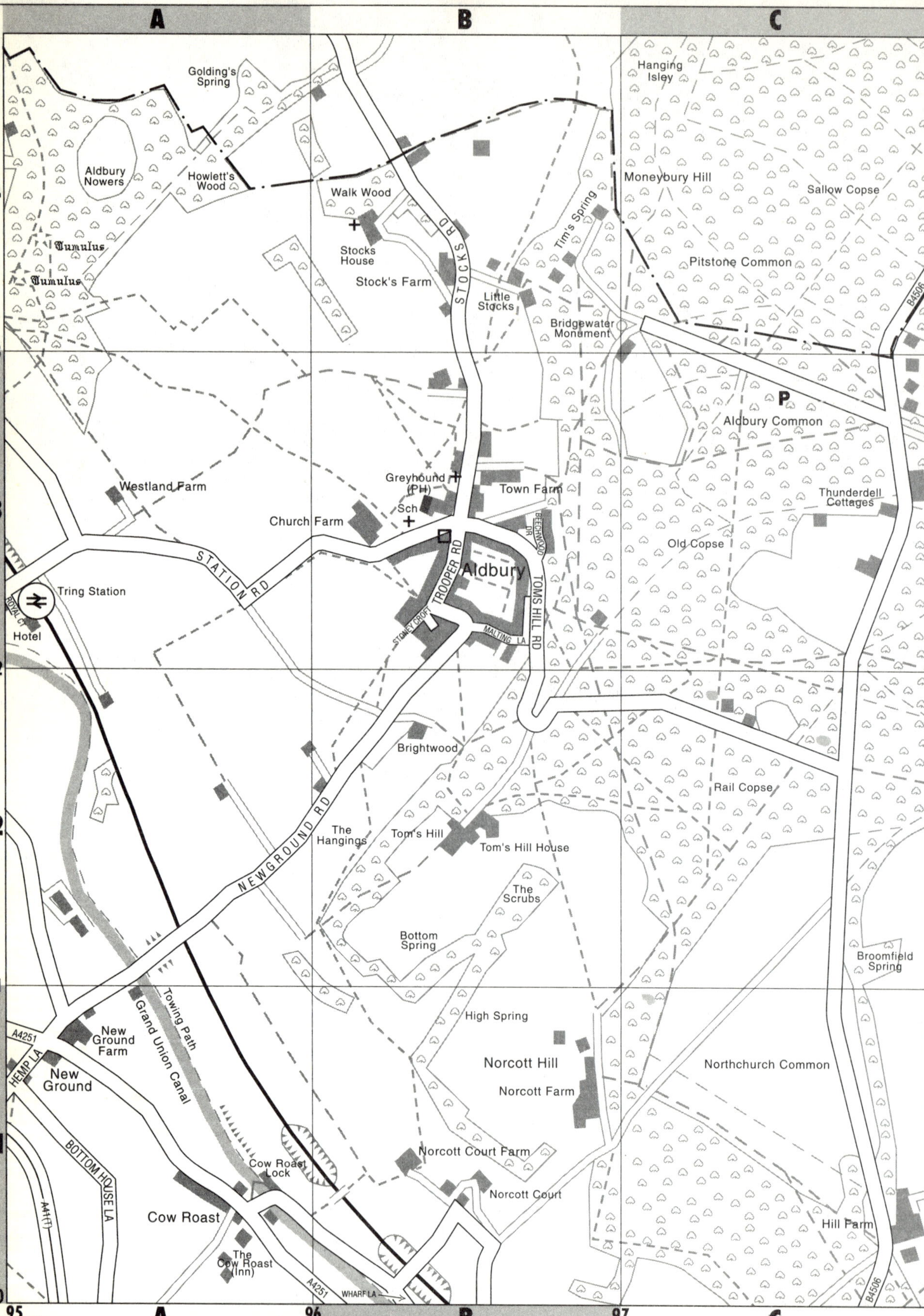

119
134

D
E
F
Church Farm
Badger Wood
ALDERTON DR
B4506
RINGSHALL DR
GATESDENE CL
Bridgewater Arms (PH)
BEDE CT
CHURCH RD
Sch
Little Gaddesden
Hudnall Common Plantation
Hudnall Common
Hudnall
HUDNALL LA
Pitstone Park Copse
Ashridge
The Green
Manor House
CHAPEL CL
Hudnall Farm
Club House
Old Park Lodge
Golf Course
Little Brownlow Farm
Golden Valley
Robin Hood Farm
Prince's Riding
Ashridge Park
Little Gaddesden House
Cromer Wood
Home Farm
Lady Grove
Thunderdell Wood
College
CROMER CL
NETTLEDEN RD
Harding's Rookery
Woodyard Cottage
Toll
Pulridge Wood
Little Coldharbour Farm
Berkhamsted Common
Coldharbour Farm
Goldon Valley Farm
Furzefield Wood
Nettleden Lodge
Webb's Copse
Ashridge
Bluebell Spring
Brickkiln Cottage
Frithsden Gardens
Frithsden Beeches
Golf Course
4
13
3
12
2
11
1
10
8
99
00
D
E
F

108

A
B
C
4
09
3
08
2
07
1
06
59
60
61
Moorbirge Brook
Clearsale
Hursthill
Wood Farm
Waterperry Common
Bernwood Forest
Commonleys Farm
Waterperry Wood
Polecat End
Drunkard's Corner
Park Farm
Park Farm House
Oxfordshire Way
Polecat End Hollows
Marsh Copse
Parson's Farm
Ledall Cottage
M40
Holton Wood
Buryhook Barn
Holton Brook
B4027
Keeper's Cottage
Warren Farm
Pond Farm
Old Park Farm
Warren Wood
Lyehill Quarries (disused)
BURYHOOK CNR
Cottage Copse
Warwick Close Farm
A40(T)
Recreation Ground
Sch
Holton
The Rectory
Holton Place
Liby
Church Farm
Moat
Garden Copse
College
PARK HILL
LONDON RD

D
E
F
Townsend
Green Lane
Bradmoor Farm
Folly Farm
Hewdon Farm
Moat
Haddenham
WOODWAYS
CHURCHWAY
Sch
Liby
F Sta
STANBRIDGE RD
Fairfields Farm
Mushroom Farm
Aston Mullins
ASTON RD
Church End
Church Farm
Dragon Tail
Manor Farm
The Manor
Aston Sandford
Stan Bridge
Wks
Aston Leys Farm
Old Farm
Kingsey
A4129
Foxhill
Dove House Farm
Foxhill Covert
Whirlbush Farm
Blackbarn Farm
Shrove Furlong Farm
4
09
3
08
2
07
1
06
75
76

127 114

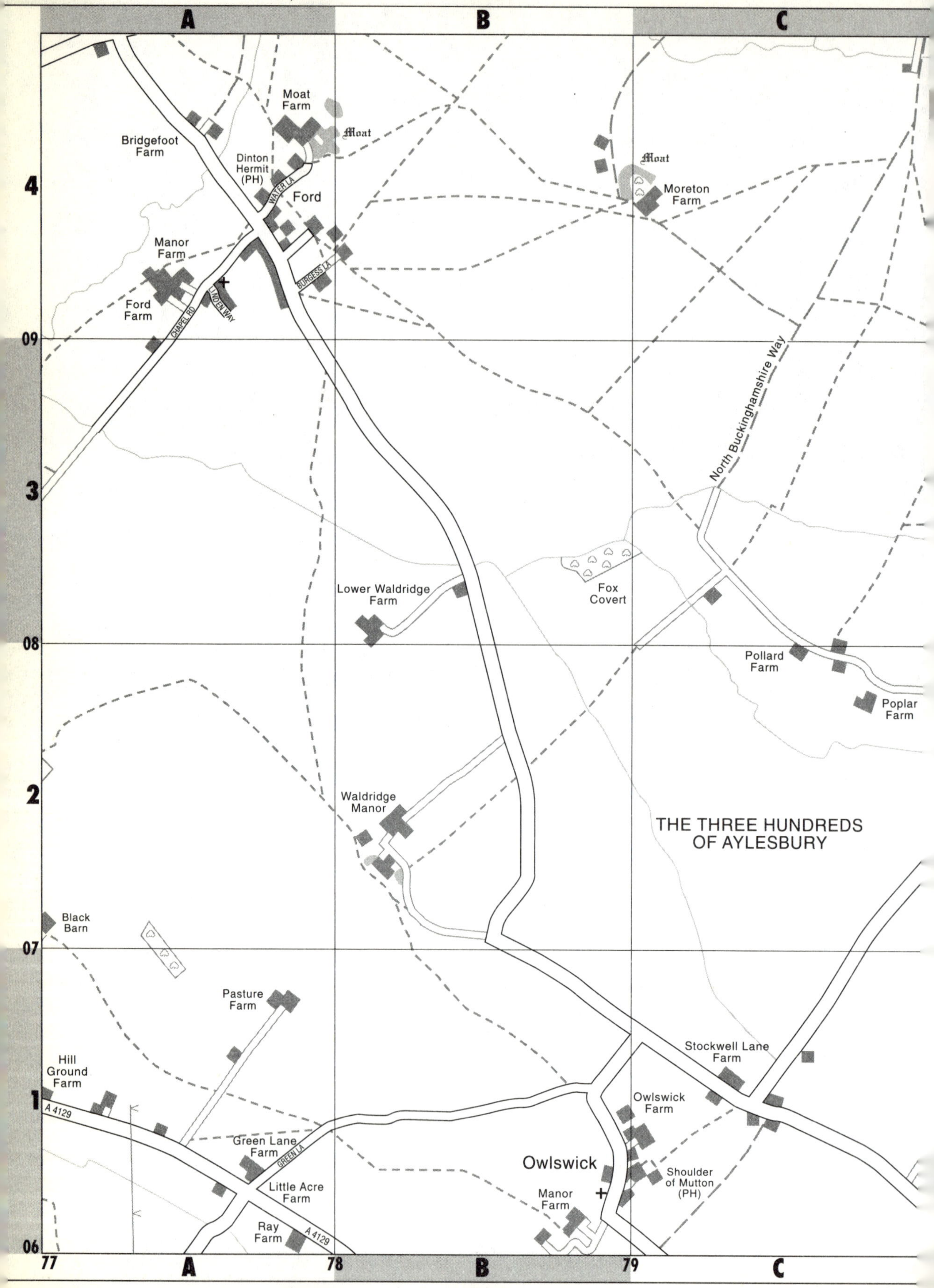

127 138

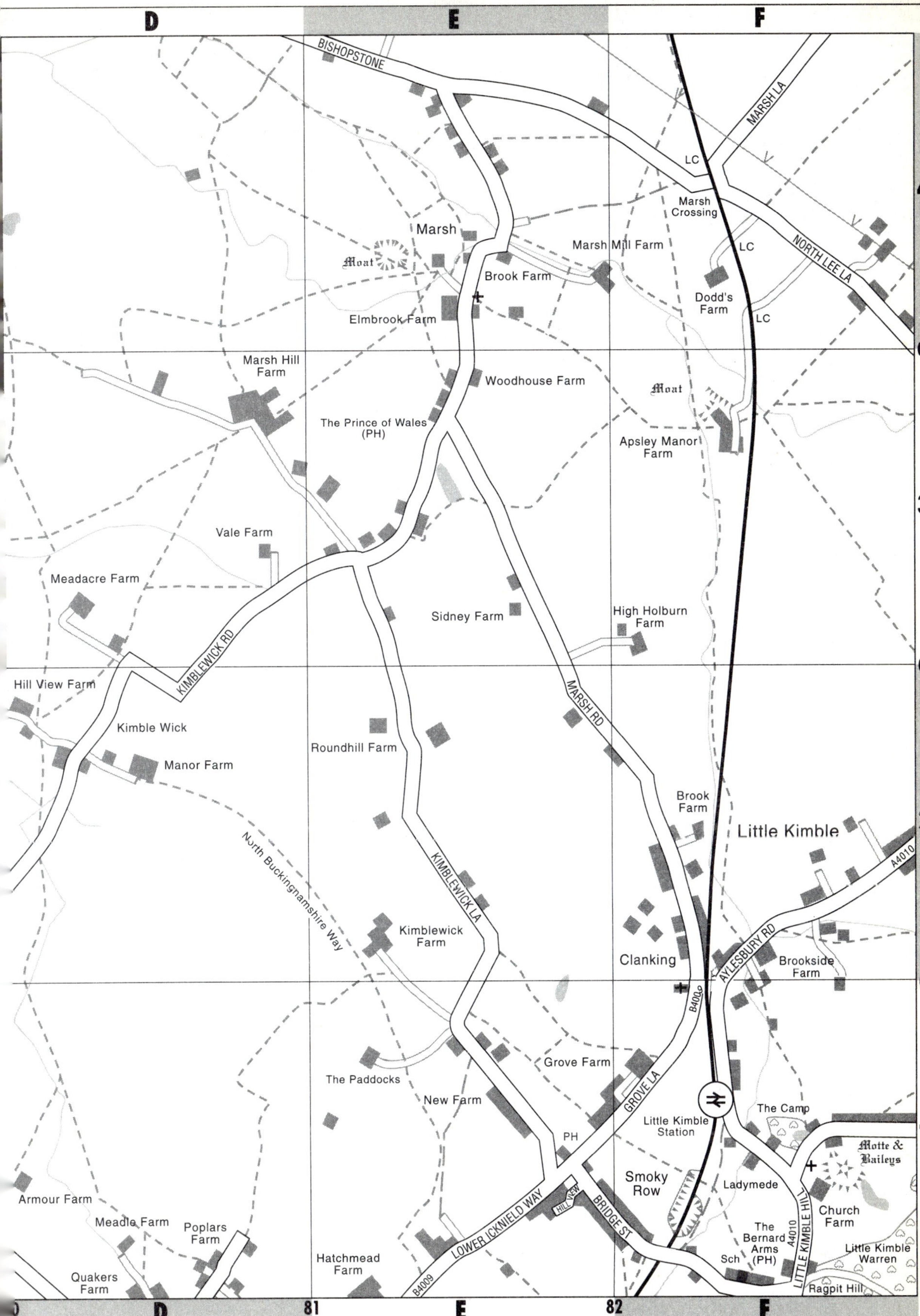
D
E
F
BISHOPSTONE
MARSH LA
LC
Marsh Crossing
NORTH LEE LA
Marsh
Moat
Brook Farm
Marsh Mill Farm
LC
Dodd's Farm
LC
Elmbrook Farm
4
09
Marsh Hill Farm
Woodhouse Farm
Moat
The Prince of Wales (PH)
Apsley Manor Farm
3
Vale Farm
Meadacre Farm
Sidney Farm
High Holburn Farm
KIMBLEWICK RD
08
Hill View Farm
MARSH RD
Kimble Wick
Manor Farm
Roundhill Farm
Brook Farm
2
Little Kimble
A4010
North Buckinghamshire Way
KIMBLEWICK LA
Kimblewick Farm
AYLESBURY RD
Brookside Farm
Clanking
B4009
07
Grove Farm
The Paddocks
New Farm
GROVE LA
The Camp
Little Kimble Station
1
PH
Motte & Baileys
Smoky Row
Ladymede
Armour Farm
Church Farm
Meadle Farm
HILL VIEW
LOWER ICKNIELD WAY
BRIDGE ST
The Bernard Arms (PH)
A4010
LITTLE KIMBLE HILL
Poplars Farm
Little Kimble Warren
Hatchmead Farm
Sch
Quakers Farm
B4009
Ragpit Hill
06
D
81
E
82
F

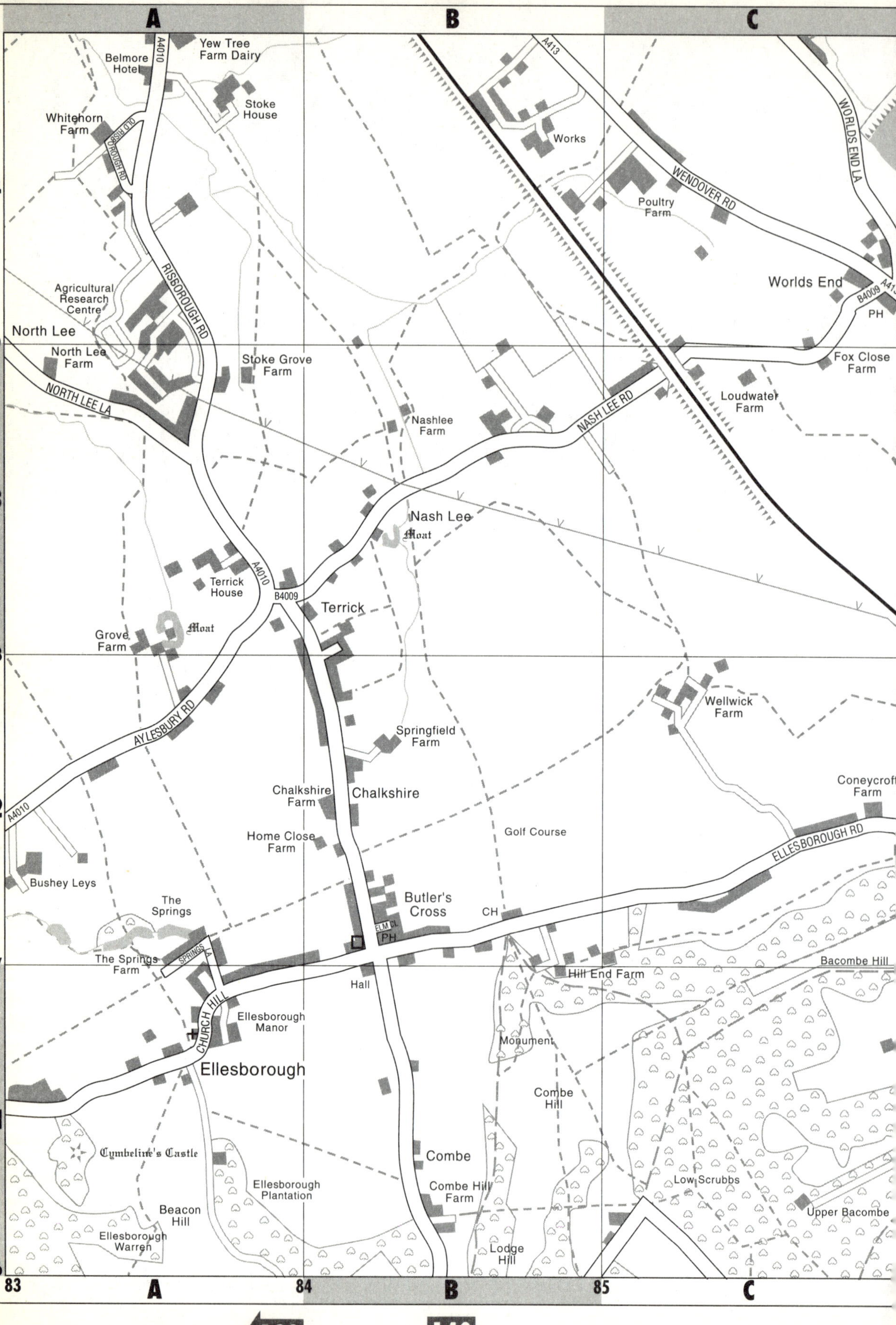
A
B
C
4
3
2
1
09
08
07
06
83
84
85
Yew Tree Farm Dairy
Belmore Hotel
A4010
Stoke House
Whitehorn Farm
OLD RISBOROUGH RD
Works
A413
WORLDS END LA
WENDOVER RD
Poultry Farm
RISBOROUGH RD
Agricultural Research Centre
Worlds End
A413
B4009
PH
North Lee
North Lee Farm
Stoke Grove Farm
Fox Close Farm
NORTH LEE LA
Loudwater Farm
NASH LEE RD
Nashlee Farm
Nash Lee
Moat
A4010
Terrick House
B4009
Terrick
Grove Farm
Moat
Wellwick Farm
AYLESBURY RD
Springfield Farm
Chalkshire Farm
Chalkshire
Coneycroft Farm
A4010
Home Close Farm
Golf Course
ELLESBOROUGH RD
Bushey Leys
The Springs
Butler's Cross
CH
ELM CL
PH
The Springs Farm
SPRINGS LA
Bacombe Hill
Hall
Hill End Farm
CHURCH HILL
Ellesborough Manor
Monument
Ellesborough
Combe Hill
Cymbeline's Castle
Combe
Ellesborough Plantation
Combe Hill Farm
Low Scrubbs
Beacon Hill
Upper Bacombe
Ellesborough Warren
Lodge Hill

D
E
F
4
09
3
08
2
07
1
06
87
88
Boat House
Weston Turville Reservoir (Grand Union Canal)
Sewage Works
Dismantled Railway
Towing Path
Grand Union Canal (Wendover Arm) (disused)
Schools
Halton Camp
Haddington Hill
Wendover Woods
Halton Wood
Picnic Site
Forest Walks
Fort
Resr (dis)
Boddington Hill
WENDOVER
Wendover Station
Bank Farm
Hospl
Sch
Sta
Path Sta
Mill
Liby
Beechwood Lane
HALE LA
HALE RD
CHURCH LA
Wellhead Farm
PH
Ridgeway
HOGTROUGH LA
Boswells Farm
Rifle Range
Road Barn Farm
LONDON RD
Smalldene Farm
Coxgrove Wood
Bacombe Hill
Tumulus
Bacombe Warren
BACOMBE LA
ELLESBOROUGH RD
LITTLE HAMPDEN CL
SOUTH ST
POUND ST
HIGH ST
AYLESBURY RD
TRING RD
UPPER ICKNIELD WAY
CHESTNUT AVE
HALTON LA
A413
A4011
Barn Wood
Concord

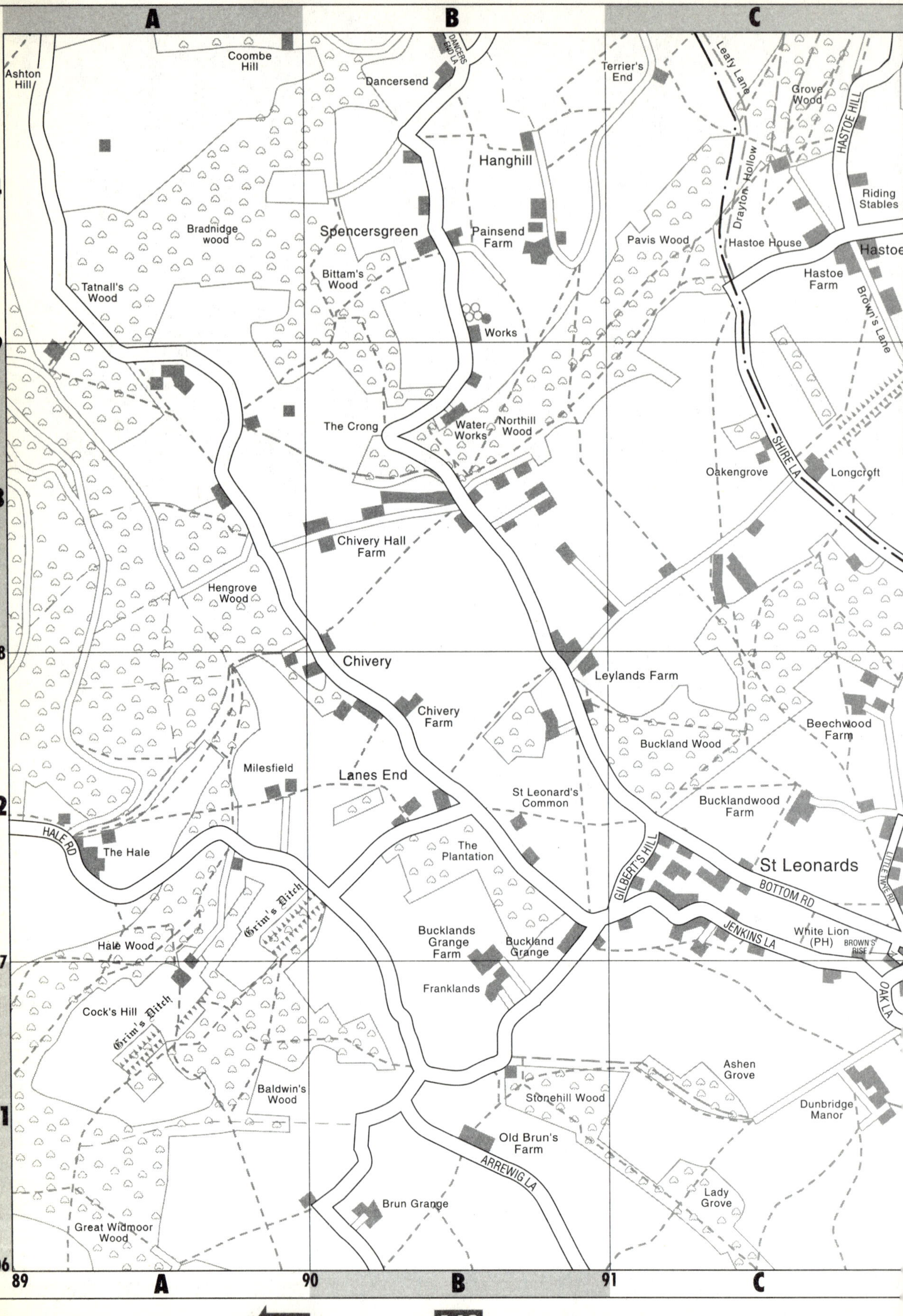
A
B
C
Coombe Hill
Ashton Hill
Dancersend
DANCERS END LA
Terrier's End
Leafy Lane
Grove Wood
HASTOE HILL
Hanghill
Riding Stables
Drayton Hollow
Bradnidge wood
Spencersgreen
Painsend Farm
Pavis Wood
Hastoe House
Hastoe
Tatnall's Wood
Bittam's Wood
Hastoe Farm
Brown's Lane
Works
The Crong
Water Works
Northill Wood
Oakengrove
SHIRE LA
Longcroft
Chivery Hall Farm
Hengrove Wood
Chivery
Leylands Farm
Chivery Farm
Beechwood Farm
Buckland Wood
Milesfield
Lanes End
St Leonard's Common
Bucklandwood Farm
HALE RD
The Hale
The Plantation
GILBERT'S HILL
St Leonards
LITTLE TWYE RD
BOTTOM RD
Grim's Ditch
Hale Wood
Bucklands Grange Farm
Buckland Grange
JENKINS LA
White Lion (PH)
BROWN'S RISE
Franklands
OAK LA
Cock's Hill
Grim's Ditch
Ashen Grove
Baldwin's Wood
Stonehill Wood
Dunbridge Manor
Old Brun's Farm
ARREWIG LA
Lady Grove
Brun Grange
Great Widmoor Wood
4
09
3
08
2
07
1
06
89
90
91

119 134

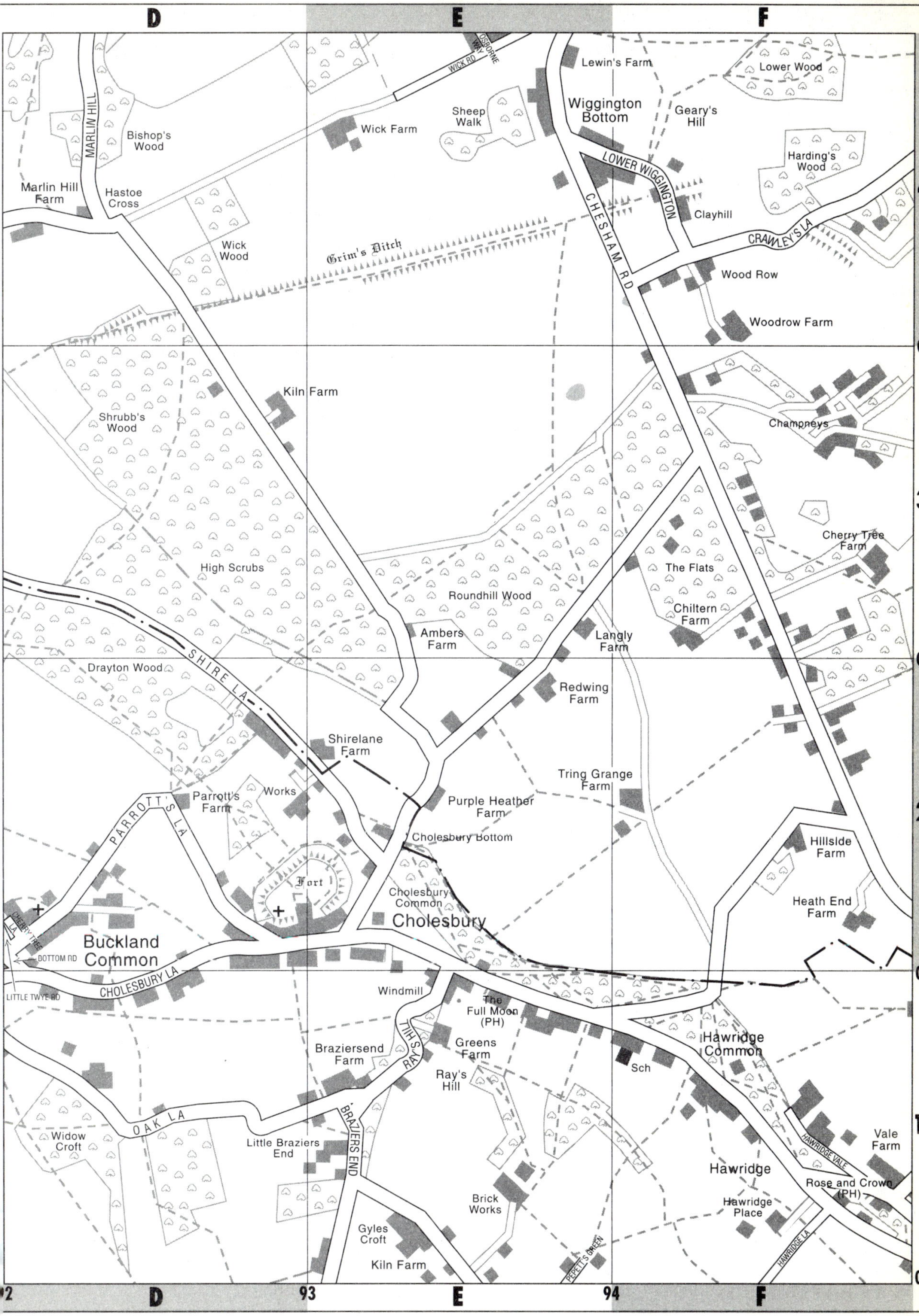

143 134

133
120

A
B
C
4
09
3
08
2
07
1
06
95
96
97
Tinkers Lodge
HOUSE LA
BOTTOM
A41(T)
CRAWLEY'S LA
A4251
WHARF LA
B4506
Northchurch Common
Gorseside
Dudswell
Grand Union Canal
River Bulbourne
Towing Path
BOSWICK LA
DUDSWELL LA
TRING RD
Hamberlins Farm
Crawley's Lane Farm
ROSSWAY LA
HAMBERLINS LA
Hamberlins House
PEA LA
White Farm
TINKERS LA
Hamberlins Wood
Grim's Ditch
LYME AVE
BIRCH RD
HOME FARM RD
DELL RD
ASHBY RD
COVERT CL
COVERT RD
ST MARY'S AVE
HIGH ST
PETER'S PL
PARK RISE
HERONS ELM
FRIARS FIELD
MANDELYNS
MERLING CROFT
KITE FIELD
BRAYNEBERY
ALYNGTON
EMERTON GARTH
EMERTON CT
NEW RD
CAREYS CROFT
STANIER RISE
CREW CURVE
ST KATHERINE'S WAY
BRIDGEWATER RD
COMPASS GDNS
DORRIEN'S CROFT
Tunnel
MORTAIN DR
SOUTH BANK RD
B4506
Sch
NORTH BRIDGE RD
THE MEADS
VALLEY RD
LOCHNELL RD
MOORE RD
BULBOURNE CL
DUNCOMBE RD
SEYMOUR RD
ALMA RD
BELL LA
GRANVILLE RD
LOXLEY RD
SALTER'S CL
Sch
Newsetts Wood
Pea Lane
DARR'S LA
Northchurch
WESTFIELD RD
A4251
FARM CL
COMBE GDNS
CHAUCER CL
DOUGLAS GDNS
Shootersway Farmhouse
THE LARCHES
BELL LA
DURRANTS RD
Lodge Farm
The Shrubbery
Grim's Ditch
Woodcock Hill
DURRANTS LA
MARLIN CL
BOURNE RD
ASHRIDGE RISE
CHILTERN RD
TRESCO RD
VERNEY CL
The Lodge
Sch
Oak Corner
RIDGEWAY
COBB RD
Tring Lodge
CHALEY CL
TOLWOOD CL
GREENWAY
Windbush
Shootersway
SHOOTERSWAY
COPPINS CL
CROSSFIELD CL
SHOOTERSWAY
WINSTON GDNS
Sch
THE HEMMINGS
SHOOTERSWAY PARK
BARNCROFT RD
CROSSWAYS
CROSS OAK RD
Cock Grove
Rossway Home Farm
Rossway
Chapel (remains of)
Marlin Chapel Farm
Moat
OAK WOOD
HOG LA
A41(T)
Heath End
Glebe Farm
Pancake Wood
HOG LA
The Old Farm
JOHNS LA
Hill Farm
Hockeridge Bottom
Hockeridge Wood
Woodfield Spring Farm
Johns Lane Farm
Hog Lane Farm
Hadden's Plantation
A416
CHESHAM RD
A416

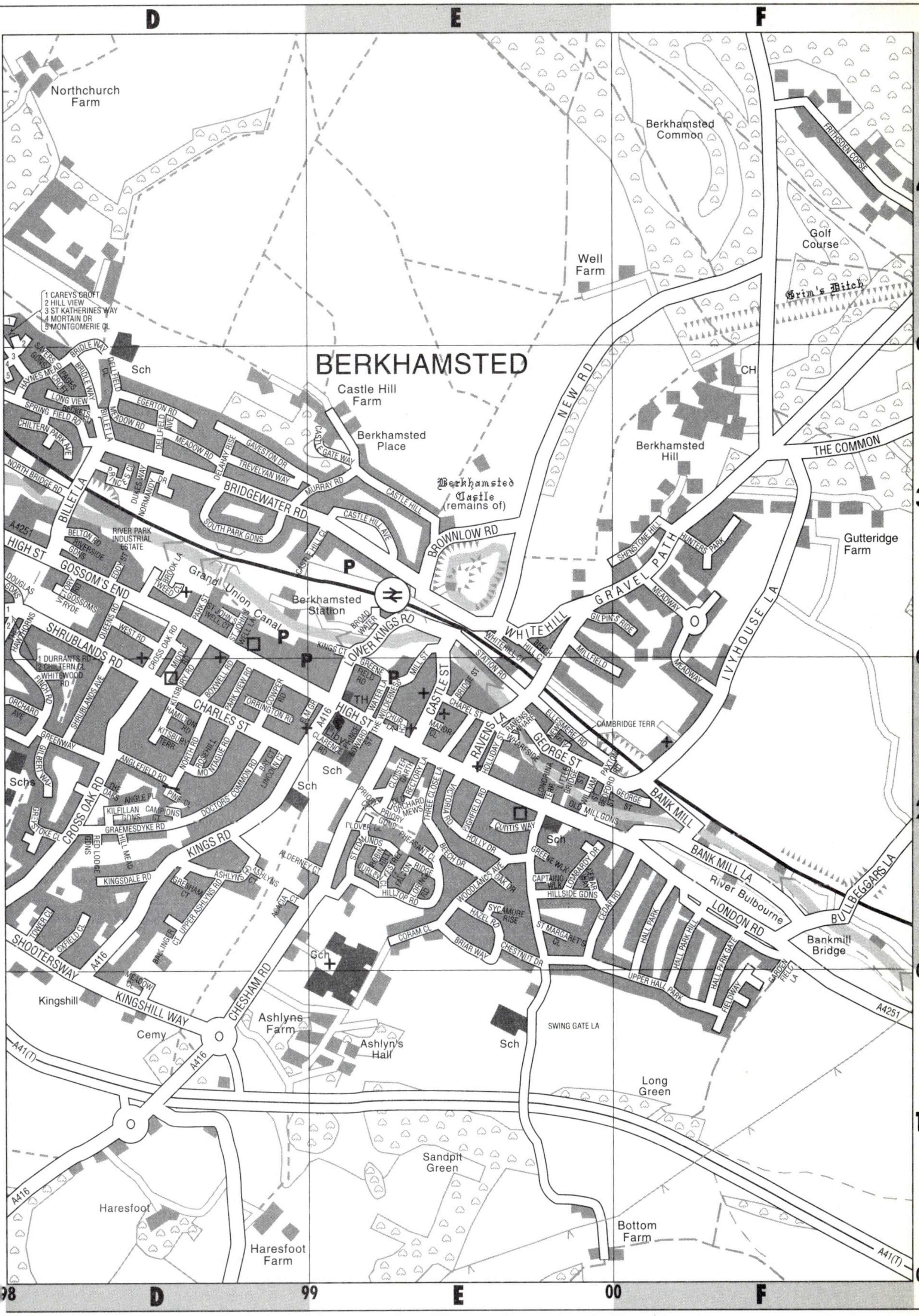
D
E
F
Northchurch Farm
Berkhamsted Common
Golf Course
Well Farm
Grim's Ditch
1 CAREYS CROFT
2 HILL VIEW
3 ST KATHERINES WAY
4 MORTAIN DR
5 MONTGOMERIE CL
BERKHAMSTED
Castle Hill Farm
Berkhamsted Place
Berkhamsted Hill
Berkhamsted Castle (remains of)
THE COMMON
NEW RD
Gutteridge Farm
BROWNLOW RD
Grand Union Canal
Berkhamsted Station
WHITEHILL
GRAVEL PATH
IVYHOUSE LA
LOWER KINGS RD
HIGH ST
GOSSOM'S END
SHRUBLANDS RD
CHARLES ST
1 DURRANTS RD
2 CHILTERN CL
WHITEWOOD RD
CAMBRIDGE TERR
GEORGE ST
BANK MILL
BANK MILL LA
River Bulbourne
LONDON RD
BULLBEGGARS LA
Bankmill Bridge
KINGS RD
CHESHAM RD
SHOOTERSWAY
KINGSHILL WAY
Kingshill
Cemy
Ashlyns Farm
Ashlyn's Hall
SWING GATE LA
Sch
Long Green
Sandpit Green
Haresfoot
Haresfoot Farm
Bottom Farm
A41(T)
A416
A4251
4
3
2
1
09
08
07
06
98
99
00

124

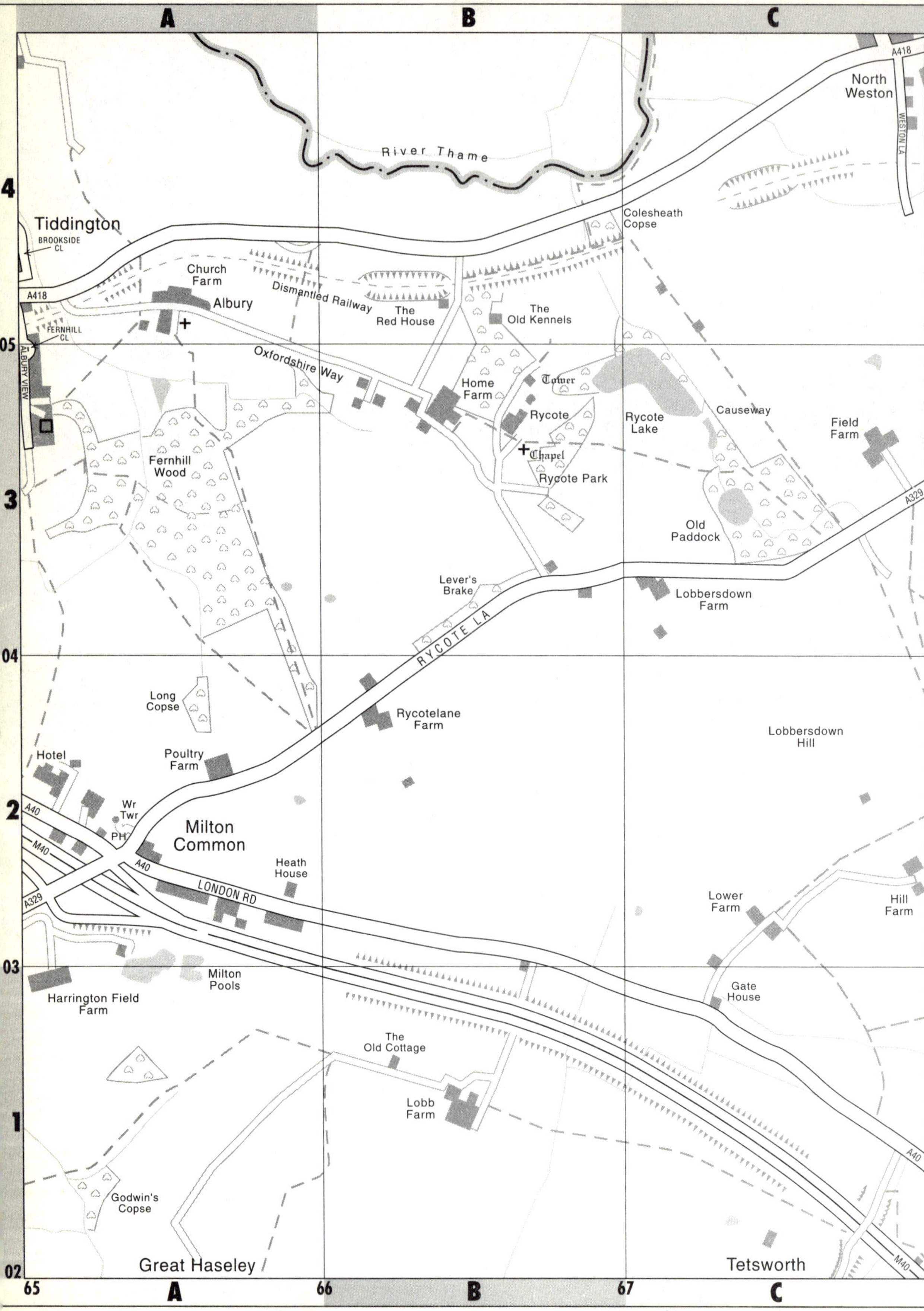
A
B
C
4
05
3
04
2
03
1
02
65
66
67
River Thame
North Weston
A418
WESTON LA
Tiddington
BROOKSIDE CL
Colesheath Copse
Church Farm
Albury
Dismantled Railway
The Red House
The Old Kennels
FERNHILL CL
ALBURY VIEW
Oxfordshire Way
Home Farm
Tower
Rycote
Rycote Lake
Causeway
Field Farm
Chapel
Rycote Park
Fernhill Wood
Old Paddock
A329
Lever's Brake
Lobbersdown Farm
RYCOTE LA
Long Copse
Rycotelane Farm
Lobbersdown Hill
Hotel
Poultry Farm
Wr Twr
PH
A40
M40
Milton Common
Heath House
LONDON RD
Lower Farm
Hill Farm
Milton Pools
Harrington Field Farm
Gate House
The Old Cottage
Lobb Farm
Godwin's Copse
Great Haseley
Tetsworth

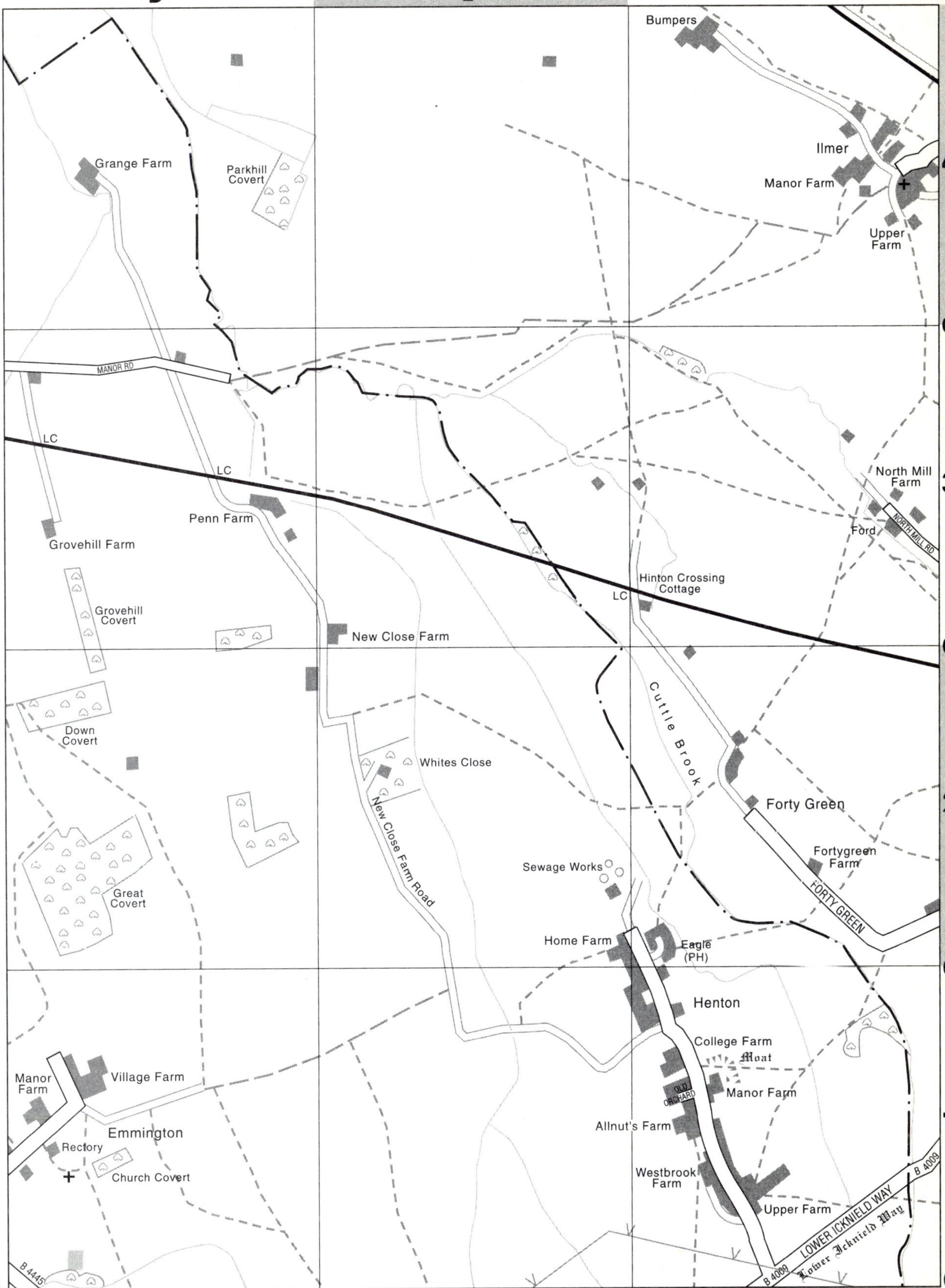
D
E
F
Bumpers
Ilmer
Manor Farm
Upper Farm
Grange Farm
Parkhill Covert
MANOR RD
LC
Penn Farm
Grovehill Farm
Grovehill Covert
New Close Farm
Hinton Crossing Cottage
North Mill Farm
Ford
NORTH MILL RD
Cuttle Brook
Down Covert
Whites Close
New Close Farm Road
Forty Green
Fortygreen Farm
FORTY GREEN
Sewage Works
Great Covert
Home Farm
Eagle (PH)
Henton
College Farm
Moat
Manor Farm
OLD ORCHARD
Allnut's Farm
Westbrook Farm
Upper Farm
LOWER ICKNIELD WAY
Lower Icknield Way
B 4009
Manor Farm
Village Farm
Emmington
Rectory
Church Covert
B 4445
4
05
3
04
2
03
1
02
74
75
76

137
128

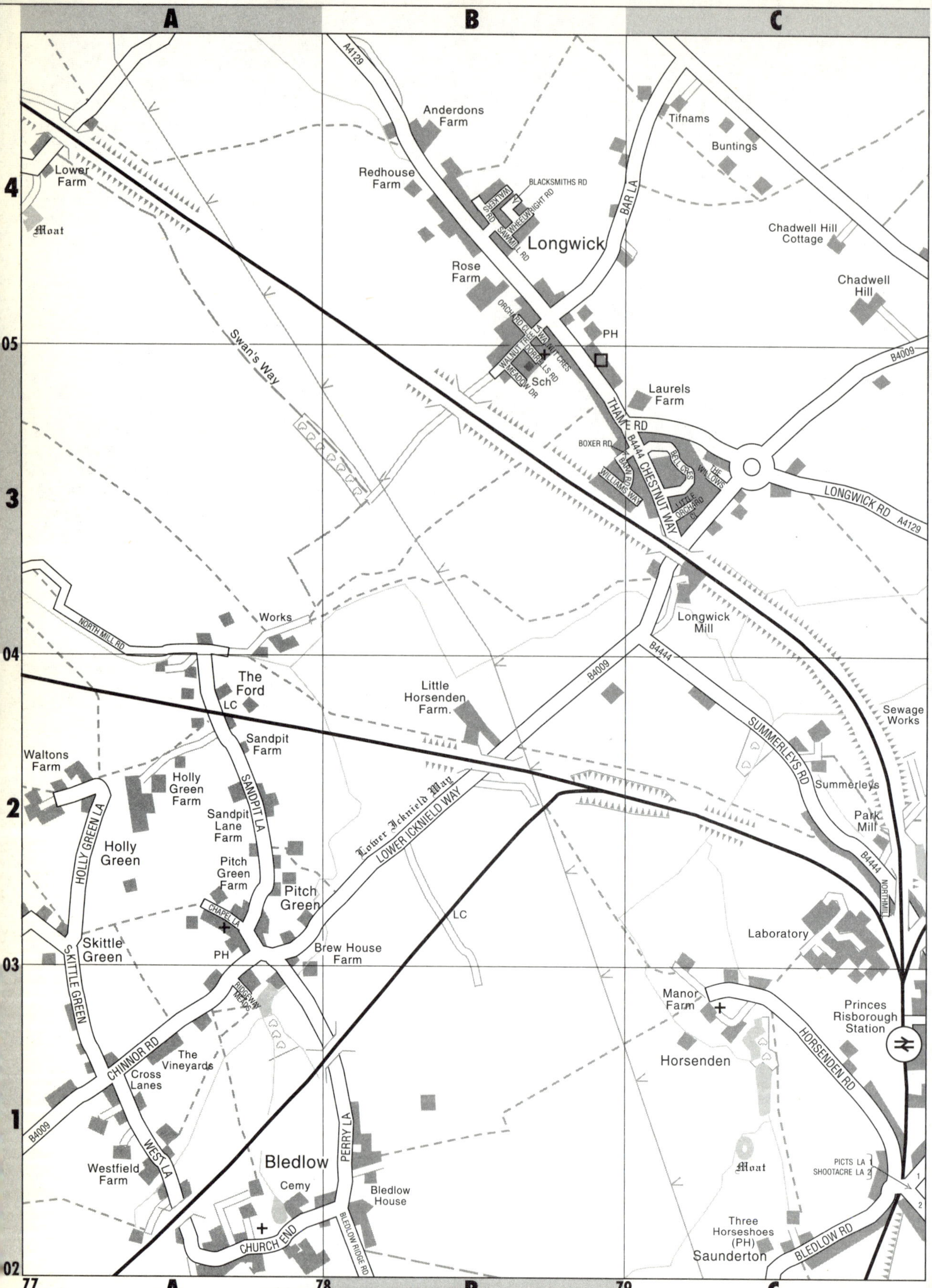

137
148

D E F

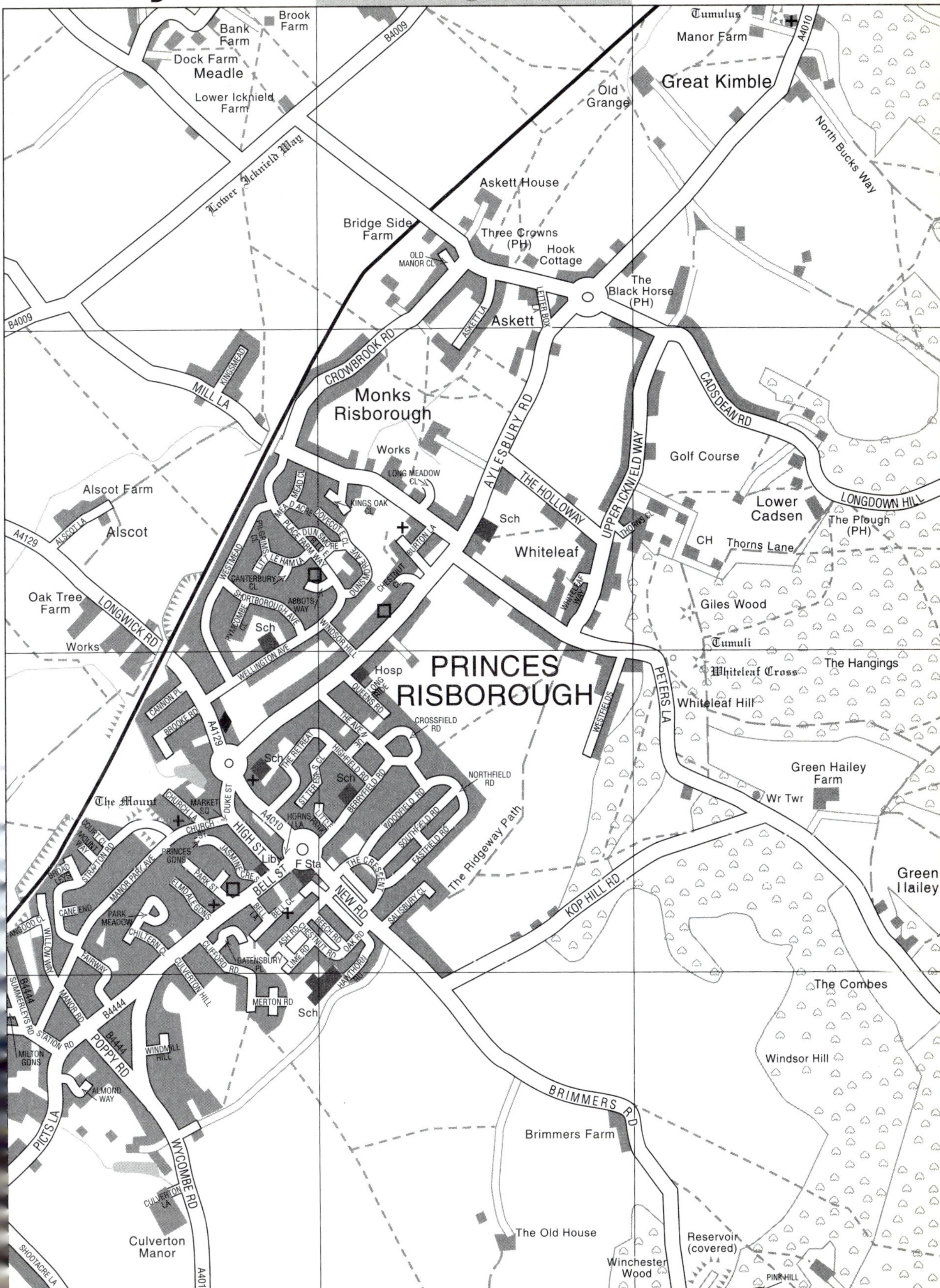
Brook Farm
Bank Farm
Dock Farm
Meadle
Lower Icknield Farm
Lower Icknield Way
B4009
Tumulus
Manor Farm
A4010
Great Kimble
Old Grange
North Bucks Way
Askett House
Bridge Side Farm
Three Crowns (PH)
Hook Cottage
OLD MANOR CL
The Black Horse (PH)
Askett
ASKETT LA
LETTER BOX LA
CROWBROOK RD
KINGSMEAD
MILL LA
Monks Risborough
AYLESBURY RD
UPPER ICKNIELD WAY
CADSDEAN RD
Golf Course
Works
LONG MEADOW CL
THE HOLLOWAY
LONGDOWN HILL
Alscot Farm
Alscot
ALSCOT LA
A4129
KINGS OAK CL
Sch
Lower Cadsen
The Plough (PH)
THORNS CL
CH
Thorns Lane
Whiteleaf
WHITELEAF WAY
Oak Tree Farm
LONGWICK RD
WESTMEAD
CANTERBURY CL
SHORTBOROUGH AVE
ABBOTS WAY
WINDSOR HILL
CHESTNUT CL
BURTON LA
Giles Wood
Tumuli
Whiteleaf Cross
The Hangings
Works
WELLINGTON AVE
Hosp
QUEENS RD
PRINCES RISBOROUGH
WESTFIELDS
PETERS LA
Whiteleaf Hill
CANNON PL
BROOKE RD
CROSSFIELD RD
THE RETREAT
HIGHFIELD RD
BERRYFIELD RD
NORTHFIELD RD
Green Hailey Farm
Wr Twr
The Mount
MARKET SQ
DUKE ST
CHURCH LA
HIGH ST
A4010
WOODFIELD RD
SOUTHFIELD RD
EASTFIELD RD
The Ridgeway Path
Green Hailey
Liby
F Sta
BELL ST
THE CRESCENT
NEW RD
SALISBURY CL
KOP HILL RD
MANOR PARK AVE
PRINCES GDNS
PARK ST
ELMODALE GDNS
CANE END
PARK MEADOW
CHILTERN CL
WILLOW WAY
FAIRWAY
GATENSBURY PL
CLIFFORD RD
CULVERTON HILL
MERTON RD
Sch
HAWTHORN RD
B4444
SUMMERLEYS RD
MANOR RD
STATION RD
POPPY RD
WINDMILL HILL
MILTON GDNS
The Combes
Windsor Hill
ALMOND WAY
BRIMMERS RD
Brimmers Farm
PICTS LA
WYCOMBE RD
CULVERTON LA
Culverton Manor
SHOOTACRE LA
The Old House
Reservoir (covered)
Winchester Wood
PINK HILL
4
05
3
04
2
03
1
02
81
82

D E F

139
130

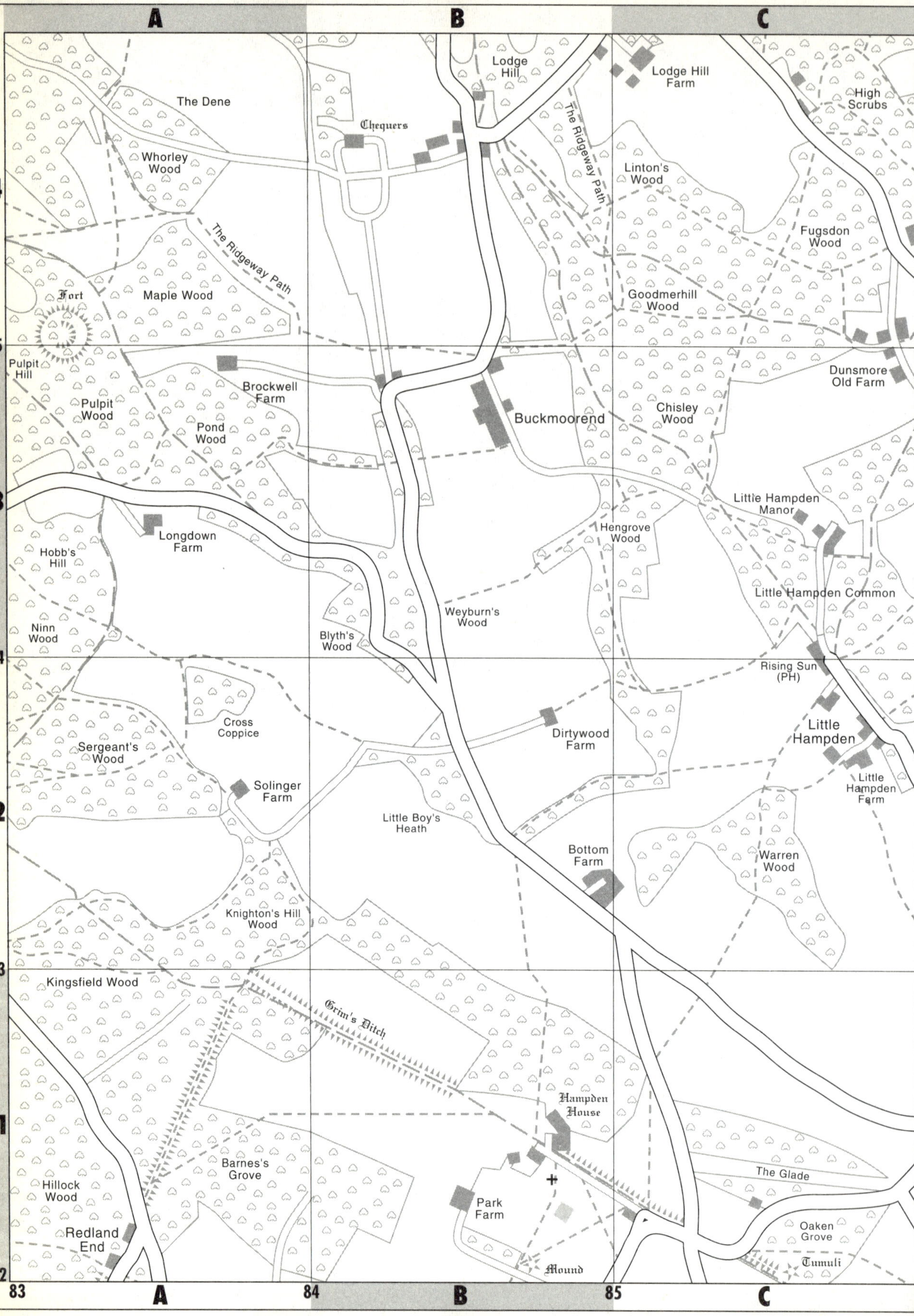

139
150

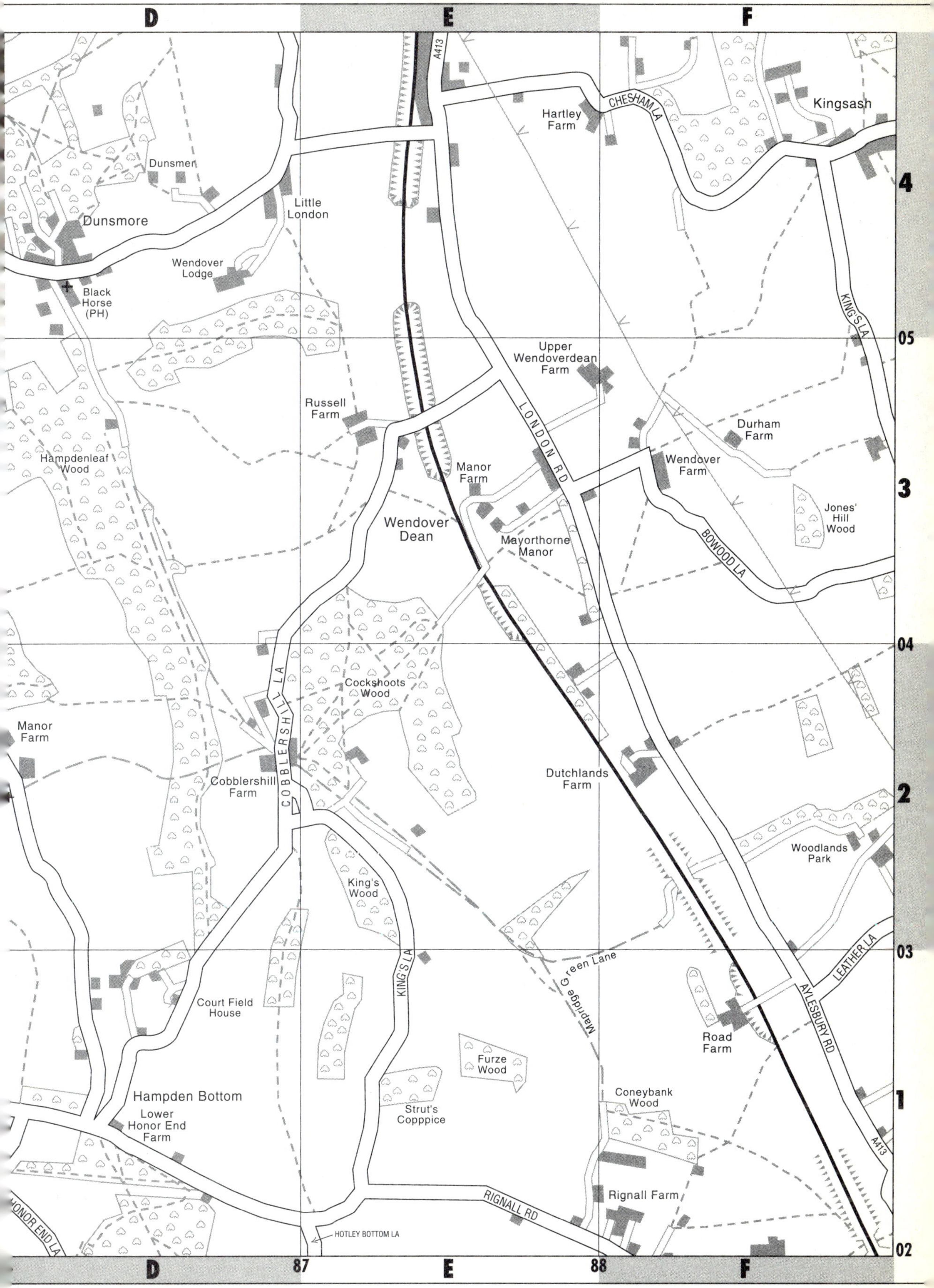
D
E
F
A413
Hartley Farm
CHESHAM LA
Kingsash
Dunsmer
Dunsmore
Little London
Wendover Lodge
Black Horse (PH)
KING'S LA
Upper Wendoverdean Farm
Russell Farm
LONDON RD
Durham Farm
Hampdenleaf Wood
Manor Farm
Wendover Farm
Jones' Hill Wood
Wendover Dean
Mayorthorne Manor
BOWOOD LA
Cockshoots Wood
COBBLERSHILL LA
Manor Farm
Cobblershill Farm
Dutchlands Farm
Woodlands Park
King's Wood
KING'S LA
LEATHER LA
Mapridge Green Lane
Court Field House
AYLESBURY RD
Road Farm
Furze Wood
Hampden Bottom
Coneybank Wood
Lower Honor End Farm
Strut's Copppice
A413
Rignall Farm
RIGNALL RD
HONOR END LA
HOTLEY BOTTOM LA
4
05
3
04
2
03
1
02
D
87
E
88
F

A
B
C
Timberley Lane
Lordling Wood
Old Swan (PH)
Furze Field
Kingswood
ARREWIG LA
Erriwig Farm
4
The Gate (PH)
Lee Gate
Kingsgate Farm
Swan Bottom
Three Gates Farm
05
Gwenfa Farm
Bray's Wood
Moat
Lownde's Wood
3
Lee Clump
The Lee
Home Farm
Leeclump Farm
Church Farm
Church (restored)
PRINCES LA
The Bugle (PH)
CROCKETTS LA
ST MARY'S LA
BOWOOD LA
Hawthorn Farm
Sch
OXFORD ST
Bassibones Farm
Cock and Rabbit (PH)
Rushmoor Wood
Lee Common
Lower Bassibones Farm
04
KING'S LA
CHERRYTREE LA
Pipers
Hunt's Green
SLY CNR
Field End Grange
Hunt's Green Farm
Grim's Ditch
2
Ballinger Bottom
CHILTERN RD
BLACKTHORNE LA
BLACKFIELD LA
P
LEATHER LA
Ballinger Common
Hammondshall Farm
03
Springfield Farm
Ballinger Farm
Ballinger Grove
Wr Twr
1
Havenfields
POTTER ROW
HERBERTS HOLE
Park Farm
Ballinger Bottom (South)
BALLINGER RD
A413
MARRIOTTS AVE
AYLESBURY RD
Bury Farm
02
89
90
91
A
B
C

133
144

153
144

143
134

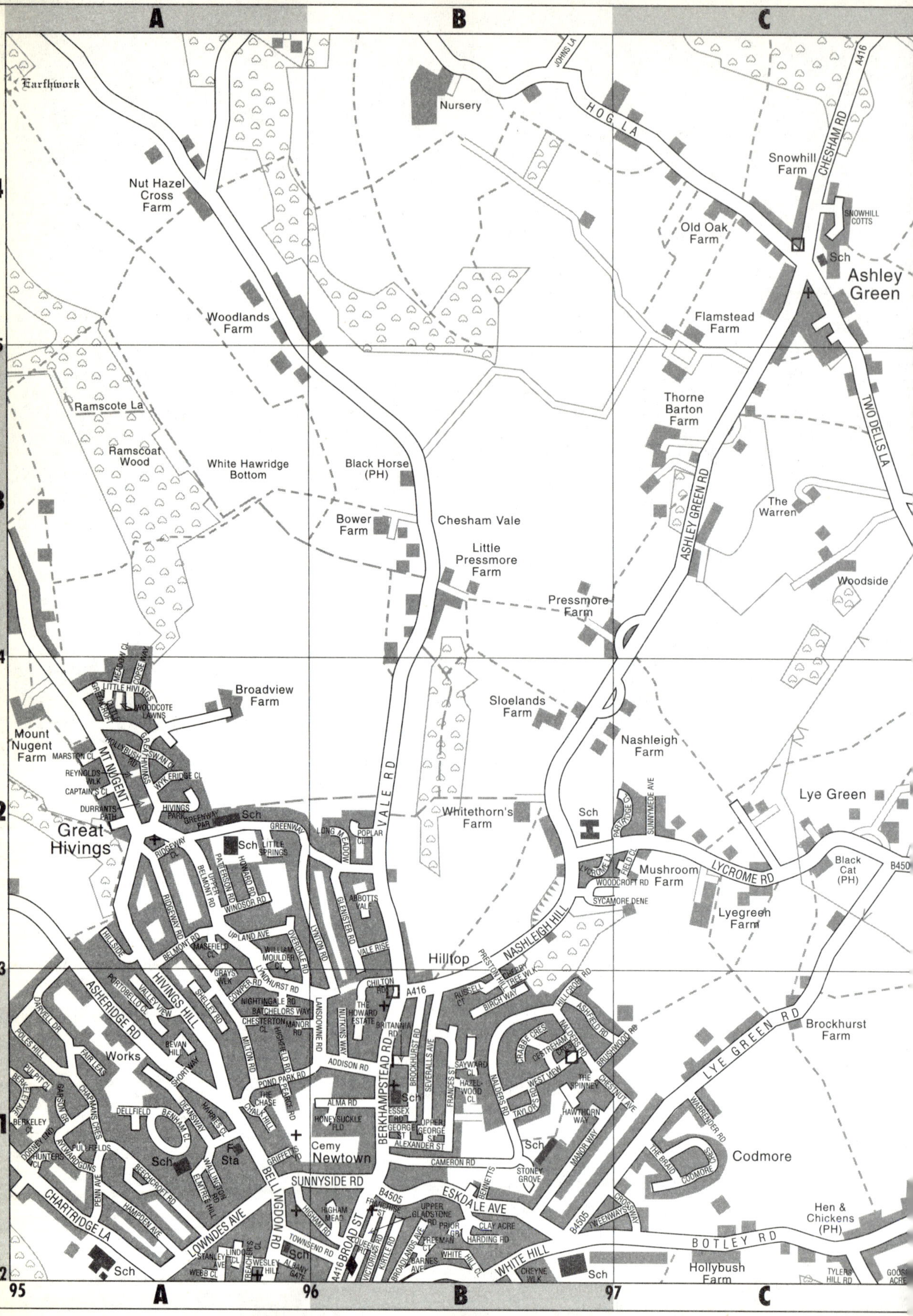
A
B
C
4
05
3
04
2
03
1
02
95
96
97
Earthwork
Nursery
HOG LA
JOHNS LA
CHESHAM RD
A416
Nut Hazel
Cross
Farm
Snowhill
Farm
SNOWHILL
COTTS
Old Oak
Farm
Sch
Ashley
Green
Woodlands
Farm
Flamstead
Farm
Ramscote La
Thorne
Barton
Farm
TWO DELLS LA
Ramscoat
Wood
White Hawridge
Bottom
Black Horse
(PH)
ASHLEY GREEN RD
The
Warren
Bower
Farm
Chesham Vale
Little
Pressmore
Farm
Woodside
Pressmore
Farm
Broadview
Farm
Sloelands
Farm
Mount
Nugent
Farm
Nashleigh
Farm
MT NUGENT
VALE RD
Lye Green
Whitethorn's
Farm
Sch
Great
Hivings
Sch
Black
Cat
(PH)
LYCROME RD
Mushroom
Farm
Lyegreen
Farm
NASHLEIGH HILL
Hilltop
A416
HIVINGS HILL
ASHERIDGE RD
Works
Brockhurst
Farm
LYE GREEN RD
BERKHAMPSTEAD RD
Sch
Codmore
Cemy
Newtown
F
Sta
Sch
SUNNYSIDE RD
ESKDALE AVE
Hen &
Chickens
(PH)
CHARTRIDGE LA
LOWNDES AVE
BELLINGDON RD
BROAD ST
WHITE HILL
BOTLEY RD
B4505
Sch
Sch
Hollybush
Farm
Sch

135
146

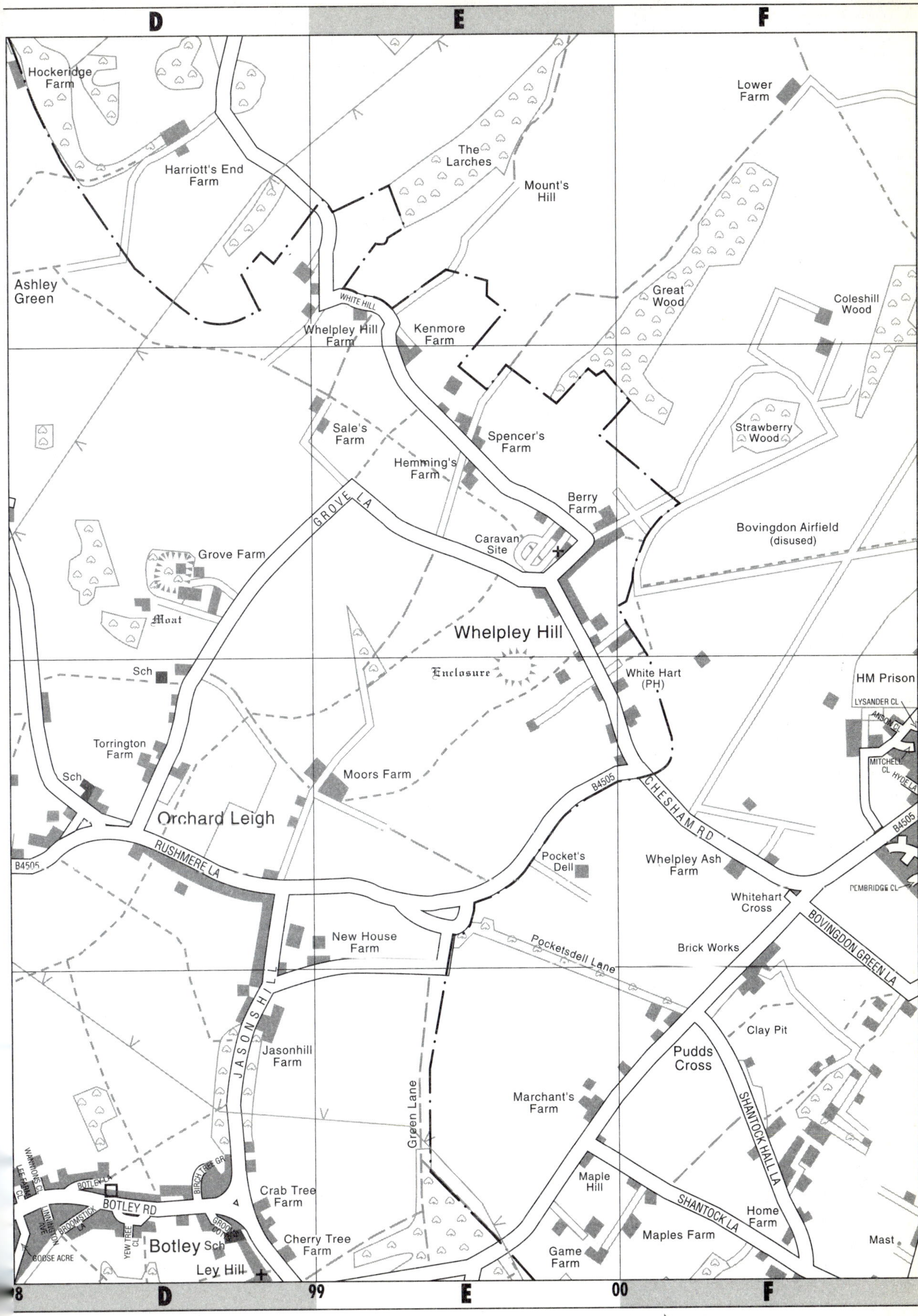

155
146

145

A
B
C
4
05
3
04
2
03
1
02
01
02
03
A41(T)
A4251
LONDON RD
A4251
FELDEN LA
B4505
Vale Farm
Golf Course
Green Croft
Feldon
Sch
COPPER BEECH CL
THE SYCAMORES
THE BIRCHES
THE LINDENS
BEECHWOOD PARK
HAWKSVIL DR
CH
Hanging Wood
BOURNE END LA
Westbrook Hay
Hay Wood
THE HAWTHORNS
THE CHESTNUTS
Sheethanger Common
Golf Course
CH
P
BOX LA
Feldon Lodge
Ramacre Wood
Bury Wood
BURY RISE
Gorsefield Wood
Mast
Mast
SHOTHANGER WAY
Longcroft Farm
BUSHFIELD RD
STONEY LA
HEMPSTEAD RD
Highcroft
Inn
Caravan Park
LONGCROFT LA
HM Prison
Duckhall Farm
Random Farm
Kingshill Dell
Valley Farm
Shortridge Wood
GRANVILLE DENE
NEWHOUSE RD
FIELD WAY
THE BOURNE
VICARAGE LA
ST LAWRENCE CL
Old Dean
Homefield Spring
LANCASTER DR
LYSANDER CL
CHESHAM RD
HOWARD AGNE CL
NEWHALL CL
HIGH ST
Schs
CHURCH LA
CHURCH ST
Bury Farm
F
Sta
PH
PH
Bovingdon
SIMON DEAN
OLD DEAN
DEAN FIELD
HYDE MEADOWS
RYDER CL
Lane Farm
B4505
HYDE LA
ORCHARD WAY
GRYMILL CL
NYE WAY
HOMEFIELD
YEW TREE CT
AUSTINS MEAD
Nuffield Farm
PEMBRIDGE LA
EASTNOR
CLAVERTON CL
FARNHAM CL
WINDSOR RD
ARDEN CL
PEMBRIDGE CHASE
LITTLE PARK
GREEN LA
CHIPPERFIELD RD
FLAUNDEN LA
BULSTRODE LA
Bovingdon Lodge
Street Farm
1 ASHRIDGE CL
2 DINMORE
3 PEMBRIDGE CL
GREEN VIEW CL
Bulstrode
Greinan Farm
Bulstrode Farm
Bovingdon Green
Cross Farm
Green Farm
HUNTERS CL
Tower Hill
THE HOLLIES
PH
Waterlane Farm
Milbaise
NEW RD
WATER LA
TOWER HILL
STONEY LA
Tenements Farm
Harts Hill Farm
Long Lane Farm
LONG LA
MIDDLE LA
Tuffs Farm
Cottingham Farm
HOLLY HEDGES LA
Chipperfield House
SCATTERDELLS LA
Meadow Way Farm
Heartsfield

145 156

D
E
F
B4445
THAME RD
B4009
LOWER ICKNIELD WAY
Lane Farm
HOLLAND CL
ELDERDENE
SPRINGFIELD GDNS
LEYBOURNE GDNS
New Farm
MALYNS CL
LOWER RD
DOVELEAT
B4445
B4009
P
PH
BENTON DR
GRATTON
HIGH ST
Sch
Schs
Chinnor
Liby
Lower Icknield Way
MILL LA
DIEMENS CL
DUCK SQ
MUSGRAVE RD
RECTORY MEADOW
Middle Farm
FORESTERS
HEDGERLEY
CHERRY TREE RD
STATION RD
CHURCH RD
KEENS LA
CLEAVERS
MILLERS TURN
HAILEY CFT
MIDDLE WAY
BEECH RD
WILLOW RD
PH
CHURCH LA
THE AVENUE
ROBINS PLATT
ASHRIDGE
HUNTERS POINT
RIDERS WAY
HILLVERKE
B4009
RAVENSMEAD
OAKLEY LA
PENLY
FLINT HOLLOW
OAKLEY RD
Works
ORCHARD WAY
GLIMBERS GR
ST ANDREW'S RD
ELM DR
GREENWOOD AVE
WHEELER RD
WOODVILLE
GREENWOOD MEADOW
MEADOW RD
WYKEHAM RISE
GOLDEN HILL
HILL RD
Oakley
Crowell End Farm
Pit (dis)
Works
Upper Icknield Way
The Ridgeway Path
Tumuli
Tumulus
Chinnor Hill
LC
Lower Wainhill
Hempton Wainhill
Bledlow Cross
HILL TOP LA
Crowell Farm
CHINNOR RD
Crowell
PH
B4009
Chalk Quarries
CHINNOR HILL
CHINNOR RD
Woodlands Farm
Oakley Hill
Manor Farm
Aston Rowant
Dismantled Railway
Sunley Wood
Venus Wood
Venus Wood
Race Course
Crowellhill Wood
Crowell Hill
Crowellhill Farm
Sprig's Alley
Grove Farm
KINGSTON HILL
SPRIGS HOLLY LA
Kingston Wood
4
01
3
00
2
99
1
98
75
76
D
E
F

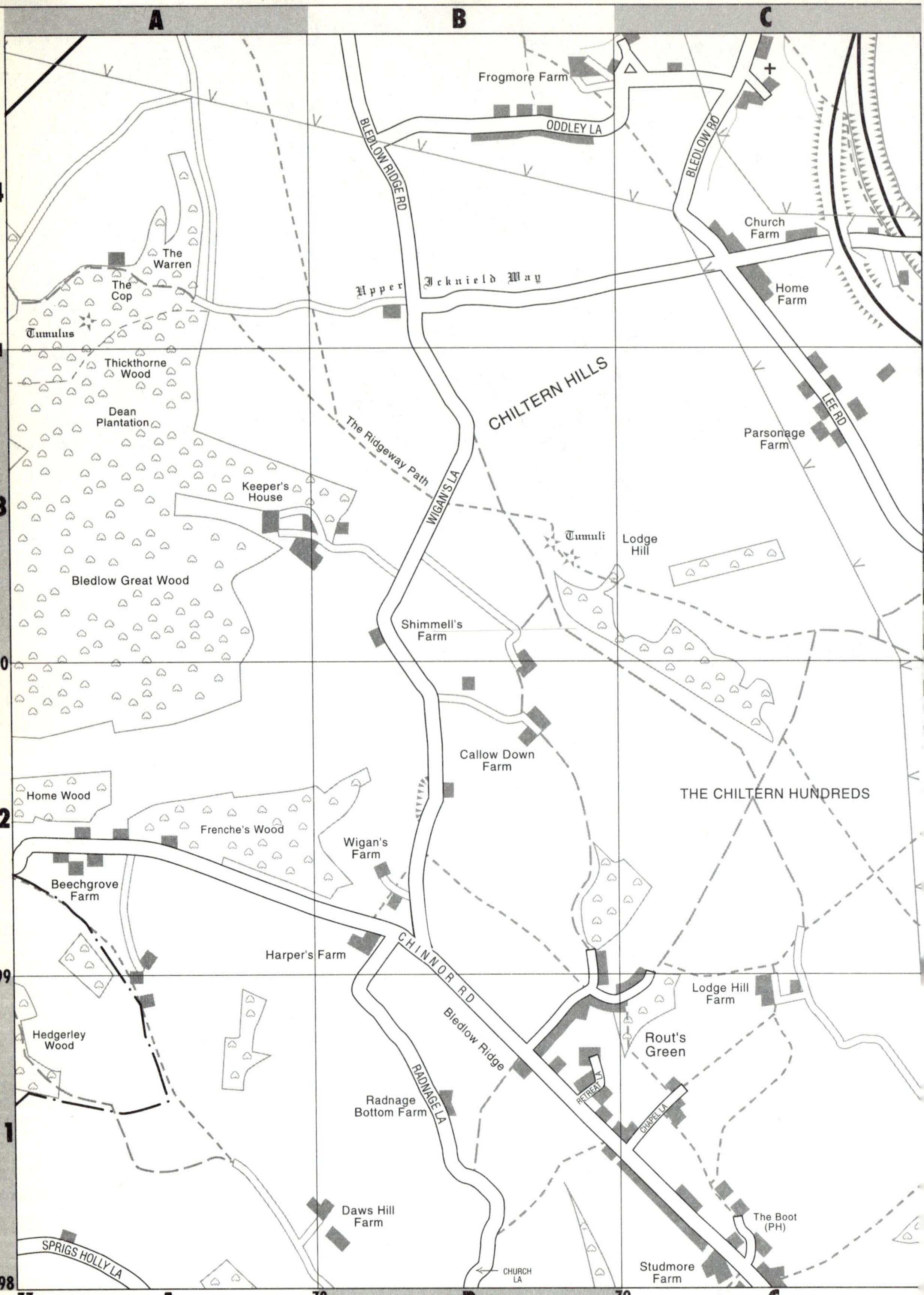
A
B
C
Frogmore Farm
ODDLEY LA
BLEDLOW RIDGE RD
BLEDLOW RD
Church Farm
Home Farm
The Warren
The Cop
Tumulus
Upper Icknield Way
Thickthorne Wood
Dean Plantation
CHILTERN HILLS
LEE RD
Parsonage Farm
The Ridgeway Path
WIGAN'S LA
Keeper's House
Tumuli
Lodge Hill
Bledlow Great Wood
Shimmell's Farm
Callow Down Farm
THE CHILTERN HUNDREDS
Home Wood
Frenche's Wood
Wigan's Farm
Beechgrove Farm
Harper's Farm
CHINNOR RD
Lodge Hill Farm
Hedgerley Wood
Bledlow Ridge
Rout's Green
RADNAGE LA
RETREAT LA
CHAPEL LA
Radnage Bottom Farm
Daws Hill Farm
The Boot (PH)
SPRIGS HOLLY LA
CHURCH LA
Studmore Farm
4
01
3
00
2
99
1
98
77
78
79

D
E
F
4
01
3
00
2
99
1
98
0
81
82
Shootacre Corner
Hemley Hill
SHOOTACRE LA
UPPER ICKNIELD WAY
A4010
WOODWAY
Wardrobes
WARDROBES LA
PINK HILL
BRIMMERS RD
The Pink and Lily (PH)
Parslow's Hillock
LILLY BOTTOM LA
PINK RD
Saunderton Tunnel
Winder Farm
The Ridgeway Path
Loosley Row
WOODWAY
LOWER RD
VIOLET CL
Collin's Farm
Windmill (disused)
Windmill Farm
The Whip (PH)
Grim's Ditch
White House Farm
KILN LA
FOUNDRY LA
LOOSLEY HILL
WOODFIELD
GREENLANDS
MAIN RD
POUNDLANDS
EASTLANDS
WESTLANDS RD
MEADOW RISE
College Farm
Lacey Green
Stocken Farm
HAMBYE CL
CHURCH LA
Sch
WYCOMBE RD
LEE RD
Pound Farm
Saunderton Lee
LITTLE LA
Manor Farm
Rose & Crown (PH)
A4010
Woodway Farm
Callows Hill
Crownfield
Promised Land Farm
Grimsdyke Farm
SLAD LA
NEW RD
Grange Farm
Munt's Wood
Bradenham Wood
SMALLDEAN LA
Small Dean Farm
Slough Glebe Farm
HAW LA
Works
Dean Farm
Slough Hill
Saunderton Station
CHILTERN WAY
A4010
Park Wood
PARKWOOD

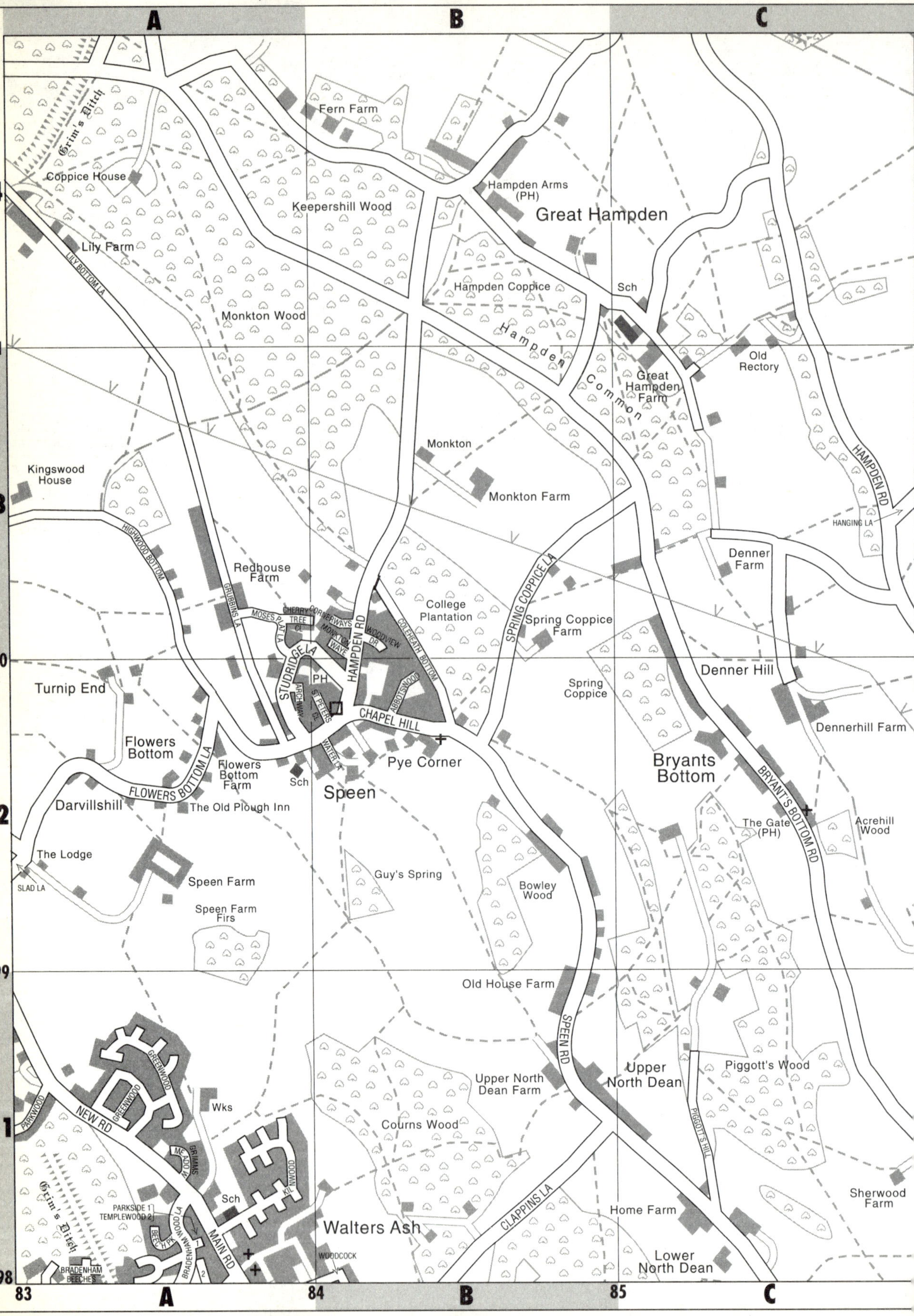
A
B
C
4
3
2
1
01
00
99
98
83
84
85
Fern Farm
Grim's Ditch
Coppice House
Keepershill Wood
Hampden Arms (PH)
Great Hampden
Lily Farm
LILY BOTTOM LA
Hampden Coppice
Sch
Monkton Wood
Hampden Common
Great Hampden Farm
Old Rectory
Monkton
HAMPDEN RD
Kingswood House
Monkton Farm
HANGING LA
HIGHWOOD BOTTOM
Redhouse Farm
SPRING COPPICE LA
Denner Farm
GRUBBINS LA
MOSES PL
CHERRY TREE CL
CORNERWAYS
MONKTON WAYE
WOODVIEW DR
HAMPDEN RD
COLEHEATH BOTTOM
College Plantation
Spring Coppice Farm
STUDRIDGE LA
PH
ARCHWAY
ST PETERS CL
ABBOTSWOOD
Denner Hill
Turnip End
Spring Coppice
CHAPEL HILL
Dennerhill Farm
Flowers Bottom
FLOWERS BOTTOM LA
WATER CT
Flowers Bottom Farm
Sch
Pye Corner
Bryants Bottom
Darvillshill
The Old Plough Inn
Speen
BRYANT'S BOTTOM RD
The Gate (PH)
Acrehill Wood
The Lodge
SLAD LA
Guy's Spring
Speen Farm
Bowley Wood
Speen Farm Firs
Old House Farm
SPEEN RD
Upper North Dean
Upper North Dean Farm
Piggott's Wood
GREENWOOD
PARKWOOD
NEW RD
Wks
Courns Wood
PIGGOTT'S HILL
Grim's Ditch
GRIMMS MEADOW
KILNWOOD
CLAPPINS LA
Sherwood Farm
PARKSIDE 1
TEMPLEWOOD 2
Sch
Home Farm
BEECH PK
BRADENHAM WOOD LA
MAIN RD
Walters Ash
BRADENHAM BEECHES
WOODCOCK
Lower North Dean

D
E
F
Monument
Honor End Farm
Hotley Bottom
Broomfield Farm
RIGNALL RD
Rignall Wood
Broomfield House
WINSLOW FIELD
Lodge Wood
Kiln Common
HOTLEY BOTTOM LA
BROOMBARN LA
BROOMFIELD HILL
UPPER HOLLIS
LITTLE HOLLIS
GRIMMS HILL
Hampden Farm
GREENLANDS LA
OVER HAMPDEN
Moat Farm
HONOR END LA
PARLIAMENT CL
JOHN HAMPDEN WAY
Sch
BROOMFIELD CL
A4128
Nanfans Farm
Wr Twr
KILN LA
KILN CL
MOAT DR
Pankridge Farm
FIRS RISE
MARTINSEND LA
CHILTERN MANOR PARK
LAUREL
THE GLEBE
LYNDON CL
MOAT LA
Prestwood Farm
Angling Spring Wood
HONORWOOD CL
CHEQUERS DR
CHEQUERS LA
FLINT WAY
PANKRIDGE DR
PETER'S CL
ROSETREE CL
MOAT CL
HIGH ST
HANGINGS LA
Michaelmas Farm
CLARENDON RD
PEPYS DR
Sch
BLACKSMITH LA
ORCHARD LA
SALMONS LA
NEW RD
Andlows Farm
GREEN PARK
GREEN LA
CLARE RD
HONOR RD
GRAEME AVE
COULSON CT
Prestwood
SIXTY ACRES RD
GRYMS DYKE
CHERRY CL
Idaho Farm
Atkins Wood
Hobbshill Wood
DRESSER RD
HILDRETH RD
HAZEL RD
WRIGHT'S LA
FAIR ACRES
SHAWS CL
STOCKLANDS WAY
GROOM RD
SHEPPARD MEADOW
STEVENS CL
GREENSIDE
WREN RD
WARDES CL
NAIRDWOOD LA
Nanfan Wood
LODGE LA
Sch
Atkins Farm
1 TULKERS CL
2 STRAWBERRY CL
3 FRIARS WLK
4 OAKENGROVE
5 CARRINGTON WAY
6 WESTRICK WLK
7 COLLINGS WLK
CHURCH PATH
WYCOMBE RD
LENMERE FIELD
DELL FIELD
NAIRDWOOD WAY
NAIRDWOOD CL
Collings Hangar Farm
Stonyrock Plantation
Stony Green
GLEBELANDS CL
NAGS HEAD LA
Stonygreen Hall
Peterley Wood
Peterley Wood Farm
Nairdwood Farm
Meadsgarden Wood
PETERLEY
Peterley Manor Farm
The Kings Head (PH)
New House farm
MEADOW GATE
PERKS LA
HAMPDEN RD
Crook's Wood
Peterley Corner Farm
Perks Lane Farm
MISSENDON RD
HEATH END RD
Long field Wood
Ninneywood Farm
Upper Warren Farm
Cherry Tree Farm
CHERRY TREE
Heath End
SPURLANDS END RD
Birchmore Wood
BRYANTS BOTTOM RD
LOWLANDS
CRES
FERNSIDE
HEATH END CL
Hatches Wood
MARGARETS GR
FAIRFIELDS
Lower Warren Farm
WARRENDENE RD
Hatches Farm
BIRCHWOOD CHASE
THE COMMON
STAG LA
COPES RD
COMMON RD
HATCHES LA
A4128
COCKPIT RD
Cockpit Hole
COCKPIT CL
RAMLEY END
4
01
3
00
2
99
1
98
87
88

151
142

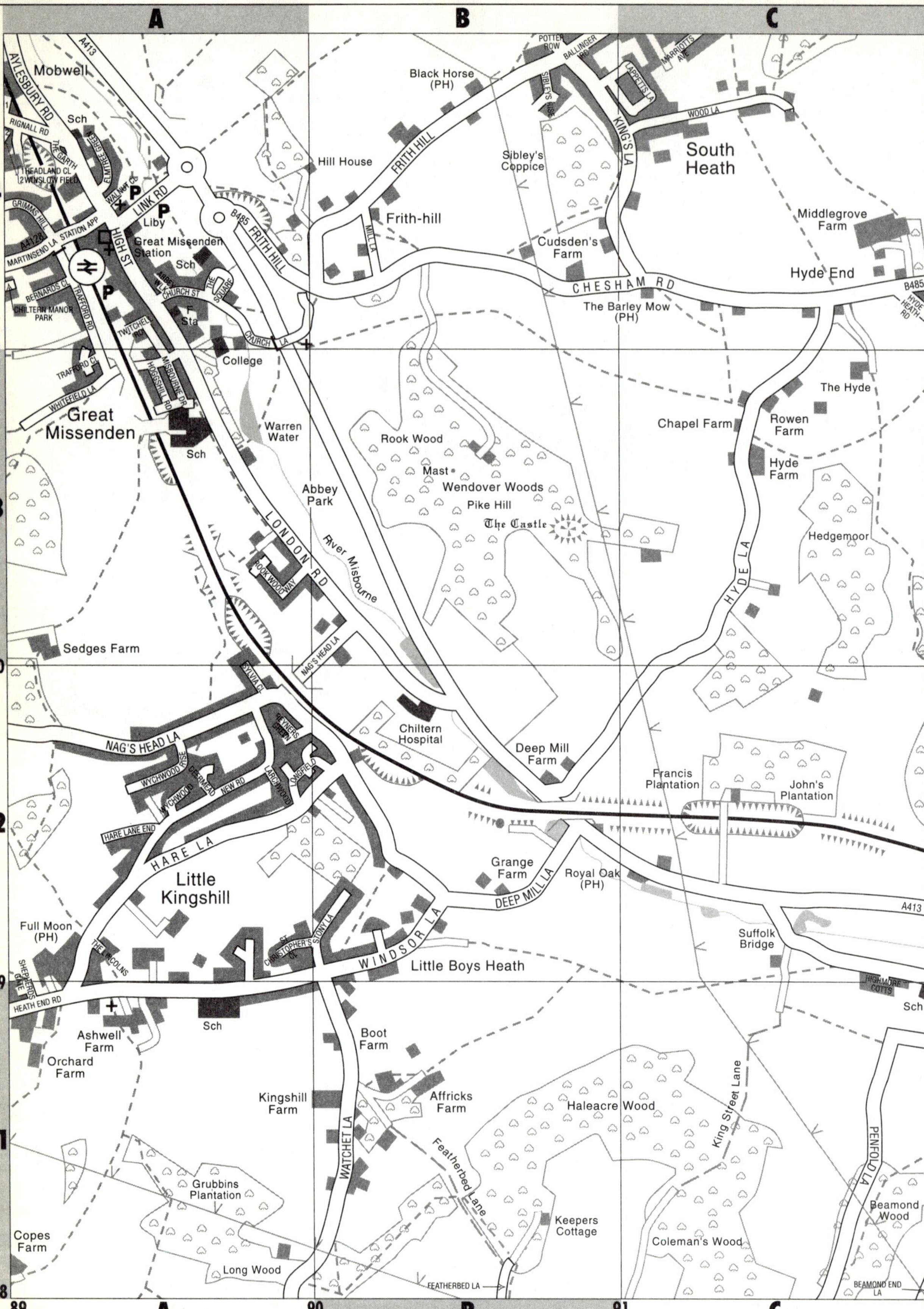

151
163

D
E
F
BLIND LA
Blind Lane
PEDNOR RD
DRYDELL LA
Willow Coppice
The Plantation
Hundridge Manor
Chapel
Devil's Den
LITTLE HUNDRIDGE LA
4
CHESHAM RD
Lower Hundridge Farm
B485
Hawthorn Farm
BROWNS RD
Halfway House Farm
MISSENDEN RD
HALFWAY HOUSE LA
B485
01
Hyde House
HYDE HEATH RD
Halfway House Lane
White's Wood
3
The Green
Monk's Wood
White House Farm
BULLBAITERS LA
Sch
Mantle's Wood
Hydeheath Common
The Plough (PH)
Hyde Heath
BRAYS LA
SAUNDERS END
HARVEST BANK
BRAYS MEADOW
MEADOW WAY
WESTFIELD
WALNUT WAY
BRAYS CL
WEEDON HILL
Weedon Hill Farm
00
COPPERKINS LA
BRAYS GREEN LA
Castle Tower
Motte & Bailey
Mantle's Farm
CHALK LA
Bray's Wood
KEEPERS LA
2
Weedonhill Farm
A413
The Vicarage
Lott's Wood
Weedonhill Wood
Ash Grove Plantation
Lime Farm
Mill End
High Spring
99
Crown (PH)
Keeper's Wood
Little Missendon
River Misbourne
Ash Grove
Ostler's Wood
Toby's Farm
Kennel Farm
New Sowed Wood
Toby's Lane
1
MOP END LA
Breaches Wood
Todd's Wood
Lower Park
SCHOOL LA
A413
98
93
94

153
144

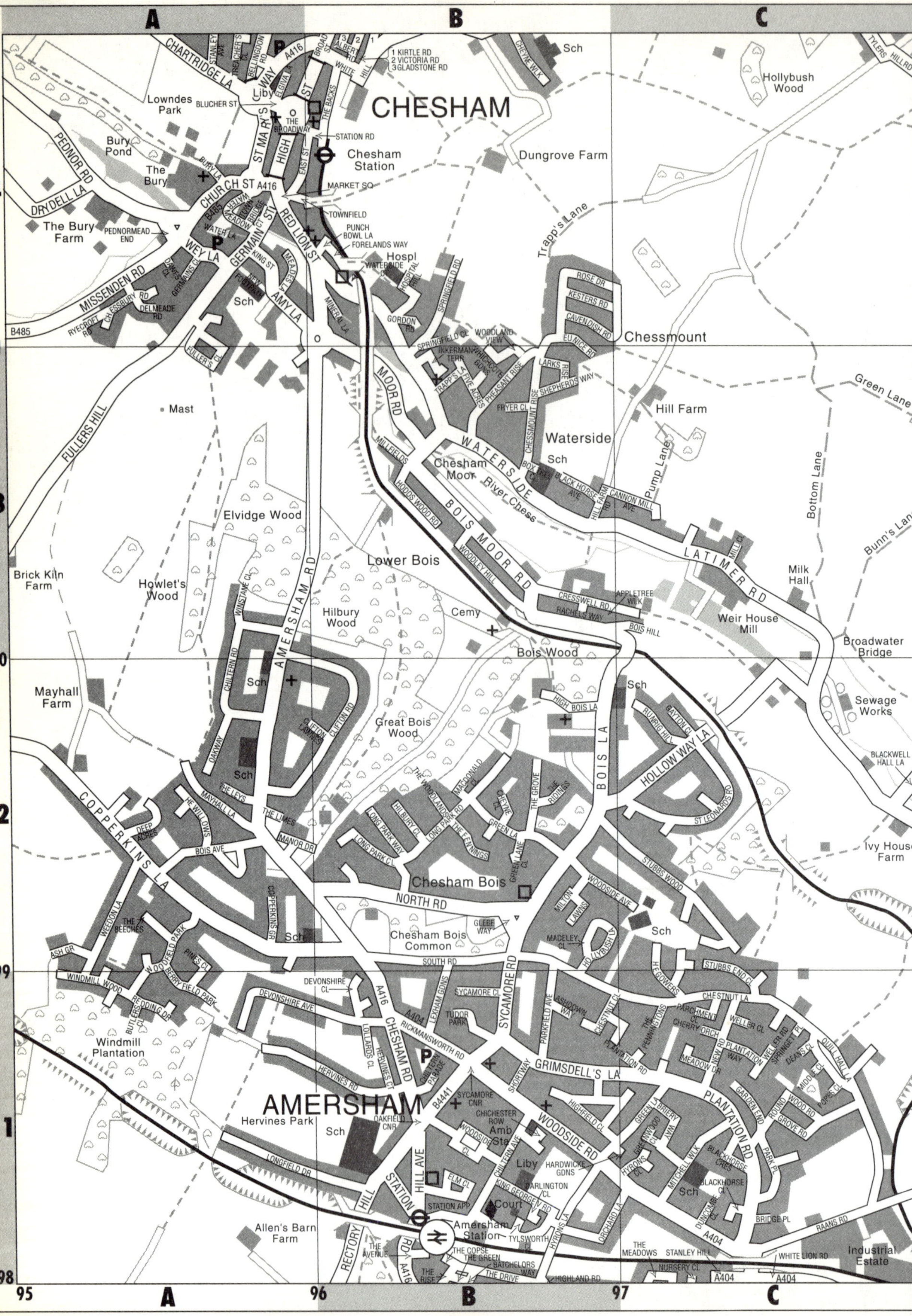

153
165

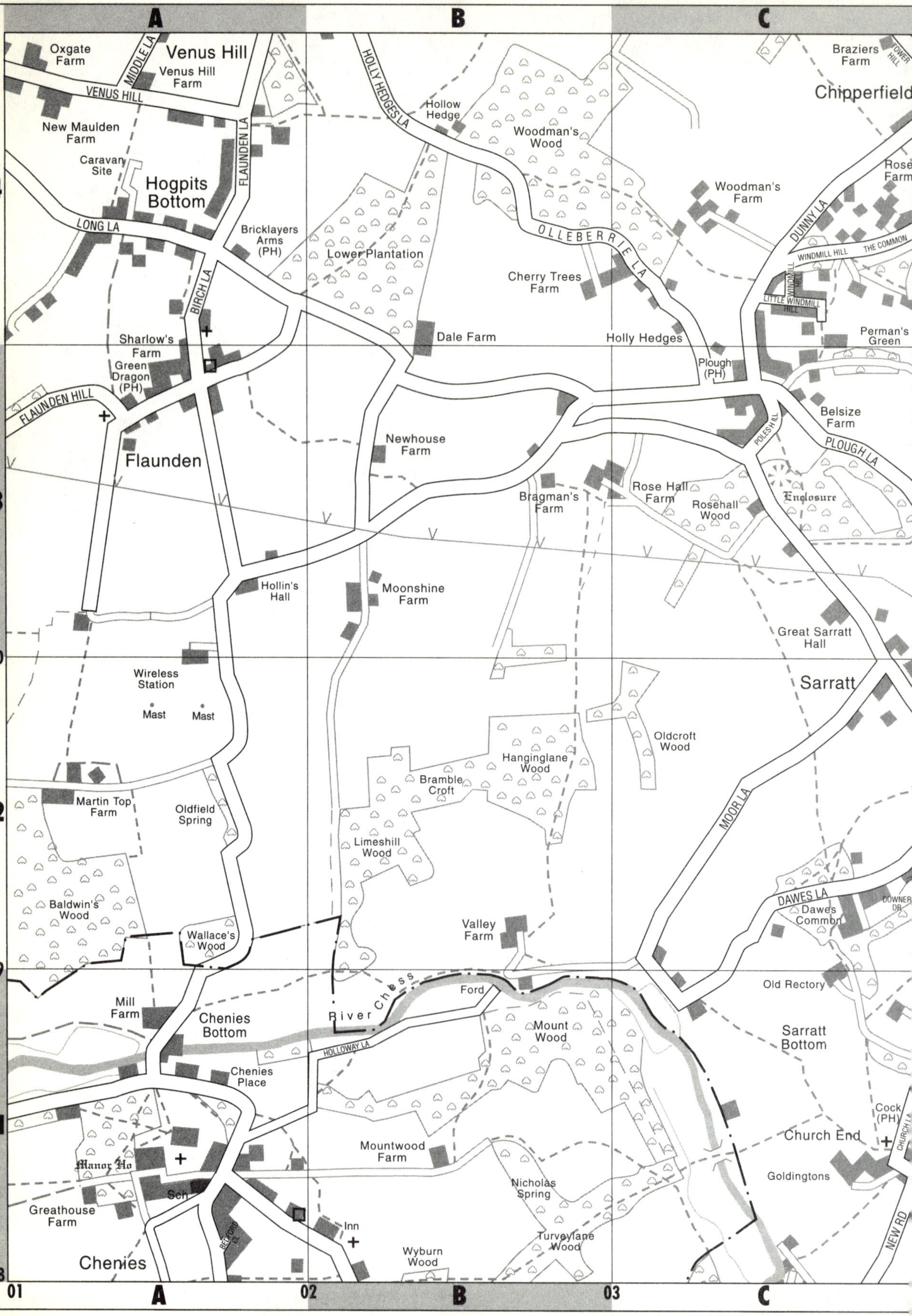
A
B
C
Oxgate Farm
Venus Hill
Venus Hill Farm
MIDDLE LA
VENUS HILL
New Maulden Farm
FLAUNDEN LA
Caravan Site
Hogpits Bottom
LONG LA
Bricklayers Arms (PH)
HOLLY HEDGES LA
Hollow Hedge
Woodman's Wood
Lower Plantation
OLLEBERRIE LA
Cherry Trees Farm
Braziers Farm
TOWER HILL
Chipperfield
Rose Farm
Woodman's Farm
DUNNY LA
WINDMILL HILL
THE COMMON
WINDMILL HILL
LITTLE WINDMILL HILL
Perman's Green
BIRCH LA
Sharlow's Farm
Green Dragon (PH)
FLAUNDEN HILL
Dale Farm
Holly Hedges
Plough (PH)
Belsize Farm
POLES HILL
PLOUGH LA
Flaunden
Newhouse Farm
Bragman's Farm
Rose Hall Farm
Rosehall Wood
Enclosure
Hollin's Hall
Moonshine Farm
Great Sarratt Hall
Wireless Station
Mast
Mast
Sarratt
Oldcroft Wood
Hanginglane Wood
Bramble Croft
MOOR LA
Martin Top Farm
Oldfield Spring
Limeshill Wood
Baldwin's Wood
DAWES LA
DOWNER DR
Dawes Common
Wallace's Wood
Valley Farm
Old Rectory
River Chess
Ford
Mill Farm
Chenies Bottom
Mount Wood
Sarratt Bottom
HOLLOWAY LA
Chenies Place
Cock (PH)
Church End
CHURCH LA
Mountwood Farm
Manor Ho
Goldingtons
Sch
Nicholas Spring
Greathouse Farm
Inn
BEDFORD CL
Turveylane Wood
Wyburn Wood
NEW RD
Chenies
4
01
3
00
2
99
1
98
01
02
03

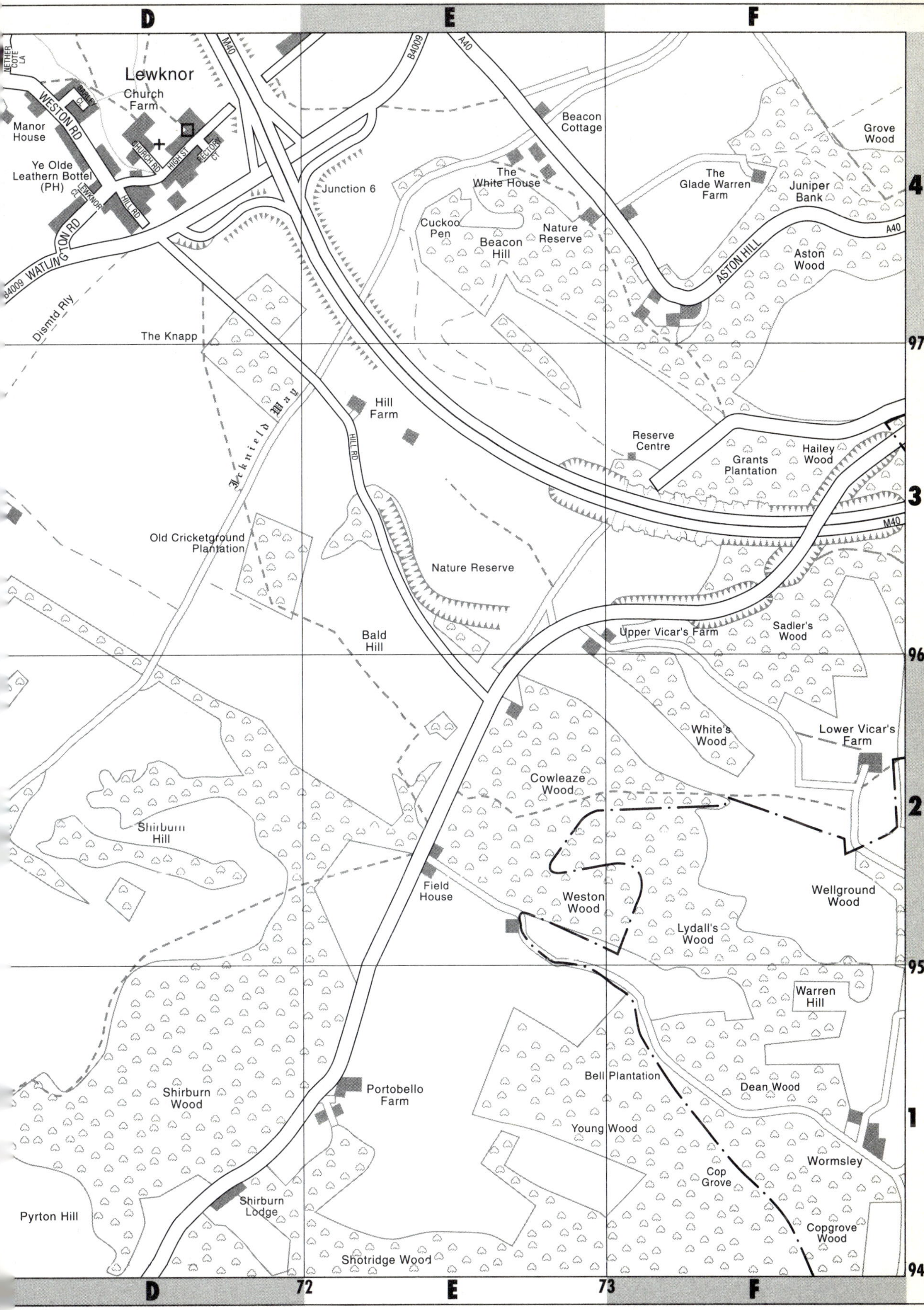
D
E
F
Lewknor
Church Farm
Manor House
Ye Olde Leathern Bottel (PH)
WESTON RD
CHURCH RD
HIGH ST
RECTORY CT
HILL RD
LEWKNOR CL
B4009 WATLING TON RD
Dismtd Rly
M40
B4009
A40
Junction 6
Beacon Cottage
The White House
Cuckoo Pen
Beacon Hill
Nature Reserve
The Glade Warren Farm
Juniper Bank
Grove Wood
ASTON HILL
Aston Wood
The Knapp
Icknield Way
Hill Farm
Reserve Centre
Grants Plantation
Hailey Wood
Old Cricketground Plantation
Nature Reserve
Bald Hill
Upper Vicar's Farm
Sadler's Wood
White's Wood
Lower Vicar's Farm
Cowleaze Wood
Shirburn Hill
Field House
Weston Wood
Lydall's Wood
Wellground Wood
Warren Hill
Bell Plantation
Dean Wood
Shirburn Wood
Portobello Farm
Young Wood
Cop Grove
Wormsley
Copgrove Wood
Pyrton Hill
Shirburn Lodge
Shotridge Wood
4
97
3
96
2
95
1
94
72
73
D
E
F

157
147

157
169

148
160

D E F

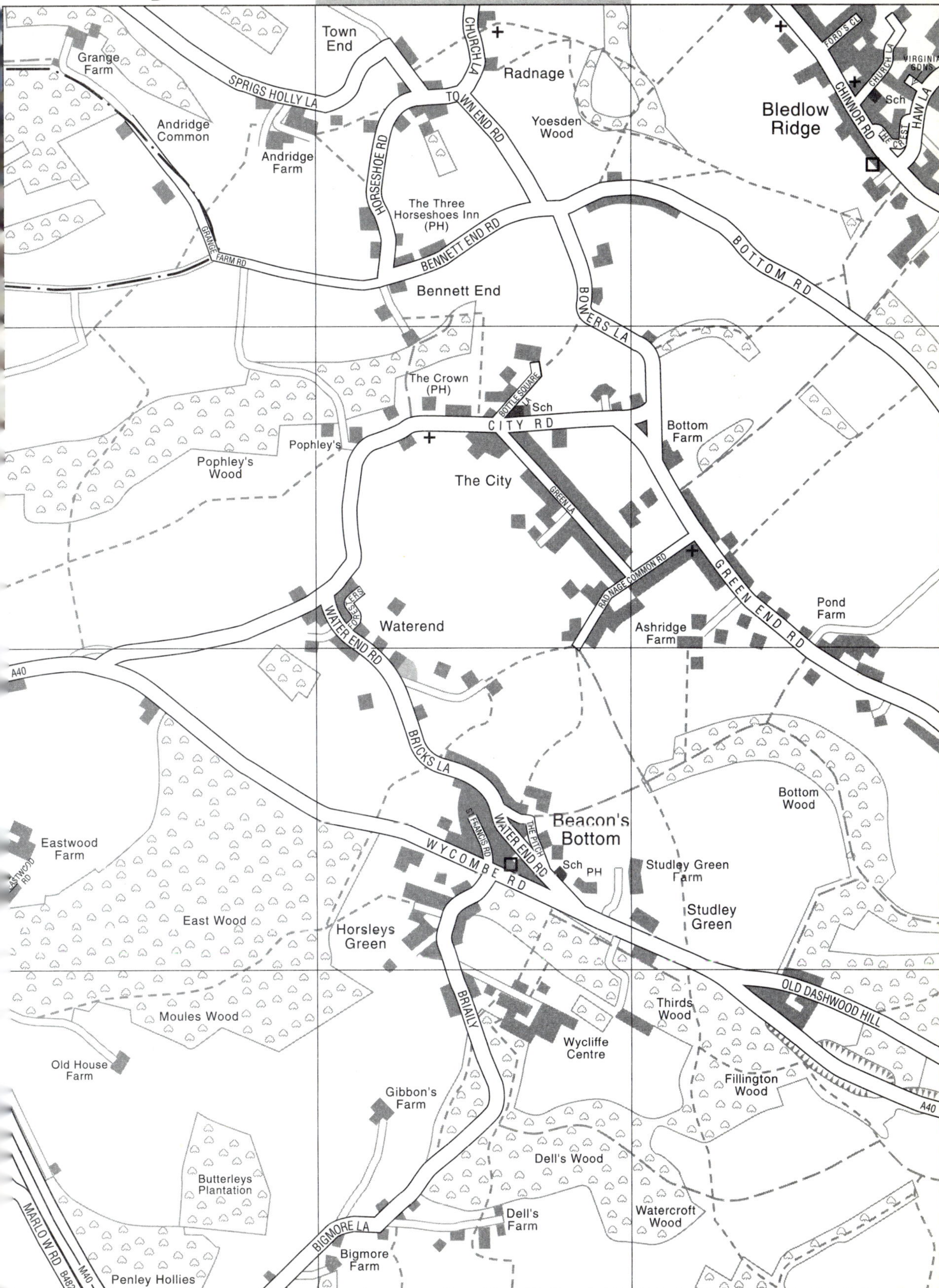

4
97
3
96
2
95
1
94

D 78 E 79 F

170
160

159
149

A
B
C
4
97
3
96
2
95
1
94
80
81
82
HAW LA
RIDGE SIDE
Orchard Farm
Works
A4010
Industrial Estate
WYCOMBE RD
Yewtree Hill Plantation
The Old House
Slough Bottom Farm
Allnutt's Wood
Piper's Hanging Wood
Bradenham
Manor Farm
The Red Lion (PH)
BRADENHAM WOOD LA
Morlands Farm
SCRUBB'S LA
Bradenham Manor
SLOUGH LA
Loxborough House
Wayside Farm
The Old Rectory
CHINNOR RD
Averingdown Farm
Hearnton Wood
BRADENHAM RD
Loxboro Wood
Wks
Nature Reserve
A4010
BOTTOM RD
Pond Wood
Chawley Manor Farm
Green End
GREEN END RD
HATCH LA
Chawley Green Farm
LOXBORO HILL
Chorley Farm
Green End Farm
Chawley Wood
Windyhaugh House
Plomer's Bottom
West Wycombe Hill
Cockshoot Farm
CHORLEY RD
Little Cockshoots Wood
Fort
Cave
WEST WYCOMBE HILL RD
Sch
A40 HIGH ST
Liby
OLD DASHWOOD HILL
A40
Great Cockshoots Wood
West Wycombe
WYCOMBE RD
Fillingdon Farm
Ham Farm
CHIPPS HILL
PH
OXFORD RD
West Wycombe House
TOWERIDGE LA
OLD OXFORD RD
PRINCES ST
QUEEN ST
KING ST
Piddington
PIDDINGTON LA
Myze Farm
BULLOCKS FARM LA
High Wood

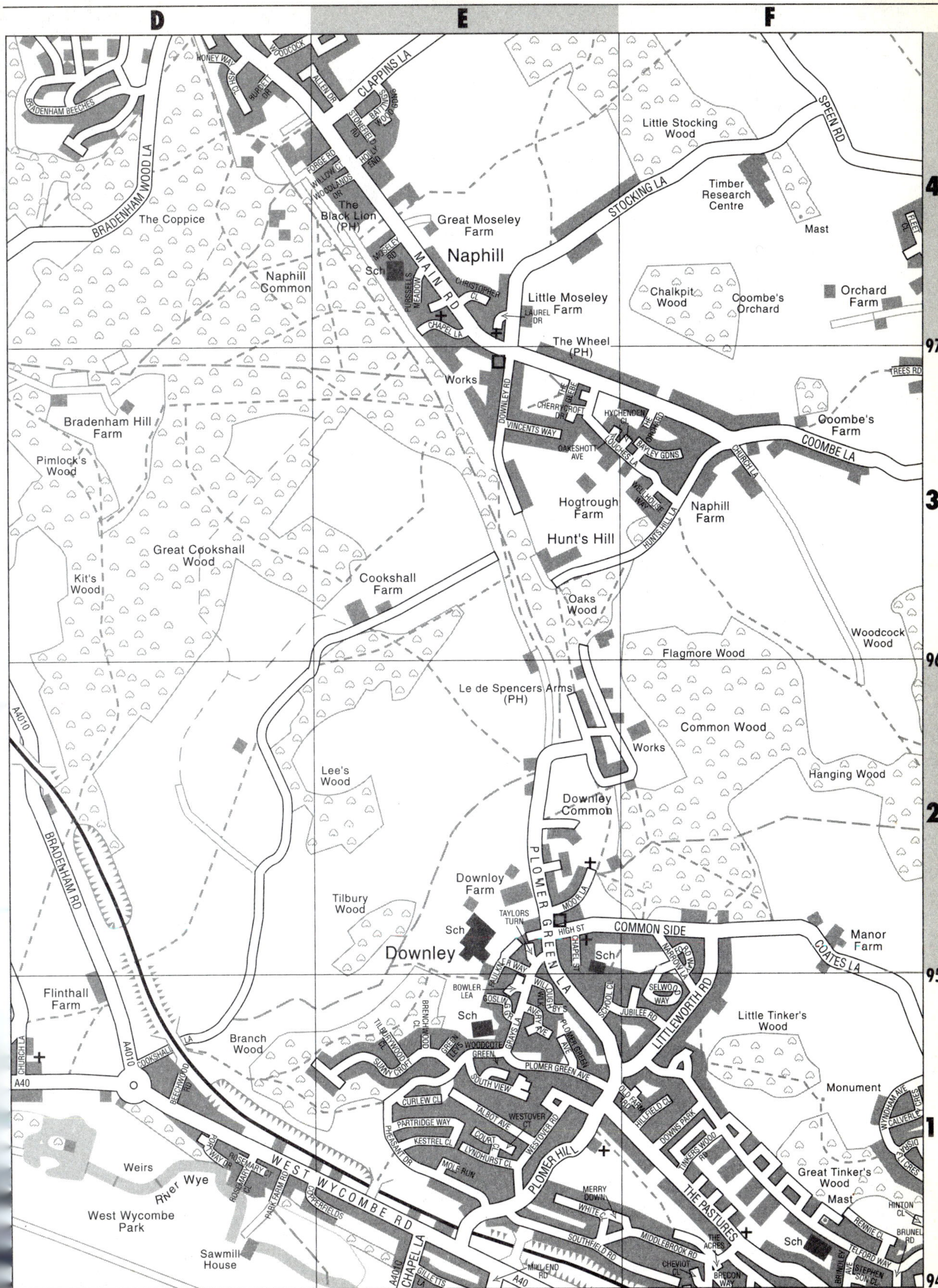
D
E
F
4
3
2
1
97
96
95
94
83
84
85
Bradenham Beeches
Honey Way
Ash Cl
Woodcock
Burdett Dr
Allen Dr
Clappins La
Stonefield Rd
Batting Wood Gdns
Holly End
Forge Rd
Willow Ct
Woodlands Dr
Bradenham Wood La
The Coppice
The Black Lion (PH)
Great Moseley Farm
Naphill
Moseley Rd
Sch
Pursells Meadow
Main Rd
Christopher Cl
Naphill Common
Chapel La
Laurel Dr
Little Moseley Farm
Little Stocking Wood
Stocking La
Timber Research Centre
Speen Rd
Mast
Fleet Cl
Chalkpit Wood
Coombe's Orchard
Orchard Farm
The Wheel (PH)
Trees Rd
Works
Downley Rd
The Glebe
Cherrycroft Dr
Hychenden Cl
The Orchard
Vincents Way
Oakeshott Ave
Louches La
Bayley Gdns
Coombe's Farm
Coombe La
Church La
Bradenham Hill Farm
Pimlock's Wood
Hogtrough Farm
Wellhouse Way
Hunts Hill La
Naphill Farm
Hunt's Hill
Great Cookshall Wood
Kit's Wood
Cookshall Farm
Oaks Wood
Woodcock Wood
Flagmore Wood
Le de Spencers Arms (PH)
A4010
Common Wood
Works
Hanging Wood
Lee's Wood
Downley Common
Bradenham Rd
Plomer Green La
Moor La
Downloy Farm
Tilbury Wood
Taylors Turn
High St
Common Side
Manor Farm
Sch
Downley
Chapel St
Narrow La
Coates La
Faulkner Way
Selwood Way
Bowler Lea
Flinthall Farm
Brenchwood Cl
Gosling Gr
Willoughby's Wlk
School Cl
Littleworth Rd
Little Tinker's Wood
Jubilee Rd
Church La
Branch Wood
Tilburywood Cl
Green Leys
Avery Ave
Plomer Green Ave
Woodcote Green
Grays La
Cookshall La
Sunny Croft
A4010
Beechwood Rd
South View
Plomer Green Ave
Old Farm Rd
Hillfield Cl
Monument
Wyndham Ave
Calverley Cres
A40
Curlew Cl
Talbot Ave
Westover Ct
Partridge Way
Kestrel Cl
Court Cl
Westover Rd
Downs Park
Tinkers Wood Rd
Osier Cres
Pheasant Dr
Lyndhurst Cl
Mole Run
Plomer Hill
Great Tinker's Wood
Weirs
Rosemary Ct
Poppyway Dr
River Wye
West Wycombe Rd
Mast
Hinton Cl
West Wycombe Park
Rosemary Cl
Park Farm Rd
Copperfields
Merry Down
White Cl
The Pastures
Rennie Cl
Brunel Rd
Southfield Rd
Middlebrook Rd
The Acres
Sch
Telford Way
Sawmill House
A4010
Chapel La
Gilletts La
Mill End Rd
A40
Cheviot Cl
Brecon Way
Brindley Ave
Stephenson Cl

161
151

161
173

152
164

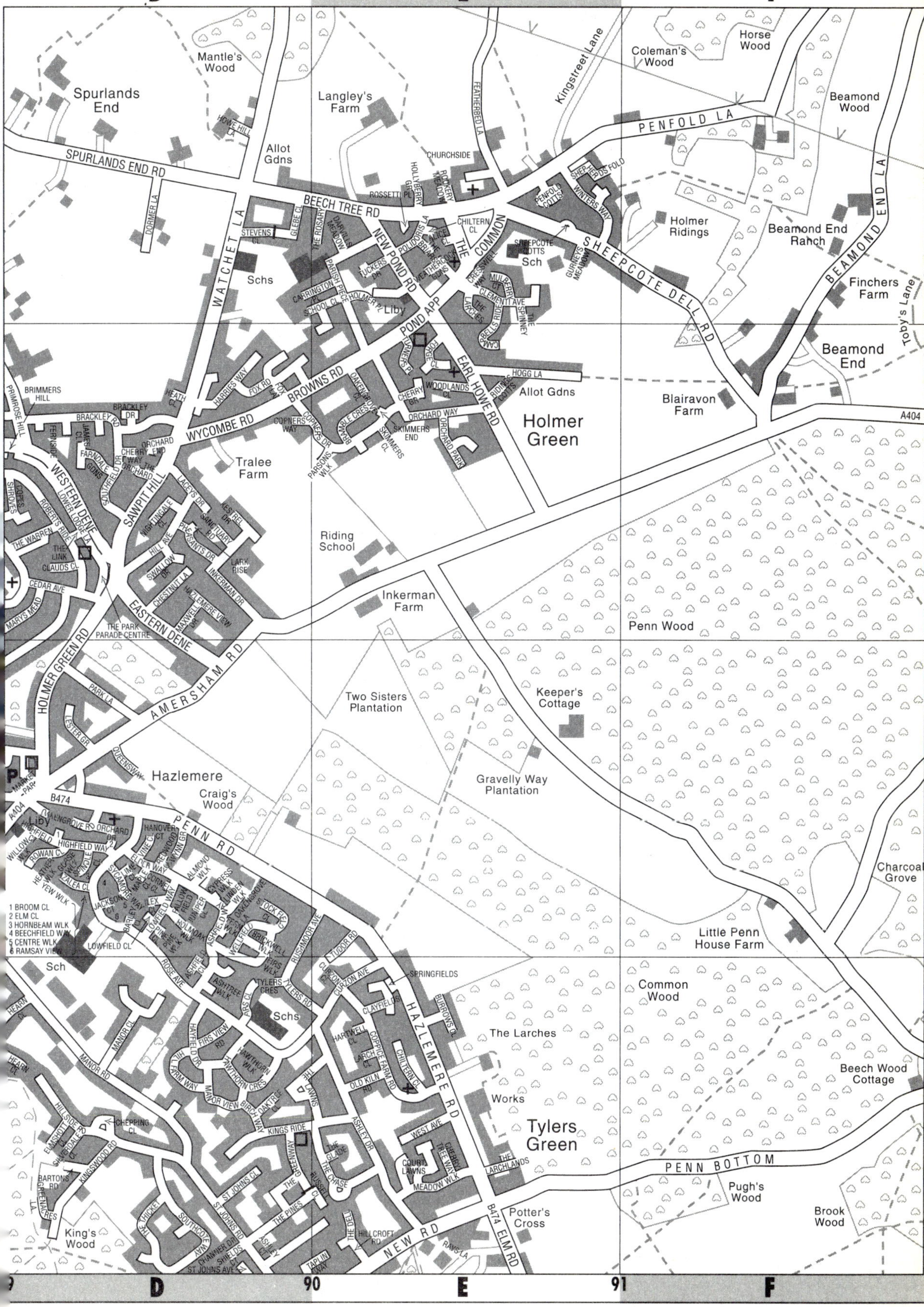

174
164

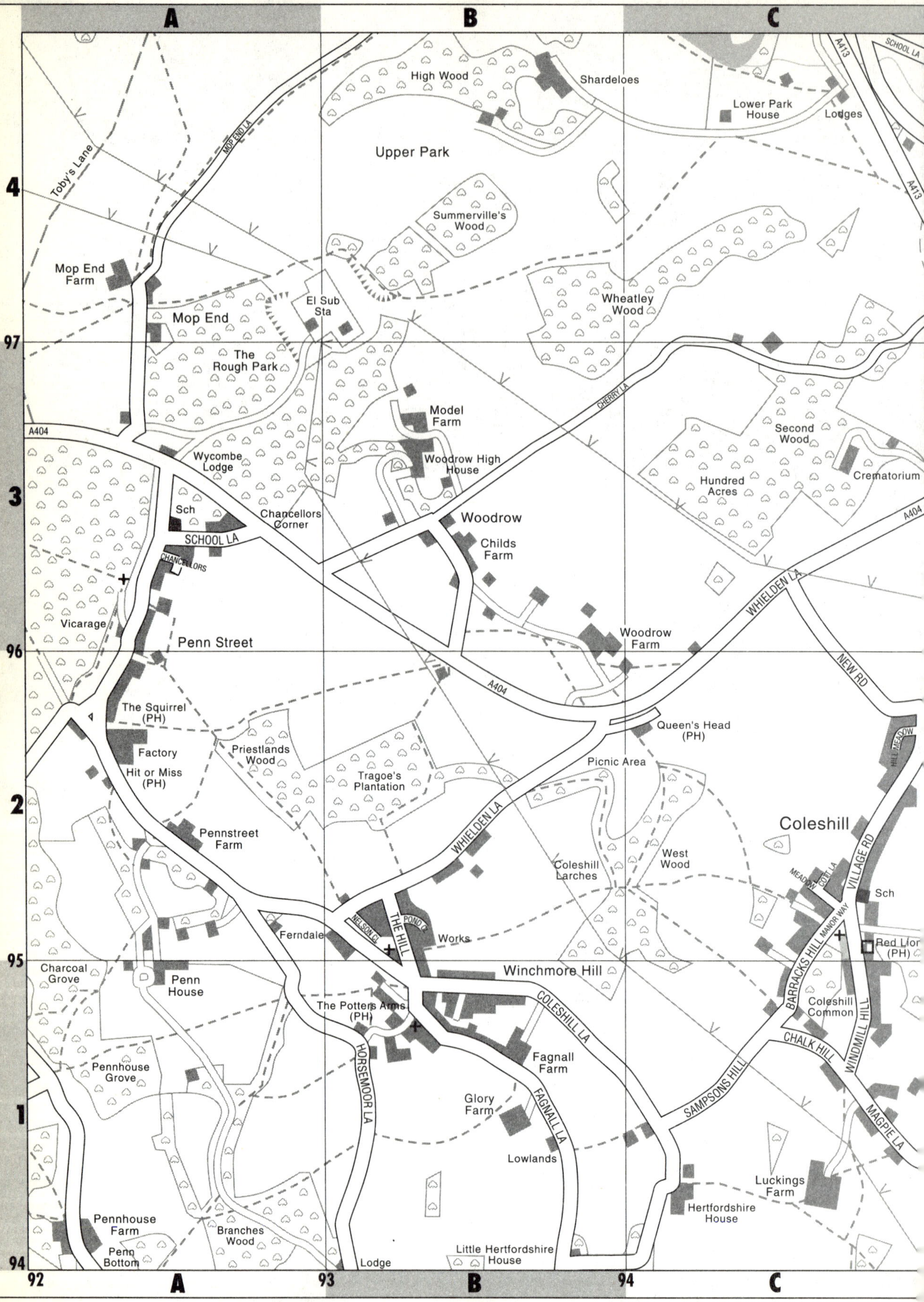
A
B
C
4
97
3
96
2
95
1
94
92
93
94
Toby's Lane
MOP END LA
High Wood
Shardeloes
Lower Park House
Lodges
A413
SCHOOL LA
Upper Park
Summerville's Wood
Mop End Farm
Mop End
El Sub Sta
Wheatley Wood
The Rough Park
Model Farm
CHERRY LA
Second Wood
A404
Wycombe Lodge
Woodrow High House
Crematorium
Hundred Acres
Sch
Chancellors Corner
Woodrow
SCHOOL LA
Childs Farm
CHANCELLORS
WHIELDEN LA
Vicarage
Penn Street
Woodrow Farm
NEW RD
A404
The Squirrel (PH)
Queen's Head (PH)
Factory
Priestlands Wood
Picnic Area
HILL MEADOW
Hit or Miss (PH)
Tragoe's Plantation
Coleshill
Pennstreet Farm
WHIELDEN LA
West Wood
Coleshill Larches
VILLAGE RD
MEADOW
COTT LA
Sch
MANOR WAY
NELSON CL
THE HILL
POND CL
Ferndale
Works
Red Lion (PH)
Charcoal Grove
Winchmore Hill
BARRACKS HILL
Penn House
COLESHILL LA
Coleshill Common
The Potters Arms (PH)
CHALK HILL
WINDMILL HILL
Fagnall Farm
Pennhouse Grove
SAMPSONS HILL
MAGPIE LA
Glory Farm
HORSEMOOR LA
FAGNALL LA
Lowlands
Luckings Farm
Hertfordshire House
Pennhouse Farm
Branches Wood
Penn Bottom
Lodge
Little Hertfordshire House

D
E
F
Mantles Green
Allot Gdns
Rectory
Sch
SCHOOL LA
MILL LA
HIGH ST
RECTORY HILL
CHURCH ST
Cemy
BROADWAY
MARKET SQ
Amersham Old Town
Hospital
WHIELDEN ST
CHERRY LA
A413
A404
A355
A416
WHIELDEN LA
Parsonage Wood
STATION RD
HIGHLAND RD
THE MEADOWS NURSERY CL
STANLEY HILL AVE
BATCHELORS WAY
WESTANLEY AVE
HAZELL PARK
BEECH GR
WESTMOUNT AVE
LONGWOOD LA
HIGHMOOR
HUNDRED ACRES LA
SHEEPFOLD LA
QUARRENDON RD
FIRST AVE
MILLSHOT DR
CHEQUERS HILL
LONDON RD W
STANLEY HILL
Amersham Common
College
Sch
CANTERBURY CL
LINCOLN PARK
YORK CL
LITTLE REEVES AVE
WHITE LION RD
POPLAR AVE
PINEAPPLE RD
ORCHARD END AVE
ST GEORGES INDUSTRIAL ESTATE
Cemy
CLARE PARK
Willow Wood
Bury End
River Misbourne
Hovel Wood
Finches Farm
BRAMBLE LA
WILLOW LA
LONDON RD E
FINCH LA
DANE CL
Gore Hill
GORE HILL
Rodger's Wood
Quarrendon Mill
Coleshill House
Coldharbour Farm
CHASE CL
TOWER RD
David's Wood
Quarrendon Farm
Sewage Works
Rushymead
Brentford Wood
Day's Wood
Rushymead Farm
High Wood
Herts Wood
AMERSHAM RD
Brentford Grange
Upper Bottom House Farm
BOTTOM HOUSE FARM LA
Brentford Grange Farm
The Larches
Hobbs Hole
Bowers Farm
MAGPIE LA
Ongar Hill Farm
BOTTRELLS LA
The Magpies (PH)
Stockings Farm
Hales Wood
Welpley's Wood
Works
Works
HILL FARM LA
95
96
97
94
4
3
2
1

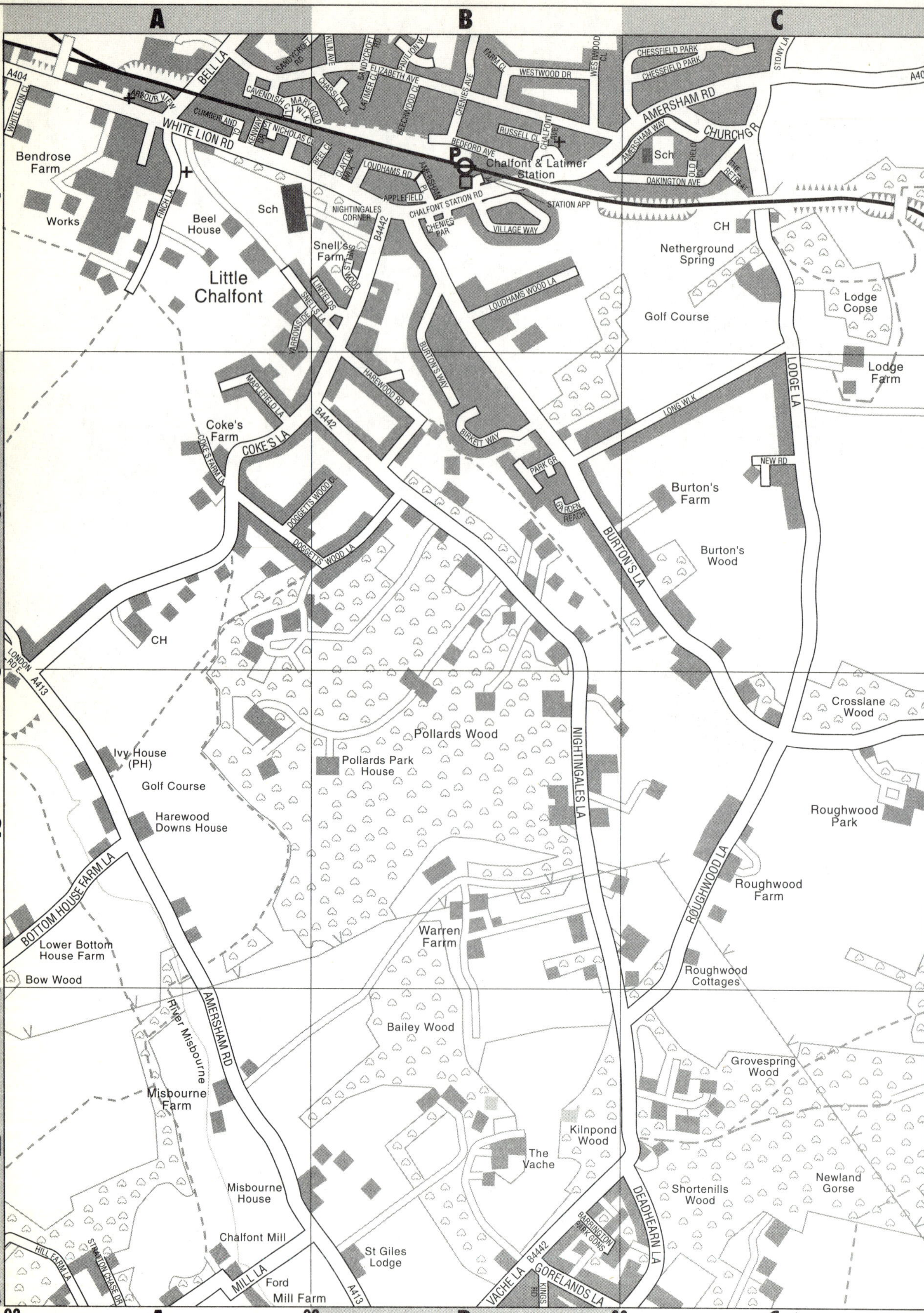
A
B
C
A404
WHITE LION CL
ARBOUR VIEW
BELL LA
CUMBERLAND CL
WHITE LION RD
KENWAY DR
ST NICHOLAS CL
CAVENDISH CL
MARYGOLD WLK
SANDYCROFT RD
KILN AVE
CHARSLEY CL
LATIMER CL
SANDYCROFT RD
ELIZABETH AVE
PAVILION W
BEECHWOOD CL
CHENIES AVE
FARM CL
WESTWOOD DR
WESTWOOD CL
RUSSELL CL
CHALFONT AVE
BEDFORD AVE
BEEL CL
CLAYTON WLK
LOUDHAMS RD
AMERSHAM PL
APPLEFIELD
CHALFONT STATION RD
Chalfont & Latimer Station
CHENIES PAR
VILLAGE WAY
STATION APP
CHESSFIELD PARK
STONY LA
AMERSHAM RD
AMERSHAM WAY
CHURCH GR
Sch
OLD FIELD CL
THE RETREAT
OAKINGTON AVE
Bendrose Farm
Works
FINCH LA
Beel House
Sch
NIGHTINGALES CORNER
B4442
Snell's Farm
STEINS WOOD CL
LINFIELDS
SNELL'S LA
YARROWSIDE
Little Chalfont
LOUDHAMS WOOD LA
CH
Netherground Spring
Golf Course
Lodge Copse
Lodge Farm
LODGE LA
LONG WLK
BURTON'S WAY
HAREWOOD RD
MAPLEFIELD LA
Coke's Farm
COKE'S FARM LA
COKE'S LA
B4442
BIRKETT WAY
PARK GR
NEW RD
DOGGETTS WOOD CL
DOGGETTS WOOD LA
GARDEN REACH
BURTON'S LA
Burton's Farm
Burton's Wood
CH
LONDON RD E
A413
Crosslane Wood
Pollards Wood
Ivy House (PH)
Pollards Park House
Golf Course
NIGHTINGALES LA
Roughwood Park
Harewood Downs House
BOTTOM HOUSE FARM LA
ROUGHWOOD LA
Roughwood Farm
Warren Farm
Lower Bottom House Farm
Bow Wood
Roughwood Cottages
River Misbourne
AMERSHAM RD
Bailey Wood
Grovespring Wood
Misbourne Farm
Kilnpond Wood
The Vache
Misbourne House
Shortenills Wood
Newland Gorse
DEADHEARN LA
BARRINGTON PARK GDNS
Chalfont Mill
HILL FARM LA
STRATTON CHASE DR
MILL LA
St Giles Lodge
B4442
VACHE LA
GORELANDS LA
KINGS RD
Ford
Mill Farm
A413
4
97
3
96
2
95
1
94
98
99
00

D
E
F
AMERSHAM RD
Sarrattmill Ho
NEW RD
Bullscroft Spring
Sarrattmill Bridge
NORTH LA
Chilton's Wood
Little Green Street Farm
Old Hanging Wood
Halsey's Wood
Great Green Street Farm
Sch
Field Study Centre
CHENIES RD
MARLINS CL
GREEN ST
Whitelands Wood
Cemy
RICKMANSWORTH RD
SOLESBRIDGE LA
Hillas Wood
Carpenter's Wood
WHITELANDS AVE
WOODLAND LA
Sch
Chorleywood Common
COMMON RD
CH
CHORLEYWOOD
Golf Course
DOG KENNEL LA
Coll
CARPENTERS WOOD DR
BEECHWOOD AVE
BRUSHWOOD DR
Sch
Newhouse Farm
ST PETERS WAY
WOOD DR
BLACKETTS
LOWER RD
Chorleywood Station
The Black Horse (PH)
Chorleywood West
CHALFONT LA
SHIRE LA
COMMON GATE RD
Philipshill Farm
QUICKLEY LA
CLEMENTS RD
BERRY LA
Berry Farm
HERONSGATE
Chorleywood Bottom
The Hall Farm
Catlips Farm Livery Stables
Penn Farm
STAG LA
Hill Farm
The Swillet
SHEPHERD'S LA
Bullsland Farm
Philipshill Wood
Shire Lane
Bullsland Lane
Heronsgate
LONG LA
Mill End
Ladywalk
Hostel
A404
A412
M25
97
96
95
94
4
3
2
1
01
02
03

157

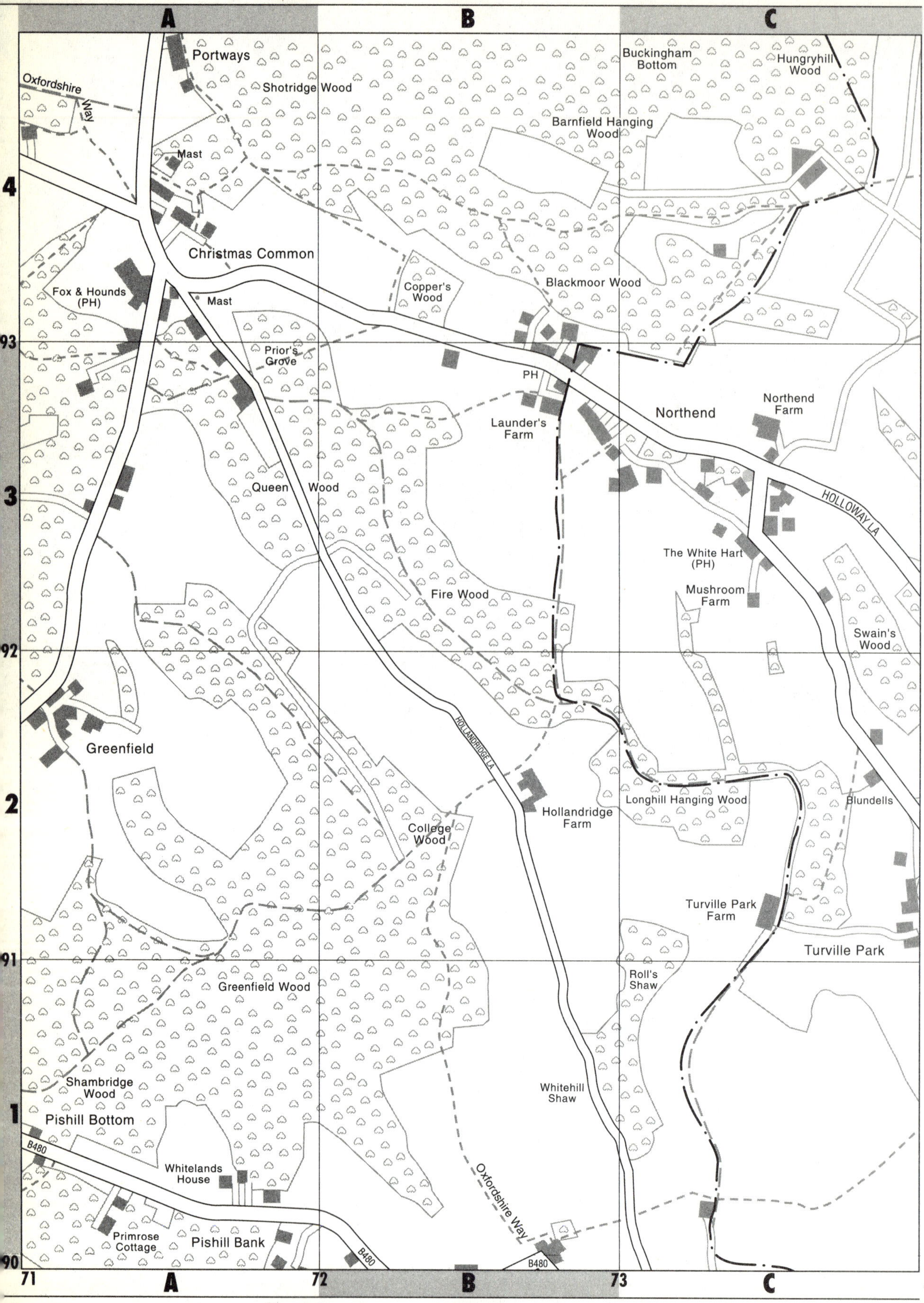
A
B
C
Portways
Shotridge Wood
Buckingham Bottom
Hungryhill Wood
Oxfordshire Way
Barnfield Hanging Wood
Mast
4
Christmas Common
Fox & Hounds (PH)
Mast
Copper's Wood
Blackmoor Wood
93
Prior's Grove
PH
Launder's Farm
Northend
Northend Farm
Queen Wood
3
HOLLOWAY LA
The White Hart (PH)
Mushroom Farm
Fire Wood
Swain's Wood
92
HOLLANDRIDGE LA
Greenfield
Longhill Hanging Wood
Blundells
2
Hollandridge Farm
College Wood
Turville Park Farm
Turville Park
91
Roll's Shaw
Greenfield Wood
Whitehill Shaw
Shambridge Wood
1
Pishill Bottom
B480
Whitelands House
Oxfordshire Way
Primrose Cottage
Pishill Bank
B480
B480
90
71
72
73
A
B
C

179

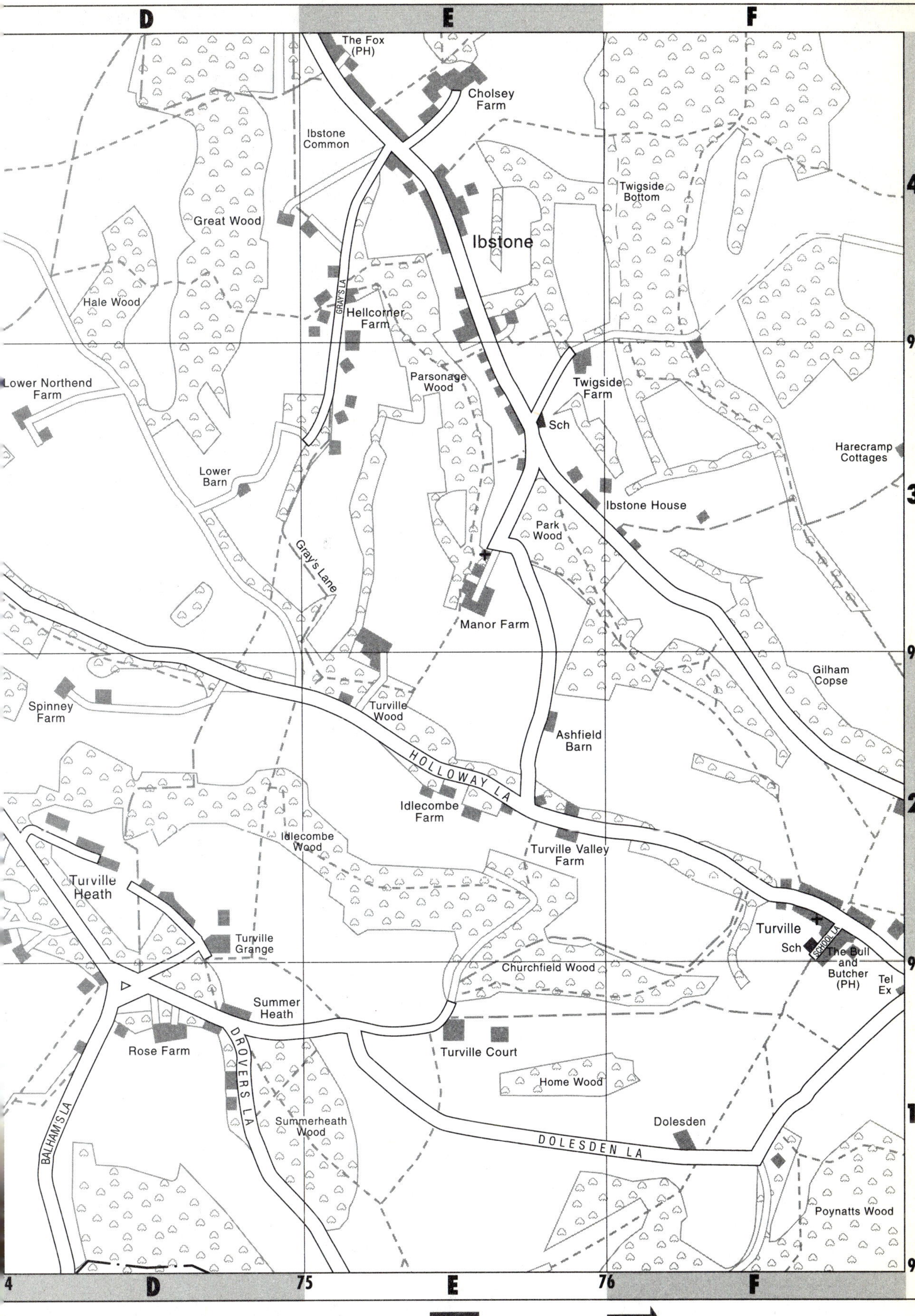
D
E
F
The Fox (PH)
Cholsey Farm
Ibstone Common
Twigside Bottom
4
Great Wood
Ibstone
Hale Wood
GRAY'S LA
Hellcorner Farm
93
Lower Northend Farm
Parsonage Wood
Twigside Farm
Sch
Harecramp Cottages
Lower Barn
Ibstone House
3
Park Wood
Gray's Lane
Manor Farm
92
Gilham Copse
Spinney Farm
Turville Wood
Ashfield Barn
HOLLOWAY LA
2
Idlecombe Farm
Idlecombe Wood
Turville Valley Farm
Turville Heath
Turville
SCHOOL LA
Turville Grange
Sch
The Bull and Butcher (PH)
91
Churchfield Wood
Tel Ex
Summer Heath
Rose Farm
DROVERS LA
Turville Court
Home Wood
1
BALHAM'S LA
Summerheath Wood
Dolesden
DOLESDEN LA
Poynatts Wood
90
4
D
75
E
76
F

169
159

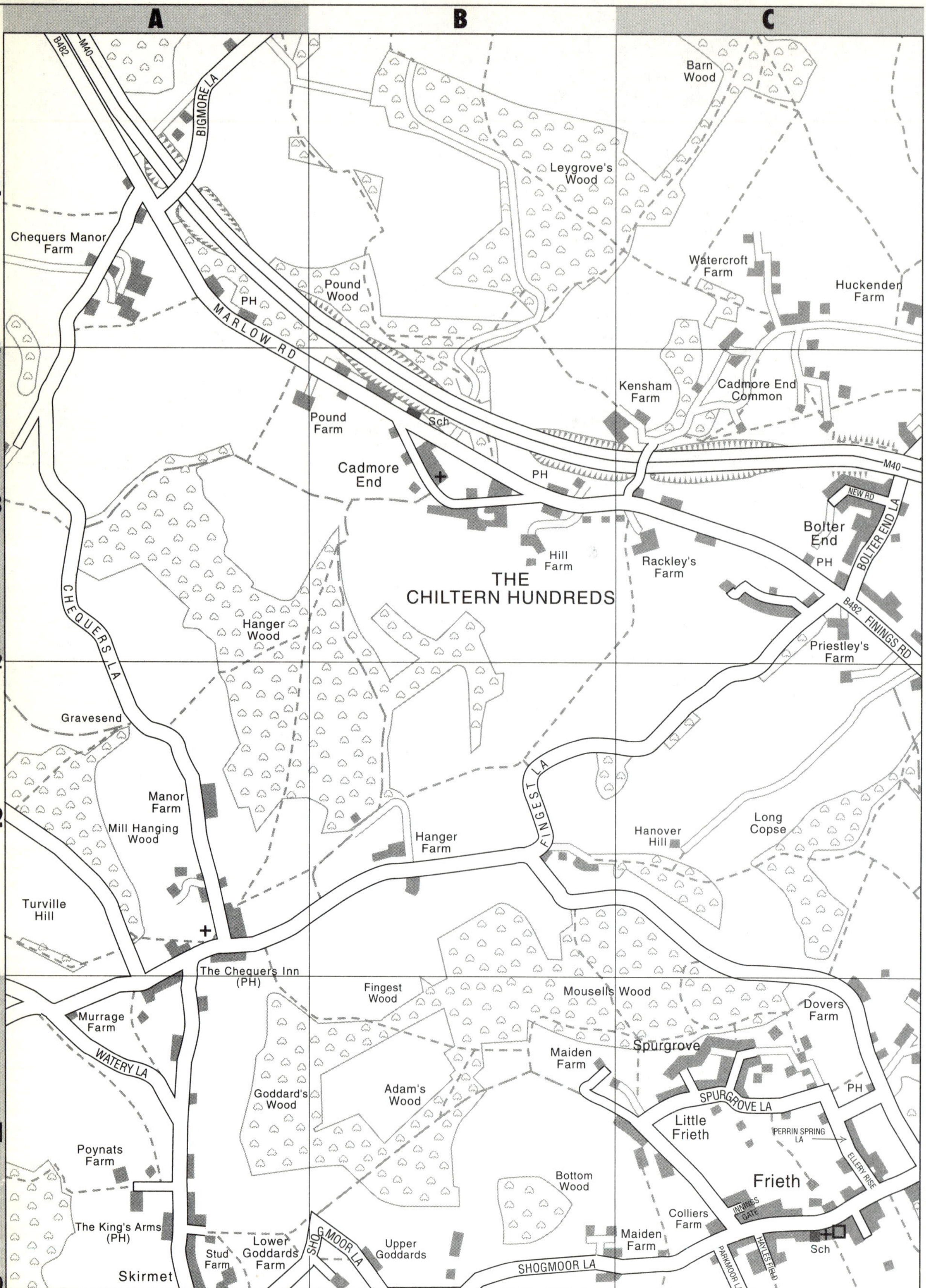

169
181

160
172

182
172

A
B
C
Park Farm
Druid's Hutt
Toweridge Lane
TOWERIDGE LA
HEATHFIELD RD
Sands Wood
Sands
COMBE RISE
HILLBOTTOM RD
Works
Football Ground
PROGRESS RD
Sunter's Wood
Round Wood
High Barber's Wood
Spring Coppice
Booker Common
Booker
Recreation Ground
HORNS LA
LANE END RD
WARWICK AVE
CARISBROOKE AVE
ARUNDEL RD
RYDAL WAY
HIGHWOOD AVE
HIGHWOOD CRES
MENTMORE RD
MENTMORE CL
FIELD RD
BOOKERHILL RD
Sch
SUNTERS WOOD CL
GRAHAM DR
HIGHFIELD AVE
SUNNINGDALE CL
BARBERS WOOD CL
SQUIRREL LA
FERNIE FIELDS
GLENISTER RD
THE COPPICE
HORNBEAM CL
HAVENFIELD RD
ASH RD
THE LAURELS
THRUSH CL
OAK CRES
ELM RD
SYCAMORE RD
SYCAMORE CT
BARRY CL
LANSDELL AVE
WILLOW AVE
GIBSON RD
PINE CHASE
NEWMER RD
LIMMER LA
LIMMER CL
THE PADDOCKS
CRESSEX RD
HOLMERS LA
REDMAN RD
BRANDON RD
SHRIMPTON RD
CULLYN RD
CHALLENER RD
ALFORD RD
HOLMERS CT
HOLMERS FARM WAY
WESTWOOD
BEACHAM RD
BEDDER RD
HARMAN WLK
BUCKMASTER RD
DAVENPORT RD
Hospl
M40
TA Centre
OLD HORNS LA
Clay Lane Farm
CLAYHILL
CLAYMOOR PARK
CLAY LA
Reading Shaw
Refuse Destructor
Hill Green
Hillgreen Wood
Old House Farm
Ragman's Castle
Hollyhill Wood
RAGMANS LA
The Blacksmiths Arms (PH)
Handy Cross Farm
WINCHBOTTOM LA
Redhouse Farm
Monkton Cottage
A404
A4010
CHAPEL LA
CARRS DR
GROVE RD
WALNUT TREE CL
STANLEY RD
PINEWOOD RD
HYLTON RD
PENMOOR CL
GALLOWS LA
MILL END RD
GILLETTS LA
River Wye
Sch
Fords
A40
PARK VIEW CT
EATON AVE
PRESTWOOD CL
FRYERS LA
GRAFTON ST
DASHWOOD AVE
BRITANNIA INDUSTRIAL ESTATE
Desborough Castle
Castlefield Wood
BARN CT
ROUNDWOOD RD
Rowliff Wood
WOODLAND CL
HIGH BEECHES
NEW RD
NEW ROAD CL
FIVE ACRE WOOD
EDMUNDS GDNS
EDMUNDS CL
WYCHWOOD GDNS
Schs
JUNIPER DR
LABURNUM RD
MAPLE CL
ALBION RD
BIRINUS CT
FRASER RD
YOUENS RD
SPEARING RD
CROSS RD
Liby
ROWLIFF RD
RUTLAND AVE
THE MIDDLEWAY
CHILTERN AVE
LONGLAND WAY
GRENFELL AVE
BURNHAM CL
BOOKER LA
PETTIFER WAY
OAKRIDGE RD
LINK RD
CHAIRBOROUGH RD
CASTLE VIEW GDNS
WHITELANDS RD
WHITELANDS WAY
DAVIES CT
MILDON WESTFIELD WAY
BUSHEY CL
CARRINGTON RD
LINCOLN PARK BUSINESS CENTRE
1 NURSERY CT
2 LINDEN CT
SHACKLETON RD
LINCOLN RD
HALIFAX RD
CORONATION RD
Cressex
TURNPIKE WAY
TURNPIKE RD
BLENHEIM RD
VERNEY AVE
YORK RD
LANCASTER RD
WELLINGTON RD
SHELBURNE CT
SHELBURNE RD
ACORN GDNS
RUPERT AVE
CLAYDON CT
ABBOTS WAY
THE HOMESTEAD
ROBINS CL
NEALE CL
CHALFONT WAY
MIERSFIELD
LITTLE CL
PINIONS WAY
REDHOUSE CL
GILLFIELD CL
DOWNE CL
Holmer's Farm
JOHN HALL WAY
CREST RD
Hotel
Sch
Schs
WEST WYCOMBE RD
BIRCHES RISE
MALVERN CL
COTSWOLD WAY
BRECON WAY
CUMBRIAN WAY
MENDIP WAY
DESBOROUGH INDUSTRIAL PARK
PARK RD
ABERCROMBY AVE
MAHONEY CT
OGILVIE RD
BEVELWOOD GDNS
COPYGROUND LA
LINDSAY AVE
OAKRIDGE RD
JUBILEE RD
UPPER GREEN ST
GREEN ST
LEIGH ST
KITCHENER RD
SHARROW VALE
PLUMER RD
SABINA CL
CONIFER RISE
MOUNT CL
BARONSMEAD RD
COLEVILLE RD
THE CHINES
DEAN CL
KNIGHTS HILL
DEEDS GR
DESBOROUGH AVE
DESBOROUGH RD
ELLSWORTH RD
WINCUP CL
VICTORIA GDNS
MARLOW RD
Sch
NUTFIELD LA
SHAFTESBURY CT
DESBOROUGH ST
VICTORIA ST
CEDAR TERR
MARLBOROUGH TRADING ESTATE
GEORGE ST
BAKER ST
RICHARDSON ST
SHORT ST
WEST END RD
WYCOMBE IND MALL
WENDOVER ST
SUFFIELD RD
BRIDLE GATE
ARCHDALE
Amb Sta
KEATS CL
KINGSLEY CRES
SHELLEY RD
CARVER HILL RD
WORDSWORTH RD
MARLOW HILL
SCHOOL CL
THE SPINNEY
FAIR RIDGE
Sports Centre
HUGHENDEN AVE
KELVIN CL
BRINDLEY AVE
BRUNEL RD
MYLNE CL
GARRATTS WAY
THE PASTURES
GIBBS CL
CAMPBELL CL
4
3
2
1
93
92
91
90
83
84
85

D E F

HIGH WYCOMBE
Totteridge
Micklefield
King's Wood
Lucas Wood
Cemy
Day Hospl
Mus
High Wycombe Station
Coll
Liby
Hospl
Courts
TH
River Wye
The Rye
The Dyke
Bassetsbury Manor
Rookery Wood
Daws Hill House
Warren Wood
Keep Hill
Funges Farm
Sewage Works
Wycombe Marsh
Deangarden Wood
High Wycombe Air Station
Mast
Myee's Plantation
Barrowcroft Wood
Abbey Barn Farm
Cobbles Farm
Lower Grounds Wood
Lower Grounds Belt
Gillfield Wood
Princess Gorse Farm
Heath End Farm
Winchbottom Farm
Ray Farm
Horton Wood
Hard to find Farm
Ford
Sch
AMERSHAM HILL
AMERSHAM RD
TOTTERIDGE RD
TOTTERIDGE LA
HUGHENDEN RD
HAMILTON RD
BELLFIELD RD
OXFORD RD
CASTLE ST
EASTON ST
QUEEN VICTORIA RD
ABBEY WAY
LILY'S WLK
MARLOW HILL
LONDON RD
BASSETSBURY LA
HATTER'S LA
HICKS FARM RISE
MICKLEFIELD RD
KINGSMEAD RD
ABBEY BARN LA
ABBEY BARN RD
DAWS HILL LA
HEATH END RD
WINCHBOTTOM LA
SPRING LA
COCK LA
M40
A40
A404
A4128
4
93
3
92
2
91
1
90
87
88

D E F

173
163

173
185

D
E
F
Branches Wood
Penn Bottom
HORSEMOOR LA
MARROD'S BOTTOM
FAGNALL LA
Great Luckings Wood
Downham Grove
Westfield Pieces
CLAY ST
Chalkpit Cottage
CROWN LA
Park Grove
Seagrave's Farm
Great Beard's Wood
Penbury Farm
Witheridge Wood
B474
WITHERIDGE LA
Sandels Wood
Wood Cottage
Penbury Grove
Sch
Knotty Green
Sandels Wood
The Grange
DREWS PARK
LATIMER WAY
WOODCHESTER PARK
SHRIMPTON CL
SHRIMPTON RD
MYNCHEN CL
MYNCHEN RD
MYNCHEN END
BERKLEY RD
Netherlands Wood
Brown's Wood
Underwood
WHICHERT CL
NATWOKE CL
HUTCHINGS RD
BEALINGS END
KNOTTOCKS END
KNOTTOCKS DR
Corkers Wood
FINCH LA
OLD FARM CL
FARM GR
PITCH POND CL
WYNGRAVE PL
OLDBURY GR
Saunder's Wood
ROBINSWOOD CL
UPPER DR
NETHERWOOD RD
HOWE DR
COPPERFIELDS
Ledborough Wood
Peggs Wood
CHURCHILL DR
PENN RD
SCOTSWOOD CL
MIDDLE DR
SANDELSWOOD END
Wilton Place
The Royal Standard (PH)
ROUNDHEADS END
RED HOUSE CL
CHERRY DR
FORTY GREEN RD
DOWER CL
EGHAMS CL
THE COPSE
COSSWAY
CAMPBELL DR
EASTERGATE
DISRAELI PARK
LOWER DR
SANDELS WAY
BROWNSWOOD RD
LEDBOROUGH WOOD
A355
WHIPASS HILL
GOMMS WOOD CL
WOODLANDS GLADE
SEELEYS RD
TOE MEADOW
SEAGRAVE RD
FOLEY CL
SHEEPCOTE CL
CURZON AVE
ASSHETON RD
RIDING LA
Forty Green
HOGBACK WOOD RD
EGHAMS WOOD RD
WOODLANDS DR
SEELEYS CL
BUSTIN CL
OWLSEARS CL
BLYTON CL
LEDBOROUGH LA
WOODSIDE AVE
MALKIN DR
HARVEY ORCHARD
HUBERT DAY CL
ORCHARD CL
REYNOLDS RD
GRENFELL RD
WILTON RD
WILTON CRES
Sch
Hogback Wood
WARWICK RD
ST MICHAEL'S GREEN
CALEDON RD
ONE TREE LA
WOODSIDE RD
BARING CRES
BARING RD
WOODSIDE CL
Beaconsfield Station
AMERSHAM RD
B474
POST OFFICE LA
MAXWELL RD
CHESTERTON GREEN
HYDE GREEN
GREGORIES RD
WALLER RD
GARVIN AVE
Holtspur Bottom Farm
CAMBRIDGE RD
STRATTON RD
BEECHWOOD RD
CHARTWELL GATE
GREGORIES FARM LA
STATION RD
CANDLEMAS MEAD
FERNHURST CL
RONALD RD
BELL CL
HAMPDEN HILL
CHILTERN HILLS RD
FURZEFIELD RD
BEECHES PARK
BURKES CRES
GROVE RD
CANDLEMAS LA
MEADOW LA
RIDING LA
HOLTSPUR TOP LA
BURGESS WOOD RD
BURKES RD
AYLESBURY END
UPPER RIDING
LOWER RIDING
BURGESS WOOD GR
WESTFIELD RD
BEACONSFIELD
WHITE HART MEADOW
ORCHARD RD
Cemy
Walk Wood
Butlers Court
Schs
MILL LA
HORSESHOE CRES
SHEPHERDS LA
YEW TREE CL
PARK LA A355
Wilton Park Farm
ROWAN CL
CHERRY TREE RD
BURGESS WOOD RD S
WALKWOOD END
BUTLERS COURT RD
WATTLETON RD
Holtspur Sch
HOLTSPUR WAY
CRAB TREE CL
ROLFE CL
OLD TOWN CL
B474
CROSSWAYS
MINERVA WAY
A40
HEATH RD
IVINS RD
CHESTNUT RD
ELLWOOD RD
TILSWORTH RD
WALK WOOD RISE
OLD LODGE DR
THE SPINNEY
A40
WYCOMBE END
LONDON END
MALTHOUSE SQ
WINDSOR END
THE FERNS
LAKES LA
EAST WAY
P
4
93
3
92
2
91
1
90
2
93
94
D
E
F

A
B
C
4
3
2
1
93
92
91
90
95
96
97
Hill's Wood
A355
BOTTOM HOUSE FARM LANE
BOTTRELLS LA
Barnhurst
Highfield Grove
Hodgemoor Woods
Red Barn Farm
Owlsears Wood
Three Households
Piggery
RAWLINGS LA
Starveacre Wood
AMERSHAM RD
Widmer Farm
Rawlings Farm
Newbarn
THREE HOUSEHOLDS
Bottom Wood
Big Copse
NEWBARN LA
Butlers Cross
South Lodge
West Riding
The Princess Marina Centre
Birchen Spring
Cleare Craft Wood
CHALFONT RD
TWITCHELL'S LA
WHIPASS HILL
HIGHLANDS RD
HOWARD CRES
HOWARD RD
Recreation Ground
BOTTOM LA
ORCHARD RD
MANOR RD
Harmony Nurseries
Blue Close Wood
Oldfields Farm
A355
CHURCH RD
ORCHARD MEWS
MANOR FARM WAY
Austens
Drummer's Yard
Seer Green
GREENWOOD CL
School
GODOLPHIN RD
FARMERS WAY
Hall Place
Young's Wood
LONG GROVE
SCHOOL LA
Cemetery
WILTON LA
PUERS LA
CRUTCHES LA
LONG WOOD DR
SEER MEAD
JORDANS WAY
School
GREEN WEST RD
NORTH RD
EAST RD
SEER GREEN LA
BAYNE HILL
Jordans
LONGBOTTOM LA
COPSE LA
JORDANS LA
Jordans Farm
Crutches Wood
BEECH LA
Golf Course
Seer Green and Jordans Station
FARM LA
WELDERS LA
Club House
DEAN WOOD RD
Meeting House
Welders House
Tumulus
The Mount
Walk Wood
Wheatsheaf Wood
Stone Dean Farm
Thirty Acre Knoll
MINERVA WAY
MAUDE RD
MAUDE CL
Wilton Park
Sports Field
Pitlands Wood
POTKILN LA
GORELL RD
WAVELL RD
DUPRE CRES
BERWICK CL
Birchland Wood
LONDON END
A40
LONDON RD
BURNHAM AVE
A40

D
E
F
Stratton Chase Drive
MILL LA
HILL FARM LA
CHASE LA
STRATTON
DODDS LA
BOTTRELLS LA
SILVER HILL
HIGH ST
Liby
P
AMERSHAM RD
A413
B4442
VACHE LA
CHERRY RISE
HIGHFIELD
KINGS CL
ELLWOOD RISE
KINGS RD
ASHWELLS WAY
PHEASANT HILL
The Pheasant Inn
Merlin's Cave (PH)
CROMWELL CL
LONDON RD
ORCHARD RD
STYLECROFT RD
VALENTINE WAY
THE BROW
OUTLOOK DR
WOODBANK DR
SILSDEN CRES
TURNERS WOOD DR
Turners Wood
Shrubs Wood
Gorelands
College
GORELANDS LA
Ashwell's Farm
Rowan Farm
Allot Gdns
BACK LA
GRAYBURN CL
ALBION CRES
ALBION RD
SUSSEX CL
UP CORNER CL
SCHOOL LA
Sch
WHITE HART CL
MILTON FIELDS
MILTON CL
SYCAMORE RD
SYCAMORE CL
SYCAMORE RISE
DEAN WAY
Mus
CROSSLEY'S HILL
TOWNFIELD LA
PARSONAGE RD
HILLSIDE CL
LAGGER CL
HEARNE CT
Sch
THREE HOUSEHOLDS
ORCHARD
BOWLER'S
TRIPPS HILL
NARCOT RD
PALLISER RD
FLEETWOOD CL
NARCOT WAY
CAPTAIN COOK CL
THE LAGGER
GORDON WAY
MIDDLE MEADOW
CROSSLEYS
SEYMOUR RD
ARAN HTS
Chalfont St Giles
Top Farm
Cemy
Dibden Hill
BOWSTRIDGE LA
AMERSHAM RD
River Misbourne
CHESHAM LA
Skipping's Farm
Chalfont Common
Chalfont Centre
GABLES CL
PHEASANT WLK
MARK DR
FOXDELL WAY
NICHOLLS AVE
TATE RD
PENN GASKELL LA
CROSS LANES
CROSS LANES CL
MID CROSS LA
RICKMANSWORTH LA
COOPERS RIDGE
NORTOFT RD
ROBERTS WOOD DR
Dibden Hill Farm
Narcot Farm
Bramleys Farm
Abattoir
Bowstridge
NARCOT LA
MISBOURNE CL
ALDERBOURNE LA
SOUTHCLIFFE DR
MISBOURNE AVE
HOLLYTREE CL
PETERHILL CL
THE DRIVE
THE PADDOCK
MONUMENT LA
CEDARS CL
NORTHDOWN RD
RAVENSMEAD
OLD MEAD
WHITE ATLEY WAY
THE DELL
DEANACRE CL
DEANCROFT RD
RICKMANSWORTH LA
THE PHYGTLE
GARDNERS END
GARDNERS RD
FERNSLEIGH CL
WHEELERS ORCHARD
Coll
Gravel Hill
DENHAM WLK
DENHAM LA
GRAVEL HILL
ROBINS ORCHARD
HILLSIDE CL
HILL HOUSE CL
COPTHALL CNR
HEDGEROW
GREENFIELD END
HIGHLANDS
GLYNSWOOD
HIGHLANDS CL
Sch
WEST HYDE LA
Outfield Farm
Windmill Farm
Woodlands Farm
Grove Farm
Farm Wood
Grove Lodge
Pond Warren Wood
Chalfont Grove
Outfield Plantation
Grove Wood
Sch
COPTHALL LA
ELMS RD
HILLFIELD RD
WHITE HOUSE CL
HILLFIELD SQ
HILL FARM RD
GRASSINGHAM END
GRASSINGHAM RD
CHESTNUT WLK
NINNINGS WAY
NINNINGS RD
JOINERS CL
ROYLE CL
JOINER'S LA
BOUNDARY RD
LOVEL END
PINETREE CL
GROVE HILL
LOVEL MEAD
TOP AND BOTTOM RD
PENNINGTON RD
OUTFIELD RD
FIELD WAY
WINDMILL RD
Allot Gdns
WELDERS LA
Sch
Leisure Centre
GLEBE CL
LAUREL RD
GORDON CL
CHURCH LA
WINKERS LA
MORRIS CL
WINKERS CL
UPWAY
LEWIS LA
CHESTNUT CL
SANDY RISE
TUNMERS END
GROVE END
LOVEL RD
VALE CL
PENN RD
Hospl
Sch
GLEBE RD
LANSDOWN RD
THE VALE
HAMPDEN RD
CHURCHFIELD RD
HIGH ST
HILTON CRES
CHILTERN HILL
Chalfont St Peter
GROVE LA
LEACHCROFT
WEEDON CL
NICOL END
ELEANOR RD
NICOL RD
NICOL CL
MARKET PL
P
Amb Sta
Liby
ORCHARD GR
GOLD HILL N
ELLIS AVE
HALF ACRE HILL
LINCOLN RD
The Ash Beds
GROVE CL
CHIPSTEAD
POND LA
Goldhill Common
GOLD HILL W
GOLD HILL E
Convent
GRANGE RD
GRANGE FIELDS
HITHER MEADOW
CROFT RD
WOODSIDE CL
WOODSIDE HILL
Great Legs Wood
Layter's Green
LAYTER'S AVE
BEECH MANOR CRES
CHERRYTREE LA
MEADOWCROFT
LOWER RD
Hogtrough Wood
LAYTER'S CL
LAYTER'S END
HILL RISE
HILL RISE CRES
Malms Wood
LAYTERS GREEN LA
Layter's Green Farm
CRISS GR
AUSTENWOOD LA
AUSTENWOOD CL
THE RUSSETS
PRIORY RD
PENSHURST CL
AUSTENWOOD LA
CLELAND RD
ST MARY'S WAY
SCHOOL LA
LAMBSCROFT WAY
ASHLEA RD
AUSTENWAY
B416
KINGSWAY
LOWER RD
A413
Gerrards Cross Golf Course
4
93
3
92
2
91
1
90
98
99
00
D
E
F

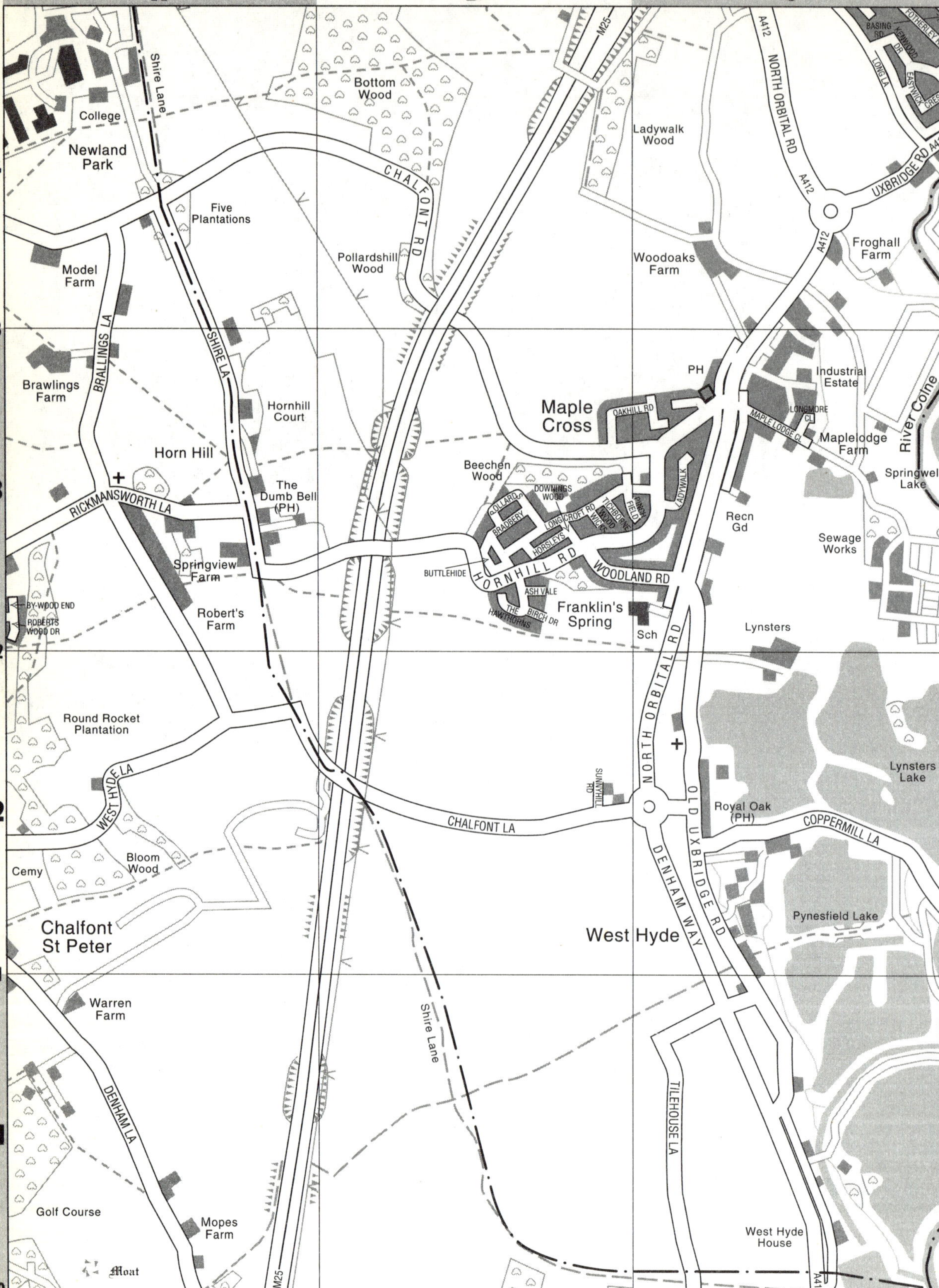
A
B
C
Shire Lane
Bottom Wood
College
Newland Park
CHALFONT RD
Five Plantations
Model Farm
Pollardshill Wood
Ladywalk Wood
NORTH ORBITAL RD
A412
UXBRIDGE RD A412
Woodoaks Farm
Froghall Farm
BRALLINGS LA
Brawlings Farm
SHIRE LA
Hornhill Court
Maple Cross
OAKHILL RD
PH
Industrial Estate
LONGMORE CL
MAPLE LODGE CL
Maplelodge Farm
River Colne
Horn Hill
Beechen Wood
DOWNINGS WOOD
Springwell Lake
The Dumb Bell (PH)
RICKMANSWORTH LA
POLLARDS
BRADBERY
LONG CROFT RD
TICHBORNE
WOOD WICKS
FINCH FIELD
LADYWALK
Recn Gd
Sewage Works
Springview Farm
BUTTLEHIDE
HORNHILL RD
HORSLEYS
WOODLAND RD
ASH VALE
BY-WOOD END
ROBERTS WOOD DR
Robert's Farm
THE BIRCH DR
HAWTHORNS
Franklin's Spring
Sch
Lynsters
Round Rocket Plantation
NORTH ORBITAL RD
WEST HYDE LA
SUNNYHILL RD
Lynsters Lake
Royal Oak (PH)
OLD UXBRIDGE RD
COPPERMILL LA
CHALFONT LA
Bloom Wood
Cemy
DENHAM WAY
Chalfont St Peter
Pynesfield Lake
West Hyde
Warren Farm
Shire Lane
DENHAM LA
TILEHOUSE LA
Golf Course
Mopes Farm
West Hyde House
Moat
M25
A412
4
93
3
92
2
91
1
90
01
02
03

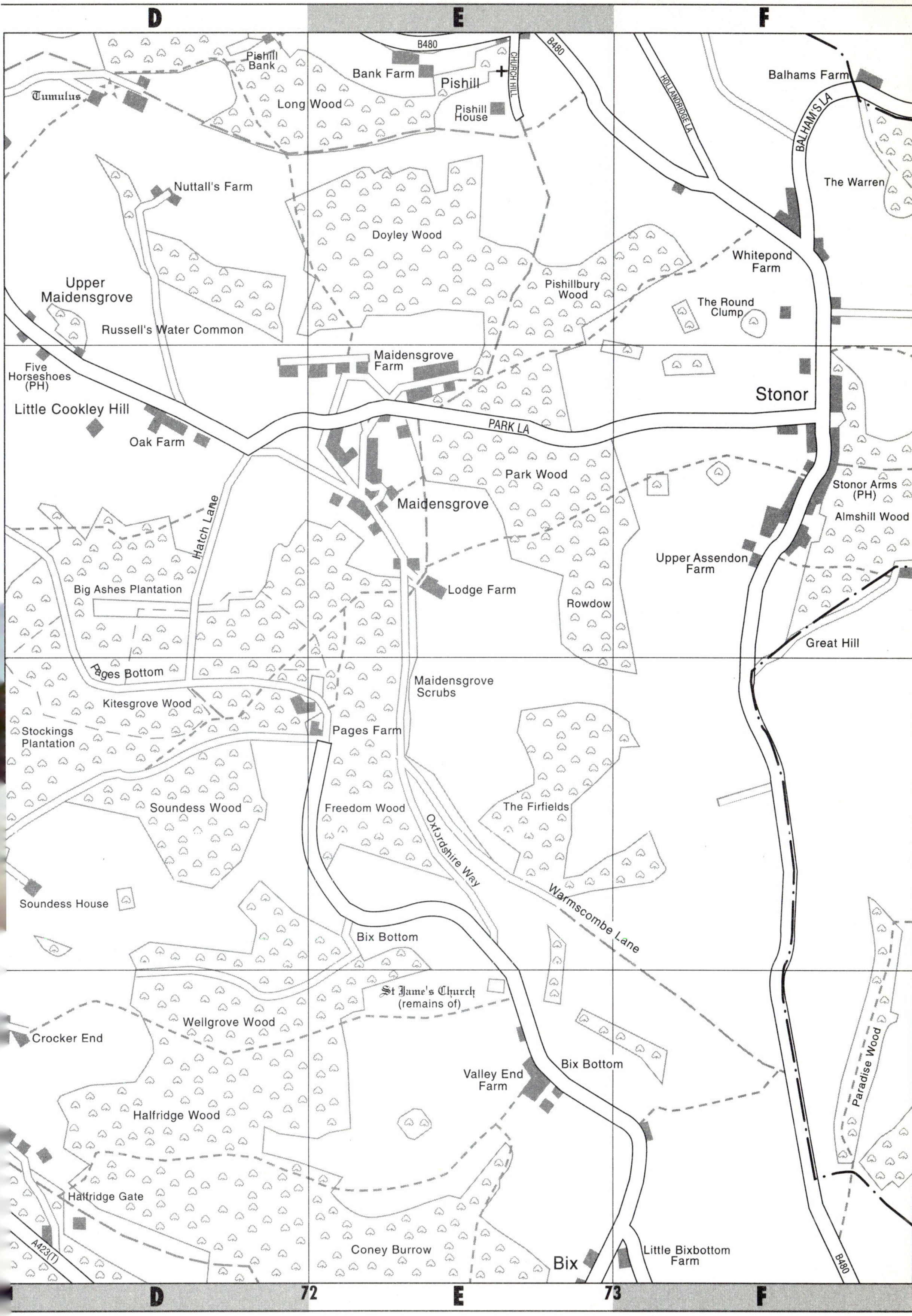
D
E
F
Pishill Bank
Tumulus
B480
Bank Farm
Pishill
CHURCH HILL
Long Wood
Pishill House
HOLLANDRIDGE LA
Balhams Farm
BALHAM'S LA
The Warren
Nuttall's Farm
Doyley Wood
Whitepond Farm
Upper Maidensgrove
Pishillbury Wood
The Round Clump
Russell's Water Common
Five Horseshoes (PH)
Maidensgrove Farm
Little Cookley Hill
Stonor
Oak Farm
PARK LA
Park Wood
Stonor Arms (PH)
Hatch Lane
Maidensgrove
Almshill Wood
Upper Assendon Farm
Big Ashes Plantation
Lodge Farm
Rowdow
Great Hill
Pages Bottom
Maidensgrove Scrubs
Kitesgrove Wood
Stockings Plantation
Pages Farm
Soundess Wood
Freedom Wood
Oxfordshire Way
The Firfields
Warmscombe Lane
Soundess House
Bix Bottom
St Jame's Church (remains of)
Wellgrove Wood
Crocker End
Valley End Farm
Bix Bottom
Paradise Wood
Halfridge Wood
Halfridge Gate
A423(T)
Coney Burrow
Bix
Little Bixbottom Farm
B480
4
3
2
1
89
88
87
86
72
73

179
169

179
191

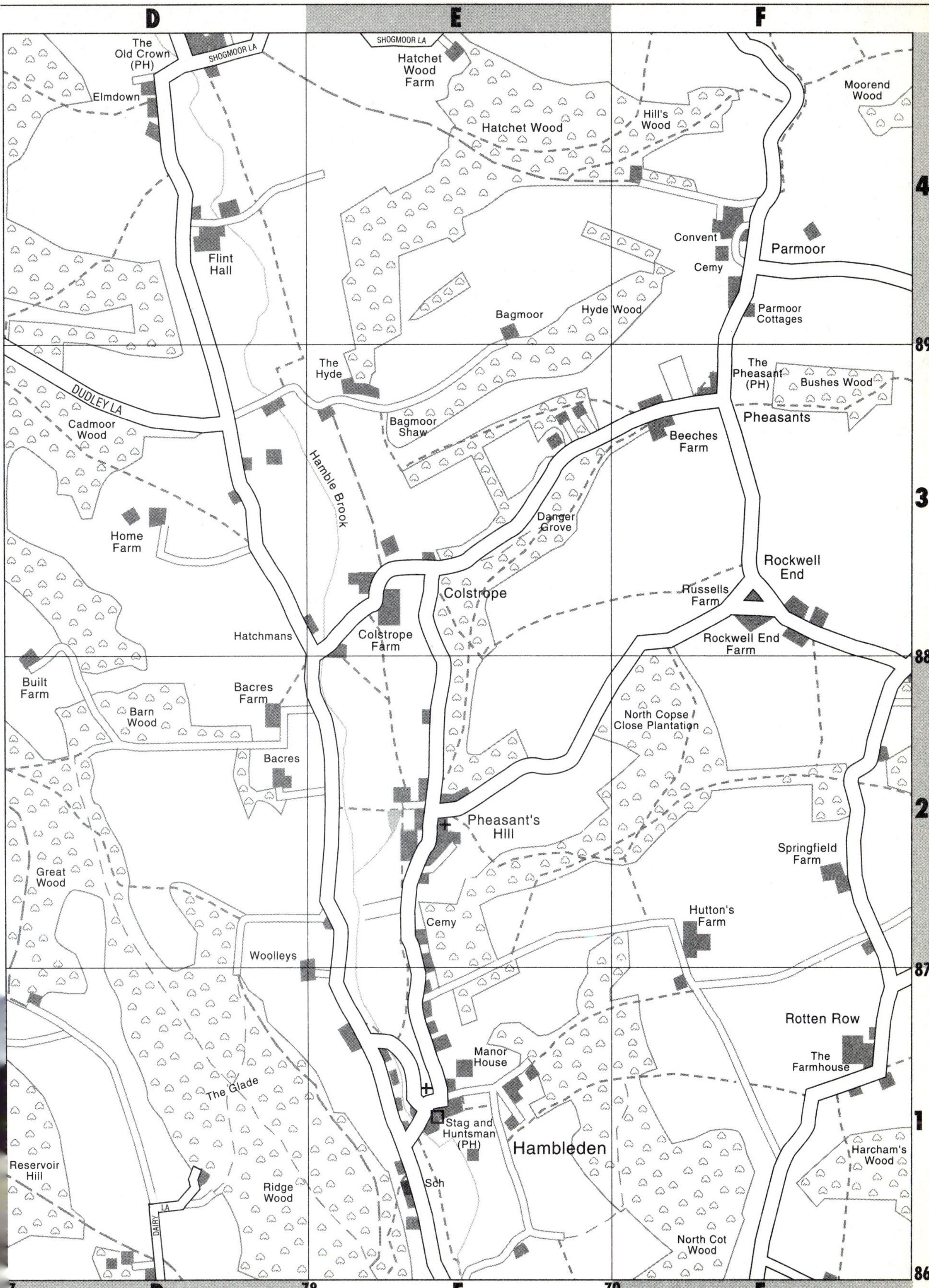
D
E
F
The Old Crown (PH)
SHOGMOOR LA
Hatchet Wood Farm
Moorend Wood
Elmdown
Hill's Wood
Hatchet Wood
4
Convent
Parmoor
Flint Hall
Cemy
Parmoor Cottages
Bagmoor
Hyde Wood
89
The Hyde
The Pheasant (PH)
Bushes Wood
DUDLEY LA
Cadmoor Wood
Bagmoor Shaw
Pheasants
Beeches Farm
Hamble Brook
3
Danger Grove
Home Farm
Rockwell End
Colstrope
Russells Farm
Hatchmans
Colstrope Farm
Rockwell End Farm
88
Built Farm
Bacres Farm
Barn Wood
North Copse Close Plantation
Bacres
2
Pheasant's Hill
Springfield Farm
Great Wood
Hutton's Farm
Cemy
Woolleys
87
Rotten Row
Manor House
The Farmhouse
The Glade
1
Stag and Huntsman (PH)
Harcham's Wood
Hambleden
Reservoir Hill
Sch
Ridge Wood
DAIRY LA
North Cot Wood
86
7
78
79

181
171

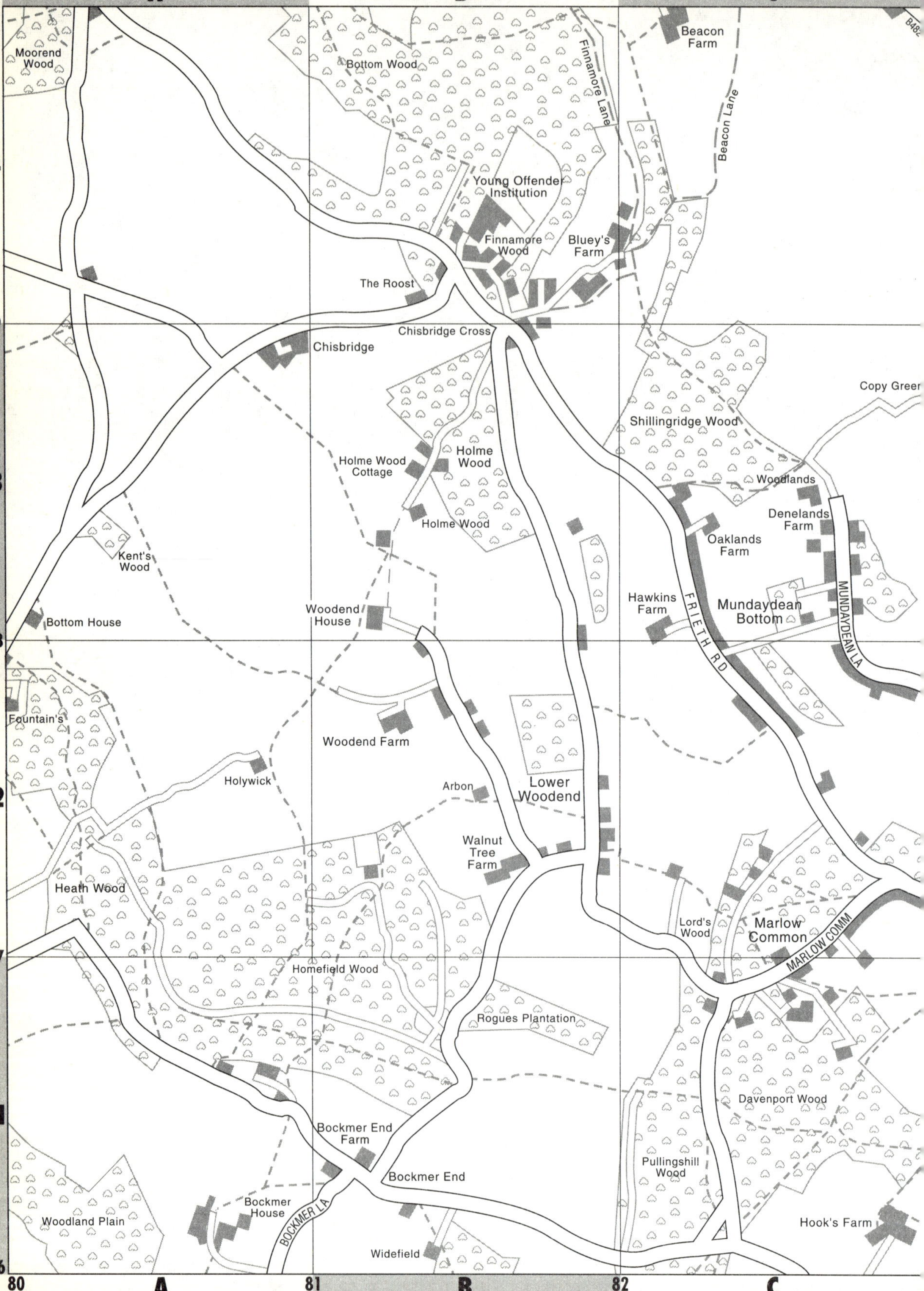

181
193

172
184

194
184

A
B
C
Horton Wood
Bloom Wood
New Farm
PH
Sheepridge
SHEEPRIDGE LA
Bloom Farm
WINCHBOTTOM LA
Merton's Hole Cottage
Pigeon House Farm
A404
Fern House
Cemy
Fern
Wilton Farm
Caravan Site
MARLOW RD
Well End
ELM LA
ABBEY RD
Coronach
Sch
SCHOOL LA
Pump Farm
The King's Head (PH)
CHURCH RD
Little Marlow
PUMP LA
PUMP LAS
POUND LA
A4155
STAPLETON CL
Manor House
COLDMOORHOLME LA
SPADE OAK MEADOW
THE AVENUE
FARM RD
The Abbey
THE DRIVE
LITTLE MARLOW RD
The Spade Oak (PH)
P
Spade Oak Farm
Abbotsbrook
LC
WILTSHIRE RD
GRATTAN CT
BUTLER CT
BRISTOW CT
DOUGLAS CT
GUNTHORPE RD
THE CHASE
THE CROFT
PARKWAY
Westhorpe House
Sewage Works
The Moor
River Thames
Westhorpe Farm
1 MARCHANT CT
2 WASHINGTON CT
SAVILL WAY
FOURTH AVE
Tumuli
Noah's House
Cock Marsh
FIRST AVE
Patches
Sewage Wks
Stone House
STONE HOUSE LA
Coney Copse
WINTER HILL
GIBRALTAR LA
RIVERWOODS DR
RIVERWOODS AVE
Winter Hill
BRADCUTTS LA
TERRY'S LA
Harvest Moon
Greythatch
Golf Course
4
89
3
88
2
87
1
86
86
87
88

187
177

187
199

D
E
F
Sch
Flackwell Heath
Parklands
Under Ridge
Westwinds
Unity House
Resr
Golf Course
Juniper Farm
Clayfield House
Old Meadows
Ronald Wood
Mill
Works
Sch
Glory Hill Farm
Wooburn Green
River Wye
Wooburn
Wooburn Park
Berghers Hill
Farm Wood
Wash Hill Wood
Mast
Cores End
Cemy
The Swilley
Widmoor
Hedsor
Hawk's Hill
The Chequers (PH)
Hedsor Farmhouse
Bourne End
Bourne End Station
Liby
Works
Hollands Farm
River Thames
Mill House
Merlins Mead
White Hill
Woodman's Wood
Church Road
Hedsor Priory
Hedsor Court
Park Top
Dismantled Railway
CHAPMAN LA
BLIND LA
GREEN DRAGON LA
STRAIGHT BIT
WHITEPIT LA
JUNIPER LA
WYCOMBE LA
WATERY LANE
GLORY MILL LA
HOLTSPUR AVE
HOLTSPUR LA
BOUNDARY RD
WHITE HILL
A40
M40
A4094
B4440
A4155
THE GREEN
WINDSOR HILL
MARLOW RD
THE PARADE
CORES END RD
STATION RD
FURLONG RD
KILN LA
HARVEST HILL
HAWKS HILL
HEDSOR HILL
HEDSOR RD
HEDSOR LA
FERRY LA
WASH HILL
TOWN LA
BROOKBANK
SHEEPCOTE LA
1 STRATHCONA CL
2 STRATHCONA WAY
4
89
3
88
2
87
1
86
90
91
9

185
175

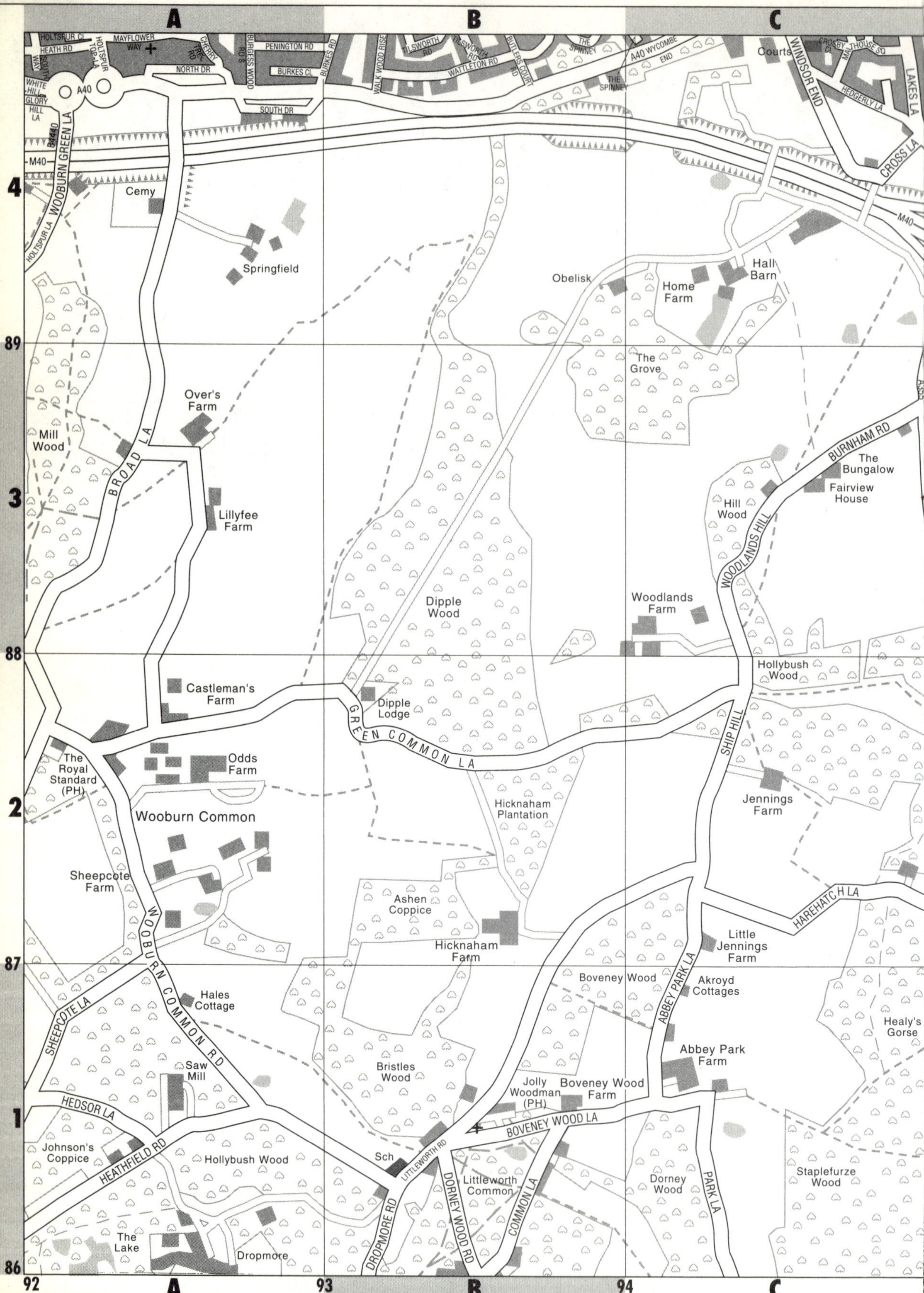

185
197

176
188

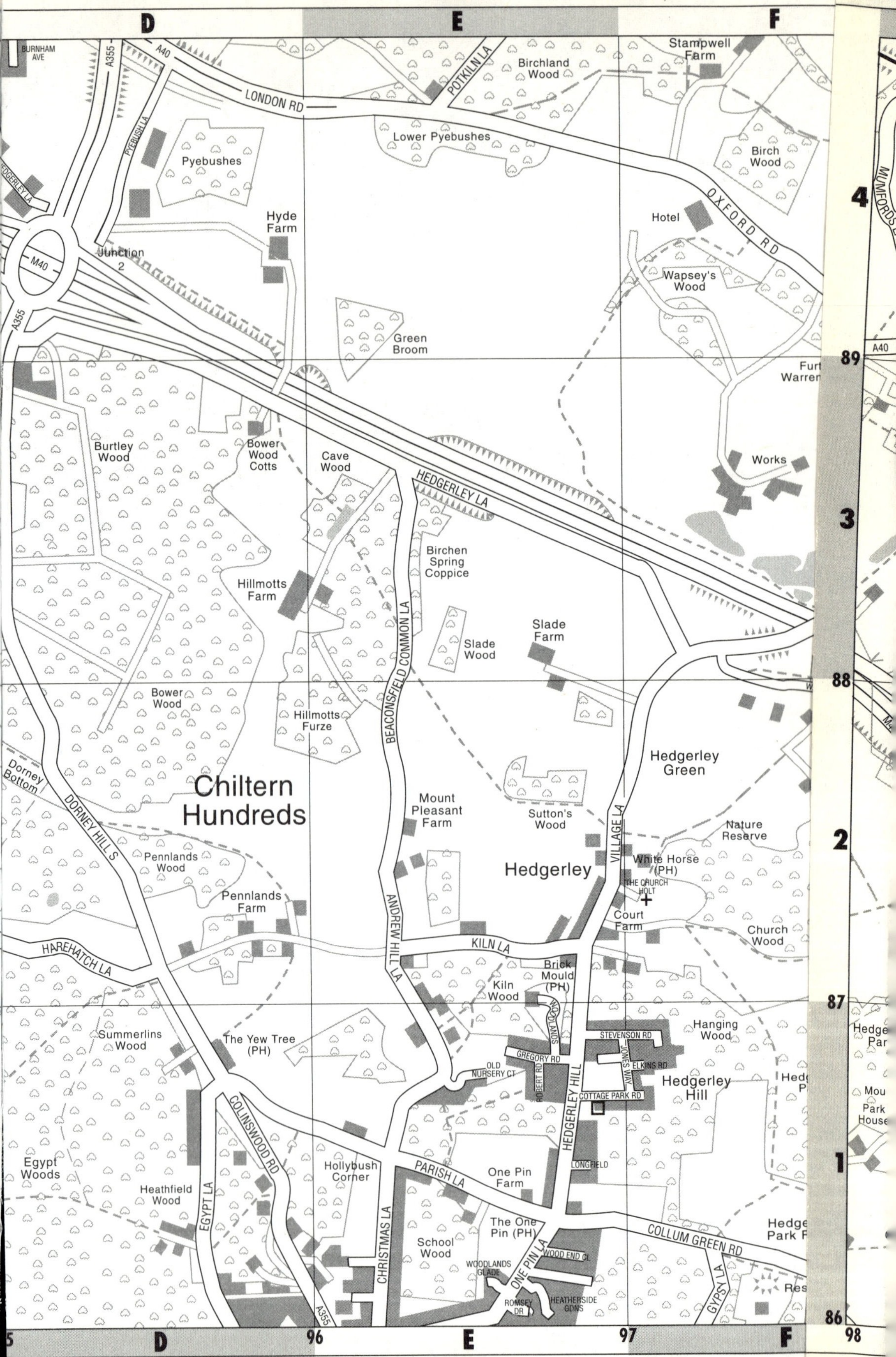

198
188

D
E
F
Chalfont Lodge
DENHAM LA
M25
Tile House
A412
Juniper Wood
Durdent Court
Nockhill Wood
Golf Course
Great Halings Wood
NORTH ORBITAL RD
Caravan Site
HALINGS LA
Weir
Coldharbour Farm
The Marish
Northmoor Hill Wood
MARISH LA
Denham Park Farm
Marish Farm
Oakend Wood
Denham Aerodrome
Denham Garden Village
Denham Marsh Wood
1 PATRONS DR
2 SUSSEX WAY
3 CONSORT WAY
4 FOUNDERS DR
5 EDINBURGH DR
6 AUXILIARIES WAY
7 GOVERNORS AVE
8 QUEEN MOTHER'S DR
Owls Oak
MIRRIE LA
TILEHOUSE LA
TRUSTEES WAY
A413
AMERSHAM RD
WOODLANDS CL
MILL LA
Isle Of Wight Farm
SLADE OAK LA
WOODHURST DR
CHAIRMANS AVE
KNOWLAND WAY
DENHAM GREEN LA
HOBARTS DR
OVER THE MISBOURNE
Golf Course
Denham Green
Sch
RANSTON CL
POLLARD AVE
Collsels Wood
CH
ST FRANCIS RD
HILLCREST WAYE
WOODHILL AVE
NIGHTINGALE WAY
PENN DR
ST MARY'S RD
GREEN TILES LA
CREST
OWYER
ASHCROFT DR
Bailey Hill
BEECH WAYE
Denham Golf Club Station
DOGGETTS FARM RD
UPPER RD
TILEHOUSE WAY
GOLDSMITH LA
STATION APP
MIDDLE CRES
MIDDLE RD
River Misbourne
LOWER RD
SIDE RD
Sewage Works
OLD RECTORY LA
The Old Rectory
Gallows Wood
Weir
Higher Denham
Moor House Farm
A40
Caps Wood
Baker's Wood
F Sta
Tatling End
NEAL CL
BROKEN GATE LA
Denham Place
DENHAM AVE
Poultry Farm
BAKERS WOOD
REDHILL
VILLAGE RD
SKYLARK RD
FULMER LA
OXFORD RD
Huntwyk
Mount Farm
FORE END
Hollybush Farm
HOLLYBUSH LA
MOUNT LA
Redhill Farm
CHEAPSIDE LA
BLACKSMITH'S LA
BRONSDON WAY
Sch
OXFORD GDNS
Alderbourne Manor
Denham Mount
FROGGY LA
Little Acres Farm
ST HUBERTS LA
Gladwin's Wood
FIELD RD
SOUTHLANDS RD
HAWKS WOOD LA
Hawk's Wood
M25
4
89
3
88
2
87
1
86
02
03

A
B
C
4
3
2
1
89
88
87
86
04
05
06
Langley Farm
Breakspear Path
Bourne Farm
Highbones
BREAKSPEAR RD N
Breakspear House
Nature Reserve
LOVETT RD
CHURCH HILL
ST MARY'S RD
ST MARY'S CL
ST ANNE'S RD
CHURCH RD
Broadwater Farm
BROADWATER LA
SEDLEY GR
HINKLEY CL
BROADWATER GDNS
Broad Water
PRIORY GDNS
PRIORY CL
PRIORY AVE
TRUESDALE DR
Park Lodge Farm
South Harefield
Bayhurst Wood (Countryside Park)
Battlesford Wood
Widewater Lock
DELLSIDE
THE FURROWS
HILLSIDE
MOORHALL RD
The Horse & Barge (PH)
Lower Lodge
A412
Harefield Moor
Grand Union Canal
Towing Path
BROADWATER PARK
1 GREEN TILES LA
2 SHEEPCOTE GDNS
3 DENHAM GREEN LA
LINK WAY
JAMES MARTIN CL
MOORFIELD RD
Green Bridge
Savay Farm
SAVAY LA
MORTEN GDNS
AM GREEN CL
PYGHTLE FOOTPATH
SAVAY CL
STATION PAR
DENH
NEWYEARS GREEN LA
Newyears Green
HARVIL RD
Highway Farm
Dews Farm
Braemar Farm
Newyears Green Covert
Denham Station
River Colne
Pyghtle Footpath
Camping Site
Research Farm
Copthall Covert
Moat
VILLAGE RD
The White House
Denham
Court Farm
Denham Court
Golf Course
CH
THE GARDENS
Harvil Farm
Copthall Farm
ASHMEAD LA
MEAD CL
ASH MEAD DR
River Misbourne
BACONSMEAD
DENHAM WAY
Priory Covert
OLD MILL RD
DENHAM CL
OXFORD GDNS
COURTFIELD GDNS
LINDSEY RD
WOLSTAN CL
WENLACK CL
CAMPION CL
PRIORY CL
OXFORD RD
A40
Fray's River
The Lea
Denham Lock
THE DRIVE
HIGHFIELD DR
LODORE GREEN
B467
Ickenham
BREAKSPEAR RD S
GREENACRE AVE
SWAKELEYS RD
VINLAKE
THREE OAKS CL
CAMPDEN RD
CHARLBURY

D
E
F
Middle Assendon Farm
FAWLEY BOTTOM RD
Crockmore Farm
DOBSON'S LA
Fawley
Benhams Wood
Oaken Grove
BENHAMS LA
Rowe Wood
4
Round Hill Farm
B480
A4155
Roothouse Wood
Fawley Court Farm
Round Hill
85
The Golden Ball (PH)
Lower Assendon
Henley Park
Great Hill
New Cottages
BIX HILL
A423(T)
B480
No Man's Hill
Oxfordshire Way
Cemy
Deer Park
3
Lambridge Hill
Fawley Court
Henley Reach
The Grove
Hospital
College
Lambridge Farm
Little Wood
Wks
84
FAIR MILE
South Lodge
Lambridge Wood
The Mount
River Thames
LAMBRIDGE WOOD RD
BARN LA
Caravan and Camping Site
Badgemore End
2
REMENHAM LA
Golf Course
Swiss Farm
MARLOW RD
Badgemore House
Beechwood
Court
NORTHFIELD END
A423(T)
Remenham Court
CLEMENTS RD
ABRAHAMS RD
BOWLING CT
PEARCES ORCH
LUKER AVE
COOPER CL
SIMMONS RD
CRISP RD
LAMBRIDGE LA
LEICESTER CL
NORTHFIELD CT
BADGEMOOR LA
PHYLLIS CT DR
RUPERT CL
RUPERT'S LA
Phyllis Court
CH
DELL LA
Sch
83
Wilminster Park
MOUNT VIEW
MOUNT VIEW
KINGS RD
BARONS MEAD
Liby
RAVENSCROFT RD
ADAM CT
BELL ST
RIDNOR CL
WHARF LA
Friar Park
Sch
HOP GDNS
CLARENCE RD
NEW ST
Church Avenue
THAMES SIDE
Lower Hernes
Hospl
YORK RD
CALDWELL
KINGS CL
MARKET
HART ST
PARKSIDE
WEST ST
TH
PL
MATSON DR
GRAVEL HILL
F Sta
DUKE ST
WHITE HILL
A4130
PACK AND PRIME LA
Parkside
MILTON CL
TOWNS LA
1
ANCASTLE GR
FRIDAY ST
PUTMAN PL
QUEEN ST
A321
PARADISE RD
DEANFIELD AVE
Coll
DEANFIELD AVE
Pack and Prime Lane
College
ALBERT RD
STATION RD
BOATHOUSE REACH
WARGRAVE RD
HENLEY-ON-THAMES
CHURCH ST
Coll
MEADOW RD
Henley-on-Thames Station
ST ANNE'S CL
GREYS RD
NORMAN AVE
READING RD
A321
VALLEY RD 1
GAINSBOROUGH RD 2
GAINSBOROUGH HILL 3
LAL
LEVER RD
DEANFIELD RD
Sch
HAMILTON AVE
WYNDALE CL
UPTON CL
Greenfield Cottages
HARCOURT CL
GREYS HILL
1 ORCHARD CL
2 GROVE RD
3 MARMION RD
HAYWARDS CL
Sch
VICARAGE RD
ST MARK'S RD
A4155
SINGER LA
PARK RD
GRANGE RD
Hernes
82
D
75
E
76
F

191
181

A
B
C
4
3
2
1
85
84
83
82
77
78
79
DAIRY LA
Greenlands Dairy Farm
Burrow Farm
Chalkpit Wood
A4155
Greenlands
Towing Path
Mill End
Hambleden Lock
Mill
Weir
Millend Farm
Binfields Wood
Temple Island
River Thames
FERRY LA
Killdown Bank
A4155
Hambleden Place
WESTFIELD COTTS
Aston
Remenham
REMENHAM LA
ASTON FERRY LA
Westfield Farm
Hotel
Culham Farm
Towing Path
Culham Court
REMENHAM CHURCH LA
ASTON LA
Culham House
Lower Culham Farm
Woodside Farm
Common Barn
Rosehill Wood
Remenham Wood
Remenham Place
Remenham Hill
Middle Culham Farm
WHITE HILL
A4130
A4130
Branfords
Parkplace Farm
Wild's Belt
CH
Aspects Park Golf Centre
Mon
Mast
Sch
Park Place
Piggots Corner
Upper Culham Farm
A321
WARGRAVE RD

182
194

D
E
F
4
85
3
84
2
83
1
82
81
82
Damaskfield Wood
Bockmer Hill House
Widefield Wood
Marlins Grove
Hog Wood
Hollowhill Wood
Hooks Farm Cottage
A4155
Rassler Wood
BOCKMER LA
Millbank Wood
Cobble Wood
NORTH CL
WEST CL
SOUTH CL
SHELLEY CL
BUCKINGHAM GATE
CHESTNUT CL
KINGS WOOD
THAMES REACH
School
The Brambles
Kings Barn Farm
Kingsbarn House
SCHOOL LA
Home Copse
Fort
Lodge Farm
A4155
Home Farm House
Millbank Wood
Dog & Badger (PH)
Caravan Site
Harleyford Manor
Danesfield
Fort
Medmenham Mill
Hurley Lock
Medmenham
FERRY LA
River Thames
LOWLACE CL
MILL LA
Caravan Site
Hurley Farm
Research Institute
Mon
Ye Olde Bell Hotel
Frogmill Spinney
Meadowcroft
SHEPHERDS LA
Hurley
HURLEY HIGH ST
BELL CT
TEMPLE PARK
Temple Park Farm
FROGMILL
Frogmill Farm
BLACK BOY LA
SHEPHERDS CL
NEW RD
Shepherds Cottage
Hurley Bottom
PROSPECT PL
A4130
HENLEY RD
The Black Boy Inn (PH)
East Arms Hotel
The Grassland Research Institute
Culham Court Lodge
Prospect Hill
A4130
Rosehill
High Wood
Garden Cottage
HONEY LA
Hodgedale Lane
ROSE LA
The Grassland Research Institute Farm
South Lodge
Channy Grove
Recreation Ground

193
183

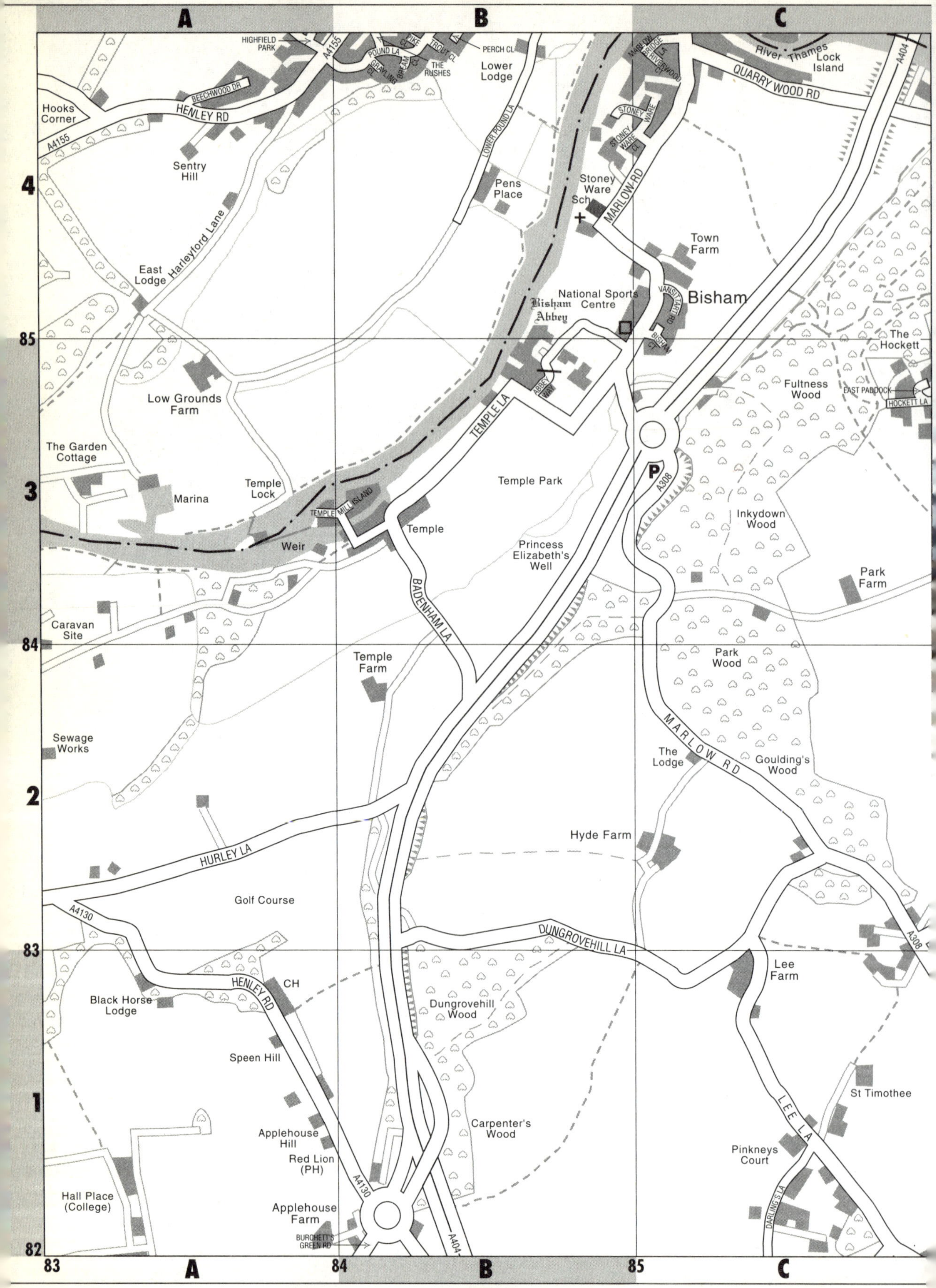
A
B
C
HIGHFIELD PARK
A4155
POUND LA
PIKE CL
TROUT CL
PERCH CL
GRAYLING CL
BREAM CL
THE RUSHES
Lower Lodge
MARLOW BRIDGE LA
RIVERWOOD CT
River Thames
Lock Island
QUARRY WOOD RD
A404
Hooks Corner
BEECHWOOD DR
HENLEY RD
A4155
Sentry Hill
LOWER POUND LA
STONEY WARE
STONEY WARE CL
Pens Place
Stoney Ware
Sch
MARLOW RD
Harleyford Lane
East Lodge
Town Farm
National Sports Centre
Bisham Abbey
Bisham
VANSITTART RD
BISHAM CT
The Hockett
Fultness Wood
EAST PADDOCK
HOCKETT LA
ABBEY WAY
Low Grounds Farm
TEMPLE LA
The Garden Cottage
Temple Park
Marina
Temple Lock
TEMPLE MILL ISLAND
Temple
A308
Inkydown Wood
Weir
Princess Elizabeth's Well
Park Farm
Caravan Site
BADENHAM LA
Temple Farm
Park Wood
Sewage Works
MARLOW RD
The Lodge
Goulding's Wood
HURLEY LA
Hyde Farm
Golf Course
A4130
DUNGROVEHILL LA
A308
HENLEY RD
CH
Black Horse Lodge
Lee Farm
Dungrovehill Wood
Speen Hill
St Timothee
LEE LA
Applehouse Hill
Carpenter's Wood
Red Lion (PH)
Pinkneys Court
A4130
DARLING'S LA
Hall Place (College)
Applehouse Farm
BURCHETT'S GREEN RD
A404
4
85
3
84
2
83
1
82
83
84
85

D E F

4 85 3 84 2 83 1 82

86 D 87 E 88 F

195
185

195
203

186
198

204
198

197
187

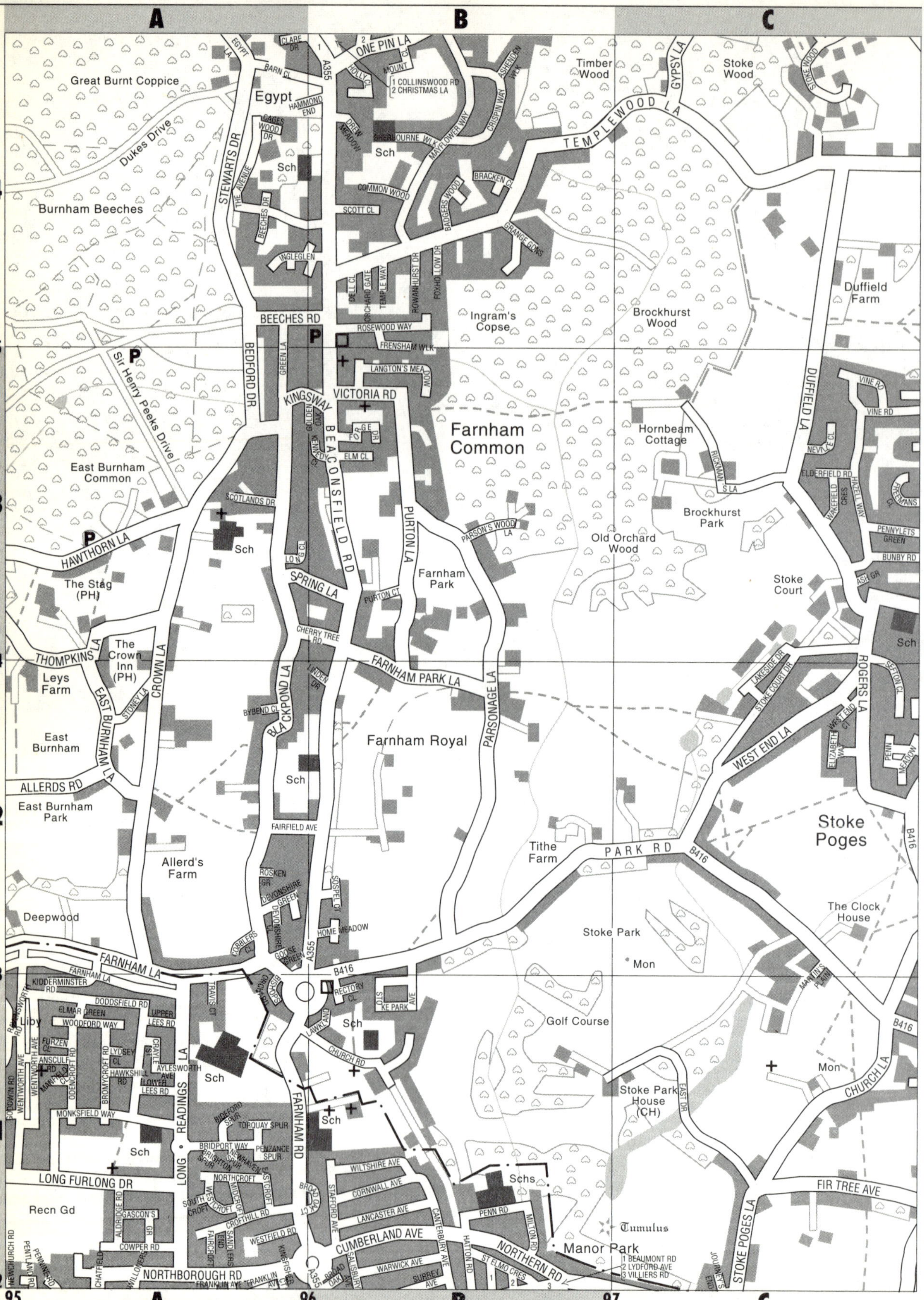

197
205

188
200

D E F

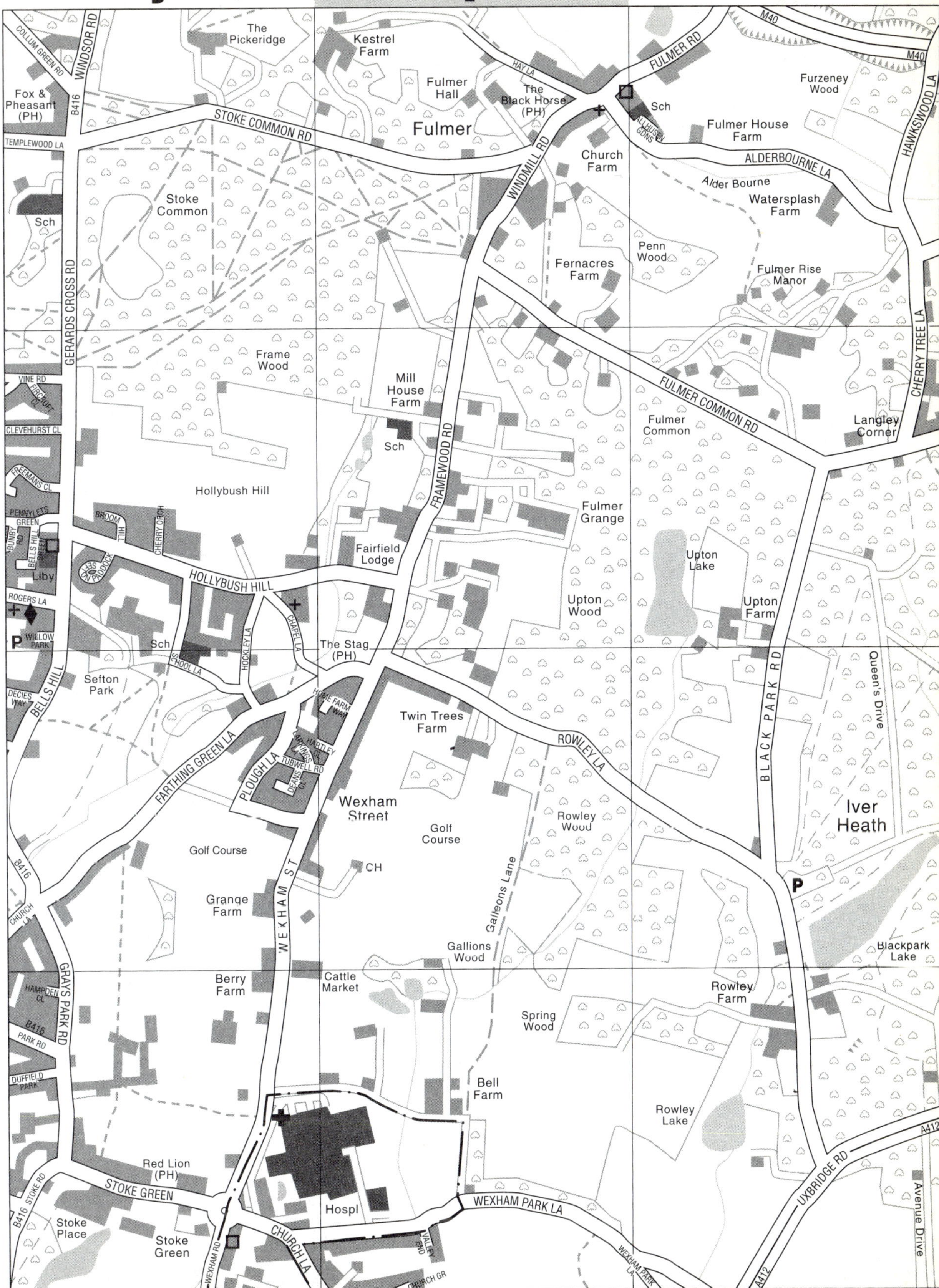

D E F

206
200

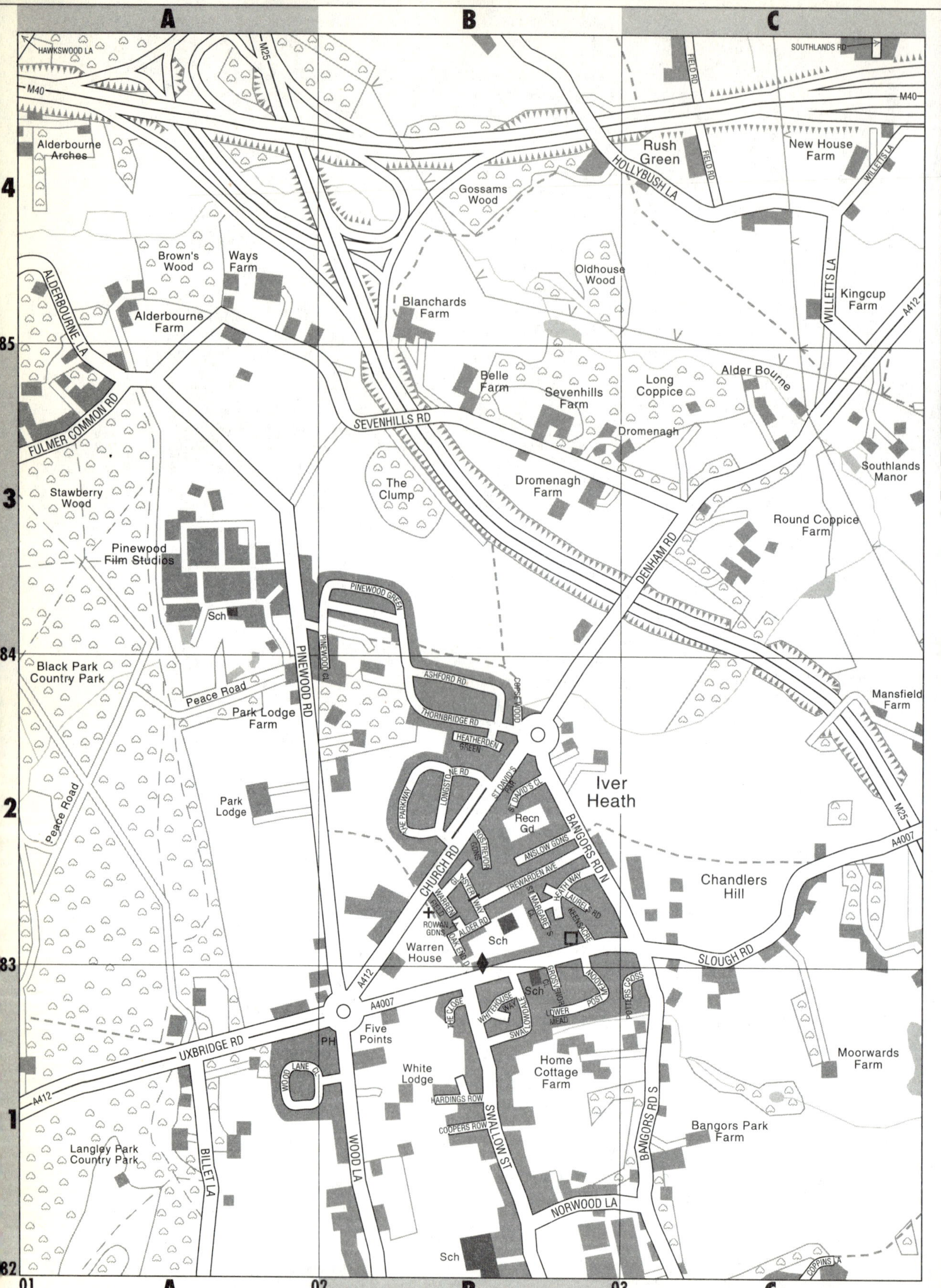
A
B
C
HAWKSWOOD LA
M25
M40
FIELD RD
SOUTHLANDS RD
Alderbourne Arches
Rush Green
New House Farm
HOLLYBUSH LA
WILLETTS LA
Gossams Wood
Brown's Wood
Ways Farm
Oldhouse Wood
ALDERBOURNE LA
Alderbourne Farm
Blanchards Farm
Kingcup Farm
A412
Belle Farm
Sevenhills Farm
Long Coppice
Alder Bourne
FULMER COMMON RD
SEVENHILLS RD
Dromenagh
Southlands Manor
Stawberry Wood
The Clump
Dromenagh Farm
Round Coppice Farm
DENHAM RD
Pinewood Film Studios
PINEWOOD GREEN
Sch
PINEWOOD CL
PINEWOOD RD
Black Park Country Park
ASHFORD RD
COPSEWOOD
Mansfield Farm
Peace Road
Park Lodge Farm
THORNBRIDGE RD
HEATHERDEN GREEN
LONGSTONE RD
ST DAVID'S PAR
ST DAVID'S CL
Iver Heath
Park Lodge
THE PARKWAY
Recn Gd
BANGORS RD N
A4007
ANSLOW GDNS
ROSTREVOR GDNS
CHURCH RD
TREWARDEN AVE
HEATH WAY
GLADSTONE WAY
WARREN FIELD
ST MARGARET'S CL
LAURELS RD
KEENSACRE
Chandlers Hill
ROWAN GDNS
ALDER RD
OAK END DR
Warren House
SLOUGH RD
POST MEADOW
POTTERS CROSS
GROSVENOR CL
Sch
LOWER MEAD
WHITEHOUSE WAY
SWALLOWDALE
THE CLOSE
Five Points
UXBRIDGE RD
PH
WOOD LANE CL
White Lodge
Home Cottage Farm
Moorwards Farm
A412
HARDINGS ROW
COOPERS ROW
SWALLOW ST
BANGORS RD S
Bangors Park Farm
Langley Park Country Park
BILLET LA
WOOD LA
NORWOOD LA
Sch
COPPINS LA
4
85
3
84
2
83
1
82
01
02
03

190

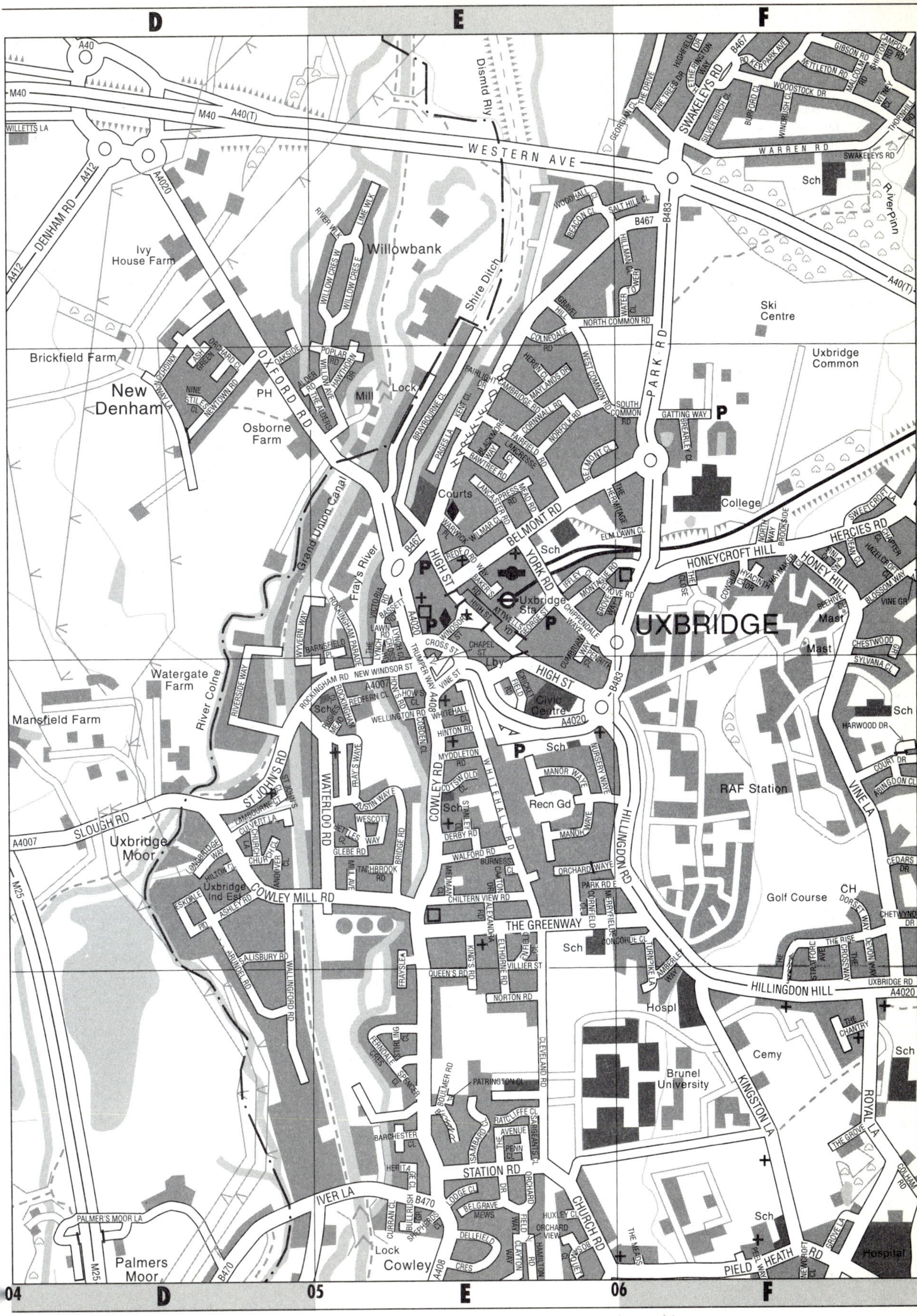
D
E
F
4
85
3
84
2
83
1
82
04
05
06
A40
M40
A40(T)
M40
WILLETTS LA
WESTERN AVE
A412
DENHAM RD
A4020
Ivy
House Farm
Brickfield Farm
New
Denham
PH
Osborne
Farm
OXFORD RD
Willowbank
Dismtd Rly
Shire Ditch
Mill
Lock
Courts
Grand Union Canal
Fray's River
River Colne
Watergate
Farm
Mansfield Farm
Uxbridge
Moor
Uxbridge
Ind Est
SLOUGH RD
A4007
M25
ST JOHN'S RD
WATERLOO RD
COWLEY MILL RD
COWLEY RD
WHITEHALL RD
HIGH ST
Uxbridge
Sta
UXBRIDGE
Civic
Centre
Lby
Sch
Recn Gd
THE GREENWAY
HILLINGDON RD
HILLINGDON HILL
A4020
Hospl
Brunel
University
Cemy
KINGSTON LA
ROYAL LA
Hospital
RAF Station
Golf Course
Mast
VINE LA
HONEYCROFT HILL
HONEY HILL
HERCIES RD
College
PARK RD
B483
B467
Ski
Centre
Uxbridge
Common
River Pinn
SWAKELEYS RD
WARREN RD
BELMONT RD
YORK RD
NORTH COMMON RD
STATION RD
IVER LA
B470
CHURCH RD
PIELD HEATH RD
Lock
Cowley
Palmers
Moor
PALMER'S MOOR LA
A408

208

195

A
B
C
4
81
3
80
2
79
1
78
86
87
88
MAIDENHEAD
Industrial Estates
Sch
Cemy
Hospl
Coll
Highway
Punt Hill
Tittle Row
Schs
Boyn Hill
Maidenhead Station
CH
Golf Course
Business Estate
Little Lowbrook Farm
Cox Green
Lillibrooke Manor
Ockwells Manor Farm
Ockwells Manor
Woodlands Business Park
The Cut
Heywood Farm
Cresswells Farm
The Bourne
PINKNEYS RD
ST MARK'S CRES
ST MARK'S RD
COURTHOUSE RD
ALL SAINTS AVE
BELMONT RD
COLLEGE RD
GRINGER HILL
NORFOLK RD
CASTLE HILL
BATH RD
KING'S GR
GRENFELL RD
BOYN HILL RD
BOYN VALLEY RD
WOOTTON WAY
LARCHFIELD RD
SHOPPENHANGER'S RD
NORREYS DR
HARVEST HILL RD
WESSEX WAY
HIGHFIELD LA
COX GREEN LA
COX GREEN RD
WOODLANDS PARK RD
OCKWELLS RD
BRAYWICK RD
A4
A308
A404(M)
A308(M)
M4
HIGHWAY AVE
MARLBOROUGH RD
NAPIER RD
FARM RD
ALWYN RD
LINCOLN RD
HALIFAX RD
SUNDERLAND RD
BLENHEIM RD
WESTFIELD RD
PENYSTON RD
RISELEY RD
VANWALL RD
NORDEN RD
LUDLOW RD
RIXMAN CL
MANOR LA
SPRING HILL
KIMBER'S LA
SHOPPENHANGER'S RD
TREESMILL DR
LAMBOURNE DR
RUSSET RD
THURLBY WAY
WOODLANDS PARK AVE
SNOWBALL HILL
HEYWOOD AVE
LOWBROOK DR
THRIFT LA

196
204

D
E
F
4
3
2
1
81
80
79
78
90
91
Dunloe Lodge
Berry Hill
Berry Hill Farm
Sports Ground
Maidenhead Bridge
The Dumb Bell (PH)
Railway Cottages
Taplow Station
F Sta Court
Liby
Sch
Sewage Works
Amerden Ponds
Fishery
Sports Centre
Green Lane
Barge Farm
River Thames
Weir
Bray Lock
Amerden House
New Thames Bridge
Bray Wick
Cemy
Bray
Hospl
The Cut
Dorney Reach
Weir Bank Stud Farm
Marina
Moor Farm
The Bourne
The Philberds
RAY MILL RD W
FLORENCE AVE
FULLBROOK CL
1 HAZELL CL
2 EVENLODE
3 WINDRUSH WAY
4 TATCHBROOK CL
CHERWELL CL
KENNET RD
HOLMAN LEAZE
BLACKAMORE LA
ST-CLOUD WAY
ST MARY'S CL
HIGH ST
BRIDGE ST
BRIDGE AVE
MOORBRIDGE RD
CROWN LA
A4
ST IVES RD
YORK RD
FORLEASE RD
FORLEASE CL
FOTHERBY CT
CEDARS RD
LANGDALE CL
WALDECK RD
REFORM RD
MOORFIELD TERR
SALTERS RD
SALTERS CL
RAY ST
BRIDGE RD
RAY DR
RAY PARK RD
RAY PARK AVE
RAY PARK LA
RAY LODGE MEWS
JUNIPER DR
LASSELL GDNS
SIMPSON CL
AUCKLAND CL
SOMERFORD CL
BRAMPTON CT
GABLES CL
RAY LEA RD
RAY LEA CL
ANDREW CL
ANDREW RD
PRINCE ANDREW RD
DEERSWOOD
THE RAY
WOODHURST RD
DEREK RD
GROSVENOR DR
LOCKBRIDGE CT
RAY MEAD RD
A4094
MILL LA
BERRY HILL
B3028
OLDFIELD RD
THE FARTHINGALES
MEDALLION PL
HORSEGUARDS DR
OLDACRES
GUARDS CLUB RD
ELLINGTON GDNS
ELLINGTON RD
ELLINGTON CT
RIVER RD
APPROACH RD
BATH RD
AMERDEN LA
AMERDEN CL
STATION RD
BOUNDARY RD
HILLMEAD CT
INSTITUTE RD
HITCHAM RD
CHAUNTRY CL
CHAUNTRY RD
DEPOT RD
LISSET RD
HOWARTH RD
THE QUADRANT
STAFFERTON WAY
GREENFIELDS
GREEN LA
CHALGROVE CL
CANNOCK CL
NEWBURY DR
CHEVIOT CL
CHILTERN RD
CLEVELAND
COTSWOLD CL
THE RUSHES
AVENUE RD
GLEBE RD
FISHERY RD
BRAY RD
CHURCH RD
MARSH LA
YE MEADS
OLD MARSH LA
GLEBE CL
M4
A308
CLIFTON CL
BRAYWICK RD
WALKER RD
OLD FORGE CL
HARVEST HILL RD
ORCHARD CL
HIBBERT RD
THE CAUSEWAY
VICARAGE WLK
VICARAGE DR
CHURCH PATH
CHURCH LA
HIGH ST
FERRY RD
BRAYBANK
BEAUFORT PL
RIVER GDNS
OLD MILL LA
BRAYFIELD RD
THE TERRACE
MEADOW WAY
OAK STUBBS LA
HARCOURT CL
HARCOURT RD
DORNEY REACH RD
A308(M)
A330
THE BRAMBLES
CANON HILL DR
CANON HILL WAY
CANNON HILL CL
HASTINGS CL
WILLOW DR
PRIORS CL
PRIORS WAY
UPPER BRAY RD
B3028
MONKEY ISLAND LA
ASCOT RD
BRAY CT
COURT CL
WINDSOR RD
ESKDALE GDNS
AYSGARTH PARK
BYLAND DR
HOLYPORT RD
EARLSFIELD
ARKLEY CT
CRESSWELLS MEAD
MOOREND
SANDY MEAD
LONSDALE WAY
SPRINGFIELD PARK
TITHE CL
STOMPITS RD
HENDONS WAY
FARM CL
BUCKLEBURY CL
TITHE BARN DR
BROADWATER PARK
WESTBROOK
HEARNE DR

204

203
197

203
209

198
206

D E F

D E F

210
206

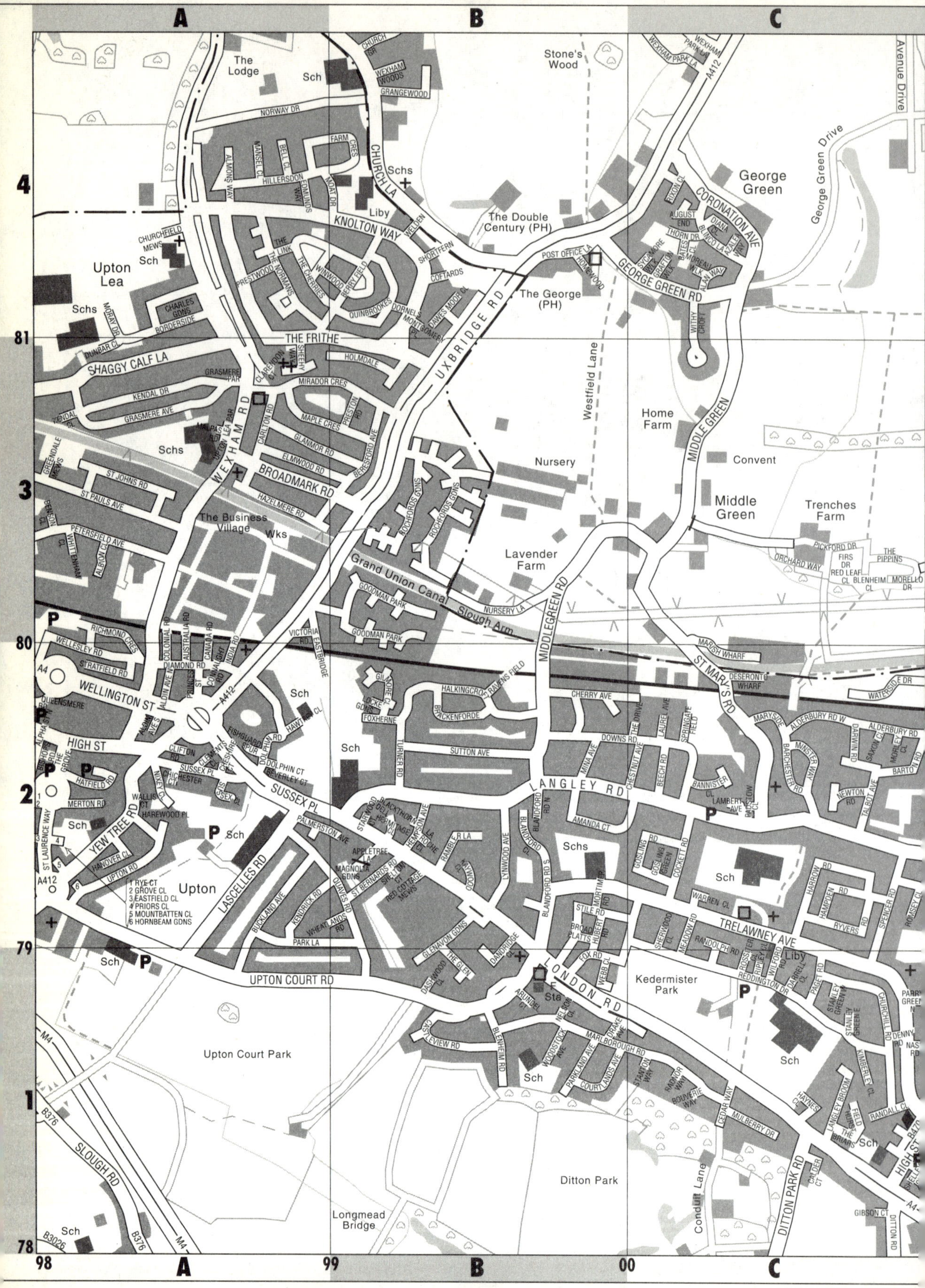
A
B
C
4
3
2
1
81
80
79
78
98
99
00
The Lodge
Sch
Stone's Wood
Avenue Drive
George Green Drive
George Green
Upton Lea
Schs
Liby
The Double Century (PH)
The George (PH)
CHURCHFIELD MEWS
NORWAY DR
GRANGEWOOD
CHURCH LA
KNOLTON WAY
WEXHAM PARK LA
A412
CORONATION AVE
GEORGE GREEN RD
POST OFFICE LA
HOMEWOOD
WITHY CROFT
UXBRIDGE RD
THE FRITHE
SHAGGY CALF LA
KENDAL DR
GRASMERE AVE
HOLMDALE
MIRADOR CRES
MAPLE CRES
GLANMOR RD
ELMWOOD RD
BROADMARK RD
HAZELMERE RD
BERESFORD AVE
PRESTON RD
CARLTON RD
WEXHAM RD
ST JOHNS RD
ST PAULS AVE
PETERSFIELD AVE
The Business Village
Wks
Westfield Lane
Home Farm
Nursery
Convent
Middle Green
MIDDLE GREEN
Trenches Farm
Lavender Farm
ROCHFORDS GDNS
Grand Union Canal
Slough Arm
GOODMAN PARK
NURSERY LA
MIDDLEGREEN RD
ORCHARD WAY
PICKFORD DR
THE PIPPINS
BLENHEIM CL
MORELLO DR
MARISH WHARF
DESERONTO WHARF
ST MARY'S RD
WATERSIDE DR
RICHMOND CRES
WELLESLEY RD
STRATFIELD RD
A4
WELLINGTON ST
QUEENSMERE
HIGH ST
COLONIAL RD
AUSTRALIA RD
CANADA RD
INDIA RD
DIAMOND RD
VICTORIA RD
EASTBRIDGE
RAVENS FIELD
HALKINGCROFT
BRACKENFORDE
CHERRY AVE
SUTTON AVE
TURNER RD
FOXHERNE
DOWNS RD
LANGLEY RD
MARYSIDE
ALDERBURY RD W
ALDERBURY RD
DARWIN RD
BARCHESTER RD
NEWTON RD
TALBOT AVE
BARTON RD
FISHGUARD SPUR
DOLPHIN RD
DOLPHIN CT
BEVERLEY CT
SUSSEX PL
HATFIELD RD
MERTON RD
YEW TREE RD
ST LAURENCE WAY
HANOVER CL
UPTON RD
Upton
1 RYE CT
2 GROVE CL
3 EASTFIELD CL
4 PRIORS CL
5 MOUNTBATTEN CL
6 HORNBEAM GDNS
LASCELLES RD
PALMERSTON AVE
BUCKLAND AVE
KENDRICK RD
WHEATLANDS RD
PARK LA
UPTON COURT RD
Schs
AMANDA CT
GOSLING RD
COCKETT RD
Sch
WARREN CL
TRELAWNEY AVE
HARROW RD
HAMPDEN RD
RYVERS RD
SPENCER RD
Kedermister Park
RANDOLPH RD
REDDINGTON DR
LONDON RD
Sta
GLENAVON GDNS
DANDRIDGE CL
BLANDFORD RD S
LYNWOOD AVE
Upton Court Park
CASTLEVIEW RD
BLENHEIM RD
WOODSTOCK AVE
PARKLAND AVE
COURTLANDS AVE
MARLBOROUGH RD
BOUVERIE WAY
CEDAR WAY
MULBERRY DR
Ditton Park
Conduit Lane
DITTON PARK RD
Longmead Bridge
SLOUGH RD
B376
B3026
M4
KIMBERLEY CL
CHURCHILL RD
LANGLEY BROOM
RANDALL CL
GIBSON CT
DITTON RD
A4

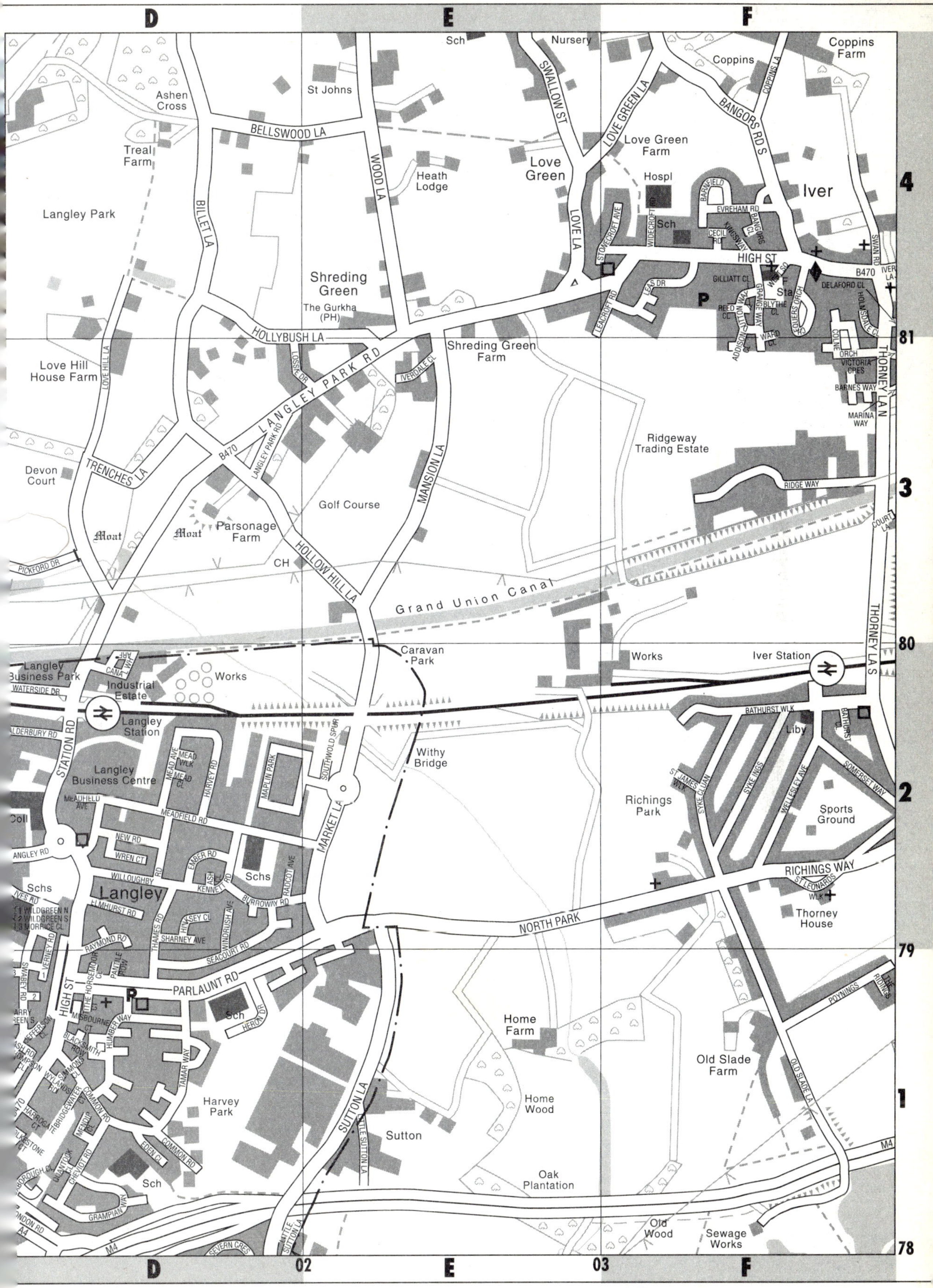
D
E
F
Sch
Nursery
Coppins Farm
Coppins
St Johns
Ashen Cross
Treal Farm
BELLSWOOD LA
SWALLOW ST
LOVE GREEN LA
BANGORS RD S
COPPINS LA
Love Green Farm
Love Green
Hospl
Heath Lodge
WOOD LA
Iver
Langley Park
BILLET LA
LOVE LA
STONECROFT AVE
WIDECROFT RD
EVREHAM RD
BANGORS CL
KINGSWAY
CECIL RD
SWAN RD
HIGH ST
B470
IVER LA
Shreding Green
The Gurkha (PH)
LEAS DR
GILLIATT CL
DELAFORD CL
HOLMSDALE CL
LEACROFT RD
GRANGE WAY
Sta
REED CL
BLYTHE CL
ADDISON CL
WARD CL
COLNE ORCH
VICTORIA CRES
BARNES WAY
MARINA WAY
THORNEY LA N
HOLLYBUSH LA
LANGLEY PARK RD
IVERDALE CL
Shreding Green Farm
Love Hill House Farm
LOVE HILL LA
Ridgeway Trading Estate
RIDGE WAY
Devon Court
TRENCHES LA
MANSION LA
Golf Course
Moat
Moat
Parsonage Farm
COURT LA
PICKFORD DR
CH
HOLLOW HILL LA
Grand Union Canal
THORNEY LA S
Caravan Park
Langley Business Park
Works
Works
Iver Station
WATERSIDE DR
Industrial Estate
Langley Station
BATHURST WLK
Liby
ALDERBURY RD
STATION RD
MEAD AVE
MEAD WLK
MEAD CL
HARVEY RD
MAPLIN PARK
SOUTHWOLD SPUR
Withy Bridge
Langley Business Centre
ST JAMES WLK
SYKE CLUAN
SYKE INGS
WELLESLEY AVE
SOMERSET WAY
MEADFIELD AVE
MEADFIELD RD
Richings Park
Sports Ground
Coll
NEW RD
WREN CT
MARKET LA
LANGLEY RD
EMBER RD
Schs
Schs
WILLOUGHBY RD
ASH
KENNET RD
RADCOT AVE
BURROWAY RD
RICHINGS WAY
ST LEONARDS WLK
Langley
ELMHURST RD
HAILSEY CL
Thorney House
NORTH PARK
RAYMOND RD
THAMES RD
SHARNEY AVE
WINDRUSH AVE
SEACOURT RD
PANTILE ROW
VERNEY RD
HIGH ST
PARLAUNT RD
POYNINGS
THE RIDINGS
MISBOURNE CT
HUMBER WAY
Sch
HERON DR
Home Farm
BLACKSMITH ROW
TAMAR WAY
Old Slade Farm
OLD SLADE LA
Harvey Park
Home Wood
COMMON RD
SUTTON LA
LITTLE SUTTON LA
Sutton
EDEN CL
M4
Oak Plantation
Sch
GRAMPIAN WAY
CHEVIOT RD
QUANTOCK CL
Old Wood
Sewage Works
M4
SEVERN CRES
LITTLE SUTTON LA
A4
4
81
3
80
2
79
1
78
02
03
D
E
F

207
201

207
213

204
210

D
E
F
Boveney Court Farm
Roasthill La
BOVENEY RD
LOCK PATH
Boveney
Boveney Court
Boveney Lock
Weir
Race Course
Yacht Basin
Oakley Court
Hotel
DOWN PL
Down Place Farm
A308
WINDSOR RD
River Thames
Caravan Site
Mill Stream
Works
PH
Windsor Marina
Caravan Park
THE HATCH
Oak View Farm
MAIDENHEAD RD
A308
B3025
77
Cemy
Community Centre
VALE RD
Willows Path
RUDDLESWAY
B3383
Bishops Farmhouse
BISHOPS FARM CL
B3024
Kimbers Lane Farm
Oakley Place Farm
PH
Fair Acres Farm
DEDWORTH RD
Dedworth
Schs
Sch
SMITH'S LA
GALLYS RD
3
4
OAKLEY GREEN RD
FAIRACRES INDUSTRIAL ESTATE
1 CHARLTON WAY
2 CHARLTON SQ
3 FURNESS SQ
4 FURNESS WAY
5 LIDDELL SQ
TINKERS LA
TARBAY LA
Oakley Green
Ye Old Red Lion (PH)
Forest Farm
B3024
76
Sch
Gale House Farm
Tarbay Farm
WOLF LA
CLEWER HILL RD
Sch
WASHINGTON DR
ILLINGWORTH
ST LEONARDS HILL
2
Darkhole Bridge
Clewer Green
B3022
Holliday's Plain
St Leonard's
St Leonard's Farm
75
WINKFIELD RD
1
Darkhole Ride
Queen Adelaide's Ride
ST LEONARD'S RD
High Standinghill Woods
Forbe's Ride
Forbe's Fields
DRIFT RD
WINKFIELD LA
Orchard Lea
Forest Park
Flemish Farm
B3022
74
92
93
94
D
E
F

210

A
B
C
ETON
College
Weir
Golf Course
River Thames
The Home Park
Recn Gd
KING EDWARD VII AVE
WINDSOR RD
B470
Race Course
SOUTH MEADOW LA
HIGH ST
Sch
Liby
MEADOW LA
The Brocas
Windsor and Eton Riverside Station
Prince Albert's Walk
Slopes Lodge
Clewer Village
Swimming Baths
STOVELL RD
River Thames
PROMENADE
BARRY AVE
DATCHET RD
North Terrace
Lime Avenue
Dutch Elm Avenue
A308
MAIDENHEAD RD
The Goswells
Windsor Castle
East Terrace
Chalk Hill
Vansittart Estate
Chapel Hill
South Terrace
Windsor and Eton Central Station
Castle Hill
Queen Victoria's Walk
Adelaide Road
MAIDENHEAD RD
ARTHUR RD
Amb Sta
A332
Schs
PARSONAGE LA
VANSITTART RD
PEASCOD ST
1 QUEEN CHARLOTTE ST
2 MARKET ST
3 CHURCH LA
4 CHURCH ST
Mus
WINDSOR
1 ATHLONE SQ
2 CAMBRIDGE HOUSE
3 MOUNTBATTEN SQ
4 CHRISTIAN SQ
5 BOWES-LYON CL
6 CHARLES HOUSE
Recn Gd
CLARENCE RD
VICTORIA ST
Golf Course
B3024
1 PENCOED PL
2 SUN PAS
3 HIBBERT'S ALLEY
SHEET ST
Queen Elizabeth's Walk
Court
GOSLAR WAY
ALMA RD
Coll
Liby
F Sta
The Home Park
Coronation Avenue
Frogmore Drive
Clewer New Town
FRANCES RD
Frogmore
Frogmore House
Royal Mausoleum
Mulberry Avenue
IMPERIAL RD
Sch
Hospl
B470
OSBORNE RD
Sch
A308
Cvt
Hospl
BOLTON AVE
ST LEONARD'S RD
B3022
KING'S RD
BOLTON RD
WINKFIELD RD
Cemy
Spital
The Long Walk
Shaw Farm
Shaw Farm
ALBERT RD
Hog Common
Moat
QUEEN ANNE'S RD
QUEEN'S GATE
A308
Queen Anne's Gate
Battle Bourne
HOLLY DR
New Cover
Review Ground
Clayhall Farm
CLAY HALL LA
Moat
Prince Consort's Drive
SHEET STREET RD
Tileplace Farm
Queen Anne's Ride
Cavalry Exercise Ground
The Gallop
Peter's Hill
Sch
Newmeadow Plantation
CRIMP HILL
Star Clump
A332
4
77
3
76
2
75
1
74
95
96
97

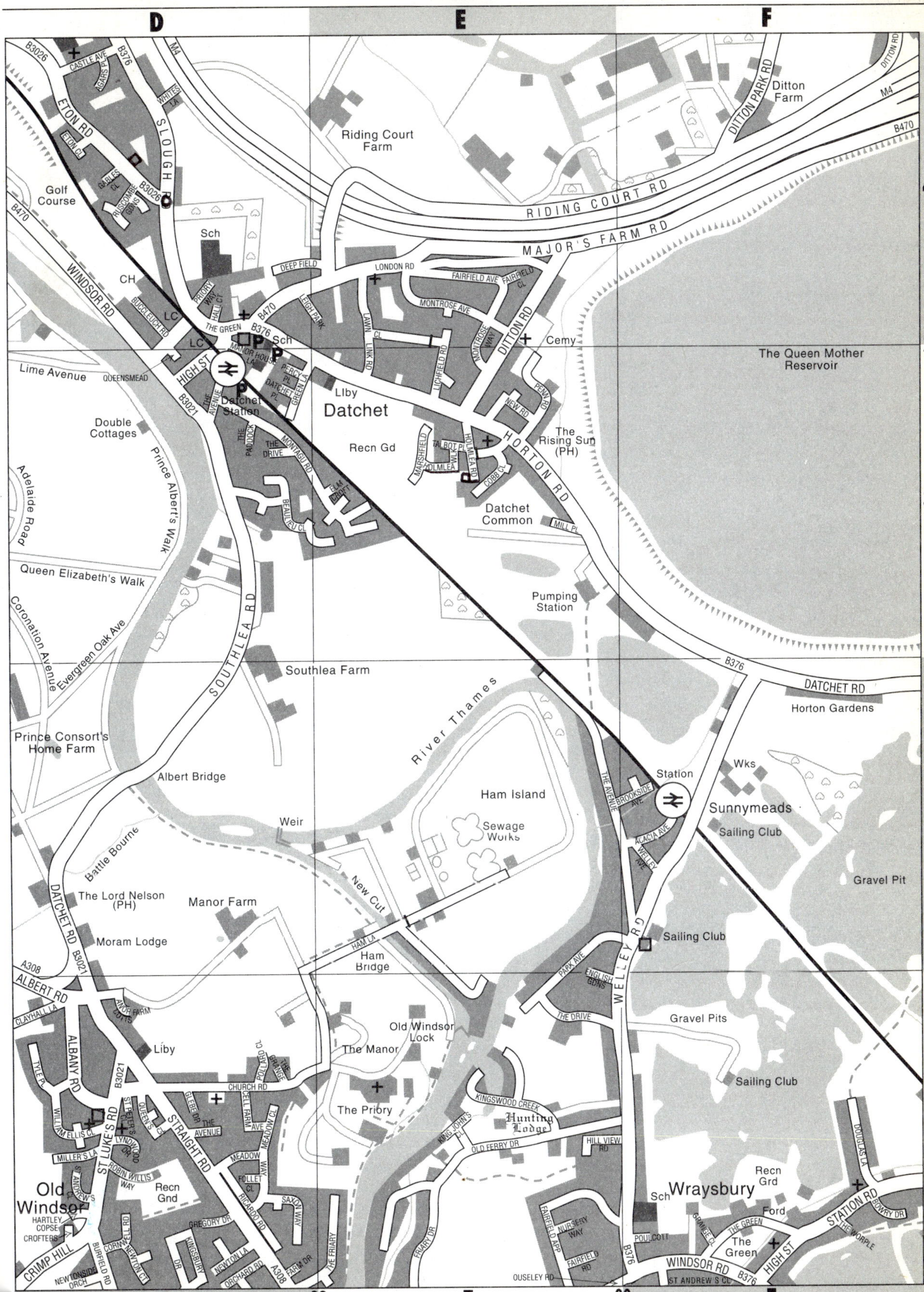
D
E
F
4
77
3
76
2
75
1
74
98
99
00
Riding Court Farm
Ditton Farm
DITTON PARK RD
M4
B470
RIDING COURT RD
MAJOR'S FARM RD
Golf Course
Sch
CH
LC
ETON RD
ETON CL
SLOUGH RD
B3026
B376
CASTLE AVE
AGARS PL
WHITES LA
GABLES CL
RUSCOMBE GDNS
WINDSOR RD
BUCCLEUCH RD
PRIORY WAY
HALL CT
THE GREEN
DEEP FIELD
LONDON RD
FAIRFIELD AVE
FAIRFIELD CL
MONTROSE AVE
MONTROSE WAY
LEIGH PARK
LAWN CL
LINK RD
LICHFIELD RD
DITTON RD
Cemy
The Queen Mother Reservoir
Lime Avenue
QUEENSMEAD
HIGH ST
MANOR HOUSE LA
PERCY PL
DATCHET PL
GREEN LA
Lliby
Datchet
Datchet Station
THE AVENUE
B3021
PENN RD
NEW RD
The Rising Sun (PH)
HORTON RD
Double Cottages
Prince Albert's Walk
Adelaide Road
THE PADDOCK
THE DRIVE
MONTAGU RD
ELM CROFT
BEAULIEU CL
Recn Gd
MARSHFIELD
TALBOT PL
HOLMLEA RD
HOLMLEA WK
COBB CL
Datchet Common
MILL PL
Queen Elizabeth's Walk
Coronation Avenue
Evergreen Oak Ave
SOUTHLEA RD
Pumping Station
Southlea Farm
B376
DATCHET RD
Horton Gardens
Prince Consort's Home Farm
River Thames
Albert Bridge
Ham Island
Station
THE AVENUE
BROOKSIDE AVE
Wks
Sunnymeads
Sailing Club
Sewage Works
Weir
Battle Bourne
ACACIA AVE
WELLEY AVE
Gravel Pit
The Lord Nelson (PH)
Manor Farm
New Cut
DATCHET RD
Moram Lodge
HAM LA
Ham Bridge
WELLEY RD
Sailing Club
PARK AVE
ENGLISH GDNS
A308
ALBERT RD
CLAYHALL LA
AMOR FARM
THE DRIVE
Gravel Pits
ALBANY RD
Liby
Old Windsor Lock
The Manor
TYLE PL
POLLARD CL
THE GRANGE
CHURCH RD
Sailing Club
WILLIAM ELLIS CL
ST LUKE'S RD
ST PETER'S CL
QUEEN'S CL
GLEBE DR
THE AVENUE
CELL FARM AVE
MEADOW CL
STRAIGHT RD
The Priory
KINGSWOOD CREEK
Hunting Lodge
KING JOHN'S CL
OLD FERRY DR
HILL VIEW RD
DOUGLAS LA
MILLER'S LA
LYNWOOD DR
ROBIN WILLIS WAY
MEADOW WAY
FOLLET CL
Recn Gnd
ST ANDREW'S CL
Old Windsor
HARTLEY COPSE
CROFTERS
CRIMP HILL
NEWTONSIDE ORCH
BURFIELD RD
CORNWELL RD
NEWTON CT
RICARDO RD
SAXON WAY
GREGORY DR
KINGSBURY DR
NEWTON LA
ORCHARD RD
A308
FARM DR
THE FRIARY
FRIARY DR
FAIRFIELD APP
NURSERY WAY
FAIRFIELD RD
OUSELEY RD
Recn Grd
Sch
Wraysbury
Ford
STATION RD
BOWRY DR
THE WORPLE
GRANGE CL
THE GREEN
The Green
HIGH ST
POULCOTT
B376
WINDSOR RD
ST ANDREW'S CL

211
207

A
B
C
4
77
3
76
2
75
1
74
01
02
03
M4
A4(T)
B470
MAJOR'S FARM RD
WELLAND CL
TORRIDGE RD
TWEED RD
TRENT RD
CHERWELL CL
SEVERN CRES
SUTTON LA
SUTTON PL
LONDON RD
HILLRISE
LABURNUM GR
LITTLE SUTTON LA
DISRAELI CT
Brands Hill
LABURNUM CRES
BRANDS RD
PEPYS CL
SPRINGFIELD RD
COLNBROOK BY-PASS
The Crown (PH)
Brook Farm
CROWN MEADOW
Mildridge Farm
ST THOMAS WALK
VICARAGE WAY
HIGH ST
MILL ST
WILLOW CL
MORELAND AVE
BROOKSIDE
DRIFT WAY
RAYNERS CL
POPES CL
BRIDGE ST
Sch
RUDSWORTH CL
Colnbrook
PARK ST
ALBANY PARK
AINTREE CL
TALL TREES
COTTESBROOKE CL
HEATHACRE
LAUREL CL
FAWSLEY CL
MYRTLE CL
COLERIDGE CRES
DAWLEY RIDE
WINCHESTER CL
RAYMOND CL
THE HAWTHORNS
RODNEY WAY
DAVENTRY CL
GALLEYMEAD RD
The Greyhound (PH)
A4(T)
LAKESIDE RD
Orlitts Lake
Coln Trading Estate
Poyle
BATH RD
LC
POPLAR CL
SHERBORNE CL
INGLESIDE
MEADOWBROOK CL
ELBOW MEADOW
MATHISEN WAY
RIVERSIDE PK
Poyle Lodge
Poyle Channel
COLNDALE RD
ARKWRIGHT RD
WILLOW RD
DAVID RD
POYLE RD
Britannia Industrial Estate
Mckay Trading Estate
PRESCOTT RD
BLACKTHORNE RD
AUGUSTINE CL
Trident Industrial Estate
Viscount Trading Estate
Poyle 14 Trading Estate
NEWLANDS DR
CALDER WAY
Skyway Trading Estate
HORTON RD
Lintell's Bridge
M25
HORTON RD
Horton Lodge
Rectory
PICKINS PIECE
Ashgood Farm
Berkyn Manor Farm
Colne Brook
DATCHET RD
DAWN REDWOOD CL
MILTON CL
PARK LA
FOUNDRY LA
Weir
Horton
BELLS LA
MILL LA
COLNE BK
STANWELL RD
A3113
AIRPORT WAY
Wraysbury River
HORTON RD
LEYLANDS LA
Manor Farm
Wks
Wraysbury Reservoir
COPPERMILL RD
COLNE REACH
MEADOW VIEW
BENEN-STOCK RD
Gravel Pit
Sailing Club
FARM WAY
HITHERMOOR RD
RUSSET CL
Nurseries
OLD STATION LA
WHITEHALL LA
STATION RD
TITHE LA
Wraysbury Station
Lower Mill Farm
King George VI Reservoir
M25

211

208

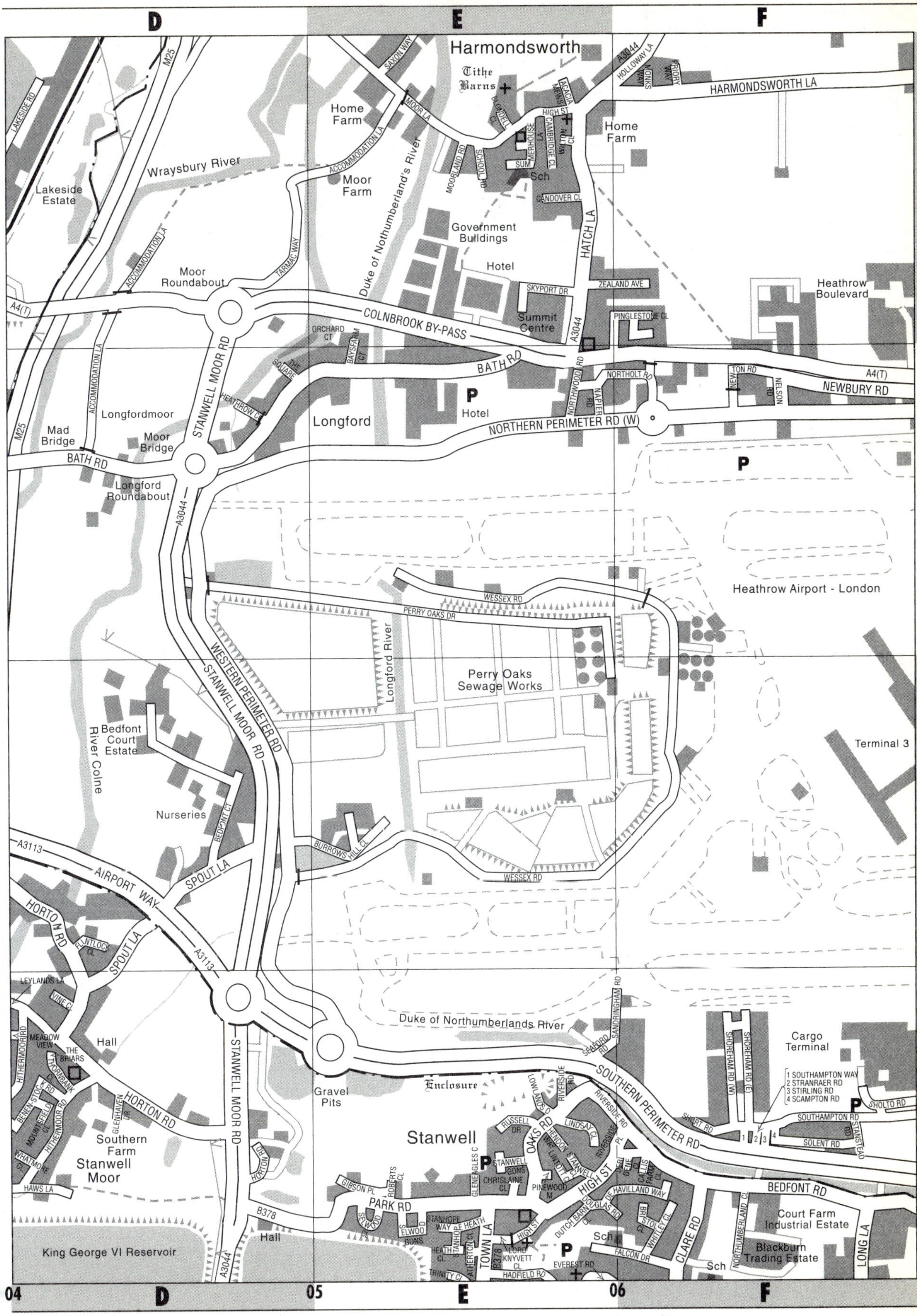
D
E
F
Harmondsworth
Tithe Barns
HARMONDSWORTH LA
SAXON WAY
MOOR LA
Home Farm
Moor Farm
ACCOMMODATION LA
Duke of Northumberland's River
Wraysbury River
Lakeside Estate
LAKESIDE RD
M25
HOLLOWAY LA
MONKS WAY
PRIORY WAY
A3044
ACACIA
NEWSTEAD
HIGH ST
BLONDELL CL
MOORLAND RD
SCHOOL RD
SUMMERHOUSE LA
CAMBRIDGE CL
WILLIAM CL
Sch
CANDOVER CL
HATCH LA
Government Buildings
Hotel
TARMAC WAY
Moor Roundabout
A4(T)
SKYPORT DR
ZEALAND AVE
Summit Centre
PINGLESTONE CL
Heathrow Boulevard
COLNBROOK BY-PASS
ORCHARD CT
BAYSFARM CT
THE SQUARE
BATH RD
STANWELL MOOR RD
HEATHROW CL
NORTHWOOD RD
NAPIER RD
NORTHOLT RD
NEWTON RD
NELSON RD
NEWBURY RD
Longfordmoor
Mad Bridge
Moor Bridge
Longford
P
NORTHERN PERIMETER RD (W)
Longford Roundabout
4
77
3
Heathrow Airport - London
WESSEX RD
PERRY OAKS DR
Longford River
Perry Oaks Sewage Works
76
WESTERN PERIMETER RD
Bedfont Court Estate
River Colne
Terminal 3
Nurseries
BEDFONT CT
BURROWS HILL CL
2
A3113
AIRPORT WAY
SPOUT LA
HORTON RD
FLINTLOCK CL
LEYLANDS LA
VINE CL
75
Hall
HITHERMOOR RD
MEADOW VIEW
THE BRIARS
TOORBANK
STOCKS RD
BENEN-STOCK RD
MOUNTSFIELD CL
GLENHAVEN DR
Southern Farm
Stanwell Moor
WHATMORE CL
HAWS LA
Duke of Northumberlands River
SANDRINGHAM RD
SEAFORD RD
Gravel Pits
Enclosure
LOWLANDS RD
RIVERSIDE RD
SOUTHERN PERIMETER RD
SHOREHAM RD (W)
SHOREHAM RD (E)
Cargo Terminal
1 SOUTHAMPTON WAY
2 STRANRAER RD
3 STIRLING RD
4 SCAMPTON RD
SHOLTO RD
SOUTHAMPTON RD
SOLENT RD
STANSTEAD RD
SHORT RD
1
Stanwell
RUSSELL DR
OAKS RD
LINDSAY CL
HENDON WAY
LIMCOTT CL
STANWELL CL
STANWELL GDNS
CHRISLAINE CL
GLENEAGLES C
PINEWOOD M
HIGH ST
DEER CL
GAINSBOROUGH
CALLIS FARM CL
HAVILLAND WAY
DOUGLAS RD
DUTCH BARN CL
BRISTOL CL
WHITLEY CL
CLARE RD
BEDFONT RD
NORTHUMBERLAND CL
Court Farm Industrial Estate
Blackburn Trading Estate
LONG LA
FALCON DR
GIBSON PL
ROBERTS CL
PARK RD
SEDWOOD PL
ELWOOD GDNS
STANHOPE WAY
HEATH CL
TANHOPE HEATH
ATHERTON CL
TRINITY CL
TOWN LA
LORD KNYVETT CL
HADFIELD RD
EVEREST RD
B378
HORTON RD
King George VI Reservoir
A3044
74
04
05
06

EXPLANATION OF THE STREET INDEX REFERENCE SYSTEM

Street names are listed alphabetically and show the locality, the page number and a reference to the square in which the name falls on the map page.

Example:	Church La. Lud...96 B4
Church La	This is the full street name, which may have been abbreviated on the map.
Lud	This is the abbreviation for the town, village or locality in which the street falls.
96	This is the page number of the map on which the street name appears.
B4	The letter and figure indicate the square on the map in which the centre of the street falls. The square can be found at the junction of the vertical column carrying the appropriate letter and the horizontal row carrying the appropriate figure.

ABBREVIATIONS USED IN THE INDEX

Road Names

Approach	App	Lane	La
Avenue	Ave	North	N
Boulevard	Bvd	Orchard	Orch
Broadway	Bwy	Parade	Par
By-Pass	By-Ps	Passage	Pas
Causeway	Cswy	Place	Pl
Common	Comm	Pleasant	Plea
Corner	Cnr	Precinct	Prec
Cottages	Cotts	Promenade	Prom
Court	Ct	Road	Rd
Crescent	Cres	South	S
Drive	Dri	Square	Sq
Drove	Dro	Street,Saint	St
East	E	Terrace	Terr
Gardens	Gdns	Walk	Wlk
Grove	Gr	West	W
Heights	Hts	Yard	Yd

Key to abbreviations of Town, Village and Rural locality names used in the index of street names.

Locality	Abbreviation	Page	Grid
Adstock	Adsk	53	F1
Akeley	Akel	42	A4
Aldbury	Ald	120	B3
Amersham	Ame	154	B1
Ashendon	Ash	97	F1
Ashley Green	Ash Gr	144	C4
Ashton	Ash	9	F4
Aspley Guise	Asp G	49	F2
Aspley Heath	Asp H	49	D1
Aston Abbots	A Abb	88	B3
Aston Clinton	Ast C	117	E3
Aston Rowant	Ast R	147	D2
Astwood	Ast	16	A2
Aylesbury	Ayl	116	B4
Beachampton	Beac	44	A3
Beacon's Bottom	B Bot	159	E2
Beaconsfield	Beac	175	E1
Beckley	Beck	108	A1
Berkhamsted	Berk	135	E3
Bierton	Bier	102	B2
Billington	Bill	91	E4
Bisham	Bish	194	C4
Blackthorn	Bktn	81	D3
Bledlow	Bled	138	A1
Bledlow Ridge	Bled R	159	F4
Botley	Bot	145	A1
Bourne End	Bou E	185	D1
Bovingdon	Bov	146	A2
Bow Brickhill	B Bkhl	48	B1
Bozeat	Boz	2	C4
Brackley	Brac	38	A4
Brill	Bri	69	A1
Buckingham	Buck	52	A4
Buckland Common	Buc Co	133	D2
Burnham	Burn	197	E2
Carlton	Carl	3	F2
Castlethorpe	Cast	19	F3
Chackmore	Chac	1	D2
Chalfont St Giles	C St G	177	E4
Chalfont St Peter	C St P	178	A2
Chartridge	Char	143	E2
Chearsley	Chea	112	A1
Cheddington	Ched	105	D4
Chenies	Chen	156	A1
Chesham	Ches	154	B4
Chicheley	Chic	23	E4
Chilton	Chil	111	D2
Chinnor	Chin	147	E3
Chipperfield	Chipf	156	C4
Cholesbury	Chol	133	E2
Chorleywood	Chor	167	B3
Clifton Reynes	C Rey	7	E2
Cold Brayfield	C Bray	8	A3
Coleshill	Cole	164	C2
Cookham	Cook	196	A4
Cosgrove	Cos	19	E1
Cranfield	Cran	25	E1
Cublington	Cub	78	A1
Cuddington	Cudd	113	D1
Dagnall	Dagn	107	E3
Datchet	Datch	211	E3
Deanshanger	Dean	31	E2
Denham	Den	190	A1
Denham Green	Den G	189	F3
Dinton	Dint	113	F1
Dorney	Dorn	204	B2
Dorton	Dor	96	C1
Drayton Beauchamp	Dra B	118	B3
Drayton Parslow	Dray P	68	B3
Dunstable	Dun	93	F4
East Claydon	E Clay	74	C4
Eaton Bray	Eat B	92	C3
Edgcott	Edgc	72	C1
Edlesborough	Edle	92	C2
Ellesborough	Elle	130	A1
Emberton	Emb	13	F4
Eton	Eton	210	B4
Farnham Common	Far C	198	B3
Fawley	Faw	180	B1
Feldon	Fel	146	C4
Finmere	Fin	50	B4
Flackwell Heath	Fla H	185	D4
Flaunden	Flau	156	A3
Frieth	Frie	170	C1
Fulmer	Fulm	199	E4
Gawcott	Gawt	51	F2
Gerrards Cross	Ger C	188	C3
Godington	Gdtn	61	F2
Grafton Regis	Graf R	9	E1
Granborough	Gran	75	F4
Great Brickhill	G Bhkl	58	E1
Great Haseley	G Has	136	A1
Great Horwood	G Hrwd	55	D1
Great Kimble	G Kim	139	F4
Great Kingshill	G Kin	162	C4
Great Missenden	G Mis	152	A3
Grendon Underwood	Gr Und	83	D4
Haddenham	Hadd	127	D3
Halton	Hal	117	E1
Hambledon	Hamb	181	E1
Hanslope	Hans	11	D2
Hardwick	Hdwk	87	D2
Harmondsworth	Harm	213	E4
Harrold	Harr	3	F4
Hartwell	Hart	10	B4
Hastoe	Has	132	C4
Haversham	Have	20	C1
Heath	Hth	60	A1
Hedgerley	Hedg	187	E2
Helmdon	Helm	26	A4
Henley-On-Thames	Hen-O-T	191	E1
High Wycombe	H Wyc	173	E3
Hoggeston	Hogg	77	D4
Holmer Green	Hol G	163	E3
Holton	Holt	122	B1
Horton	Hor	4	C4
Horton	Hort	212	A2
Horton-cum-Studley	Hor-c-S	108	A3
Hughenden Valley	Hgh V	162	A4
Hurley	Hurl	193	F2
Hyde Heath	H Hea	153	E3
Ibstone	Ibst	169	E4
Ickenham	Ick	190	C1
Ickford	Ick	124	A2
Iver	Iver	207	F4
Iver Heath	Iver H	200	B2
Ivinghoe	Ivin	105	F3
Lacey Green	Lac G	149	F3
Lane End	La En	171	F2
Lathbury	Lath	22	B4
Latimer	Lat	155	F2
Lavendon	Lave	7	F4
Leckhampstead	Leck	42	B4
Lee Common	Lee C	142	B3
Leighton Buzzard	L Buzz	80	C3
Lewknor	Lewk	157	D4
Lillingstone Lovell	Lill L	30	A3
Little Brickhill	L Bkhl	58	F3
Little Chalfont	L Chal	155	D1
Little Chalfont	L Chal	166	A4
Little Gaddesden	L Gad	121	E4
Little Horwood	L Hrwd	55	F1
Little Kingshall	L Kin	152	A2
Little Marlow	Lit M	184	B3
Long Crendon	L Cre	125	D3
Long Marston	Lon M	104	A2
Longwick	Lgwk	138	B4
Loudwater	Loud	174	B1
Ludgershall	Lud	96	B4
Maidenhead	Maid	202	C2
Maids Moreton	M Mor	41	F2
Maple Cross	Map Cr	178	B3
Marlow	Mar	183	D1
Marlow Bottom	Mar B	183	E3
Marsh Gibbon	M Gib	71	F2
Marsworth	Mars	105	D1
Medmenham	Medm	193	D3
Mentmore	Men	90	B2
Milton Keynes	M Keyn	46	B2
Milton Keynes Village	M K Vil	35	F2
Moulsoe	Moul	36	B4
Murcott	Mur	94	A2
Mursley	Mur	67	E3
Nash	Nash	44	B1
New Denham	N Den	201	D3
Newport Pagnell	N Pag	22	B3
Newton Blossomville	New B	8	A2
Newton Longville	Nwtn L	57	E2
Newton Purcell	Nwtn P	50	A1
North Crawley	N Craw	24	A3
North Marston	N Mar	76	A1
Northchurch	Nthch	134	C3
Oakley	Oak	109	E3
Oakley Green	Oak G	209	D3
Old Stratford	Old S	32	A4
Old Windsor	Old W	211	D1
Olney	Oln	6	C2
Oving	Oving	86	B4
Padbury	Pad	53	D1
Paulerspury	Paul	17	D4
Piddington (Bucks)	Pidd (B)	95	F4
Piddington (Northants)	Pid (N)	4	A4
Pitstone	Pit	105	E2
Potterspury	Pott	18	B1
Poundon	Pndn	71	F4
Preston Bissett	Pres B	62	A4
Prestwood	Pres	151	E3
Princes Risborough	P Ris	139	E2
Puttenham	Put	103	F1
Quainton	Qntn	85	D3
Ravenstone	Rav	5	E1
Remenham Hill	Rem H	192	B1
Ringshall	Rin	107	D1
Salford	Sal	37	E2
Sarratt	Sar	156	C2
Seer Green	Se Gr	176	B2
Shabbington	Shab	124	B2
Shalstone	Shal	39	F3
Shenley Brook End	She B E	46	A2
Shenley Church End	She C E	45	F3
Sherington	Sher	14	A1
Slapton	Slap	91	E3
Slough	Slough	205	F3
Soulbury	Soul	69	F2
South Harefield	S Har	190	B3
South Heath	S Hea	152	C4
St Leonard	St Le	132	C2
Stagsden	Stag	16	C3
Stanwell	Stan	213	E1
Steeple Claydon	Stp Cl	63	E2
Stewkley	Stew	68	C1
Stoke Bruerne	S Bru	9	D4
Stoke Goldington	S Gol	12	A3
Stoke Hammond	S Ham	69	F4
Stoke Mandeville	S Man	116	A1
Stoke Poges	Sto P	198	C2
Stokenchurch	Skch	158	C3
Stone	Sto	114	B3
Stoner	Ston	179	F3
Stratton Audley	S Adly	61	D1
Swanbourne	Swan	67	D2
Syresham	Syr	27	D4
Taplow	Tapl	196	C1
Tetsworth	Tet	136	A1
Thame	Tha	126	A1
Thornborough	Thrn	54	A4
Tiddington	Tidd	136	A4
Tingewick	Ting	51	D4
Totternhoe	Tott	93	D4
Tring	Tri	119	D2
Turvey	Turv	8	C3
Turweston	Turw	38	B4
Twyford	Twyf	62	B1
Tylers Green	Ty Gr	163	E1
Upper Arncott	U Arn	94	C4
Uxbridge	Uxb	201	E3
Waddesdon	Wadd	99	D4
Walter's Ash	Wal A	150	B1
Walton	Walt	48	A3
Warrington	Warr	7	D4
Water Stratford	W Str	40	A1
Waterperry	Wtpy	123	D1
Wavendon	Wave	48	C4
Weedon	Wedn	87	E1
Wendover	Wen	131	E2
West Drayton	W Dra	208	B2
Westbury	West	39	D2
Westcott	Wcot	98	B4
Weston Turville	W Tur	117	D1
Weston Underwood	W Und	6	A1
Whaddon	Whad	45	D1
Whitchurch	Whit	87	D3
Whitfield	Whit	26	B2
Wicker	Wick	31	D2
Wigginton	Wigg	119	E1
Wilstone	Wils	104	B1
Windsor	Wind	210	C3
Wing	Wing	79	F1
Wingrave	Win	89	E2
Winslow	Wins	66	A2
Woburn	Wbrn	60	C4
Woburn Sands	Wbn S	49	D3
Wooburn Green	Woo G	185	F4
Woodburn Green	Woo G	185	F4
Worminghall	Worm	123	F3
Wotton Underwood	W Und	97	E2
Wraysbury	Wray	211	F1
Yardley Gobion	Yard G	18	C3
Yardley Hastings	Y Has	1	A3

Abbey Barn La. H Wyc 173 F2
Abbey Barn La. Lit M 173 F2
Abbey Barn Rd. H Wyc 173 F2
Abbey Cl. Slough 204 C3
Abbey Park. Burn 186 C2
Abbey Rd. Ayl 101 D1
Abbey Rd. Bou E 184 C3
Abbey Rd. M Keyn 34 A2
Abbey Rd. M Keyn 47 F3
Abbey Rd. Syr 27 E4
Abbey Terr. N Pag 22 B2
Abbey Way. Bish 194 B3
Abbey Way. H Wyc 173 D3
Abbey Way. M Keyn 34 A3
Abbey Way. Rav 5 F1
Abbey Wlk. S Hea 152 A4
Abbot Ridge. L Cre 125 E3
Abbot Wlk. L Cre 125 E3
Abbot's Wlk. Wind 209 F3
Abbots Cl. M Keyn 34 A3
Abbots Way. Lit M 172 B2
Abbots Way. P Ris 139 E3
Abbotsfield. M Keyn 47 D4
Abbotswood. Lac G 150 B2
Abbott's Cl. Uxb 208 B4
Abbotts Cl. Ayl 101 F1
Abbotts Rd. Ayl 101 F1
Abbotts Vale. Ches 144 B2
Abbotts Way. Burn 204 B3
Abbotts Way. Win 89 D2
Abercromby Ave. H Wyc 172 C4
Aberdeen Ave. Slough 205 D3
Aberdeen Cl. M Keyn 46 C1
Abingdon Cl. Uxb 201 F2
Abingdon Wlk. Maid 195 F2
Abney Court Dr. Bou E 185 D1
Abraham Cl. M Keyn 35 E3
Abrahams Rd. Hen-O-T 191 E2
Abstacle Hill. Tri 118 C2
Acacia Ave. W Dra 208 C3
Acacia Ave. Wray 211 F2
Acacia Gr. Berk 135 D2
Acacia Mews. Harm 213 E4
Accommodation La. Harm 213 D4
Ackerman Cl. Buck 52 C4
Acorn Cl. H Wyc 173 E4
Acorn Gdns. H Wyc 172 C2
Acorn Wlk. M Keyn 34 C1
Acre Pas. Wind 210 B3
Acre The. Mar 183 F1
Acrefield Rd. Ger C 188 B4
Acres End. Ame 165 F4
Acres The. H Wyc 161 F1
Adam Cl. Ayl 116 A2
Adam Cl. H Wyc 173 E4
Adam Cl. Slough 205 D3
Adams Cl. Buck 41 E1
Adams Ct. M Keyn 47 E4
Adams Way. Tri 119 D3
Addington Cl. Wind 210 A2
Addington Rd. Buck 41 E1
Addison Cl. Iver 207 F3
Addison Ct. Maid 196 A1
Addison Rd. Ches 144 B1
Addison Rd. Stp Cl 63 E1
Adelaide Cl. Slough 205 D2
Adelaide Rd. H Wyc 162 B1
Adelaide Sq. Wind 210 B3
Adelphi Gdns. Slough 205 F2
Adelphi St. M Keyn 34 C2
Adwell Sq. Hen-O-T 191 E1
Agars Pl. Datch 211 D4
Ailward Rd. Ayl 101 D1
Ainsdale Cl. M Keyn 46 B1
Aintree Cl. M Keyn 57 E3
Aintree Cl. Stan 212 C3
Airport Way. Stan 213 D2
Aiston Pl. Ayl 101 F1
Ajax Ave. Slough 205 D3
Akeman St. Tri 119 D2
Akerman Cl. M Keyn 33 D3
Akister Cl. Buck 52 C4
Alan Wlk. Slough 206 C4
Albany Ct. M Keyn 34 B4
Albany Gate. Ches 144 A1
Albany Park. Iver 212 B4
Albany Pl. Ayl 101 D1
Albany Rd. Old W 211 D1
Albany Rd. Wind 210 B3
Albert Cl. Slough 205 F2
Albert Rd. Ches 154 B4
Albert Rd. Hen-O-T 191 F1
Albert Rd. Old W 211 D1
Albert Rd. W Dra 208 C3
Albert Rd. Wind 210 C2
Albert St. Ayl 116 A4
Albert St. H Wyc 173 E4
Albert St. M Keyn 58 B4
Albert St. Maid 202 C4
Albert St. Slough 205 F2
Albert St. Tri 119 D2
Albert St. Wind 210 A3
Albion Cl. Slough 206 A3
Albion Cres. C St G 177 D4
Albion Pl. M Keyn 35 D2
Albion Rd. C St G 177 D4
Albion Rd. H Wyc 172 B3
Albion Rd. Pit 105 E3
Albion St. Ayl 115 F4
Albury Ct. M Keyn 33 F1
Albury View. Tidd 136 A3
Aldborough Spur. Slough 205 F4
Aldbourne Rd. Burn 204 A4
Aldbury Rd. Chor 167 F1
Aldebury Rd. Maid 195 F1
Alden View. Wind 209 E3
Aldene Rd. Hans 11 D2
Aldenham. M Keyn 47 E3
Alder Cl. Slough 204 C3
Alder Rd. Iver H 200 B2
Alder Rd. N Den 201 E3
Alderbourne La. Fulm 200 A4
Alderbury Rd W. Slough 206 C2
Alderbury Rd. Slough 206 C2
Aldergill. M Keyn 34 B3
Aldermead. M Keyn 33 F3
Alderney Ct. Berk 135 E2
Alders The. N Den 201 E3
Alderson Cl. Ayl 101 D1
Alderton Dr. Rin 121 D4
Aldin Ave N. Slough 206 A2
Aldin Ave S. Slough 206 A2
Aldrich Dr. M Keyn 35 F4
Aldridge Rd. Slough 198 A1
Aldwick Dr. Maid 202 B3
Aldwycks Cl. She C E 45 F3
Alexander Rd. Ayl 101 E1
Alexander St. Ches 144 B1
Alexandra Dr. N Pag 22 B1
Alexandra Park. H Wyc 173 D3
Alexandra Rd. H Wyc 173 F3
Alexandra Rd. Maid 202 B4
Alexandra Rd. Slough 205 E2
Alexandra Rd. Uxb 201 E2
Alexandra Rd. Wind 210 B3
Alford Rd. H Wyc 172 B2
Alham Rd. Ayl 115 E3
Alice Cl. Hol G 163 E4
Alice La. Burn 197 D1
All Saints View. M Keyn 46 A4
All Saints' Ave. Maid 202 B4
Alladale Pl. M Keyn 33 E2
Allanson Rd. Mar 183 F2
Allen Cl. M Keyn 58 B3
Allen Dr. Wal A 161 E4
Allenby Rd. Maid 202 A4
Allerds Rd. Burn 198 A2
Alleyns La. Cook 195 E4
Allhusen Gdns. Fulm 199 F4
Allison Ct. M Keyn 35 E1
Allkins Ct. Wind 210 B3
Allonby Way. Ayl 116 A4
Allyn Cl. H Wyc 173 E4
Alma Rd. Berk 134 C3
Alma Rd. Ches 144 B1
Alma Rd. Eton 204 C1
Alma Rd. Wind 210 B3
Almond Cl. N Pag 22 A2
Almond Cl. Wind 210 A3
Almond Rd. Burn 197 E1
Almond Way. P Ris 139 D1
Almond Wlk. Ty Gr 163 D2
Almons Way. Slough 206 A4
Alnwick Rd. Lon M 103 F4
Alpha Ct. Ame 165 D4
Alpha St N. Slough 206 A2
Alpha St S. Slough 205 F2
Alscot La. P Ris 139 D3
Alston Dr. M Keyn 33 F2
Althorpe Cres. M Keyn 34 A3
Altona Rd. Loud 174 B1
Altona Way. Slough 205 D4
Altwood Bailey. Maid 202 A3
Altwood Cl. Maid 202 A3
Altwood Cl. Slough 204 C4
Altwood Dr. Maid 202 A3
Alverton. M Keyn 34 C4
Alvista Ave. Burn 204 A4
Alwin Cl. Ayl 115 E2
Alwyn Rd. Maid 202 A4
Alyngton. Berk 134 C4
Amanda Ct. Slough 206 B2
Amberley Ct. Maid 196 B2
Amberley Rd. Slough 204 C4
Amberley Way. Uxb 201 F1
Amblers Way. Pad 53 D1
Ambleside. Ayl 116 A3
Ambrose Ct. M Keyn 35 E1
Amelias La. M Keyn 35 D2
Amerden Cl. Tapl 203 E4
Amerden La. Tapl 203 E4
Amerden Way. Slough 205 D2
Amersham Hill Dr. H Wyc 173 E4
Amersham Hill Gds H Wyc 173 E4
Amersham Hill. H Wyc 173 D4
Amersham Pl. L Chal 166 B4
Amersham Rd. Beac 176 A3
Amersham Rd. C St G 166 A1
Amersham Rd. C St P 177 E3
Amersham Rd. Char 154 A3
Amersham Rd. Ches 154 A3
Amersham Rd. Chor 166 C4
Amersham Rd. Den G 189 D2
Amersham Rd. Hol G 163 D2
Amersham Rd. L Chal 166 C4
Amersham Way. L Chal 166 C4
Amherst Ct. M Keyn 35 E4
Amy La. Ches 154 A4
Ancastle Gr. Hen-O-T 191 E1
Andermans. Wind 209 E3
Anderson Cl. Skch 158 C2
Anding Way. Oln 6 C2
Andover Cl. Uxb 201 D2
Andrew Hill La. Hedg 187 E2
Andrews Cl. Soul 69 F2
Andrews Croft. M Keyn 34 C4
Andrews Way. Mar B 183 E4
Anershall. Win 89 D2
Angel Cl. M Keyn 35 D4
Angela Ct. Walt 48 A3
Angell Rd. M Keyn 32 C3
Angle Pl. Berk 135 D2
Anglefield Rd. Berk 135 D2
Anglesey Ct. M Keyn 46 A4
Angood Cl. P Ris 139 D2
Angstrom Cl. She B E 46 A3
Angus Dr. M Keyn 46 C1
Anne Cl. Maid 195 F1
Annes Gr. M Keyn 21 E1
Annesley Rd. N Pag 22 A2
Anns Cl. Ayl 116 A2
Anns Cl. Tri 118 C2
Ansculf Rd. Slough 198 A1
Anslow Gdns. Iver H 200 B2
Anslow Pl. Burn 204 B4
Anson Cl. Ayl 115 F2
Anson Cl. Bov 145 F2
Anson Rd. M Keyn 33 E3
Anstey Brook. W Tur 117 D2
Anstey Cl. Wadd 99 D3
Anthony Ct. M Keyn 32 B3
Anthony Way. Burn 204 B3
Anton Way. S Man 115 E2
Anxey Cl. Hadd 126 C3
Aplin Rd. Ayl 116 B3
Apple Tree Ave. Uxb 208 C4
Apple Tree Ave. W Dra 208 C4
Appleacres. S Ham 69 E4
Appleby Heath. M Keyn 58 B3
Applecroft. Berk 134 C3
Applecroft. Maid 202 B2
Applecroft. Nwtn L 57 E2
Applefield. L Chal 166 B4
Appletree La. Slough 206 B2
Appletree Wlk. Ches 154 B3
Appleyard Pl. M Keyn 34 C1
Approach Rd. Tapl 203 F4
Approach The. M Keyn 33 F1
Aran Heights. C St G 177 D3
Arborfield Cl. Slough 205 F2
Arbour View. L Chal 166 A4
Arbroath Cl. M Keyn 46 C2
Arbrook Ave. M Keyn 34 B2
Arcade The. H Wyc 173 D4
Arcadia La. M Keyn 35 D2
Archdale. H Wyc 173 D3
Archer Cl. Maid 202 B4
Archers Way. La En 171 D3
Archers Wells. M Keyn 47 D1
Archway. Lac G 150 A2
Arden Cl. Bov 146 A2
Arden Park. M Keyn 33 D4
Ardenham La. Ayl 101 E1
Ardenham St. Ayl 101 E1
Ardwell La. M Keyn 33 D3
Argyle Ave. Ayl 101 D1
Argyll Ave. Slough 205 D3
Arkley Ct. Holy 203 E1
Arkwright Rd. Stan 212 C3
Arlington Ct. M Keyn 46 C2
Arlott Cres. M Keyn 46 C4
Armourer Dr. M Keyn 34 C3
Armstrong Cl. She C E 45 F3
Arncliffe Dr. M Keyn 34 A3
Arncott Rd. Pidd (B) 95 E4
Arncott Wood Rd. U Arn 94 C3
Arne La. Walt 48 B3
Arnison Ave. H Wyc 162 B1
Arnold Cl. S Man 116 B1
Arnold Ct. Ayl 115 F3
Arrewig La. Dra B 132 B1
Arrewig La. St Le 142 C4
Arrow Pl. M Keyn 58 B2
Arthur Rd. Slough 205 E2
Arthur Rd. Wind 210 B3
Arundel Cl. Maid 202 A4
Arundel Ct. Slough 206 B1
Arundel Gr. M Keyn 57 F4
Arundel Rd. H Wyc 172 A3
Arundel Rd. Uxb 201 D1
Ascot Dr. L Buzz 80 B3
Ascot Rd. Holy 203 D1
Ascot Rd. Maid 203 D1
Ascott Ct. Ayl 101 F1
Ascott Rd. Ayl 101 F1
Ash Cl. Ayl 102 A1
Ash Cl. Slough 207 D2
Ash Cl. Wal A 161 D4
Ash Gr. Ame 154 A2
Ash Gr. Ayl 116 A4
Ash Gr. Sto P 198 C3
Ash Gr. W Dra 208 C3
Ash Green. N Den 201 D3
Ash Hill Rd. N Pag 22 A2
Ash La. Wind 209 E3
Ash Mead Dr. Den 190 A1
Ash Rd. H Wyc 172 B2
Ash Rd. P Ris 139 D2
Ash Rd. Tri 118 C2
Ash Vale. Map Cr 178 B3
Ashbourne End. Ayl 115 E2
Ashbourne Gr. Maid 202 B2
Ashburnham Cl. M Keyn 46 B1
Ashburnham Cres. L Buzz 80 C3
Ashby Rd. Berk 134 B4
Ashby. M Keyn 47 D4
Ashcroft Ct. Burn 197 D2
Ashcroft Dr. Den G 189 F2
Ashcroft Rd. Maid 202 B4
Ashcroft Terr. Tri 119 D3
Ashdown Cl. M Keyn 35 D4
Ashdown Rd. H Wyc 174 A4
Ashdown Way. Ame 154 B1
Ashdown. Maid 196 A2
Ashenden Wlk. Far C 198 B4
Ashendon Rd. Wcot 98 B3
Asheridge Rd. Ches 144 A1
Ashfield Cl. Ty Gr 163 D1
Ashfield Gr. M Keyn 58 B4
Ashfield Rd. Ches 144 B1
Ashfield Way. Ty Gr 163 D2
Ashfield. M Keyn 34 B4
Ashford Cl. Ayl 116 A3
Ashford La. Dorn 204 A2
Ashford Rd. Iver H 200 B2
Ashford Rise. Oak 109 E3
Ashgrove Gdns. Oving 86 C4
Ashgrove. Stp Cl 63 E1
Ashlea Rd. Ger C 177 F1
Ashlea. Oln 6 C2
Ashleigh Cl. Ame 165 F4
Ashley Cl. Ched 105 D4
Ashley Ct. Ty Gr 163 D1
Ashley Dr. Ty Gr 163 E1
Ashley Green Rd. Ash Gr 144 C3
Ashley Park. Maid 196 A1
Ashley Rd. Uxb 201 D2
Ashley Row. Ayl 102 A1
Ashleys. Chor 167 F1
Ashlyns Ct. Berk 135 D2
Ashlyns Rd. Berk 135 D2
Ashmead La. Den 190 A1
Ashotts La. Char 143 D3
Ashpole Furlong. M Keyn 46 A4
Ashridge Cl. Bov 146 A2
Ashridge Cl. M Keyn 57 E4
Ashridge La. Bot 155 E4
Ashridge Rise. Berk 134 C3
Ashridge. Chin 147 D3
Ashton Pl. Maid 202 A3
Ashton Rd. S Bru 9 E4
Ashtree Wlk. Ty Gr 163 D1
Ashwell St. L Buzz 80 C4
Ashwells Manor Dr. Ty Gr 174 B4
Ashwells Way. C St G 177 E4
Ashwells. Ty Gr 174 A4
Ashwood. M Keyn 34 A4
Askett La. P Ris 139 E4
Aspen Cl. Ayl 102 A1
Aspen Cl. Slough 205 D4
Aspen Cl. W Dra 208 C3
Asplands Cl. Wbn S 49 D2
Aspley Hill. Asp G 49 E2
Aspley La. Asp G 49 F1
Aspreys. Oln 6 C3
Assheton Rd. Beac 175 F2
Astlethorpe. M Keyn 33 F1
Astley Rd. Tha 126 A1
Aston Abbotts Rd. Cub 78 B1
Aston Abbotts Rd. Wedn 87 F1
Aston Clinton Rd. W Tur 116 C4
Aston Ferry La. Rem H 192 B3
Aston Hill. Ast R 157 F4
Aston La. Rem H 192 B2
Aston Mead. Wind 209 F3
Aston Rd. Hadd 127 D3
Astrope La. Lon M 104 A2
Astwood Rd. Cran 25 E4
Atherstone Ct. M Keyn 33 E1
Atherton Cl. Stan 213 E1
Athlone Cl. Maid 195 F1
Atkins Cl. M Keyn 34 A2
Atterbrook. M Keyn 34 A2
Attingham Hill. M Keyn 34 A1
Attwells Yd. Uxb 201 E3
Auckland Cl. Maid 203 D4
Auckland Dr. H Wyc 173 F3
Auckland Park. M Keyn 47 E2
Auden Cl. N Pag 22 A3
Audley Mead. M Keyn 34 A2
August End. Slough 206 C4
Augustine Cl. Stan 212 C2
Augustus Rd. M Keyn 32 B2
Austen Ave. Oln 7 D2
Austen Ave. Oln 7 D2
Austen Pl. Ayl 100 C1
Austenway. Ger C 188 C4
Austenwood Cl. Ger C 177 E1
Austenwood Cl. H Wyc 173 D2
Austenwood La. Ger C 188 B4
Austin Wray. Uxb 201 E2
Austins Mead. Bov 146 A2
Australia Ave. Maid 202 C4
Australia Rd. Slough 206 A2
Autumn Cl. Slough 204 C3
Autumn Wlk. Maid 202 A3
Auxiliaries Way. Den G 189 F3
Avalon Rd. Bou E 185 D3
Avebury Bvd. M Keyn 34 C1
Avebury. Slough 205 D3
Aveling Rd. H Wyc 173 E3
Avenue Cl. W Dra 208 B2
Avenue Rd. M Mor 41 F2
Avenue Rd. Maid 203 D3
Avenue Rd. Wins 65 F2
Avenue The. Ame 154 B1
Avenue The. Bou E 185 D2
Avenue The. Chin 147 E3
Avenue The. Datch 211 D3
Avenue The. Dun 93 F4
Avenue The. Far C 198 A4
Avenue The. Maid 196 B2
Avenue The. Old W 211 D1
Avenue The. P Ris 139 D2
Avenue The. Uxb 201 E1
Avenue The. Whit 26 B2
Avenue The. Worm 123 F3
Avenue The. Wray 211 F2
Averil Ct. Slough 204 B4
Avery Ave. H Wyc 161 E1
Avington. M Keyn 33 F1
Avon Cl. N Pag 22 B2
Avon Cl. Slough 204 C3
Avon Gr. M Keyn 57 F4
Avon Pl. Ayl 115 E2
Avonbury Ct. Brac 38 A3
Avondale. Maid 195 E1
Awling Field. L Buzz 80 B4
Aylesbury Bsness Cen. Ayl 101 D1
Aylesbury Cres. Slough 205 E4
Aylesbury End. Beac 175 F1
Aylesbury Rd. Ast C 117 D3
Aylesbury Rd. Bier 102 A2
Aylesbury Rd. Chea 112 A1
Aylesbury Rd. Cudd 113 D2
Aylesbury Rd. Dra B 118 C1
Aylesbury Rd. Elle 129 F2
Aylesbury Rd. G Kim 129 F2
Aylesbury Rd. Hadd 126 B3
Aylesbury Rd. P Ris 139 E3
Aylesbury Rd. Tha 126 B3
Aylesbury Rd. Tri 118 C1
Aylesbury Rd. Wen 131 D3
Aylesbury Rd. Wing 79 F1
Aylesbury St W. M Keyn 33 E3
Aylesbury St. M Keyn 33 E3
Aylesbury St. M Keyn 58 C4
Aylesbury St. M Keyn 101 F2 (see note)
Ayleswater. Ayl 101 F2
Aylesworth Ave. Slough 198 A1
Aylward Gdns. Ches 144 A1
Aynho Ct. M Keyn 45 F4
Ayr Way. M Keyn 46 C1
Aysgarth Park. Holy 203 D1
Azalea Cl. Ty Gr 163 D2
Azalea Way. Slough 206 C4

Babington Rd. Wen 131 E3
Baccara Gr. M Keyn 58 B4
Bachelors Acre. Wind 210 B3
Back Dr. Emb 12 C2
Back La. Gawt 51 F2
Back La. C St G 177 D4
Back St. Skch 158 C3
Back St. Thrn 54 A4
Back St. Wen 131 D2
Backs The. Ches 154 B4
Bacombe La. Wen 131 D2
Bacon Hill. Oln 6 C2
Baconsmead. Den 190 A1
Bad Godesberg Way. Maid 202 C4
Bader Gdns. Slough 205 D2
Badgebury Rise. Mar B 183 E4
Badgemoor La. Hen-O-T 191 E2
Badgemore Ct. M Keyn 33 E1
Badger Cl. Maid 202 B2
Badgers Oak. M K Vil 48 A4
Badgers Way. Buck 52 C4
Badgers Way. Mar B 183 E4
Badgers Wood. Far C 198 B4
Badminton Rd. Maid 202 A3
Badminton View. M Keyn 34 A1
Bagley Cl. W Dra 208 C2
Bailey Cl. H Wyc 173 E4
Bailey Cl. Maid 202 C4
Bailey Cl. Wind 210 A3
Baird Cl. Slough 205 D2
Baker St. H Wyc 172 C4
Baker St. Wadd 99 D3
Baker's Rd. Uxb 201 E3
Bakers La. S Bru 9 D4
Bakers Walk. W Tur 116 C1
Bakers Wood. Den G 189 E2
Bakery Cl. Gr Und 83 D3
Bala Cl. M Keyn 58 B3
Bala Way. M Keyn 58 B3
Baldways Cl. Win 89 E2
Baldwin Cres. N Pag 22 A2

Baldwin Rd. Beac 176 A1
Baldwin Rd. Burn 197 E1
Baldwin's Shore. Eton 210 B4
Balfour Pl. Mar 183 F2
Balham's La. Ibst 179 F4
Balham's La. Ston 179 F4
Ballard Cl. Ayl 116 A3
Ballard Green. Wind 209 F4
Ballinger Ct. Berk 135 D2
Ballinger Rd. S Hea 142 C1
Balmoral Cl. Slough 204 C4
Balmoral Gdns. Wind 210 B2
Balmoral. Maid 195 D1
Bamfords La. Turv 8 C3
Bamfords Yd. Turv 8 C3
Bampton Cl. M Keyn 46 C1
Banburies Cl. M Keyn 47 D1
Banbury Ave. Slough 204 C4
Bangors Cl. Iver 207 F4
Bangors Rd N. Iver H 200 B2
Bangors Rd S. Iver 207 F4
Bangors Rd S. Uxb 200 C1
Bank Green. Char 143 E4
Bank Mill La. Berk 135 F2
Bank Mill. Berk 135 F2
Bank Rd. Ty Gr 174 B4
Bank St. H Wyc 174 A2
Banks Rd. Hadd 127 D3
Banks Spur. Slough 205 D2
Banktop Pl. M Keyn 46 B2
Bannard Rd. Maid 202 A3
Bannister Cl. Slough 206 C2
Bar La. Lgwk 138 C4
Barbers Mews. M Keyn 34 C3
Barbers Wk. Tri 118 C2
Barbers Wood Cl. H Wyc 172 A2
Barbers Wood Rd. H Wyc 172 A3
Barbury Ct. M Keyn 35 D4
Barchester Cl. Uxb 201 E1
Barchester Rd. Slough 206 C2
Bardney Cl. Maid 202 B2
Bardon Green. Ayl 101 F1
Barford. M Keyn 32 C2
Bargeman Rd. Maid 202 C3
Baring Cres. Beac 175 E2
Baring Rd. Beac 175 E2
Baring Rd. H Wyc 173 F4
Barkers Croft. M Keyn 33 E2
Barkestone Cl. M Keyn 46 B1
Barkham Cl. Ched 104 C4
Barlee Cres. Uxb 208 B4
Barley Cl. Lewk 157 D4
Barley Cl. Ty Gr 163 D2
Barley Cl. W Tur 116 C1
Barley Cres. S Man 115 E2
Barley Fields. Woo G 185 F4
Barleycroft. M Keyn 46 C2
Barlow Rd. Wen 131 E3
Barn Cl. Far C 198 A4
Barn Cl. Maid 195 F1
Barn Ct. H Wyc 172 B4
Barn Dr. Maid 202 A2
Barn La. Hen-O-T 191 E2
Barn Rd. Lgwk 138 C3
Barnabas Rd. L Buzz 80 B3
Barnacre Cl. Uxb 208 B4
Barnard Cres. Ayl 115 F3
Barnards Hill. Mar 183 B1
Barncroft Rd. Berk 134 C2
Barncroft. Turv 8 C3
Barnes Ave. Ches 144 B1
Barnes Pl. M Keyn 46 C4
Barnes Way. Iver 207 F3
Barnett Way. Bier 102 A2
Barnfield Dr. M Keyn 47 E3
Barnfield. Iver 207 F4
Barnfield. Slough 204 B3
Barnhill Cl. Mar 183 E2
Barnhill Gdns. Mar 183 E2
Barnhill Rd. Mar 183 E2
Barnsbury Ave. Ayl 116 A4
Barnsbury Gdns. N Pag 22 B2
Barnsfield Pl. Uxb 201 E3
Barnstable Ct. M Keyn 46 B2
Barons Cl. M Keyn 58 B4
Barons Mead. Hen-O-T 191 E1
Baronsmead Rd. H Wyc 172 C3
Barr's Rd. Burn 204 A4
Barrack Hill. Cudd 112 C3
Barrack La. Wind 210 B3
Barracks Hill. Cole 164 C1
Barracks Rd. H Wyc 173 D3
Barrards Way. Se Gr 176 B2
Barrie Cl. Ayl 100 C1
Barrington Mews. M Keyn 34 C1
Barrington Park Gdns. C St G 166 B1
Barry Ave. Eton 210 B4
Barry Ave. M Keyn 34 B4
Barry Cl. H Wyc 172 B2
Bartelotts Rd. Slough 197 F1
Bartholomew Cl. Walt 48 A3
Bartlett Pl. Buck 41 F1
Barton Rd. M Keyn 58 B3
Barton Rd. Slough 206 C2
Bartons Rd. Ty Gr 163 D1
Bascote. M Keyn 47 E3
Base Cl. Ayl 101 F1
Basford Way. Wind 209 E2
Basildon Ct. M Keyn 45 F4
Basing Rd. Chor 167 F1
Baskerfield Gr. M Keyn 47 E4
Bass Mead. Cook 195 F3
Basset Rd. La En 171 E2
Bassetsbury La. H Wyc 173 F2
Bassett Rd. L Buzz 80 C4
Bassett Rd. Uxb 201 E3
Bassett Way. Slough 197 F1
Batchelor Cl. Ayl 101 F1
Batchelor Way. Ame 165 E4
Batchelors Way. Ches 144 A1
Bateman Dr. Ayl 115 F3
Bates Cl. Gran 75 F4
Bates Cl. M Keyn 35 E4
Bates Cl. Slough 206 C4
Bates Gdns. Dray P 68 B3
Bates La. W Tur 116 C1
Bath La. Buck 52 B4
Bath Rd. Burn 204 B3
Bath Rd. Harm 213 E3
Bath Rd. Stan 212 C3
Bathurst Cl. Iver 207 F2
Bathurst Wlk. Iver 207 F2
Batt Furlong. S Man 115 F2
Battersby Mews. Ayl 115 E4
Battings Wood Gdns. Wal A 161 E4
Battle Cl. Emb 13 F4
Battlemead Cl. Maid 196 B2
Baulk The. Ched 104 C4
Baulk The. Ivin 105 F3
Bawtree Rd. Uxb 201 E3
Baxter Cl. She C E 45 F4
Bay La. Rav 5 E1
Bay Tree Cl. Loud 174 A1
Bay Tree Cl. Nwtn L 57 E2
Bayard Ave. M Keyn 34 C3
Bayley Cres. Burn 204 A4
Bayley Gdns. Wal A 161 F3
Baylis Rd. Slough 205 F3
Bayne Hill Cl. Se Gr 176 B2
Bayne Hill. Se Gr 176 B2
Baynham Mead. M K Vil 48 A4
Baysfarm Ct. Harm 213 E3
Beacham Rd. H Wyc 172 B2
Beacon Ave. Dun 93 F4
Beacon Cl. Uxb 201 E4
Beacon Ct. M Keyn 46 B1
Beacon Hill. Ty Gr 174 B4
Beacon La. Mar B 171 F1
Beacon Rd. Ivin 106 C1
Beacon Rd. Rin 106 C1
Beacon Way. Tri 119 E3
Beaconsfield Ave. H Wyc 162 A1
Beaconsfield Com La. Hedg 187 E3
Beaconsfield Pl. N Pag 22 B2
Beaconsfield Rd. Ast C 117 F2
Beaconsfield Rd. Ayl 115 F4
Beaconsfield Rd. Far C 198 B3
Beaconsfield Rd. Tri 118 C2
Beadlemead. M Keyn 47 E3
Beales La. Walt 48 A3
Bealings End. Beac 175 E3
Beamish Way. Wins 66 A3
Beamond End La. H Hea 163 F4
Beamond End La. Hol G 163 F4
Beanfare. M Keyn 47 D2
Beauchamp Cl. M Keyn 34 C3
Beaufort Cl. Ayl 116 B4
Beaufort Cl. Mar 183 F1
Beaufort Dr. M Keyn 35 E4
Beaufort Gdns. Mar 183 F1
Beaufort Pl. Maid 203 E2
Beaulieu Cl. Datch 211 D3
Beaumaris Gr. She C E 46 A3
Beaumont Cl. Maid 202 A2
Beaumont Rd. Slough 205 E4
Beaumont Rd. Wind 210 B3
Beaumont Rise. Mar 183 F1
Beaumont Way. Ty Gr 162 C2
Beaver Cl. Buck 52 C4
Beaverbrook Ct. M Keyn 46 C1
Bec La. M Keyn 35 D4
Beckets Sq. Berk 135 D3
Beckins Way. Fla H 185 E4
Beckinsale Gr. She C E 45 F4
Bedder Rd. H Wyc 172 B2
Bede Ct. L Gad 121 E4
Bedfont Ct. Stan 213 D2
Bedfont Rd. Stan 213 F1
Bedford Ave. L Chal 166 B4
Bedford Ave. Slough 205 D4
Bedford Cl. Chen 156 A1
Bedford Cl. Maid 202 A2
Bedford Dr. Far C 198 A3
Bedford Rd E. Y Has 1 B3
Bedford Rd W. Y Has 1 A3
Bedford Rd. Asp G 49 F3
Bedford Rd. C Bray 8 A3
Bedford Rd. Cran 25 E1
Bedford Rd. Sher 14 A1
Bedford St. Hth 60 C4
Bedford St. M Keyn 33 E3
Bedford St. M Keyn 58 B4
Bedgebury Pl. M K Vil 48 A4
Bedgrove. Ayl 116 B3
Bedlam La. Chic 14 B1
Bedwins La. Cook 195 E3
Bedwyn Wlk. Ayl 115 E2
Beech Ave. La En 171 E3
Beech Ave. Oln 6 C2
Beech Cl. Bier 102 A2
Beech Cl. Buck 41 E1
Beech Cl. Fla H 174 A1
Beech Cl. H Wyc 173 F2
Beech Cl. Skch 158 C2
Beech Dr. Berk 135 E2
Beech Fern. Walt 48 A3
Beech Gr. Ame 165 E4
Beech Gr. Ayl 115 D3
Beech Gr. L Buzz 80 C4
Beech Green. Ayl 115 E3
Beech Hill Ct. Berk 135 E3
Beech House Dr. Pott 18 C2
Beech La. Pres 151 D4
Beech La. Se Gr 176 C2
Beech Leys. Stp Cl 63 F2
Beech Park. L Chal 155 D1
Beech Park. Wal A 150 A1
Beech Rd. Chin 147 E3
Beech Rd. H Wyc 173 F2
Beech Rd. N Pag 22 A2
Beech Rd. P Ris 139 E2
Beech Rd. Slough 206 C2
Beech Tree Rd. Hol G 163 E4
Beech Waye. Den G 189 D2
Beech Wlk. Tri 119 E2
Beechams The. Mur 67 E3
Beechcroft Rd. Ches 144 A1
Beechcroft Rd. M Keyn 57 F3
Beeches Dr. Far C 198 A4
Beeches Park. Beac 175 E1
Beeches Rd. Far C 198 A4
Beeches The. Ame 154 A2
Beeches The. Dean 31 F2
Beeches The. Tri 119 E2
Beeches Way. Burn 197 D1
Beechfield Way. Ty Gr 163 D2
Beechingstoke. Mar 183 F2
Beechtree Ave. Mar B 183 E3
Beechwood Ave. Chor 167 D3
Beechwood Ave. L Chal 155 E1
Beechwood Ave. Uxb 208 C4
Beechwood Cl. L Chal 166 B4
Beechwood Ct. Dun 93 F4
Beechwood Dr. Ald 120 B3
Beechwood Dr. Maid 202 A3
Beechwood Dr. Mar 194 A4
Beechwood Gdns. Slough 205 F2
Beechwood La. Wen 131 E3
Beechwood Park. Fel 146 C4
Beechwood Rd. Beac 175 E1
Beechwood Rd. H Wyc 161 D1
Beechwood Rd. Slough 205 E4
Beechwood Way. Ast C 117 F3
Beecroft Way. Dun 93 F4
Beehive Cl. Uxb 201 F3
Beel Cl. L Chal 166 B4
Beeward Cl. M Keyn 33 D3
Bekonscot Ct. M Keyn 21 F1
Belfast Ave. Slough 205 E4
Belgrave Mews. Uxb 201 E1
Belgrave Rd. Ayl 101 D2
Belgrave Rd. Slough 205 F3
Bell Alley. Wins 65 F2
Bell Ave. W Dra 208 C2
Bell Cl. Beac 175 F1
Bell Cl. Cub 78 A1
Bell Cl. Dray P 68 A3
Bell Cl. P Ris 139 D2
Bell Cl. Slough 206 A4
Bell Cl. Tha 125 F1
Bell Cres. Lgwk 138 C3
Bell Ct. Hurl 193 F2
Bell La. Berk 134 C3
Bell La. Eton 204 C1
Bell La. Hen-O-T 191 F2
Bell La. L Chal 155 E1
Bell La. P Ris 139 D2
Bell La. Syr 27 D4
Bell La. Tha 125 E1
Bell Leys. Win 89 D2
Bell St. Hen-O-T 191 F1
Bell St. Maid 202 C3
Bell St. P Ris 139 D2
Bell View Cl. Wind 209 F3
Bell View. Wind 209 F3
Bellamy Rd. H Wyc 173 E4
Bellclose Rd. W Dra 208 C2
Belle Vue. Sto 114 B3
Bellfield Rd. H Wyc 173 D4
Bellis Gr. M Keyn 47 E4
Bells Hill Green. Sto P 199 D3
Bells Hill. Sto P 199 D2
Bells La. Hort 212 A2
Bells Meadow. M Keyn 35 D4
Bellswood La. Iver 207 D4
Bellway. Wave 49 D3
Bellwether. M Keyn 33 D2
Bellwood Rise. H Wyc 173 D2
Belmers Rd. Wigg 119 E1
Belmont Cl. Uxb 201 E3
Belmont Cres. Maid 202 B4
Belmont Ct. M Keyn 33 E1
Belmont Dr. Maid 202 B4
Belmont Park Ave. Maid 202 B4
Belmont Park Rd. Maid 202 B4
Belmont Rd. Ches 144 A2
Belmont Rd. Maid 202 B4
Belmont Rd. Uxb 201 E3
Belmont Vale. Maid 202 B4
Belmont. Slough 205 D4
Belsize Ave. M Keyn 35 D1
Belton Rd. Berk 135 D3
Belvoir Ave. M Keyn 46 B1
Bembridge Ct. Slough 205 F2
Benbow Ct. M Keyn 46 A4
Benbow Way. Uxb 208 B4
Bench Manor Cres. Ger C 177 E1
Bencombe Rd. Mar B 183 F3
Benen-stock Rd. Stan 213 D1
Benham Cl. Ches 144 A1
Benhams La. Faw 180 B1
Benjamin Rd. H Wyc 173 D4
Benjamins Footpath. H Wyc 173 D4
Bennet Cl. M Keyn 32 B2
Bennett End Rd. Bled R 159 E4
Bennett's Hill. Swan 76 B4
Bennetts Cl. Slough 205 D3
Bennetts La. Wind 102 C4
Bennetts. Ches 144 B1
Benning Ave. Dun 93 F4
Benning Cl. Wind 209 E2
Benson Cl. Slough 206 A3
Benson Cl. Uxb 208 C4
Bentall Cl. M Keyn 35 E4
Bentinck Cl. Ger C 188 B3
Bentinck Rd. W Dra 208 B3
Bentley Park. Burn 197 E2
Bentley Rd. Slough 205 D3
Benton Dr. Chin 147 E4
Benwell Cl. M Keyn 33 F3
Benwells. Chin 147 E3
Berakspear Rd N. S Har 190 C4
Berberis Cl. Walt 48 A3
Berberis Wlk. W Dra 208 C1
Bercham. M Keyn 33 F1
Beresford Ave. Ayl 101 E2
Beresford Ave. Slough 206 B3
Beresford Rd. Chor 167 F1
Beretun. M Keyn 33 F1
Bergamot Gdns. Walt 48 A3
Berkeley Cl. Ches 144 A1
Berkeley Ave. Ches 143 F1
Berkeley Cl. S Gol 12 A3
Berkeley Mews. Mar 183 F1
Berkeley Rd. Loud 174 B1
Berkeley Rd. Tha 126 A1
Berkeley Rise. Ayl 101 D1
Berkhampstead Rd. Ches 144 B1
Berkley Cl. Maid 202 A4
Berkley Rd. Beac 175 E3
Berks Hill. Chor 167 E2
Berkshire Ave. Slough 205 D4
Berling Rd. M Keyn 33 F1
Bernard Cl. Cudd 112 C1
Bernard's Cl. Chea 112 A1
Bernards Cl. S Hea 152 A4
Bernards Way. Fla H 174 A1
Bernay Gdns. M Keyn 35 D4
Berners Cl. Slough 204 C3
Bernewood Cl. L Cre 125 E4
Berries Rd. Cook 196 A4
Berry Field Park. Ame 154 A1
Berry Field. Slough 206 B4
Berry Hill. Tapl 203 E4
Berry La. Asp G 49 F3
Berry La. Chor 167 F2
Berry Way. Nwtn L 57 F2
Berryfield Rd. Ayl 101 D2
Berryfield Rd. P Ris 139 D2
Berryfield. Ched 104 C4
Berrystead. B Bkhl 48 A2
Berwick Ave. Slough 205 D3
Berwick Cl. Beac 176 A1
Berwick Cl. Mar 183 E2
Berwick La. Mar 183 E2
Berwick Rd. Mar 183 E2
Bessemer Ct. M Keyn 22 A1
Bessimer Cres. Ayl 100 C1
Bestobell Rd. Slough 205 E4
Bettles Cl. Uxb 201 E2
Betty's Cl. Nwtn L 57 E2
Betty's La. Tri 119 D2
Bevan Hill. Ches 144 A1
Bevelwood Gdns. H Wyc 172 B4
Beverley Cl. Mar 183 B1
Beverley Ct. Slough 206 A2
Beverley Gdns. Maid 195 D1
Beverley Pl. M Keyn 35 D1
Bewdley Rd. L Buzz 80 B4
Bexley St. Wind 210 B3
Beyners Green. L Kin 152 A2
Bicester Rd. Ayl 101 D1
Bicester Rd. L Cre 125 E3
Bicester Rd. Lud 96 B4
Bicester Rd. M Gib 71 F2
Bicester Rd. Oak 109 E3
Bicester Rd. Twyf 62 B1
Bickleigh Cres. She B E 46 B2
Biddlesden Rd. West 39 D3
Bideford Green. L Buzz 80 B4
Bideford Spur. Slough 198 A1
Bierton Rd. Ayl 101 F1
Bigfrith La. Cook 195 D3
Biggs La. Dint 113 F1
Bigmore La. B Bot 170 A1
Biko Way. Uxb 208 B4
Billet La. Berk 135 D3
Billet La. Iver 207 D4
Billingwell Pl. M Keyn 35 D1
Billwell. L Cre 125 E3
Bilton Rd. M Keyn 47 E1
Bingham Cl. M Keyn 46 B1
Bingham Rd. Burn 204 A4
Binghams The. Maid 203 D2
Birch Ave. W Dra 208 C4
Birch Ct. Ayl 115 E3
Birch Gr. Slough 205 D4
Birch Gr. Wind 209 E3
Birch La. Flau 156 A4
Birch Rd. Berk 134 B4
Birch Tree Gr. Bot 145 D1
Birch Way. Ches 144 B1
Birch Way. Ty Gr 163 D1
Birchdale. Ger C 188 B2
Birches Rise. H Wyc 172 C4
Birches The. Fel 146 C4
Birchfield Gr. M Keyn 58 B4
Birchington Rd. Wind 210 A3
Birchwood Chase. G Kin 151 E1
Birdlip La. M K Vil 48 A4
Birdlip. Walt 48 A3
Birds La. S Gol 12 A3
Birfield Rd. Loud 174 B1
Birinus Ct. H Wyc 172 B3
Birkdale Cl. M Keyn 57 E4
Birkett Way. L Chal 166 B3
Birley Rd. Slough 205 E4
Bisham Ct. Bish 194 C3
Bishop Ct. Maid 202 B3
Bishops Farm Cl. Oak G 209 D3
Bishops Orch. Far C 198 A1
Bishops Wlk. Ayl 115 F3
Bishops Wlk. Bou E 185 F3
Bishopstone Rd. Sto 114 B3
Bishopstone. M Keyn 34 A3
Bishopstone. Sto 115 D1
Bishors Meadow. Bier 102 A2
Bissley Dr. Maid 202 A2
Bit The. Wigg 119 E1
Bittenham Cl. Sto 114 C2
Bix Hill. Faw 191 D3
Black Acre Cl. Ame 165 F4
Black Boy La. Hurl 193 E2
Black Butts Cotts. Cook 196 A4
Black Horse Ave. Ches 154 B3
Black Horse Cl. Wind 209 E3
Black Park Rd. Fulm 199 F2
Black Park Rd. Iver H 199 F2
Blackberry Ct. Walt 48 A3
Blackdown. M Keyn 32 C2
Blacketts Wood Dr. Chor 167 D3
Blackfield La. S Hea 142 C2
Blackham Ct. M Keyn 46 C4
Blackheath Cres. M Keyn 34 B2
Blackhill Dr. M Keyn 33 D3
Blackhorse Cl. Ame 154 C1
Blackhorse Cres. Ame 154 C1
Blackmoor Gate. M Keyn 46 B1
Blackmore Way. Uxb 201 E3
Blackpond La. Far C 198 A2
Blacksmith La. Pres 151 E3
Blacksmith How. Slough 207 D1
Blacksmith's La. Den 189 E1
Blacksmiths Rd. Lgwk 138 B4
Blackthorn Cl. Bktn 81 D2
Blackthorn Dell. Slough 206 B2
Blackthorn Gr. Wbn S 49 D2
Blackthorne La. S Hea 142 C2
Blackthorne Rd. Stan 212 C2
Blackwater Dr. Ayl 115 E2
Blackwell End. Pott 18 B2
Blackwell Hall La. Bot 155 D3
Blackwell Hall La. Lat 155 D3
Blackwell Rd. La En 171 D3
Blackwood Cres. M Keyn 33 F3
Blair Rd. Slough 205 F3
Blairmont St. M Keyn 34 C2
Blake Way. Tha 126 A1
Blakedown Rd. L Buzz 80 B4
Blandford Cl. Slough 206 B2
Blandford Rd N. Slough 206 B2
Blandford Rd S. Slough 206 B2
Blatherwick Ct. She C E 45 F4
Blaydon Cl. M Keyn 57 E3
Bleasdale. M Keyn 34 B3
Bledlow Ridge Rd. Bled 148 B4
Bledow Rd. Bled 148 C4
Bledow Ridge Rd. Bled 148 B4
Blenheim Ave. M Keyn 32 C2
Blenheim Cl. Slough 206 C3
Blenheim Pl. Ayl 115 F3
Blenheim Pl. Syr 27 E4
Blenheim Rd. H Wyc 172 B2
Blenheim Rd. Maid 202 A4
Blenheim Rd. Slough 206 B1
Bletcham Way. B Bkhl 48 A2

Bletcham Way. M Keyn 47 F1
Bletcham Way. Walt 48 A2
Bletchley Rd. Nwtn L 57 E3
Bletchley Rd. She B E 46 A2
Bletchley Rd. Stew 68 B2
Blinco La. Slough 206 C4
Blind La. Bou E 185 D3
Blind La. Char 153 D4
Blind La. Fla H 185 D3
Bliss Ave. Cran 25 E1
Blisworth. M Keyn 47 E3
Blondell Cl. Harm 213 E4
Bloomfield Rd. Maid 202 A3
Bloomsbury Cl. Hth 60 C3
Blossom Way. Uxb 201 F3
Blucher St. Ches 154 A4
Blumfield Cres. Slough 204 C4
Blumfield Ct. Slough 197 E1
Blundells Rd. M Keyn 34 B3
Blyth Cl. Ayl 115 E3
Blythe Cl. Iver 207 F4
Blythe Cl. N Pag 22 B2
Blyton Cl. Beac 175 E2
Boarlands Cl. Slough 204 C3
Boathouse Reach. Hen-on-T 191 F1
Bobmore La. Mar 183 F2
Bockmer La. Medm 193 D4
Boddington Rd. Wen 131 E2
Bodenham Cl. Buck 52 C4
Bodiam Cl. She C E 46 A3
Bodle Cl. M Keyn 35 D3
Bodmin Ave. Slough 205 D4
Bois Ave. Ame 154 A2
Bois Hill. Ches 154 C3
Bois La. Ame 154 B2
Bois Moor Rd. Ches 154 B3
Bolan Ct. She C E 45 F3
Bolter End La. La En 171 D3
Bolton Ave. Wind 210 B2
Bolton Cl. M Keyn 47 D1
Bolton Cres. Wind 210 B2
Bolton Rd. Wind 210 B2
Bond Ave. M Keyn 47 E2
Bond Cl. W Dra 208 C4
Bonham Carter Rd. Hal 131 F4
Bonnards Rd. Nwtn L 57 E2
Bonnersfield. L Cre 125 E4
Booker La. H Wyc 172 B4
Booker Ave. M Keyn 34 B2
Bookerhill Rd. H Wyc 172 B3
Boot La. Dint 113 F1
Booth Pl. Eat B 92 C3
Borderside. Slough 206 A4
Borough Rd. Brac 38 A3
Borough Wlk. M Keyn 34 C2
Bosanquet Cl. Uxb 201 E1
Boss La. Hgv V 162 A4
Bossiney Pl. M Keyn 34 C1
Bossington La. L Buzz 80 C4
Boston Gr. Slough 205 E4
Boswell Ct. Buck 41 F1
Boswell La. Dean 31 F2
Boswick La. Berk 134 B4
Bosworth Cl. M Keyn 46 C1
Botley La. Bot 145 D1
Botley Rd. Ches 144 C1
Bottesford Cl. M Keyn 46 B1
Bottle Square La. Bled R 159 E3
Bottom Ho Fm La. Ame 165 F1
Bottom House La. Wigg 120 A1
Bottom La. Se Gr 176 B3
Bottom Rd. Bled R 160 A3
Bottom Rd. Buc Co 133 D2
Bottom Rd. Dra B 132 C2
Bottrells La. Ame 176 C4
Bottrells La. C St G 176 C4
Bottrells La. Cole 176 B4
Botyl Rd. E Clay 74 C3
Boulmer Rd. Uxb 201 E1
Boulters Cl. Maid 196 B1
Boulters Cl. Slough 205 D2
Boulters Ct. Maid 196 B1
Boulters Gdns. Maid 196 B1
Boulters La. Maid 196 B1
Boundary Cres. M Keyn 32 C3
Boundary Pl. Woo G 185 E4
Boundary Rd. Brac 38 A3
Boundary Rd. Ger C 177 E2
Boundary Rd. Tapl 203 F4
Boundary Rd. Woo G 185 E4
Boundary The. M Keyn 46 C4
Bounds Croft. M Keyn 33 D2
Bounty St. M Keyn 33 F4
Bourbon St. Ayl 115 E4
Bourne Ave. Wind 210 B2
Bourne Cl. Bou E 185 D3
Bourne End La. Heml H 146 A4
Bourne End Rd. Bou E 196 C4
Bourne End Rd. Cran 25 E2
Bourne End Rd. Tapl 196 C4
Bourne Rd. Berk 134 C3
Bourne Rd. Slough 205 E2
Bourne The. Bov 146 A2
Bourton Low. Walt 48 A3
Bourton Rd. Buck 52 C4
Bourtonville. Buck 52 B4
Bouverie Way. Slough 206 C1
Boveney Cl. Slough 205 D2
Boveney New Rd. Eton 204 C1
Boveney Rd. Dorn 204 B1
Boveney Wood La. Burn 186 B1
Bovingdon Green La. Bov 145 F2
Bovingdon Hts. Mar 183 A1
Bow Brickhill Rd. Wbn S 48 C2
Bow Brickhill Rd. Wbn S 48 C2
Bowden La. H Wyc 173 E3
Bowen Cl. Walt 48 B3
Bower Cl. Eat B 92 C3
Bower La. Eat B 92 C3
Bower Way. Slough 204 C3
Bowerdean Rd. H Wyc 173 E4
Bowers La. Bled R 159 E4
Bowes Cl. N Pag 22 B2
Bowler Lea. H Wyc 161 E1
Bowler Rd. Ayl 115 F2
Bowler Rd. Ayl 115 F2
Bowler's Orch. C St G 177 D4
Bowles Pl. M Keyn 47 E4
Bowling Alley. Oving 86 B4
Bowling Ct. Hen-O-T 191 E2
Bowling Gr. Skch 158 B3
Bowling Green Rd. Cran 25 E1
Bowmans Cl. Burn 197 D2
Bowmont Dr. S Man 115 E2
Bowood Ct. M Keyn 33 F1
Bowry Dr. Wray 211 F1
Bowstridge La. C St G 177 E3
Bowyer Cres. Den G 189 F3
Bowyer Dr. Slough 204 C3
Bowyers Mews. M Keyn 34 C3
Box La. Fel 146 C4
Box Tree Cl. Ches 154 B3
Boxberry Gdns. Walt 48 A3
Boxer Rd. Lgwk 138 C3
Boxwell Rd. Berk 135 D2
Boxwood Cl. W Dra 208 C2
Boyce Cres. Walt 48 B3
Boycott Ave. M Keyn 34 C1
Boyn Hill Ave. Maid 202 B3
Boyn Hill Cl. Maid 202 B3
Boyn Hill Rd. Maid 202 B3
Boyn Valley Rd. Maid 202 B3
Boyndon Rd. Maid 202 B4
Bozenham Mill La. Ash 9 F3
Bozenham Mill La. Graf R 9 F2
Bracken Cl. Far C 198 B4
Bracken Rd. Maid 202 B2
Bracken Way. Fla H 185 D4
Brackenforde. Slough 206 B2
Brackens The. H Wyc 173 E3
Brackley Dr. Hol G 163 D3
Brackley La. Twyf 73 D3
Brackley Rd. Buck 41 D1
Brackley Rd. Chac 41 D1
Brackley Rd. Hol G 163 D3
Brackley Rd. West 39 D3
Bradbery. Map Cr 178 B3
Bradbourne Dr. B Bkhl 48 A2
Bradbury Cl. M Keyn 34 A2
Bradcutts La. Cook 195 F4
Braddenham Wlk. Ayl 115 F2
Braden Cl. Ayl 116 A3
Bradenham Beeches. Wal A 161 D4
Bradenham La. Bish 194 B3
Bradenham Rd. H Wyc 161 D2
Bradenham Wd La. Bled. R 161 D4
Bradfield Ave. Buck 41 E1
Bradford Rd. Chor 167 E1
Bradford Rd. Slough 205 D4
Bradley Cl. Oak 109 E3
Bradley Rd. Slough 205 F3
Bradshaw Cl. Wind 209 F3
Bradshaw Rd. H Wyc 173 F3
Bradshawe Waye. Uxb 208 C4
Bradvue Cres. M Keyn 34 A3
Bradwell Cmn Bvd. M Keyn 34 B2
Bradwell Rd. M Keyn 34 A3
Bradwell Rd. M Keyn 46 A4
Brae Hill Cl. Bri 110 A4
Brae Hill. Bri 110 A4
Braemar Gdns. Slough 205 D2
Bragenham La. L Buzz 70 B3
Bragenham La. Soul 70 B3
Bragenham Side. S Ham 69 F4
Brahms Cl. Walt 48 B3
Braid The. Ches 144 C1
Brakynbery. Berk 134 C4
Brallings La. C St P 178 A3
Bramber Cl. M Keyn 57 F4
Bramber Ct. Slough 205 D3
Bramble Ave. M Keyn 34 C2
Bramble Cl. Uxb 208 C4
Bramble Cres. Hol G 163 E3
Bramble Dr. Maid 202 A2
Bramble La. Ame 165 F3
Brambles The. W Dra 208 C1
Bramcote Cl. Ayl 116 B4
Bramley Cl. Maid 202 B2
Bramley End. Hgh V 151 D1
Bramley Grange. M Keyn 58 B2
Bramley Rd. M Keyn 47 E2
Brammas Cl. Slough 205 E2
Brampton Ct. M Keyn 34 A3
Brampton Ct. Maid 203 D4
Branch Rd. Loud 174 A1
Brandon Rd. H Wyc 172 A2
Brands Hill Ave. H Wyc 162 B1
Brands Rd. Slough 212 A4
Brandville Rd. W Dra 208 C2
Bransgill Ct. M Keyn 34 A2
Bransworth Ave. M K Vil 48 B4
Braunston. M Keyn 47 E3
Bravenfield. Pad 53 E1
Bray Cl. Maid 203 E2
Bray Ct. Holy 203 E1
Bray Rd. Maid 203 D3
Braybank. Maid 203 E2
Braybourne Cl. Uxb 201 B1
Braybrooke Dr. M Keyn 46 C2
Brayfield Rd. Maid 203 E2
Brays Cl. H Hea 153 E2
Brays Green La. H Hea 153 E2
Brays La. H Hea 153 E3
Brays Meadow. H Hea 153 E2
Brayton Ct. She B E 46 B3
Braywick Rd. Maid 203 D2
Braziers End. Buc Co 133 E1
Breachwell Pl. Men 91 D1
Breakspear Rd S. Ick 190 C1
Bream Cl. Mar 194 B4
Breamore Ct. M Keyn 45 F4
Brearley Ave. M Keyn 46 C4
Brearley Cl. Uxb 201 F3
Brecon Way. H Wyc 172 C4
Bredward Cl. Burn 197 D1
Brenchwood Cl. H Wyc 161 E1
Brendon Ct. M Keyn 46 B1
Brent Rd. Bou E 185 D2
Brent. M Keyn 47 E3
Brentwood Way. Ayl 116 A3
Breton. M Keyn 32 C3
Brewhouse La. Win 88 C1
Briaily. B Bot 159 E1
Briar Cl. Burn 204 A4
Briar Dene. Maid 195 E1
Briar Glen. Cook 195 F3
Briar Hill. M Keyn 33 F2
Briar Way. Berk 135 E2
Briar Way. Slough 205 D4
Briars The. H Wyc 173 E3
Briars The. Hol G 163 E4
Briars The. Slough 206 C1
Briars The. Stan 213 D1
Briary View. Whad 56 A4
Brices Meadow. She B E 46 A2
Brick Cl. M Keyn 33 E1
Brick Hill. Ash 97 F1
Brick Kiln La. Bier 102 A2
Brickfield La. Burn 197 D2
Brickhill Manor Ct. L Bkhl 59 E3
Brickhill St. B Bkhl 48 A2
Brickhill St. M K Vil 35 F1
Brickhill St. M Keyn 35 E3
Brickhill St. Walt 48 A3
Bricks La. Bled R 159 E2
Brickwell Wlk. Ty Gr 163 D2
Bricstock. A Abb 88 B2
Briden's Way. Hadd 126 C3
Bridge Ave. Cook 195 F3
Bridge Ave. Maid 203 D4
Bridge Bank Cl. Loud 174 A2
Bridge Cl. Slough 204 C3
Bridge Pl. Ame 154 C1
Bridge Rd. Cast 19 F1
Bridge Rd. Ick 123 F1
Bridge Rd. Maid 203 D4
Bridge Rd. Uxb 201 E2
Bridge St. Berk 135 E2
Bridge St. Buck 52 B4
Bridge St. G Kim 129 E1
Bridge St. H Wyc 173 D4
Bridge St. Iver 212 B4
Bridge St. L Buzz 80 C4
Bridge St. M Keyn 33 F4
Bridge St. Maid 203 D4
Bridge St. Oln 6 C2
Bridge St. Thrn 54 A4
Bridge St. Turv 8 B3
Bridge Turn Ave. M Keyn 33 E4
Bridgeford Ct. M Keyn 46 C4
Bridgegate Bsnss Pk. Ayl 101 D1
Bridgeman Dr. Wind 210 A3
Bridgestone Dr. Bou E 185 E2
Bridgewater Ct. Slough 207 D1
Bridgewater Rd. Berk 134 C4
Bridgewater Rd. Berk 135 D3
Bridgewater Terr. Wind 210 B3
Bridgewater Way. Wind 210 B3
Bridgeway. Cudd 112 C2
Bridgeway. M Keyn 34 A4
Bridle Cl. M Keyn 34 A3
Bridle Cl. Maid 195 F1
Bridle Gate. H Wyc 172 C3
Bridle Rd. Maid 195 F1
Bridle Way. Berk 135 D3
Bridleway. W Tur 116 C1
Bridlington Spur. Slough 205 D2
Bridport Way. Slough 198 A1
Briery Way. Ame 154 C1
Brighton Spur. Slough 198 A1
Brightwell Ave. Tott 93 E4
Brill Cl. Maid 202 B2
Brill Cl. Mar 183 B1
Brill Pl. M Keyn 34 B2
Brill Rd. Chl 111 D2
Brill Rd. Lud 96 A4
Brill Rd. Oak 109 F3
Brimmers Hill. Hol G 162 C3
Brimmers Rd. P Ris 139 E1
Brindlebrook. M Keyn 33 F1
Brindley Ave. H Wyc 161 F1
Bristle Hill. Buck 52 B4
Bristol Cl. Stan 213 F1
Bristol Way. Slough 205 F3
Bristow Cl. M Keyn 47 F1
Bristow Ct. Mar 184 A2
Britannia Ind Est. H Wyc 172 B4
Britannia Rd. Ches 144 B1
Britannia St. Ayl 115 F4
Britten Gr. Walt 48 B3
Brittons La. Sal 37 E2
Britwell Rd. Burn 197 E1
Broad Arrow Cl. M Keyn 34 C4
Broad Dean. M Keyn 47 D4
Broad La. Beac 186 A3
Broad Leys. P Ris 139 D2
Broad Oak Ct. Slough 198 B1
Broad Oak. Slough 198 B1
Broad Piece. M Keyn 35 D4
Broad Platts. Slough 206 B2
Broad St. Ches 144 B1
Broad St. N Pag 22 B2
Broad St. Syr 27 D4
Broadfields. Ayl 101 D1
Broadlands Ave. Ches 144 B1
Broadlands. M Keyn 47 D3
Broadmark Rd. Slough 206 A3
Broadwater Gdns. S Har 190 B4
Broadwater La. S Har 190 B4
Broadwater Park. Den G 190 A3
Broadwater Park. Holy 203 F1
Broadwater. Berk 135 E3
Broadwater. M Keyn 47 E3
Broadway Ave. M Keyn 21 F1
Broadway Cl. Ame 165 D4
Broadway The. Ches 154 A4
Broadway. Ame 165 D4
Broadway. Maid 202 C4
Brocas St. Eton 210 B4
Brocas Terr. Eton 210 B4
Brocas Way. Slap 91 D2
Brock La. Maid 202 C4
Brockhampton. M Keyn 35 D3
Brockhurst Rd. Ches 144 B1
Brockwell. N Pag 22 B2
Broken Furlong. Eton 205 D1
Broken Gate La. Den G 189 E2
Bromham Mill. M Keyn 21 F1
Bromley. Lon M 104 A2
Brompton Cl. Ayl 101 D1
Brompton Cres. Ayl 101 D1
Brompton Dr. Maid 195 E1
Bromycroft Rd. Slough 198 A1
Bronsdon Way. Den 189 F1
Bronte Cl. Ayl 100 C1
Brook Cl. Lud 96 B4
Brook Cres. Slough 204 C4
Brook End. N Craw 24 A3
Brook End. W Tur 117 D2
Brook La. Berk 135 D3
Brook La. Harr 3 F4
Brook La. New B 8 A2
Brook La. Tha 125 F1
Brook Path. Slough 204 C3
Brook St. Ast C 117 E3
Brook St. Edle 92 C2
Brook St. H Wyc 173 D4
Brook St. Tri 119 D2
Brook St. Wind 210 B3
Brookbank. Bou E 185 E2
Brookdene Cl. Maid 195 F1
Brooke Cl. M Keyn 57 F4
Brooke Rd. P Ris 139 D2
Brookfield Cl. Tri 119 D2
Brookfield Farm. Ast C 117 D2
Brookfield La. Buck 52 B4
Brookfield Rd. Bou E 185 E2
Brookfield Rd. Have 20 B1
Brookfield Rd. Nwtn L 57 E2
Brookhouse Dr. Bou E 185 E2
Brooklands Rd. M Keyn 58 B4
Brooklyn Way. W Dra 208 B2
Brooks Ct. Buck 52 B4
Brookside Ave. Wray 211 F2
Brookside Cl. Old S 32 A3
Brookside Cl. Tidd 136 A4
Brookside. Hal 117 E1
Brookside. Iver 212 B4
Brookside. Lill L 30 A3
Brookside. M Keyn 33 E2
Brookside. Oak 109 E3
Brookside. Tha 125 F1
Brookside. Uxb 201 F3
Brookside. Dean 31 F2
Broom Cl. Ty Gr 163 D2
Broom Hill. Cook 195 F3
Broom Hill. Sto P 199 D3
Broombarn La. G Mis 151 F4
Broomfield Cl. G Mis 151 F4
Broomfield Hill. G Mis 151 F4
Broomfield. M Keyn 33 E2
Broomlee. M Keyn 34 A3
Broomstick La. Bot 145 D1
Brora Cl. M Keyn 58 B3
Brotheridge Ct. Ayl 115 D3
Brough Cl. She C E 46 A3
Broughton Ave. Ayl 116 A4
Broughton Cl. Bier 102 A2
Broughton La. Ayl 116 B4
Broughton La. Bier 116 B4
Broughton Rd. Sal 37 E2
Brow The. C St G 177 E4
Brown Cl. N Pag 22 A2
Brown's Rise. Dra B 132 C2
Brownbaker Ct. M Keyn 34 C3
Browne Wills Cl. M Keyn 58 B4
Brownfield Gdns. Maid 202 C3
Browning Cres. M Keyn 58 A4
Brownlow Ave. Edle 92 C2
Brownlow La. Ched 105 D4
Brownlow Rd. Berk 135 E3
Brownlow Rise. Tott 93 D4
Browns Rd. Char 153 D4
Browns Rd. Hol G 163 E3
Browns Way. Asp G 49 F3
Brownsfield Rd. Yard G 18 C3
Brownswood Dr. Pott 18 B2
Brownswood Rd. Beac 175 F2
Broxbourne Cl. M Keyn 21 F1
Bruce Cl. Slough 205 D3
Bruckner Gdns. Walt 48 B3
Brudenell Dr. M K Vil 48 B4
Brudenell Dr. S Man 116 A1
Brudenell. Wind 209 F2
Brunel Cl. Maid 202 C3
Brunel Rd. Ayl 100 C1
Brunel Rd. H Wyc 161 F1
Brunel Rd. Maid 202 B3
Brunel Way. Slough 205 F3
Brunleys. M Keyn 33 D2
Brunswick Cl. Ayl 101 D2
Brushford Cl. M Keyn 46 B2
Brushwood Dr. Chor 167 E3
Brushwood Rd. Ches 144 B1
Bryans Cres. N Craw 24 A3
Bryanston Ave. Ayl 101 F1
Bryant Ave. Slough 205 F4
Bryant's Bottom Rd. Wal A 150 C2
Bryants Acre. Wen 131 D3
Bryer Pl. Wind 209 E2
Bryne La. Pad 53 D1
Bryony Cl. Uxb 208 C4
Bryony Pl. M Keyn 34 C3
Buccleuch Rd. Datch 211 D4
Buchan Cl. Uxb 201 E1
Buchanan Rd. U Arn 94 C4
Buckby. M Keyn 47 E3
Buckfast Ave. M Keyn 47 D1
Buckingham Ave E. Slough 205 E4
Buckingham Ave. Slough 205 D4
Buckingham Cl. H Wyc 174 A4
Buckingham Gate. M Keyn 35 D1
Buckingham Gate. Medm 193 E4
Buckingham Gdns. Slough 205 F2
Buckingham Rd. Brac 38 A3
Buckingham Rd. Dean 31 F1
Buckingham Rd. Edgc 72 C1
Buckingham Rd. Gawt 52 A3
Buckingham Rd. M Keyn 57 E4
Buckingham Rd. She B E 57 E4
Buckingham Rd. Stp Cl 63 F2
Buckingham Rd. Tri 118 C2
Buckingham Rd. Wick 31 F1
Buckingham Rd. Wins 65 F3
Buckingham St. Ayl 101 E1
Buckingham St. M Keyn 33 E4
Buckingham St. Ting 51 D3
Buckingham Way. Fla H 174 A1
Buckland Ave. Slough 206 A2
Buckland Cres. Wind 209 F3
Buckland Dr. M Keyn 47 E3
Buckland Rd. Dra B 118 A2
Bucklebury Cl. Holy 203 E1
Buckley Ct. M Keyn 32 C2
Buckman Cl. M Keyn 33 D3
Buckmaster Rd. H Wyc 172 B2
Buckthorn. M Keyn 33 F3
Budge Rd. Yard G 18 C3
Buffins. Tapl 196 C1
Bulbourne Cl. Berk 134 C3
Bulbourne Rd. Tri 119 E4
Bulkeley Ave. Wind 210 A2
Bull La. Ger C 188 B4
Bull La. H Wyc 173 D4
Bullbaiters La. H Hea 153 D3
Bullbeggars La. Berk 135 F2
Bullfinch Gdns. Ayl 101 F2
Bullington End Rd. Cast 20 A3
Bullocks Farm La. H Wyc 171 F4
Bullocks Farm La. La En 171 D4
Bullrush Gr. Uxb 201 E1
Bulls La. Ick 124 A2
Bullsland Gdns. Chor 167 D2
Bullsland La. Chor 167 D2

Bulstrode Ct. Ger C 188 B3
Bulstrode La. Chipf 146 C2
Bulstrode Way. Ger C 188 B3
Bunby Rd. Sto P 198 C3
Bunces Cl. Eton 205 D1
Bunhill Cl. Dun 93 F4
Bunkers La. L Buzz 80 B3
Bunstrux. Tri 119 D2
Bunten Meade. Slough 205 D3
Bunyan Cl. Tri 119 D3
Burano Cl. Walt 48 B3
Burchard Cres. She C E 46 A3
Burchett's Green Rd. Bish 194 B1
Burcot Gdns. Maid 195 F2
Burcott Cl. Bier 102 A2
Burcott La. Bier 102 B2
Burdett Dr. Wal A 161 D4
Burdock Ct. N Pag 21 F2
Burewelle. M Keyn 33 E1
Burfield Rd. Chor 167 E2
Burfield Rd. Old W 211 D1
Burford Cl. Ick 201 F4
Burford Cl. Mar B 183 E3
Burford Gdns. Burn 204 B4
Burgess Gdns. N Pag 22 A1
Burgess La. Dint 128 A4
Burgess Wood Gr. Beac 175 D1
Burgess Wood Rd S. Beac 175 D1
Burgess Wood Rd. Beac 175 D1
Burgett Rd. Slough 205 D2
Burghley Ct. M Keyn 45 F4
Burkes Cl. Beac 186 A4
Burkes Cres. Beac 175 E1
Burkes Rd. Beac 175 E1
Burleigh Piece. Buck 52 C4
Burleys Rd. Wins 65 F2
Burlington Ave. Slough 205 F2
Burlington Rd. Burn 197 D1
Burlington Rd. Slough 205 F2
Burma Cl. H Wyc 173 F3
Burn Wlk. Burn 197 D1
Burners La S. M Keyn 33 D2
Burners La. M Keyn 33 D2
Burness Cl. Uxb 201 E2
Burnetts Rd. Wind 209 F3
Burnham Ave. Beac 176 A1
Burnham Cl. Bou E 185 D2
Burnham Cl. H Wyc 172 B3
Burnham Cl. Wind 209 E3
Burnham Dr. M Keyn 34 B2
Burnham Field. W Tur 116 C4
Burnham La. Slough 204 C4
Burnham Pl. Syr 27 D4
Burnham Rd. Beac 186 C3
Burnham Rd. Hgh V 162 A3
Burnham Rd. Wcot 98 A4
Burnhams The. Shab 124 B2
Burnmoor Cl. M Keyn 58 B2
Burns Cl. L Cre 125 E4
Burns Cl. N Pag 22 A2
Burns Rd. M Keyn 58 A4
Burnt Oak. Cook 195 F4
Burroughs Cres. Bou E 185 D2
Burroway Rd. Slough 207 D2
Burrows Cl. Asp G 49 D3
Burrows Cl. Ty Gr 163 E1
Burrows Hill Cl. Stan 213 E2
Burt's La. L Cre 125 E3
Burton La. P Ris 139 E3
Burton Way. Wind 209 F2
Burton's La. L Chal 166 B3
Burton's Way. L Chal 166 B4
Burtree Cl. M Keyn 33 F3
Bury Ave. N Pag 22 B2
Bury Cl. N Pag 22 B2
Bury La. Ches 154 A4
Bury Rise. Fel 146 B3
Bury St. N Pag 22 B2
Buryhook Cnr. Holt 122 B1
Busby Cl. Buck 41 F1
Buscot Pl. M Keyn 45 F4
Bush The. Hadd 126 C3
Bushel Wharf. Tri 119 D3
Bushes La. Pres B 51 E1
Bushey Cl. Buck 41 F1
Bushey Cl. H Wyc 172 C4
Bushfield Rd. Bov 146 B3
Bushmead Rd. Whit 87 D3
Bushy Cl. M Keyn 47 D2
Buslins La. Char 143 F2
Bute Brae. M Keyn 46 C1
Butler Ct. Mar 184 A2
Butlers Cl. Ame 154 A1
Butlers Cl. Wind 209 E3
Butlers Court Rd. Beac 175 E1
Butlers Gr. M Keyn 34 B4
Butterfield Cl. M Keyn 35 E1
Butterfield. Bou E 185 E2
Butterfly Rd. Skch 158 C2
Buttermere Ave. Burn 204 B4
Buttermere Cl. M Keyn 58 B3
Buttermere. Ayl 116 A4
Buttfurlong. Hadd 127 D4
Buttlehide. Map Cr 178 B3
Buzzacott La. M Keyn 46 B2
By-wood End. C St P 178 A3
Bybend Cl. Far C 198 A2
Bycell Rd. M Mor 41 E3
Bye Green. W Tur 117 D2
Byerly Pl. M Keyn 34 C3
Byford Way. Wins 65 F2
Byland Dr. Holy 203 D1
Byrd Cres. Walt 48 B3
Byron Cl. M Keyn 57 F4
Byron Cl. Mar 183 C2
Byron Dr. N Pag 22 A2
Byron Rd. Ayl 115 F3
Byron Way. W Dra 208 C1
Byward Cl. M Keyn 34 C4
Byways. Burn 204 A4

Cadman Gate. She B E 46 B3
Cadsdean Rd. P Ris 139 F3
Cadwell Dr. Maid 202 B2
Caernarvon Cres. M Keyn 57 F4
Caesars Cl. M Keyn 34 A3
Caesers Gate. Brac 38 A3
Cages Wood Dr. Far C 198 A4
Cairngorm Gate. M Keyn 46 B4
Cairnside. H Wyc 173 F3
Caithness Ct. M Keyn 46 C1
Calbroke Rd. Slough 197 F1
Caldecote La. N Pag 22 C1
Caldecote St. N Pag 22 B2
Caldecotte Lake Dr. B Bkhl 48 A1
Calder Cl. Maid 195 F1
Calder Ct. Maid 195 E1
Calder Ct. Slough 206 C1
Calder Gdns. L Buzz 80 A4
Calder Vale. M Keyn 46 C1
Calder Way. Stan 212 C2
Caldewell. M Keyn 33 E1
Caldicot Cl. Ayl 116 A3
Caledon Cl. Beac 175 F2
Caledon Rd. Beac 175 F2
Caledonian Rd. M Keyn 33 F4
Calewen. M Keyn 33 F1
Callis Farm Cl. Stan 213 F1
Calluna Dr. M Keyn 47 D2
Calvards Croft. M Keyn 33 E2
Calverleigh Cres. M Keyn 46 B2
Calverley Cres. H Wyc 161 F1
Calverton La. She C E 33 D1
Calverton Rd. M Keyn 32 B2
Calves Cl. She B E 46 A2
Cam Ct. M Keyn 57 F4
Cam Mead. Ayl 116 A3
Camber Cl. M Keyn 57 F4
Camberton Rd. L Buzz 80 C3
Camborne Ave. Ayl 116 A3
Cambridge Ave. Burn 197 D2
Cambridge Ave. Slough 205 D4
Cambridge Cl. Ayl 101 F1
Cambridge Cl. Harm 213 E4
Cambridge Cres. H Wyc 173 F4
Cambridge Pl. Ayl 115 F4
Cambridge Rd. Beac 175 E1
Cambridge Rd. Mar 183 E1
Cambridge Rd. Uxb 201 E3
Cambridge St. Ayl 101 F1
Cambridge St. M Keyn 33 E3
Cambridge St. M Keyn 58 B4
Cambridge Terr. Berk 135 E2
Cambron. M Keyn 33 E1
Camden Pl. Bou E 185 D2
Camden Rd. Maid 195 E1
Cameron Rd. Ches 144 B1
Camley Gdns. Maid 202 A4
Camm Ave. Wind 209 F2
Camp Rd. Ger C 188 B2
Campbell Cl. Buck 52 C4
Campbell Cl. H Wyc 172 C4
Campbell Dr. Beac 175 E3
Campbells Ride. Hol G 163 E4
Campden Rd. Ick 190 C1
Camperdown. Maid 196 A1
Campion Cl. Ayl 116 B4
Campion Cl. Den 190 A1
Campion Cl. Uxb 208 C4
Campion Rd. Hol G 162 C3
Campion. M Keyn 21 F1
Campions Ct. Berk 135 D2
Canada Rd. Slough 206 A2
Canal Wharf. Slough 207 D2
Candlemas La. Beac 175 F1
Candlemas Mead. Beac 175 F1
Candover Cl. Harm 213 E4
Candytuft Green. Hol G 162 C3
Cane End. P Ris 139 D2
Canford Ct. Ayl 115 F3
Cannock Cl. Maid 203 D3
Cannock Rd. Ayl 101 F2
Cannon Court Rd. Cook 195 E2
Cannon Court Rd. Maid 195 E2
Cannon Hill Cl. Maid 203 E1
Cannon La. Maid 202 A3
Cannon Mill Ave. Ches 154 C3
Cannon Pl. P Ris 139 D2
Cannon's Hill. Cudd 112 B3
Cannondown Rd. Cook 195 F3
Canon Hill Dr. Maid 203 D2
Canon Hill Way. Maid 203 D1
Canterbury Ave. Slough 198 B1
Canterbury Cl. Ame 165 F4
Canterbury Cl. P Ris 139 D3
Cantilupe Cl. Eat B 92 B3
Cantle Ave. M Keyn 35 D3
Cantley Cl. Ayl 101 F1
Capel Dr. M Keyn 34 C3
Capell Ave. Chor 167 E2
Capell Rd. Chor 167 E2
Capell Way. Chor 167 E2
Capps La. Char 143 D3
Capron. M Keyn 47 D3
Captain Cook Cl. C St G 177 D3
Captain's Cl. Ches 144 A2
Captains Wlk. Berk 135 E2
Caraway Cl. B Bkhl 48 A2
Cardigan Cl. M Keyn 46 C1
Cardinals Wlk. Slough 204 B4
Carey Cl. Ayl 115 E2
Carey Cl. Wind 210 A2
Carey Way. Oln 7 D2
Careys Croft. Berk 135 D4
Carhampton Ct. M Keyn 46 B2
Carisbrooke Ave. H Wyc 172 A3
Carisbrooke Cl. Maid 202 B3
Carisbrooke Ct. Buck 41 F1
Carisbrooke Ct. Slough 205 F3
Carleton Gate. M Keyn 35 F4
Carlina Pl. M Keyn 34 B2
Carlisle Rd. Slough 205 E3
Carlton Cl. Ayl 101 D1
Carlton Cl. N Pag 22 C2
Carlton Rd. Slough 206 A3
Carlton Rd. Turv 8 C4
Carlyle Ave. Ayl 115 F4
Carlyle Cl. N Pag 22 A2
Carmarthen Rd. Slough 205 F3
Carne The. M Keyn 32 C3
Carnoustie Cl. M Keyn 57 E4
Caroline Cl. W Dra 208 B2
Caroline Ct. Mar 183 F2
Carolus Creek. M Keyn 35 D4
Carpenter Ct. M Keyn 34 C3
Carpenters Wood Dr. Chor 167 D3
Carpenters Yard. Tri 119 D2
Carr Cl. Ayl 101 D1
Carrick Rd. M Keyn 34 C1
Carrington Ave. Fla H 185 D4
Carrington Cl. Hogg 77 F3
Carrington Cres. Wen 131 D4
Carrington Pl. Hol G 163 E4
Carrington Pl. Tri 119 D3
Carrington Rd. Ayl 115 E3
Carrington Rd. H Wyc 172 B3
Carrington Rd. N Pag 22 A2
Carrington Rd. Slough 205 F3
Carrington Way. Pres 151 E3
Carroll Cl. N Pag 22 A3
Carron Cl. L Buzz 80 A4
Carrs Dr. H Wyc 172 B4
Carter Cl. Wind 210 A3
Carter Wlk. Ty Gr 174 B4
Carter's La. N Mar 75 F1
Carteret Cl. M Keyn 35 F4
Carters Cl. Sher 13 F1
Carters La. L Cre 125 D4
Carters La. M Keyn 33 D2
Carters La. Qntn 85 F3
Carters Meadow. N Mar 76 A1
Carters Ride. S Man 116 A1
Cartmel Cl. M Keyn 57 E3
Cartwright Pl. M Keyn 46 C4
Carver Hill Rd. H Wyc 172 C3
Carvers Mews. M Keyn 34 C3
Cascadia Cl. Loud 174 A1
Casterton Cl. M Keyn 34 B2
Castle Ashby Rd. Y Has 1 A4
Castle Ave. Datch 211 D4
Castle Ave. W Dra 208 C3
Castle Cl. Tott 93 D4
Castle Cl. Wing 79 F2
Castle Ct. M Gib 72 A2
Castle Ct. Maid 202 B4
Castle Dr. Maid 202 B4
Castle Gate Way. Berk 135 E3
Castle Hill Ave. Berk 135 E3
Castle Hill Ct. Berk 135 E3
Castle Hill Rd. Tott 93 D4
Castle Hill Terr. Maid 202 C4
Castle Hill. Berk 135 E3
Castle Hill. Maid 202 C4
Castle La. Whit 86 C3
Castle Meadow Cl. N Pag 22 C2
Castle Mews. Berk 135 E2
Castle Mews. Maid 202 C4
Castle Park Rd. Wen 131 D3
Castle Rose. M Keyn 47 E3
Castle St. Ayl 115 E4
Castle St. Berk 135 E2
Castle St. Buck 52 B4
Castle St. H Wyc 173 D4
Castle St. M Gib 72 A2
Castle St. Slough 205 F2
Castle St. Win 89 D2
Castle View Gdns. H Wyc 172 B4
Castlesteads. M Keyn 33 F3
Castlethorpe Rd. Hans 11 D1
Castleton Ct. Mar 183 F1
Castleview Rd. Slough 206 B1
Caswell La. Hth 60 C4
Catchpole Cl. M Keyn 33 D3
Cater Rd. La En 171 E2
Cathay Cl. M Keyn 58 A4
Catherine Ct. Buck 41 F1
Catherines Cl. W Dra 208 B2
Causeway The. Maid 203 E2
Causeway The. Mar 183 F1
Cautley Cl. Qntn 85 D3
Cavalier Rd. Tha 126 A1
Cavalry Cres. Wind 210 B2
Cavendish Cl. Burn 204 A4
Cavendish Cl. L Chal 166 A4
Cavendish Cl. Wen 131 D3
Cavendish Rd. Ches 154 B4
Cavendish Wlk. Tha 126 A1
Cavenham. M Keyn 33 F1
Caversham Green. Ayl 101 E1
Cawardon. M Keyn 34 B4
Cawcott Dr. Wind 209 F3
Caxton Dr. Uxb 201 E2
Caxton Rd. M Keyn 33 D4
Ceadr Rd. Berk 135 F2
Cecil Rd. Iver 207 F4
Cecil Way. Slough 197 F1
Cedar Ave. Hol G 163 D3
Cedar Ave. W Dra 208 C3
Cedar Chase. Maid 196 B1
Cedar Cl. Ayl 102 A1
Cedar Ct. Mar 183 F1
Cedar Dr. Mar B 183 E4
Cedar Gr. Ame 165 E4
Cedar Gr. Char 143 E4
Cedar Lodge Dr. M Keyn 33 E4
Cedar Terr. H Wyc 172 C4
Cedar Way. Berk 135 E2
Cedar Way. Slough 206 C1
Cedars Cl. Akel 41 F4
Cedars Cl. C St P 177 F3
Cedars Dr. Uxb 201 F2
Cedars Rd. Maid 203 D4
Cedars The. Wen 131 D3
Cedars Way. L Buzz 80 C3
Cedars Way. N Pag 22 B2
Ceely Rd. Ayl 115 E3
Celina Cl. M Keyn 58 B4
Cell Farm Ave. Old W 211 D1
Central Ave. Cran 24 C1
Central Dr. Slough 204 C3
Centre Wlk. Ty Gr 163 D2
Century Ave. M Keyn 46 C4
Cestreham Cres. Ches 144 B1
Chadbone Cl. Ayl 115 E4
Chadds La. M Keyn 47 E4
Chadwell Path. Ayl 116 B3
Chadwick Dr. M Keyn 47 D4
Chadwick St. H Wyc 162 B1
Chaffinch. Ayl 101 F2
Chaffron Way. M K Vil 35 E1
Chaffron Way. M Keyn 47 D4
Chaffron Way. She B E 46 B3
Chairborough Rd. H Wyc 172 B3
Chairmans Ave. Den G 189 F3
Chalcot Pl. M Keyn 45 F4
Chalet Cl. Berk 134 C2
Chalfont Ave. L Chal 166 B4
Chalfont Cl. M Keyn 34 A3
Chalfont La. Chor 167 D2
Chalfont La. Map Cr 178 B2
Chalfont Rd. Map Cr 178 B4
Chalfont Rd. Se Gr 176 B3
Chalfont Station Rd. L Chal 166 B4
Chalfont Way. Lit M 172 B2
Chalford. Woo G 185 F3
Chalgrove Cl. Maid 203 D3
Chalgrove End. S Man 116 A1
Chalgrove Rd. Tha 126 A1
Chalgrove Wlk. Ayl 115 E3
Chalk Farm Rd. Skch 158 B3
Chalk Hill. Ches 144 A1
Chalk Hill. Cole 164 C1
Chalk La. H Hea 153 D2
Chalk Pit La. Burn 197 D2
Chalkdell Dr. She B E 45 F2
Chalklands. Bou E 185 D2
Chalkpit La. Mar 183 D2
Challacombe. M Keyn 46 B1
Challener Rd. H Wyc 172 B2
Challow Ct. Maid 195 E1
Chalmers Ave. Have 20 B1
Chaloner Cl. Ayl 115 E3
Chaloner Rd. Ayl 115 E3
Chaloners Hill. Stp Cl 63 E2
Chalvey Gdns. Slough 205 F2
Chalvey Gr. Slough 205 D2
Chalvey Park. Slough 205 F2
Chalvey Rd E. Slough 205 F2
Chalvey Rd W. Slough 205 E2
Chamberlain Rd. Ayl 101 D1
Champflower. M Keyn 46 B2
Chancellors. Ty Gr 164 A3
Chancery Cl. M Keyn 34 A3
Chandlers Ct. M Keyn 47 F3
Chandos Cl. Buck 52 B4
Chandos Cl. L Chal 155 E1
Chandos Pl. M Keyn 58 B4
Chandos Rd. Buck 52 B4
Channer Dr. Ty Gr 174 A4
Chantry Cl. W Dra 208 B3
Chantry Cl. Wbn S 49 D3
Chantry Cl. Wind 210 A3
Chantry Rd. Ayl 101 E2
Chantry The. Uxb 201 F1
Chapel Cl. Akel 41 F4
Chapel Cl. L Gad 121 E3
Chapel Dr. Ast C 117 F3
Chapel End La. Wils 118 B4
Chapel Hill. Soul 69 F2
Chapel La. Akel 41 F4
Chapel La. Bled 138 A2
Chapel La. Bled R 148 C1
Chapel La. Chil 111 D2
Chapel La. Dray P 68 A3
Chapel La. H Wyc 172 B4
Chapel La. Lon M 104 A2
Chapel La. S Bru 9 D4
Chapel La. S Man 116 A1
Chapel La. Sto P 199 D3
Chapel La. Thrn 54 A4
Chapel La. Tott 92 C4
Chapel La. Turw 38 A4
Chapel La. Wal A 161 E4
Chapel La. Wen 131 D2
Chapel La. Whit 26 B2
Chapel Rd. Dint 128 A4
Chapel Rd. Edle 92 A3
Chapel Rd. Fla H 185 D4
Chapel Sq. Stew 68 C1
Chapel St. Berk 135 E2
Chapel St. H Wyc 161 E2
Chapel St. Mar 183 F1
Chapel St. Slough 205 F2
Chapel St. Tri 118 C2
Chapel St. Uxb 201 E2
Chapel St. Wbn S 49 D2
Chaplin Gr. She C E 45 E4
Chapman Ave. M Keyn 35 D3
Chapman Cl. W Dra 208 C2
Chapman La. Bou E 185 D3
Chapman La. Fla H 185 D3
Chapmans Cres. Ches 144 A1
Chapter Cl. Uxb 201 F3
Chapter. M Keyn 47 D3
Chardacre. M Keyn 33 F1
Charlbury Rd. Ick 190 C1
Charles Cl. Ayl 116 A2
Charles Dr. Tha 126 A1
Charles Gdns. Slough 206 A4
Charles St. Berk 135 D2
Charles St. Tri 119 D2
Charles St. Wind 210 B3
Charles Way. N Pag 22 B2
Charlton Cl. Slough 205 D2
Charlton Cl. Swan 66 C2
Charlton Sq. Oak G 209 E3
Charlton Way. Oak G 209 E3
Charlton. Oak G 209 E3
Charmfield Rd. Ayl 116 A3
Charnwood Cl. H Wyc 173 F3
Charsley Cl. L Chal 166 B4
Charter Cl. Slough 205 F2
Charter Rd. Slough 204 C3
Chartridge Grange Dr. Char 143 E2
Chartridge La. Char 143 F1
Chartridge La. Ches 143 F1
Chartwell Gate. Beac 175 E1
Chartwell Rd. N Pag 22 C2
Chase Ave. Walt 48 A2
Chase Cl. Cole 165 D2
Chase Park Rd. Y Has 1 A3
Chase The. Ches 144 A1
Chase The. Mar 184 A2
Chase The. Nwtn L 57 E2
Chase The. Ty Gr 163 E1
Chaseside Cl. Ched 105 D4
Chatfield. Slough 205 D4
Chatsworth Cl. Maid 202 B3
Chatsworth. M Keyn 33 F1
Chaucer Cl. Berk 134 C3
Chaucer Cl. N Pag 22 A2
Chaucer Dr. Ayl 115 F3
Chaucer Rd. M Keyn 58 A4
Chauntry Rd. Maid 203 D3
Chawton Cres. M Keyn 33 F1
Cheapside La. Den 189 F1
Chearsley Rd. L Cre 125 E4
Cheddington La. Lon M 104 B3
Cheddington La. Mars 104 B3
Cheddington Rd. Pit 105 E2
Chelsea Green. L Buzz 80 B3
Cheltenham Gdns. M Keyn 57 E3
Cheney Cl. Cub 78 A1
Cheney Way. Ayl 101 F1
Cheneys Wlk. M Keyn 47 D1
Chenies Ave. L Chal 166 B4
Chenies Par. L Chal 166 B4
Chenies Rd. Chor 167 E4
Chepping Cl. Ty Gr 163 D1
Chepstow Dr. M Keyn 57 E3
Chequers Cl. Pit 105 E2
Chequers Ct. Ayl 115 F2
Chequers End. Wins 66 A2
Chequers Hill. Ame 165 E4
Chequers La. Ibst 170 A3
Chequers La. La En 170 A2

Chequers La. N Craw 24 A3
Chequers La. Pit 105 E3
Chequers La. Pres 151 E3
Chequers Orch. Iver 207 F4
Chequers The. Cast 19 F3
Cherington Gate. Maid 195 D1
Cheriton. M Keyn 46 C2
Cherleton. M Keyn 33 F1
Cherries The. Slough 206 A4
Cherry Ave. Slough 206 B2
Cherry Cl. Fla H 185 D4
Cherry Cl. Pres 151 E3
Cherry Dr. Beac 175 D2
Cherry Gdns. Tri 118 C2
Cherry Gr. Hol G 163 E3
Cherry La. Ame 164 B3
Cherry La. W Dra 208 C1
Cherry Leys. Stp Cl 63 F2
Cherry Orch. Ame 154 C1
Cherry Orch. Oln 6 C2
Cherry Orch. Sto P 199 D3
Cherry Orch. W Dra 208 C2
Cherry Rd. N Pag 22 A2
Cherry Rise. C St G 177 E4
Cherry Rise. Fla H 185 D4
Cherry St. H Wyc 174 A2
Cherry Tree Ave. W Dra 208 C4
Cherry Tree Cl. G Kin 151 E1
Cherry Tree Cl. Hgh V 162 A4
Cherry Tree Cl. Lac G 150 A3
Cherry Tree La. Buc Co 133 D2
Cherry Tree La. Chor 167 E1
Cherry Tree La. Fulm 199 F3
Cherry Tree La. Lee C 142 C2
Cherry Tree Rd. Chin 147 E3
Cherry Tree Rd. Far C 198 B3
Cherry Tree Way. Ty Gr 163 E1
Cherry Tree Wlk. Ches 144 B1
Cherry Tree Wlk. L Buzz 80 C4
Cherry Way. Hol G 163 D3
Cherrycroft Dr. Wal A 161 E3
Cherrytree La. Ger C 177 E1
Cherrywood Cl. Se Gr 176 B3
Cherrywood Gdns. Fla H 185 D4
Cherwell Cl. Maid 203 D4
Cherwell Cl. Slough 212 A4
Cherwell Rd. Ayl 115 E3
Cherwell Rd. Bou E 185 D2
Chesham Ave. M Keyn 34 B2
Chesham La. C St P 177 F3
Chesham Rd. Ame 154 B1
Chesham Rd. Ash Gr 135 D2
Chesham Rd. Berk 135 D2
Chesham Rd. Bov 145 F2
Chesham Rd. Char 143 F4
Chesham Rd. Char 153 E4
Chesham Rd. Wigg 133 E4
Cheshire Ct. Slough 206 A2
Cheslyn Gdns. M Keyn 35 D4
Chesney Wold. M Keyn 46 C3
Chess Cl. Lat 155 E2
Chess Cl. S Man 115 E2
Chessbury Rd. Ches 154 A4
Chessfield Park. L Chal 166 C4
Chessmount Rise. Ches 154 B3
Chester Cl. M Keyn 57 E4
Chester Rd. Slough 205 E4
Chesterfield Cres. Wing 79 F2
Chesterfield Pl. Ayl 115 D4
Chesterholm. M Keyn 33 F3
Chesterton Cl. Ches 144 A1
Chesterton Green. Beac 175 F2
Chestnut Ave. Ches 144 B1
Chestnut Ave. H Wyc 173 E3
Chestnut Ave. Slough 206 C2
Chestnut Ave. W Dra 208 C3
Chestnut Cl. Ame 154 B1
Chestnut Cl. Ast C 117 F3
Chestnut Cl. C St P 177 F1
Chestnut Cl. Dag 107 E3
Chestnut Cl. M Keyn 32 B3
Chestnut Cl. Maid 196 A1
Chestnut Cl. Medm 193 E4
Chestnut Cl. Nwtn L 57 E1
Chestnut Cl. P Ris 139 E3
Chestnut Cl. Wadd 99 D3
Chestnut Cres. Ayl 115 F3
Chestnut Cres. M Keyn 58 B4
Chestnut Dr. Berk 135 E2
Chestnut Dr. Wind 209 F2
Chestnut Hill. L Buzz 80 B4
Chestnut La. Ame 154 C1
Chestnut La. Hol G 163 D3
Chestnut Leys. Stp Cl 63 F2
Chestnut Rd. Beac 175 D1
Chestnut Rd. P Ris 139 E2
Chestnut Rd. Yard G 18 C3
Chestnut Rise. L Buzz 80 B4
Chestnut View. E Clay 74 C4
Chestnut Way. Hal 131 E4
Chestnut Way. Lgwk 138 C3
Chestnut Way. S Man 116 A1
Chestnut Wlk. C St P 177 F2
Chestnuts The. Fel 146 C4
Chestnuts The. Shab 124 B2
Chestwood Gr. Uxb 201 F3
Chetwode Ave. M K Vil 36 A1
Chetwode Cl. Buck 41 F1
Chetwynd Dr. Uxb 201 F2
Chevalier Gr. She C E 45 E4
Cheveley Gdns. Burn 197 E2
Cheviot Cl. H Wyc 161 F1
Cheviot Cl. L Buzz 80 B4
Cheviot Cl. Maid 203 D3
Cheviot Rd. Slough 207 D1
Cheyne Cl. Ame 154 B2
Cheyne Cl. Buck 41 F1
Cheyne Cl. Ger C 188 C2
Cheyne Cl. Pit 105 E2
Cheyne Wlk. Ches 154 B4
Chicheley Hill. Sher 23 D4
Chicheley Rd. Chic 23 F4
Chicheley Rd. N Craw 23 F4
Chicheley St. N Pag 22 C2
Chichester Cl. H Wyc 173 E3
Chichester Ct. Slough 206 A2
Chichester Row. Ame 154 B1
Chievely Ct. M Keyn 46 B1
Childs Way. M Keyn 46 B4
Childs Way. She B E 46 A2
Chillery Leys. M Keyn 35 F4
Chiltern Ave. Ame 154 B1
Chiltern Ave. Edle 92 C2
Chiltern Ave. H Wyc 172 B3
Chiltern Ave. Sto 114 B3
Chiltern Cl. Berk 135 D3
Chiltern Cl. Hol G 163 E4
Chiltern Cl. P Ris 139 D2
Chiltern Cl. Sto 114 B3
Chiltern Cl. Ty Gr 163 E1
Chiltern Cl. Wen 131 D3
Chiltern Ct. Wins 65 F2
Chiltern Dr. Chor 167 F1
Chiltern Green. Fla H 185 D4
Chiltern Hill. C St P 177 F1
Chiltern Hills Rd. Beac 175 E1
Chiltern Manor Park.
S Hea 152 A4
Chiltern Parade. Ame 154 B1
Chiltern Park Ave. Berk 135 D3
Chiltern Rd. Ame 154 A2
Chiltern Rd. Burn 204 A4
Chiltern Rd. Maid 203 D3
Chiltern Rd. Mar 183 B1
Chiltern Rd. S Hea 142 C2
Chiltern Rd. Wen 131 D3
Chiltern Rd. Win 89 D2
Chiltern Ridge. Skch 158 B2
Chiltern St. Ayl 115 F3
Chiltern View Rd. Uxb 201 E2
Chiltern View. Bled R 149 E1
Chiltern Way. Ast C 117 F1
Chiltern Way. Tri 119 E3
Chilterns Cl. Fla H 185 D4
Chilterns Park. Bou E 185 D3
Chilterns The. H Wyc 173 D4
Chilton Rd. Chea 112 A2
Chilton Rd. Ches 144 B1
Chilton Rd. L Cre 125 E4
Chilwick Rd. Slough 197 F1
Chimes The. H Wyc 172 C3
Chinalls Cl. Fin 50 B3
Chingle Croft. She B E 46 A1
Chinner Hill. Chin 147 F2
Chinner Rd. Chin 147 D3
Chinnor Rd. Bled 138 A1
Chinnor Rd. Bled R 148 B2
Chippendale Cl. H Wyc 162 B1
Chippendale Waye. Uxb 201 E3
Chippenham Dr. M K Vil 36 B1
Chipperfield Cl. M Keyn 34 A4
Chipperfield Rd. Bov 146 B2
Chipping Vale. She B E 46 B1
Chipps Hill. La En 171 D4
Chipstead. Ger C 177 E1
Chislehampton. M Keyn 35 E2
Choke La. Cook 195 D2
Cholesbury La. Buc Co 133 D1
Chorley Rd. H Wyc 160 C2
Chorleywood Bottom.
Chor 167 E2
Chrislaine Cl. Stan 213 E1
Christchurch Rd. Tri 118 C2
Christian Ct. M Keyn 35 E4
Christie Cl. N Pag 22 A3
Christmas La. Far C 187 E1
Christopher Cl. Wal A 161 E4
Church Green. L Cre 125 E4
Church Way. Sto 114 B3
Church Cl. Ast C 117 E3
Church Cl. Cudd 112 C2
Church Cl. Eton 210 B4
Church Cl. M Mor 41 F2
Church Cl. Maid 202 B3
Church Cl. Uxb 201 D2
Church Cl. W Dra 208 C2
Church Cl. Wick 31 D2
Church Croft. Edle 92 C2
Church Dr. Maid 203 E2
Church End Rd. She B E 46 A2
Church End. Adsk 53 F1
Church End. Bled 138 A1
Church End. Nwtn L 57 E2
Church End. Pott 18 C2
Church End. Sher 14 A1
Church End. Stp Cl 63 D3
Church End. Syr 27 E4
Church End. Wave 48 C4
Church Farm Cres.
M Keyn 34 C4
Church Gr. L Chal 166 C4
Church Gr. Slough 206 B4
Church Green Rd. M Keyn 58 A4
Church Green. Tott 93 D4
Church Headland La. Whit 87 D3
Church Hill. Akel 41 F4
Church Hill. Asp G 49 F3
Church Hill. Ched 105 D4
Church Hill. Elle 130 A1
Church Hill. M Keyn 33 F1
Church Hill. S Har 190 B4
Church Hill. Ston 179 E4
Church Hill. Whad 45 D1
Church Holt The. Hedg 187 E2
Church La. Ast C 117 E2
Church La. Berk 135 E2
Church La. Bled R 159 E4
Church La. Bled R 159 F4
Church La. Bov 146 A2
Church La. Brac 38 B1
Church La. Chea 112 A1
Church La. Ched 105 D4
Church La. Chin 147 E3
Church La. Dean 31 F2
Church La. Eat B 92 C3
Church La. Edgc 72 C1
Church La. Emb 13 F4
Church La. G Hrwd 55 D2
Church La. Ger C 177 E1
Church La. Graf R 9 D1
Church La. Graf R 9 E1
Church La. Gran 75 F3
Church La. H Wyc 161 D1
Church La. Hol G 162 B2
Church La. Hor-c-S 108 A3
Church La. Lac G 149 F2
Church La. Lud 96 B4
Church La. M Keyn 34 A1
Church La. Maid 203 E2
Church La. Mars 104 C1
Church La. Mur 67 E3
Church La. N Pag 22 B4
Church La. Oving 86 B4
Church La. P Ris 139 D2
Church La. Pad 53 E1
Church La. Pott 18 C2
Church La. S Bru 9 D4
Church La. S Gol 12 A4
Church La. S Hea 152 A4
Church La. Slough 206 B4
Church La. Soul 69 F1
Church La. Sto P 198 C1
Church La. Ting 51 D3
Church La. Uxb 201 D2
Church La. W Tur 116 C1
Church La. Wal A 161 F3
Church La. Wen 131 E2
Church La. Whad 45 D1
Church La. Whit 87 D3
Church La. Wick 31 D2
Church La. Wind 210 B3
Church Lees. M Keyn 21 E1
Church Passage. N Pag 22 B2
Church Path. Maid 203 E2
Church Path. Pres 151 E3
Church Path. Skch 158 B3
Church Rd. B Bkhl 48 B1
Church Rd. Brac 38 A4
Church Rd. Chin 147 E3
Church Rd. Chl 111 D2
Church Rd. Cook 195 D3
Church Rd. Far C 198 B1
Church Rd. Ick 123 F2
Church Rd. Iver H 200 B2
Church Rd. Ivin 105 F3
Church Rd. L Buzz 80 C3
Church Rd. L Gad 121 E4
Church Rd. La En 171 D2
Church Rd. Lewk 157 D4
Church Rd. Lit M 184 B3
Church Rd. Maid 203 D3
Church Rd. Old W 211 D1
Church Rd. Pit 105 F2
Church Rd. S Ham 69 E4
Church Rd. S Har 190 B4
Church Rd. Se Gr 176 B2
Church Rd. Sher 13 F1
Church Rd. Skch 158 B3
Church Rd. Slap 91 E3
Church Rd. Tha 125 F1
Church Rd. Tott 93 D3
Church Rd. Ty Gr 174 C4
Church Rd. Uxb 201 E1
Church Rd. W Dra 208 C2
Church Sq. H Wyc 173 D4
Church Sq. L Buzz 80 C3
Church St. Ame 165 D4
Church St. Asp G 49 F3
Church St. Ayl 115 E4
Church St. Bov 146 A2
Church St. Bri 110 A4
Church St. Buck 52 B4
Church St. Burn 197 E1
Church St. Ches 154 A4
Church St. Gawt 52 A2
Church St. H Wyc 173 D4
Church St. Hen-O-T 191 E1
Church St. L Hrwd 55 F1
Church St. M Gib 71 F2
Church St. M Keyn 33 E4
Church St. M Keyn 33 F4
Church St. M Keyn 47 F1
Church St. M Mor 41 F2
Church St. N Mar 76 A1
Church St. Oln 7 D2
Church St. P Ris 139 D2
Church St. Qntn 85 D3
Church St. S Hea 152 A4
Church St. Skch 158 C3
Church St. Slough 205 E2
Church St. Slough 205 F2
Church St. Twyf 62 B1
Church St. Win 89 D1
Church St. Wind 210 B3
Church St. Wing 79 F2
Church St. Wins 65 F2
Church View. Hal 117 E1
Church View. Lon M 104 A2
Church View. Stp Cl 63 F1
Church Views. Maid 202 C4
Church Walk. W Tur 116 C1
Church Way. E Clay 74 C4
Church Wlk. M Keyn 57 F4
Church Wlk. N Craw 24 A3
Church Yard. Tri 119 D2
Churchfield Mews.
Slough 206 A4
Churchfield Rd. Ger C 177 E1
Churchill Ave. Ayl 115 E3
Churchill Cl. Fla H 185 D4
Churchill Dr. Beac 175 E3
Churchill Dr. Mar 183 F2
Churchill Rd. Slough 206 C1
Churchmere Wlk. Ayl 115 E3
Churchside. Hol G 163 E4
Churchway. Hadd 127 D4
Cinnamon Gr. Walt 48 A3
Cippenham Cl. Slough 204 C3
Cippenham La. Slough 205 D3
City Rd. Bled R 159 E3
Clailey Ct. M Keyn 32 C3
Clammas Way. Uxb 208 B4
Clapham Pl. M Keyn 34 B1
Clappers Meadow. Maid 196 B1
Clappins La. Wal A 161 E4
Clapton App. Woo G 185 E4
Clare Rd. Pres 151 E3
Clare Dr. Far C 198 A4
Clare Park. Ame 165 F4
Clare Rd. Maid 202 B3
Clare Rd. Slough 204 B4
Clare Rd. Stan 213 F1
Clarefield Dr. Maid 195 D1
Claremont Ave. M Keyn 32 C2
Claremont Cl. Ayl 115 F3
Claremont Gdns. Mar 183 F1
Claremont Rd. Mar 183 F1
Claremont Rd. Wind 210 B3
Clarence Cres. Wind 210 B3
Clarence Rd. Berk 135 E2
Clarence Rd. Hen-O-T 191 E1
Clarence Rd. M Keyn 32 C3
Clarence Rd. Wind 210 A3
Clarendon Ct. Slough 206 A3
Clarendon Dr. M Keyn 33 F1
Clarendon Dr. Tha 126 A1
Clarendon Rd. H Wyc 173 F3
Clarendon Rd. Pres 151 D3
Claridge Dr. M K Vil 36 A1
Clarke Ct. Ayl 101 F1
Clarke Dr. H Wyc 174 A3
Clarke Rd. M Keyn 47 E2
Clarke's Spring. Tri 119 F3
Clarkes Dr. W Dra 208 C4
Clarkes Field Cl. Bri 110 A4
Classon Cl. W Dra 208 C2
Clauds Cl. Hol G 163 D3
Claverton Cl. Bov 146 A2
Clay Acre. Ches 144 B1
Clay Cl. Fla H 185 D4
Clay Hall La. Wind 210 C1
Clay Hill. M Keyn 33 F1
Clay La. Mar B 172 A1
Clay La. Wen 131 E3
Clay St. Cole 175 E4
Claydon Cl. Ayl 115 E3
Claydon Ct. H Wyc 172 C2
Claydon End. Ger C 188 C4
Claydon La. Ger C 188 C4
Claydon Path. Ayl 115 F2
Clayfield Rd. Hal 131 E4
Clayfields. Ty Gr 163 E1
Clayhill. Mar B 172 A1
Claymoor Park. Mar B 172 A1
Clays The. Hadd 127 D4
Clayton Gate. M Keyn 35 D4
Clayton Way. Uxb 201 E1
Clayton Wlk. L Chal 166 B4
Claytons Meadow. Bou E 185 D2
Clearbrook Cl. Loud 174 A2
Cleavers Ave. M Keyn 34 C2
Cleavers. Chin 147 D3
Cleeve Cres. M Keyn 47 D1
Clegg Sq. She B E 46 A3
Cleland Rd. Ger C 177 E1
Clementi Ave. Hol G 163 E4
Clements Cl. Slough 206 A2
Clements La. M Gib 71 F1
Clements Pl. Tri 119 D2
Clements Rd. Chor 167 E2
Clements Rd. Hen-O-T 191 E2
Clerkenwell Pl. M Keyn 35 D2
Cleve Ct. Wind 209 F2
Clevehurst Cl. Sto P 199 D3
Cleveland Cl. Maid 203 D3
Cleveland Dr. L Buzz 80 B4
Cleveland Park.Ayl 101 F2
Cleveland Rd. Ayl 101 F2
Cleveland Rd. Uxb 201 E1
Cleveland. M Keyn 34 A3
Clewer Ave. Wind 210 A3
Clewer Ct Rd. Wind 210 A4
Clewer Fields. Wind 210 B3
Clewer Hill Rd. Wind 209 F2
Clewer New Town. Wind 210 A3
Clewer Park. Wind 210 A4
Clifden Rd. Worm 123 E3
Clifford Ave. M Keyn 58 B4
Clifford Rd. P Ris 139 D2
Clifford Way. Bou E 185 D3
Clifton Cl. Maid 203 D2
Clifton Green. Ayl 101 D1
Clifton Lawnes. Ame 154 B2
Clifton Rd. Ame 154 B2
Clifton Rd. New B 7 F2
Clifton Rd. Slough 206 A2
Clifton Rise. Wind 209 E3
Clinkard Cl. La En 171 D2
Clinton Cres. Ayl 116 A4
Clive Ct. Slough 205 E2
Cliveden Mead. Maid 196 B1
Cliveden Rd. Tapl 196 C2
Clivemont Rd. Maid 202 C4
Cloister Garth. Berk 135 E2
Cloisters The. H Wyc 162 B1
Clonmel Way. Burn 197 D1
Close The. Ash 97 F1
Close The. Bier 102 A2
Close The. Bou E 185 D3
Close The. Burn 204 B3
Close The. G Hrwd 55 D2
Close The. Iver H 200 B1
Close The. M Keyn 34 A2
Close The. M Keyn 47 E4
Close The. Oln 6 A1
Close The. Uxb 201 F3
Close The. Whit 87 D2
Closes The. Hadd 127 D4
Cloudberry. Walt 48 A3
Cloutsham Cl. M Keyn 46 B2
Clover Cl. M Keyn 46 A4
Clover La. Ayl 115 F3
Clyde Pl. M Keyn 46 C1
Clydesdale Pl. M Keyn 34 C2
Coach Ride. Mar 183 E2
Coachmaker Ct. M Keyn 34 C3
Coat Wicks. Se Gr 176 B2
Coates La. H Wyc 162 A1
Coates Way. Wing 79 F2
Cobb Cl. Datch 211 E3
Cobb Hall. Nwtn L 57 E2
Cobb Rd. Berk 134 C2
Cobbetts Mount. Stp Cl 63 E1
Cobbetts Ride. Tri 118 C2
Cobblers Cl. Far C 198 A2
Cobblers Wick. Win 89 D2
Cobbs Gdn. Oln 6 C2
Cobden Cl. Uxb 201 E2
Coberley Cl. M Keyn 35 D3
Cochran Cl. She C E 45 F4
Cock La. H Wyc 174 A3
Cockett Rd. Slough 206 C2
Cockpit Cl. G Kin 151 F1
Cockpit Rd. G Kin 162 B4
Coddimoor La. Whad 56 B4
Codmore Wood Rd. Lat 155 E3
Coe Spur. Slough 205 D2
Coftards. Slough 206 B4
Cogan Ct. She C E 45 F4
Cogdells Cl. Char 143 D2
Cogdells La. Char 143 D2
Coggeshall Gr. M K Vil 48 B4
Coke's Farm La. L Chal 166 A3
Coke's La. Ame 166 A3
Coke's La. L Chal 166 A3
Colborne Rd. H Wyc 173 E4
Coldeaton La. She B E 46 A2
Coldmoorholme La.
Bou E 184 C2
Cole Rd. Ayl 115 E3
Coleheath Bottom. Lac G 150 B2
Colenorton Cres. Eton 204 C1
Coleridge Cl. M Keyn 58 A4
Coleridge Cl. N Pag 21 F2
Coleridge Cres. Stan 212 C3
Coleridge Way. W Dra 208 C1
Colesbourne Dr. M Keyn 35 D3
Coleshill La. Cole 164 B1
Coleshill Pl. M Keyn 34 B2
Colet Rd. Wen 131 E3

Coleville Rd. H Wyc 172 C3
Colgrain St. M Keyn 35 D2
Colham Ave. W Dra 208 C3
Colham Mill Rd. W Dra 208 B3
Colham Rd. Uxb 201 F1
Colin Way. Slough 205 D2
Colinswood Rd. Beac 187 D1
Colinswood Rd. Far C 187 D1
Colinswood Rd. Hedg 187 D1
College Ave. Maid 202 C4
College Ave. Slough 205 F2
College Cres. Oak 109 F2
College Cres. Wind 210 B3
College Glen. Maid 202 B4
College Rd. Ast C 117 E4
College Rd. Cran 24 C1
College Rd. Maid 202 C4
College Rd. Slough 204 C3
College Rise. Maid 202 B4
Colley Hill La. Hedg 187 F1
Colley Hill. M Keyn 34 A2
Colley Land. Chor 167 E3
Collier Cl. Maid 195 F1
Collings Walk. Pres 151 E3
Collingwood Cl. H Wyc 174 A3
Collins Wlk. N Pag 22 A2
Collum Green Rd. Far C 187 F1
Collum Green Rd. Sto P 187 F1
Collyer Rd. Skch 158 C2
Coln Cl. Maid 202 C4
Colnbrook By-Pass. Iver 212 B4
Colnbrook By-Pass. Slough 212 B4
Colndale Rd. Stan 212 C3
Colne Ave. W Dra 208 B2
Colne Bank. Hort 212 B2
Colne Orch. Iver 207 F3
Colne Rd. H Wyc 173 F4
Colne Reach. Stan 212 C1
Colne. M Keyn 47 E3
Colnedale Rd. Uxb 201 E4
Colonial Rd. Slough 206 A2
Colspie Croft. M Keyn 33 E2
Colston Bassett. M Keyn 46 B1
Coltman Ave. L Cre 125 E3
Colts Holm Rd. M Keyn 33 E4
Coltsfoot Pl. M Keyn 34 B2
Columbia Pl. M Keyn 35 D2
Columbine Rd. Hol G 162 C3
Combe Martin. M Keyn 46 B2
Combe Rise. H Wyc 172 A4
Combermere Cl. Wind 210 A3
Comfrey Cl. Walt 48 A3
Comfrey The. Ayl 101 F2
Common Field. Wigg 119 E1
Common Gate Rd. Chor 167 F2
Common La. Burn 186 B1
Common La. Eton 205 E1
Common La. M Keyn 34 A2
Common Rd. Chor 167 E3
Common Rd. Dag 107 F2
Common Rd. Dorn 204 B1
Common Rd. Eton 205 D1
Common Rd. Fla H 185 D4
Common Rd. G Kin 151 F1
Common Rd. Slough 207 D1
Common Side. H Wyc 161 F2
Common St. Rav 5 E1
Common The. Berk 135 F3
Common The. Chipf 156 C4
Common The. Fla H 185 D4
Common The. G Kin 151 E1
Common The. Hol G 163 E4
Common Wood. Far C 198 B4
Como Rd. Ayl 116 A4
Comp The. Eat B 92 C3
Compton Ct. Slough 204 C4
Compton Dr. Maid 202 A4
Compton Rd. Wen 131 E3
Concorde Cl. Uxb 201 F2
Concorde Way. Slough 205 E2
Concourse The. M Keyn 58 B4
Concra Park. Asp G 49 E2
Condor Cl. M Keyn 47 D4
Conegar Ct. Slough 205 F3
Conegra Rd. H Wyc 173 E4
Coneygere. Oln 7 D2
Congreve. M Keyn 47 E3
Conifer Rise. H Wyc 172 C3
Conigre. Chin 147 D3
Coningsby Cl. Maid 202 B2
Coningsby Rd. H Wyc 162 A1
Coniston Cres. Burn 204 B4
Coniston Green. Ayl 101 E2
Coniston Rd. L Buzz 80 B4
Coniston Way. M Keyn 58 B3
Connaught Cl. Maid 195 F1
Connaught Gdns. Berk 134 C4
Connaught Rd. Ayl 116 B4
Connaught Rd. Slough 206 A2
Conniburrow Bvd. M Keyn 34 C2
Conniston Cl. Mar 183 A1
Consort Way. Den G 189 F3
Constable Cl. M Keyn 34 C4
Constable Pl. Ayl 100 C1
Constable's Croft. U Arn 94 C4
Constantine Way. M Keyn 33 F3
Convent Rd. Wind 210 A3
Conway Cl. Ayl 115 F4
Conway Cl. Loud 174 B1
Conway Cl. M Keyn 57 F4
Conway Cres. M Keyn 57 F4
Conway Rd. Burn 204 A4
Cook Cl. Walt 48 A2
Cook's Meadow. Edle 92 C2
Cookerell Gr. She B E 46 B3
Cookfield Cl. Dun 93 F4
Cookham Dean Bm La. Cook 195 E4
Cookham Rd. Maid 195 F2
Cooks Cl. Ash 9 F4
Cooks La. Mur 67 F3
Coombe Ave. Wen 131 D2
Coombe Cl. S Man 116 B1
Coombe Dr. Dun 93 F4
Coombe Gdns. Berk 134 C3
Coombe Gdns. Hgh V 162 A3
Coombe La. Wal A 161 F3
Coombe Vale. Ger C 188 C2
Cooper Rd. Hen-O-T 191 E2
Cooper Ridge. C St P 177 F3
Cooper Way. Slough 205 D2
Cooper's Court Rd. Skch 158 B3
Cooper's Yd. Ayl 101 E1
Coopers Mews. M Keyn 34 C3
Coopers Row. Iver H 200 B1
Coots Cl. Buck 52 C4
Copeland Cl. Walt 48 B3
Copes Rd. G Kin 151 F1
Copes Shroves. Hol G 162 C3
Copmans Wick. Chor 167 E2
Copners Dr. Hol G 163 E3
Copners Way. Hol G 163 D3
Copper Beech Cl. Fel 146 C4
Copper Beech Cl. Wind 209 E3
Copperfields. Beac 175 F3
Copperfields. H Wyc 161 D1
Copperkins Gr. Ame 154 A2
Copperkins La. Ame 154 A2
Coppermill La. Map Cr 178 C2
Coppermill Rd. Hort 212 A1
Coppermill Rd. Wray 212 A1
Coppice Cl. Ayl 102 A1
Coppice Farm Rd. Ty Gr 163 E1
Coppice The. H Wyc 172 A2
Coppice The. W Dra 208 C4
Coppice Way. Ayl 102 A1
Coppidwell Dr. Ayl 116 A3
Coppin La. M Keyn 34 A2
Coppins Cl. Berk 134 C2
Coppins La. Iver 207 F4
Copse Cl. Mar 183 B1
Copse Cl. W Dra 208 B2
Copse Gate. Wins 66 A2
Copse La. Se Gr 176 C2
Copse The. Ame 154 B1
Copse The. Beac 175 E2
Copse Way. Ches 144 A2
Copse Wood. Iver H 200 B2
Copthall Cl. C St P 177 F2
Copthall Cnr. C St P 177 F2
Copthall La. C St P 177 F2
Copthorn Cl. Maid 202 A2
Copyground La. H Wyc 172 C4
Coral Cl. Eat B 92 C3
Coram Cl. Berk 135 E2
Corbet Ride. L Buzz 80 B4
Corbett Cl. M Keyn 35 E4
Cordwainer Ct. M Keyn 34 C3
Cordwallis Rd. Maid 202 C4
Cordwallis St. Maid 202 C4
Cores End Rd. Bou E 185 D2
Corfe Cl. Ayl 116 A3
Corfe Cres. M Keyn 57 F4
Corfe Gdns. Slough 205 D3
Corfe Pl. Maid 202 B4
Coriander Ct. Walt 48 A3
Corin Cl. M Keyn 58 B3
Corin Way. M Keyn 58 B3
Corn Hill. M Keyn 33 F1
Corn Market. H Wyc 173 D4
Cornbrook Rd. Ayl 115 E3
Cornbury Cres. M Keyn 35 D3
Corncrake. Ayl 101 F2
Cornel Cl. Ty Gr 163 D2
Cornelia Cl. M Keyn 58 B3
Cornerways. Lac G 150 B3
Cornfield Cl. Uxb 201 E2
Cornwall Ave. Slough 198 B1
Cornwall Cl. Eton 204 C1
Cornwall Cl. Maid 195 F1
Cornwall Gr. M Keyn 46 C1
Cornwall Rd. Uxb 201 E3
Cornwell Rd. Old W 211 D1
Coronation Cres. La En 171 E3
Coronation Ave. Slough 206 C4
Coronation Pl. Stp Cl 63 E1
Coronation Rd. Cran 25 D1
Coronation Rd. H Wyc 172 B2
Coronation Rd. M Keyn 32 C3
Coronation Villas. Ayl 115 F4
Corporation St. H Wyc 173 D4
Corrigan Cl. M Keyn 58 A4
Corsham Ct. M Keyn 33 F1
Cosgrove Rd. Old S 32 B4
Cotman Cl. M Keyn 33 D3
Cotswold Cl. L Buzz 80 B4
Cotswold Cl. Maid 203 D3
Cotswold Cl. Slough 205 E2
Cotswold Cl. Uxb 201 E2
Cotswold Green. Ayl 101 F1
Cotswold Way. H Wyc 172 C4
Cottage Grounds. Sto 114 B3
Cottage Park Rd. Hedg 187 E1
Cottesbrooke Cl. Stan 212 B3
Cottesloe Cl. Wing 79 F2
Cottesloe Ct. M Keyn 32 C3
Cottesloe Rd. Ayl 115 F3
Cottingham Gr. M Keyn 58 A4
Cottisford Cres. M Keyn 21 F1
Cottland Clay. Hadd 127 D4
Coulson Way. Burn 204 A4
Countisbury. M Keyn 46 B1
County Rd. Brac 38 A3
Cours La Ville Cl. Wins 65 F2
Court Cl. Ayl 115 F4
Court Cl. Holy 203 E1
Court Cl. P Ris 139 D2
Court Cnr. Oln 6 C2
Court Cres. Slough 205 E4
Court Dr. Maid 196 B2
Court Dr. Uxb 201 F2
Court La. Burn 197 E1
Court La. Dorn 204 A2
Court La. Iver 207 F3
Court Lawns. Ty Gr 163 E1
Court Rd. Cran 25 D1
Court Rd. Maid 196 B2
Court The. Sal 37 E2
Courtfield Dr. Maid 202 B3
Courtfield Gdns. Den 190 A1
Courthouse Cl. Wins 65 F3
Courthouse Rd. Maid 202 B4
Courtlands Ave. Slough 206 B1
Courtlands. Maid 202 C3
Cousins Cl. W Dra 208 C3
Coventon Rd. Ayl 101 E1
Coverdale Way. Slough 197 F1
Coverdale. M Keyn 34 B3
Covert Cl. Berk 134 B3
Covert Rd. Berk 134 B3
Cow La. Edle 92 C2
Cow La. Gawt 51 F2
Cow La. Tri 119 E2
Cowdray Cl. M Keyn 35 E2
Cowleaze. Chin 147 D3
Cowley Cl. Bier 102 A2
Cowley Cres. Uxb 208 B4
Cowley Mill Rd. Uxb 201 D2
Cowley Rd. Uxb 201 E2
Cowper Cl. N Pag 22 A2
Cowper Rd. Berk 135 D2
Cowper Rd. Ches 144 A1
Cowper Rd. Oln 6 C2
Cowper Rd. Slough 198 A1
Cowper St. Oln 7 D3
Cowpers Orch. W Und 6 A1
Cowslip Cl. Uxb 201 F3
Cowslip Rd. Hol G 162 C4
Cox Green La. Maid 202 B2
Cox Green Rd. Maid 202 B2
Coxborrow Cl. Cook 195 F4
Coxwell Cl. Buck 41 F1
Crab Tree Cl. Beac 175 D1
Crab Tree Cl. Oln 6 C3
Crabbe Cres. Ches 144 D1
Crabtree Rd. Hadd 127 D3
Craddocks Cl. M Keyn 34 A2
Cradley Wlk. Ayl 101 F2
Craigmore Ave. M Keyn 57 F4
Craigwell Ave. Ayl 116 B4
Cranberry Cl. Walt 48 A3
Cranbourne Ave. Wind 209 F3
Cranbourne Cl. Slough 205 E3
Cranbourne Rd. Slough 205 E3
Cranbrook Dr. Maid 195 E1
Crane Way. Cran 25 E1
Cranes Cl. Turv 8 C3
Cranesbill Pl. M Keyn 34 C2
Cranfield Rd. Ast 16 A1
Cranfield Rd. Cran 25 F2
Cranfield Rd. Moul 36 C4
Cranfield Rd. Sal 37 E3
Cranfield Rd. Wave 49 D4
Craufurd Rise. Maid 202 C4
Craven The. M Keyn 34 B2
Crawley Rd. Cran 25 D2
Crawley Rd. Hth 60 C4
Crawley's La. Wigg 133 F4
Crayle St. Slough 198 A1
Creed St. M Keyn 33 E4
Creighton Rd. W Und 83 F1
Crendon Rd. Chea 112 A1
Crendon St. H Wyc 173 D3
Crescent Dr. Maid 202 C4
Crescent The. Cran 24 C1
Crescent The. H Wyc 173 F4
Crescent The. Have 20 C1
Crescent The. M Keyn 21 F1
Crescent The. M Keyn 47 E1
Crescent The. Maid 202 C4
Crescent The. Mars 105 D1
Crescent The. P Ris 139 E2
Crescent The. Pit 105 E2
Crescent The. Slough 205 F2
Creslow Ct. M Keyn 32 C3
Cress Rd. Slough 205 D2
Cressex Rd. H Wyc 172 B2
Cressey Ave. She B E 46 A2
Cressington Pl. Bou E 185 D2
Cresswell Rd. Ches 154 B3
Cresswell Way. Hol G 163 E4
Cresswells Mead. Holy 203 E1
Crest Rd. Lit M 172 B2
Crest The. Bled R 159 F4
Creswick Meadow. Ayl 116 A3
Crew Curve. Berk 134 C4
Cricket Field Rd. Uxb 201 E2
Cricket Ground. Skch 158 B3
Cricketers Row. Wins 66 A2
Cricketfield Rd. W Dra 208 B1
Cricklebeck. M Keyn 34 A3
Crimp Hill. Old W 211 D1
Crisp Rd. Hen-O-T 191 E2
Crispin Cl. Beac 175 E2
Crispin Field. Pit 105 E2
Crispin Rd. M Keyn 34 A4
Crispin Way. Far C 198 B4
Crispin Way. H Wyc 173 D2
Criss Gr. Ger C 177 E1
Crocketts La. Lee C 142 B3
Crocus Dr. Ayl 115 D3
Croft Courtyard. Hadd 126 C3
Croft Green. Dun 93 F4
Croft Rd. Ayl 115 F4
Croft Rd. Ger C 177 F1
Croft The. Hadd 126 C3
Croft The. Maid 202 B3
Croft The. Mar 184 A2
Crofters. Old W 211 D1
Crofthill Rd. Slough 198 A1
Crofts End. Sher 14 A1
Crofts La. Nwtn L 57 F2
Croftwood. H Wyc 173 F4
Cromarty Ct. M Keyn 46 C2
Cromer Cl. L Gad 121 F2
Cromhamstone. Sto 114 B3
Cromwell Ave. Ayl 101 E1
Cromwell Ave. N Pag 22 A2
Cromwell Ave. Tha 126 A1
Cromwell Cl. C St G 177 E4
Cromwell Ct. Buck 41 F1
Cromwell Dr. Slough 205 F4
Cromwell Gdns. Mar 183 F1
Cromwell Rd. H Wyc 173 F3
Cromwell Rd. Maid 202 B4
Cromwell Rd. Mar 183 F1
Cropredy Ct. Buck 41 F1
Cropwell Bishop. M Keyn 46 B1
Crosby Cl. Beac 186 C4
Crosby Ct. She C E 45 F3
Crosland Rd. Ayl 116 A3
Cross End. Wave 48 C4
Cross La. Beac 186 C4
Cross La. Ting 51 D3
Cross La. W Und 6 A1
Cross Lanes Cl. C St P 177 F3
Cross Lanes. C St P 177 F3
Cross Meadow. Ches 143 F1
Cross Oak Rd. Berk 135 D2
Cross Oak. Wind 210 A3
Cross Rd. H Wyc 172 B3
Cross Rd. Uxb 201 E3
Cross St. N Pag 22 B2
Cross St. Uxb 201 E3
Cross Tree Rd. Wick 31 D2
Crossfield Cl. Berk 134 C2
Crossfield Rd. P Ris 139 D2
Crosshills. M Keyn 32 B2
Crosslands. M Keyn 34 C4
Crossley's Hill. C St G 177 E4
Crossleys. C St G 177 E4
Crossway The. Uxb 201 F2
Crossway. Ches 144 C1
Crossways. Beac 175 F1
Crossways. Berk 134 C2
Crosthwaite Way. Slough 204 B4
Crow La. Wave 49 D4
Crow Piece La. Burn 197 F2
Crowborough La. M K Vil 48 A4
Crowbrook Rd. P Ris 139 E3
Crown La. Burn 198 A2
Crown La. H Wyc 173 D3
Crown La. Maid 203 D4
Crown La. Ty Gr 174 C4
Crown Meadow. Iver 212 A4
Crown Rd. Mar 183 E1
Crown Way. W Dra 208 C3
Crown Wlk. M Keyn 34 C2
Crowther Ct. She B E 46 B3
Croxley Rise. Maid 202 B3
Cruickshank Gr. She C E 45 F4
Crummock Cl. Slough 204 B4
Crummock Pl. M Keyn 58 B3
Crutches La. Se Gr 176 C2
Cryers Hill La. G Kin 162 B3
Cubb Field. Ayl 115 D4
Cublington Rd. A Abb 88 B3
Cuddington Hill. Cudd 112 C2
Cuddington Rd. Dint 113 F2
Cuff La. G Bkhl 59 E1
Culbertson La. M Keyn 33 F3
Culham Dr. Maid 195 F1
Cullen Pl. M Keyn 58 B3
Cullern's Pass. Maid 202 C3
Culley Way. Maid 202 A2
Cullyn Rd. H Wyc 172 B2
Culmstock Cl. M Keyn 46 B1
Culrain Pl. M Keyn 33 E2
Culvers Croft. Se Gr 176 B2
Culvert La. Uxb 201 D2
Culverton Hill. P Ris 139 D2
Culverton La. P Ris 139 D1
Cumberland Ave. Slough 198 B1
Cumberland Cl. Ayl 116 A4
Cumberland Cl. L Chal 166 A4
Cumbria Cl. M Keyn 46 C1
Cumbria Cl. Maid 202 B2
Cumbrian Way. H Wyc 172 C4
Cumbrian Way. Uxb 201 E3
Curlew Cl. Berk 135 E2
Curlew Cl. H Wyc 161 E1
Curlew. Ayl 101 F2
Curls La. Maid 202 C2
Curls Rd. Maid 202 B2
Curran Cl. Uxb 201 E1
Currier Dr. M Keyn 34 C3
Curriers La. Burn 197 E4
Curtis Way. Berk 135 E2
Curzon Ave. Beac 175 E2
Curzon Ave. Ty Gr 163 E1
Curzon Cl. Ty Gr 163 E1
Cutlers Mews. M Keyn 34 C3
Cuttlebrook Gdns. Tha 125 E1
Cypress Wlk. Ty Gr 163 D2
Cypress. N Pag 22 A2

D'ville Ct. She C E 46 A3
Dacre Rd. Hal 131 F4
Dadbrook Cl. Cudd 112 C1
Dadbrook. Cudd 112 C1
Dadfield Cl. Cudd 112 C1
Dag Lane. S Gol 12 A4
Dagmar Rd. Wind 210 B3
Dagnall Cres. Uxb 208 B4
Dagnall Rd. Eat B 93 E1
Dagnall Rd. Oln 6 C2
Dairy La. Hamb 192 A4
Dale Cl. Brac 38 A4
Dale Ct. Slough 205 E2
Dale Side. Ger C 188 C1
Dalesford Rd. Ayl 116 A2
Dalgin Pl. M Keyn 35 D2
Dalston Cl. Ayl 101 F1
Dalvina Pl. M Keyn 33 E2
Daly Way. Ayl 116 A4
Dancers End La. Dra B 118 B1
Dandridge Cl. Slough 206 B1
Dandridge Dr. Bou E 185 E2
Dane Cl. Ame 165 F3
Dane Ct. Ayl 115 E2
Dane Rd. M Keyn 47 F1
Daniels Welch. M Keyn 47 D3
Danstead Way. She C E 45 E4
Dansteed Way. M Keyn 34 B2
Danvers Croft. Tri 119 E3
Darin Ct. She C E 45 F4
Dark La. Chea 112 A1
Dark La. Oving 86 B4
Dark La. Win 89 E1
Darley Cl. Ayl 116 A3
Darley Gate. M Keyn 35 D3
Darley's Cl. Gr Und 83 D3
Darling's La. Bish 194 C1
Darlington Cl. Ame 154 B1
Darnel Cl. M Keyn 47 D3
Darr's La. Berk 134 B3
Darrell Cl. Slough 206 C1
Dart Cl. Ayl 115 E3
Dart Cl. N Pag 22 B2
Dart Cl. Slough 212 A4
Dartmouth Rd. Oln 6 C2
Darvell Dr. Ches 144 A1
Darvill Rd. Sto 114 A3
Darvill's La. Slough 205 E2
Darvills Meadow. Hol G 163 E4
Darwin Rd. Slough 206 C2
Dashfield Gr. Hol G 162 C3
Dashwood Ave. H Wyc 172 B4
Dashwood Cl. Slough 206 B1
Datchet Pl. Datch 211 D3
Datchet Rd. Datch 205 F1
Datchet Rd. Eton 205 F1
Datchet Rd. Hort 211 F2
Datchet Rd. Old W 211 D2
Datchet Rd. Wind 210 B4
Daubeney Gate. She C E 45 F3
Daventry Cl. Stan 212 C3
David Cl. Ayl 116 A2
David Rd. Stan 212 C3
Davies Cl. Ayl 115 E4
Davies Ct. H Wyc 172 B3
Davis Cl. Mar 183 F1
Davy Ave. M Keyn 46 B3
Dawes Cl. Ches 154 A4
Dawes East Rd. Burn 197 E1
Dawes La. Sar 156 C2
Dawes Moor Cl. Slough 206 B4
Dawley Ride. Stan 212 C3
Dawn Redwood Cl. Hort 212 A2

Daws Hill La. H Wyc 173 D2
Daws Lea. H Wyc 173 D2
Dawson Cl. Wind 210 A3
Dawson Rd. M Keyn 47 E2
Daylesford Ct. M Keyn 35 D3
De Clare Ct. Buck 41 F1
De Havilland Way. Stan 213 F1
Deacon Cl. H Wyc 172 A2
Deadhearn La. C St G 166 C1
Deal Ave. Slough 204 C4
Dean Cl. Ayl 116 A3
Dean Cl. H Wyc 172 C3
Dean Cl. Uxb 201 F3
Dean Cl. Wind 209 E2
Dean Farm La. Soul 69 F2
Dean Field. Bov 146 A2
Dean La. Cook 195 E4
Dean Rd. Stew 68 A1
Dean St. Mar 183 E1
Dean The. Win 89 D2
Dean Way. C St G 177 D4
Dean Wood Rd. Se Gr 176 B1
Dean's Rd. M Keyn 33 E4
Deanacre Cl. C St P 177 F2
Deancroft Rd. C St P 177 F2
Deanfield Ave. Hen-O-T 191 E1
Deanfield Cl. Bled R 149 E1
Deanfield Cl. Mar 183 E2
Deanfield Rd. Hen-O-T 191 E1
Deangarden Rise. H Wyc 173 F2
Deans Cl. Ame 154 C1
Deans Cl. Sto P 199 D2
Deans Cl. Tri 119 D2
Deans Furlong. Tri 119 D2
Deans Meadow. Dag 107 E3
Deanshanger Rd. Old S 32 A3
Deanshanger Rd. Wick 31 D2
Deansway. Ches 144 A1
Dearing Cl. Ayl 101 F1
Deben Cl. N Pag 22 C2
Decies Way. Sto P 199 D2
Dedmere Ct. Mar 183 F1
Dedmere Rd. Mar 183 F1
Dedmere Rise. Mar 183 F1
Dedworth Dr. Wind 209 F3
Dedworth Rd. Wind 209 E3
Deena Cl. Slough 204 C3
Deep Acres. Ame 154 A2
Deep Field. Datch 211 D4
Deep Mill La. L Kin 152 B2
Deepdale. M Keyn 34 B3
Deerfern Cl. M Keyn 21 F1
Deerfield Cl. Buck 52 C4
Deermead. L Kin 152 A2
Deerswood. Maid 196 A1
Deethe Cl. Wbn S 49 D3
Delaford Cl. Iver 207 F4
Delahay Rise. Berk 135 D3
Delamere Cl. Ayl 101 F1
Delamere Gdns. L Buzz 80 B4
Delaware Dr. M Keyn 35 D4
Dell Cl. Far C 198 B4
Dell Field. Pres 151 E3
Dell Lees. Se Gr 176 B2
Dell Rd. Berk 134 B4
Dell Rd. W Dra 208 C2
Dell The. Ayl 102 A1
Dell The. C St P 177 F2
Dell The. Maid 202 A1
Dell The. Ty Gr 163 E1
Dellfield Ave. Berk 135 D3
Dellfield Cl. Berk 135 D3
Dellfield Cres. Uxb 201 E1
Dellfield. Ches 144 A1
Dells. Oln 6 C2
Dellside. S Har 190 B3
Delmeade Rd. Ches 154 A4
Deltic Ave. M Keyn 34 A1
Demoram Cl. Wins 65 F2
Denbigh Hall Dr. M Keyn 46 C2
Denbigh Hall. M Keyn 46 C2
Denbigh Rd. M Keyn 47 D1
Denbigh Rd. Tha 126 A1
Denbigh Way. M Keyn 47 E1
Denborough Cres. Maid 202 B3
Denby Walk. Ayl 116 A4
Denchworth Ct. She B E 46 B1
Dene Cl. Asp G 49 E2
Dene Cl. Wins 66 A2
Dene The. Stp Cl 63 E2
Denewood. H Wyc 173 F4
Denham Ave. Den G 189 F2
Denham Cl. Den 190 A1
Denham Cl. M Keyn 57 E4
Denham Cl. Maid 202 B3
Denham Green Cl. Den G 190 A2
Denham Green La. Den G 189 F3
Denham La. C St P 178 A1
Denham Rd. Iver H 200 C3
Denham Rd. La En 171 E3
Denham View. Gran 75 F3
Denham Way. Den 190 A1
Denham Way. Map Cr 178 C2
Denham Wlk. C St P 177 F2
Denmark St. H Wyc 173 D4
Denmark St. M Keyn 58 C4
Denmark St. Maid 202 C4
Denmead Cl. Ger C 188 C2
Denmead. M Keyn 33 F1
Dennis Way. Slough 204 B3
Denny Rd. Slough 206 C1
Depot Rd. Maid 203 D3
Derby Rd. Uxb 201 E2
Dere Pl. M Keyn 58 C2
Derehams Ave. Loud 174 B2
Derehams La. Loud 174 B2
Derek Rd. Maid 203 E4
Deri Dene Cl. Stan 213 F1
Derwent Cl. N Pag 22 B2
Derwent Dr. Burn 204 B4
Derwent Dr. M Keyn 57 F4
Derwent Dr. Maid 202 B4
Derwent Rd. L Buzz 80 A4
Desborough Ave. H Wyc 172 C3
Desborough Green. Ayl 101 E1
Desborough Ind Pk.
H Wyc 172 C4
Desborough Park Rd.
H Wyc 172 C4
Desborough Rd. H Wyc 172 C4
Desborough St. H Wyc 172 C4
Deseronto Wharf. Slough 206 C2
Develin Cl. M Keyn 34 C4
Devereux Pl. Ayl 101 D1
Devereux Rd. Wind 210 B3
Deverill Rd. S Man 115 E2
Devon Ave. Slough 205 E4
Devon Cl. M Keyn 46 C1
Devon Way. Uxb 201 F2
Devonshire Ave. Ame 154 A1
Devonshire Cl. Ame 154 B1
Devonshire Cl. Far C 198 A2
Devonshire Green. Far C 198 A2
Dexter Ave. M Keyn 46 C4
Dhoon Rise. Maid 202 C3
Diamond Rd. Slough 206 A2
Diana Cl. Slough 206 C4
Dickens Rd. M Keyn 33 E4
Dickens Way. Ayl 100 C1
Dicks Way. Ayl 100 C2
Diddington Cl. M Keyn 58 B2
Dingle Dell. L Buzz 70 C1
Dingledery. Oln 6 C2
Dinmore. Bov 145 F2
Disraeli Cres. H Wyc 161 F1
Disraeli Ct. Slough 212 A4
Disraeli Park. Beac 175 E2
Ditchingham Cl. Ayl 115 D4
Ditton Park Rd. Datch 211 F4
Ditton Rd. Datch 211 E3
Ditton Rd. Slough 211 F4
Dixie La. Walt 48 B3
Dobbins La. Wen 131 D3
Dobson's La. Faw 191 E4
Doctors' Common Rd.
Berk 135 D2
Dodkin. M Keyn 47 D3
Dodsfield Rd. Slough 198 A1
Dog Kennel La. Chor 167 F3
Doggett St. L Buzz 80 C4
Doggetts Farm Rd.
Den G 189 E2
Doggetts Wood Cl.
L Chal 166 B3
Doggetts Wood La.
L Chal 166 B3
Dolben Ct. M Keyn 35 E4
Dolesden La. Ibst 169 E1
Dollicot. Hadd 126 C4
Dolphin Ct. Slough 206 A2
Dolphin Rd. Slough 206 A2
Dolphin Sq. Tri 119 D2
Don The. M Keyn 46 B1
Donnay Cl. Ger C 188 B3
Donnington. M Keyn 34 A3
Doon Way. M Keyn 58 B3
Dorchester Cl. S Man 116 A1
Dorchester Ave. M Keyn 47 D1
Dorchester Cl. Maid 195 D1
Doreen Cl. M Keyn 58 B4
Dormans Cl. M K Vil 36 A1
Dormer Ave. Wing 79 F2
Dormer Cl. Ayl 115 D3
Dormer Ct. Ayl 101 F1
Dormer La. Hol G 163 D4
Dornels. Slough 206 B4
Dorney End. Ches 144 A1
Dorney Hill S. Hedg 187 D2
Dorney Pl. M Keyn 34 B2
Dorney Reach Rd. Dorn 203 F2
Dorney Wood Rd. Burn 197 E3
Dorrells Rd. Lgwk 138 B3
Dorrien's Croft. Berk 134 C4
Dorset Cl. Berk 134 C3
Dorset Cl. M Keyn 46 C1
Dorset Pl. Ayl 116 B3
Dorset Rd. Wind 210 B3
Dorset Way. Uxb 201 F2
Dorton Cl. M Keyn 33 F1
Douglas Ct. Mar 184 A2
Douglas Gdns. Berk 135 D3
Douglas La. Wray 211 F1
Douglas Pl. M Keyn 46 C4
Douglas Rd. Ayl 102 A1
Douglas Rd. Slough 205 E4
Douglas Rd. Stan 213 E1
Dove Acre. Ayl 101 F2
Dove Cl. Ayl 115 E3
Dove Cl. Buck 52 C4
Dove Cl. N Pag 22 B2
Dove House Cl. Edle 92 C2
Dove House Cl. Wins 66 A2
Dove House Cres.
Slough 197 F1
Dove Park. Chor 167 D2
Dove St. Stew 78 C4
Dovecot Rd. H Wyc 173 D4
Dovecote Cl. Hadd 126 C3
Dovecote Cl. P Ris 139 E3
Dovecote. Hadd 126 C3
Dovecote. N Pag 22 B2
Dovehouse Ct. Dean 31 F2
Doveleat. Chin 147 E4
Dover Gate. M Keyn 57 F4
Dover Hedge. Ayl 116 B4
Dover Rd. Slough 204 C4
Dower Cl. Beac 175 E3
Dower Park. Wind 209 F2
Down Pl. Oak G 209 D4
Downdean. M Keyn 47 D4
Downer Cl. Buck 52 C4
Downham Rd. Wbn S 49 E2
Downing Path. Burn 197 F1
Downings Wood. Map Cr 178 B3
Downland. M Keyn 33 F1
Downley Ave. M Keyn 34 B2
Downley Rd. Wal A 161 E3
Downs Park. H Wyc 161 F1
Downs Rd. Slough 206 B2
Downs View. B Bkhl 48 B1
Drake Ave. Slough 206 B1
Drake's Rd. Ame 165 F4
Drakeloe Cl. Hth 60 C4
Drakes Mews. She C E 45 F4
Drakewell Rd. B Bkhl 48 B1
Drayton Gdns. W Dra 208 C2
Drayton Rd. Ayl 101 E1
Drayton Rd. M Keyn 58 B3
Drayton Rd. Nwtn L 57 E1
Dresser Rd. Pres 151 E3
Drew Meadow. Far C 198 B4
Drews Park. Beac 175 E3
Drey The. C St P 177 F3
Drift Rd. Oak G 209 D1
Drift Way. Iver 212 B4
Drive The. Ame 154 B1
Drive The. Bou E 184 C2
Drive The. C St P 177 F2
Drive The. Cran 24 B1
Drive The. Datch 211 D3
Drive The. Ick 190 C1
Drive The. Slough 206 C2
Drive The. Wray 211 E1
Dropmore Rd. Burn 197 E3
Drovers Croft. M Keyn 33 D2
Drovers La. Ibst 169 D1
Drovers Way. Dun 93 F4
Drovers Way. Se Gr 176 B2
Druids Wlk. Chin 147 E3
Drummond Ride. Tri 119 D3
Drummond Way. M Keyn 35 E4
Drydell La. Ches 153 F4
Dryden Cl. Ayl 101 F1
Dryden Cl. N Pag 22 A2
Du Pre Wlk. Bou E 185 E2
Duchess Gr. M K Vil 48 B4
Duck End. G Bkhl 59 E1
Duck La. Hth 60 C4
Duck La. Lud 96 B4
Duck Sq. Chin 147 E3
Duckmore La. Tri 118 C1
Dudley Hill. She C E 46 A3
Dudley La. Frie 181 D3
Dudswell La. Berk 134 B4
Duffield La. Sto P 198 C3
Duffield Park. Sto P 199 D1
Duke St. Asp G 49 E2
Duke St. Eton 210 B4
Duke St. H Wyc 173 E3
Duke St. Hen-O-T 191 F1
Duke St. P Ris 139 D2
Dukes Cl. Ger C 188 B2
Dukes Cl. Shab 124 B1
Dukes Dr. M Keyn 47 E1
Dukes La. Ger C 188 C2
Dukes Piece. Buck 52 C4
Dukes Pl. Mar 183 E1
Dukes Ride. Ger C 188 C2
Dukes Ride. L Buzz 70 C2
Dukes Way. Berk 135 D3
Dukes Wood Ave. Ger C 188 C2
Dukes Wood Dr. Ger C 188 B2
Dulverton Dr. She B E 46 B2
Dulwich Cl. N Pag 22 B1
Dumfries Cl. M Keyn 46 C2
Dunbar Cl. M Keyn 57 E4
Dunbar Cl. Slough 206 A3
Dunbar Dr. Tha 126 A1
Duncan Gr. She C E 45 F3
Duncan Rd. Cran 24 C1
Duncannon Cres. Wind 209 E2
Dunchurch Dale. Walt 48 A3
Duncombe Cl. Ame 154 C1
Duncombe Rd. Berk 134 C3
Duncombe St. M Keyn 58 B4
Duncroft. Wind 209 F2
Dundale Rd. Tri 119 D2
Dundee Rd. Slough 205 D4
Dungrovehill La. Bish 194 B2
Dunholme End. Maid 202 B2
Dunkery Beacon. M Keyn 46 B2
Dunny La. Chipf 156 C4
Dunsby Rd. M Keyn 47 D2
Dunsham La. Ayl 101 F1
Dunsley Pl. Tri 119 D2
Dunsmore Ave. P Ris 139 E3
Dunsmore Ride. P Ris 139 E3
Dunstable Rd. Dag 107 E4
Dunstable Rd. Eat B 93 D3
Dunstable Rd. Tott 93 E4
Dunster Ct. M Keyn 46 C2
Dunster Gdns. Slough 205 D3
Dunston Hill. Tri 119 D2
Dunton Rd. Stew 78 B3
Dunvedin Pl. M Keyn 33 E2
Dunvegan Cl. M Keyn 58 B2
Duparc Cl. Walt 48 B3
Dupre Cres. Beac 176 A1
Durgate. M K Vil 48 A4
Durham Ave. Slough 205 D4
Durrans Ct. M Keyn 47 F1
Durrants La. Berk 134 C3
Durrants Path. Ches 144 A2
Durrants Rd. Berk 134 C3
Durrell Cl. L Buzz 80 C4
Dutch Barn Cl. Stan 213 E1
Dutton Way. Iver 207 F4
Dyers Mews. M Keyn 34 C3
Dyersdale. M Keyn 34 B3
Dyson Cl. Wind 210 A2

Eagle Wlk. M Keyn 34 C2
Eagles Rd. Ayl 116 A4
Eames Cl. Ayl 101 F2
Earl Cl. H Wyc 162 A1
Earl Howe Rd. Hol G 163 E3
Earls Cl. M Keyn 58 B4
Earls Willow. M Keyn 34 A4
Earlsfield. Holy 203 E1
Earlswood Cl. Ayl 116 A3
Easington La. Chil 111 D1
East Burnham La. Burn 198 A2
East Common. Ger C 188 C3
East Cres. Wind 209 F3
East Dales. M Keyn 34 B3
East Dr. H Wyc 173 F4
East Dr. Sto P 198 C1
East Hills. Cran 25 D1
East Paddock. Bish 194 C3
East Rd. Cran 24 C1
East Rd. Maid 202 C4
East Rd. W Dra 208 C1
East Ridge. Bou E 185 D2
East St. Adsk 53 F1
East St. Ches 154 A4
East St. Oln 6 C2
East Way. Beac 175 D1
Eastbourne Rd. Slough 205 D4
Eastbridge. Slough 206 A3
Eastbrook Cl. Pidd (B) 95 F4
Eastbury Ct. M Keyn 46 B1
Eastcote Rd. Ayl 116 A2
Eastcourt Dr. Hol G 162 C3
Eastcroft. Slough 198 A1
Eastergate. Beac 175 E2
Eastern Dene. Hol G 163 D3
Eastern Dr. Bou E 185 E2
Eastern St. Ayl 101 F1
Eastfield Cl. Slough 206 A2
Eastfield Cres. Yard G 18 C3
Eastfield Dr. Hans 11 D2
Eastfield Rd. Ayl 116 A4
Eastfield Rd. Burn 204 A4
Eastfield Rd. P Ris 139 E2
Eastlands. Lac G 149 F3
Eastnor. Bov 146 A2
Easton St. H Wyc 173 D3
Easton Terr. H Wyc 173 E3
Eastwick Cres. Chor 178 C4
Eastwood Rd. Skch 158 C2
Eaton Ave. H Wyc 172 B4
Eaton Ave. M Keyn 58 B4
Eaton Bray Rd. Edle 92 B3
Eaton Bray Rd. Tott 92 C4
Eaton Park. Eat B 92 C3
Eaton Rd. Ayl 115 E4
Ebble Cl. Ayl 115 E2
Ebsworth Cl. Maid 196 B2
Eddington Ct. M Keyn 46 B1
Eddy St. Berk 135 D3
Eden Cl. S Man 115 E2
Eden Cl. Slough 207 D1
Eden Wlk. M Keyn 46 C1
Edgar Rd. W Dra 208 C3
Edge Hill Ct. Buck 41 F1
Edgecombe Rd. Ayl 116 A3
Edgecote. M Keyn 46 A4
Edgehill. Tha 125 F1
Edgewood. H Wyc 173 E3
Edinburgh Ave. Slough 205 D4
Edinburgh Dr. Den G 189 F3
Edinburgh Rd. Maid 195 F1
Edinburgh Rd. Mar 183 F2
Edison Sq. She B E 46 B3
Edith Rd. Maid 202 A4
Edlyn Cl. Berk 134 C3
Edmonds Cl. Buck 41 F1
Edmonds Rd. La En 171 D2
Edmund Ct. She C E 45 F4
Edmunds Cl. H Wyc 172 B3
Edmunds Gdns. H Wyc 172 B3
Edmunds Way. Slough 206 A4
Edrich Ave. M Keyn 46 C4
Edward Cl. Ayl 116 A2
Edward Walk. Ayl 116 A2
Edwards Ct. Slough 205 F2
Edwin Cl. B Bkhl 48 B1
Edy Ct. M Keyn 34 A1
Eelbrook Ave. M Keyn 34 B1
Eeles Cl. Ayl 100 C2
Egerton Cl. Brac 38 A4
Egerton Gate. She B E 46 A2
Egerton Rd. Berk 135 D3
Egerton Rd. Slough 197 F1
Eghams Cl. Beac 175 E2
Eghams Wood Rd. Beac 175 E2
Egmont Ave. M Keyn 32 C3
Egremont Gdns. Slough 205 D3
Egypt La. Burn 187 D1
Eight Acres. Burn 197 D1
Eight Acres. Tri 119 D2
Elbow Meadow. Stan 212 C3
Elder Cl. Loud 174 A2
Elder Gate. M Keyn 34 B1
Elder Way. Ty Gr 163 D2
Elderdene. Chin 147 E4
Elderfield Rd. Sto P 198 C3
Eleanor Cl. Hth 60 C4
Eleanor Gdns. Ayl 115 F3
Eleanor Rd. Ger C 177 E1
Eleanor Wlk. Hth 60 C4
Elfords. M Keyn 47 D3
Elgar Gr. Walt 48 B2
Elgiva La. Ches 154 A4
Elham Way. Ayl 116 A2
Eliot Cl. Ayl 100 C1
Eliot Cl. N Pag 21 F3
Elizabeth Cl. Ayl 116 A2
Elizabeth Dr. Tri 119 D3
Elizabeth Rd. Mar 183 F2
Elizabeth Rd. Skch 158 C2
Elizabeth Way. Sto P 198 C2
Elkins Rd. Hedg 187 F1
Ellen Pl. Ayl 115 E3
Ellen Rd. Ayl 115 E3
Ellenstow. M Keyn 34 A2
Ellerburn Pl. She B E 46 A2
Ellery Rise. Frie 170 C1
Ellesborough Rd. Wen 131 D2
Ellesmere Cl. Tott 93 E3
Ellesmere Rd. Berk 135 E2
Elliman Ave. Slough 205 F3
Ellington Ct. Tapl 203 E4
Ellington Gdns. Tapl 203 E4
Ellington Park. Maid 195 F1
Ellington Rd. Tapl 203 E4
Elliot Dr. Mar 183 F2
Ellis Ave. C St P 177 F1
Ellis Ave. Slough 205 F2
Ellisgill Ct. M Keyn 34 A2
Ellison Cl. Wind 209 F2
Ellsworth Rd. H Wyc 172 C2
Ellwood Rd. Beac 175 D1
Ellwood Rise. C St G 177 E4
Elm Brook Cl. Chea 112 B1
Elm Cl. Ame 154 B1
Elm Cl. Chin 147 E3
Elm Cl. Elle 130 B2
Elm Cl. Far C 198 B3
Elm Cl. Nwtn L 57 E1
Elm Cl. Ty Gr 163 D2
Elm Cl. W Tur 116 C1
Elm Croft. Datch 211 E3
Elm Dr. Chin 147 E3
Elm Dr. Dean 31 E3
Elm Farm Rd. Ayl 116 A3
Elm Gr. Berk 135 E2
Elm Gr. Maid 202 C4
Elm Gr. W Dra 208 C3
Elm Gr. Wbn S 49 D2
Elm Green. Ayl 115 E4
Elm La. Bou E 184 C3
Elm Lawn Cl. Uxb 201 F3
Elm Rd. H Wyc 172 B2
Elm Rd. Ty Gr 174 B4
Elm Rd. Wind 210 A2
Elm St. Buck 52 B4
Elm Tree Wlk. Tri 119 D3
Elm Trees. L Cre 125 D4
Elmar Green. Slough 198 A1
Elmdale Gdns. P Ris 139 D2
Elmers Cl. Beac 44 A3
Elmers Park. M Keyn 58 A4
Elmfields Gate. Wins 66 A2
Elmhurst Cl. M Keyn 46 C2
Elmhurst Rd. Ayl 101 F1
Elmhurst Rd. Slough 207 D2
Elmlea Dr. Oln 6 C2
Elms Dr. Bou E 185 E2
Elms Rd. C St P 177 F2

Elms The. M Keyn 57 F4
Elmshott Cl. Ty Gr 163 D1
Elmshott La. Slough 204 C3
Elmside. Wins 66 A2
Elmtree Green. S Hea 152 A4
Elmtree Hill. Ches 144 A1
Elmwood Cl. Oak 109 E3
Elmwood Park. Ger C 188 C2
Elmwood Rd. Slough 206 A3
Elmwood. Turv 8 C3
Elora Rd. H Wyc 173 F4
Elruge Cl. W Dra 208 B2
Elsmore Cl. Ayl 116 A2
Elthorne Rd. Uxb 201 E2
Elthorne Way. N Pag 22 B1
Elton Dr. Maid 202 B4
Elton. M Keyn 47 E4
Elwes Rd. La En 171 E2
Ely Ave. Slough 205 E4
Ely Cl. Ame 165 F4
Ember Path. Ayl 115 E2
Ember Rd. Slough 207 D2
Emberton Gdns. M Keyn 32 C3
Emerald Cl. E Clay 74 C4
Emerald Ct. Slough 205 F2
Emerton Ct. Berk 134 C4
Emerton Garth. Berk 134 C4
Emlyns Bldgs. Eton 210 B4
Emma Rothschild Cl. Tri 119 D3
Empingham Cl. M Keyn 58 B2
Enborne Cl. S Man 115 E2
Enfield Cl. Uxb 201 E2
Engaine Dr. She C E 45 F4
English Gdns. Wray 211 E1
Enmore Gate. M Keyn 35 D2
Ennell Gr. M Keyn 58 B3
Ennerdale Cl. M Keyn 58 B3
Ennerdale Cres. Burn 204 B4
Enstone Rd. Ick 190 C1
Enterprise La. M Keyn 35 D2
Epsom Gr. M Keyn 57 E3
Eriboll Cl. L Buzz 80 A4
Erica Cl. Slough 204 C3
Erica Rd. M Keyn 33 F2
Errington Dr. Wind 210 A3
Esk Way. M Keyn 46 C1
Eskdale Ave. Ches 144 B1
Eskdale Gdns. Holy 203 D1
Eskdale Rd. S Man 116 A1
Eskdale Rd. Uxb 201 D2
Essenden Ct. M Keyn 32 C3
Essex Ave. Slough 205 E4
Essex Cl. M Keyn 46 C1
Essex Rd. Ches 144 B1
Eston Ct. M Keyn 34 A3
Estover Way. Chin 147 D3
Etheridge Ave. M K Vil 48 B4
Ethorpe Cl. Ger C 188 C3
Ethorpe Cres. Ger C 188 C3
Ethorpe. M Keyn 33 F1
Eton Cl. Datch 211 D4
Eton Cres. M Keyn 33 E3
Eton Ct. Eton 210 B4
Eton Pl. Mar 183 B1
Eton Rd. Datch 211 D4
Eton Sq. Eton 210 B4
Eton Wick Rd. Eton 205 D1
Eunice Rd. Ches 154 B4
Evans Cl. Ayl 116 A2
Evans Gate. M Keyn 46 C4
Evelyn Cl. Wing 79 F1
Evelyns Cl. Uxb 208 C4
Evenlode Cl. Ayl 115 E3
Evenlode Rd. Bou E 185 D2
Evenlode. Maid 202 C4
Everard Ave. Slough 205 F2
Everest Cl. H Wyc 173 E3
Everest Rd. H Wyc 173 F3
Everglade. M Keyn 47 D4
Everley Cl. M Keyn 46 B2
Evreham Rd. Iver 207 F4
Exchange St. Ayl 115 F4
Exmoor Gate. M Keyn 46 C1
Eyethrope Rd. Sto 114 A3
Eynsford Terr. W Dra 208 C4
Eynsham Ct. M Keyn 35 E1

Fadmoor Pl. She B E 46 A2
Fagnall La. Cole 164 B1
Fair Acres. Pres 151 E3
Fair Leas. Ches 144 A1
Fair Meadow. Wins 66 A2
Fair Mile. Ayl 116 A4
Fair Mile. Hen-O-T 191 E2
Fair Ridge. H Wyc 172 C2
Fairacre. Maid 202 B3
Fairacres Ind Est. Wind 209 E3
Faircroft. Slough 198 A1
Fairfax Cres. Ayl 101 F1
Fairfax Mews. Ame 165 D4
Fairfax. M Keyn 34 B3
Fairfield App. Wray 211 E1
Fairfield Ave. Datch 211 E4
Fairfield Cl. Datch 211 E4
Fairfield Cl. Oln 7 D2
Fairfield La. Far C 198 A2
Fairfield Rd. Burn 197 E1
Fairfield Rd. Paul 17 D4
Fairfield Rd. Uxb 201 E3
Fairfield Rd. W Dra 208 C3
Fairfield Rd. Wray 211 E1
Fairfields. G Kin 151 F1
Fairford Cres. M Keyn 35 D3
Fairford Rd. Maid 202 C4
Fairlawn Pk. Wind 209 F2
Fairlea. Maid 202 A2
Fairlie Rd. Slough 205 D4
Fairlight Ave. Wind 210 B3
Fairlight Dr. Uxb 201 E3
Fairthorn Cl. Tri 118 C2
Fairview La. Fla H 174 A1
Fairview Rd. Burn 204 A4
Fairview Rd. Slough 197 F1
Fairway Ave. W Dra 208 B3
Fairway Cl. W Dra 208 B3
Fairway The. Burn 197 E2
Fairway The. Fla H 185 E4
Fairway The. Maid 202 A2
Fairway The. Uxb 201 F2
Fairway. P Ris 139 D1
Fairways. M Keyn 33 E1
Falcon Ave. M Keyn 35 D1
Falcon Dr. Stan 213 F1
Falcon Ridge. Berk 135 E2
Falcons Croft. Woo G 185 F4
Falling La. W Dra 208 C3
Fallow Field. Ty Gr 163 D2
Falmouth Pl. M Keyn 34 C1
Falmouth Rd. Slough 205 D4
Fane Way. Maid 202 B3
Fantail La. Tri 118 C2
Far Furlong Cl. S Man 115 E2
Faraday Cl. Slough 205 D4
Faraday Dr. She B E 46 B3
Faraday Rd. Ayl 101 D1
Faraday Rd. Slough 205 D4
Farinton. M Keyn 33 F1
Farm Cl. H Wyc 174 A4
Farm Cl. Holy 203 E1
Farm Cl. L Chal 166 B4
Farm Cl. Maid 202 A4
Farm Cl. Stew 78 C4
Farm Cres. Slough 206 B4
Farm Dr. Old W 211 D1
Farm Gr. Beac 175 E3
Farm La. Beac 176 B2
Farm Lea. Woo G 185 F4
Farm Pl. Berk 134 C3
Farm Rd. Bou E 184 C2
Farm Rd. Brac 38 A3
Farm Rd. Chor 167 D3
Farm Rd. Maid 202 A4
Farm Way. Stan 212 C1
Farm Yd. Wind 210 B4
Farmborough Cl. Ayl 102 A1
Farmborough. M Keyn 47 E3
Farmers Cl. Maid 202 A2
Farmers Way. Maid 202 A2
Farmers Way. Se Gr 176 B2
Farnburn Ave. Slough 205 D4
Farndale Gdns. Hol G 163 D3
Farnham Cl. Bov 146 A2
Farnham Ct. M Keyn 33 F1
Farnham La. Slough 198 A2
Farnham Park La. Far C 198 B2
Farnham Rd. Slough 205 E4
Farnley Rd. Ayl 101 F1
Farrer Cl. Whit 26 B2
Farrier Pl. M Keyn 35 D3
Farthing Gr. M Keyn 47 E3
Farthing Green La. Sto P 199 D2
Farthingales The. Maid 203 D4
Fassets Rd. Loud 174 A1
Faulkner Way. H Wyc 161 E2
Faulkner's Way. L Buzz 80 C4
Favell Dr. M Keyn 46 C2
Faversham Cl. Tri 119 D2
Fawcett Rd. Wind 210 A3
Fawley Bottom La. Faw 180 A1
Fawley Cl. Maid 195 E1
Fawsley Cl. Iver 212 C4
Featherbed La. Hol G 163 E4
Featherstone Rd. M Keyn 33 D3
Felbridge. M K Vil 48 A4
Felden La. Fel 146 C4
Fells Cl. L Cre 125 E3
Fences La. Emb 13 D1
Fennel Dr. M Keyn 34 C2
Fennels Farm Rd. Fla H 174 A1
Fennels Rd. H Wyc 174 A2
Fennels Way. Fla H 174 A1
Fennimore Cl. Oak 109 E2
Fennings The. Ame 154 B2
Fenny Rd. S Ham 69 F4
Fennymere. M Keyn 33 E1
Fenton Ct. M Keyn 45 F4
Fern Dr. Burn 204 A4
Fern Gr. M Keyn 58 B3
Fern La. Hadd 127 D3
Fern La. Hadd 127 D4
Fern Wlk. Ty Gr 163 D2
Fernborough Haven.
She B E 46 B1
Ferndale Cl. Skch 158 C2
Ferndale Cres. Uxb 201 E1
Ferndale. M Keyn 35 D1
Fernes Cl. Uxb 208 B4
Fernhill Cl. Tidd 136 A4
Fernhurst Cl. Beac 175 F1
Fernie Fields. H Wyc 172 B2
Fernley Ct. Maid 195 E1
Ferns The. Beac 175 F1
Fernside. G Kin 151 F1
Fernside. Hol G 163 D3
Fernsleigh Cl. C St P 177 F2
Ferrers Ave. W Dra 208 B2
Ferry La. Bou E 185 D1
Ferry La. Hamb 192 B3
Ferry La. Medm 193 D3
Ferry Rd. Maid 203 E2
Field Rd. Mur 94 A3
Field Cl. Ayl 102 A1
Field Cl. Ches 144 C2
Field Cl. Ick 124 A2
Field Cl. Sher 14 A1
Field End. L Cre 125 F3
Field End. Tri 119 D3
Field Hurst. Slough 206 C1
Field La. M Keyn 33 D3
Field Rd. Den 189 F1
Field Rd. H Wyc 172 A3
Field Way. Ayl 102 A1
Field Way. Bov 146 A3
Field Way. Ger C 177 E2
Field Way. Uxb 201 E1
Field Wlk. M Keyn 34 C2
Fieldhead Gdns. Bou E 185 D2
Fieldhouse Ind Est. Mar 183 F1
Fieldhouse La. Mar 183 F1
Fieldhouse Way. Mar 183 F1
Fielding Rd. Maid 202 A4
Fields The. Slough 205 E2
Fieldway. Ame 165 D3
Fieldway. Berk 135 F1
Fieldway. Wigg 119 E1
Filey Spur. Slough 205 D2
Filmer Rd. Wind 209 E3
Finch Cl. M Keyn 35 F2
Finch Cres. L Buzz 80 C3
Finch Ct. Maid 202 B3
Finch End. Ty Gr 174 B4
Finch La. Ame 166 A4
Finch La. Beac 175 E3
Finch La. L Chal 166 A4
Finch Rd. Berk 135 D2
Findlay Way. M Keyn 58 B4
Fingest La. Frie 170 C2
Fingest La. La En 170 B2
Fingle Dr. M Keyn 33 F4
Finians Cl. Uxb 201 F3
Finings Rd. La En 171 D2
Finmere Cres. Ayl 116 B3
Fir Tree Ave. Sto P 198 C1
Fircroft Cl. Sto P 199 D3
Fire La. Nwtn L 57 E2
Firs Ave. Wind 209 F2
Firs Cl. H Wyc 173 F4
Firs Cl. La En 171 E3
Firs Cl. Ty Gr 163 D1
Firs Cl. Whit 87 D3
Firs Ct. Bier 102 B2
Firs Dr. Slough 206 C3
Firs End. Ger C 188 B4
Firs Rise. G Mis 151 F4
Firs The. Bier 102 B2
Firs The. Bri 110 A4
Firs The. Wigg 119 E1
Firs View Rd. Ty Gr 163 D1
Firs Wlk. Ty Gr 163 D1
First Ave. Ame 165 E4
First Ave. M Keyn 47 E1
First Ave. Mar 184 A1
First Cres. Slough 205 E4
Firview Cl. Mar 183 F1
Fish Ponds La. Tha 125 E1
Fisherman's Way. Bou E 185 D2
Fishermans Cl. Oln 6 C2
Fishermans Retreat. Mar 183 F1
Fishermead Bvd. M Keyn 35 D1
Fishers Field. Buck 52 B4
Fishery Rd. Maid 203 D3
Fishguard Spur. Slough 206 A2
Fishweir. Stew 68 B1
Five Acre Wood. H Wyc 172 B3
Five Acres. Ches 154 B3
Five Acres. Woo G 185 F4
Flaggs Meadow. Oln 6 C2
Flambard Cl. M Keyn 35 D4
Flamborough Spur.
Slough 205 D2
Flaunden Bottom. Lat 155 F2
Flaunden Hill. Flau 156 A3
Flaunden La. Bov 146 B2
Flavius Gate. Brac 38 A4
Fleet Cl. Buck 41 F1
Fleet Cl. Wal A 161 F4
Fleet St. Ayl 101 E1
Fleet The. M Keyn 35 D1
Fleetwood Cl. C St G 177 D3
Fleetwood Rd. Slough 205 F3
Fleetwood Way. Tha 125 F1
Fleming Dr. M Keyn 47 D3
Fletcher Cl. Ayl 100 C2
Fletchers Mews. M Keyn 34 C3
Flint Hollow. Chin 147 D3
Flint St. Hadd 127 D3
Flint Way. Pres 151 E4
Flintlock Cl. Stan 213 D2
Flitcroft Lea. H Wyc 173 D4
Flitton Ct. M Keyn 32 C3
Flora Thompson Dr. N Pag 21 F3
Florence Ave. Maid 203 D4
Florin Cl. M Keyn 35 D4
Flowers Bottom La. Lac G 150 A2
Foley Cl. Beac 175 E2
Foliejohn Way. Maid 202 A1
Folkestone Ct. Slough 207 D1
Follet Cl. Old W 211 D1
Folley La. N Craw 24 A3
Folly La. Hart 10 B4
Folly Rd. Dean 31 E2
Fontwell Cl. Maid 202 A4
Fontwell Dr. M Keyn 57 E3
Forches Cl. M Keyn 46 B1
Ford La. Iver 208 A4
Ford St. Buck 52 B4
Ford St. H Wyc 173 F2
Ford Way. H Wyc 161 F2
Ford's Cl. Bled R 159 F4
Fordcombe Lea. M K Vil 48 A4
Fore End. Den 189 F1
Forelands Way. Ches 154 B4
Forest Cl. Wen 131 D2
Forest Rd. Hans 10 C3
Forest Rd. Pid (N) 4 A4
Forest Rd. Wind 209 F3
Forest Rise. M Keyn 47 D4
Forest Way. H Wyc 174 A4
Foresters. B Bot 159 E3
Foresters. Chin 147 D3
Foresters. Oak 109 E3
Forfar Dr. M Keyn 46 C1
Forge Cl. Hol G 163 E3
Forge Cl. Hor-c-S 108 A3
Forge Cl. Stp Cl 63 F2
Forge Dr. Far C 198 B3
Forge End. Ame 165 D4
Forge Rd. Wal A 161 E4
Forge The. Emb 13 F4
Forgetts Rd. La En 171 E2
Forlease Cl. Maid 203 D3
Forlease Dr. Maid 203 D3
Forlease Rd. Maid 203 D3
Formby Cl. M Keyn 57 E4
Forrabury Ave. M Keyn 34 B2
Fortescue Dr. She C E 46 A3
Fortuna Ct. Walt 48 B3
Forty Green Dr. Mar 183 A1
Forty Green Rd. Beac 175 E2
Forty Green. Bled 137 F2
Foscote Rd. M Mor 41 F2
Foscott Way. Buck 41 F1
Foster Ave. Wind 209 F2
Foster Cl. Ayl 101 F1
Fosters La. M Keyn 34 A2
Fosters Path. Slough 197 F1
Fotherby Ct. Maid 203 D3
Fotheringay Gdns.
Slough 205 D3
Fotherley Rd. Chor 178 C4
Founders Dr. Den G 189 F3
Founders Mews. M Keyn 34 C3
Foundry La. Hort 212 A2
Foundry La. Lac G 149 E3
Fountain Gdns. Wind 210 B2
Fountaine Cl. M Keyn 34 C4
Four Ashes Rd. G Kin 162 B3
Fourth Ave. Mar 184 A1
Fowler Rd. Ayl 115 D4
Fowler. M Keyn 34 B4
Fowlers Farm Rd. Skch 158 C2
Fox Cl. Wigg 119 E1
Fox Cover. Chin 147 E3
Fox Covert Rd. She B E 45 F2
Fox Field. Hol G 162 C3
Fox Hill Cl. H Wyc 162 A1
Fox La. Hol G 163 D3
Fox Rd. Hol G 163 D3
Fox Rd. Slough 206 B1
Fox Rd. Wigg 119 E1
Fox Way. Buck 52 C4
Foxborough Cl. Slough 207 D1
Foxdell Way. C St P 177 F3
Foxes Piece. Mar 183 F2
Foxgate. N Pag 22 A2
Foxherne. Slough 206 B2
Foxhill. Oln 6 C3
Foxhollow Dr. Far C 198 B4
Foxhunter Dr. M Keyn 34 C3
Foxleigh. H Wyc 173 D2
Foxton. M Keyn 47 E3
Framewood Rd. Sto P 199 E3
France Furlong. M Keyn 34 C4
Frances Ave. Maid 196 B1
Frances Rd. Wind 210 B3
Frances St. Ches 144 B1
Franchise St. Ches 144 B1
Francis Way. Burn 204 B3
Frank Lunnon Cl. Bou E 185 E2
Franklin Ave. Slough 205 E4
Franklin Cl. Hadd 127 D4
Franklin Rd. Dun 93 F4
Franklin Rd. Hadd 127 D4
Franklins Croft. M Keyn 33 E3
Franklyn Cres. Wind 209 E2
Frankston Ave. M Keyn 32 C3
Frascati Way. Maid 202 C4
Fraser Rd. H Wyc 172 B3
Fray's Waye. Uxb 201 E2
Frays Ave. W Dra 208 B2
Frays Cl. W Dra 208 B2
Frayslea. Uxb 201 E2
Frederick St. Wadd 99 D4
Freeman Cl. M Keyn 33 D3
Freeman Ct. Ches 144 B1
Freemans Cl. Sto P 199 D3
Freemans Gdns. Oln 7 D2
Freemantle Rd. Ayl 115 F3
Fremantle Rd. H Wyc 162 C1
Frenchum Gdns. Slough 204 C3
Frensham Dr. M Keyn 58 B4
Frensham Wlk. Far C 198 B3
Friarage Rd. Ayl 115 E4
Friars Field. Berk 134 C4
Friars Furlong. L Cre 125 E4
Friars Gdns. Hgh V 162 A4
Friars Walk. Pres 151 E3
Friars Wlk. Tri 119 D2
Friary Dr. Wray 211 E1
Friary Gdns. N Pag 22 B1
Friary The. Old W 211 E1
Friday St. Hen-O-T 191 F1
Friday St. L Buzz 80 C4
Frieth Rd. Mar 182 C3
Frieth Rd. Mar B 182 C3
Frith Hill. S Hea 152 A4
Frithe The. Slough 206 A4
Frithsden Copse. Berk 135 F4
Frithwood Cres. M K Vil 48 A4
Frog La. Cudd 112 C2
Froggy La. Den 189 E1
Frogmill. Hurl 193 E2
Frogmoor. H Wyc 173 D4
Frogmore Cl. Hgh V 162 A4
Frogmore Cl. Slough 205 D2
Frogmore St. Tri 119 D2
Frome Cl. Ayl 115 E3
Fromer Rd. Bou E 185 E2
Froxfield Ct. M Keyn 46 B1
Fryday St. M Keyn 46 C4
Fryer Cl. Ches 154 B3
Fryers La. H Wyc 172 B4
Frymley Hill. Wind 209 E3
Fullbrook Cl. Maid 203 D4
Fuller's Cl. Ches 154 A3
Fullers Hill. Char 154 A3
Fullers Hill. Ches 154 A3
Fullers Slade La. M Keyn 33 D2
Fulmer Common Rd.
Fulm 199 F3
Fulmer Dr. Ger C 188 B1
Fulmer La. Ger C 189 D1
Fulmer Rd. Ger C 188 C1
Fulmer St. She B E 46 B2
Fulmer St. She C E 45 E3
Fulmer Way. Ger C 188 C3
Fulwell Rd. West 39 D2
Fulwoods Dr. M Keyn 47 D4
Furlong Cl. Bou E 185 D2
Furlong Cres. Sto 115 D1
Furlong La. Tott 93 E4
Furlong Rd. Bou E 185 D2
Furness Sq. Oak G 209 E3
Furness Way. Oak G 209 E3
Furness. Oak G 209 E3
Furnival Ave. Slough 205 D4
Furrow Cl. S Man 115 E2
Furrow Way. Maid 202 A2
Furrows The. S Har 190 B3
Furtho La. Pott 18 C2
Fury Ct. She C E 45 F4
Furze La. Wins 65 F3
Furze Platt Rd. Maid 195 D1
Furze Rd. Maid 195 E1
Furze View. Chor 167 E2
Furze Way. M Keyn 33 E3
Furzefield Rd. Beac 175 E1
Furzeham Rd. W Dra 208 C2
Furzen Cl. Slough 198 A1
Fuzzens Wlk. Wind 209 F3
Fyfield Barrow. Walt 48 B3

Gable Thorne. Walt 48 B3
Gables Cl. C St P 177 F3
Gables Cl. Datch 211 D4
Gables Cl. Maid 203 D4
Gables Cl. Wen 131 D2
Gables The. Hadd 127 D3
Gables The. L Buzz 80 C3
Gabriel Cl. Walt 48 B3
Gaddesden Cres. Walt 48 B3
Gadge Cl. Tha 125 F1
Gadsden Cl. Cran 25 E2
Gadsden Ct. S Ham 69 F4
Gage Cl. Maid 202 C2
Gainsborough Dr. Maid 202 B2
Gainsborough Hill.
Hen-O-T 191 E1
Gainsborough Pl. Ayl 100 C2
Gainsborough Rd. Ayl 115 F2

Gainsborough Rd. Hen-O-T 191 E1
Gainsborough Cl. Cook 195 F3
Gairloch Ave. M Keyn 58 B3
Galahad Cl. Slough 205 D2
Galley Hill. M Keyn 32 C3
Galley La. G Bkhl 59 D2
Galley La. L Bkhl 59 D2
Galleymead Rd. Stan 212 C3
Galloway Cl. M Keyn 46 C1
Gallows La. H Wyc 172 B4
Gallys Rd. Wind 209 E3
Galsworthy Pl. Ayl 100 C1
Galvin Rd. Slough 205 E3
Gamnel Terr. Tri 119 D3
Gandon Vale. H Wyc 173 D4
Ganton Cl. M Keyn 46 B1
Garamonde Dr. M Keyn 33 F1
Garbo Cl. She C E 45 E4
Garden Cl. Maid 202 A3
Garden Field La. Berk 135 F1
Garden Reach. L Chal 166 B3
Gardens The. Adsk 53 F1
Gardens The. Ick 190 C1
Gardiner Ct. M Keyn 33 F3
Gardner Rd. Maid 195 F1
Gardner's Cl. Dun 93 F4
Garland Way. Ast C 117 F3
Garners Cl. C St P 177 F2
Garners End. C St P 177 F2
Garners Rd. C St P 177 F2
Garnet Cl. Slough 205 D2
Garnet Ct. Mar 183 E1
Garrard Rd. Slough 197 F1
Garratts Way. H Wyc 173 D4
Garraways. M Keyn 47 D3
Garron Cl. S Man 115 E2
Garrowmore Gr. M Keyn 58 B3
Garry Cl. M Keyn 58 B3
Garson Gr. Ches 144 A1
Garston. M Keyn 33 F1
Garth The. S Hea 152 A4
Garvin Ave. Beac 175 F1
Gascon's Gr. Slough 198 A1
Gaskin Ct. M Keyn 35 D3
Gatcombe. M Keyn 33 F1
Gatehouse Cl. Ayl 101 E1
Gatehouse Rd. Ayl 101 E1
Gatehouse Way. Ayl 101 D1
Gatensbury Pl. P Ris 139 D2
Gatesdene Cl. L Gad 121 E4
Gatewick Cl. Slough 205 F3
Gatewick La. B Bkhl 48 A2
Gatting Way. Uxb 201 F3
Gatward Ave. Maid 202 A2
Gaveston Dr. Berk 135 D3
Gaveston Rd. Slough 197 F1
Gaviots Cl. Ger C 188 C2
Gaviots Green. Ger C 188 C2
Gaviots Way. Ger C 188 C2
Gawcott Rd. Buck 52 A3
Gayhurst Rd. H Wyc 173 F4
Gayton Cl. Ame 154 C2
Gell Cl. Ick 190 C1
George Cl. Mar 183 F2
George Green Rd. Slough 206 C4
George Inn Pl. S Gol 12 A3
George Rd. Skch 158 C3
George St. Ayl 115 E4
George St. Berk 135 E2
George St. Ches 144 B1
George St. H Wyc 172 C4
George St. Hth 60 C4
George St. M Keyn 47 F1
George St. Uxb 201 E3
George St. Wing 79 F1
Georges Dr. Fla H 185 E4
Georges Hill. Hol G 162 C3
Georgian Cl. Ick 201 F4
Geralds Rd. H Wyc 162 B1
Gerards Cross Rd. Sto P 199 D4
Germain St. Ches 154 A4
Germains Cl. Ches 154 A4
Germander Pl. M Keyn 34 B2
Gibbings Cl. N Mar 76 A2
Gibbs Cl. H Wyc 172 C4
Gibbwin. M Keyn 34 C4
Gibraltar La. Cook 184 B1
Gibson Ct. Slough 206 C1
Gibson La. Hadd 127 D3
Gibson Pl. Stan 213 E1
Gibson Rd. H Wyc 172 A2
Gibson Rd. Ick 201 F4
Gibsons Green. M Keyn 34 B2
Giffard Rd. M Keyn 58 B3
Giffard Way. L Cre 125 E4
Gifford Gate. M Keyn 34 C4
Gifford Pl. Buck 41 F1
Gilbert Cl. M Keyn 58 A4
Gilbert Scott Rd. Buck 41 E1
Gilbert Way. Berk 135 D2
Gilbert's Hill. Dra B 132 C2
Gilbey Wlk. Bou E 185 E2
Gilders Mews. M Keyn 34 C3
Gilletts La. H Wyc 161 E1
Gillfield Cl. H Wyc 172 C2
Gilliat Rd. Slough 205 F3
Gilliatt Cl. Iver 207 F4
Gilman Cres. Wind 209 E2
Gilmore Cl. Slough 206 B2
Gilmore Rd. Ayl 101 F2
Gilpin Way. Oln 7 D2
Gilpin's Ride. Berk 135 F3
Gingers Cl. Ast C 117 F3
Gisburn Cl. M Keyn 34 A3
Glade Rd. Mar 183 F1
Glade The. Ger C 188 B1
Gladstone Cl. N Pag 22 B2
Gladstone Rise. H Wyc 173 F3
Gladstone Way. Slough 205 D3
Glaisyer Way. Iver H 200 B2
Glamorgan Cl. M Keyn 46 C1
Glanmor Rd. Slough 206 A3
Glasgow Rd. Slough 205 D4
Glastonbury Cl. M Keyn 47 D1
Glaven Rd. Ayl 115 E2
Glazier Dr. M Keyn 34 C3
Glebe Cl. Dorn 203 F2
Glebe Cl. Ger C 177 E2
Glebe Cl. Hol G 163 D4
Glebe Cl. M Mor 41 F2
Glebe Cl. Pit 105 E3
Glebe Dr. Brac 38 A4
Glebe Dr. Old W 211 D1
Glebe La. Hans 10 C3
Glebe Rd. Dean 31 F3
Glebe Rd. Ger C 177 E1
Glebe Rd. Maid 203 D3
Glebe Rd. Uxb 201 E2
Glebe The. Lave 7 F4
Glebe The. Pres 151 E4
Glebe The. Sto 114 B3
Glebe The. W Dra 208 C1
Glebe The. W Tur 116 C1
Glebe The. Wal A 161 E3
Glebe Way. Ame 154 B2
Glebelands Cl. Pres 151 F2
Gledfield Pl. M Keyn 33 E2
Gleeman Cl. M Keyn 33 D3
Glen The. Slough 206 B1
Glenavon Gdns. Slough 206 B2
Gleneagles Cl. M Keyn 57 E4
Gleneagles Cl. Stan 213 E1
Glenfield Cl. Ayl 116 A3
Glenham Rd. Tha 126 A1
Glenhaven Dr. Stan 213 D1
Glenister Rd. Ches 144 B2
Glenister Rd. H Wyc 172 A2
Glenmore Cl. Fla H 174 A1
Glentworth Pl. Slough 205 E3
Glenwoods. N Pag 22 B2
Glimbers Gr. Chin 147 E3
Globe La. L Buzz 70 C1
Glory Hill La. Beac 185 F4
Glory Mill La. Woo G 185 F4
Glory Cl. Woo G 185 F4
Glory Hill La. Beac 186 A4
Gloucester Ave. Slough 205 E4
Gloucester Pl. Wind 210 B3
Gloucester Rd. M Keyn 33 E3
Gloucester Rd. Maid 195 F1
Glovers Ct. Ayl 101 F1
Glovers La. M Keyn 34 A2
Glyn Sq. M Keyn 33 E4
Glyn St. M Keyn 34 A4
Glynswood Rd. Buck 41 E1
Glynswood. C St P 177 F2
Glynswood. Chin 147 E3
Glynswood. H Wyc 162 A1
Goathland Croft. She B E 46 A1
Goddards Croft. M Keyn 33 E3
Goddington Rd. Bou E 185 D3
Godolphin Rd. Se Gr 176 B2
Godolphin Rd. Slough 205 E3
Godwin Cl. M K Vil 48 B4
Gogh Rd. Ayl 100 C1
Gold Crest. Ayl 101 F2
Gold Hill E. Ger C 177 E1
Gold Hill N. Ger C 177 E1
Gold Hill W. Ger C 177 E1
Gold Oak Wlk. M Keyn 34 C2
Gold St. Hans 11 D1
Golden Ball La. Maid 195 D2
Golden Dr. M Keyn 47 D4
Golden Hill. Chin 147 E3
Golden Oak. Far C 198 B3
Golden Riddy. L Buzz 80 C4
Golder's Cl. Ick 123 F2
Goldfield Rd. Tri 118 C2
Goldilocks. Walt 48 A3
Goldlake Ct. Den G 189 F2
Goldmark Cl. Walt 48 B3
Goldsmith Dr. N Pag 21 F2
Goldsworthy Way. Slough 204 B4
Gomm Rd. H Wyc 174 A2
Gomms Wood Cl. Beac 175 D2
Good Intent. Edle 92 C2
Goodman Gdns. M Keyn 47 E4
Goodman Park. Slough 206 B3
Goodwin Meadows. Woo G 185 F3
Goodwin Rd. Ayl 115 E4
Goodwin Rd. Slough 197 F1
Goodwins Mead. Ched 105 D4
Goodwood Rise. Mar B 183 E4
Goodwood. M Keyn 45 F4
Goose Acre. Bot 145 D1
Goose Acre. Ched 105 D4
Goose Green. Far C 198 A2
Goosen Green. Ayl 116 B3
Goran Ave. M Keyn 32 C2
Gordale. M Keyn 34 B3
Gordon Cl. Ger C 177 F1
Gordon Rd. Ches 154 B4
Gordon Rd. H Wyc 173 E3
Gordon Rd. Maid 202 B4
Gordon Rd. W Dra 208 C3
Gordon Rd. Wind 209 F3
Gordon Way. C St G 177 D4
Gore Hill. Ame 165 D3
Gore Rd. Burn 197 D1
Gorelands La. C St P 177 F4
Gorell Rd. Beac 176 A1
Goring. M Keyn 34 B4
Gorman Pl. M Keyn 58 C2
Gorrell Cl. Ting 51 D3
Gorricks. M Keyn 32 B2
Gorse Meade. Slough 205 D3
Gorse Rd. Cook 195 F3
Gorse Wlk. Ty Gr 163 D2
Gorse Wlk. W Dra 208 C4
Goslar Way. Wind 210 A3
Gosling Gr. H Wyc 161 E1
Gosling Green. Slough 206 C2
Gosling Rd. Slough 206 C2
Goslington. M Keyn 47 E1
Goss Ave. Wadd 99 D3
Gossmore Cl. Mar 183 F1
Gossmore La. Mar 183 F1
Gossmore Wlk. Mar 183 F1
Gossom's End. Berk 135 D3
Gossoms Ryde. Berk 135 D3
Goswell Hill. Wind 210 B3
Goswell Rd. Wind 210 B3
Governors Ave. Den G 189 F3
Gowers The. Ame 154 C1
Goya Pl. Ayl 100 C1
Grace Ave. M Keyn 46 C4
Graces Cl. Cran 25 E2
Graces Maltings. Tri 119 D2
Graeme Ave. Pres 151 E3
Graemesdyke Rd. Berk 135 D2
Grafham Cl. M Keyn 35 D4
Grafton Cl. Maid 195 F1
Grafton Cl. Pott 18 C2
Grafton Cl. Slough 206 C4
Grafton Gate. M Keyn 34 B1
Grafton Orch. Chin 147 E4
Grafton Park. M Keyn 34 B1
Grafton Rd. Ayl 101 D1
Grafton Rd. Yard G 18 C4
Grafton St. H Wyc 172 B4
Grafton St. M Keyn 34 A2
Grafton St. M Keyn 46 C4
Graham Cl. Maid 202 B3
Graham Dr. H Wyc 172 A3
Graham Rd. Cook 195 F3
Grampian Gate. M Keyn 46 C4
Grampian Way. Slough 207 D1
Gramwell. She C E 45 F4
Granborough Rd. N Mar 76 A1
Granborough Rd. Wins 65 F1
Granes End. M Keyn 34 C4
Grange Cl. Ger C 177 F1
Grange Cl. L Buzz 80 B3
Grange Cl. M Mor 41 F2
Grange Cl. Wray 211 F1
Grange Dr. Bou E 185 E2
Grange Farm Rd. Bled R 159 D4
Grange Fields. Ger C 177 F1
Grange Gdns. Far C 198 B4
Grange Gdns. Wen 131 D3
Grange La. Cook 195 F4
Grange Rd. Cook 195 F4
Grange Rd. Ger C 177 F1
Grange Rd. Hen-O-T 191 F1
Grange Rd. Hol G 162 C3
Grange Rd. M Keyn 57 F4
Grange Rd. Pit 105 E3
Grange Rd. Tri 119 E2
Grange Rd. Ty Gr 162 C2
Grange Rd. Wils 104 B1
Grange The. Burn 197 E1
Grange The. Old W 211 D1
Grange Way. Iver 207 F4
Grangers Croft. M Keyn 33 E2
Grangewood. Slough 206 B4
Grant Ave. Slough 205 F4
Grantham Ct. She B E 46 B3
Granville Ave. Slough 205 E4
Granville Dene. Bov 146 A2
Granville Pl. Ayl 115 E4
Granville Rd. Berk 134 C3
Granville Sq. M Keyn 35 E4
Granville St. Ayl 115 E4
Grapevine Cl. H Wyc 173 F2
Grasmere Ave. Slough 206 A3
Grasmere Par. Slough 206 A3
Grasmere Way. L Buzz 80 B4
Grasmere Way. M Keyn 58 B3
Grasmere. Ayl 116 A3
Grass Hays. Ayl 116 B4
Grasscroft. M Keyn 46 C2
Grassingham End. C St P 177 F2
Grassingham Rd. C St P 177 F2
Grassington. M Keyn 34 A3
Grasslands. Ayl 102 A1
Grassy La. Maid 202 C4
Grattan Ct. Mar 184 A2
Gratton Dr. Wind 209 F2
Gravel Hill. C St P 177 F2
Gravel Hill. Hen-O-T 191 E1
Gravel Hill. Uxb 201 E4
Gravel Path. Berk 135 F3
Gravel Wlk. Emb 13 F4
Graveney Pl. M Keyn 35 D1
Gray's La. Ibst 169 E4
Gray's Pl. Slough 205 F3
Gray's Rd. Slough 205 F3
Grayburn Cl. C St G 177 D4
Grayling Cl. Mar 194 B4
Grays Cl. Paul 17 E4
Grays La. H Wyc 161 E1
Grays La. Paul 17 E4
Grays La. Yard G 18 C3
Grays Park Rd. Sto P 199 D1
Grays Wlk. Ches 144 A1
Great Benty. W Dra 208 C1
Great Brickhill La. L Bkhl 59 E3
Great Denson. M Keyn 47 D4
Great Ground. M Keyn 34 C4
Great Hill Cres. Maid 202 B3
Great Hivings. Ches 144 A2
Great Horwood Rd. G Hrwd 65 F4
Great La. Bier 102 A2
Great Monks St. M Keyn 33 E3
Great Stone. Cudd 112 C2
Greaves Rd. H Wyc 173 E3
Grecian St. Ayl 116 A4
Green Acre. Ayl 116 A4
Green Acres Cl. Whit 86 C4
Green Cl. Burn 204 A4
Green Cl. Maid 195 F1
Green Common La. Beac 186 B2
Green Cres. Fla H 185 E4
Green Dragon La. Fla H 185 D4
Green East Rd. Se Gr 176 C2
Green End Rd. Bled R 159 F3
Green End St. Ast C 117 F3
Green End. Gran 76 A4
Green Farm Rd. N Pag 22 B2
Green Hill Cl. H Wyc 162 B1
Green Hill. H Wyc 162 A1
Green La. Ame 154 C1
Green La. Asp G 49 F2
Green La. Bled R 159 E3
Green La. Bov 146 A2
Green La. Burn 197 E2
Green La. Datch 211 D3
Green La. Eat B 92 B4
Green La. Far C 198 A3
Green La. Ivin 105 F3
Green La. Lat 155 D3
Green La. Lgwk 128 A1
Green La. M Keyn 33 E3
Green La. Maid 203 D3
Green La. Pres 151 F3
Green La. Skch 158 B3
Green La. U Arn 94 C4
Green La. Wind 210 A3
Green Lane Cl. Ame 154 B2
Green Lane Ct. Burn 197 E1
Green Leys. H Wyc 161 E1
Green North Rd. Se Gr 176 C2
Green Park Dr. N Pag 22 B2
Green Park. Pres 151 E3
Green Rd. H Wyc 162 B1
Green St. Chor 167 E3
Green St. H Wyc 172 C4
Green St. Ty Gr 162 C2
Green The. A Abb 88 B3
Green The. Ame 154 B1
Green The. Burn 197 D1
Green The. Cast 19 F1
Green The. Chea 112 A1
Green The. Ched 105 D4
Green The. Cran 24 C1
Green The. Cudd 112 C2
Green The. Datch 211 D4
Green The. Dean 31 F2
Green The. Edle 92 C2
Green The. G Hrwd 55 D2
Green The. Hans 11 D1
Green The. Hor-c-S 108 A3
Green The. M Keyn 46 A4
Green The. M Keyn 47 E4
Green The. N Pag 22 B2
Green The. Paul 17 D4
Green The. Pit 105 E2
Green The. Qntn 85 D3
Green The. Slough 205 E2
Green The. Thrn 54 A4
Green The. Turv 8 C3
Green The. W Dra 208 B2
Green The. Woo G 185 F3
Green The. Wray 211 F1
Green Tiles La. Den G 189 F3
Green Verges. Mar 183 F2
Green View Cl. Bov 146 A1
Green View. Ayl 102 A1
Green Way. Nwtn L 57 E2
Green West Rd. Se Gr 176 C2
Greenacre. Wind 209 F3
Greenacres Ave. Ick 190 C1
Greenacres La. Ty Gr 163 D1
Greenacres. Pit 105 E2
Greenbury Cl. Chor 167 E3
Greendale Mews. Slough 206 A3
Greene Field Rd. Berk 135 E2
Greene Wlk. Berk 135 E2
Greenfern Ave. Slough 204 B4
Greenfield End. C St P 177 F2
Greenfield Rd. N Pag 22 A2
Greenfields. Adsk 53 F1
Greenfields. Maid 203 D3
Greenfields. U Arn 94 C4
Greenhill Cl. M Keyn 46 A4
Greenlands Cl. N Pag 22 A2
Greenlands La. Pres 151 D4
Greenlands. Fla H 185 D4
Greenlands. Lac G 149 E3
Greenlaw Pl. M Keyn 47 D2
Greenleys La. M Keyn 33 E2
Greenock Rd. Slough 205 D4
Greenridge. Ty Gr 174 A4
Greenside. Bou E 185 D3
Greenside. Pres 151 E3
Greenside. Slough 205 D4
Greenway Par. Ches 144 A2
Greenway The. Ger C 188 B4
Greenway The. H Wyc 173 D4
Greenway The. Slough 204 B3
Greenway The. Tri 118 C3
Greenway The. Ty Gr 163 D1
Greenway The. Uxb 201 E2
Greenway Wlk. Buck 41 F1
Greenway. Berk 135 D2
Greenway. Ches 144 A2
Greenway. G Hrwd 55 D1
Greenway. Hadd 126 C3
Greenways Dr. Maid 202 A4
Greenways. B Bkhl 48 B1
Greenways. Eat B 92 B4
Greenwich Gdns. N Pag 22 B1
Greenwood Ave. Chin 147 E3
Greenwood Cl. Ame 154 C1
Greenwood Cl. Se Gr 176 B2
Greenwood Meadow. Chin 147 E3
Greenwood Pl. Stp Cl 63 E2
Greenwood. Wal A 150 A1
Greenyard The. Y Has 1 A4
Greetham Rd. Ayl 116 B3
Gregories Dr. Walt 48 B3
Gregories Farm La. Beac 175 E1
Gregories Rd. Beac 175 E2
Gregory Dr. Old W 211 D1
Gregory Rd. Hedg 187 E1
Grenadine Way. Tri 119 D3
Grendon Rd. Edgc 72 C1
Grendon Rd. Gr Und 83 E2
Grendon Way. Bier 102 A2
Grenfell Ave. H Wyc 172 B4
Grenfell Ave. Maid 202 C
Grenfell Pl. Maid 202 C
Grenfell Rd. Beac 175 F2
Grenfell Rd. Maid 202 C
Grenville Ave. Wen 131 D
Grenville Cl. Burn 197 D
Grenville Ct. Chor 167 E
Grenville Green. Ayl 115 E
Grenville Rd. Ayl 115 E
Grenville Rd. Buck 41 E
Grenville Way. Tha 126 A
Gresham Ct. Berk 135 D
Gresham Rd. Slough 205 D
Greyhound La. Tha 125 F
Greyhound La. Wins 66 A
Greys Hill. Hen-O-T 191 E
Greys Rd. Hen-O-T 191 E
Greys The. M Keyn 47 E
Greystoke Cl. Berk 135 D
Greystoke Rd. Slough 204 C
Griffetts Yd. Ches 144 A
Griffin Cl. Maid 202 C
Griffin Cl. Slough 205 E
Griffin Industrial Mall. Ayl 101 D
Griffin La. Ayl 101 D
Griffith Gate. M K Vil 36 A
Griffon Cl. M Keyn 47 D
Griggs Gdn. Sher 14 A
Grimbald Ct. M Keyn 35 E
Grimmer Cl. Ayl 100 C
Grimms Hill. G Mis 151 F
Grimms Meadow. Wal A 150 A
Grimsdell's La. Ame 154 B
Grimsdyke Rd. Wigg 119 E
Gringer Hill. Maid 202 C
Grizedale. M Keyn 34 A
Groom Rd. Pres 151 E
Groombridge. M K Vil 48 A
Grooms Cottages. Bot 145 D
Groomsby Dr. Ivin 105 F
Grosmont Cl. She B E 46 A
Grosvenor Cl. Iver H 200 B
Grosvenor Dr. Maid 203 B
Groundsel Cl. Walt 48 A
Grove Ash. M Keyn 47 B

Grove Cl. Ger C 177 E1
Grove Cl. Slough 206 A2
Grove Ct. Bier 102 B3
Grove End. Ger C 177 E1
Grove Gdns. Tri 119 D3
Grove Hill. Ger C 177 E2
Grove La. Ash Gr 145 E3
Grove La. G Kim 129 F1
Grove La. Ger C 177 E1
Grove La. Uxb 201 F1
Grove Park. Tri 119 E3
Grove Rd. Ame 154 C1
Grove Rd. Beac 175 F1
Grove Rd. Burn 197 F2
Grove Rd. H Wyc 172 B4
Grove Rd. Hen-O-T 191 F1
Grove Rd. Maid 202 C4
Grove Rd. Tri 119 E3
Grove Rd. Turv 8 C3
Grove Rd. Ty Gr 162 C2
Grove Rd. Uxb 201 E3
Grove Rd. Wind 210 B3
Grove The. Ame 154 B2
Grove The. Lat 155 E2
Grove The. M Keyn 34 A2
Grove The. M Keyn 58 A4
Grove The. N Pag 22 A2
Grove The. Slough 206 A2
Grove The. Tri 119 E3
Grove The. Uxb 201 F1
Grove The. Wadd 99 D3
Grove Way. Uxb 201 E3
Grove Way. Wadd 99 D3
Groves Cl. Bou E 185 E2
Groves Rd. Hal 131 F4
Groves Way. Cook 195 F3
Grovesbrook. B Bkhl 48 B1
Groveway. M K Vil 47 E3
Groveway. M Keyn 47 E3
Groveway. Walt 47 E3
Grovewood Cl. Chor 167 D2
Grubbins La. Lac G 150 A3
Grubwood La. Cook 195 D4
Gryms Dyke. Pres 151 E3
Guards Club Rd. Maid 203 E4
Guards Rd. Oak G 209 E3
Guest Gdns. M Keyn 34 A4
Guillemot Way. Ayl 101 F2
Guinea Orch. Oln 6 C2
Guinions Rd. H Wyc 173 F3
Gull Way. Ayl 101 F2
Gun La. Sher 14 A1
Gunmaker Ct. M Keyn 34 C3
Gunthorpe Rd. Mar 184 A2
Gurnard Cl. W Dra 208 B3
Gurnards Ave. M Keyn 35 D1
Gurnells Rd. Se Gr 176 B3
Gurney Cl. Ayl 101 F1
Gurneys Meadow. Hol G 163 E4
Gwendale. Maid 195 E1
Gweneth Ct. Mar 183 E2
Gwent Cl. Maid 202 A2
Gwynne Cl. Tri 119 D3
Gwynne Cl. Wind 209 F3
Gynant Rd. H Wyc 173 F3
Gypsy La. Asp G 49 F2
Gypsy La. Mar 183 F2
Gypsy La. Sto P 187 F1

Haberley Mead. M Keyn 34 A2
Habuchin La. Wins 66 A2
Hackett Pl. N Craw 24 A3
Haddington Cl. M Keyn 46 C1
Haddington Cl. Wen 131 E3
Haddington Way. Ayl 102 A1
Haddon Rd. Chor 167 E2
Haddon Rd. Maid 202 B3
Haddon. M Keyn 45 F4
Hadfield Rd. Stan 213 E1
Hadley Pl. M Keyn 34 B2
Hadlow Ct. Slough 205 E3
Hadrians Dr. M Keyn 34 A3
Hadrians Gate. Brac 38 A4
Hag Hill La. Burn 204 A4
Hag Hill Rise. Burn 204 A4
Haglis Dr. Wen 131 D3
Haig Dr. Slough 205 D2
Hailey Cft. Chin 147 D3
Hainault Ave. M Keyn 22 A1
Haines Cl. Ayl 100 C1
Haines Rd. Hol G 162 C3
Haithwaite. M Keyn 33 E1
Haldene. M Keyn 33 F1
Hale Ave. M Keyn 32 C3
Hale La. Wen 131 F2
Hale Rd. Wen 131 E2
Hale St. Ayl 115 F4
Hales Croft. Ayl 116 A2
Halfacre Hill. C St P 177 F1
Halfway House La. Ches 153 F4
Halifax Cl. Maid 202 A4
Halifax Rd. Chor 167 E1
Halifax Rd. H Wyc 172 B3
Halifax Rd. Maid 202 A4
Halifax Way. Maid 202 A4
Halings La. Den G 189 F4
Halkingcroft. Slough 206 B2
Hall Cl. M Mor 41 F2
Hall Ct. Datch 211 D4
Hall La. Chic 23 E4
Hall Meadow. Burn 197 D2
Hall Park Gate. Berk 135 F2
Hall Park Hill. Berk 135 F2
Hall Park. Berk 135 F2
Halldore Hill. Cook 195 F4
Halls Corner. Fla H 174 A1
Halton La. Hal 131 D4
Halton La. Wen 131 D4
Halton Wood Rd. Wen 131 E3
Haltonchesters. M Keyn 33 F3
Haly Cl. M Keyn 34 A2
Ham La. Old W 211 E2
Hamberlins La. Berk 134 A4
Hamble Dr. Ayl 115 E3
Hambleton Gr. She B E 46 A1
Hambling Pl. Dun 93 F4
Hambye Cl. Lac G 149 F2
Hamilton Ave. Hen-O-T 191 F1
Hamilton Gdns. Burn 197 D1
Hamilton La. M Keyn 57 E3
Hamilton Mead. Bov 146 A2
Hamilton Rd. Berk 135 D2
Hamilton Rd. H Wyc 162 B1
Hamilton Rd. Slough 205 D4
Hamilton Rd. Tha 126 A1
Hamilton Rd. Uxb 201 E1
Hamlins. M Keyn 47 D3
Hammersley La. Ty Gr 174 A3
Hammerwood Gate.
M K Vil 48 A4
Hammond Cres. M Keyn 35 D3
Hammond End. Far C 198 A4
Hampden Ave. Ches 144 A1
Hampden Cl. Ayl 115 E3
Hampden Cl. Sto P 199 D1
Hampden Gdns. Ayl 115 E3
Hampden Hill. Beac 175 D1
Hampden Rd. Ayl 115 E3
Hampden Rd. Ger C 177 E1
Hampden Rd. H Wyc 173 D4
Hampden Rd. Hgh V 151 D2
Hampden Rd. Lac G 150 B3
Hampden Rd. Maid 202 A4
Hampden Rd. Pres 151 D2
Hampden Rd. S Man 116 A1
Hampden Rd. Slough 206 C2
Hampden Rd. Wen 131 E3
Hampshire Ave. Slough 205 E4
Hampson Cl. M Keyn 34 A3
Hampstead Gate. M Keyn 34 B2
Hampton. M Keyn 46 A4
Hanbury Cl. Burn 204 A4
Handel Mead. Walt 48 B3
Handley Page Cl. Cran 24 C2
Hanging Croft Cl. H Wyc 173 F3
Hangings La. Pres 151 D3
Hanley Cl. Wind 160 E3
Hanmer Rd. M Keyn 47 F3
Hannon Rd. Ayl 115 E3
Hanover Cl. Slough 206 A2
Hanover Cl. Wind 209 F3
Hanover Ct. L Buzz 80 B4
Hanover Ct. M Keyn 34 B4
Hanover Ct. Ty Gr 163 D2
Hanover Way. Wind 209 F3
Hanscomb Cl. M Keyn 35 E1
Hanslope Rd. Cast 19 F3
Hanson Way. Ayl 116 A2
Harborne Ct. M Keyn 33 E1
Harborough Cl. Slough 204 B3
Harbourne Cl. S Man 115 E2
Harby Cl. M Keyn 46 B1
Harcourt Cl. Dorn 203 F2
Harcourt Cl. Hen-O-T 191 E1
Harcourt Cl. L Buzz 80 C4
Harcourt Green. Ayl 101 D1
Harcourt Rd. Dorn 203 F2
Harcourt Rd. Skch 158 C2
Harcourt Rd. Tri 119 E2
Harcourt Rd. Wind 209 F3
Harcourt. M Keyn 34 A2
Hardenwaye. H Wyc 162 C1
Harding Rd. Ches 144 B1
Harding Rd. M K Vil 48 B4
Hardings Row. Iver H 200 B1
Hardmead Rd. New B 8 A2
Hardwick Cl. Maid 202 A4
Hardwick Pl. Wbn S 49 D2
Hardwick Rd. Wbn S 49 D2
Hardwicke Gdns. Ame 154 C1
Hardy Cl. Ayl 115 F4
Hardy Cl. Slough 205 D3
Hare Cl. Buck 52 C4
Hare La. L Kin 152 A2
Hare Lane End. L Kin 152 A2
Hare Shoots. Maid 202 C3
Harebell Cl. Walt 48 A3
Harebell Wlk. Hol G 162 C3
Harefield Rd. Maid 202 A4
Harefield Rd. Uxb 201 E3
Harehatch La. Burn 186 C2
Harewood Pl. Slough 206 A2
Harewood Rd. L Chal 166 B3
Hargrave Rd. Maid 202 B4
Hargreaves Nook. M Keyn 22 A1
Harkness Cl. M Keyn 58 B3
Harkness Rd. Burn 204 A4
Harlans Cl. M Keyn 47 D4
Harlech Pl. M Keyn 57 F4
Harlestone Ct. M Keyn 22 A1
Harling Rd. Eat B 93 D2
Harlow Rd. H Wyc 173 E3
Harman Wlk. H Wyc 172 B2
Harmondsworth La. Harm 213 F4
Harmondsworth Rd.
W Dra 208 C1
Harper Cl. U Arn 94 B4
Harpers La. M Keyn 34 C4
Harrier Cl. Ayl 101 F2
Harrier Ct. M Keyn 47 D4
Harrier Dr. M Keyn 47 D4
Harries Cl. Ches 144 A1
Harries Way. Hol G 163 D3
Harrington Cl. Wind 209 F2
Harris Ct. Ayl 101 F1
Harris Rd. La En 171 D3
Harrison Cl. M Keyn 46 B3
Harrison Pl. Tha 125 F1
Harrison Way. Burn 204 B3
Harroell. L Cre 125 E3
Harrogate Ct. Slough 207 D1
Harrold Rd. Lave 8 A4
Harrow Cl. Ayl 115 F2
Harrow Cl. Maid 195 F1
Harrow La. Maid 195 F1
Harrow Rd. Slough 206 C2
Harrow Yard. Tri 119 D2
Harrowden. M Keyn 34 A4
Hart St. Hen-O-T 191 F1
Hartdames. She B E 46 A2
Harthmoor Cl. Skch 158 C2
Hartland Cl. Slough 205 E3
Hartley Cl. Sto P 199 E2
Hartley Copse. Old W 211 D1
Hartley. M Keyn 34 C4
Harts Rd. Hadd 127 D3
Hartwell Cl. Ty Gr 163 E1
Hartwell End. Ayl 115 D4
Hartwell Rd. Ash 9 F4
Hartwell Rd. Hans 10 C3
Hartwort Cl. Walt 48 A3
Harvard Cl. M Keyn 21 F1
Harvest Bank. H Hea 153 E2
Harvest Hill Rd. Maid 202 C2
Harvest Hill. Bou E 185 E1
Harvester Cl. M Keyn 33 D3
Harvey Orch. Beac 175 E2
Harvey Rd. Ayl 115 F3
Harvey Rd. Dun 93 E4
Harvey Rd. Slough 207 D2
Harvil Rd. Den G 190 C2
Harvil Rd. Ick 190 C2
Harwich Rd. Slough 205 D4
Harwood Dr. Uxb 201 F2
Harwood Rd. Mar 183 E1
Harwood St. M Keyn 34 A4
Hasgill Ct. M Keyn 34 A2
Haslemere Rd. Wind 210 A3
Haslow Ct. M Keyn 33 F2
Hasting Cl. Maid 203 E1
Hastings. M Keyn 32 C3
Hastoe Hill. Dra B 102 C4
Hastoe Hill. Has 119 D1
Hastoe La. Tri 119 D1
Hastoe Park. Ayl 101 F1
Hatch La. Bled R 100 A2
Hatch La. Harm 213 E4
Hatch La. Wind 210 A3
Hatch The. Oak G 209 E4
Hatches La. Hgh V 162 A4
Hatchgate Gdns. Burn 197 E1
Hatchlands. M Keyn 33 F1
Hatfield Cl. Maid 202 B3
Hatfield Rd. Slough 206 A2
Hatter's La. H Wyc 173 F4
Hatton Ave. Slough 198 B1
Hatton Ct. Wind 210 B3
Hatton Gr. W Dra 208 B2
Hatton. M Keyn 47 E3
Havelock Cres. Maid 202 A4
Havelock Rd. Maid 202 A4
Havelock St. Ayl 101 E1
Haven Shaw Cl. Ayl 116 A3
Havenfield Rd. H Wyc 172 B2
Haversham Rd. Have 20 B1
Haversham Rd. M Keyn 21 F1
Haw La. Bled R 149 D1
Hawfinch. Ayl 101 F2
Hawkins Cl. M Keyn 32 B3
Hawkmoor Cl. M Keyn 47 D4
Hawkridge. M Keyn 46 C2
Hawks Hill. Bou E 185 E1
Hawkshill Dr. Fel 146 C4
Hawkshill Rd. Slough 198 A1
Hawkslade Furlong. S Man 115 E2
Hawksmoor Cl. H Wyc 173 D4
Hawkswood La. Fulm 199 F4
Hawkswood. Oln 6 C3
Hawkwell Dr. Tri 119 E2
Hawkwell Estate. Old S 32 A4
Hawleys La. Whit 87 D3
Hawridge La. Char 143 F4
Hawridge La. Chol 143 F4
Hawridge Vale. Chol 133 F1
Haws La. Stan 213 D1
Hawthorn Ave. M Keyn 58 C4
Hawthorn Cl. Ayl 101 F1
Hawthorn Cl. Mar 183 F2
Hawthorn Cl. Turv 8 C3
Hawthorn Cres. Ty Gr 163 D1
Hawthorn Dr. N Den 201 E3
Hawthorn La. Burn 198 A3
Hawthorn Pl. Ty Gr 174 B4
Hawthorn Rd. P Ris 139 E2
Hawthorn Way. Ches 144 B1
Hawthorn Wlk. Ty Gr 163 D1
Hawthorne Cres. Slough 205 F4
Hawthorne Cres. W Dra 208 C2
Hawthorne Gdns. Fla H 174 A1
Hawthorne Rd. H Wyc 174 A3
Hawthorne Way. Wing 79 F2
Hawthorns The. Berk 135 D3
Hawthorns The. Cran 25 D1
Hawthorns The. Fel 146 C4
Hawthorns The. Map Cr 178 B3
Hawthorns The. Stan 212 C3
Hawtrey Cl. Slough 206 A2
Hawtrey Rd. Wind 210 B3
Hay La. Fulm 199 E4
Haydock Cl. M Keyn 57 E3
Haydon Rd. Ayl 101 E1
Hayes Pl. Mar 183 E1
Hayes Rd. Dean 31 F3
Hayfield Dr. Ty Gr 163 D1
Hayles Field. Frie 170 C1
Haymaker Cl. Uxb 201 F3
Haymill Rd. Slough 197 E1
Haynes Cl. Slough 206 C1
Haynes Mead. Berk 135 D3
Haynes Way. B Bkhl 48 B1
Hayse Hill. Wind 209 E3
Haystacks The. H Wyc 173 D4
Haythorp Cl. M Keyn 35 D3
Haywards Cl. Hen-O-T 191 E1
Haywards Croft. M Keyn 33 D3
Haywards Mead. Eton 204 C1
Haywood Park. Chor 167 F2
Haywood Park. Stew 68 B2
Haywood Way. Ayl 100 C2
Hazel Ave. Ayl 116 A4
Hazel Cl. Mar B 183 E3
Hazel Gr. M Keyn 58 B4
Hazel Rd. Berk 135 E2
Hazel Rd. Pres 151 E3
Hazelbury Rd. H Wyc 173 E3
Hazelcroft Cl. Uxb 201 F3
Hazelhurst Dr. Ayl 116 A3
Hazelhurst Rd. Burn 197 E2
Hazell Cl. Maid 203 D4
Hazell Park. Ame 165 E4
Hazell Way. Sto P 198 C3
Hazelmere Rd. Slough 206 A3
Hazelwood Cl. Ches 144 B1
Hazelwood. M Keyn 34 C4
Hazely. Tri 119 E2
Hazlemere Rd. Ty Gr 163 E1
Hazlemere View. Hol G 163 D3
Hazlerig Cl. Ayl 115 F3
Hazlerig Cl. Ayl 115 F3
Hazley Wlk. Buck 41 F1
Headington Cl. Maid 202 A4
Headington Rd. Maid 202 A4
Headland Cl. S Hea 152 A4
Healey Ave. H Wyc 173 E4
Heaney Cl. N Pag 22 A3
Hearn Cl. Ty Gr 162 C1
Hearn's Meadow. Se Gr 176 B2
Hearne Ct. C St G 177 D4
Hearne Dr. Holy 203 D1
Hearne Pl. M Keyn 46 C4
Hearne's Cl. Se Gr 176 B3
Heath Cl. Asp G 49 E2
Heath Cl. Ayl 116 A3
Heath Cl. Hol G 163 D3
Heath Cl. Stan 213 E1
Heath Ct. L Buzz 70 C2
Heath End Cl. G Kin 151 F1
Heath End Rd. Fla H 173 E1
Heath End Rd. G Kin 151 F1
Heath End Rd. L Kin 151 F1
Heath End Rd. Lit M 173 E1
Heath La. Asp H 49 D1
Heath Rd. Beac 185 F4
Heath Rd. G Bkhl 59 E1
Heath The. L Buzz 70 C2
Heath Way. Iver H 200 B2
Heathacre. Stan 212 C3
Heathcote Way. W Dra 208 B3
Heathcroft. M Keyn 34 C4
Heather Cl. W Dra 208 C4
Heather La. W Dra 208 C4
Heather Mead. Eat B 92 C3
Heather Wlk. Ayl 115 D3
Heather Wlk. Ty Gr 163 D2
Heatherden Green. Iver H 200 B2
Heatherside Gdns. Far C 187 E1
Heathfield Rd. H Wyc 172 A4
Heathfield Rd. Tapl 186 A1
Heathfield. M Keyn 33 F2
Heathlands Dr. Maid 202 A3
Heathrow Cl. Harm 213 D3
Heavens Lea. Bou E 185 E1
Hedge Lea. Woo G 185 E4
Hedgerley Hill. Hedg 187 E1
Hedgerley La. Beac 187 E3
Hedgerley La. Ger C 187 E3
Hedgerley. Chin 147 D3
Hedgerows The. M Keyn 46 C2
Hedingham Mews. Maid 202 B4
Hedley Rd. Fla H 185 D4
Hedsor Hill. Bou E 185 E1
Hedsor La. Bou E 185 F1
Hedsor La. Tapl 186 A1
Hedsor Rd. Bou E 185 D1
Helena Rd. Wind 210 B3
Helford Cl. Ayl 115 E2
Helford Pl. M Keyn 35 D1
Hellyer Way. Bou E 185 E2
Helston La. Wind 210 A3
Helston Pl. M Keyn 34 C1
Hemel Hempstead Rd.
Dag 107 F1
Hemingway Rd. Ayl 100 C1
Hemmings The. Berk 134 C2
Hemmingway Cl. N Pag 21 F3
Hemp La. Wigg 119 E1
Hempson Ave. Slough 206 B2
Hempstead Rd. Bov 146 A3
Hemwood Rd. Wind 209 E2
Hencroft St N. Slough 205 F2
Hencroft St S. Slough 205 F2
Henders. M Keyn 32 C3
Hendon Way. Stan 213 E1
Hendons Way. Holy 203 D1
Hendrix Dr. She C E 45 E4
Henley Rd. Bish 194 A1
Henley Rd. Hurl 193 E2
Henley Rd. Mar 194 A4
Henley Rd. Slough 204 C4
Hennerton Way. H Wyc 173 F3
Henrietta Rd. Tha 126 A1
Henry Rd. Ayl 116 A4
Henry Rd. Slough 205 E2
Henson Cl. Cran 24 C2
Hepleswell. M Keyn 33 F1
Hepplewhite Cl. H Wyc 173 E4
Herbert Rd. H Wyc 174 A4
Herberts Hole. S Hea 142 C1
Hercies Rd. Uxb 201 F3
Herd's Hill. Stp Cl 64 A2
Herdman Cl. M Keyn 33 D3
Heritage Cl. Uxb 201 E1
Hermitage Cl. Slough 206 B2
Hermitage La. Wind 210 A2
Hermitage The. Uxb 201 E3
Heron Cl. Ayl 116 B4
Heron Cl. Uxb 201 E3
Heron Dr. Slough 207 D1
Heron The. Ayl 101 F2
Herons Elm. Berk 134 C4
Herons Pl. Mar 183 F2
Heronsgate Dr. Chor 167 D2
Herriot Cl. N Pag 22 A3
Herschel Park Dr. Slough 205 F2
Herschel St. Slough 205 F2
Herston Cl. Ayl 116 A3
Hertford Pl. M Keyn 46 C1
Hervines Ct. Ame 154 B1
Hervines Rd. Ame 154 B1
Hesketh Rd. Yard G 18 C3
Het's Orch. Lac G 149 F3
Hetherington Cl. Slough 197 F1
Hetherington Way. Ick 201 F4
Hetton Cl. M Keyn 34 B2
Heusden Way. Ger C 188 C2
Hever Cl. Maid 202 B3
Hexham Gdns. M Keyn 57 E3
Heybridge Cres. B Bkhl 48 A2
Heywood Ave. Maid 202 A1
Heywood Court Cl. Maid 202 A1
Heywood Gdns. Maid 202 A1
Hibbert Rd. Maid 203 D2
Hibbert's Alley. Wind 210 B3
Hibberts Way. Ger C 188 B3
Hickmans Cl. Ting 51 D3
Hicks Farm Rise. H Wyc 173 F4
Hide The. M Keyn 47 E3
Higgs Ct. M Keyn 46 A4
High Beeches. Ger C 188 B1
High Beeches. H Wyc 172 B3
High Bois La. Ame 154 B2
High Coppice. Ame 165 E4
High Heavens Wood.
Mar B 183 E1
High Land Cl. Bri 96 A1
High Moors. Hal 131 D4
High Rd. Cook 195 F3
High Rd. Soul 69 F1
High Rd. Uxb 208 B4
High St N. Stew 68 B1
High St S. Oln 6 C2
High St S. Stew 78 C4
High St The. M Keyn 33 E1
High St. Ame 165 D4
High St. Ayl 115 F4
High St. Berk 134 C3
High St. Bov 146 A2
High St. Bri 110 A4
High St. Buck 41 E1
High St. Burn 197 E1

High St. C St G 177 E4
High St. Ched 105 D4
High St. Ches 154 A4
High St. Chin 147 E4
High St. Colnbrook 212 B4
High St. Cook 196 A4
High St. Cran 25 D1
High St. Cub 78 A1
High St. Datch 211 D3
High St. Dean 31 F2
High St. Dint 113 F1
High St. Eat B 92 C3
High St. Edle 92 C2
High St. Emb 13 F4
High St. Eton 210 B4
High St. G Hrwd 55 D2
High St. Ger C 177 F1
High St. H Wyc 161 E2
High St. H Wyc 173 D3
High St. Hadd 126 C3
High St. Harm 213 E4
High St. Harr 3 F3
High St. Have 21 D2
High St. Hth 60 C4
High St. Iver 207 F4
High St. Ivin 105 F3
High St. L Buzz 80 C3
High St. L Cre 125 E3
High St. La En 171 D2
High St. Lave 7 F4
High St. Lewk 157 D4
High St. Lud 96 A4
High St. M Keyn 21 F1
High St. M Keyn 33 F4
High St. M Keyn 58 C4
High St. Maid 202 C4
High St. Maid 203 E2
High St. Mar 183 F1
High St. N Craw 24 A3
High St. N Mar 76 A1
High St. N Pag 22 B2
High St. Nash 44 B1
High St. Oln 6 C2
High St. P Ris 139 D2
High St. Paul 17 E4
High St. Pott 18 B2
High St. Pres 151 E3
High St. S Gol 12 A3
High St. S Hea 152 A4
High St. Sher 13 F1
High St. Slough 205 F2
High St. Slough 207 D1
High St. Stan 213 E1
High St. Syr 27 D4
High St. Tapl 196 C1
High St. Tha 125 E1
High St. Thrn 54 A4
High St. Tri 119 D2
High St. Turv 8 C3
High St. Uxb 201 E3
High St. W Dra 208 C3
High St. W Und 6 A1
High St. Wadd 99 D3
High St. Wbn S 49 D2
High St. Wcot 98 A4
High St. Wedn 87 E1
High St. Wen 131 D2
High St. Whad 45 D1
High St. Whit 87 D3
High St. Wind 210 B3
High St. Wing 79 E2
High St. Wing 79 F1
High St. Wins 65 F3
High St. Wray 211 F1
High St. Y Has 1 A3
High St. Yard G 18 C3
High Town Rd. Maid 202 C4
High Trees. M Keyn 47 D4
High View Cl. Mar B 183 E4
Higham Cross Rd. Hans 10 C2
Higham Mead. Ches 144 B1
Higham Rd. Ches 144 B1
Highbeeches Cl. Mar B 183 E4
Highbridge Rd. Ayl 115 F4
Highbridge Wlk. Ayl 115 F4
Highbury La. M Keyn 35 D2
Highcroft Cl. Yard G 18 C3
Highfield Ave. H Wyc 172 A3
Highfield Cl. Ame 154 B1
Highfield Cl. M Keyn 47 D1
Highfield Cl. N Pag 22 C2
Highfield Ct. Ty Gr 163 D2
Highfield Dr. Ick 190 C1
Highfield La. Maid 202 A2
Highfield Park. Mar 183 D1
Highfield Park. Mar 194 A4
Highfield Rd. Berk 135 E2
Highfield Rd. Bou E 185 D2
Highfield Rd. Ches 144 A1
Highfield Rd. Fla H 185 D4
Highfield Rd. Maid 202 A4
Highfield Rd. P Ris 139 D2
Highfield Rd. Tri 118 C2
Highfield Rd. Wigg 119 E1
Highfield Rd. Wind 209 F2
Highfield Rd. Wins 65 F3
Highfield Way. Ty Gr 163 D2
Highfield Way. Y Has 1 A3
Highfield. C St G 177 E4
Highfield. L Cre 125 E4
Highgate Over. Walt 48 A3
Highgrove Hill. M Keyn 45 F4
Highgrove Park. Maid 202 C4
Highland Cl. M Keyn 46 C2
Highland Rd. Ame 165 E4
Highlands Cl. C St P 177 F2
Highlands End. C St P 177 F2
Highlands La. C St P 177 F2
Highlands Rd. Buck 41 F1
Highlands Rd. Se Gr 176 B3
Highlands. Fla H 185 D4
Highlea Ave. Fla H 185 D4
Highmoor. Ame 165 E4
Highmore Cotts. H Hea 152 C2
Highover Park. Ame 165 E4
Highview. Dean 31 F3
Highway Ave. Maid 202 A3
Highway. Dray P 68 B3
Highwood Ave. H Wyc 172 A3
Highwood Bottom. Lac G 150 A3
Highwood Cres. H Wyc 172 A3
Highwoods Cl. Mar B 183 E4
Highwoods Dr. Mar B 183 E4
Highworth Cl. H Wyc 162 C1
Hilbury Cl. Ame 154 B2
Hiljon Cres. Ger C 177 F1
Hill Ave. Ame 154 B1
Hill Ave. Hol G 163 D3
Hill Cl. Woo G 185 F4
Hill Farm App. Woo G 185 F4
Hill Farm La. C St G 166 A1
Hill Farm Rd. C St P 177 F2
Hill Farm Rd. Ches 154 B3
Hill Farm Rd. Mar B 183 F3
Hill Farm Rd. Tapl 196 C1
Hill Farm Way. Ty Gr 163 D1
Hill Farm. N Mar 76 A1
Hill House Cl. C St P 177 F2
Hill Mead. Berk 135 D2
Hill Meadow. Cole 164 C2
Hill Rd. Chin 147 E3
Hill Rd. Lewk 157 D4
Hill Rd. Lewk 157 E3
Hill Rise Cres. Ger C 177 F1
Hill Rise. Ger C 177 E1
Hill Side. Ched 104 C4
Hill St. H Wyc 174 A3
Hill The. Cole 164 B2
Hill The. Syr 27 D4
Hill Top Dr. Mar 183 A1
Hill Top La. Chin 147 F2
Hill View Rd. Wray 211 E1
Hill View. Berk 135 D3
Hill View. G Kim 129 E1
Hill View. Oak 109 E3
Hill Waye. Ger C 188 C2
Hillary Cl. Ayl 116 A3
Hillary Cl. H Wyc 173 F3
Hillary Rd. H Wyc 173 F3
Hillary Rd. Slough 206 C2
Hillbottom Rd. H Wyc 172 A4
Hillcrest Ave. Cook 195 F3
Hillcrest Cl. M Keyn 46 A3
Hillcrest Waye. Ger C 188 C2
Hillcrest. Cran 25 E1
Hillcroft Rd. Ches 144 B1
Hillcroft Rd. Ty Gr 163 E1
Hillersdon Chase. S Ham 69 E4
Hillersdon. Slough 206 A4
Hillesden Way. Buck 41 F1
Hillfield Cl. H Wyc 161 F1
Hillfield Rd. C St P 177 F2
Hillfield Sq. C St P 177 F2
Hilliard Dr. M Keyn 34 A2
Hilliards Rd. Uxb 208 B4
Hillier Rd. S Man 115 E2
Hillingdon Hill. Uxb 201 F1
Hillingdon Rd. Uxb 201 F2
Hillington Cl. Ayl 115 D4
Hillman Cl. Uxb 201 F4
Hillmead Ct. Tapl 203 F4
Hillrise. Slough 212 A4
Hills Cl. M Keyn 34 C4
Hills La. Cook 195 E4
Hillside Cl. C St G 177 D4
Hillside Cl. C St P 177 F2
Hillside Cl. U Arn 94 C4
Hillside Gdns. Berk 135 E2
Hillside Gdns. H Wyc 173 E4
Hillside Rd. Chor 167 E2
Hillside Rd. Mar 183 F2
Hillside Rd. Ty Gr 163 D1
Hillside. Ches 144 A2
Hillside. Gawt 51 F2
Hillside. H Wyc 173 E4
Hillside. Maid 202 B3
Hillside. S Har 190 B3
Hillside. Slough 205 F2
Hilltop Ave. Buck 41 F1
Hilltop Rd. Berk 135 E2
Hilltop. L Cre 125 E3
Hillview Rd. H Wyc 173 E4
Hillview. Sher 14 A1
Hillway. Ame 165 D3
Hillway. Wave 49 D3
Hillwerke. Chin 147 E3
Hilperton Rd. Slough 205 F2
Hilton Ave. Ayl 101 F1
Hilton Cl. Uxb 201 D2
Himley Green. L Buzz 80 B3
Hindemith Gdns. Walt 48 B3
Hindhead Knoll. Walt 48 A3
Hinkley Cl. S Har 190 B4
Hinksey Cl. Slough 207 D2
Hinton Cl. H Wyc 162 A1
Hinton Rd. Slough 204 C3
Hinton Rd. Uxb 201 E2
Hipwell Ct. Oln 6 C2
Hisbourne Dr. G Mis 152 A3
Hitcham La. Burn 197 D1
Hitcham La. Tapl 196 C1
Hitcham Rd. Burn 204 A4
Hither Meadow. Ger C 177 F1
Hithercroft Rd. H Wyc 161 F1
Hithermoor Rd. Stan 213 D1
Hivings Hill. Ches 144 A1
Hivings Park. Ches 144 A2
Hoathly Mews. M K Vil 48 A4
Hobart Cl. H Wyc 162 C1
Hobart Cres. M Keyn 35 D4
Hobart Ct. Mar 184 A2
Hobart Rd. H Wyc 162 B1
Hobarts Dr. Den G 189 F3
Hobbis Dr. Maid 202 A3
Hobbs Rd. La En 171 E2
Hobsons Wk. Tri 118 C3
Hockett La. Bish 195 D3
Hockett La. Cook 195 D3
Hockley La. Sto P 199 D3
Hockliffe Brae. Walt 48 A3
Hodder La. She B E 46 B1
Hodds Wood Rd. Ches 154 B3
Hodge Lea La. M Keyn 33 E2
Hodgemore Ct. M Keyn 21 F1
Hoe Meadow. Beac 175 E2
Hog Hall La. Dag 107 D3
Hog La. Ash Gr 144 B4
Hog La. Berk 134 E1
Hogarth Cl. Slough 204 C3
Hogarths Ct. M Keyn 33 F1
Hogback Wood Rd. Beac 175 D2
Hogfair La. Burn 197 E1
Hogg La. Hol G 163 E3
Hoggshill Rd. G Mis 152 A3
Hogshaw Rd. Gran 75 F3
Hogtrough La. Wen 131 E1
Holdom Ave. M Keyn 47 E1
Holes La. Oln 6 C2
Holiday La. Hans 10 C2
Holland Cl. Chin 147 E4
Holland Cl. Wen 131 D2
Holland Rd. Ayl 101 D1
Holland Rd. Mar 183 F2
Holland Way. N Pag 22 B2
Hollandridge La. Ston 168 B2
Holliday Cl. She C E 45 F4
Holliday St. Berk 135 E2
Hollies The. Bov 146 A1
Hollies The. Chor 167 E1
Hollies The. Tri 119 D2
Hollies The. Wigg 119 E1
Hollin La. M Keyn 33 F2
Hollingdon Rd. Soul 69 E2
Hollington. L Cre 125 D1
Hollinwell Cl. M Keyn 46 B1
Hollis Rd. H Wyc 173 F4
Hollow Hill End. Gran 75 F4
Hollow Hill La. Iver 207 E3
Hollow Rise. H Wyc 162 A1
Hollow Way La. Ame 154 C2
Hollow Way La. Ches 154 C2
Hollow Way. Ches 143 F1
Hollow Wood. Oln 6 C2
Holloway Cl. W Dra 208 C1
Holloway La. Chen 156 B1
Holloway La. Ibst 169 E2
Holloway La. W Dra 208 C1
Holloway The. Dra B 118 B2
Holloway The. P Ris 139 E3
Holly Wlk. Asp H 49 D1
Holly Cl. Far C 198 B4
Holly Cl. She C E 45 F3
Holly Cres. Wind 209 E3
Holly Dr. Berk 135 E2
Holly Dr. Maid 202 C4
Holly Dr. Wind 210 C1
Holly End. Wal A 161 E4
Holly Gdns. W Dra 208 C2
Holly Green La. Bled 138 A2
Holly Hedges La. Bov 156 B4
Holly Tree Cl. Bot 155 D4
Holly Tree La. Cudd 112 C2
Hollyberry Gr. Hol G 163 E4
Hollybush Hill. Sto P 199 D3
Hollybush La. Ame 154 B2
Hollybush La. Cook 195 D3
Hollybush La. Den 200 C4
Hollybush La. Iver 207 D4
Hollybush Rd. Ches 144 A2
Hollyfield Cl. Tri 119 E3
Hollyfield. Tri 119 E3
Hollytree Cl. C St P 177 F3
Holm Gate. M Keyn 46 A4
Holman St. Ayl 101 E1
Holmanleaze. Maid 203 D4
Holmdale. Slough 206 B3
Holmer Green Rd. Ty Gr 163 D2
Holmer La. H Wyc 172 B2
Holmer Pl. Hol G 163 E4
Holmers Ct. H Wyc 172 A2
Holmers Farm Way. H Wyc 172 B2
Holmers Farm Way. Lit M 172 B2
Holmers Farm Way. Mar B 172 B2
Holmewood. M Keyn 46 C2
Holmlea Rd. Datch 211 E3
Holmlea Wlk. Datch 211 E3
Holmoak Wlk. Ty Gr 163 D2
Holmsdale Cl. Iver 207 F4
Holmwood Cl. Maid 202 A3
Holst Cres. Walt 48 B2
Holt The. Buck 52 C4
Holton Hill. She B E 46 B1
Holton Rd. Buck 41 E1
Holts Green. G Bkhl 59 E1
Holtspur Ave. Woo G 185 F4
Holtspur Cl. Beac 186 A4
Holtspur La. Woo G 185 F3
Holtspur Top La. Beac 175 D1
Holtspur Way. Beac 175 D1
Holyport Rd. Holy 203 D1
Holyrood. M Keyn 45 F4
Holythorne. She C E 46 A3
Holywell Pl. M Keyn 35 E1
Home Cl. M Keyn 47 D1
Home Cl. W Tur 116 C1
Home Farm La. G Bkhl 59 E1
Home Farm Rd. Berk 134 B4
Home Farm Way. Sto P 199 E2
Home Farm. Nwtn L 57 E2
Home Meadow Dr. Fla H 185 D4
Home Meadow. Far C 198 B2
Home Way. Chor 167 F1
Homefield Cl. Skch 158 C2
Homefield. Bov 146 A2
Homelands Gdns. G Kin 162 B4
Homeridings House. M Keyn 34 A2
Homers Rd. Wind 209 E3
Homestall Cl. M Keyn 46 A4
Homestead Farm. Dint 114 A2
Homestead Rd. Maid 202 B2
Homestead The. Lit M 172 B2
Homestead The. She C E 46 A3
Homestead Way. Pott 18 C2
Homeward Ct. M Keyn 46 A4
Homewood. Slough 206 B4
Hondur Cl. Bier 102 A1
Honey Hill. Uxb 201 F3
Honey La. Hurl 193 F1
Honey Way. Wal A 161 D4
Honeycroft Hill. Uxb 201 F3
Honeypot Cl. M Keyn 34 A2
Honeysuckle Fld. Ches 144 B1
Honeysuckle Rd. Hol G 162 C4
Honeywick La. Eat B 92 C4
Honor End La. Pres 151 D4
Honor Rd. Pres 151 E3
Honorwood Cl. Pres 151 D4
Hoods Farm Cl. Bier 102 B2
Hooper Gate. M Keyn 35 E4
Hop Gdns. Hen-O-T 191 E1
Hopcraft Cl. U Arn 94 C4
Hopkins Cl. M K Vil 36 A1
Hopkins Ct. Ayl 101 F1
Hoppers Meadow. M Keyn 46 A4
Hoppers Way. G Kin 162 B4
Hopton Rd. Tha 126 A1
Horn La. M Keyn 32 B3
Horn St. Wins 65 F2
Hornbeam Cl. H Wyc 172 A2
Hornbeam Gdns. Slough 206 A2
Hornbeam Wlk. Ty Gr 163 D2
Hornbeam. N Pag 22 A2
Hornbill Cl. Uxb 208 B4
Horners Croft. M Keyn 33 E3
Hornhill Rd. Map Cr 178 B3
Horns La. H Wyc 172 A2
Horns La. P Ris 139 D2
Horse Hill. Bot 155 E4
Horseguards Dr. Maid 203 D4
Horsemoor Cl. Slough 207 D1
Horsemoor La. Cole 164 B1
Horsenden Rd. Bled 138 C1
Horsenden Rd. H Wyc 173 F3
Horseshoe Cl. Ched 105 D4
Horseshoe Cres. Beac 175 F1
Horseshoe Hill. Burn 197 D4
Horseshoe Rd. Bled R 159 E4
Horsleys. Map Cr 178 B3
Horton Bridge Rd. W Dra 208 C3
Horton Cl. Maid 196 B1
Horton Cl. W Dra 208 C3
Horton Gate. M Keyn 21 F1
Horton Rd. Datch 211 E3
Horton Rd. Hort 212 A3
Horton Rd. Ivin 91 D1
Horton Rd. Slap 91 E3
Horton Rd. Stan 213 D2
Horton Rd. W Dra 208 C3
Hortonsfield Rd. Yard G 18 C3
Horwood Ct. M Keyn 47 E1
Hospital Circular Rd. Wen 131 E3
Hospital Hill. Ches 154 B4
Hotch Croft. Cran 25 E2
Hotley Bottom La. Pres 151 E4
Houghton Ct. M Keyn 45 F4
Housman Cl. N Pag 22 A3
How's Cl. Uxb 201 E2
How's Rd. Uxb 201 E2
Howard Agne Cl. Bov 146 A2
Howard Ave. Ayl 116 A3
Howard Ave. Slough 205 F4
Howard Cres. Se Gr 176 B3
Howard Rd. Ches 144 A2
Howard Rd. Se Gr 176 B3
Howard Way. N Pag 23 D2
Howards Thicket. Ger C 188 B1
Howards Wood Dr. Ger C 188 B1
Howarth Rd. Maid 203 D3
Howe Dr. Beac 175 F3
Howe Hill La. Hol G 163 D4
Howland Pl. Hth 60 C4
Hoylake Cl. M Keyn 57 E4
Hubbard Cl. Buck 41 F1
Hubbards Rd. Chor 167 E2
Hubert Day Cl. Beac 175 E2
Hubert Rd. Slough 206 B2
Huckleberry Cl. Walt 48 A3
Hudnall La. L Gad 121 F4
Hudson La. She C E 45 E4
Hughenden Ave. H Wyc 173 D4
Hughenden Green. Ayl 115 F2
Hughenden Rd. H Wyc 162 A1
Hughenden Rd. Slough 205 E4
Hughendon Cl. Maid 202 B3
Hulbert End. Ayl 116 B3
Hulcombe Wlk. Ayl 101 F1
Hull Cl. Ayl 115 F3
Hull Cl. Slough 205 E2
Hulton Dr. Emb 13 F4
Humber Dr. Ayl 115 E3
Humber Way. M Keyn 46 C1
Humber Way. Slough 207 D1
Hundred Acres La. Ame 165 E4
Hungerford Ave. Slough 205 F4
Hungerford Dr. Maid 195 F2
Hunstanton Way. M Keyn 57 E4
Hunt Rd. H Wyc 173 F3
Hunt's La. Tapl 196 C2
Hunter Dr. M Keyn 58 B3
Hunter St. Buck 52 B4
Huntercombe Cl. Burn 204 B4
Huntercombe La N. Slough 204 B4
Huntercombe La S. Burn 204 B3
Hunters Cl. Bov 146 A1
Hunters Cl. Ches 144 A1
Hunters Cl. Tri 119 D3
Hunters Hill. H Wyc 173 F3
Hunters Mews. Wind 210 B3
Hunters Park. Berk 135 F3
Hunters Point. Chin 147 E3
Hunters Reach. M Keyn 34 A2
Huntingbrooke. M Keyn 45 F4
Huntingdon Cres. M Keyn 57 E3
Huntley Cl. H Wyc 162 B1
Hunts Hill La. Wal A 161 F3
Huntsman Gr. M Keyn 22 A1
Huntsmans. Dag 107 E3
Huntswood La. Burn 196 C2
Huntswood La. Tapl 196 C2
Hurley High St. Hurl 193 F2
Hurley La. Bish 194 A2
Hurley La. Hurl 194 A2
Hurlstone Gr. M Keyn 46 B2
Hurst Rd. Slough 204 B4
Hurstfield Dr. Burn 204 A4
Hutchings Cl. M Keyn 46 A4
Hutchings Rd. Beac 175 E3
Hutton Ave. M Keyn 34 C1
Hutton Way. Asp G 49 D3
Huxley Cl. N Pag 21 F2
Huxley Cl. Uxb 201 E1
Hyacinth Dr. Uxb 201 F3
Hychenden Cl. Wal A 161 F3
Hyde Cl. N Pag 22 B1
Hyde Green. Beac 175 F2
Hyde Green. Mar 183 F1
Hyde Heath Rd. S Hea 153 D3
Hyde La. Bov 146 A2
Hyde La. S Hea 152 C3
Hyde Meadows. Bov 146 A2
Hyde The. W Tur 116 C1
Hylle Cl. Wind 209 F3
Hylton Rd. H Wyc 172 B4
Hyrons Cl. Ame 154 C1
Hyrons La. Ame 154 B1
Hythe The. M Keyn 33 F2

Ibstone Ave. M Keyn 34 B2
Ibstone Rd. Skch 158 B2
Ickford Rd. Shab 124 B1
Ickford Rd. Worm 123 F3
Icknield Cl. Chin 147 D2
Icknield Cl. Wen 131 E3
Icknield Cres. Tri 119 D3
Icknield Way. Eat B 93 E2
Icknield Way. Tri 118 C2

Iffley Cl. Uxb 201 E3
Ilchester Cl. Maid 202 B3
Ilex Cl. Ty Gr 163 D2
Illingworth Pl. M Keyn 46 C4
Illingworth. Wind 209 F2
Imperial Rd. Wind 210 A3
In The Ray. Maid 203 D4
India Rd. Slough 206 A2
Ingleglen. Far C 198 A4
Ingleside. Stan 212 C3
Ingleton Cl. M Keyn 34 B2
Ingram Ave. Ayl 116 B3
Inholder Ct. M Keyn 34 C3
Inkerman Dr. Hol G 163 D3
Inkerman Rd. Eton 204 C1
Inkerman Terr. Ches 154 B3
Inn Farm Ct. N Pag 22 B4
Innings Gate. Frie 170 C1
Institute Rd. Burn 203 F4
Institute Rd. Mar 183 F1
Institute Rd. Tapl 203 F4
Intalbury Ave. Ayl 101 D1
Inverness Cl. M Keyn 46 C1
Inwood Cl. Cook 195 D3
Iona Cres. Slough 204 C4
Ipswich Rd. Slough 205 D4
Ireton Ct. Tha 125 F1
Iris Cl. Ayl 115 D3
Ironmonger Ct. M Keyn 34 C3
Irvine Dr. S Man 116 A1
Irving Cres. Ched 105 D4
Isaacson Dr. Walt 48 B3
Isambard Cl. Uxb 201 E1
Isis Cl. S Man 115 E2
Isis Way. Bou E 185 D2
Isis Wlk. M Keyn 46 C1
Island The. Stp Cl 63 E1
Islet Park Dr. Maid 196 B2
Islet Park. Maid 196 B2
Islet Rd. Maid 196 B2
Ivanhoe Cl. Uxb 208 B4
Iver La. Iver 208 A4
Iver La. Uxb 201 E1
Iver La. Uxb 208 A4
Iverdale Cl. Iver 207 E3
Ives Rd. Slough 207 D2
Ivinghoe View. Ayl 102 A1
Ivinghoe Way. Edle 92 C1
Ivins Rd. Beac 175 D1
Ivy Cl. N Pag 22 C2
Ivy Cres. Slough 204 C3
Ivy La. Bier 102 A1
Ivy La. G Bhkl 70 A4
Ivy La. Nwtn L 57 E2
Ivy La. Stew 68 C1
Ivy La. Wing 79 E2
Ivy Pl. La En 171 E3
Ivyhouse La. Berk 135 F3

Jack's La. Turv 8 C3
Jacks Cl. Lave 7 F4
Jackson Ct. Ty Gr 163 D2
Jackson Rd. Ayl 101 D2
Jacksons Cl. Edle 92 C2
Jacob Cl. Wind 209 F3
Jacobs Cl. M Keyn 34 B4
Jamaica. M Keyn 47 D3
James Cl. Hol G 163 D3
James Cl. Mar 183 F2
James Martin Cl. Den G 190 A3
James Rd. La En 171 D2
James St. Wind 210 B3
James Way. M Keyn 47 D1
Jane Cl. Ayl 116 A2
Jansel Sq. Ayl 116 A3
Jarry Ct. Mar 183 F2
Jarvis Cl. Ayl 116 A3
Jasmine Cl. Ayl 116 A2
Jasmine Cres. P Ris 139 D2
Jasons Hill. Bot 145 D1
Jeeves Cl. M Keyn 47 E4
Jefferson Cl. Slough 207 D1
Jeffries Ct. Bou E 185 D1
Jellicoe Cl. Slough 205 D2
Jenkins Cl. She C E 45 F3
Jenkins La. Dra B 132 C2
Jenna Way. N Pag 23 D2
Jenner Rd. Ayl 115 F3
Jennery La. Burn 197 E1
Jennings Field. Fla H 185 E4
Jennings Wharf. Wind 210 B4
Jennings. M Keyn 34 B4
Jerome Cl. Mar 183 F2
Jersey Rd. M Keyn 33 E3
Jesse's La. L Cre 125 E3
Job's La. Cook 195 D4
John Hall Way. H Wyc 172 B2
John Hall Way. Lit M 172 B2
John Hampden Way. Pres 151 D4
John Taylor Ct. Slough 205 E3
Johns La. Ash Gr 134 C1
Johnson Rd. La En 171 D3
Johnston Pl. M Keyn 46 C4
Joiner's Cl. C St P 177 F2
Joiner's La. C St P 177 F2
Joiners Way. C St P 177 F2
Joiners Way. Lave 7 F4
Jonathans. M Keyn 47 D3
Jones Way. Hedg 187 E1
Jordans La. Se Gr 176 C2
Jordans Way. Se Gr 176 C2
Joules Ct. She B E 46 B3
Jourdelay's Pas. Eton 210 B4
Journeys End. Slough 205 F4
Jubilee Rd. H Wyc 161 F1
Jubilee Rd. H Wyc 172 C4
Jubilee Rd. Skch 158 C2
Judge's La. L Buzz 80 C3
Judy's Pas. Eton 205 E1
Juniper Cl. Ty Gr 163 D2
Juniper Dr. H Wyc 172 B3
Juniper Dr. Maid 203 D4
Juniper Gdns. Walt 48 A4
Juniper La. Fla H 185 E4
Juniper Rd. Mar B 183 E3

Kaplan Cl. She B E 46 A3
Katherine Cl. Ty Gr 174 B4
Katrine Pl. M Keyn 58 B3
Kaybridge Cl. H Wyc 173 F3
Kaywoo Cl. Slough 206 B2
Keach Cl. Wins 66 A3
Keaton Cl. She C E 45 E4
Keats Cl. H Wyc 172 C3
Keats Cl. N Pag 22 A2
Keats La. Eton 210 B4
Keats Way. M Keyn 57 F4
Keats Way. W Dra 208 C1
Keble Cl. Ayl 115 D4
Keble Rd. Maid 202 C4
Keel Dr. Slough 205 E2
Keeler Cl. Wind 209 F2
Keen's Cl. H Wyc 162 C1
Keens La. Chin 147 E3
Keensacre. Iver H 200 B2
Keep Hill Dr. H Wyc 173 E2
Keep Hill Rd. H Wyc 173 E3
Keepers Farm Cl. Wind 209 F3
Keepers La. Ame 153 E2
Keinches La. Whit 87 D3
Kellan Dr. M Keyn 35 D1
Kelpatrick Rd. Slough 204 B4
Kelsey Cl. Maid 202 B2
Kelso Cl. M Keyn 57 E3
Kelvin Cl. H Wyc 172 C4
Kelvin Dr. She B E 46 B3
Kemble Ct. M Keyn 35 D3
Kempton Gdns. M Keyn 57 E3
Kenchester. M Keyn 33 F3
Kendal Cl. Ayl 116 A3
Kendal Cl. Slough 206 A3
Kendal Dr. Slough 206 A3
Kendal Gdns. L Buzz 80 B4
Kendalls Cl. H Wyc 173 F3
Kendrick Rd. Slough 206 A2
Keneally. Oak G 209 E3
Kenilworth Ct. Slough 205 F2
Kenilworth Dr. Ayl 101 E1
Kenilworth Dr. M Keyn 57 F4
Kennedy Cl. Far C 198 B3
Kennedy Cl. Maid 202 B3
Kennedy Cl. Mar 183 F2
Kennel La. Cook 195 E4
Kennet Cl. Ayl 115 E2
Kennet Cl. H Wyc 162 B1
Kennet Dr. M Keyn 57 F4
Kennet Pl. M Keyn 57 F4
Kennet Rd. Maid 202 C4
Kennett Rd. Bou E 185 D2
Kennett Rd. Slough 207 D2
Kennington Cl. N Pag 22 B2
Kennish Cl. Wins 65 F2
Kensington Dr. M Keyn 33 F1
Kent Ave. Slough 205 E4
Kent Cl. Uxb 201 E3
Kent Way. Maid 195 F1
Kentmere Rd. Ayl 116 A4
Kenton Cl. Mar 183 F1
Kenton's La. Wind 209 F3
Kents Rd. M Keyn 34 B4
Kenway Dr. L Chal 166 A4
Kenwell Ct. M Keyn 35 E2
Kenwood Gate. M Keyn 35 D1
Kenwood Cl. Maid 202 A4
Kenwood Dr. Chor 178 C4
Keppel Ave. Have 20 B1
Keppel St. Wind 210 B3
Kepwick. M Keyn 33 F1
Kercroft. M Keyn 33 F1
Kernow Cres. M Keyn 35 D1
Kerria Pl. M Keyn 47 D2
Kersey. M Keyn 34 B4
Kesters Rd. Ches 154 B4
Kestrel Cl. Berk 135 E2
Kestrel Cl. H Wyc 161 E1
Kestrel Dr. Hol G 163 D3
Kestrel Path. Slough 197 F1
Kestrel Way. Ayl 101 F2
Kestrel Way. Buck 52 C4
Keswick Ct. Slough 205 F3
Keswick Rd. Hans 11 D1
Ketchmere Cl. L Cre 125 E3
Ketton Cl. M Keyn 35 E4
Kew Ct. M Keyn 33 F1
Kew Gr. H Wyc 173 D2
Keyes Way. Buck 41 F1
Keynes Cl. N Pag 22 C2
Keys La. Maid 202 C3
Khasiaberry. Walt 48 A3
Kidd Cl. She C E 45 F3
Kidderminster Rd. Slough 198 A2
Kidwells Cl. Maid 202 C4
Kidwells Park Dr. Maid 202 C4
Kildonan Pl. M Keyn 33 E2
Kilfillan Gdns. Berk 135 D2
Killarney Dr. Maid 202 C4
Kiln Ave. L Chal 155 E1
Kiln Cl. Pres 151 E4
Kiln La. Bot 155 D4
Kiln La. Bou E 185 E2
Kiln La. Hedg 187 E2
Kiln La. Lac G 149 F3
Kiln La. Pres 151 D4
Kiln Pl. Maid 195 D2
Kilner Rd. Ayl 115 F3
Kilnwood. Wal A 150 A1
Kilpin Green. N Craw 24 A3
Kimbells Cl. Shab 124 B1
Kimber Cl. Wind 210 A2
Kimber's La. Maid 202 C2
Kimberley Cl. Slough 206 C1
Kimbers Dr. Burn 197 E1
Kimblewick La. G Kim 129 E2
Kimbolton Ct. M Keyn 35 D4
Kincardine Dr. M Keyn 46 C2
Kindleton. M Keyn 34 C4
King Charles Cl. Buck 41 F1
King Edward Ave. Ayl 116 A4
King Edward St. M Keyn 33 F4
King Edward St. Slough 205 E2
King Edward VII Ave. Wind 210 C4
King George Cres. M Keyn 32 C3
King George V Rd. Ame 154 B1
King John's Cl. Wray 211 E1
King St. Ches 154 A4
King St. H Wyc 160 B1
King St. M Keyn 32 C3
King St. Tri 119 D2
King Stable St. Eton 210 B4
King's Gr. Maid 202 C3
King's La. Lee C 142 A2
King's La. S Hea 152 C4
King's Rd. Ayl 115 F4
King's Rd. H Wyc 173 F2
King's Rd. Slough 205 F2
King's Rd. Uxb 201 E2
King's Rd. Wind 210 B2
Kingfisher Ct. Slough 198 A1
Kingfisher Rd. Buck 52 C4
Kingfisher. Ayl 101 F2
Kinghorn Park. Maid 195 E2
Kings Cl. C St G 177 E4
Kings Cl. Hen-O-T 191 E1
Kings Cl. Worm 123 E3
Kings Ct. Berk 135 E3
Kings Farm Rd. Chor 167 E2
Kings Hall Par. Wen 131 D2
Kings La. Cook 195 D4
Kings Mead. Edle 92 C2
Kings Meadow. Bier 102 B2
Kings Oak Cl. P Ris 139 E3
Kings Rd. Berk 135 D2
Kings Rd. C St G 177 E4
Kings Rd. Hen-O-T 191 E1
Kings Rd. W Dra 208 C2
Kings Ride. Ty Gr 163 D1
Kings Sq. H Wyc 173 F2
Kings St. Maid 202 C3
Kings Wood. Medm 193 E4
Kingsbridge. M Keyn 46 B1
Kingsbury Dr. Old W 211 D1
Kingsbury. Ayl 115 E4
Kingsdale Rd. Berk 135 D2
Kingsey Rd. Tha 126 B1
Kingsfield. Wind 209 E3
Kingsfold. M Keyn 34 A4
Kingshill Rd. H Wyc 162 B1
Kingshill Rd. Hol G 162 B2
Kingshill Way. Berk 135 D1
Kingshorn La. Maid 195 E2
Kingsland Rd. Ayl 116 A2
Kingsley Cl. N Pag 21 F2
Kingsley Cres. H Wyc 172 C3
Kingsley Dr. Mar B 183 E3
Kingsley Wlk. Tri 119 D2
Kingsmead Rd. H Wyc 173 F2
Kingsmead Rd. Loud 173 F2
Kingsmead. P Ris 139 D3
Kingston Ave. M Keyn 32 C3
Kingston Ave. W Dra 208 C3
Kingston La. Uxb 201 F1
Kingston La. W Dra 208 C2
Kingston Rd. H Wyc 162 B1
Kingstone Hill. Ast R 158 A4
Kingsway. Far C 198 B3
Kingsway. Ger C 188 C4
Kingsway. Iver 207 F4
Kingswood Ave. Ty Gr 174 A4
Kingswood Creek. Wray 211 E1
Kingswood Ct. Maid 202 C3
Kingswood La. W Und 96 C3
Kingswood Rd. Ty Gr 163 D1
Kinloch Pl. M Keyn 58 C3
Kinnaird Cl. Slough 204 B4
Kinnear Cl. She C E 45 F4
Kinross Dr. M Keyn 46 C1
Kinson Green. Ayl 101 F2
Kipling Dr. N Pag 21 F2
Kipling Rd. M Keyn 58 A4
Kirk Cl. She C E 46 A3
Kirkeby Cl. M Keyn 34 B3
Kirkstall Pl. M Keyn 46 C4
Kirkwall Spur. Slough 205 F4
Kirtle Rd. Ches 144 B1
Kirtlington. M Keyn 35 D3
Kitchener Rd. H Wyc 172 C4
Kite Field. Berk 134 C4
Kite Hill. M Keyn 47 D4
Kitsbury Rd. Berk 135 D2
Kitsbury Terr. Berk 135 D2
Kittiwake. Ayl 101 F2
Klondyke. Mar 183 E1
Knapp Gate. She C E 45 F4
Knaves Beech Way. Loud 174 B1
Knaves Beech. Loud 174 B1
Knaves Hill. L Buzz 80 B4
Knaves Hollow. Woo G 174 B1
Knebworth Gate. N Pag 22 A1
Knighton Way La. N Den 201 D3
Knights Cl. Eat B 92 C3
Knights Cl. G Bkhl 59 E1
Knights Cl. Wind 209 E3
Knights Hill. H Wyc 172 C3
Knights Templar W. H Wyc 173 D2
Knolls Cl. Win 89 D2
Knolton Way. Slough 206 B4
Knottocks Cl. Beac 175 E3
Knottocks Dr. Beac 175 E3
Knottocks End. Beac 175 E3
Knowl Gate. M Keyn 46 B4
Knowland Way. Den G 189 F3
Knowles Cl. W Dra 208 C3
Knowles Green. M Keyn 58 B4
Knowsley Cl. Maid 195 D1
Kop Hill Rd. P Ris 139 E2
Kop Hill Rd. Pres 139 E2
Krohn Cl. Buck 52 C4
Krypton Cl. She B E 46 B3
Kynaston Ave. Ayl 115 F2

La Roche Cl. Slough 206 B2
Laburnham Rd. Maid 202 C3
Laburnum Ave. W Dra 208 C3
Laburnum Cl. Mar 183 F2
Laburnum Cres. Slough 212 A4
Laburnum Gr. M Keyn 58 C4
Laburnum Gr. Slough 212 A4
Laburnum Rd. H Wyc 172 B3
Lace Mews. Oln 7 D2
Lacemakers. Chin 147 E3
Lacemakers. L Cre 125 E4
Laceys Dr. Hol G 163 D3
Lacy Dr. M Keyn 35 D4
Ladbroke Cl. Ayl 101 F1
Ladbrooke Rd. Slough 205 E2
Ladymead Cl. Whad 56 A4
Ladysmith Rd. Ivin 106 F3
Ladywalk. Map Cr 178 B3
Laggan Rd. Maid 195 F1
Laggan Sq. Maid 195 F1
Laggan Ct. M Keyn 58 B2
Lagger Cl. C St G 177 D4
Lagger The. C St G 177 D4
Lagonda Cl. N Pag 22 C2
Laiden Cl. M Keyn 58 B2
Lake Ave. Slough 205 E3
Lake Cl. Wins 66 A3
Lake End Rd. Burn 204 A3
Lakes La. Beac 186 C4
Lakes La. N Pag 22 A3
Lakeside Dr. Sto P 198 C2
Lakeside Rd. Iver 212 C4
Lakeside. Maid 196 A1
Lakeside. Tri 119 D3
Lamb Cl. N Pag 22 A2
Lamb La. M K Vil 48 B4
Lambe Rd. Wen 131 E3
Lamberhurst Gr. M K Vil 48 A4
Lambert Ave. Slough 206 C2
Lambert Wlk. Tha 125 F1
Lamberts Croft. M Keyn 33 E3
Lambourn Ct. M Keyn 46 B1
Lambourne Ave. S Man 115 E2
Lambourne Ct. Uxb 201 D2
Lambourne Dr. Maid 202 B2
Lambridge La. Hen-O-T 191 E2
Lambridge Wd R. Hen-O-T 191 D2
Lambscroft Way. Ger C 177 F1
Lambtons Way. Wins 66 A3
Lammas Ave. Wind 210 B3
Lammas Ct. Wind 210 B3
Lammas Rd. Ched 105 D4
Lammas Rd. Slough 204 B4
Lammas Way. La En 171 D2
Lammas Way. Loud 174 B1
Lammas. M Keyn 47 D3
Lampets Cross. M Keyn 47 D3
Lamport Ct. M Keyn 46 A4
Lamva Ct. M Keyn 32 C3
Lancaster Ave. Slough 198 B1
Lancaster Dr. Bov 146 A2
Lancaster Gate. M Keyn 57 F4
Lancaster Rd. Ayl 116 A3
Lancaster Rd. H Wyc 172 C2
Lancaster Rd. Maid 202 A4
Lancaster Rd. Uxb 201 E3
Lancaster Ride. Ty Gr 174 A4
Lancastria Mews. Maid 202 B4
Lance Way. H Wyc 174 A3
Lancelot Cl. Slough 205 D2
Lanchester Rd. Cran 24 B1
Lancot Ave. Dun 93 F4
Lancot Dr. Dun 93 F4
Lancotbury Cl. Tott 93 D4
Lancresse Cl. Uxb 201 E3
Lander Rd. Ayl 100 C2
Landsborough Gate. M Keyn 35 E4
Lane End Rd. H Wyc 172 A3
Lane The. Graf R 9 E1
Lane The. Mur 67 E3
Lane Wood Cl. Ame 165 F4
Lanercost Cres. M K Vil 36 A1
Lanfranc Gdns. M Keyn 35 D4
Langcliffe Dr. M Keyn 34 B3
Langdale Cl. M Keyn 58 B2
Langdale Cl. Maid 203 D3
Langdon Ave. Ayl 116 A3
Langdon St. Tri 119 D2
Langland Rd. M Keyn 47 E3
Langlands. Lave 7 F4
Langley Broom. Slough 206 C1
Langley Park Rd. Iver 207 E3
Langley Rd. Slough 206 B2
Langley Way. Mar 183 B1
Langston Cl. Slough 204 B3
Langstone Cl. Ayl 101 F2
Langton Cl. Maid 202 B4
Langton Dr. M Keyn 33 F2
Langton's Meadow. Far C 198 B3
Lanner Wlk. M Keyn 47 D4
Lansdell Ave. H Wyc 172 A2
Lansdown Rd. Ger C 177 E1
Lansdown Way. H Wyc 172 C2
Lansdowne Ave. Slough 205 F3
Lansdowne Ct. Slough 205 F3
Lansdowne Rd. Ayl 101 E1
Lansdowne Rd. Ches 144 B1
Lanthorn Cl. M Keyn 34 C3
Lappetts La. S Hea 152 C4
Larch Cl. Ayl 102 A1
Larch Cl. Slough 205 D4
Larch Cl. Ty Gr 163 E1
Larch Gr. M Keyn 58 C4
Larches The. Berk 134 B3
Larches The. Hol G 163 E4
Larchfield Rd. Maid 202 C3
Larchlands The. Ty Gr 163 E1
Larchwood. L Kin 152 A2
Lark Cl. Buck 52 C4
Lark Rise. Hol G 163 D3
Lark Vale. Ayl 101 F2
Larkfield Cl. H Wyc 162 C1
Larkin Cl. N Pag 22 A3
Larkings La. Sto P 199 D2
Larks Rise. Ches 154 B3
Larkspur Way. Hol G 162 C3
Larvic Rd. Ayl 115 E3
Larwood Pl. M Keyn 34 C1
Lasborough Rd. M K Vil 36 B1
Lascelles Cl. M Keyn 35 D4
Lascelles Rd. Slough 206 A2
Laser Cl. She B E 46 B3
Lashlake Rd. Tha 125 F1
Lassell Gdns. Maid 203 D4
Lastingham Gr. She B E 46 A1
Latchmoor Ave. Ger C 188 B4
Latchmoor Gr. Ger C 188 B4
Latchmoor Way. Ger C 188 B4
Latimer Cl. L Chal 166 B4
Latimer Rd. Ches 155 E1
Latimer Rd. Lat 155 E1
Latimer Way. Beac 175 E3
Latimer. M Keyn 32 C2
Laud's Cl. Hen-O-T 191 E1
Launceston Ct. She C E 46 A3
Launde. M K Vil 36 A1
Laurel Ave. Slough 206 C2
Laurel Cl. Iver 212 C4
Laurel Cl. Pres 151 D4
Laurel Cl. She C E 45 E4
Laurel Dr. Loud 174 A2
Laurel Dr. Wal A 161 E4
Laurel La. W Dra 208 C1
Laurel Rd. Ger C 177 E1
Laurels Rd. Iver H 200 B2
Laurels The. H Wyc 172 B2
Laurels The. M Keyn 47 E1
Lautrec Way. Ayl 100 C1
Lavender Gr. Walt 48 A3
Lavender Rd. Uxb 208 C4
Lavender Way. Hol G 162 C4
Lavender Wlk. Ayl 115 D3
Lavendon Rd. Oln 7 D3
Lawford Ave. Chor 167 E2
Lawford Cl. Chor 167 E2

Lawkland. Far C 198 B1
Lawn Ave. W Dra 208 B2
Lawn Cl. Datch 211 E4
Lawn Hill. Edgc 73 D1
Lawn Rd. Uxb 201 E3
Lawns The. Bri 96 A1
Lawns The. Ty Gr 163 D1
Lawnsmead Gdns. N Pag 22 B3
Lawrence Ct. Wind 210 B3
Lawrence Way. Slough 204 B4
Laws Cl. Turv 8 C3
Lawsone Rise. H Wyc 162 A1
Laxton Green. Maid 202 B2
Lay Rd. Ayl 101 D1
Layter's Ave. Ger C 177 E1
Layter's Cl. Ger C 177 E1
Layter's End. Ger C 177 E1
Layters Green La. Ger C 177 D1
Layters Way. Ger C 188 B3
Lea Cl. Mar B 183 E3
Leach Rd. Ayl 115 E4
Leachcroft. Ger C 177 D1
Leacroft Cl. W Dra 208 C4
Leacroft Rd. Iver 207 F4
Leaders Cl. Win 89 D2
Leafield Rise. M Keyn 33 E1
Leaholme Gdns. Slough 204 B4
Leapingwell La. Wins 66 A3
Leas Cl. H Wyc 173 F4
Leas Dr. Iver 207 F4
Leaside. S Gol 12 A3
Leather La. G Mis 142 A2
Leaver Rd. Hen-O-T 191 E1
Leckhampstead Rd. Akel 42 A4
Leckhampstead Rd. Wick 31 D2
Ledborough La. Beac 175 F2
Ledborough Wood. Beac 175 F2
Ledburn Gr. L Buzz 80 C3
Ledbury. M Keyn 21 E1
Ledger's Rd. Slough 205 E2
Lee Cres. Sto 114 B3
Lee Farm Cl. Bot 145 D1
Lee La. Bish 194 C1
Lee La. Maid 194 C1
Lee Rd. Ayl 115 E3
Lee Rd. Bled R 148 C3
Lee Rd. Qntn 85 D3
Leeches Way. Ched 105 D4
Leeds Rd. Slough 205 F3
Lees Cl. Maid 202 A3
Lees Gdns. Maid 202 A3
Lees Wlk. Mar 183 B1
Leeson Gdns. Eton 204 C1
Leicester Cl. Hen-O-T 191 E2
Leigh Hill. M Keyn 46 B1
Leigh Park. Datch 211 D4
Leigh Rd. Slough 205 D3
Leigh Sq. Wind 209 E3
Leigh St. H Wyc 172 C4
Leighton Gdns. Maid 196 A1
Leighton Rd. Edle 92 B2
Leighton Rd. L Buzz 80 C4
Leighton Rd. S Ham 69 F4
Leighton Rd. Soul 70 A1
Leighton Rd. Win 89 E2
Leighton Rd. Wing 80 A2
Leighton St. Hth 60 C3
Leiston Spur. Slough 205 F4
Lembrook Wlk. Ayl 115 E3
Lenborough Cl. Buck 52 B4
Lenborough Ct. M Keyn 35 E1
Lenborough Rd. Buck 52 B4
Lennon Dr. She C E 45 F4
Lennox Rd. M Keyn 58 B4
Lent Green La. Burn 197 D1
Lent Rise Rd. Burn 197 D1
Lenthall Cl. M Keyn 34 A2
Leon Ave. M Keyn 58 B4
Leonards Cl. Edgc 72 C1
Leopard Dr. M Keyn 35 D4
Leopold Rd. L Buzz 80 B4
Lerwick Dr. Slough 205 F4
Lester Gr. Ty Gr 163 D2
Lesters Rd. Cook 195 E3
Letchfield. Bot 155 D4
Letter Box La. P Ris 139 E4
Leven Cl. L Buzz 80 A4
Leven Cl. M Keyn 58 B3
Levings Cl. Ayl 101 D2
Lewins Rd. Ger C 188 B4
Lewins Way. Slough 204 C3
Lewis Cl. N Pag 21 F3
Lewis La. C St P 177 F1
Lewknor Cl. Lewk 157 D4
Lexham Gdns. Ame 154 B1
Lexington Ave. Maid 202 B3
Leybourne Gdns. Chin 147 E4
Leyburne Cl. Men 90 B4
Leyfield Rd. Ayl 115 F3
Leyland Pl. M Keyn 34 C1
Leylands La. Stan 212 C2
Leys Rd. M Keyn 46 A4
Leys The. Ame 154 A2
Leys The. Tri 119 D2
Leys The. Wbn S 49 D2
Leys View. Sher 13 F1
Leywood Cl. Ame 165 F4
Lichfield Down. Walt 48 A3
Lichfield Rd. Datch 211 E3
Liddall Way. W Dra 208 C3
Liddell Sq. Oak G 209 E3
Liddell. Oak G 209 E3
Lightlands La. Cook 195 F3
Ligo Ave. S Man 116 B1
Lilac Pl. W Dra 208 C3
Lillac Cl. Nwtn L 57 E2
Lillibrooke Cres. Maid 202 A2
Lilly Bottom La. Lac G 150 A4
Lily's Wlk. H Wyc 173 D3
Limbaud Cl. Walt 48 A3
Lime Ave. Buck 52 C4
Lime Ave. H Wyc 173 E3
Lime Ave. W Dra 208 C3
Lime Cl. N Pag 22 A2
Lime Cl. Ty Gr 163 D2
Lime Gr. Chin 147 E3
Lime Gr. L Buzz 80 C4
Lime Gr. Wbn S 49 D2
Lime Rd. P Ris 139 D2
Lime Rd. Yard G 18 C3
Lime St. Oln 6 C2
Lime Tree Cl. G Kin 162 B4
Lime Tree Wlk. Ame 165 F4
Lime Wlk. Maid 202 A4
Lime Wlk. N Den 201 E4
Limerick La. M Keyn 35 D2
Limes Ave. Ayl 116 A4
Limes The. Ame 154 A2
Limes The. M Keyn 32 C3
Limes The. M Keyn 58 C4
Limmer La. H Wyc 172 A2
Limmers La. G Kin 162 B4
Linceslade Gr. M Keyn 46 A4
Linchfield. H Wyc 173 F4
Lincoln Ct. Berk 135 D2
Lincoln Hatch La. Burn 197 E1
Lincoln Park Bs Cntr. H Wyc 172 B3
Lincoln Park. Ame 165 F4
Lincoln Rd. C St P 177 F1
Lincoln Rd. H Wyc 172 C3
Lincoln Rd. Maid 202 A4
Lincoln Way. Slough 204 B3
Lincoln. M Keyn 34 B4
Lincolns The. L Kin 152 A2
Lincroft. Cran 25 D1
Linden Ave. Maid 195 E1
Linden Ct. H Wyc 172 B3
Linden Dr. Far C 198 B2
Linden End. Ayl 115 F3
Linden Gr. M Keyn 34 C4
Linden Way. Dint 128 A4
Linden Wlk. Ty Gr 163 D2
Lindens The. Fel 146 C4
Lindo Cl. Ches 144 A1
Lindsay Ave. H Wyc 172 C4
Lindsay Cl. Stan 213 E1
Lindsey Rd. Den 190 A1
Lines Hill. A Abb 88 A2
Lines Rd. La En 171 D3
Lines The. A Abb 88 B2
Linfields. L Chal 166 B4
Linford Ave. N Pag 22 A2
Linford La. M Keyn 35 E2
Linford La. M Keyn 35 E4
Lingfield Cl. H Wyc 174 A3
Lingfield. M Keyn 33 F2
Lingholm Cl. Maid 202 B3
Link Rd. Datch 211 E3
Link Rd. H Wyc 172 B3
Link Rd. S Hea 152 A4
Link The. Hol G 163 D3
Link The. Slough 206 A4
Link Way. Den G 190 A3
Links Rd. Fla H 185 E4
Links Way. Fla H 185 D4
Linkswood Rd. Burn 197 E2
Linnet Cl. H Wyc 172 A2
Linnet Dr. Wcot 98 B3
Linnington Ave. Bot 145 D1
Linslade Rd. L Buzz 70 C2
Lintlaw Pl. M Keyn 47 D2
Linton Cl. M Keyn 34 B2
Lintott Ct. Stan 213 E1
Linx The. M Keyn 47 D1
Lionel Ave. Wen 131 D3
Lionel Cl. Wen 131 D3
Lipscomb La. M Keyn 46 A4
Lipscome Dr. Buck 41 F1
Lisle Rd. H Wyc 162 A1
Lisleys Field. G Kin 162 B4
Lissel Rd. M Keyn 47 F3
Lisset Rd. Maid 203 D3
Lister Green. Ayl 115 F3
Liston Rd. Mar 183 E1
Litcham Spur. Slough 205 E4
Little Benty. W Dra 208 B1
Little Bridge St. Berk 135 E2
Little Britain. Wadd 99 D4
Little Buntings. Wind 209 F2
Little Cl. Fla H 185 D3
Little Cl. H Wyc 172 C2
Little Greencroft. Ches 144 A2
Little Habton. She B E 46 A1
Little Ham La. P Ris 139 D3
Little Hame. M Keyn 35 F2
Little Hampden Cl. Wen 131 D2
Little Hill. Chor 167 E2
Little Hivings. Ches 144 A2
Little Hollis. G Mis 151 F4
Little Hoo. Tri 118 C2
Little Horwood Rd. G Hrwd 55 E2
Little Horwood Rd. L Hrwd 55 E2
Little Hundridge La. Char 153 D4
Little Kimble Hill. G Kim 129 F1
Little La. Bled R 149 E2
Little La. Lac G 149 E2
Little La. Y Has 1 A4
Little Linford La. Have 21 E2
Little London Green. Oak 109 F3
Little London. Dean 31 F2
Little London. Whit 87 D3
Little Marlow Rd. Mar 183 F2
Little Meadow. M Keyn 46 B4
Little Mollards. Win 89 D2
Little Orchard Cl. Lgwk 138 C3
Little Orchard. Ayl 101 F2
Little Park. Bov 146 A2
Little Park. P Ris 139 E2
Little Reeves Ave. Ame 165 F4
Little Shardeloes. Ame 165 D4
Little Spinney. Cran 25 E2
Little Springs. Ches 144 A2
Little St. Y Has 1 A3
Little Stanton. M Keyn 34 B4
Little Stocking. She B E 46 A2
Little Sutton La. Slough 207 E1
Little Sutton La. Slough 212 A4
Little Tring Rd. Tri 118 C3
Little Twye Rd. Dra B 132 C2
Little Windmill Hill. Sar 156 C4
Little Woodlands. Wind 209 F2
Littlebrook Ave. Slough 204 C4
Littlecote. M Keyn 34 A1
Littledown Rd. Slough 205 F3
Littlemere. M Keyn 33 E1
Littleport Spur. Slough 205 F4
Littlewood. Skch 158 C3
Littleworth Rd. Burn 186 B1
Littleworth Rd. H Wyc 161 F1
Littleworth. Wing 79 F2
Liverpool Rd. Slough 205 D4
Livesey Hill. She B E 46 A3
Lloyds. M Keyn 47 D4
Loakes Rd. H Wyc 173 D3
Lochinvar Cl. Slough 205 D2
Lochnell Rd. Berk 134 C3
Lock Ave. Maid 196 B1
Lock Bridge Rd. Bou E 185 D2
Lock La. Maid 202 B2
Lock Mead. Maid 196 B1
Lock Path. Dorn 209 E4
Lock Rd. Mar 183 F1
Lock Rd. Mar 183 F1
Lock View La. M Keyn 47 F1
Lockbridge Ct. Maid 203 E4
Locke Gdns. Slough 206 B2
Locke Rd. M Keyn 58 B4
Lockets Cl. Wind 209 E3
Lockton Ct. She B E 46 A2
Lodden Cl. S Man 115 E2
Loddon Dr. Maid 202 B4
Loddon Rd. Bou E 185 D2
Loddon Spur. Slough 205 F4
Lodge Cl. Mar 183 F1
Lodge Cl. Pad 53 E1
Lodge Cl. Slough 205 E2
Lodge Cl. Uxb 201 E1
Lodge Gate. M Keyn 34 C4
Lodge La. L Chal 166 C3
Lodge La. Pres 151 E3
Lodge La. S Ham 69 F4
Lodge Park The. N Pag 22 B2
Lodge Way. Wind 209 F2
Lodore Green. Ick 190 C1
Lollards Cl. Ame 154 B1
Lombardy Dr. Berk 135 E2
Lomond Dr. L Buzz 80 B4
Lomond Dr. M Keyn 58 B2
London End La. B Bkhl 48 B1
London End. Beac 175 F1
London End. Hth 60 C3
London End. Nwtn L 57 E2
London Rd E. Ame 165 F3
London Rd W. Ame 165 E4
London Rd. Beac 187 D4
London Rd. Berk 135 F2
London Rd. Buck 52 C3
London Rd. C St G 177 E4
London Rd. Datch 211 E4
London Rd. Dra B 118 A2
London Rd. Fel 146 C4
London Rd. G Has 136 A2
London Rd. G Mis 152 A3
London Rd. H Wyc 173 F3
London Rd. Holt 122 A1
London Rd. L Kin 152 A3
London Rd. Loud 173 F3
London Rd. M K Vil 36 A3
London Rd. M Keyn 46 A4
London Rd. N Pag 22 C1
London Rd. Old S 32 B4
London Rd. Slough 206 C1
London Rd. Tri 119 E2
London Rd. Wen 131 E1
Londrina Terr. Berk 135 E2
Long Cl. Far C 198 A3
Long Crendon Rd. Shab 124 B2
Long Croft Rd. Map Cr 178 B3
Long Dr. Burn 197 E1
Long Furlong Dr. Slough 197 F1
Long Furlong. Hadd 126 C3
Long Furlong. Sto 114 A3
Long Grove. Se Gr 176 B2
Long La. Bov 155 F4
Long La. Chor 167 E1
Long La. Cook 195 E3
Long La. Flau 155 F4
Long La. Oln 6 C2
Long Ley. Ched 105 D4
Long Lional. Ayl 115 E4
Long Marston Rd. Mars 104 C1
Long Massey. Oln 6 C3
Long Meadow Cl. P Ris 139 E3
Long Meadow. Ayl 116 A3
Long Meadow. Ches 144 B2
Long Park Cl. Ame 154 B2
Long Park Rd. Ame 154 B2
Long Park Way. Ame 154 B2
Long Plough. Ast C 117 E3
Long Readings La. Slough 198 A1
Long Ride. P Ris 139 D2
Long Row. Leck 30 C1
Long Street Rd. Hans 11 D2
Long View. Berk 135 D3
Long Wlk. L Chal 166 C3
Long Wood Dr. Se Gr 176 C2
Longbottom La. Beac 176 A2
Longbottom La. Se Gr 176 B2
Longbridge Cl. Tri 119 D3
Longbridge Way. Uxb 201 D2
Longcroft Ave. Wen 131 E3
Longcroft La. Bov 146 B3
Longcroft. Ast C 117 F3
Longcross. M Keyn 35 D3
Longdown Hill. P Ris 139 F3
Longfellow Dr. N Pag 22 A2
Longfield Dr. Ame 154 A1
Longfield Gdns. Tri 118 C2
Longfield Rd. Ches 143 F1
Longfield Rd. Tri 118 C2
Longfield. Hedg 187 E1
Longfield. L Kin 152 A2
Longfoot La. Paul 17 E4
Longland Way. H Wyc 172 B3
Longlands Ct. Wins 66 A3
Longlands Wlk. Wins 66 A3
Longleat Ct. M Keyn 33 F1
Longleat Gdns. Maid 202 B3
Longmead La. Burn 197 E3
Longmead. Wind 209 F3
Longstone Rd. Iver H 200 B2
Longview. Beac 185 F4
Longville. M Keyn 33 D4
Longwick Rd. Lgwk 139 D3
Longwick Rd. P Ris 139 D3
Longwood La. Ame 165 E4
Longworth Dr. Maid 196 B1
Lonsdale Cl. Maid 196 A1
Lonsdale Way. Holy 203 E1
Loosen Dr. Maid 202 A2
Loosley Hill. Lac G 149 E3
Lord Knyvetts Cl. Stan 213 E1
Lords Cl. M Keyn 47 E1
Lordsmead. Cran 25 E1
Loriner Pl. M Keyn 35 D3
Loring Rd. Berk 135 F2
Loring Rd. Dun 93 F4
Loring Rd. Wind 209 F3
Lorne Cl. Slough 205 D2
Lorraine Cl. H Wyc 173 F4
Loseley Ct. M Keyn 33 F1
Losfield Rd. Wind 209 F3
Lothersdale. M Keyn 34 A3
Lothian Cl. M Keyn 46 C1
Lott Meadow. S Man 115 E2
Lott Wlk. S Man 115 E2
Louches La. Wal A 161 E3
Loudhams Rd. L Chal 166 B4
Loudhams Wood La. L Chal 166 B4
Loughton Rd. M Keyn 34 A2
Lovat St. N Pag 22 B2
Lovatt Dr. M Keyn 57 F4
Love Green La. Iver 207 F4
Love Hill La. Iver 207 D3
Love La. Iver 207 E4
Lovejoy La. Wind 209 E3
Lovel End. Ger C 177 E2
Lovel Mead. Ger C 177 E2
Lovel Rd. Ger C 177 E1
Lovelace Cl. Hurl 193 F3
Lovett Gdns. Maid 196 B2
Lovett Rd. S Har 190 B4
Lovibonds Ave. W Dra 208 C4
Lowbrook Cl. Ayl 116 A2
Lowbrook Dr. Maid 202 A2
Lowdell Cl. W Dra 208 C4
Lowdon Cl. H Wyc 173 E2
Lower Boyndon Rd. Maid 202 C3
Lower Britwell Rd. Slough 197 E1
Lower Church St. Cudd 112 C2
Lower Church St. Skch 158 C3
Lower Cippenham La. Slough 204 C3
Lower Cl. Ayl 115 D4
Lower Cookham Rd. Maid 196 B1
Lower Dr. Beac 175 E3
Lower Eighth St. M Keyn 34 C1
Lower End Rd. Wave 49 D4
Lower End. Ash 97 F1
Lower End. Pidd (B) 95 F4
Lower End. Thrn 53 F4
Lower End. Win 89 D1
Lower Farm Cl. Shab 124 B2
Lower Farm Gate. Dint 114 A2
Lower Fourth St. M Keyn 34 B1
Lower Furney Cl. H Wyc 173 E4
Lower Green La. Chea 112 B1
Lower Green. Wcot 98 B4
Lower Icknield Way. Ast C 117 F2
Lower Icknield Way. Bled 38 B2
Lower Icknield Way. Chin 147 E4
Lower Icknield Way. Dra B 118 B4
Lower Icknield Way. G Kim 129 E1
Lower Icknield Way. Mars 118 B4
Lower Icknield Way. P Ris 138 B2
Lower Icknield Way. Wils 118 B4
Lower King's Rd. Berk 135 E3
Lower Lees Rd. Slough 198 A1
Lower Lodge La. Hol G 163 D3
Lower Mead. Iver H 200 B1
Lower Ninth St. M Keyn 34 C1
Lower Pound La. Mar 183 E1
Lower Rd. Bktn 81 D2
Lower Rd. Chin 147 E4
Lower Rd. Chor 167 E3
Lower Rd. Cook 195 F4
Lower Rd. Den G 189 E2
Lower Rd. Ger C 188 C4
Lower Rd. Lac G 149 E3
Lower Rd. S Man 115 F2
Lower Rd. Whit 87 D2
Lower Ridge. Bou E 185 D2
Lower Riding. Beac 175 D1
Lower Second St. M Keyn 34 B1
Lower St. Paul 17 D4
Lower St. Qntn 85 D3
Lower Stonehayes. M Keyn 34 C4
Lower Tenth St. M Keyn 34 C1
Lower Third St. M Keyn 34 B1
Lower Way. G Bkhl 59 E1
Lower Way. Pad 53 E1
Lower Wiggington. Wigg 133 F4
Lowes Cl. Skch 158 B3
Lowfield Cl. Ty Gr 163 D2
Lowfield Way. Ty Gr 163 D2
Lowlands Cres. G Kin 151 E1
Lowlands Dr. Stan 213 E1
Lowman Way. Ayl 115 E2
Lowndes Ave. Ches 144 A1
Lownes Gr. She C E 45 F4
Loxbeare Dr. She B E 46 B2
Loxboro Hill. Bled R 160 B2
Loxley Rd. Berk 134 C3
Lucas Pl. M Keyn 47 E4
Lucky La Or Cock La. Ayl 101 E1
Lucy La. M Keyn 46 A4
Ludgate. M Keyn 46 C4
Ludgate. Tri 118 C2
Ludgershall Rd. Pidd (B) 95 F4
Ludlow Cl. M Keyn 57 F4
Ludlow Mews. H Wyc 174 A2
Ludlow Pl. Ayl 116 B4
Ludlow Rd. Maid 202 C3
Luff Cl. Wind 209 F2
Lufford Park. M Keyn 34 C4
Luker Ave. Hen-O-T 191 E2
Lukes La. Lon M 104 B2
Lukes Lea. Mars 105 D1
Lullingston Dr. M Keyn 33 F3
Lumber La. Paul 17 D4
Lundholme. M Keyn 34 A3
Lupin Cl. W Dra 208 B1
Lutman La. Maid 195 F1
Lutyens Gr. Walt 48 B3
Lycrome La. Ches 144 B2
Lycrome Rd. Ches 144 C2
Lydford Ave. Slough 205 E4
Lydiard Cl. Ayl 116 A2
Lydiard. M Keyn 33 F1
Lydsey Cl. Slough 198 A1
Lye Green Rd. Ches 144 C1
Lyell. Oak G 209 E3
Lyme Ave. Berk 134 B4
Lynch Cl. Uxb 201 E3
Lynch Hill La. Slough 197 F1
Lynch The. Uxb 201 E3
Lyndhurst Ave. Cook 195 F3
Lyndhurst Cl. H Wyc 161 E1
Lyndhurst Rd. Ches 144 A1
Lyndon Cl. Pres 151 E4

Lyndon Gdns. H Wyc 173 F4
Lyndwood Dr. Old W 211 D1
Lyneham Gdns. Maid 195 D1
Lynher Cl. Ayl 115 E2
Lynmouth Cres. She B E 46 B2
Lynott Cl. She C E 45 F3
Lynton Green. Maid 202 C4
Lynton Rd. Ches 144 B2
Lynwood Ave. Slough 206 B2
Lynwood Rd. Ayl 116 A3
Lyon Rd. M Keyn 47 D1
Lysander Cl. Bov 146 A2

Macdonald Cl. Ame 154 B2
Mackenzie St. Slough 205 F2
Maclaren Ct. M Keyn 46 C4
Madeira Wlk. Wind 210 B3
Madeley Cl. Ame 154 B2
Madeley Rd. Ayl 115 F3
Magdalen Cl. M Keyn 32 B3
Magdalen Cl. Syr 27 E4
Magenta Cl. M Keyn 58 B3
Magnolia Dene. Ty Gr 162 C1
Magnolia Gdns. Slough 206 B2
Magnolia St. W Dra 208 B1
Magpie Cl. Fla H 174 A1
Magpie La. Cole 165 D1
Magpie La. Fla H 174 A1
Magpie La. Loud 174 A2
Magpie Way. Slough 197 F1
Magpie Way. Wins 66 A3
Mahler Cl. Walt 48 B3
Mahoney Ct. H Wyc 172 C4
Maidenhead Ave. M Keyn 34 B2
Maidenhead Crt Pk. Maid 196 A2
Maidenhead Rd. Cook 195 F3
Maidenhead Rd. Oak G 209 F4
Maidenhead Rd. Wind 209 F4
Maidstone Rd. M K Vil 36 B1
Main Dr. Ger C 188 B3
Main Par. Chor 167 E3
Main Rd N. Dag 107 D3
Main Rd S. Dag 107 E2
Main Rd. Ast 16 A2
Main Rd. Dray P 68 A3
Main Rd. Gr Und 83 D3
Main Rd. Lac G 149 F3
Main Rd. Syr 27 E4
Main Rd. Wadd 99 D1
Main Rd. Wal A 161 E4
Main St. Adsk 53 F1
Main St. Ash 97 F1
Main St. Beac 44 A3
Main St. Cast 19 F1
Main St. Chac 41 D2
Main St. Gawt 51 F2
Main St. Mur 67 E3
Main St. Pad 53 D1
Main St. Pres B 62 A4
Main St. Shal 39 F3
Main St. Ting 51 D3
Main St. Turw 38 B4
Main St. Twyf 62 B1
Main St. Twyf 72 C3
Main St. W Tur 116 C1
Main St. West 39 D2
Maitland Dr. H Wyc 173 D4
Maitland Rd. Hal 131 E4
Major's Farm Rd. Datch 211 E4
Malborough Way. Yard G 18 C3
Malcolm Rd. Ick 201 F4
Malders La. Cook 195 E2
Malders La. Maid 195 E2
Malins Gate. M Keyn 34 C4
Malkin Dr. Beac 175 E2
Mallard Cl. Ayl 101 F2
Mallard Dr. Slough 204 C3
Malletts Cl. M Keyn 32 C3
Mallow Gate. M Keyn 34 C2
Mallow Park. Maid 195 E1
Malmers Well Rd. H Wyc 173 D4
Malpas Rd. Slough 206 A3
Malt La. Syr 27 E4
Malting Cl. S Gol 12 A3
Malting La. Ald 120 B3
Malting La. Dag 107 E3
Maltings Cl. Cran 25 D1
Maltings The. Chac 41 D2
Maltings The. Oln 7 D2
Maltmans La. Ger C 188 B4
Malton Ave. Slough 205 D3
Malvern Cl. H Wyc 172 C4
Malvern Dr. L Buzz 80 B4
Malvern Dr. M Keyn 32 C2
Malvern Rd. Ayl 116 B4
Malvern Rd. Maid 195 E1
Malyns Cl. Chin 147 E4
Mandelyns. Berk 134 C4
Mandeville Dr. M K Vil 36 B1
Mandeville Rd. Ayl 115 F3
Mandeville Rd. Pres 151 D4
Manfield Cl. Slough 198 A1
Manifold La. She B E 46 A2
Manor Cl. Berk 135 E2
Manor Cl. Cast 19 F1
Manor Cl. Hans 11 D1
Manor Cl. M Keyn 35 F2
Manor Cl. Sal 37 E2
Manor Cl. Ty Gr 163 D1
Manor Cres. Se Gr 176 B3
Manor Cres. Wen 131 E3
Manor Ct. Mar 183 E2
Manor Dr. Ame 154 A2
Manor Dr. Ayl 101 F1
Manor Dr. Have 20 C1
Manor Dr. Stew 78 C4
Manor Farm Cl. Sto 114 B3
Manor Farm Cl. W Tur 116 C1
Manor Farm Cl. Wind 209 F2
Manor Farm Cotts. Old W 211 D1
Manor Farm La. Men 90 B4
Manor Farm Way. Se Gr 176 B2
Manor Gdns. H Wyc 162 A1
Manor Gdns. Woo G 185 F3
Manor House Cl. Ayl 101 F1
Manor House La. Datch 211 D3
Manor La. Ger C 188 B2
Manor La. Maid 202 C2
Manor Park Ave. P Ris 139 D2
Manor Park. M Mor 41 F2
Manor Pound Rd. Ched 105 D4
Manor Rd. Akel 41 F4
Manor Rd. Ayl 101 F1
Manor Rd. Ched 104 C4
Manor Rd. Ches 144 A1
Manor Rd. Have 20 C1
Manor Rd. M Keyn 33 D4
Manor Rd. Maid 202 C2
Manor Rd. N Pag 22 A2
Manor Rd. Nwtn L 57 E2
Manor Rd. Oak 109 E3
Manor Rd. Oving 86 B4
Manor Rd. P Ris 139 D1
Manor Rd. Se Gr 176 B3
Manor Rd. Tow 137 D3
Manor Rd. Tri 119 D3
Manor Rd. Ty Gr 163 D1
Manor Rd. Wen 131 E3
Manor Rd. Wind 209 F3
Manor Rd. Wing 102 B4
Manor St. Berk 135 E2
Manor St. Buck 52 B4
Manor View. Ty Gr 163 D1
Manor Way. Ches 144 B1
Manor Way. Cole 164 C2
Manor Way. Yard G 18 C3
Manor Waye. Uxb 201 E2
Manorfields Rd. Old S 32 A3
Mansard Cl. Tri 119 D2
Manse Cl. M Keyn 32 B3
Mansel Cl. Cast 19 F1
Mansel Cl. Slough 206 A4
Mansell Cl. She C E 46 A3
Mansell Cl. Wind 209 F3
Manshead Ct. M Keyn 32 C3
Mansion Dr. Tri 119 D2
Mansion Hill. Hal 131 F4
Mansion La. Harr 3 F3
Mansion La. Iver 207 E3
Maple Ave. W Dra 208 C3
Maple Cl. H Wyc 172 B3
Maple Cl. Maid 202 B3
Maple Cl. Ty Gr 163 D2
Maple Cres. Slough 206 A3
Maple Gr. M Keyn 58 C4
Maple Gr. Wbn S 49 D2
Maple Leys. Stp Cl 63 F2
Maple Lodge Cl. Map Cr 178 B2
Maple Pl. W Dra 208 C3
Maple Rise. Mar 183 F2
Mapledean. M Keyn 33 F2
Mapledurham Wlk. Maid 195 F2
Maplefield La. L Chal 166 A3
Maplin Park. Slough 207 D2
Marbeck Cl. Wind 209 E3
March Edge. Buck 41 F1
March Pl. Ayl 115 D4
Marchant Ct. Mar 184 A2
Mardle Rd. L Buzz 80 C3
Mare Leys. Buck 52 C4
Maree Cl. L Buzz 80 B4
Maree Cl. M Keyn 58 B3
Marefield Rd. Mar 183 B1
Marescroft Rd. Slough 197 F1
Margarets Gr. G Kin 151 F1
Marigold Pl. M Keyn 34 C2
Marigold Wlk. Hol G 162 C3
Marina Dr. Dun 93 F4
Marina Dr. M Keyn 33 E3
Marina Way. Burn 204 B3
Marina Way. Iver 208 A3
Marish La. Den G 189 E4
Marish Wharf. Slough 206 C2
Marjoram Pl. M Keyn 34 C2
Mark Dr. C St P 177 E3
Market Hill. M Keyn 47 D4
Market Hill. Whit 86 C3
Market La. Slough 207 E2
Market Par. Ty Gr 163 D2
Market Pl. Ger C 177 E1
Market Pl. Hen-O-T 191 E1
Market Pl. Hth 60 C4
Market Pl. Oln 6 C2
Market Sq. Ame 165 D4
Market Sq. Ayl 115 E4
Market Sq. Ches 154 A4
Market Sq. Hans 11 D1
Market Sq. P Ris 139 D2
Market Sq. Wins 65 F2
Market St. Ayl 115 E4
Market St. Maid 202 C4
Market St. Wind 210 B3
Marlborough Cl. Maid 202 A3
Marlborough Gate. M Keyn 34 C2
Marlborough Rd. Ayl 115 F2
Marlborough Rd. Maid 202 A3
Marlborough Rd. Slough 206 C1
Marlborough St. M Keyn 34 C3
Marlborough Tdng Es.
H Wyc 172 C4
Marley Gr. She C E 45 F4
Marlin Cl. Berk 134 C3
Marlin Ct. Mar 183 E1
Marlin Hill. Has 133 D4
Marlins Cl. Chor 167 F4
Marlow Bottom. Mar B 183 E3
Marlow Bridge La. Bish 194 C4
Marlow Comm. Mar 182 C2
Marlow Dr. N Pag 22 A2
Marlow Hill. H Wyc 173 D3
Marlow Mill. Mar 183 F1
Marlow Rd. B Bot 170 A1
Marlow Rd. Bish 194 C2
Marlow Rd. Bou E 184 B3
Marlow Rd. H Wyc 172 C2
Marlow Rd. Hen-O-T 191 F2
Marlow Rd. La En 171 E1
Marlow Rd. Lit M 184 B3
Marlow Rd. Maid 202 C4
Marlow Rd. Mar B 171 F1
Marmion Rd. Hen-O-T 191 F1
Marquis Ct. Hth 60 C4
Marram Cl. M Keyn 47 D3
Marriotts Ave. S Hea 142 C1
Marriotts Cl. Hadd 126 C3
Marriotts La. Hadd 126 C3
Marriotts Way. Hadd 126 C3
Marrod's Bottom. Cole 175 E4
Marron La. M Keyn 33 E3
Marroway. S Man 116 B1
Marroway. W Tur 116 B1
Marsh Dr. M Keyn 21 F1
Marsh End Rd. N Pag 22 B2
Marsh La. Tapl 203 F3
Marsh Lane. S Man 129 F4
Marsh Rd. G Kim 129 E2
Marsh Rd. Shab 124 B2
Marshalls La. M Keyn 35 E1
Marshalls Lea. Bier 102 B2
Marsham Cl. Ayl 116 A2
Marsham La. Ger C 188 C3
Marsham Lodge. Ger C 188 C3
Marsham Way. Ger C 188 C3
Marshcroft La. Tri 119 E3
Marshfield. Datch 211 E3
Marshworth. M Keyn 47 E3
Marston Cl. Ches 144 A2
Marston Ct. Lon M 104 A2
Marston Hill. Cran 25 F1
Marston Hill. Oving 86 B4
Marston Rd. Gran 75 F3
Marston Rd. Tha 126 A1
Marstonfields Rd. N Mar 76 A1
Marsworth Rd. Pit 105 E2
Martin Cl. Buck 52 C4
Martin Cl. M Keyn 34 C3
Martin Cl. Wind 209 E3
Martin Rd. Maid 202 C4
Martin Rd. Slough 205 F2
Martin's Plain. Sto P 198 C2
Martingale Pl. M Keyn 34 C3
Martins Dr The. L Buzz 80 C4
Martinsend La. G Mis 151 F4
Marunden Green. Slough 197 F1
Marwood Cl. M Keyn 46 B2
Mary Macmanus Dr. Buck 41 E1
Marygold Wlk. L Chal 166 B4
Maryland Rd. M Keyn 35 D4
Marys Mead. Hol G 163 D3
Maryside. Slough 206 C2
Mascoll Path. Slough 197 F1
Masefield Cl. Ches 144 A2
Masefield Cl. N Pag 22 A2
Masefield Gr. M Keyn 58 A4
Maslin Dr. M Keyn 47 D3
Mason's Ct. Ayl 115 D4
Mason. M Keyn 34 B4
Masons Rd. Slough 204 C3
Massie Cl. M Keyn 35 D3
Mathieson Rd. M Keyn 34 A3
Mathisen Way. Stan 212 C3
Matilda Gdns. She C E 46 A3
Matlock Rd. Ayl 101 F1
Matson Dr. Hen-O-T 191 F1
Matthew Ct. She C E 46 A3
Matthews Cl. Ayl 101 F1
Maud Jane's Cl. Ivin 105 F3
Maude Cl. Beac 176 A1
Maude Rd. Beac 176 A1
Maudsley Cl. She B E 46 B3
Mauduit Cl. Hans 11 D2
Maulden Gdns. M Keyn 35 D4
Maurice Mount. Hol G 162 C3
Maxham. She B E 46 A2
Maxwell Dr. Hol G 163 D3
Maxwell Rd. Beac 175 F2
Maxwell Rd. W Dra 208 C1
May Cl. Eat B 92 C3
May Rd. Turv 8 C3
May Tree Cl. Mar B 183 E3
Maybrook Gdns. H Wyc 173 E4
Maybury Cl. Slough 204 B4
Maybush Wlk. Oln 6 C3
Mayditch Pl. M Keyn 34 B2
Mayer Gdns. She B E 46 B3
Mayfield Ave. Ger C 188 B4
Mayfield Rd. Woo G 185 F3
Mayflower Cl. Sto 114 C3
Mayflower Way. Beac 186 A4
Mayflower Way. Far C 198 B4
Maygoods Cl. Uxb 208 B4
Maygoods Green. Uxb 208 B4
Maygoods La. Uxb 208 B4
Mayhall La. Ame 154 A2
Mayhew Cres. H Wyc 173 E4
Maylands Dr. Uxb 201 E3
Maynard Cl. M Keyn 34 A2
Maypole Rd. Burn 204 A4
Mays Way. Pott 18 B2
McConnell Dr. M Keyn 33 F3
Mcewen Ride. Hal 117 E1
Mckenzie Cl. Buck 52 B4
Mead Acre. P Ris 139 D3
Mead Ave. Slough 207 D2
Mead Cl. Den 190 A1
Mead Cl. Mar 183 F2
Mead Cl. P Ris 139 D3
Mead Cl. Slough 207 D2
Mead Platt. Skch 158 B3
Mead Rd. Uxb 201 E3
Mead St. H Wyc 174 A2
Mead The. Soul 69 F2
Mead Way. H Wyc 173 F2
Mead Way. Slough 204 B4
Mead Wlk. Slough 207 D2
Meades La. Ches 154 A4
Meadfield Ave. Slough 207 D2
Meadfield Rd. Slough 207 D2
Meadow Bank. S Man 116 B1
Meadow Cl. Ayl 102 A1
Meadow Cl. Berk 135 D1
Meadow Cl. Ches 144 A2
Meadow Cl. Cub 78 B1
Meadow Cl. H Wyc 173 F2
Meadow Cl. Mar 183 F1
Meadow Cl. Oak 109 E2
Meadow Cl. Old W 211 D1
Meadow Cott La. Cole 164 C2
Meadow Dr. Ame 154 C1
Meadow Dr. Lgwk 138 B3
Meadow Gate. Pad 53 D1
Meadow Gate. Pres 151 E2
Meadow Gdns. Buck 52 C3
Meadow La. Beac 175 F1
Meadow La. Eton 210 B4
Meadow La. M K Vil 36 A2
Meadow La. Pit 105 F2
Meadow Rd. Berk 135 D3
Meadow Rd. Chin 147 E3
Meadow Rd. Hen-O-T 191 F1
Meadow Rd. Mar B 183 F3
Meadow Rd. Slough 206 C2
Meadow Rise. Lac G 149 F3
Meadow Row. Buck 41 E1
Meadow Side. Se Gr 176 C2
Meadow View. L Cre 125 F2
Meadow View. Pott 18 B2
Meadow View. Stan 213 D1
Meadow Way. Ayl 102 A1
Meadow Way. Dorn 203 F2
Meadow Way. H Hea 153 E2
Meadow Way. Old W 211 D1
Meadow Way. Tha 125 F1
Meadow Way. Wing 79 F2
Meadow Wlk. Buck 41 E1
Meadow Wlk. Ty Gr 163 E1
Meadoway. Sto 114 C3
Meadoway. Stp Cl 63 F2
Meadowbank Cl. L Cre 125 E4
Meadowbrook Cl. Stan 212 C3
Meadowcroft. Ayl 101 D2
Meadowcroft. Ger C 177 E1
Meadows The. Ame 154 C1
Meadows The. Fla H 185 D4
Meadowsweet. Walt 48 A3
Meads Cl. M Keyn 34 A4
Meads The. Berk 134 C3
Meads The. Eat B 92 C3
Meads The. Tri 119 D2
Meads The. Uxb 201 F1
Meadway The. M Keyn 46 A4
Meadway. Berk 135 F3
Meadway. Buck 52 C3
Meadway. Dun 93 F4
Meadway. Oving 76 C1
Meare Estate. Woo G 185 F4
Meavy Cl. Loud 174 A2
Medale Rd. M Keyn 47 D3
Medallion Pl. Maid 203 D4
Medeswell. M Keyn 46 C2
Medhurst. M Keyn 33 F1
Medland. M Keyn 47 E4
Medley Cl. Eat B 92 C3
Medman Cl. Uxb 201 E2
Medway Cl. N Pag 22 C2
Meeting Oak La. Wins 66 A3
Megdale Pl. Ayl 101 E1
Melbourne Ave. Slough 205 E4
Melbourne Cl. Ayl 115 F3
Melbourne Rd. H Wyc 173 F3
Melford Green. Ayl 101 E2
Melfort Dr. L Buzz 80 A4
Melfort Dr. M Keyn 58 B2
Melick Rd. M Keyn 47 D2
Mellstock Rd. Ayl 115 F3
Melrose Ave. M Keyn 47 D1
Melrose Ct. H Wyc 162 A1
Melrose Wlk. Ayl 115 F3
Melton Ct. Maid 202 C3
Melton. M Keyn 34 B4
Mendelssohn Gr. Walt 48 B2
Mendip Cl. Slough 207 D1
Mendip Way. H Wyc 172 C4
Mendy St. H Wyc 173 D4
Menmarsh Rd. Worm 123 F3
Menteith Cl. M Keyn 58 B3
Mentmore Cl. H Wyc 172 A3
Mentmore Ct. M Keyn 45 F4
Mentmore Gdns. L Buzz 80 C3
Mentmore Green. Ayl 115 F2
Mentmore Rd. Ched 104 C4
Mentmore Rd. H Wyc 172 A3
Mentmore Rd. L Buzz 80 C3
Mentmore View. Tri 118 C3
Mentone Ave. Asp G 49 E2
Mercers Dr. M Keyn 34 A3
Merchant La. Cran 24 C1
Merchant La. Cran 25 D1
Mercia Rd. Maid 202 B2
Mercian Way. Slough 204 B3
Mere Cl. Mar 183 F1
Mere Rd. Slough 205 F2
Meredith Dr. Ayl 100 C1
Merlewood Cl. H Wyc 173 D2
Merlewood Dr. She B E 45 F2
Merlin Cl. Slough 212 A4
Merlin Wlk. M Keyn 47 D4
Merling Croft. Berk 134 C4
Merrivale Mews. W Dra 208 B3
Merry Down. H Wyc 161 E1
Merryfields. Uxb 201 E2
Mersey Cl. M Keyn 46 C1
Mersey Way. M Keyn 46 C1
Merton Cl. Maid 202 B2
Merton Dr. M Keyn 47 D2
Merton Rd. P Ris 139 D1
Merton Rd. Slough 206 A2
Merwin Way. Wind 209 E2
Messenger Cl. Ayl 116 A3
Metcalfe Gr. M Keyn 22 A1
Michael Rd. Maid 202 B3
Michigan Dr. M Keyn 35 D4
Michigan Dr. N Pag 22 B1
Micholls Ave. C St P 177 F3
Micklefield Rd. Ty Gr 174 A4
Mickleton. M Keyn 35 D3
Mid Cross La. C St P 177 F3
Midcot Way. Berk 104 C3
Midcroft. Slough 198 A1
Middle Cl. Ame 154 C1
Middle Cres. Den G 189 E2
Middle Dr. Beac 175 E3
Middle Field. W Tur 116 C2
Middle Green. Slough 206 C3
Middle La. Bov 146 A1
Middle Meadow. C St G 177 E4
Middle Rd. Ayl 116 A4
Middle Rd. Berk 135 D2
Middle Rd. Den G 189 E2
Middle Walk. Burn 197 E1
Middle Way. Chin 147 D3
Middlebrook Rd. H Wyc 161 F1
Middlefield Cl. Buck 41 F1
Middlegreen Rd. Slough 206 B3
Middlesex Dr. M Keyn 46 C1
Middleton. M Keyn 34 C4
Middleway The. H Wyc 172 B3
Midhurst Cl. Ayl 116 A3
Midland Rd. Oln 7 D3
Midsummer Arc. M Keyn 34 C2
Midsummer Bvd. M Keyn 34 C1
Miersfield. Lit M 172 B2
Mikern Cl. M Keyn 58 B4
Milburn Ave. M Keyn 46 C4
Milburn Dr. W Dra 208 C3
Mildenhall Rd. Slough 205 F4
Mildun Way. H Wyc 172 B3
Mile Elm. Mar 184 A2
Milebush. L Buzz 80 B4
Milecastle. M Keyn 34 A3
Miles Cl. Ayl 116 A4
Miles Cl. M Keyn 22 A2
Milesmere. M Keyn 33 E1
Milfoil Ave. M Keyn 34 C2
Milford Ave. M Keyn 32 C2
Mill Ave. Uxb 201 E2
Mill Cl. Ches 154 C3
Mill Cl. W Dra 208 B2
Mill Cl. Win 89 D2
Mill Ct. W Dra 208 B2

Mill End Rd. H Wyc 172 B4
Mill Gdns. Tri 119 D2
Mill Green. Turv 8 B3
Mill La. Ame 165 D4
Mill La. Asp G 49 E3
Mill La. Beac 175 F1
Mill La. Brac 38 A4
Mill La. Buck 52 B4
Mill La. C St G 177 D4
Mill La. Chin 147 D4
Mill La. Cook 196 B4
Mill La. Ger C 188 C3
Mill La. Hadd 126 A2
Mill La. Hor-c-S 108 A3
Mill La. Hort 212 A2
Mill La. Hurl 193 F2
Mill La. M Keyn 34 A4
Mill La. M Keyn 35 E2
Mill La. P Ris 139 D3
Mill La. S Hea 152 B4
Mill La. Sal 37 E2
Mill La. Skch 158 B3
Mill La. Tapl 203 E4
Mill La. Twyf 62 B1
Mill La. U Arn 94 C4
Mill La. W Tur 117 D1
Mill La. West 39 D2
Mill La. Win 89 E1
Mill La. Wind 210 A4
Mill Mead. Wen 131 D3
Mill Pl. Datch 211 E3
Mill Rd. Cran 25 E1
Mill Rd. L Buzz 80 C4
Mill Rd. M Keyn 58 C4
Mill Rd. Mar 183 F1
Mill Rd. Oak 109 E2
Mill Rd. Skch 158 B3
Mill Rd. Slap 91 E4
Mill Rd. W Dra 208 B2
Mill Rd. Whit 26 C2
Mill St. Ayl 101 F1
Mill St. Berk 135 E2
Mill St. H Wyc 172 C4
Mill St. Iver 212 B4
Mill St. N Pag 22 B3
Mill St. Slough 205 F3
Mill Tower. Eat B 92 C3
Mill View Rd. Tri 118 C2
Mill Way. Asp G 49 E3
Mill Way. Ayl 115 E4
Mill Way. Chor 167 F1
Millards Cl. Cran 25 E1
Millbank Pl. M K Vil 48 A4
Millbank. L Buzz 80 C4
Millbank. Mar 183 F1
Millboard Rd. Bou E 185 D2
Miller Pl. Ger C 188 C4
Miller's La. Old W 211 D1
Millers Turn. Chin 147 D3
Millers Way. M Keyn 33 E3
Millfield Ave. M Gib 71 F2
Millfield Cl. Cran 25 D1
Millfield. Berk 135 E2
Millfields. Ches 154 B3
Millhayes. M Keyn 34 C4
Milliers The. Ayl 101 F1
Millington Gate. M Keyn 35 E4
Mills Ct. M Keyn 33 D3
Millshot Dr. Ame 165 E4
Millside. Bou E 185 E2
Millstream La. Slough 204 C3
Millstream Way. Woo G 185 F4
Milner Rd. Burn 204 A4
Milton Ave. Ger C 188 B4
Milton Cl. Hen-O-T 191 E1
Milton Cl. Hort 212 A2
Milton Dr. N Pag 22 C2
Milton Fields. C St G 177 D4
Milton Gdns. P Ris 139 D1
Milton Gr. M Keyn 57 F4
Milton Hill. C St G 177 D4
Milton Lawns. Ame 154 B2
Milton Rd. Ast C 117 F3
Milton Rd. Ayl 115 F3
Milton Rd. Ches 144 A1
Milton Rd. M Keyn 35 E4
Milton Rd. M Keyn 47 F4
Milton Rd. Slough 198 B1
Milton Way. W Dra 208 C1
Milverton Cl. Maid 202 A2
Mina Ave. Slough 206 B2
Mineral La. Ches 154 B4
Minerva Gdns. M K Vil 48 B4
Minerva Way. Beac 176 A1
Minniecroft Rd. Burn 197 D1
Minshull Cl. Buck 41 E1
Minster Way. Slough 206 C2
Minstrel Ct. M Keyn 34 A4
Minton Rise. Burn 204 A4
Mirador Cres. Slough 206 B3
Mirrie La. Den G 189 E3
Misbourne Ave. C St P 177 F3
Misbourne Ave. H Wyc 173 F3
Misbourne Cl. S Man 115 E2
Misbourne Ct. Slough 207 D1
Missenden Gdns. Burn 204 A4
Missenden Rd. Ches 154 A4
Missenden Rd. G Kin 151 E1
Missenden Rd. Wins 65 F2
Miswell La. Tri 118 C2
Mitcham Pl. M Keyn 34 B2
Mitcham Wlk. Ayl 101 D1
Mitchell Cl. Bov 145 F2
Mitchell Cl. Slough 205 D2
Mitchell Cl. Tha 125 F1
Mitchell Rd. Cran 24 C1
Mitchell Wlk. Ame 154 C1
Mithras Gdns. Walt 48 B3
Mitre St. Buck 52 B4
Moat Cl. Pres 151 E3
Moat Dr. Pres 151 E4
Moat Dr. Slough 206 B4
Moat End. Bier 102 A2
Moat La. A Abb 88 B2
Moat La. M Gib 71 F1
Moat La. Pres 151 E4
Moat La. Win 89 D1
Moffy Hill. Maid 195 F1
Mole Run. H Wyc 161 E1
Monellan Gr. B Bkhl 48 A1
Monellan Gr. B Bkhl 48 A2
Monet Pl. Ayl 100 C1
Money La. W Dra 208 B2
Monkey Island La. Holy 203 F1
Monks Hollow. Mar B 183 F3
Monks Rd. Wind 209 E3
Monks Way. Harm 213 F4
Monks Way. M Keyn 34 B3
Monksfield Way. Slough 198 A1
Monkton Waye. Lac G 150 B3
Monmouth Cl. Ayl 101 D1
Monro Ave. She C E 45 F4
Montabaur Rd. Brac 38 A4
Montagu Dr. M Keyn 47 D4
Montagu Rd. Datch 211 D3
Montague Rd. Ayl 115 E4
Montague Rd. Berk 135 D2
Montague Rd. Slough 205 F3
Montague Rd. Uxb 201 E3
Montem La. Slough 205 E2
Montgomerie Cl. Berk 135 D3
Montgomery Cres. M Keyn 35 D4
Montgomery Pl. Slough 206 B4
Montpelier Ct. Wind 210 B3
Montrose Ave. Datch 211 E4
Montrose Ave. Slough 205 D4
Montrose Dr. Maid 202 A3
Montrose Way. Datch 211 E4
Monument La. C St P 177 F3
Monycrower Dr. Maid 202 C4
Moon St. M Keyn 33 E3
Moor End Cl. Eat B 92 C2
Moor End La. Eat B 92 C3
Moor End. Eat B 92 C3
Moor End. Holy 203 E1
Moor La. H Wyc 161 E2
Moor La. Harm 213 E4
Moor La. Maid 195 F1
Moor La. Sar 156 C2
Moor Park. Hal 131 D4
Moor Park. M Keyn 57 E4
Moor Rd. Ches 154 B3
Moorbridge Rd. Maid 203 D4
Moore Cl. Slough 205 D2
Moore Rd. Berk 134 C3
Moorend La. Tha 125 F1
Moorend La. Tha 126 A1
Moorend Rd. Yard G 18 C3
Moores Hill. Oln 6 C3
Moores La. Eton 204 C1
Moorfield Rd. Den G 190 A3
Moorfield Rd. Uxb 208 B4
Moorfield Terr. Maid 203 D4
Moorfield. Nwtn L 57 E2
Moorfoot. M Keyn 33 D2
Moorgate. M Keyn 46 C4
Moorhall Rd. S Har 190 A3
Moorhen Ct. Ayl 101 F2
Moorhills Cres. Wing 79 F2
Moorhills Rd. Wing 79 F2
Moorland Rd. Harm 213 E4
Moorlands Rd. Wing 79 E2
Moorlands. Wing 79 F2
Moorside Cl. Maid 195 F1
Moorside. Woo G 185 F4
Moorstown Ct. Slough 205 F2
Mop End La. H Hea 164 A4
Morar Cl. L Buzz 80 B4
Moray Dr. Slough 206 A4
Moray Pl. M Keyn 46 C1
Mordaunt Cl. Turv 8 C3
Mordaunts Cl. M Keyn 35 E1
More Ave. Ayl 115 E4
Moreau Wlk. Slough 206 C4
Morebath Gr. M Keyn 46 B2
Morefields. Tri 119 D3
Moreland Ave. Iver 212 B4
Morelands Dr. Ger C 188 C2
Morello Dr. Slough 206 C3
Moreton Dr. Buck 41 F1
Moreton La. Sto 115 D1
Moreton Rd. Buck 41 E1
Moreton Way. Slough 204 B3
Morley Cl. Slough 206 C2
Morley Cres. Walt 48 B2
Morrel Cl. She C E 46 A3
Morrice Cl. Slough 207 D1
Morris Cl. C St P 177 F1
Morris Wlk. N Pag 22 A2
Morrison Ct. She C E 45 F3
Mortain Cl. B Bkhl 48 A2
Mortain Dr. Berk 134 C3
Morten Gdns. Den G 190 A2
Mortens Wood. Ame 165 F4
Mortimer Hill. Tri 119 D2
Mortimer Rd. Slough 206 B2
Mortimer Rise. Tri 119 D2
Morton Cl. N Mar 76 A1
Morton Cl. Pit 105 E2
Mortons Fork. M Keyn 33 F3
Moseley Rd. Wal A 161 E4
Moses Plat La. Lac G 150 A3
Mossdale. M Keyn 34 A3
Mossway. Beac 175 E3
Mossy Vale. Maid 195 E1
Mount Ave. M Keyn 47 F2
Mount Cl. Ast C 117 F2
Mount Cl. Far C 198 B4
Mount Cl. H Wyc 172 C3
Mount Hill La. Hedg 188 A1
Mount La. Den 189 E1
Mount Pleasant Cl. Buck 52 B4
Mount Pleasant. Asp G 49 F2
Mount Pleasant. Ayl 101 E1
Mount Pleasant. La En 171 D3
Mount Pleasant. M Keyn 47 E2
Mount Pleasant. S Gol 12 A4
Mount Pleasant. Soul 69 F2
Mount Pleasant. Stp Cl 63 F1
Mount Pleasant. Yard G 18 C3
Mount St. Ayl 115 E4
Mount The. Asp G 49 E2
Mount The. M Keyn 47 F2
Mount View. Hen-O-T 191 E1
Mount Way. P Ris 139 D2
Mountain Ash. Mar B 183 E3
Mountbatten Cl. Slough 206 A2
Mounthill Ave. Old S 32 A4
Mountsfield Cl. N Pag 22 B2
Mountsfield Cl. Stan 213 D1
Mowbray Rd. Ayl 101 E1
Mowhills. Harr 3 F3
Moyleen Rise. Mar 183 B1
Mozart Cl. Walt 48 B2
Mt Nugent. Ches 144 A2
Mt Pleasant. Whit 86 C4
Muirfield Dr. M Keyn 46 B1
Mulberry Cl. Tri 119 D3
Mulberry Ct. Hol G 163 E4
Mulberry Dr. Slough 206 C1
Mullen Ave. M Keyn 34 C2
Mullins Way. Ayl 100 C1
Mullion Pl. M Keyn 35 D1
Mumfords La. Ger C 188 A4
Munces Rd. Mar B 183 E3
Mundaydean La. Mar 183 D2
Mundesley Spur. Slough 205 F4
Murcott Rd. U Arn 94 B3
Murray Rd. Berk 135 E3
Murrey Cl. She B E 46 B3
Murrin Rd. Maid 202 B4
Mursley C. M Keyn 32 C3
Mursley Rd. L Hrwd 55 F1
Mursley Rd. Mur 67 D2
Musgrave Rd. Chin 147 E1
Myddleton Rd. Uxb 201 E2
Mylne Cl. H Wyc 172 C4
Mynchen Cl. Beac 175 E3
Mynchen End. Beac 175 E3
Mynchen Rd. Beac 175 E3
Myrke The. Datch 205 F1
Myrtle Bank. M Keyn 33 F3
Myrtle Cl. Stan 212 C3
Myrtle Cl. W Dra 208 C4
Myrtle Cres. Slough 205 F3

Nag's Head La. G Kin 152 A2
Nag's Head La. L Kin 152 A2
Nailzee Cl. Ger C 188 C2
Nairdwood Cl. Pres 151 F2
Nairdwood La. Pres 151 E3
Nairdwood Way. Pres 151 F2
Nairn Ct. M Keyn 46 C1
Naisby Dr. G Bkhl 59 E1
Nalders Rd. Ches 144 B1
Nan Aires. Win 89 D2
Nancy Hall Ct. H Wyc 172 B2
Naphill Pl. M Keyn 34 B2
Napier Cl. W Dra 208 C2
Napier Rd. Harm 213 E3
Napier St. M Keyn 58 B4
Nappin Cl. Ayl 101 D2
Nappins Cl. L Cre 125 E3
Narberth Dr. Ayl 116 A4
Narcot La. C St G 177 D3
Narcot La. Ger C 177 D3
Narcot Rd. C St G 177 D4
Narcot Way. C St G 177 D3
Narrow La. Asp H 49 D2
Narrow La. H Wyc 161 F2
Naseby Cl. N Pag 22 A2
Naseby Cl. Tha 126 A1
Naseby Ct. Buck 41 F1
Naseby Ct. M Keyn 34 A3
Nash Cl. Ayl 116 A2
Nash Lee Rd. Elle 130 A3
Nash Rd. G Hrwd 55 D2
Nash Rd. Slough 207 D1
Nash Rd. Thrn 54 A4
Nash Rd. Whad 45 D1
Nashdom La. Burn 197 D3
Nashleigh Hill. Ches 144 B2
Nathaniel Cl. She C E 46 A3
Nathaniel Wlk. Tri 119 D3
Natwoke Cl. Beac 175 E3
Neal Cl. Den G 189 D2
Neale Cl. Lit M 172 B2
Neapland. M Keyn 47 D3
Near Town Gdns. Oln 7 D2
Neath Cres. M Keyn 47 D1
Needham Cl. Wind 209 F3
Needlemakers. L Cre 125 E4
Neilson Ct. Walt 48 B3
Nelson Cl. Cole 164 B2
Nelson Cl. H Wyc 173 F3
Nelson Cl. She C E 45 F3
Nelson Cl. Slough 206 B1
Nelson Ct. Buck 52 B4
Nelson Rd. Dag 107 E3
Nelson Rd. Harm 213 F3
Nelson Rd. Wind 209 F2
Nelson St. Buck 52 B4
Nelson Terr. Ayl 115 E4
Nene Cl. Ayl 115 E2
Nene Cl. N Pag 22 B2
Nene Dr. M Keyn 57 F4
Ness Way. M Keyn 58 B3
Nether Cl. Brac 38 A4
Netherby Cl. Tri 119 E3
Nethercote La. Lewk 157 D4
Netherwood Rd. Beac 175 E3
Nettlecombe. M Keyn 46 B2
Nettleden Rd. L Gad 121 F2
Nettleton Rd. Ick 201 F4
Nevill Cl. Hans 11 D1
Neville Cl. Sto P 198 C3
Nevis Cl. L Buzz 80 B4
Nevis Gr. M Keyn 58 C2
New College Ct. Chac 41 D2
New Ct. Mar 183 E1
New Dr. H Wyc 173 F4
New Footpath. Ches 154 A4
New Garden Dr. W Dra 208 C2
New Inn La. Gawt 51 F2
New Par. Chor 167 E3
New Peachey La. Uxb 208 B4
New Pond Rd. Hol G 163 E4
New Rd. Ame 154 C1
New Rd. Ast C 117 F3
New Rd. Ayl 116 C3
New Rd. Berk 134 C4
New Rd. Berk 135 E3
New Rd. Bou E 185 D2
New Rd. Cast 19 F3
New Rd. Chipf 146 C1
New Rd. Cole 164 C2
New Rd. Cook 195 F4
New Rd. Datch 211 E3
New Rd. Dint 113 F1
New Rd. Dray P 68 B3
New Rd. G Kin 162 B4
New Rd. H Wyc 172 B3
New Rd. Harr 3 F3
New Rd. Hurl 193 F2
New Rd. L Buzz 80 C4
New Rd. L Chal 166 C3
New Rd. L Kin 152 A2
New Rd. La En 170 C3
New Rd. Lac G 149 F2
New Rd. Mar B 183 E3
New Rd. P Ris 139 E2
New Rd. Pres 151 E3
New Rd. Sar 156 C1
New Rd. Skch 158 C2
New Rd. Slough 207 D2
New Rd. Tri 119 D3
New Rd. Ty Gr 163 E1
New Rd. Wal A 150 A1
New Rd. Wedn 101 D4
New Rd. Wils 118 B4
New Road Cl. H Wyc 172 B3
New Road Gdns. H Wyc 172 B3
New St. Ayl 101 E1
New St. Berk 135 E2
New St. Ched 104 C4
New St. Hen-O-T 191 F1
New St. M Keyn 32 B3
New St. Ting 51 D3
New St. Wadd 99 D4
New Windsor St. Uxb 201 E2
Newark Ct. B Bkhl 48 A2
Newbarn La. Se Gr 176 C3
Newberry Cres. Wind 209 E3
Newbery Way. Slough 205 E2
Newbolt Cl. Paul 17 D4
Newbridge Oval. She B E 46 A2
Newbury Ct. M Keyn 57 E3
Newbury Dr. Maid 203 D3
Newbury Rd. Harm 213 F3
Newchurch Rd. Slough 204 C4
Newcombe Rise. W Dra 208 C4
Newcourt. Uxb 208 B4
Newcroft Cl. Uxb 208 C4
Newell Cl. Ayl 116 A3
Newells Hedge. Pit 105 E3
Newfield Gdns. Mar 183 F2
Newfield Rd. Mar 183 F2
Newground Rd. Ald 120 A2
Newhall Cl. Bov 146 A2
Newhaven Spur. Slough 198 A1
Newhouse Rd. Bov 146 A3
Newlands Dr. Maid 202 A4
Newlands Dr. Stan 212 C2
Newlands Gdns. Wing 79 F1
Newlyn Pl. M Keyn 35 D1
Newmarket Ct. M K Vil 36 B1
Newmer Rd. H Wyc 172 A2
Newport Pagnell Rd. Stag 16 B2
Newport Rd. Ast 15 E1
Newport Rd. Emb 13 F4
Newport Rd. Hans 11 D1
Newport Rd. Hth 60 C4
Newport Rd. M K Vil 36 B1
Newport Rd. M Keyn 35 E1
Newport Rd. Moul 36 B4
Newport Rd. Slough 197 F1
Newport Rd. Wave 48 C4
Newton Cl. Slough 206 C2
Newton Ct. Old W 211 D1
Newton La. Old W 211 D1
Newton Rd. Dray P 68 B4
Newton Rd. Harm 213 F3
Newton Rd. M Keyn 57 F3
Newton Rd. Turv 8 C3
Newton St. Oln 7 D2
Newtonside Orch. Old W 211 D1
Newtown Rd. Mar 183 F2
Newtown Rd. N Den 201 D3
Newtown Rd. S Ham 69 E4
Newville. Wedn 87 E1
Newyears Green La. S Har 190 C3
Neyland Dr. Ayl 101 E2
Nicholas Gdns. H Wyc 173 E4
Nicholas Mead. M Keyn 34 C4
Nicholls. Oak G 209 E3
Nicholsons La. Maid 202 C4
Nicol Cl. Ger C 177 E1
Nicol End. Ger C 177 E1
Nicol Rd. Ger C 177 E1
Nightingale Cl. Hol G 163 D3
Nightingale Cl. Stp Cl 63 F1
Nightingale Park. Burn 197 F3
Nightingale Pl. Buck 41 F1
Nightingale Rd. Ayl 115 F3
Nightingale Rd. Ches 144 A1
Nightingale Rd. Wen 131 D3
Nightingale Way. Den G 189 F3
Nightingales Corner. L Chal 166 B4
Nightingales La. C St G 166 B2
Nightingales La. L Chal 166 B2
Nine Elms Ave. Uxb 208 B4
Nine Elms Cl. Uxb 208 B4
Nine Stiles Cl. N Den 201 D3
Ninnings Rd. C St P 177 F2
Ninnings Way. C St P 177 F2
Nixey Cl. Slough 206 A2
Noble Cl. M Keyn 35 D4
Nooke The. M Keyn 35 E4
Norbrek. M Keyn 33 F1
Norden Cl. Maid 202 B2
Norden Rd. Maid 202 B3
Norfolk Ave. Slough 205 E4
Norfolk Park Cotts. Maid 202 C4
Norfolk Rd. Maid 202 C4
Norfolk Rd. Turv 8 C3
Norfolk Rd. Uxb 201 E3
Norfolk Terr. Ayl 101 F1
Norgrove Park. Ger C 188 C4
Norman Ave. Hen-O-T 191 F1
Norman Way. Dun 93 F4
Normandy Dr. Berk 135 D3
Normandy Way. M Keyn 46 C1
Normans Cl. Uxb 208 C4
Normans The. Slough 206 A4
Normill Terr. Ast C 117 D3
Norreys Dr. Maid 202 B2
Norrington. M Keyn 33 F1
Norris Ct. Ayl 115 E2
Norris Rd. U Arn 94 C4
North Bridge Rd. Berk 135 D3
North Burnham Cl. Burn 197 D2
North Cl. Dray P 68 B3
North Cl. Medm 193 E4
North Cl. Wind 209 F3
North Common Rd. Uxb 201 F4
North Crawley Rd. Moul 23 E2
North Crawley Rd. N Craw 23 E2
North Crawley Rd. N Pag 23 E2
North Croft. Wins 66 A2
North Croft. Woo G 185 F3
North Dr. Ayl 115 F3
North Dr. Beac 186 A4
North Dr. H Wyc 173 F4
North Eastern Rd. Ayl 101 E1
North Eighth St. M Keyn 34 C2
North Eleventh St. M Keyn 34 C2
North End Rd. Qntn 85 D3
North End Rd. Stp Cl 63 E2

North Field Ct. Hen-on-T 191 E2
North Fifth St. M Keyn 34 B1
North Fourth St. M Keyn 34 B1
North Gate. M Keyn 47 E1
North Green. Maid 195 F1
North Green. Slough 205 F3
North La. Chor 167 F4
North Lee La. S Man 129 F4
North Lines Rd. Fla H 174 A1
North Mill Rd. Bled 138 A3
North Ninth St. M Keyn 34 C2
North Orbital Rd. Den G 189 F4
North Orbital Rd. Map Cr 178 C2
North Park. Ger C 188 C4
North Park. Iver 207 E2
North Rd. Ame 154 B2
North Rd. Berk 135 D2
North Rd. Chor 167 E2
North Rd. Hol G 162 B3
North Rd. Maid 202 C4
North Rd. W Dra 208 C2
North Ridge. M Keyn 35 D1
North Row. M Keyn 34 C2
North Second St. M Keyn 34 B1
North Seventh St. M Keyn 34 B1
North Sixth St. M Keyn 34 B1
North Sq. N Pag 22 B3
North St. Cast 19 F3
North St. M Keyn 34 A4
North St. M Keyn 47 E1
North St. Tha 125 E1
North Star La. Maid 202 B3
North Tenth St. M Keyn 34 C2
North Third St. M Keyn 34 B1
North Thirteenth St. M Keyn 34 C2
North Town Cl. Maid 195 F1
North Town Mead. Maid 195 F1
North Town Moor. Maid 195 F1
North Town Rd. Maid 195 F1
North Twelfth St. M Keyn 34 C2
North Way. Dean 31 F3
North Way. Pott 18 C1
North Way. Uxb 201 F3
Northall Cl. Eat B 92 B3
Northall Rd. Eat B 92 B3
Northampton Ave. Slough 205 E4
Northampton Rd. Brac 26 A1
Northampton Rd. Cast 19 E1
Northampton Rd. Graf R 9 E2
Northampton Rd. Lath 22 B3
Northampton Rd. Lave 7 F4
Northampton Rd. Y Has 1 A3
Northborough Rd. Slough 198 A1
Northcliffe. Eat B 92 C3
Northcroft. She B E 46 B3
Northcroft. Slough 198 A1
Northcroft. Wedn 87 E1
Northdean. Maid 195 F1
Northdown Rd. C St P 177 F2
Northend Cl. Fla H 185 E4
Northend Sq. Buck 41 E1
Northend. Rav 5 F2
Northern Hts. Bou E 185 D3
Northern Per R (W). Harm 213 F3
Northern Rd. Ayl 101 E1
Northern Rd. Slough 198 B1
Northern Woods. Fla H 185 E4
Northfield Dr. M Keyn 35 F3
Northfield End. Hen-O-T 191 E2
Northfield Rd. Ayl 116 A4
Northfield Rd. Eton 204 C1
Northfield Rd. Maid 195 F1
Northfield Rd. P Ris 139 E2
Northlands Dr. Burn 197 E2
Northlands Rd. Adsk 53 F1
Northleigh. M Keyn 46 B1
Northmead Rd. Slough 204 C4
Northmill. P Ris 138 C2
Northolt Rd. Harm 213 F3
Northumberland Ave. Ayl 116 A3
Northumberland Cl. Stan 213 F1
Northumbria Rd. Maid 202 A2
Northwich. M Keyn 47 E4
Northwood Rd. Harm 213 E3
Nortoft Rd. C St P 177 F3
Norton Rd. Uxb 201 E1
Norvic Rd. Mars 105 D1
Norway Dr. Slough 206 A4
Norwood Cl. Ayl 101 F1
Norwood La. N Pag 22 B2
Norwood La. Uxb 200 B1
Norwood Rd. Loud 174 A1
Norwoods Ct. Ame 165 D4
Nottingham Rd. Chor 167 E1
Novello Croft. Walt 48 B2
Nugent Cl. Mar 183 F2
Nup End Cl. Win 89 D2
Nup End La. Win 89 D2
Nurseries The. Eat B 92 C3
Nursery Cl. Ame 165 F4
Nursery Cl. Ty Gr 174 B4
Nursery Ct. H Wyc 172 B3
Nursery Dr. La En 171 D3
Nursery Gdns. M Keyn 34 A2
Nursery Gdns. Tri 119 D2
Nursery La. Slough 206 B3
Nursery La. Ty Gr 174 B4
Nursery Rd. Burn 204 A4
Nursery Way. Wray 211 E1
Nursery Waye. Uxb 201 E2
Nursery Wlk. Mar 183 A2
Nutfield La. H Wyc 172 C4
Nuthatch. Ayl 101 F2
Nutkins Way. Ches 144 B1
Nutmeg Cl. Walt 48 A3
Nye Way. Bov 146 A2

O'Grady Way. Ayl 101 D2
Oadman Sq. She B E 46 B3
Oak Barn Cl. Cran 25 D1
Oak Cres. H Wyc 172 B2
Oak Dr. Berk 135 E2
Oak End Dr. Iver H 200 B2
Oak End Way. Chin 147 E3
Oak End Way. Ger C 188 C3
Oak Green. Ayl 115 E4
Oak La. Buc Co 133 D1
Oak La. Wind 210 A3
Oak Rd. P Ris 139 E2
Oak Stubbs La. Dorn 203 F2
Oak Tree Ave. Mar 183 E2
Oak Tree Cl. Mar 183 E2
Oak Tree Dr. La En 171 E3
Oak Tree Rd. Mar 183 E2
Oak View. G Kin 162 B4
Oak Way. Wins 66 A2
Oak Wood. Berk 134 C2
Oakdown Cres. Oln 6 C2
Oaken Gr. Maid 195 E1
Oakengrove Cl. Hol G 163 E3
Oakengrove La. Ty Gr 163 D2
Oakengrove Rd. Ty Gr 163 D2
Oakengrove. Pres 151 E3
Oakeshott Ave. Wal A 161 E3
Oakfield Ave. Slough 205 D3
Oakfield Cnr. Ame 154 B1
Oakfield Rd. Ayl 116 A4
Oakfield Rd. Bou E 185 D2
Oakfield. Chor 167 F1
Oakhill Rd. Map Cr 178 B3
Oakhill Rd. She C E 45 F3
Oakhurst. Maid 196 A2
Oakington Ave. L Chal 166 C4
Oakland Way. Fla H 174 A1
Oakley Cres. Slough 205 F3
Oakley Gdns. M Keyn 35 D3
Oakley Green Rd. Oak G 209 D3
Oakley La. Chin 147 D3
Oakley Rd. Chin 147 E3
Oakridge Ct. H Wyc 172 B3
Oakridge Rd. H Wyc 172 C4
Oakridge. M Keyn 46 C2
Oaks Rd. Stan 213 E1
Oaks The. Berk 135 D2
Oakside. N Den 201 D3
Oaktree Cl. Ty Gr 163 D1
Oakway. Ame 154 A2
Oakwell Cl. Dun 93 F4
Oakwood Dr. M Keyn 58 C4
Oakwood. Fla H 174 A1
Oatlands Dr. Slough 205 E4
Oban Ct. Slough 205 E2
Ockwells Rd. Maid 202 B2
Octagon Par. H Wyc 173 D4
Octavian Dr. M Keyn 33 F3
Octavian Way. Brac 38 A4
Oddley La. Bled 148 B4
Odell Cl. M Keyn 47 E4
Odencroft Rd. Slough 198 A1
Odney La. Cook 196 A4
Offas La. Wins 66 A3
Ogilvie Rd. H Wyc 172 C4
Okeford Dr. Tri 118 C2
Okeley La. Tri 118 C2
Old Barn Cl. Gawt 52 A2
Old Burrs. S Man 115 E2
Old Coach Dr. H Wyc 174 A2
Old Court Cl. Maid 202 A2
Old Dashwood Hill. La En 159 F1
Old Dean. Bov 146 A2
Old End. Pad 53 D1
Old Farm Cl. Beac 175 E3
Old Farm Cl. Worm 123 E3
Old Farm Rd. H Wyc 161 F1
Old Farm Rd. W Dra 208 B2
Old Farm. Pit 105 E2
Old Ferry Dr. Wray 211 E1
Old Field Cl. L Chal 166 C4
Old Forge Cl. Maid 203 D2
Old Forge Cl. Ting 51 D3
Old Forge Gdns. Bier 102 A2
Old Forge Rd. Loud 174 B1
Old Groveway. M Keyn 47 E3
Old Hardenwaye. H Wyc 162 C1
Old Horns La. Mar B 172 A2
Old Kiln Rd. Fla H 185 D4
Old Kiln Rd. Ty Gr 163 E1
Old Linslade Rd. L Buzz 70 C2
Old Lodge Dr. Beac 175 F1
Old Manor Cl. P Ris 139 E4
Old Manor Cl. Whad 45 D1
Old Marsh La. Dorn 203 F2
Old Marsh La. Tapl 203 F2
Old Mead. C St P 177 F2
Old Mill Cl. Hadd 127 D3
Old Mill Furlong. Wins 66 A3
Old Mill Gdns. Berk 135 E2
Old Mill La. Uxb 208 A4
Old Mill Rd. Den 190 A1
Old Nursery Ct. Hedg 187 E1
Old Orchard Mews. Berk 135 E2
Old Orchard. Bier 102 A2
Old Orchard. Chin 137 F1
Old Oxford Rd. La En 160 B1
Old Plough Cl. Chea 112 A1
Old Post Office La. Maid 202 C4
Old Rd. L Buzz 80 C4
Old Rectory La. Den G 189 F2
Old Risborough Rd. S Man 130 A4
Old Sax La. Char 143 E2
Old School Cl. Hal 117 E1
Old School Cl. Skch 158 C2
Old School Ct. Eat B 92 C3
Old School Yd. Stp Cl 63 E2
Old Slade La. Iver 207 F1
Old Station La. Wray 212 A1
Old Station Way. Bou E 185 F3
Old Stoke Rd. Ayl 115 E3
Old Town Cl. Beac 175 F1
Old Town. Brac 38 A4
Old Vicarage Way. Bou E 185 F4
Old Watery La. Woo G 185 F4
Old Windmill Way. L Cre 125 E4
Old Wolverton Rd. M Keyn 33 E4
Oldacres. Maid 203 D4
Oldbrook Bvd. M Keyn 46 C4
Oldbury Gr. Beac 175 E3
Olde Bell Cl. S Ham 69 F4
Olde Bell La. M Keyn 46 A4
Oldershaw Mews. Maid 202 A4
Oldfield Rd. Maid 203 D4
Oldhams Meadow. Bier 102 A1
Oldhouse Cl. H Wyc 172 C2
Oldway La. Burn 204 B3
Oliffe Cl. Ayl 101 E2
Oliffe Way. Ayl 101 E2
Oline Ct. She C E 45 F3
Oliver Rd. M Keyn 58 B4
Oliver's Paddock. Mar B 183 E3
Olleberrie La. Sar 156 B4
Olney Rd. Emb 13 F4
Olney Rd. Lave 7 F4
One Pin La. Far C 187 E1
One Tree La. Beac 175 F2
Onslow Ct. B Bkhl 48 A2
Onslow Dr. Tha 126 A1
Opendale Rd. Burn 204 A4
Orchard Ave. Slough 204 B4
Orchard Ave. Berk 135 D2
Orchard Ave. Wind 210 A3
Orchard Cl. Ayl 101 F2
Orchard Cl. Beac 175 E2
Orchard Cl. Chor 167 E3
Orchard Cl. Cran 25 D1
Orchard Cl. Hen-O-T 191 F1
Orchard Cl. Hgh V 162 A4
Orchard Cl. Lgwk 138 B4
Orchard Cl. M Keyn 57 F4
Orchard Cl. Maid 203 D2
Orchard Cl. N Den 201 D3
Orchard Cl. Oak 109 E2
Orchard Cl. S Man 116 A1
Orchard Cl. Wadd 99 D4
Orchard Cl. Wen 131 D3
Orchard Cl. Win 89 D2
Orchard Cl. Yard G 18 C3
Orchard Ct. Harm 213 E4
Orchard Dr. Ast C 117 F2
Orchard Dr. Bou E 185 E2
Orchard Dr. Chor 167 E3
Orchard Dr. L Buzz 80 B3
Orchard Dr. Ty Gr 163 D2
Orchard Dr. Uxb 201 E1
Orchard End Ave. Ame 165 F4
Orchard End. Edle 92 C2
Orchard End. Hol G 163 D3
Orchard Gate. Far C 198 B4
Orchard Gr. Fla H 185 D4
Orchard Gr. Ger C 177 E1
Orchard Gr. Maid 202 B4
Orchard La. Ame 154 B1
Orchard La. Harr 3 F4
Orchard La. Pres 151 E3
Orchard La. Stew 78 C4
Orchard Mews. Se Gr 176 B2
Orchard Park. Hol G 163 E3
Orchard Pl. West 39 D2
Orchard Rd. Beac 175 F1
Orchard Rd. C St G 177 E4
Orchard Rd. H Wyc 174 A2
Orchard Rd. Old W 211 D1
Orchard Rd. Se Gr 176 B3
Orchard Ri. Oln 6 C2
Orchard The. Ast C 117 F3
Orchard The. Fla H 185 D4
Orchard The. Hal 131 E4
Orchard The. Hol G 163 D3
Orchard The. Mar 183 F2
Orchard The. Pott 18 B2
Orchard The. Wal A 161 F3
Orchard View. Uxb 201 E1
Orchard Way. Ayl 101 F1
Orchard Way. Bov 146 A2
Orchard Way. Chin 147 E3
Orchard Way. Cran 25 D1
Orchard Way. E Clay 74 C3
Orchard Way. Hal B 92 C3
Orchard Way. Hol G 163 E3
Orchard Way. Ivin 105 F2
Orchard Way. N Craw 24 A3
Orchard Way. Slough 206 C3
Orchard Waye. Uxb 201 E2
Orchard Wlk. Lave 7 F4
Orchards The. Eat B 92 C4
Orchards The. Tri 118 C2
Orchardville. Burn 197 D1
Orchehill Ave. Ger C 188 B4
Orchehill Rise. Ger C 188 C3
Orkney Cl. M Keyn 46 C1
Orkney Cl. Stew 78 C4
Ormesby Cl. Ayl 116 A3
Ormond Rd. Tha 126 A1
Ormonde. M Keyn 34 B4
Ormsgill Ct. M Keyn 34 A3
Orne Gdns. M Keyn 35 D4
Ortensia Ave. M K Vil 48 B4
Orwell Cl. Ayl 115 E2
Orwell Cl. N Pag 21 F3
Orwell Cl. Wind 210 B2
Orwell Dr. Ayl 115 E2
Orwell Dr. S Man 115 E2
Osborn's Ct. Oln 6 C2
Osborne Mews. Wind 210 B3
Osborne Rd. Wind 210 B2
Osborne St. M Keyn 58 B4
Osborne St. Slough 205 F2
Osborne Way. Wigg 119 E1
Osbourne Ct. Wind 210 B3
Osbourne St. M Keyn 33 E3
Osier Way. Ayl 115 F4
Osmington Pl. Tri 118 C2
Osney Rd. Maid 195 F1
Osprey Cl. M Keyn 47 D4
Osprey Cl. W Dra 208 C2
Osprey The. Ayl 101 F2
Osprey Wlk. Ayl 101 F2
Osprey Wlk. Buck 52 C4
Ostler Gate. Maid 195 E1
Ostlers La. M Keyn 32 B3
Otter Cl. M Keyn 46 B1
Otterfield Rd. W Dra 208 C3
Otters Brook. Buck 52 C4
Otway Cl. S Man 115 F2
Oulton Cl. Ayl 116 A3
Ousebank St. N Pag 22 B3
Ousebank Way. M Keyn 32 B3
Ouseley Rd. Wray 211 E1
Outfield Rd. Ger C 177 E2
Outlook Dr. C St G 177 E4
Ouzel Cl. M Keyn 46 C1
Oval Way. Ger C 188 C4
Over Hampden. Pres 151 E4
Over The Misbourne. Den G 189 D3
Overdale Rd. Ches 144 A2
Overdales. Ty Gr 162 C2
Overend Cl. M Keyn 34 A2
Overgate. M Keyn 35 D2
Overn Ave. Buck 41 E1
Overn Cl. Buck 41 E1
Overn Cres. Buck 41 E1
Oversley Ct. M Keyn 22 A1
Overstrand. Ast C 117 F3
Overstreet. M Keyn 35 D4
Overton Dr. Tha 126 A1
Oving Rd. Oving 86 C4
Oving Rd. Whit 86 C4
Ovitts Cl. Wins 66 A3
Owl Cl. Ayl 101 F2
Owlsears Cl. Beac 175 E2
Oxendon Ct. L Buzz 70 C1
Oxfield Cl. Berk 135 D2
Oxford Ave. Burn 197 D2
Oxford Ave. Slough 204 C4
Oxford Gdns. Den 190 A1
Oxford Rd E. Wind 210 B3
Oxford Rd. Ayl 115 D4
Oxford Rd. Den 189 E1
Oxford Rd. Ger C 188 B3
Oxford Rd. H Wyc 173 D4
Oxford Rd. La En 160 B1
Oxford Rd. Mar 183 E1
Oxford Rd. N Den 201 D3
Oxford Rd. Oak 109 E3
Oxford Rd. Skch 158 B3
Oxford Rd. Sto 114 B3
Oxford Rd. Sto 115 D4
Oxford Rd. Tha 125 E1
Oxford Rd. Wind 210 B3
Oxford St. H Wyc 173 D4
Oxford St. Lee C 142 B3
Oxford St. M Keyn 32 B3
Oxford St. M Keyn 33 E3
Oxford St. M Keyn 58 B4
Oxleys. Oln 6 C2
Oxman La. M Keyn 33 D3

Pack & Prime L. Hen-O-T 191 E1
Packet Boat La. W Dra 208 B4
Packhorse Rd. Ger C 188 C3
Padcroft Rd. W Dra 208 B3
Paddock Cl. Maid 202 A1
Paddock The. Ayl 116 B4
Paddock The. C St P 177 F3
Paddock The. Datch 211 D3
Paddock The. Emb 13 F4
Paddock The. Maid 195 E1
Paddock Way. M Keyn 47 E1
Paddocks The. Fla H 185 D4
Paddocks The. H Wyc 172 A2
Paddocks The. Hadd 127 D3
Paddocks The. L Buzz 80 C4
Paddocks The. Stp Cl 63 F2
Paddocks The. Wen 131 D3
Padstow Ave. M Keyn 34 C1
Padstow Cl. Ayl 101 F1
Padstow Cl. Slough 206 C2
Page Hill Ave. Buck 41 F1
Pages Croft. Berk 135 D3
Pages La. Uxb 201 E3
Paget Cl. Mar 183 F2
Paget Dr. Maid 202 A2
Paget Rd. Slough 206 C1
Pagoda The. Maid 196 A1
Paines Orch. Ched 105 D4
Palace Sq. M Keyn 46 C4
Palliser Rd. C St G 177 D4
Palmer Ave. Ayl 115 E4
Palmer Ave. U Arn 94 C4
Palmer's Moor La. Uxb 201 D1
Palmers Cl. Maid 202 A2
Palmers Moor. Thrn 54 A4
Palmers Rd. Oln 7 D2
Palmerston Ave. Slough 206 A2
Pankridge Dr. Pres 151 E4
Pannier Pl. M Keyn 35 D3
Pantile Row. Slough 207 D1
Paprika Ct. Walt 48 A3
Parade The. Bou E 185 D2
Paradise Rd. Hen-O-T 191 E1
Paradise. Nwtn L 57 E2
Parchment Cl. Ame 154 C1
Parish La. Far C 187 E1
Parish Piece. Hol G 163 E4
Park Ave. N Pag 22 A2
Park Ave. Tott 93 D4
Park Ave. Wray 211 E2
Park Cl. Cast 19 F1
Park Cl. Hogg 77 F3
Park Cl. La En 171 E3
Park Cl. Wind 210 B3
Park Cnr. Wind 209 F2
Park Farm Rd. H Wyc 161 D1
Park Farm Way. La En 171 E3
Park Gate. Wing 79 F1
Park Gdns. M Keyn 47 D1
Park Gr. L Chal 166 B3
Park Hill. Holt 122 A1
Park La. Beac 175 F1
Park La. Burn 197 F4
Park La. Eat B 92 B3
Park La. Hort 212 A2
Park La. La En 171 E3
Park La. Paul 17 D4
Park La. Skch 158 C3
Park La. Slough 206 A2
Park La. Ston 179 E3
Park La. Ty Gr 163 D2
Park Meadow. P Ris 139 D2
Park Par Cntr The. Hol G 163 D3
Park Pl. Ame 154 C1
Park Rd E. Uxb 201 E2
Park Rd S. Wins 65 F2
Park Rd. Far C 108 B2
Park Rd. Gr Und 82 C4
Park Rd. Gran 76 F3
Park Rd. Hans 11 D1
Park Rd. Hart 10 B4
Park Rd. Hen-O-T 191 F1
Park Rd. M Keyn 32 B3
Park Rd. Sher 14 A1
Park Rd. Stan 213 E1
Park Rd. Sto P 198 B2
Park Rd. Tri 118 C1
Park Rd. Uxb 201 F3
Park Rd. Wins 65 F3
Park Rise. Berk 134 C3
Park St. Ayl 115 F4
Park St. Berk 135 D3
Park St. H Wyc 173 E3
Park St. Hth 60 C4
Park St. Maid 202 C4
Park St. P Ris 139 D2
Park St. Slough 205 F2
Park St. Stan 212 B3
Park St. Tri 119 D2
Park St. Wind 210 B3
Park View Ct. H Wyc 172 B4
Park View Rd. Berk 135 D2
Park View. N Pag 22 B2
Parker Cl. M Keyn 34 A3
Parkfield Ave. Ame 154 B1
Parkfield. Chor 167 F3
Parkgate. Burn 197 E1
Parkland Ave. Slough 206 B1
Parklands. M Keyn 21 E1
Parkmoor La. Frie 170 C1

Parkside. Ger C 188 C4
Parkside. Hen-on-T 191 E1
Parkside. M Keyn 46 C2
Parkside. Maid 195 E1
Parkside. Wal A 150 A1
Parkview Chase. Slough 204 C4
Parkview. Fla H 185 D4
Parkway The. Iver H 200 B2
Parkway. B Bkhl 48 B1
Parkway. Mar 184 A2
Parkway. Wave 49 D3
Parkwood. Wal A 150 A1
Parlaunt Rd. Slough 207 D1
Parliament Cl. Pres 151 D4
Parliament La. Burn 196 C3
Parliament Rd. Tha 125 F1
Parneleys. M Keyn 35 F2
Parrock La. M K Vil 36 A1
Parrot Cl. Ayl 115 D3
Parrott's La. Buc Co 133 D2
Parrs Rd. Skch 158 C2
Parry Green N. Slough 206 C1
Parry Green S. Slough 207 D1
Parsley Cl. Walt 48 A3
Parslow Cl. S Man 115 E2
Parson's Fee. Ayl 115 E4
Parson's Wood La. Far C 198 B3
Parsonage Cl. H Wyc 173 E3
Parsonage Cl. Tri 119 D2
Parsonage Ct. Tri 119 D2
Parsonage Gdns. Mar 183 F1
Parsonage La. Far C 198 B2
Parsonage La. Wind 210 A3
Parsonage Pl. Tri 119 D2
Parsonage Rd. C St G 177 D4
Parsons Cl. Stew 78 C4
Parsons Cl. Wins 65 F2
Parsons Cres. She B E 46 B3
Parsons La. Bier 102 A2
Parsons Wlk. Hol G 163 E3
Parton Cl. Wen 131 D3
Parton Rd. Ayl 116 A4
Partridge Cl. Buck 52 C4
Partridge Cl. Ches 144 C2
Partridge Mead. Maid 195 F1
Partridge Piece. Cran 25 E2
Partridge Way. Ayl 101 F2
Partridge Way. H Wyc 161 E1
Pascomb Rd. Dun 93 F4
Passalewe La. Walt 48 B4
Passmore. M Keyn 47 E3
Pastern Pl. M Keyn 35 D3
Pastures The. Ayl 102 A1
Pastures The. Edle 92 C2
Pastures The. H Wyc 161 F1
Patches Field. Mar B 183 F3
Paterson Rd. Ayl 115 E3
Patricia Cl. Slough 204 C3
Patrick Haugh Rd. U Arn 94 C4
Patrick Way. Ayl 116 A2
Patrick's La. Dean 31 F2
Patrington Cl. Uxb 201 E1
Patriot Dr. M Keyn 34 A1
Patrons Dr. Den G 189 F3
Patterson Rd. Ches 144 A2
Pattison La. M Keyn 35 E2
Paul's Row. H Wyc 173 D3
Pauls Hill. Ty Gr 174 C3
Pavers Ct. S Man 115 E2
Pavilion Way. L Chal 166 B4
Paxton Ave. Slough 205 E2
Paxton Cl. Oln 6 C2
Paxton Cres. She B E 46 A3
Paxton Rd. Berk 135 E2
Paynes Dr. M Keyn 46 A4
Pea La. Berk 134 B4
Peach Meadow. Hal 131 D4
Peach Tree Ave. W Dra 208 C4
Peachey Cl. Uxb 208 B4
Peachey La. Uxb 208 B4
Peacock Rd. Mar 184 A2
Pear Tree Ave. W Dra 208 C4
Pear Tree Cl. Se Gr 176 B2
Pearce Cl. Ayl 115 F2
Pearce Cl. Maid 195 F1
Pearce Rd. Ches 144 A1
Pearce Rd. Maid 195 F1
Pearces Orch. Hen-O-T 191 E2
Pearl Gdns. Slough 205 D3
Pearse Gr. Walt 48 A2
Peascod St. Wind 210 B3
Peascroft. L Cre 125 E3
Pebble La. Ayl 115 E4
Pebblemoor. Edle 92 C2
Peckover Ct. M Keyn 33 F1
Pednor Bottom. Char 143 D2
Pednor Rd. Ches 143 F1
Pednormead End. Ches 154 A4
Peebles Pl. M Keyn 46 C2
Peel Cl. Wind 210 A2
Peel Ct. Slough 205 D4
Peel Rd. M Keyn 33 E3
Peel Way. Uxb 208 C4
Peerless Dr. S Har 190 B4
Peers Dr. Asp G 49 F2
Peers La. She C E 46 A3
Pelham Pl. M Keyn 34 C3
Pelham Rd. Tha 126 A1
Pelton Ct. She B E 46 B3
Pemberton Cl. Ayl 115 F3
Pemberton Rd. Slough 197 F1
Pembridge Chase. Bov 146 A2
Pembridge Cl. Bov 146 A2
Pembridge Rd. Bov 146 A2
Pembroke Rd. Ayl 101 F1
Pencarrow Pl. M Keyn 35 D1
Pencoed Pl. Wind 210 B3
Penfold Cotts. Hol G 163 E4
Penfold La. H Hea 152 C1
Penfold La. Hol G 152 C1
Penfold. W Tur 116 C1
Penington Rd. Beac 186 A4
Penling Cl. Cook 195 F3
Penly Cl. Chin 147 D3
Penmoor Cl. H Wyc 172 B4
Penn Ave. Ches 144 A1
Penn Bottom. Ty Gr 163 F1
Penn Cl. Chor 167 E2
Penn Cl. Uxb 201 E1
Penn Dr. Den G 189 F3
Penn Gaskell La. C St P 177 F3
Penn Meadow. Sto P 198 C2
Penn Rd. Ayl 115 E4
Penn Rd. Beac 175 E3
Penn Rd. Chor 167 F1
Penn Rd. Ger C 177 E1
Penn Rd. M Keyn 58 C4
Penn Rd. Slough 198 B1
Penn Rd. Ty Gr 163 D2
Penn Way. Chor 167 E2
Pennia Cl. M Keyn 46 B1
Pennine Rd. Slough 205 D4
Pennington Pl. Tha 126 A1
Pennington Rd. Ger C 177 E2
Pennington Rd. H Wyc 173 F3
Penningtons The. Ame 154 C1
Pennycress Way. N Pag 21 F2
Pennylets Green. Sto P 199 D3
Pennyroyal. Walt 48 A4
Penrith Cl. Uxb 201 E3
Penrith Way. Ayl 116 A4
Penryn Ave. M Keyn 35 D1
Penshurst Cl. Ger C 177 E1
Penshurst Rd. Maid 202 B3
Pentewan Gate. M Keyn 34 C1
Pentland Rd. Ayl 115 F3
Pentland Rd. Slough 205 D4
Pentlands The. H Wyc 174 A2
Pentlands. M Keyn 32 C2
Penwood Ct. Maid 202 A4
Penwood La. Mar 183 E1
Penyston Rd. Maid 202 B4
Penzance Spur. Slough 198 A1
Peplow Cl. W Dra 208 B3
Peppard Meadow. Pres 151 E3
Peppet's Green. Char 143 E4
Peppiatts The. Edle 92 A3
Pepys Cl. Slough 212 A4
Pepys Dr. Pres 151 E3
Perch Cl. Mar 194 B4
Percheron Pl. M Keyn 34 C3
Percy Pl. Datch 211 D3
Percy Terr. C St G 177 D4
Peregrine Cl. M Keyn 47 D4
Perks La. Pres 151 E2
Permayne. M Keyn 34 A4
Perracombe. M Keyn 46 C2
Perran Ave. M Keyn 35 D1
Perrin Springs La. Frie 170 C1
Perry Hill. Edgc 73 D1
Perry La. Bled 138 B1
Perry Oaks Dr. Harm 213 E3
Perry St. Wen 131 D3
Perrycroft. Wind 209 F2
Perryfields Way. Burn 197 D1
Perryman Way. Slough 197 F1
Perth Ave. Slough 205 D4
Perth Cl. M Keyn 46 C1
Perth Rd. H Wyc 173 E4
Peter's Cl. Pres 151 E3
Peter's Pl. Berk 134 C3
Peterborough Ave.
H Wyc 173 E4
Peterborough Gate.
M Keyn 35 E3
Peterhill Cl. C St P 177 F3
Peterley. Pres 151 F2
Peters La. P Ris 139 F2
Peters La. Pres 139 F2
Petersfield Ave. Slough 206 A3
Petersham Cl. N Pag 22 B1
Pettifer Way. H Wyc 172 B3
Pettingrew Cl. Walt 48 A3
Petty Pl. Maid 202 B2
Petworth Ct. Wind 210 A3
Petworth. M Keyn 33 F1
Pevensey Cl. Ayl 116 A3
Pevensey Cl. M Keyn 57 F4
Pevensey Rd. Slough 205 D4
Peverel Dr. M Keyn 47 D2
Peveril Cl. Ayl 116 A3
Pevers La. W Und 6 A1
Pheasant Cl. Berk 135 E2
Pheasant Cl. Tri 119 D3
Pheasant Dr. H Wyc 161 E1
Pheasant Hill. C St G 177 E4
Pheasant Rise. Ches 154 B3
Pheasant Wlk. C St P 177 F3
Pheasants Croft. Maid 202 A3
Pheasants Dr. Hol G 163 D3
Philip Ct. She C E 46 A3
Philip Dr. Fla H 185 E4
Philip Rd. H Wyc 173 E4
Phillimore Cl. M Keyn 35 D4
Philpots Cl. W Dra 208 B3
Phipps Cl. Maid 202 A1
Phipps Rd. Slough 204 C4
Phoebe La. Wave 48 C3
Phoenix Dr. M Keyn 46 C4
Phygtle The. C St P 177 F2
Phyllis Ct Dr. Hen-O-T 191 F2
Picasso Pl. Ayl 100 C1
Pickering Dr. She B E 46 A1
Pickford Dr. Slough 206 C3
Pickford Dr. Slough 207 D3
Picts La. P Ris 139 D1
Piddington La. La En 171 D4
Piddington Rd. Lud 96 A4
Pield Heath Rd. Uxb 201 F1
Pierson Rd. Wind 209 E3
Pigeon Farm Rd. Skch 158 C3
Piggott's Hill. Wal A 150 C1
Piggotts End. Ame 165 D4
Piggotts Orch. Ame 165 D4
Pightle Cres. Buck 41 E1
Pightle The. Buck 41 E1
Pightle The. M Mor 41 F2
Pightle The. Oving 86 B4
Pigott Dr. She C E 46 A3
Pigott Orch. Qntn 85 D3
Pike Cl. Mar 194 B4
Pike Corner. Ayl 116 B3
Pilch La. Adsk 54 B3
Pilch La. G Hrwd 54 B2
Pilch La. Thrn 54 B3
Pilgrim St. M Keyn 35 D2
Pilgrims Cl. P Ris 139 D3
Pimms Cl. H Wyc 174 A3
Pimms Gr. H Wyc 174 A3
Pimpernel Gr. Walt 48 A3
Pinchfield. Map Cr 178 B3
Pinders Croft. M Keyn 33 D3
Pine Chase. H Wyc 172 A2
Pine Cl. Berk 135 D2
Pine Cl. Maid 202 A4
Pine Cl. Ty Gr 163 D2
Pine Crest Mews. L Buzz 80 C3
Pine Gr. Wbn S 49 D2
Pine Hill. Ty Gr 162 C2
Pine Road. Edle 106 C4
Pine Trees Dr. Ick 201 F4
Pine Wlk. Ty Gr 163 D2
Pineapple Rd. Ame 165 F4
Pinecroft. Mar 183 E2
Pinels Way. H Wyc 172 C2
Pines Cl. Ame 154 A1
Pines The. Ty Gr 163 D1
Pinetree Cl. Ger C 177 E2
Pinewood Ave. Uxb 208 C4
Pinewood Cl. Ger C 188 C2
Pinewood Cl. Iver H 200 B3
Pinewood Dr. M Keyn 58 C4
Pinewood Green. Iver H 200 B3
Pinewood Mews. Stan 213 E1
Pinewood Rd. H Wyc 172 B4
Pinewood Rd. Iver H 200 A2
Pinfold. Walt 48 A3
Pinglestone Cl. Harm 213 F4
Pinions Rd. H Wyc 173 F3
Pink Hill. Lac G 149 F4
Pink La. Burn 197 D2
Pink Rd. Lac G 149 F4
Pinkard Ct. M Keyn 47 E4
Pinkneys Dr. Maid 195 D1
Pinkneys Rd. Maid 202 A4
Pinn Cl. Uxb 208 B4
Pipard. M Keyn 34 C4
Pipers Cl. Burn 197 E1
Pipers Croft. Dun 93 F4
Pipers La. G Kin 162 B4
Pipit Gdns. Ayl 101 F2
Pippins Cl. W Dra 208 B2
Pippins The. Slough 206 C3
Pipston Green. M K Vil 48 A4
Pitch Pond Cl. Beac 175 E3
Pitch The. B Bot 159 E2
Pitchcott Rd. Oving 86 B4
Pitcher La. M Keyn 46 A4
Pitfield. M Keyn 33 D2
Pitt Green. Buck 41 F1
Pitts Rd. Slough 205 E3
Place Farm Way. P Ris 139 D3
Plackett Way. Slough 204 B3
Plaiters Cl. Tri 119 D2
Plantain Ct. Walt 48 A3
Plantation Rd. Ame 154 C1
Plantation Rd. H Wyc 174 A4
Plantation Rd. L Buzz 70 C2
Platt The. Ame 165 D4
Pleasaunce The. Ast C 117 F3
Pleshey Cl. She C E 46 A3
Plested Ct. S Man 116 B1
Plomer Green Ave.
H Wyc 161 E1
Plomer Green La. H Wyc 161 E2
Plomer Hill. H Wyc 161 E1
Plough Cl. S Man 115 F2
Plough La. Sar 156 C3
Plough La. Sto P 199 D2
Ploughlees La. Slough 205 F3
Ploughley Rd. U Arn 94 C4
Plover Cl. Buck 52 C4
Plover Cl. N Pag 22 C2
Plover The. Ayl 101 F2
Plover Wlk. Ayl 101 F2
Plowman Cl. M Keyn 33 D3
Plum Park La. Paul 17 E4
Plumer Rd. H Wyc 172 C4
Plumstead Ave. M Keyn 34 B2
Plym Cl. Ayl 115 E3
Plymouth Rd. Slough 204 C4
Pococks La. Eton 205 F1
Poets Chase. Ayl 115 F3
Points The. Maid 202 A2
Poles Hill. Ches 144 A1
Poles Hill. Sar 156 C3
Polidoris La. Hol G 163 E4
Polish Ave. Hal 131 F4
Pollard Ave. Den G 189 F3
Pollard Cl. Old W 211 D1
Pollards. Map Cr 178 B3
Pollywick Rd. Wigg 119 E1
Polruan Pl. M Keyn 35 D1
Pomander Cres. Walt 48 A4
Pomeroy Cl. Ame 165 E4
Pond App. Hol G 163 E4
Pond Cl. Cole 164 B2
Pond Cl. Nwtn L 57 E1
Pond La. Ger C 177 D1
Pond Park Rd. Ches 144 A1
Pondgate. M K Vil 48 A4
Pondwicks. Ame 165 D4
Pool La. Slough 205 F3
Poolmans Rd. Wind 209 E2
Pope Way. Ayl 115 F2
Popes Acre. Hadd 126 C3
Popes Cl. Ame 154 C1
Popes Cl. Iver 212 B4
Popes La. Cook 195 E4
Poplar Ave. Ame 165 F4
Poplar Ave. W Dra 208 C3
Poplar Cl. Ayl 102 A1
Poplar Cl. Stan 212 C3
Poplar Rd. Ayl 102 A1
Poplar Rd. Buck 52 B4
Poplar Rd. N Den 201 E3
Poplars Gr. Maid 196 A1
Poplars The. Wen 131 E3
Poppy Rd. P Ris 139 D1
Porlock La. M Keyn 46 B2
Portal Rd. Wen 131 E3
Portchester Ct. M Keyn 33 F1
Porter's Cl. Dean 31 F2
Porters Way. W Dra 208 C2
Portfield Cl. Buck 52 C4
Portfield Way. Buck 52 C4
Portfields Rd. N Pag 22 A2
Porthleven Pl. M Keyn 35 D1
Portland Cl. Slough 197 E1
Portland Dr. M Keyn 35 E4
Portlands. Mar 183 E1
Portlock Rd. Maid 202 B4
Portmarnock Cl. M Keyn 57 E4
Portobello Cl. Ches 144 A1
Portrush Cl. M Keyn 57 E4
Portway Dr. H Wyc 161 D1
Portway Rd. Twyf 62 B1
Portway. M K Vil 34 B2
Portway. M Keyn 35 E3
Portway. N Mar 76 A1
Portway. She C E 34 B2
Portway. Sto 114 C2
Post Meadow. Iver H 200 B1
Post Office La. Beac 175 E2
Post Office La. Slough 206 B4
Post Office La. Whit 87 D3
Potash La. Lon M 104 A3
Potkiln La. Ger C 176 B1
Potter Row. S Hea 142 B1
Potters Cross. Iver H 200 C1
Potters La. M Keyn 33 D2
Poulcott. Wray 211 F1
Pound Cl. Stp Cl 63 E2
Pound Cl. Wick 31 D2
Pound Cres. Mar 183 E1
Pound Hill. G Bkhl 59 E1
Pound La. Lit M 184 B2
Pound La. Mar 183 E1
Pound La. N Craw 24 A4
Pound La. Pres B 62 A4
Pound St. Wen 131 D2
Pound The. Cook 195 F4
Pound The. Syr 27 D4
Poundfield La. Cook 195 F4
Poundfield Rd. Pott 18 C1
Poundlands. Lac G 149 F3
Pounds Cl. Cran 25 D1
Powis Cl. Maid 202 A2
Powney Rd. Maid 202 B4
Poyle La. Burn 197 D2
Poyle Rd. Stan 212 C3
Poynings. Iver 207 F1
Prebendal Ave. Ayl 115 E4
Precedent Dr. M Keyn 34 A2
Precincts The. Burn 197 E1
Prescott Rd. Stan 212 C3
Presley Way. She C E 45 F4
Press Rd. Uxb 201 E3
Preston Ct. M Keyn 35 D4
Preston Hill. Ches 144 B1
Preston Rd. Slough 206 B3
Prestwick Cl. M Keyn 57 E4
Prestwood Cl. H Wyc 172 B4
Prestwood. Slough 206 A4
Pretoria Rd. H Wyc 173 E4
Primatt Cres. She C E 46 A3
Primrose Dr. Ayl 115 D3
Primrose Green. Hol G 162 C3
Primrose Hill. Hol G 162 C4
Prince Andrew Cl. Maid 196 A1
Prince Andrew Rd. Maid 196 A1
Prince Consort Cotts.
Wind 210 B3
Prince Edward St. Berk 135 E2
Prince Philip Ave. Cran 24 B1
Prince's Rd. Ayl 115 F4
Princes Cl. Berk 135 D3
Princes Cl. Chil 111 D2
Princes Cl. Eton 204 C1
Princes Ct. L Buzz 80 C4
Princes Gdns. P Ris 139 D2
Princes La. Lee C 142 B3
Princes Rd. Bou E 185 E2
Princes Rd. La En 160 A1
Princes St. Slough 206 A2
Princes Way. M Keyn 58 B4
Princess Ave. Wind 210 A2
Princess St. Maid 202 C3
Printers End. Ayl 101 D1
Prior Gr. Ches 144 B1
Priors Cl. Maid 203 D1
Priors Cl. Slough 206 A2
Priors Park. M Keyn 46 B1
Priors Rd. Wind 209 E2
Priors Way. Maid 203 D1
Priory Ave. H Wyc 173 D4
Priory Ave. S Har 190 B4
Priory Cl. Ayl 101 E1
Priory Cl. Den 190 A1
Priory Cl. Hor-c-S 108 A3
Priory Cl. N Pag 22 C2
Priory Cl. S Har 190 B4
Priory Ct. Berk 135 E2
Priory Gdns. Berk 135 E2
Priory Gdns. S Har 190 B4
Priory Rd. Burn 204 B4
Priory Rd. Ger C 188 B4
Priory Rd. H Wyc 173 D4
Priory St. N Pag 22 C2
Priory Way. Datch 211 D4
Priory Way. Ger C 188 B4
Priory Way. Harm 213 F4
Pritchard Ct. M Keyn 34 C4
Progress Rd. H Wyc 172 A4
Promenade. Eton 210 B4
Prospect Cl. Dray P 68 B3
Prospect Ct. La En 171 D3
Prospect Pl. Cast 19 F3
Prospect Pl. Hurl 193 F2
Prospect Pl. Wing 79 F1
Prospect Rd. M Keyn 32 B3
Prospect Rd. Mar 183 B1
Providence Pl. Maid 202 C4
Providence Rd. W Dra 208 C3
Puers La. Se Gr 176 C2
Puffin Way. Ayl 101 F2
Pulborough Cl. M Keyn 46 B1
Pulford Rd. L Buzz 80 C3
Pullfields. Ches 144 A1
Pulpit Cl. Ches 144 A1
Pulpit La. Oving 76 B1
Pump La N. Lit M 183 F3
Pump La S. Lit M 184 A2
Pumpkin Hill. Burn 197 F3
Pumpus Green. Wins 66 A2
Punch Bowl La. Ches 154 B4
Purbeck Cl. Ayl 116 A3
Purbeck. M Keyn 34 B3
Purcel Dr. N Pag 22 A2
Pursell Cl. Maid 202 A2
Pursells Meadow. Wal A 161 E4
Purton Ct. Far C 198 B3
Purton La. Far C 198 B3
Pury Rd. Graf R 9 D1
Pusey Way. La En 171 E3
Putman Pl. Hen-O-T 191 F1
Putnams Dr. Ast C 117 E3
Puxley Rd. Dean 31 E3
Pyebush La. Beac 187 D4
Pyghtle Footpath. Den G 190 A2
Pyghtle The. Oln 6 C2
Pyghtle The. Turv 8 C3
Pyghtles The. Qntn 85 D3
Pym Wlk. Tha 125 F1
Pymcombe Cl. P Ris 139 D3
Pyxe Ct. Walt 48 A2

Quadrangle The. H Wyc 173 F4
Quadrans Cl. M Keyn 35 D4
Quadrant The. H Wyc 162 C1

Quadrant The. Maid 203 D3
Quainton Rd. N Mar 76 A1
Quainton Rd. Wadd 99 D4
Quaker's Mead. W Tur 116 C2
Quaker's Mede. Hadd 127 D3
Quantock Cl. Slough 207 D1
Quantock Cres. M Keyn 46 B1
Quarrendon Ave. Ayl 101 D1
Quarrendon Rd. Ame 165 F4
Quarry Cl. L Cre 125 E4
Quarrydale Dr. Mar 183 F1
Quaves Rd. Slough 206 B2
Quebec Rd. H Wyc 173 F3
Queen Alexandra R. H Wyc 173 D3
Queen Anne St. M Keyn 33 F4
Queen Anne's Rd. Wind 210 B2
Queen Catherine Rd. Stp Cl 63 F1
Queen Charlotte St. Wind 210 B3
Queen Cl. Hen-O-T 191 F1
Queen Eleanor St. M Keyn 32 B3
Queen Mother's Dr. Den G 189 F3
Queen Sq. H Wyc 173 D4
Queen St. Ayl 116 A4
Queen St. H Wyc 173 E4
Queen St. Hen-O-T 191 F1
Queen St. L Buzz 80 C4
Queen St. La En 160 A1
Queen St. M Keyn 32 C3
Queen St. Maid 202 C4
Queen St. Pit 105 E2
Queen St. Tri 119 D2
Queen St. Wcot 98 C3
Queen Victoria St. H Wyc 173 D3
Queen's Acre. Wind 210 B2
Queen's Cl. Old W 211 D1
Queen's Ct. Slough 205 F3
Queen's Dr The. Chor 167 F1
Queen's Gate. Wind 210 B2
Queen's La. Maid 202 C4
Queen's Pk. Ayl 115 F4
Queen's Rd. H Wyc 173 E3
Queen's Rd. Mar 183 B1
Queen's Rd. Slough 205 F3
Queen's Rd. Uxb 201 E1
Queen's Rd. Wind 210 B3
Queens Ave. N Pag 22 B2
Queens Cl. Tha 125 F1
Queens Mead. Ayl 116 B4
Queens Rd. Berk 135 D3
Queens Rd. Ches 144 B1
Queens Rd. Eton 204 C1
Queens Rd. P Ris 139 D2
Queens Rd. W Dra 208 C2
Queensmead Rd. Loud 174 B1
Queensmead. Datch 211 D3
Queensmere Rd. Slough 206 A2
Queensway The. Ger C 188 B4
Queensway. M Keyn 58 B4
Queensway. Maid 195 F1
Queensway. Ty Gr 163 D2
Quickberry Pl. Ame 165 E4
Quickley Brow. Chor 167 D2
Quickley La. Chor 167 E2
Quickley Rise. Chor 167 D2
Quill Hall La. Ame 154 C1
Quinbrookes. Slough 206 B4
Quince Cl. Walt 48 A3
Quinton Dr. M Keyn 34 A2
Quoiting Sq. Mar 183 E1
Quoitings Dr. Mar 183 B1

Raans Rd. Ame 154 C1
Rabans Cl. Ayl 100 C1
Rabans La. Ayl 100 C1
Rachels Way. Ches 154 B3
Rackstraw Gr. Walt 48 B3
Radcliffe St. M Keyn 33 E3
Radclive Rd. Gawt 51 F3
Radcot Ave. Slough 207 D2
Radcot Cl. Maid 195 F2
Radman Gr. M Keyn 33 D3
Radnage Com R. Bled R 159 E3
Radnage La. Bled R 148 B1
Radnor Cl. Hen-O-T 191 F1
Radnor End. Ayl 101 F1
Radnor Way. Slough 206 C1
Radworthy. M Keyn 46 B2
Raeside Cl. Se Gr 176 B3
Ragmans Cl. Mar B 183 E4
Ragmans La. Mar B 172 B1
Ragnall's La. Hor-c-S 108 A3
Ragstone Rd. Slough 205 F2
Railway St. Ayl 115 F4
Railway Terr. Slough 205 F3
Rainborough Gdns. Ayl 101 F1
Rainbow Dr. M Keyn 46 C4
Rains Rd. L Chal 154 C1
Rainsborough Chase. Maid 202 A2
Rainsborough. M Keyn 35 D4
Rake Way. S Man 115 E2
Raleigh Cl. Slough 205 D3
Ralphs Retreat. Hol G 162 C2
Rambler Cl. Burn 204 A4
Rambler La. Slough 206 B2
Ramsay View. Ty Gr 163 D2
Ramsgill Ct. M Keyn 34 B3
Ramsons Ave. M Keyn 34 C2
Ramsthorn Gr. Walt 48 A3
Ramworth Way. Ayl 116 A3
Randall Cl. Slough 206 C1
Randolph Rd. Slough 206 C2
Ranelagh Gdns. N Pag 22 B1
Rangers Ct. M Keyn 33 F1
Rannal Dr. Chin 147 E3
Rannoch Cl. M Keyn 58 B3
Rannock Gdns. L Buzz 80 B4
Ranston Cl. Den G 189 F3
Rashleigh Pl. M Keyn 46 C4
Ratcliffe Cl. Uxb 201 E1
Rathbone Cl. She C E 45 F4
Raven Cl. Ayl 101 F2
Raven Cres. Wcot 98 B3
Raven Rd. Skch 158 C2
Ravens Field. Slough 206 B2
Ravens La. Berk 135 E2
Ravens Wharf. Berk 135 E2
Ravensbourne Pl. M Keyn 35 D1
Ravenscroft Rd. Hen-O-T 191 E1
Ravenshoe Cl. Bou E 185 D2
Ravensmead. C St P 177 F3
Ravensmead. Chin 147 E3
Ravenstone Mill Rd. Rav 12 C4
Ravensworth Rd. Slough 198 A1
Ravigill P. M Keyn 33 E2
Rawling Rd. M Keyn 34 A2
Rawlings La. Se Gr 176 B4
Ray Dr. Maid 203 D4
Ray Lea Cl. Maid 203 D4
Ray Lea Rd. Maid 203 D4
Ray Lodge Mews. Maid 203 D4
Ray Mead Ct. Maid 196 B1
Ray Mead Rd. Maid 203 E4
Ray Mill Rd E. Maid 196 A1
Ray Mill Rd W. Maid 203 D4
Ray Park Ave. Maid 203 D4
Ray Park La. Maid 203 D4
Ray Park Rd. Maid 203 D4
Ray St. Maid 203 D4
Ray's Hill. Buc Co 133 E1
Ray's Hill. Chol 133 E1
Raylands Mead. Ger C 188 B3
Rayleigh Cl. She C E 46 A3
Raymond Cl. Stan 212 C3
Raymond Rd. Maid 202 B4
Raymond Rd. Slough 207 D2
Rayners Ave. Loud 174 A2
Rayners Cl. Iver 212 B4
Rays Ave. Wind 209 F4
Rays La. Ty Gr 163 E1
Read Dr. Bier 102 B2
Reading Cl. Ayl 101 D2
Reading Rd. Hen-O-T 191 F1
Readings The. Chor 167 F3
Reads La. Cub 78 B1
Recreation Rd. Bou E 185 D2
Rectory Ave. H Wyc 173 E4
Rectory Cl. Far C 198 B1
Rectory Cl. Slap 91 E3
Rectory Cl. Wind 210 A3
Rectory Ct. H Wyc 173 F3
Rectory Ct. Lewk 157 D4
Rectory Dr. Wadd 99 D3
Rectory Fields. M Keyn 35 E2
Rectory Hill. Ame 165 E4
Rectory La. Ame 165 D4
Rectory La. Berk 135 E2
Rectory La. Y Has 1 A4
Rectory Meadow. Chin 147 F1
Rectory Orch. Lave 7 F4
Rectory Rd. Tapl 196 C1
Red Cottage Mews. Slough 206 B2
Red Ct. Slough 205 F3
Red House Cl. Beac 175 D2
Red House Cl. Nwtn L 57 E2
Red Leaf Cl. Slough 206 C3
Red Lion Cl. Cran 25 D1
Red Lion Dr. Skch 158 B3
Red Lion St. Ches 154 B4
Red Lion Way. Woo G 185 F3
Red Lodge Gdns. Berk 135 D2
Redbourne Ct. M Keyn 32 C3
Redbridge. M Keyn 34 B4
Redcliffe Wlk. Ayl 101 D1
Redcote Manor. Walt 48 A2
Redding Dr. Ame 154 A1
Redding Gr. She C E 45 F3
Reddington Dr. Slough 206 C1
Redfern Cl. Uxb 201 E2
Redfield Cl. Dun 93 F4
Redford Rd. Wind 209 E3
Redford Way. Uxb 201 E3
Redhill. Den G 189 E2
Redhouse Cl. H Wyc 172 C2
Redhuish Cl. She B E 46 B2
Redland Dr. M Keyn 46 B4
Redland Way. Ayl 116 A2
Redman Rd. H Wyc 172 A2
Redriff Cl. Maid 202 B3
Redshaw Cl. Buck 41 F1
Redshots Cl. Mar 183 F2
Redvers Gate. M Keyn 35 D4
Redwing. Ayl 101 F2
Redwood Cl. Ty Gr 163 D2
Redwood Dr. Wing 79 F1
Redwood Gate. She B E 46 B2
Redwood Gdns. Slough 205 E3
Redwood Glade. L Buzz 70 C2
Redwood. Burn 197 D2
Reed Cl. Iver 207 F4
Reeves Croft. M Keyn 33 E2
Reform Rd. Maid 203 D4
Regal Ct. Tri 119 D2
Regent Ct. Maid 202 C4
Regent Ct. Wind 210 B3
Regent Rd. Ayl 116 A4
Regent St. M Keyn 58 B4
Reid Ave. Maid 202 C3
Reliance La. M Keyn 35 D2
Rembrandt End. Ayl 100 C1
Remenham Ch L. Rem H 192 A2
Remenham La. Rem H 191 F2
Remus Gate. Brac 38 A3
Rendlesham Way. Chor 167 E2
Rendlesham. M Keyn 35 E2
Renfrew Way. M Keyn 46 C2
Rennie Cl. H Wyc 161 F1
Repton Cl. Maid 202 B2
Retreat La. Bled R 148 B1
Retreat The. L Chal 166 C4
Retreat The. P Ris 139 D2
Revel Rd. Woo G 185 E4
Revesby Cl. Maid 202 B2
Reynold Dr. Bier 102 A1
Reynolds Cl. Cran 24 C2
Reynolds Cl. H Wyc 173 F4
Reynolds Rd. Beac 175 E2
Reynolds Wlk. Ches 144 A2
Rhondda Cl. M Keyn 47 F1
Rhuddlan Cl. She C E 45 F4
Rhymer Cl. Hans 10 C2
Ribble Cl. N Pag 22 C2
Ribble Cres. M Keyn 57 E4
Ribstone Rd. Maid 202 A2
Ricardo Rd. Old W 211 D1
Richard Gdns. H Wyc 173 F4
Richardson Pl. M Keyn 34 C1
Richardson St. H Wyc 172 C4
Richborough. M Keyn 34 A3
Richings Way. Iver 207 F2
Richmond Cl. M Keyn 46 B1
Richmond Cres. Slough 206 A3
Richmond Rd. Ayl 116 B4
Richmond Way. N Pag 22 B2
Rickard Cl. S Man 115 E2
Rickard Cl. W Dra 208 B2
Rickford's Hill. Ayl 115 E4
Rickley La. M Keyn 58 A4
Rickman's La. Sto P 198 C3
Rickmansworth La. C St P 177 F2
Rickmansworth Rd. Ame 154 B1
Rickmansworth Rd. Chor 167 F3
Rickyard Cl. M Keyn 34 A2
Ride The. Tott 93 D3
Riders Way. Chin 147 E3
Ridge Cl. S Man 115 E2
Ridge Side. Bled R 160 A4
Ridge View. Tri 119 E3
Ridge Way. H Wyc 162 B1
Ridge Way. Iver 207 F3
Ridgebank. Slough 204 C3
Ridgemount End. C St P 177 F3
Ridgeway Cl. Ches 144 A2
Ridgeway Cl. Mar 183 F2
Ridgeway Meads. Bled 138 A1
Ridgeway Rd. Ches 144 A2
Ridgeway The. Ger C 188 C4
Ridgeway The. Mar 183 F2
Ridgeway. Berk 134 C2
Ridgeway. M Keyn 32 C2
Ridgeway. M Keyn 33 D3
Ridgeway. Wing 79 F2
Ridgmont Cl. Dean 31 F3
Ridgmont. Dean 31 F3
Ridgway. Wbn S 49 D3
Riding Court Rd. Datch 211 E4
Riding La. Beac 174 C2
Riding The. Dean 31 F3
Ridings Cotts. Hol G 163 E3
Ridings The. Ame 154 B2
Ridings The. Lat 155 E2
Ridings The. Maid 202 A3
Ridings Way. Cub 78 A1
Rignall Rd. G Mis 151 F4
Riley Rd. Mar 183 E1
Rillington Gdns. She B E 46 A2
Rimsdale Ct. M Keyn 58 B2
Ring Rd. Fla H 173 E1
Ringshall Dr. L Gad 121 D4
Ringshall Rd. Dag 107 D2
Ringshall Rd. Rin 107 D1
Ringstead Way. Ayl 116 A3
Ripley Cl. Slough 206 C1
Ripon St. Ayl 101 E1
Risborough Rd. Elle 130 A4
Risborough Rd. Maid 202 C4
Risborough Rd. S Man 130 A4
Rise The. Ame 165 E4
Rise The. Gawt 51 F2
Rise The. Loud 174 A2
Rise The. Uxb 201 F2
Riseley Rd. Maid 202 B4
River Cl. N Pag 22 B2
River Gdns. Maid 203 E2
River Park Ind Est. Berk 135 D3
River Rd. Tapl 203 E4
River St. Wind 210 B4
River View. Fla H 185 D4
River Wlk. N Den 201 E4
Rivercrest Rd. Old S 32 A3
Riverpark Dr. Mar 183 F1
Riverside Gdns. Berk 135 D3
Riverside Park. Stan 212 C3
Riverside Pl. Stan 213 F1
Riverside Rd. Stan 213 E1
Riverside Way. Uxb 201 D2
Riverside Wlk. Oln 7 D3
Riverside. N Pag 22 B2
Riverwood Ct. Bish 194 C4
Riverwoods Ave. Mar 184 A1
Riverwoods Dr. Mar 184 A1
Rivetts Cl. Oln 6 C2
Rixband Cl. B Bkhl 48 A2
Rixman Cl. Maid 202 B3
Rixon Cl. Slough 206 C4
Roade Hill. Ash 9 F4
Robert Rd. Hedg 187 E1
Robert's Dr. Ayl 101 E1
Roberts Cl. Stan 213 E1
Roberts Cl. W Dra 208 C3
Roberts Rd. H Wyc 173 D4
Roberts Rd. Hadd 127 D3
Roberts Ride. Hol G 163 D3
Roberts Wood Dr. C St P 177 F3
Roberts Wood Dr. Map Cr 178 B2
Robertson Cl. She C E 45 F4
Robin Cl. Ayl 101 F2
Robin Cl. Buck 52 C4
Robin Hill. Berk 135 E2
Robin Hood Cl. Slough 204 C3
Robin Willis Way. Old W 211 D1
Robins Cl. Lit M 172 B2
Robins Cl. Uxb 208 B4
Robins Hill. M Keyn 47 D3
Robins Orchard. C St P 177 F2
Robins Platt. Chin 147 D3
Robinson Rd. Loud 174 A2
Robinswood Cl. Beac 175 E3
Robinswood Cl. L Buzz 70 C1
Roblin Cl. Ayl 115 F2
Robson Cl. C St P 177 F3
Roche Gdns. M Keyn 58 A4
Rochester Pl. Ayl 115 D4
Rochford Way. Burn 204 A4
Rochfords Gdns. Slough 206 B3
Rochfords. M Keyn 46 C3
Rock Cl. L Buzz 80 B3
Rock La. L Buzz 80 B4
Rockingham Cl. Uxb 201 E2
Rockingham Dr. M Keyn 34 C3
Rockingham Parade. Uxb 201 E3
Rockingham Rd. Uxb 201 E2
Rockspray Gr. Walt 48 A3
Rodney Way. Stan 212 C3
Rodwell Gdns. Walt 48 B2
Roebuck Ave. H Wyc 173 F3
Roebuck Green. Slough 204 C3
Rogers Croft. M Keyn 47 E4
Rogers La. Sto P 198 C2
Roker Park Ave. Ick 201 F4
Rokesby Rd. Slough 197 F1
Rolfe Cl. Beac 175 F1
Rolvenden Gr. M K Vil 48 A4
Roman Lea. Cook 195 F4
Roman Way. Bou E 185 D2
Roman Way. Brac 38 A4
Romar Ct. M Keyn 47 E1
Romney Ct. Mar 183 F2
Romney Rd. Ayl 115 F2
Romsey Cl. Slough 206 C2
Romsey Dr. Far C 187 E1
Romsey Way. H Wyc 173 D2
Romulus Way. Brac 38 A3
Ronald Rd. Beac 175 F1
Ronaldsay Spur. Slough 205 F4
Rook Rd. Bou E 185 E2
Rook Wood Way. L Kin 152 A3
Rookery Ct. Mar 183 E1
Rookery La. Edgc 72 C1
Rookery Meadow. Hol G 163 E4
Rookery Way. Stp Cl 63 F2
Rosary The. Hol G 163 E4
Rose Ave. Ayl 101 E1
Rose Ave. Ty Gr 163 D1
Rose Corner. Skch 158 C3
Rose Dr. Ches 154 B4
Rose Hill. Burn 197 D3
Rose La. Know H 193 D1
Rose Wlk. Slough 205 D4
Roseary Cl. W Dra 208 B1
Rosebank Cl. Cook 195 F4
Rosebay Cl. Walt 48 A3
Rosebery Ave. H Wyc 173 F3
Rosebery Ave. L Buzz 80 C4
Rosebery Rd. Ast C 117 F3
Rosebery Way. Tri 119 D3
Rosehill Cl. Twyf 62 B1
Rosehill. Berk 135 D2
Roseleigh Cl. Maid 202 A4
Rosemary Cl. H Wyc 161 D1
Rosemary Ct. Walt 48 A3
Rosemary La. Hadd 127 D4
Rosemead. Ast C 117 F1
Rosery The. Bou E 185 D2
Roses Cl. Cub 78 A1
Roses La. Wind 209 E3
Rosetree Cl. Pres 151 E3
Rosewood Way. Far C 198 B4
Rosken Gr. Far C 198 A2
Roslyn Ct. M Keyn 35 E4
Ross Rd. A Abb 88 B3
Ross Rd. Maid 202 C2
Ross Way. M Keyn 46 C1
Rossal Pl. M Keyn 33 E2
Rossetti Pl. Hol G 163 E4
Rossey Pl. Eton 205 E1
Rossiter Cl. Slough 206 C1
Rossway La. Berk 134 A4
Rostrevor Gdns. Iver H 200 B2
Rothersthorpe. M Keyn 35 D4
Rothesay Cl. Ayl 101 F1
Rothschild Ave. Ast C 117 F3
Rothschild Rd. L Buzz 80 C4
Rothschild Rd. Wing 79 F1
Rotten Row. G Bkhl 59 E1
Roughwood La. C St G 166 C2
Round Hill. Sto 114 B3
Round Wood Rd. Ame 154 C1
Roundhead Dr. Tha 125 F1
Roundheads End. Beac 175 D2
Roundwood Rd. H Wyc 172 B4
Rovelley Ct. M Keyn 32 C3
Row The. La En 171 D2
Rowan Ave. H Wyc 173 E4
Rowan Cl. Ayl 115 F2
Rowan Cl. Beac 175 D1
Rowan Cl. Ty Gr 163 D2
Rowan Dr. Have 20 B1
Rowan Gdns. Iver H 200 B2
Rowan Rd. W Dra 208 B1
Rowan Way. Slough 205 D4
Rowanhurst Dr. Far C 198 B4
Rowans The. Ger C 188 B4
Rowborough Rd. Hal 131 E4
Rowland Cl. Wind 209 E2
Rowland Way. Ayl 115 D4
Rowlands Cl. M Keyn 58 C4
Rowle Cl. M Keyn 34 C4
Rowley Furrows. L Buzz 80 B4
Rowley La. Iver H 199 E2
Rowley La. Sto P 199 E2
Rowlheys Pl. W Dra 208 C2
Rowliff Rd. H Wyc 172 B3
Rowsham Dell. M Keyn 21 F1
Rowsham Rd. Bier 102 B3
Roxburgh Way. M Keyn 46 C2
Roxwell Cl. Slough 204 C3
Royal Cl. W Dra 208 C4
Royal Ct. Tri 120 A3
Royal La. Uxb 208 C4
Royal La. W Dra 208 C4
Royce Cl. Dun 93 F4
Royce Rd. Cran 24 B2
Royle Cl. C St P 177 F2
Royston Way. Slough 204 B4
Rubbra Cl. Walt 48 B3
Rubens Cl. Ayl 100 C1
Ruby Cl. Slough 205 D2
Ruckles Way. Ame 165 E4
Rudchesters. M Keyn 33 F3
Rudd's La. Hadd 127 D4
Ruddlesway. Wind 209 E3
Rudds Cl. Wins 66 A3
Rudsworth Cl. Iver 212 B4
Rugwood Rd. Fla H 173 E1
Rumptons Paddock. Gr Und 82 C3
Run Furrow. Hadd 127 D4
Runford Ct. She B E 46 B3
Runnymead. M Keyn 21 F1
Runrig Hill. Ame 154 C2
Rupert Ave. H Wyc 172 C2
Rupert Cl. Hen-O-T 191 F2
Rupert Way. Tha 126 A1
Rupert's La. Hen-O-T 191 F2
Ruscombe Gdns. Datch 211 D4
Rushall Rd. Tha 126 A1
Rushbrooke Cl. H Wyc 162 C1
Rushburn. Woo G 185 F3
Rushendon Furlong. Ivin 105 E3
Rushes Mead. Uxb 201 E2
Rushes The. Maid 203 D3
Rushington Ave. Maid 202 C3
Rushmere Cl. B Bkhl 48 B1
Rushmere La. Ash Gr 145 D2
Rushmoor Ave. Ty Gr 163 D2
Rushton Ct. M Keyn 45 F4
Ruskin Ct. N Pag 22 B1
Ruskin Way. Ayl 101 E1
Rusland Cir. M Keyn 46 B2
Russell Ave. Ayl 115 E3
Russell Cl. L Chal 166 B4
Russell Cl. Ty Gr 163 D1
Russell Ct. Ches 144 B1

Russell Ct. Maid 202 C4
Russell Dr. Stan 213 E1
Russell St. M Keyn 32 B3
Russell St. Wbn S 49 D2
Russell St. Wind 210 B3
Russet Cl. Stan 212 C1
Russet Rd. Maid 202 B2
Russets The. Ger C 177 E1
Russett Hill. Ger C 188 C4
Rutherford Rd. Ayl 115 F2
Ruthven Cl. M Keyn 58 B2
Rutland Ave. H Wyc 172 B3
Rutland Ave. Slough 205 E4
Rutland Pl. Maid 202 B3
Rutland Rd. Maid 202 B3
Rutland St. H Wyc 173 D3
Ryans Mount. Mar 183 B1
Rycote La. G Has 136 B3
Rycroft. M Keyn 46 C2
Rycroft. Wind 209 F2
Rydal Way. H Wyc 172 A3
Rydal Way. M Keyn 58 B3
Ryder Cl. Bov 146 A2
Rydings. Wind 209 F2
Rye Cl. Ayl 115 E2
Rye Cl. Maid 202 A2
Rye Ct. Slough 206 A2
Rye The. Eat B 92 A4
Rye View. H Wyc 173 E4
Ryecroft Rd. Ches 154 A4
Ryeland Cl. W Dra 208 C4
Ryeland. M Keyn 32 C3
Rylstone Cl. M Keyn 34 A2
Rylstone Cl. Maid 202 B2
Ryman Ct. Chor 167 E2
Rymill Cl. Bov 146 A2
Ryton Pl. M Keyn 46 B2
Ryvers Rd. Slough 206 C2

Sabina Cl. H Wyc 172 C3
Saddington. M Keyn 47 E3
Saddlers Green. Asp G 49 D3
Saddlers Pl. M Keyn 35 D3
Saffron Rd. H Wyc 173 E3
Saffron Rise. Eat B 92 C3
Saffron St. M Keyn 58 B4
Saham Croft Cl. Wins 65 F2
St Adrian's Cl. Maid 202 A2
St Aidan's Cl. M Keyn 57 F3
St Alban's Rd. Wins 65 F2
St Alban's St. Wind 210 B3
St Andrew's Ave. Wind 209 F3
St Andrew's Cl. H Wyc 162 C1
St Andrew's Cl. Old W 211 D1
St Andrew's Cl. Wray 211 F1
St Andrew's Cres. Wind 209 F3
St Andrew's Rd. Chin 147 E3
St Andrew's Rd. M Keyn 57 F4
St Andrew's Way. Slough 204 B3
St Andrews Way In Es. Ayl 101 E1
St Anne's Cl. Hen-O-T 191 E1
St Anne's Cl. Wen 131 D3
St Anne's Rd. Ayl 115 D4
St Anne's Rd. S Har 190 B4
St Anthony's Cl. Ayl 115 D4
St Bees. M K Vil 36 A1
St Bernards Rd. Slough 206 B2
St Birinus. Fla H 174 A1
St Catherine's Ave. M Keyn 57 E3
St Catherine's Ct. Ayl 115 D4
St Chad's Rd. Maid 202 A2
St Christopher Rd. Uxb 208 B4
St Christopher's Cl. L Kin 152 A2
St Clement Cl. Uxb 208 B4
St Clement's Dr. M Keyn 57 E3
St Columba's Cl. Maid 202 A2
St David Cl. Uxb 208 B4
St David's Cl. Iver H 200 B2
St David's Cl. Maid 202 A2
St David's Par. Iver H 200 B2
St David's Rd. M Keyn 57 F3
St Dunstans. M Keyn 47 D3
St Edmund's Cl. Ayl 115 D4
St Edmunds. Berk 135 E2
St Edwards Ct. M Keyn 34 C4
St Elmo Cres. Slough 198 B1
St Faith's Cl. Nwtn L 57 E2
St Francis Rd. B Bot 159 E2
St Francis Rd. Den G 189 F3
St George's Cl. H Wyc 173 E4
St George's Cl. Wind 209 F3
St George's Cres. Burn 204 B3
St George's Dr. Ick 190 C1
St George's Rd. M Keyn 57 F3
St Georges Ind Est. Ame 165 F4
St Georges Way. M Keyn 33 E4
St Giles Mews. M Keyn 32 B3
St Giles St. M Keyn 33 F4
St Helen Cl. Uxb 208 B4
St Hilda's Ct. Ayl 115 D4
St Hilda's Way. Fla H 174 A1
St Huberts Cl. Ger C 188 C1
St Huberts La. Ger C 188 C1
St Hugh's Ave. H Wyc 173 F3
St Hugh's Pl. Skch 158 C2
St Ives Rd. Maid 203 D4
St James Cl. Hans 11 D1
St James Pl. Slough 204 B4
St James St. M Keyn 33 F4
St James Way. Bier 102 A2
St James Wlk. Iver 207 F2
St John St. N Pag 22 B2
St John's Ave. Ty Gr 174 A4
St John's Cl. Uxb 201 D2
St John's La. Wick 31 D2
St John's Rd. Ayl 101 F1
St John's Rd. M Keyn 57 F3
St John's Rd. Ty Gr 162 C1
St John's Rd. Uxb 201 D2
St John's St. Ayl 101 F1
St John's Terr. N Pag 22 B2
St John's Well Ct. Berk 135 D3
St John's Well La. Berk 135 D3
St Johns Cl. Ty Gr 163 D1
St Johns Cres. M Keyn 33 E3
St Johns Dr. Wind 210 A3
St Johns Rd. Slough 206 A3
St Johns Rd. Ty Gr 163 D1
St Johns Rd. Wind 210 A3
St Josephs Cl. Oln 6 C2
St Katherine's Way. Berk 134 C4
St Laurence Cl. Uxb 208 B4
St Laurence Rd. Wins 65 F2
St Laurence Way. Slough 206 A2
St Lawrence Cl. Bov 146 A2
St Lawrence View. M Keyn 34 A2
St Leger Dr. M Keyn 34 C4
St Leonard's Rd. Oak G 209 E1
St Leonard's Rd. Wind 210 B2
St Leonard's Way. Edle 92 C1
St Leonards Hill. Wind 209 F2
St Leonards Rd. Ame 154 C2
St Leonards Wlk. Iver 207 F2
St Luke Cl. Uxb 208 B4
St Luke's Rd. Maid 202 C4
St Luke's Rd. Old W 211 D1
St Margaret Ct. M Keyn 58 C4
St Margaret's Cl. Berk 135 E2
St Margaret's Cl. Iver H 200 B2
St Margaret's Rd. Maid 202 A4
St Margarets Cl. N Pag 22 C2
St Mark's Cres. Maid 202 A4
St Mark's Pl. Wind 210 B3
St Mark's Rd. Ayl 115 E4
St Mark's Rd. Hen-O-T 191 F1
St Mark's Rd. Maid 202 B4
St Mark's Rd. Wind 210 B3
St Martin Cl. Uxb 208 B4
St Martin's Cl. W Dra 208 B2
St Martin's Rd. W Dra 208 B2
St Martin's St. M Keyn 58 B4
St Mary St. H Wyc 173 D3
St Mary St. M Keyn 33 F4
St Mary's Ave. Berk 134 B3
St Mary's Ave. M Keyn 32 C3
St Mary's Ave. M Keyn 57 F4
St Mary's Cl. Maid 203 D4
St Mary's Cl. S Har 190 A4
St Mary's Cl. Wave 48 C4
St Mary's Glebe. Edle 92 C2
St Mary's La. Lee C 142 B3
St Mary's Rd. Den G 189 F3
St Mary's Rd. S Har 190 A4
St Mary's Rd. Slough 206 C2
St Mary's Sq. Ayl 115 E4
St Mary's Way. Ches 154 A4
St Mary's Way. Ger C 177 E1
St Mary's Way. L Buzz 80 C4
St Mary's Wlk. Maid 202 C4
St Marys Cl. E Clay 74 C4
St Marys Cl. Mur 67 E3
St Marys Ct. Ting 51 D4
St Marys Rd. E Clay 74 C4
St Matthew Cl. Uxb 208 B4
St Matthews Ct. M Keyn 57 F3
St Michael's Cl. Hal 117 E1
St Michael's Ct. Slough 197 E1
St Michael's Green. Beac 175 F4
St Michael's Way. Stp Cl 63 F2
St Michaels Cl. Stew 68 C1
St Nicholas Cl. Cub 78 A1
St Nicholas Cl. L Chal 166 A4
St Nicholas Cl. Uxb 208 B4
St Patrick's Cl. Maid 202 A2
St Patrick's Way. M Keyn 57 F3
St Paul Cl. Uxb 208 B4
St Paul's Rd. M Keyn 57 F3
St Pauls Ave. Slough 206 A3
St Pauls Ct. M Keyn 32 B3
St Pauls Yd. N Pag 22 B2
St Peter St. Mar 183 F1
St Peter's Ave. Ayl 101 E2
St Peter's Cl. Burn 197 D1
St Peter's Cl. Old W 211 D1
St Peter's Hill. Tri 119 D2
St Peter's Rd. Brac 38 A4
St Peter's Rd. Maid 195 E1
St Peter's Rd. Uxb 208 B4
St Peters Cl. Lac G 150 B2
St Peters Cl. Loud 174 A1
St Peters Gate. Brac 38 A4
St Peters Way. Chor 167 D3
St Peters Way. M Keyn 34 A4
St Rumbolds La. Buck 52 B4
St Stephen's Rd. W Dra 208 B3
St Stephens Dr. M Keyn 35 D4
St Teresas Cl. P Ris 139 D2
St Thomas Walk. Iver 212 B4
St Vincents. Asp G 49 E2
St-cloud Way. Maid 203 D4
Salden Cl. Dray P 68 B3
Salden Cl. She C E 46 A3
Salford Rd. Asp G 49 E4
Salisbury Ave. Slough 205 E4
Salisbury Cl. Ame 165 F4
Salisbury Cl. P Ris 139 E2
Salisbury Gr. M Keyn 21 F1
Salisbury Rd. H Wyc 162 B1
Salisbury Rd. Uxb 201 D2
Salmons La. Pres 151 E3
Salt Hill Ave. Slough 205 E3
Salt Hill Cl. Uxb 201 F4
Salt Hill Dr. Slough 205 E3
Salt Hill Way. Slough 205 E3
Saltash Cl. Loud 174 A2
Salter's Cl. Berk 134 C3
Salters Cl. Maid 203 D4
Salters La. Lud 96 B4
Salters Mews. M Keyn 34 C3
Salters Rd. Maid 203 D4
Salton Link. She B E 46 A1
Samphire Ct. Walt 48 A3
Sampsons Green. Slough 197 F1
Sampsons Hill. Cole 164 C1
San Remo Rd. Asp G 49 F2
Sanctuary Rd. Hol G 163 D3
Sandage Rd. La En 171 D3
Sandbrier Cl. Walt 48 A3
Sandbrook La. Wils 104 B1
Sandels Way. Beac 175 E2
Sandelswood End. Beac 175 E3
Sanders La. Pott 18 B2
Sandford Gdns. H Wyc 173 D2
Sandhill Rd. E Clay 74 C4
Sandholme. Stp Cl 63 F2
Sandhurst Dr. Buck 52 B4
Sandisplatt Rd. Maid 202 A3
Sandlers End. Slough 198 A1
Sandon Cl. Tri 118 C2
Sandown Ct. M Keyn 57 E3
Sandown Rd. Slough 204 C4
Sandpit Hill. Ting 50 C3
Sandpit La. Bled 138 A2
Sandpits La. Ty Gr 174 B4
Sandringham Ct. Slough 204 B4
Sandringham Pl. M Keyn 58 B4
Sandringham Rd. Maid 195 F1
Sandringham Rd. Stan 213 F1
Sands Farm Dr. Burn 197 E1
Sandwell Ct. M Keyn 33 E1
Sandy Cl. Buck 52 C4
Sandy Cl. M Keyn 34 B4
Sandy La. Asp H 49 D1
Sandy La. L Buzz 70 C2
Sandy La. L Cre 125 D3
Sandy Mead. Holy 203 E1
Sandy Rise. C St P 177 F1
Sandycroft Rd. L Chal 155 E1
Sandygate Cl. Mar 183 E2
Sandygate Rd. Mar 183 E2
Sandywell Dr. M Keyn 35 D3
Santen Gr. M Keyn 58 B2
Sargeants Cl. Uxb 201 B1
Saunders End. H Hea 153 E3
Saunders Wd Cps. Skch 158 C2
Savay Cl. Den G 190 A2
Savay La. Den G 190 A3
Savernake Rd. Ayl 101 E2
Savill Way. Mar 183 F1
Sawmill Rd. Lgwk 138 B4
Sawpit Hill. Hol G 163 D3
Sawyer's Cl. Wind 209 F4
Sawyers Cl. Maid 202 A1
Sawyers Cres. Maid 202 A1
Saxhorn Rd. La En 171 E2
Saxon Cl. Dun 93 F4
Saxon Cl. Slough 206 C2
Saxon Cl. Uxb 208 C4
Saxon Gdns. Maid 196 B1
Saxon St. M Keyn 34 B3
Saxon St. M Keyn 47 E2
Saxon Way. Harm 213 E4
Saxon Way. Old W 211 D1
Saye & Sele Cl. Gr Und 82 C3
Sayers Gdns. Berk 135 D3
Sayward Cl. Ches 144 B1
Scafell Rd. Slough 204 C4
Scampton Rd. Stan 213 F1
Scarborough Way. Slough 205 D2
Scarlett Ave. Wen 131 E3
Scars The. Edle 92 A3
Scatterdells La. Chipf 146 C1
Scatterill Cl. M Keyn 34 A2
School Cl. G Kin 162 B3
School Cl. H Wyc 161 E1
School Cl. H Wyc 173 D2
School Cl. Hol G 163 E4
School Cl. Ick 124 A2
School Dr. Nwtn L 57 E2
School End. G Hrwd 54 C2
School Hill. N Mar 76 A1
School Hill. Twyf 73 D3
School La. Ame 165 D4
School La. Buck 52 B4
School La. C St G 177 D4
School La. Cast 19 F3
School La. Chea 112 A1
School La. Cook 196 A4
School La. Eat B 92 C3
School La. Ger C 177 E1
School La. Ibst 169 F2
School La. Lit M 184 B3
School La. M Keyn 46 A4
School La. Maid 195 F1
School La. Medm 193 D3
School La. Oak 109 E3
School La. Pres B 62 A4
School La. S Ham 69 F4
School La. Se Gr 176 B2
School La. Sher 14 A1
School La. Sto P 199 D2
School La. Twyf 61 B1
School La. Ty Gr 164 A3
School La. W Tur 116 C1
School La. Wadd 99 D1
School La. Wadd 99 D3
School La. Yard G 18 C3
School Rd. Harm 213 E4
School Rd. Ty Gr 174 B4
School Rd. Woo G 185 F3
School St. M Keyn 33 F4
School Way. Loud 174 A1
Schorne La. N Mar 76 A1
Schuman Cl. Walt 48 B2
Scotlands Dr. Far C 198 A3
Scotswood Cl. Beac 175 E3
Scott Cl. Far C 198 B4
Scott Cl. W Dra 208 C1
Scott Dr. N Pag 22 A3
Scott End. Ayl 100 C1
Scott Evans Ct. Wins 66 A3
Scotts Cl. M Gib 72 A2
Scotts La. Adsk 53 F1
Scriveners La. Paul 17 D4
Scrubb's La. Bled R 160 A4
Seacourt Rd. Slough 207 D1
Seaford Rd. Stan 213 E1
Seagrave Ct. Walt 48 A2
Seagrave Rd. Beac 175 E2
Seaton Dr. Ayl 115 E2
Secklow Gate. M Keyn 34 C2
Second Ave. M Keyn 47 E1
Second Cres. Slough 205 E4
Sedgemere. M Keyn 33 E1
Sedgemoor Dr. Tha 126 A1
Sedgmoor Gdns. Fla H 185 D4
Sedgmoor La. Fla H 185 D4
Sedgmoor Rd. Fla H 185 D4
Sedley Gr. S Har 190 B4
Sedrup La. Sto 114 C2
Seeleys Cl. Beac 175 E2
Seeleys Rd. Beac 175 E2
Seer Green La. Se Gr 176 C2
Seer Mead. Se Gr 176 B2
Sefton Paddock. Sto P 199 D3
Sefton Way. Uxb 208 B4
Selbourne Ave. M Keyn 57 F4
Selby Gr. She C E 46 A3
Selkirk Ave. Ayl 101 E1
Selkirk Gr. M Keyn 46 C1
Selwood Cl. Stan 213 E1
Selwood Gdns. Stan 213 E1
Selwood Way. H Wyc 161 F1
Selworthy. She B E 46 B2
Serjeants Green. M Keyn 34 C3
Serles Cl. M Keyn 47 D3
Seven Acres. L Cre 125 D4
Sevenhills Rd. Iver H 200 B3
Severalls Ave. Ches 144 B1
Severn Cres. Slough 212 A4
Severn Dr. N Pag 22 C2
Severn Way. M Keyn 46 C1
Sewell Cl. Ayl 100 C1
Seymour Cl. Fla H 173 E1
Seymour Cl. Maid 202 A2
Seymour Court La. Mar B 183 D3
Seymour Court Rd. Mar 183 E2
Seymour Court Rd. Mar B 183 E2
Seymour Park Rd. Mar 183 E2
Seymour Plain. Mar 183 E3
Seymour Plain. Mar B 183 E3
Seymour Rd. Berk 134 C3
Seymour Rd. Slough 205 E2
Shackleton Pl. M Keyn 34 C1
Shackleton Rd. H Wyc 172 C3
Shackleton Rd. Slough 205 F3
Shaftesbury Cres. M Keyn 47 D1
Shaftesbury St. H Wyc 172 C4
Shaggy Calf La. Slough 206 A3
Shakespear Cl. N Pag 22 A3
Shakespeare Orch. Gr Und 82 C3
Shamrock Cl. Walt 48 A3
Shannon Ct. M Keyn 35 D3
Shantock Hall La. Bov 145 F1
Shantock La. Bov 145 F1
Sharman Wlk. M Keyn 34 A2
Sharney Ave. Slough 207 D2
Sharp Cl. Ayl 115 F3
Sharp's Cl. Wadd 99 D3
Sharrow Vale. H Wyc 172 C4
Shaw Cl. N Pag 22 A3
Shaw Ct. S Man 115 F2
Shaw Ct. S Man 115 F2
Shaw The. Cook 195 F3
Shaws Cl. Pres 151 E3
Shearmans. M Keyn 33 D2
Sheehy Way. Slough 206 A3
Sheep St. Wins 66 A2
Sheepcote Cl. Beac 175 E2
Sheepcote Cotts. Hol G 163 E4
Sheepcote Dell Rd. Hol G 163 F4
Sheepcote Gdns. Den G 190 A3
Sheepcote La. Tapl 186 A1
Sheepcote Rd. Eton 205 D1
Sheepcote Rd. Wind 209 F3
Sheepfold La. Ame 165 E4
Sheephouse Rd. Maid 196 A1
Sheepridge La. Bou E 184 C4
Sheepridge La. Fla H 184 C4
Sheerstock. Hadd 126 C3
Sheerwater. Ayl 101 F2
Sheet St. Wind 210 B3
Sheet Street Rd. Wind 210 B1
Sheffield Dr. Ayl 115 F3
Sheffield Rd. Slough 205 E4
Shelburne Ct. H Wyc 172 C2
Shelburne Rd. H Wyc 172 C2
Sheldon Ct. M Keyn 33 F1
Sheldon Rd. Ick 124 A2
Shelduck Cl. Ayl 101 F2
Shelley Cl. Medm 193 E4
Shelley Cl. N Pag 22 A2
Shelley Cl. Slough 206 C1
Shelley Dr. M Keyn 57 F4
Shelley Rd. Ches 144 A1
Shelley Rd. H Wyc 172 C3
Shelley Rd. Mar 183 C2
Shellin Gr. M Keyn 58 B2
Shelsmore. M Keyn 35 D4
Shelton Ct. Slough 206 B2
Sheney Rd. M Keyn 57 F4
Shenley Rd. M Keyn 46 C1
Shenley Rd. She C E 46 A3
Shenley Rd. Whad 56 A4
Shenstone Dr. Slough 197 E1
Shenstone Hill. Berk 135 F3
Shepherd's La. Chor 167 F1
Shepherds Cl. Hurl 193 F2
Shepherds Cl. Uxb 201 E1
Shepherds Fold. Hol G 163 E4
Shepherds Gate. L Kin 152 A1
Shepherds La. Beac 175 F1
Shepherds La. Hol G 162 C3
Shepherds La. Hurl 193 F2
Shepherds Row. Wins 66 A2
Shepherds Way. Ches 154 B3
Shepherds. M Keyn 33 D2
Sheppards Cl. N Pag 22 B2
Shepperds Cl. N Mar 76 A1
Shepperton Cl. Cast 19 F3
Sheraton Dr. H Wyc 162 B1
Sherborne Cl. Stan 212 C3
Sherbourne Dr. B Bkhl 48 A2
Sherbourne Dr. Maid 202 B2
Sherbourne Dr. Wind 209 F2
Sherbourne Wlk. Far C 198 B4
Shergold Way. Cook 195 F3
Sheridan Cl. S Man 115 E2
Sheriff Cl. Ayl 115 D4
Sherington Rd. Lath 22 C4
Sherington Rd. Sher 22 C4
Sherman Rd. Slough 205 F4
Shernfold. M K Vil 48 A4
Sherwood Cl. Slough 206 C2
Sherwood Dr. M Keyn 47 D1
Sherwood Dr. Maid 202 A3
Shields Ct. Ty Gr 163 D1
Shifford Cres. Maid 195 F2
Shilling Cl. M Keyn 35 D4
Ship Hill. Burn 186 C2
Ship Rd. L Buzz 80 C3
Ship St E. H Wyc 173 D4
Shipley Rd. N Pag 22 A2
Shipman Ct. M Keyn 35 D4
Shipton Hill. M Keyn 34 A3
Shipton Rd. Ick 201 F4
Shire Ct. M Keyn 35 D3
Shire La. C St P 178 A3
Shire La. Chol 133 D2
Shire La. Chor 167 E2
Shire La. Has 133 D2
Shire La. N Craw 24 C2
Shires Rd. Brac 38 A3
Shirley Ave. Wind 209 F3
Shirley Rd. Maid 202 B3
Shogmoor La. Frie 170 B1
Sholto Rd. Stan 213 F1
Shootacre La. Lac G 149 D4
Shootacre La. P Ris 149 D4
Shootersway La. Berk 134 C2
Shootersway Park. Berk 134 C2
Shootersway. Berk 134 C2
Shop La. Y Has 1 A3
Shoppenhanger's Rd. Maid 202 C2
Shorediche Cl. Ick 190 C1
Shoreham Rd (E). Stan 213 F1

Shoreham Rd (W). Stan 213 F1
Shoreham Rise. Slough 197 E1
Shorham Rise. M Keyn 33 F1
Short Massey. Oln 6 C3
Short Rd. Stan 213 F1
Short St. H Wyc 172 C4
Shortborough Ave. P Ris 139 D3
Shortfern. Slough 206 B4
Shortway. Ame 154 B1
Shortway. Ches 144 A1
Shotfield Rd. La En 171 E2
Shothanger Way. Fel 146 B3
Shouler Cl. She C E 46 A3
Shrimpton Cl. Beac 175 E3
Shrimpton Rd. Beac 175 E3
Shrimpton Rd. H Wyc 172 A2
Shrubbery Rd. H Wyc 173 D4
Shrublands Ave. Berk 135 D2
Shrublands Rd. Berk 135 D3
Shugars Green. Tri 119 D3
Shutlanger Rd. S Bru 9 D4
Shuttleworth Gr. Walt 48 B3
Sibleys Rise. S Hea 152 B4
Side Rd. Den G 189 E2
Sidlow Ct. M Keyn 32 C2
Sidney Terr. Wen 131 D3
Silbury Arc. M Keyn 34 C2
Silbury Bvd. M Keyn 34 B1
Silco Dr. Maid 202 C3
Silicon Ct. She B E 46 B3
Silk Mill Way. Tri 119 D3
Silk St. Wadd 99 D3
Sillswood. Oln 6 C2
Silsden Cres. C St G 177 E4
Silver Birch Cl. Ick 201 F4
Silver Cl. Maid 202 A3
Silver Hill. C St G 177 D4
Silver St. Ayl 115 E4
Silver St. Cub 78 A1
Silver St. N Pag 22 B2
Silverbirches La. Asp H 49 D1
Silverdale Cl. Ayl 101 E1
Silverdale Cl. Ty Gr 163 D1
Silvermead. Worm 123 E3
Silvertrees Dr. Maid 202 A3
Silverweed Ct. Walt 48 A3
Simdims. Cran 25 D1
Simmons Cl. Slough 207 D1
Simmons Ct. Ayl 115 F2
Simmons Rd. Hen-O-T 191 E2
Simmons Way. La En 171 E2
Simmons Way. Tha 125 F1
Simnel. M Keyn 47 D3
Simon Dean. Bov 146 A2
Simons Lea. M Keyn 34 A2
Simonsbath. M Keyn 46 B1
Simpson Cl. Maid 203 D4
Simpson Dr. M Keyn 47 F3
Simpson Pl. Ayl 115 F3
Simpson Rd. M Keyn 47 F2
Simpson Rd. Walt 47 F2
Sinclair Ct. M Keyn 47 D2
Singer La. Hen-O-T 191 F1
Sipson Rd. W Dra 208 C2
Sipthorp Cl. Walt 48 B3
Sitwell. N Pag 21 F3
Sixty Acres Rd. Pres 151 E3
Skeats Wharf. M Keyn 35 D4
Skeldon Gate. M Keyn 35 D2
Skene Cl. M Keyn 58 B2
Skimmers Cl. Hol G 163 E3
Skimmers End. Hol G 163 E3
Skimmers Field. Hol G 163 E3
Skippon Way. Tha 125 F1
Skipton Cl. M Keyn 35 E3
Skittle Green. Bled 138 A1
Skydmore Path. Slough 197 F1
Skylark Rd. Den G 189 E2
Skyport Dr. Harm 213 E4
Slad La. Lac G 149 F2
Slade La. M Keyn 33 D2
Slade Oak La. Den G 189 E3
Slade Rd. Skch 158 C2
Slade The. Nwtn L 57 E2
Slapton La. Edle 91 F3
Slated Row. M Keyn 33 D4
Slater St. H Wyc 173 E3
Slattenham Cl. Ayl 115 D4
Slave Hill. Hadd 126 C3
Slayter Rd. La En 171 E2
Slickett's La. Edle 92 C2
Slipe The. Ched 105 D4
Slough Rd. Datch 211 D4
Slough Rd. Eton 205 F1
Slough Rd. Iver H 200 C2
Slough Rd. Slough 205 F1
Sly Cnr. Lee C 142 C2
Smabridge Wlk. M Keyn 35 E4
Small Cres. Buck 52 C4
Smalldean La. Bled R 149 D1
Smeaton Cl. Ayl 100 C1
Smeaton Cl. M Keyn 22 A1
Smith Cl. Ayl 116 A4
Smith's La. Wind 209 F3
Smithergill Ct. M Keyn 34 B3
Smithfield End. Swan 66 C2
Smithfield Rd. Maid 202 A2
Smithsons Pl. M Keyn 35 D2
Snaith Cres. M Keyn 46 A4
Snakeley Cl. Loud 174 B1
Snape Spur. Slough 205 F4
Snells Wood Ct. L Chal 166 B4
Snelshall St. She B E 56 C4
Snowball Hill. Maid 202 A1
Snowberry Cl. M Keyn 33 E3
Snowden Cl. Wind 209 E2
Snowdon Dr. M Keyn 46 B4
Snowdrop Way. Hol G 162 C4
Snowhill Cotts. Ash Gr 144 C4
Snowshill Ct. M Keyn 21 F1
Soardale. M Keyn 34 B3
Soho Cres. Bou E 185 E2
Sokeman Cl. M Keyn 33 D3
Solar Ct. M Keyn 21 F1
Solent Rd. Stan 213 F1
Solesbridge Ct. Chor 167 F3
Solesbridge La. Chor 167 F3
Solters Cl. Lud 96 B4
Somerford Cl. Maid 203 D4
Somersby Cres. Maid 202 C2
Somerset Cl. M Keyn 46 C1
Somerset Way. Iver 207 F2
Somerville Rd. Eton 205 E1
Somerville Way. Ayl 115 D4
Sorrell Dr. N Pag 21 F2
Soskin Dr. M Keyn 34 B3
Sospel Ct. Far C 198 B2
Soulbury Rd. L Buzz 80 B4
Soulbury Rd. Stew 68 C1
Soulbury Rd. Wing 79 E2
South Bank Rd. Berk 134 C3
South Cl. Burn 204 B3
South Cl. Medm 193 E4
South Cl. W Dra 208 C2
South Common Rd. Uxb 201 F3
South Cott Dr. Chor 167 F2
South Cott Gdns. Chor 167 F2
South Dr. Beac 186 A4
South Dr. H Wyc 173 E4
South Eighth St. M Keyn 34 C1
South End La. Edle 92 A2
South End. Hadd 126 C3
South Field Cl. Dorn 204 B2
South Fifth St. M Keyn 34 C1
South Fourth St. M Keyn 34 B1
South Green. Slough 205 F3
South Lawne. M Keyn 57 F4
South Maundin. Hgh V 162 A4
South Meadow La. Eton 210 B4
South Ninth St. M Keyn 34 C1
South Park Ave. Chor 167 F2
South Park Cres. Ger C 188 C4
South Park Dr. Ger C 188 C4
South Park Gdns. Berk 135 D3
South Park View. Ger C 188 C4
South Park. Ger C 188 C3
South Path. Wind 210 B3
South Rd. Ame 154 B2
South Rd. Chor 167 E2
South Rd. Maid 202 C3
South Rd. W Dra 208 C2
South Row. M Keyn 34 C1
South Second St. M Keyn 34 B1
South Seventh St. M Keyn 34 C1
South Side. Ger C 188 B4
South Sixth St. M Keyn 34 C1
South St. Cast 19 F3
South St. Wen 131 D2
South Tenth St. M Keyn 34 C1
South Terr. M Keyn 58 B4
South Vale. Y Has 1 A3
South View Rd. Ger C 188 B4
South View. H Wyc 161 E1
South Way. Beac 186 A4
Southampton Rd. Stan 213 F1
Southampton Way. Stan 213 F1
Southbourne Dr. Bou E 185 D2
Southcliffe Dr. C St P 177 F3
Southcote Way. Ty Gr 163 D1
Southcott Village. L Buzz 80 B3
Southcourt Ave. L Buzz 80 B3
Southcourt Rd. L Buzz 80 B4
Southcroft. Slough 198 A1
Southern Per Rd. Stan 213 E1
Southern Rd. Ayl 101 E1
Southern Rd. Tha 125 E1
Southern Way. M Keyn 33 E3
Southfield Cl. M Keyn 35 F4
Southfield Dr. Hol G 163 D3
Southfield Gdns. Burn 204 A4
Southfield Rd. Ayl 116 A4
Southfield Rd. Fla H 174 A1
Southfield Rd. H Wyc 161 E1
Southfield Rd. P Ris 139 E2
Southlea Rd. Datch 211 D3
Southview Rd. Mar 183 F2
Southwick Ct. M Keyn 45 F4
Southwold Cl. Ayl 116 A3
Southwold Spur. Slough 207 E2
Southwood Gdns. Cook 195 F3
Southwood Rd. Cook 195 F3
Sovereign Dr. M Keyn 35 D4
Spackmans Way. Slough 205 E2
Spade Oak Meadow. Bou E 184 C2
Spark Way. N Pag 21 F3
Sparow Cl. Ayl 101 F2
Sparsholt Cl. She B E 46 B1
Spearing Rd. H Wyc 172 B3
Spearmint Cl. Walt 48 A3
Specklands. M Keyn 46 A4
Speedwell Pl. M Keyn 34 C2
Speen Rd. Wal A 150 B1
Speldhurst Ct. M K Vil 48 A4
Spencer Cl. Uxb 201 E1
Spencer Rd. Slough 206 C2
Spencer St. M Keyn 33 F4
Spencer. M Keyn 34 B4
Spencers Cl. Maid 202 B4
Spencers La. Cook 195 F3
Spencers Rd. Maid 202 B4
Spenlows Rd. M Keyn 47 D2
Spenser Rd. Ayl 115 F3
Sperling Rd. Maid 195 F1
Spickett's La. Cudd 113 D2
Spier's La. M Gib 71 F1
Spiert The. Sto 114 B3
Spindle Cl. Ty Gr 163 D2
Spinfield La W. Mar 183 E1
Spinfield Mount. Mar 183 A1
Spinfield Park. Mar 183 E1
Spinners Wlk. Mar 183 E1
Spinners Wlk. Wind 210 B3
Spinney Cl. Stp Cl 63 F1
Spinney Cl. W Dra 208 C3
Spinney Cres. Dun 93 F4
Spinney Hill Rd. Oln 6 C2
Spinney La. Asp G 49 F2
Spinney The. Beac 175 F1
Spinney The. Ches 144 B1
Spinney The. H Wyc 173 D2
Spinney The. Hol G 163 E4
Spinney The. M Keyn 34 A2
Spinney The. Wins 66 A3
Spinney. Slough 205 D3
Spinneys The. Ty Gr 174 A4
Spittal St. Mar 183 E1
Spoondell. Dun 93 F4
Spoonley Wood. M Keyn 33 F3
Sportsman Cl. Stp Cl 63 E2
Spout La. Stan 213 D2
Spout Rd N. Stan 213 D2
Sprigs Holly La. Bled R 159 D4
Spring Cl. Lat 155 E2
Spring Cl. Maid 195 F1
Spring Coppice La. Pres 150 B3
Spring Coppice La. Wal A 150 B3
Spring Coppice. H Wyc 171 F3
Spring Field Rd. Berk 135 D3
Spring Gardens Rd.
H Wyc 173 F3
Spring Gdns. Bou E 185 D2
Spring Gdns. Mar 183 F2
Spring Gdns. N Pag 22 B2
Spring Gdns. Woo G 185 F4
Spring Hill. Maid 202 C2
Spring La. Cook 195 E3
Spring La. Emb 7 E2
Spring La. Far C 198 B3
Spring La. Fla H 173 F2
Spring La. G Hrwd 55 D1
Spring La. Graf R 9 D1
Spring La. Oln 6 C2
Spring La. Slough 204 C3
Spring Meadow. Dor 97 D1
Spring Valley Dr. Hgh V 162 A4
Springate Field. Slough 206 C2
Springett Pl. Ame 154 C1
Springfield Bvd. M Keyn 35 D1
Springfield Cl. Ches 154 B4
Springfield Cl. Wind 210 A3
Springfield Gdns. Chin 147 E4
Springfield Gdns. Dean 31 F2
Springfield Park. Holy 203 E1
Springfield Rd. L Buzz 80 C4
Springfield Rd. Skch 158 C2
Springfield Rd. Slough 212 A4
Springfield Rd. Wind 210 A3
Springfield. Oln 6 C2
Springfields Cl. Pad 53 E1
Springfields Ct. Pad 53 E1
Springfields Way. Cran 25 E1
Springfields. Pad 53 E1
Springfields. Ty Gr 163 E1
Springhill Rd. Gr Und 83 D4
Springs La. Elle 130 A2
Spruce Dene. Ty Gr 162 C1
Spur The. Slough 204 B4
Spurgrove La. Frie 170 C1
Spurlands End Rd. G Kin 162 C4
Spurt La. Cudd 112 C2
Square The. Asp G 49 F2
Square The. Harm 213 D3
Square The. L Cre 125 E3
Square The. M Keyn 33 E3
Square The. Pres B 62 A4
Square The. S Hea 152 A4
Squires Cl. M Keyn 47 D3
Squirrel La. H Wyc 172 B3
Squirrel Rise. Mar B 183 E3
Squirrels Way. Buck 52 C4
Stable La. Se Gr 176 B2
Stable Rd. Hal 131 F4
Stablebridge Rd. Ast C 117 F2
Stables Ct. Mar 183 A1
Stacey Ave. M Keyn 33 E3
Stafferton Way. Maid 203 D3
Stafford Ave. Slough 198 B1
Stafford Cl. Burn 204 A4
Stafford Gr. She C E 46 A3
Stag La. Chor 167 E2
Stag La. G Kin 151 E1
Stainby Cl. W Dra 208 C2
Stainton Dr. M Keyn 34 B2
Stamford Ave. M Keyn 35 D1
Stamford Rd. Maid 202 B3
Stanbridge Cl. Hadd 127 D4
Stanbridge Ct. M Keyn 32 C3
Stanbridge Rd. Hadd 127 D3
Standing Way. M Keyn 47 E4
Standing Way. She B E 47 D4
Stanhope Cl. Wen 131 D4
Stanhope Heath. Stan 213 E1
Stanhope Rd. Ayl 116 A4
Stanhope Rd. Slough 204 B4
Stanhope Way. Stan 213 E1
Stanier Rise. Berk 134 C4
Stanley Ave. Ches 154 A4
Stanley Cl. Mar 183 F2
Stanley Cl. Uxb 201 E2
Stanley Cotts. Slough 205 F3
Stanley Ct. Oln 6 C2
Stanley Gdns. Tri 118 C2
Stanley Green E. Slough 206 C1
Stanley Green W. Slough 206 C1
Stanley Hill Ave. Ame 165 F4
Stanley Hill. Ame 165 F4
Stanley Rd. H Wyc 172 B4
Stanmore Gdns. M Keyn 22 A1
Stanton Ave. M Keyn 34 A3
Stanton Gate. M Keyn 34 B4
Stanton Way. Slough 206 C1
Stanway Cl. M Keyn 35 D3
Stanwell Cl. Stan 213 E1
Stanwell Gdns. Stan 213 E1
Stanwell Moor Rd. Harm 213 D2
Stanwell Moor Rd. Stan 213 D2
Stanwell Rd. Hort 212 B2
Stanwell Rd. Stan 212 B2
Staple Hall Rd. M Keyn 47 F1
Stapleton Cl. Mar 183 F2
Stars La. Dint 113 F1
Startins La. Cook 195 E4
Starwood Ct. Slough 206 B2
Staters Pound. M Keyn 35 D4
Statham Pl. M Keyn 46 C4
Station App. Ame 154 B1
Station App. Chor 167 E3
Station App. Den G 189 E2
Station App. Ger C 188 C3
Station App. L Chal 166 B4
Station App. Mar 183 F1
Station App. S Hea 152 A4
Station App. W Dra 208 C3
Station App. Wen 131 D2
Station Hill. Cook 195 F4
Station Par. Den G 190 A2
Station Rd. Ald 120 A3
Station Rd. Ame 165 E4
Station Rd. B Bkhl 48 B1
Station Rd. Beac 175 F1
Station Rd. Berk 135 E2
Station Rd. Bktn 81 D2
Station Rd. Bou E 185 D2
Station Rd. Buck 52 D4
Station Rd. Cast 19 F3
Station Rd. Ches 154 B4
Station Rd. Chin 147 E3
Station Rd. Cook 195 F4
Station Rd. Ger C 188 C3
Station Rd. H Wyc 173 E3
Station Rd. Hadd 126 C3
Station Rd. Hen-O-T 191 F1
Station Rd. Ivin 105 F3
Station Rd. L Buzz 80 C4
Station Rd. Lon M 104 A2
Station Rd. Loud 174 B1
Station Rd. M Gib 71 F2
Station Rd. Mar 183 F1
Station Rd. Men 91 D1
Station Rd. Mur 67 D4
Station Rd. N Pag 22 B2
Station Rd. P Ris 139 D1
Station Rd. Pad 53 D1
Station Rd. Qntn 85 D2
Station Rd. S Man 116 A1
Station Rd. Slough 204 C4
Station Rd. Slough 207 D2
Station Rd. Tapl 203 F4
Station Rd. Tri 119 E2
Station Rd. Uxb 201 E1
Station Rd. W Dra 208 C2
Station Rd. Wbn S 49 D3
Station Rd. Wins 66 A3
Station Rd. Wray 212 A1
Station Rise. Mar 183 F1
Station Terrace. M Keyn 21 F1
Station Way. Ayl 115 E4
Staunton Rd. Slough 205 E4
Staveley Cl. Ayl 116 B3
Staying La. M Keyn 34 C3
Stephenson Cl. Ayl 115 D4
Stephenson Cl. H Wyc 161 F1
Stephenson Dr. Wind 210 A4
Stepnells. Mars 105 D1
Stevens Cl. Hol G 163 D4
Stevens Cl. Pres 151 E3
Stevens Field. Walt 48 B3
Stevenson Rd. Hedg 187 E1
Stewart Ave. Slough 205 F4
Stewarts Dr. Far C 198 A4
Stewarts Way. Mar B 183 E4
Stewkley La. Mur 67 F2
Stewkley Rd. Cub 78 B1
Stewkley Rd. Soul 69 E1
Stewkley Rd. Wing 79 D2
Stile Rd. Slough 206 B2
Stilebrook Rd. Oln 6 C3
Stirling Ave. Ayl 101 F1
Stirling Cl. M Keyn 35 D3
Stirling Cl. Uxb 201 E1
Stirling Cl. Wind 209 E3
Stirling Rd. Slough 205 D4
Stirling Rd. Stan 213 F1
Stock Field Cl. Ty Gr 163 D2
Stock La. Whad 45 D1
Stockdale. M Keyn 34 B3
Stockdales Rd. Eton 204 C1
Stocken Cl. Oln 6 C2
Stockhall Cres. Stew 68 B1
Stocking Green Cl. Hans 11 D2
Stocking La. Wal A 161 F4
Stocklake. Ayl 101 F1
Stocklake. Bier 101 F1
Stocklands Way. Pres 151 E3
Stockleys La. Ting 51 D3
Stockport Rd. Chor 167 E1
Stocks Rd. Ald 120 B4
Stocks The. Cast 19 F1
Stockway. Wedn 87 E1
Stockwell Furlong. Hadd 127 D3
Stockwell La. Wave 48 B4
Stoke Common Rd. Fulm 199 D4
Stoke Common Rd. Sto P 199 D4
Stoke Court Dr. Sto P 198 C2
Stoke Farm La. Ayl 115 F2
Stoke Gdns. Slough 205 F3
Stoke Green. Sto P 199 D1
Stoke La. G Bkhl 59 E1
Stoke Park Ave. Far C 198 B1
Stoke Poges La. Slough 205 F4
Stoke Rd. Ash 9 F4
Stoke Rd. Ayl 115 F3
Stoke Rd. L Buzz 70 C1
Stoke Rd. M Keyn 58 C3
Stoke Rd. Nwtn L 57 F2
Stoke Rd. Slough 205 F4
Stoke Wood. Sto P 198 C4
Stokenchurch Pl. M Keyn 34 B2
Stokes Croft. Hadd 127 D4
Stokes End. Hadd 127 D4
Stokes La. Hadd 127 D4
Stokesay. Slough 205 F3
Stomp Rd. Burn 204 A4
Stompits Rd. Holy 203 E1
Stone Cl. W Dra 208 C3
Stone Croft. Sto 114 B3
Stone Ct. Emb 13 F4
Stone Hill. M Keyn 33 F1
Stone House La. Cook 184 B1
Stone View. Oving 86 B4
Stonebridge Field. Eton 205 D1
Stonebridge Rd. Ayl 101 D2
Stonechat. Ayl 101 F2
Stonecroft Ave. Iver 207 F4
Stonecrop Pl. M Keyn 34 C2
Stonefield Park. Maid 202 B4
Stonefield Rd. Wal A 161 E4
Stonegate. M Keyn 34 A3
Stonehaven Rd. Ayl 101 D1
Stoney Croft. Ald 120 B3
Stoney Grove. Ches 144 B1
Stoney La. Bov 146 B3
Stoney La. Burn 198 A2
Stoney La. Chipf 146 C1
Stoney Meade. Slough 205 D3
Stoney Ware Cl. Bish 194 C4
Stoney Ware. Bish 194 C4
Stonor Ct. M Keyn 45 F4
Stony La. Chen 155 F1
Stony La. L Chal 166 C4
Stony La. L Kin 152 B2
Stookslade. Win 89 D2
Stork Cl. Ayl 101 F2
Stotfold Ct. M Keyn 32 C2
Stour Cl. M Keyn 57 F4
Stour Cl. N Pag 22 C2
Stour Cl. Slough 205 D2
Stovell Rd. Wind 210 A4
Stowe Ave. Chac 41 D2
Stowe Cl. Buck 41 E1
Stowe Ct. M Keyn 34 B4
Stowe Rd. Slough 204 C3
Stowe Rise. Buck 41 E1
Stowe View. Ting 51 D4
Straight Bit. Fla H 185 D4
Straight Rd. Old W 211 D1
Strand La. Cook 195 F3
Strand The. Qntn 85 D3
Strangers La. Ting 51 D3
Strangford Dr. M Keyn 58 B2

Stranraer Rd. Stan 213 F1
Stratfield Ct. M Keyn 33 F1
Stratfield Rd. Slough 206 A2
Stratford Ave. Uxb 201 F2
Stratford Cl. Slough 197 E1
Stratford Dr. Ayl 115 D3
Stratford Dr. Bou E 185 E2
Stratford Gdns. Maid 202 B2
Stratford Rd. Buck 41 F1
Stratford Rd. Cast 19 E1
Stratford Rd. M Keyn 33 E4
Stratford Rd. M Mor 42 B1
Stratford Rd. Nash 44 B1
Stratford Rd. Whad 45 D1
Strathcona Cl. Fla H 185 E4
Strathcona Way. Fla H 185 E4
Strathnaver Pl. M Keyn 33 E2
Stratton Chase Dr. C St G 166 A1
Stratton Green. Ayl 116 A3
Stratton Rd. Beac 175 D1
Stratton Rd. P Ris 139 D2
Strauss Gr. Walt 48 B2
Strawberry Cl. Pres 151 E3
Streamside Wlk. Ayl 115 E3
Streatham Pl. M Keyn 34 B1
Stretton Cl. Ty Gr 174 B4
Stringfellow Cl. Cran 24 C1
Strong Ct. Slough 204 B3
Stroud Cl. Wind 209 E2
Strudwick Dr. M Keyn 46 C4
Stuart Cl. M Keyn 47 E1
Stuart Cl. Wind 209 F3
Stuart Rd. H Wyc 173 E3
Stuart Way. Tha 126 A1
Stuart Way. Wind 209 F3
Stubbles La. Cook 195 D3
Stubbs End Cl. Ame 154 C1
Stubbs Wood. Ame 154 C2
Studdridge Ct. Skch 158 B2
Studham La. Dag 107 E2
Studland Cl. Ayl 116 A3
Studley Knapp. Walt 48 A3
Studridge La. Lac G 150 A3
Sturges Cl. Walt 48 A3
Stylecroft Rd. C St G 177 E4
Suffield Rd. H Wyc 172 C4
Suffolk Cl. M Keyn 46 C1
Suffolk Cl. Slough 204 C4
Suffolk Ct. M Gib 71 F2
Suffolk Rd. Maid 202 B2
Sulby Cl. Ayl 115 E3
Sulgrave Cres. Tri 119 E3
Sulgrave Ct. M Keyn 45 F4
Sullivan Cres. Walt 48 B3
Sumburgh Way. Slough 205 F4
Summergill Ct. M Keyn 34 B3
Summerhayes. M Keyn 34 C4
Summerhouse La. Harm 213 E4
Summerlea. Slough 205 D3
Summerleaze Rd. Maid 196 A1
Summerleys Rd. Lgwk 138 C2
Summerleys Rd. P Ris 138 C2
Summerleys. Eat B 92 C2
Summers Rd. Burn 197 E1
Summerson Rd. M Keyn 46 C3
Sun Cres. Oak 109 E3
Sun La. Maid 202 C4
Sun Pas. Wind 210 B3
Sunbury Cl. M Keyn 34 A3
Sunbury Rd. Eton 210 B4
Sunderland Rd. Maid 202 A4
Sunningdale Cl. H Wyc 172 A3
Sunningdale Way. M Keyn 57 E4
Sunny Bank. Ched 104 C4
Sunny Bank. Hol G 162 C3
Sunny Croft. H Wyc 161 E1
Sunnybank. Mar 183 E2
Sunnybrook Cl. Ast C 117 E3
Sunnyhill Rd. Map Cr 178 B2
Sunnymede Ave. Ches 144 C2
Sunnyside Rd. Ches 144 B1
Sunray Ave. W Dra 208 B2
Sunridge Cl. N Pag 22 B2
Sunrise Parkway. M Keyn 34 C3
Sunset Cl. M Keyn 58 B4
Sunters Wood Cl. H Wyc 172 A3
Surly Hall Wlk. Wind 209 F3
Surrey Ave. Slough 198 B1
Surrey Pl. M Keyn 46 C1
Surrey Pl. Tri 119 D2
Surrey Rd. M Keyn 46 C1
Sussex Cl. C St G 177 D4
Sussex Cl. H Wyc 162 B1
Sussex Cl. Slough 206 A2
Sussex Pl. Slough 206 A2
Sussex Rd. M Keyn 46 C1
Sussex Way. Den G 189 F3
Sutcliffe Ave. M Keyn 34 C1
Sutherland Gr. M Keyn 46 C2
Sutherland Wlk. Ayl 115 F3
Sutton Ave. Slough 206 B2
Sutton Cl. Cook 196 A4
Sutton Cl. Maid 202 B3
Sutton Cl. Tri 119 D3
Sutton Ct. M Keyn 46 B1
Sutton La. Slough 207 E1
Sutton Pl. Slough 212 A4
Sutton Rd. Cook 196 A3
Swabey Rd. Slough 207 D1
Swains Cl. W Dra 208 C2
Swains La. Fla H 174 A1
Swakeleys Rd. Ick 201 F4
Swale Rd. Ayl 115 E3
Swallow Cl. Buck 52 C4
Swallow Dr. Hol G 163 D3
Swallow La. S Man 116 A1
Swallow St. Iver 207 E4
Swallow St. Iver H 200 B1
Swallowdale. Iver H 200 B1
Swallowfield. M Keyn 33 F1
Swan Cl. Ayl 101 F2
Swan Cl. Buck 52 C4
Swan Cl. Ches 144 A2
Swan Cl. Ivin 92 A1
Swan Cl. Whit 87 D3
Swan Ct. Oln 7 D2
Swan La. M Gib 72 A2
Swan Rd. Iver 207 F4
Swan Rd. W Dra 208 B2
Swan Yd. M Keyn 32 B3
Swan's Way. N Mar 75 E1
Swanbourne Rd. Mur 67 E2
Swann Rd. Hal 131 E4
Swansons. Edle 92 C2
Sweetcroft La. Uxb 201 F3
Swift Cl. Ayl 101 F2
Swift Cl. N Pag 22 A3
Swinden Ct. M Keyn 34 A2
Swinfens Yd. M Keyn 32 B3
Swing Gate La. Berk 135 E1
Switchback Cl. Maid 195 E1
Switchback Rd N. Cook 195 F2
Switchback Rd N. Maid 195 F2
Switchback Rd S. Maid 195 E1
Switchback Rd. Cook 195 F2
Switchback The. Maid 195 E1
Sycamore Ave. M Keyn 58 C4
Sycamore Cl. Ame 154 B1
Sycamore Cl. Buck 52 C4
Sycamore Cl. C St G 177 D4
Sycamore Cl. L Cre 125 E3
Sycamore Cl. Stew 68 B1
Sycamore Cl. W Dra 208 C3
Sycamore Cnr. Ame 154 B1
Sycamore Ct. H Wyc 172 B2
Sycamore Ct. Wind 210 B2
Sycamore Dene. Ches 144 B2
Sycamore Dr. Mar B 183 E3
Sycamore Dr. Tri 119 D2
Sycamore Leys. Stp Cl 63 F2
Sycamore Rd. Ame 154 B1
Sycamore Rd. C St G 177 D4
Sycamore Rd. H Wyc 172 B2
Sycamore Rise. Berk 135 E2
Sycamore Rise. C St G 177 D4
Sycamore Way. Ty Gr 163 D2
Sycamore Wlk. Slough 206 C4
Sycamores The. Fel 146 C4
Sydney Gr. Slough 205 E4
Syke Cluan. Iver 207 F2
Syke Ings. Iver 207 F2
Sykes Rd. Slough 205 D4
Sylvana Cl. Uxb 201 F2
Sylvester Rd. Maid 195 F1
Sylvia Cl. L Kin 152 A2
Symington Ct. She B E 46 A3
Syon Gdns. N Pag 22 B1

Tabard Gdns. N Pag 22 B1
Tachbrook Rd. Uxb 201 E2
Tadmarton. M Keyn 35 D3
Tadmere. M Keyn 33 E1
Talbot Ave. H Wyc 161 E1
Talbot Ave. Slough 206 C2
Talbot Pl. Datch 211 E3
Talbot Rd. Ast C 117 F3
Talbots Dr. Maid 202 A3
Talbots Hyde. Oln 6 C2
Tall Trees. Stan 212 C3
Talland Ave. M Keyn 34 C1
Tallis La. Walt 48 B3
Tamar Cl. Ayl 115 E2
Tamar Cl. Loud 174 A2
Tamar Way. Slough 207 D1
Tamarisk Ct. Walt 48 A3
Tamarisk Way. Slough 205 D2
Tamworth Stubb. Walt 48 A3
Tancred Rd. H Wyc 162 A1
Tandra. M Keyn 47 D3
Tandys Cl. Turv 8 C3
Tangier La. Eton 210 B4
Tank House Rd. Wins 66 A3
Tanners Dr. M Keyn 22 A1
Tannery Rd. H Wyc 174 A2
Tansman La. Walt 48 B3
Taplin Way. Ty Gr 163 E1
Taplow Common Rd. Burn 197 D3
Taplow Common Rd. Tapl 197 D3
Taplow Rd. Burn 204 A4
Tapping Rd. La En 171 E3
Taranis Cl. M K Vil 48 B4
Tarbay La. Oak G 209 D3
Tarbert Cl. M Keyn 58 B3
Tarmac Way. Harm 213 D4
Task The. Oln 7 D2
Taskers Row. Edle 92 C2
Tatchbrook Cl. Maid 203 D4
Tate Rd. C St P 177 F3
Tathams La. Mur 67 D2
Tatling Gr. Walt 48 A3
Tattam Cl. M Keyn 35 E1
Tattenhoe La. M Keyn 57 E4
Tattenhoe La. M Keyn 57 F4
Tattenhoe St. She C E 45 F2
Tattershall Cl. She C E 46 A3
Tattlers Hill. Win 89 D2
Taunton Deane. M Keyn 46 B1
Taurus Cl. Stp Cl 63 E1
Tavelhurst. M Keyn 33 F1
Tavistock Cl. Maid 202 A4
Tavistock Cl. Wbn S 49 D3
Tavistock Rd. W Dra 208 B3
Tavistock St. M Keyn 47 E1
Tay Rd. M Keyn 46 C1
Taylor Rd. Ayl 115 E3
Taylor's Cl. Mar 183 F1
Taylor's Ride. L Buzz 70 C1
Taylors Mews. M Keyn 34 C3
Taylors Rd. Ches 144 B1
Taylors Turn. H Wyc 161 E2
Taymouth Pl. M Keyn 35 D2
Teale Cl. U Arn 94 C4
Teasel Ave. M Keyn 34 C3
Tedder Rd. Wen 131 E3
Tees Way. M Keyn 46 B1
Teesdale Rd. Slough 204 C4
Teign Cl. N Pag 22 B2
Telford Cl. Ayl 100 C1
Telford Dr. Slough 205 D2
Telford Way. H Wyc 162 A1
Telford Way. M Keyn 22 A1
Telston Cl. Bou E 185 D3
Temperance Terr. M Keyn 32 B3
Temple Cl. Buck 41 F1
Temple Cl. M Keyn 57 E4
Temple End. H Wyc 173 D4
Temple La. Bish 194 B3
Temple Mill Island. Bish 194 B3
Temple Park. Hurl 193 F2
Temple Rd. Wind 210 B3
Temple Sq. Ayl 115 E4
Temple St. Ayl 115 E4
Temple St. Bri 96 A1
Temple St. H Wyc 173 D4
Temple Way. Far C 198 B4
Temple. M Keyn 34 B4
Templewood La. Far C 198 B4
Templewood. Wal A 150 A1
Ten Acres. She C E 45 F3
Tennyson Dr. N Pag 22 A2
Tennyson Gr. M Keyn 57 F4
Tennyson Rd. H Wyc 173 D3
Tennyson Way. Slough 197 F1
Tenterden Cres. M K Vil 48 A4
Tenzing Dr. H Wyc 173 F3
Terrace The. Asp G 49 F3
Terrace The. Maid 203 E2
Terrace The. Tri 119 D2
Terrington Hill. Mar 183 A1
Terry Dr. Ayl 101 E2
Terry Orch. H Wyc 173 E4
Terry Rd. H Wyc 173 E4
Terry's La. Cook 195 F4
Terryfield Rd. H Wyc 173 F3
Tess Rd. Ayl 115 E3
Testwood Rd. Wind 209 E3
Tetherdown. Pres 151 E3
Tews End La. Paul 17 E4
Thackeray End. Ayl 100 C1
Thame Rd. Ayl 115 E4
Thame Rd. Bktn 81 D2
Thame Rd. Bri 110 A4
Thame Rd. Chil 111 D2
Thame Rd. Chin 147 D4
Thame Rd. Hadd 126 B3
Thame Rd. L Cre 125 E2
Thame Rd. Lgwk 138 C3
Thame Rd. Pidd (B) 95 E3
Thames Ave. Wind 210 B4
Thames Cl. Bou E 185 D2
Thames Cl. M Keyn 57 F4
Thames Cres. Maid 196 A1
Thames Dr. N Pag 22 C2
Thames Ind Est. Mar 183 F1
Thames Mead. Wind 209 F3
Thames Rd. Slough 207 D2
Thames Reach. Medm 193 E3
Thames Side. Hen-O-T 191 F1
Thames Side. Wind 210 B4
Thames St. Wind 210 B4
Thamesfield Gdns. Mar 183 F1
Thane Ct. M Keyn 34 B4
Thatcher Cl. W Dra 208 C2
Thatchers Dr. Maid 202 A3
The Chyne. Ger C 188 C3
The Ridings. Iver 207 F1
Theydon Ave. Wbn S 49 D2
Thicket The. Ty Gr 163 D1
Thicket The. W Dra 208 C4
Third Ave. M Keyn 47 D1
Third Ave. Mar 183 F1
Third Cres. Slough 205 E4
Thirkleby Cl. Slough 205 E3
Thirlby La. She C E 46 A3
Thirlmere Ave. Burn 204 B4
Thirlmere Ave. M Keyn 58 B3
Thirsk Gdns. M Keyn 57 E3
Thomas Dr. N Pag 22 A3
Thomas Rd. Bou E 185 E2
Thompkins La. Burn 198 A3
Thompson Cl. Iver 207 D1
Thompson St. M Keyn 34 A4
Thomson Cl. Ayl 115 D3
Thomson Wlk. Ayl 115 D3
Thorn Dr. Slough 206 C4
Thorn Tree Dr. Tri 118 C2
Thornbank Cl. Stan 213 D1
Thornborough Rd. Nash 55 D4
Thornborough Rd. Nash 55 D4
Thornbridge Rd. Iver H 200 B2
Thorncliffe. M Keyn 33 E1
Thorndike. Slough 205 D4
Thorne Rd. La En 171 E2
Thorne Way. Ayl 101 F1
Thorney La N. Iver 207 F3
Thorney La S. Iver 207 F3
Thorney Mill La. Iver 208 A2
Thorney Mill Rd. W Dra 208 A2
Thorneycroft La. M Keyn 35 D3
Thornhill Cl. Ame 165 D4
Thornhill Rd. Ick 201 F4
Thornhill. Thrn 54 A4
Thornlea Croft. Oln 6 C2
Thorns Cl. P Ris 139 E3
Thornton Ave. W Dra 208 C2
Thornton Cl. W Dra 208 C2
Thornton Cres. Wen 131 D3
Thornton Rd. Nash 44 A1
Thorpe Cl. Ayl 116 A2
Thorwold Pl. M Keyn 46 A3
Thrasher Rd. Ayl 115 E3
Three Close La. Berk 135 E2
Three Households. C St G 176 C3
Three Oaks Cl. Ick 190 C1
Three Points La. Stp Cl 74 A3
Thresher Gr. M Keyn 33 D3
Thrift La. Maid 202 B1
Thrupp Cl. Cast 20 A3
Thrush Cl. Ayl 101 F2
Thrush Cl. H Wyc 172 B2
Thurlby Way. Maid 202 B2
Thurne Cl. N Pag 22 C2
Thursby Cl. M Keyn 35 E4
Thurston Rd. Slough 205 F4
Tibbys La. Cudd 112 C2
Ticehirst Cl. M K Vil 48 A4
Tichborne. Map Cr 178 B3
Tickford St. N Pag 22 C2
Tidbury Cl. Wbn S 49 D2
Tiffany Cl. M Keyn 58 B3
Tilburywood Cl. H Wyc 161 E1
Tilecotes Cl. Mar 183 B1
Tilehouse Way. Den G 189 F2
Tilehouse La. Den G 189 F3
Tilers Rd. M Keyn 33 D1
Tilling Cres. H Wyc 174 A4
Tilman Cl. M Keyn 33 E3
Tilstone Ave. Eton 204 C1
Tilstone Cl. Eton 204 C1
Tilsworth Rd. Beac 175 E1
Timber La. Hth 60 C4
Timbold Dr. M K Vil 48 A4
Tindal Rd. Ayl 101 F1
Tingewick Rd. Buck 52 A4
Tingewick Rd. Chac 51 F4
Tinkers La. Berk 134 A3
Tinkers La. Wind 209 E3
Tinkers Wood Rd. H Wyc 161 F1
Tintagel Ct. M Keyn 47 D4
Tintern Cl. Slough 205 E2
Tinterne Cl. Ayl 116 B3
Tippings. Skch 158 C3
Titchmarsh Ct. M Keyn 46 C4
Tithe Barn Dr. Holy 203 E1
Tithe Cl. Holy 203 E1
Tithe Ct. Slough 207 D1
Tithe La. Wray 212 A1
Titmus Rd. Hal 131 F4
Tiverton Cres. Ayl 101 E2
Tockley Way. Burn 197 D1
Todd Cl. Ayl 115 D3
Tolcarne Ave. M Keyn 35 D1
Tollgate Cl. Chor 167 F3
Tollgate. Maid 202 A3
Tomlin Rd. Slough 197 F1
Tompion Rd. Ayl 100 C1
Tompkins La. M Gib 71 F1
Toms Hill Rd. Ald 120 B3
Toms Turn. Hol G 162 C3
Tongwell La. N Pag 22 B1
Tongwell St. M K Vil 48 A4
Tongwell St. M Keyn 35 F3
Tongwell St. M Keyn 35 F4
Tongwell St. Walt 48 B3
Top Park. Ger C 188 B3
Topaz Cl. Slough 205 D3
Topland Rd. Ger C 177 E2
Torquay Spur. Slough 198 A1
Torre Cl. M Keyn 47 D1
Torridge Rd. Ayl 115 E2
Torridge Rd. Slough 212 A4
Torrington Rd. Berk 135 D2
Torwood Cl. Berk 134 C2
Totteridge Ave. H Wyc 173 E3
Totteridge Dr. H Wyc 162 C1
Totteridge La. H Wyc 162 C1
Totteridge Rd. H Wyc 173 E4
Totternhoe Rd. Dun 93 F4
Totternhoe Rd. Eat B 92 B4
Towan Ave. M Keyn 35 D1
Towcester Dr. Pott 18 A2
Towcester Rd. Old S 32 A4
Tower Cl. Berk 135 D2
Tower Cl. Fla H 185 E4
Tower Cotts. Mur 67 E4
Tower Cres. M Keyn 34 C3
Tower Dr. M Keyn 34 C4
Tower Hill. Chipf 146 C1
Tower Rd. Cole 165 D2
Tower St. H Wyc 162 B1
Toweridge La. H Wyc 160 C1
Toweridge La. H Wyc 172 B4
Towersey Way. Ayl 115 D4
Town Bridge Ct. Ches 154 A4
Town Cl. Fin 50 B3
Town End Cres. S Gol 12 A3
Town End Rd. Bled R 159 E4
Town Field La. C St G 177 E4
Town La. Bou E 185 E2
Town La. Stan 213 E1
Townfield Rd. H Wyc 173 E4
Townfield. Ches 154 B4
Townsend Cotts. G Hrwd 55 D2
Townsend Gr. M Keyn 34 A4
Townsend Piece. Ayl 101 E1
Townsend Rd. Ches 144 B1
Townsend. M Gib 71 F1
Townside. Edle 92 C2
Townside. Hadd 126 C3
Tozer Wlk. Wind 209 E2
Trafalgar Ave. M Keyn 46 C1
Trafford Cl. G Mis 152 A3
Trafford Rd. S Hea 152 A4
Tramhill. Bri 96 A1
Tranlands Brigg. M Keyn 34 A2
Trapp's La. Ches 154 B3
Travell Ct. M Keyn 34 A2
Travic Rd. Slough 197 F1
Travis Ct. Slough 198 A1
Treacher's Cl. Ches 154 A4
Treadaway Hill. Fla H 174 A1
Treadaway Hill. Loud 174 A1
Treadaway Rd. Fla H 174 A1
Treborough. M Keyn 46 B1
Tredington Gr. B Bkhl 48 A2
Tredington La. B Bkhl 48 A2
Treehanger Cl. Tri 119 D2
Trees Ave. Hgh V 162 A3
Trees Rd. Bou E 185 D2
Trees Rd. Hgh V 162 A3
Treeside Cl. W Dra 208 B1
Treesmill Dr. Maid 202 B2
Trelawney Ave. Slough 206 C2
Tremayne Ct. M Keyn 47 D4
Trenchard Ave. Wen 131 E3
Trenches La. Iver 207 D3
Trent Dr. N Pag 22 B2
Trent Rd. M Keyn 46 C1
Trent Rd. Slough 212 A4
Trentishoe Cres. M Keyn 46 B2
Tresco Rd. Berk 134 C3
Trevelyan Way. Berk 135 D3
Treves Green. Ayl 115 F3
Trevithick La. She B E 46 A3
Trevone Ct. M Keyn 47 D4
Trewarden Ave. Iver H 200 B2
Tring Ford Rd. Tri 119 D4
Tring Hill. Dra B 118 B2
Tring Rd. Ayl 116 A4
Tring Rd. Berk 134 B4
Tring Rd. Dun 93 F4
Tring Rd. Edle 106 C4
Tring Rd. Lon M 104 A2
Tring Rd. Wen 131 E3
Tring Rd. Win 89 E1
Trinity Ave. Mar 183 E2
Trinity Cl. Stan 213 E1
Trinity Pl. Wind 210 B3
Trinity Rd. M Keyn 33 D4
Trinity Rd. Mar 183 E1
Trinity Rd. Ty Gr 162 C2
Tripps Hill Cl. C St G 177 D4
Trispen Ct. M Keyn 47 D4
Trooper Rd. Ald 120 B3
Trout Cl. Mar 194 B4
Trout La. W Dra 208 B3
Trout Rd. W Dra 208 B3
Troutbeck. M Keyn 47 E4
Trubys Gdn. M Keyn 47 D4
Trueman Pl. M Keyn 46 C4
Truesdale Dr. S Har 190 B4
Trumper Way. Uxb 201 E2
Trumpton La. M K Vil 48 B4
Trunk Furlong Estate. Asp G 49 E3
Truro Cl. Maid 202 A4
Trustees Way. Den G 189 F3

Tubwell Rd. Sto P 199 D2
Tucker Cl. H Wyc 173 E4
Tuckers Dr. Hol G 163 E4
Tudeley Hale. M K Vil 48 A4
Tudor Dr. Woo G 185 E4
Tudor Gdns. Burn 204 B4
Tudor Gdns. M Keyn 32 C2
Tudor Park. Ame 154 B1
Tudor Rd. Ty Gr 163 E2
Tudor Way. Wind 209 F3
Tuffnell Cl. M Keyn 35 F4
Tulkers Cl. Pres 151 E3
Tulla Ct. M Keyn 58 B2
Tummell Way. M Keyn 58 B3
Tunmers End. Ger C 177 E1
Tuns La. Hen-O-T 191 F1
Tuns La. Slough 205 E2
Turnberry Cl. M Keyn 57 E4
Turnbridge Gr. M K Vil 48 A4
Turner Cl. Ayl 101 F2
Turner Rd. Slough 206 B2
Turners Dr. H Wyc 173 F4
Turners Mews. M Keyn 34 C3
Turners Pl. Hol G 163 E3
Turners Wood Dr. C St G 177 E4
Turnfields. Ick 124 A2
Turnfurlong La. Ayl 116 A3
Turnfurlong. Ayl 115 F4
Turnip Cl. Chea 112 A1
Turnmill Ave. M Keyn 35 D1
Turnoak Park. Wind 209 F2
Turnpike La. Uxb 201 F1
Turnpike Rd. H Wyc 172 B2
Turnpike The. Oak 109 E3
Turnpike Way. H Wyc 172 B2
Turnstone Way. Ayl 101 F2
Turpins Green. Maid 202 A3
Turton Way. Slough 205 E2
Turvey Cl. Ast C 117 F3
Turvey Mill. Turv 8 B3
Turvey Rd. Ast 15 F3
Turvey Rd. Carl 3 F1
Turville Rd. Ayl 116 B3
Turweston Rd. Brac 26 A1
Tweed Cl. Berk 135 D3
Tweed Dr. M Keyn 46 B1
Tweed Rd. Slough 212 A4
Tweenways. Ches 144 C1
Twelve Leys. Win 89 D2
Twinches La. Slough 205 D3
Twinflower. Walt 48 A3
Twist The. Wigg 119 E1
Twitchell La. Ast C 117 F3
Twitchell Rd. S Hea 152 A4
Twitchell's La. C St G 176 C3
Twitchen La. She B E 46 B2
Two Dells La. Ash Gr 145 D2
Two Gates La. Char 143 E4
Twyford La. Walt 48 B3
Twynham Rd. Maid 202 A4
Tyburn Ave. M Keyn 35 D1
Tyle Pl. Old W 211 D1
Tylers Cres. Ty Gr 163 D1
Tylers Green. M Keyn 34 B2
Tylers Hill Rd. Bot 154 C4
Tylers Rd. Ty Gr 163 D1
Tylsworth Cl. Ame 154 B1
Tyne Rd. Ayl 115 E2
Tyne Sq. M Keyn 46 B1
Tyneham Cl. Ayl 116 A2
Tyrell Cl. Buck 52 B4
Tyrell Gdns. Wind 209 F2
Tyrells Gdns. S Ham 69 F4
Tyrells Rd. S Ham 69 F4
Tyrill. M Keyn 34 B4
Tyson Pl. M Keyn 46 C4
Tythe Cl. Stew 78 C4
Tythe Gdns. Stew 78 C4
Tythe Mews. Edle 92 C2
Tyzack Rd. H Wyc 162 C1

Ullswater Cl. Burn 204 B4
Ullswater Dr. L Buzz 80 B4
Ulverscroft. M K Vil 36 A1
Ulyett Pl. M Keyn 46 C4
Umberville Way. Slough 197 F1
Underhill Cl. Maid 202 C3
Underwood Pl. M Keyn 46 C4
Underwood Rd. H Wyc 173 E4
Union St. H Wyc 173 D4
Union St. N Pag 22 B3
Up Corner Cl. C St G 177 D4
Upcroft. Wind 210 A2
Upland Ave. Ches 144 A2
Uplands Cl. Ger C 188 C2
Uplands Cl. H Wyc 173 F4
Uplands The. Ger C 188 C1
Uplands. Mar B 183 E3
Upper Abbotts Hill. Ayl 115 D4
Upper Ashlyns Rd. Berk 135 D2
Upper Belmont Rd. Ches 144 A2
Upper Bray Rd. Maid 203 E2
Upper Church St. Cudd 112 C2
Upper Coombe. L Buzz 80 C4
Upper Dr. Beac 175 E3
Upper Fifth St. M Keyn 34 B1
Upper Fourth St. M Keyn 34 B1
Upper George St. Ches 144 B1
Upper Gladstone Rd. Ches 144 B1
Upper Hall Park. Berk 135 F1
Upper Hollis. G Mis 151 F4
Upper Hundreds. Ayl 115 F4
Upper Ickenfield Way. P Ris 149 D4
Upper Icknield Way. Ast C 117 F1
Upper Icknield Way. Bled 149 D4
Upper Icknield Way. Dra B 117 F1
Upper Icknield Way. Hal 117 F1
Upper Icknield Way. P Ris 139 E3
Upper Icknield Way. Pit 105 F1
Upper Icknield Way. Pris 149 D4
Upper Lees Rd. Slough 198 A1
Upper Lodge La. Hol G 162 C3
Upper Rd. Den G 189 E2
Upper Riding. Beac 175 D1
Upper Second St. M Keyn 34 B1
Upper St. Qntn 85 D3
Upper St. Ting 51 D3
Upper Stonehayes. M Keyn 34 C4
Upper Third St. M Keyn 34 B1
Upper Way. G Bkhl 59 E1
Upton Cl. Hen-O-T 191 F1
Upton Cl. Slough 205 F2
Upton Court Rd. Slough 206 A1
Upton Gr. She B E 46 B2
Upton Lea Par. Slough 206 A3
Upton Park. Slough 205 F2
Upton Rd. Dint 114 A2
Upton Rd. Slough 206 A2
Upway. C St P 177 F1
Uxbridge R. Uxb 201 F1
Uxbridge Rd. Slough 206 B3

Vache La. C St G 177 E4
Vache La. She C E 45 F3
Vale Cl. Ger C 177 E1
Vale Gr. Slough 205 F2
Vale Ind Centre The. Ayl 101 E1
Vale Rd. Ayl 101 F1
Vale Rd. Ches 144 B2
Vale Rd. Wind 209 F3
Vale Rise. Ches 144 B2
Vale The. Ger C 177 E1
Valens Cl. She C E 45 F4
Valentine Way. C St G 177 E4
Valley Centre The. H Wyc 173 E3
Valley Cl. Brac 38 A4
Valley Cres. Brac 38 A4
Valley End. Iver H 199 E1
Valley Rd. Berk 134 C3
Valley Rd. Brac 38 A4
Valley Rd. Buck 52 C4
Valley Rd. Fin 50 B3
Valley Rd. Hen-O-T 191 E1
Valley Rd. Hgh V 162 A3
Valley Rise. Brac 38 A4
Valley View. Ches 144 A1
Valley Way. Ger C 188 B3
Van Der Bilt Ct. M Keyn 33 F3
Van Diemens Cl. Chin 147 E4
Vandyke Cl. Wbn S 49 D3
Vane Rd. Tha 126 A1
Vansittart Rd. Bish 194 C4
Vansittart Rd. Wind 210 A3
Vantage Rd. Slough 205 D3
Vanwall Bsns Pk. Maid 202 B3
Vanwall Rd. Maid 202 B2
Vaughan Copse. Slough 205 E1
Vaughan Way. Slough 197 F1
Vauxhall. M Keyn 34 A3
Vellan Ave. M Keyn 35 D1
Venables La. M Keyn 35 D4
Venetian Ct. M K Vil 48 B4
Ventfield Cl. Hor-c-S 108 A3
Venus Hill. Bov 156 A4
Verbena Cl. W Dra 208 B1
Verdi Cl. Walt 48 B3
Verdon Dr. M Keyn 35 D4
Verity Pl. M Keyn 34 C1
Verley Cl. M Keyn 47 E4
Vermont Rd. Slough 197 F1
Verney Ave. H Wyc 172 B2
Verney Cl. Berk 134 C3
Verney Cl. Buck 41 E1
Verney Cl. Mar 183 E1
Verney Cl. Tri 119 E3
Verney Farm Cl. E Clay 74 C4
Verney Rd. Slough 207 D1
Verney Rd. Wins 65 F2
Verney Wlk. Ayl 115 E3
Verona Cl. Uxb 208 B4
Verwood Rd. Ayl 101 F1
Veryan Pl. M Keyn 35 D1
Vicarage Cl. Cook 196 A4
Vicarage Cl. Stp Cl 63 E1
Vicarage Cl. Wen 131 D3
Vicarage Cl. Yard G 18 C3
Vicarage Dr. Maid 203 E2
Vicarage Gdns. L Buzz 80 C3
Vicarage Gdns. M Keyn 34 A2
Vicarage Gdns. Mars 105 D1
Vicarage La. Bov 146 A2
Vicarage La. Ivin 105 F3
Vicarage La. Pidd (B) 95 F3
Vicarage La. Stp Cl 63 E1
Vicarage La. Wing 79 F1
Vicarage Rd. Ayl 115 E3
Vicarage Rd. Hen-O-T 191 F1
Vicarage Rd. L Buzz 80 C3
Vicarage Rd. M Keyn 32 B3
Vicarage Rd. M Keyn 34 A2
Vicarage Rd. M Keyn 58 C4
Vicarage Rd. Maid 202 C4
Vicarage Rd. Mars 105 D1
Vicarage Rd. Pit 105 E2
Vicarage Rd. Whad 56 A4
Vicarage Rd. Wigg 119 E1
Vicarage Rd. Wins 65 F2
Vicarage St. Wbn S 49 E2
Vicarage Way. Ger C 188 C3
Vicarage Way. Iver 212 B4
Vicarage Wlk. M Keyn 32 B3
Vicarage Wlk. Maid 203 E2
Vickery Way. Ayl 115 F3
Victor Rd. Wind 210 B2
Victoria Cres. Iver 208 A3
Victoria Gdns. H Wyc 172 C2
Victoria Rd. Berk 135 E2
Victoria Rd. Ches 144 B1
Victoria Rd. Eton 204 C1
Victoria Rd. Far C 198 B3
Victoria Rd. L Buzz 80 C3
Victoria Rd. M Keyn 47 F1
Victoria Rd. Mar 183 F1
Victoria Rd. Slough 206 A3
Victoria Rd. Uxb 201 E3
Victoria St. Ayl 115 F4
Victoria St. H Wyc 172 C4
Victoria St. M Keyn 33 E3
Victoria St. Slough 205 F2
Victoria St. Wind 210 B3
Victory Rd. Berk 135 D3
Victory Rd. Stp Cl 63 E1
Victory Rd. Wen 131 D3
Vienna Gr. M Keyn 33 F3
Village Cl. Sher 13 F1
Village La. Hedg 187 E2
Village Rd. Cole 164 C2
Village Rd. Den 190 A2
Village Rd. Dorn 204 A2
Village Way. L Chal 166 B4
Villier St. Uxb 201 E2
Villiers Cl. Buck 41 F1
Villiers Rd. Slough 205 E4
Vincent Ave. She C E 45 F4
Vincent Cl. Ayl 101 D2
Vincents Way. Wal A 161 E3
Vine Cl. Stan 213 D1
Vine Cl. Ty Gr 163 D2
Vine Gr. Uxb 201 F3
Vine Rd. Sto P 198 C3
Vine St. Uxb 201 E2
Vine The. Shab 124 B2
Vinetrees. Wen 131 D2
Vinlake Ave. Ick 190 C1
Vintners Mews. M Keyn 34 C3
Violet Ave. Uxb 200 C4
Violet Ave. W Dra 208 C4
Violet Cl. Lac G 149 E3
Virginia Gdns. Bled R 159 F4
Virginia. M Keyn 47 D4
Viscount Way. M Keyn 47 E1
Vivien Cl. Cook 195 F3
Voles Cl. N Craw 24 A3
Vyne Cres. M Keyn 33 F1

Waborne Rd. Bou E 185 D2
Waddesdon Hill. Wadd 99 E2
Wade Dr. Slough 205 D3
Wadesmill La. B Bkhl 48 A2
Wadesmill La. Walt 48 A2
Wadhurst La. M K Vil 48 A4
Wagner Cl. Walt 48 B2
Wainers Croft. M Keyn 33 D2
Wainwrights. L Cre 125 E3
Waits Green. Chea 112 A1
Waivers Way. Ayl 116 A3
Wakefield Cl. M Keyn 34 C4
Wakefield Cres. Sto P 198 C3
Wakelins End. Cook 195 F4
Wakeman Rd. Bou E 185 D2
Walbrook Ave. M Keyn 35 D2
Waldeck Rd. Maid 203 D4
Waldens Cl. Bou E 185 D2
Walducks Cl. Stew 78 C4
Walford Rd. Uxb 201 E2
Walgrave Dr. M Keyn 34 A2
Walk House Cl. Cran 25 D1
Walk The. Eton 205 D1
Walk The. Wins 65 F2
Walk Wood Rise. Beac 186 B4
Walker Rd. Maid 203 D2
Walkers Rd. Lgwk 138 B4
Walkham Cl. Loud 174 A2
Walkhampton Ave. M Keyn 34 B2
Walkwood End. Beac 175 E1
Wallace Cl. Mar 183 F2
Wallace Dr. Eat B 92 C3
Wallace End. Ayl 116 A3
Wallace Mews. Eat B 92 C3
Wallace St. M Keyn 33 F4
Wallbridge Cl. Ayl 115 D4
Waller Rd. Beac 175 F1
Wallinger Dr. She B E 46 A2
Wallingford Gdns. H Wyc 173 D2
Wallingford Rd. Uxb 201 D1
Wallingford. M Keyn 34 A3
Wallington Rd. Ches 144 A1
Wallis Ct. Slough 206 A2
Wallmead Gdns. M Keyn 46 A4
Walnut Cl. N Pag 22 A2
Walnut Cl. S Hea 152 A4
Walnut Cl. S Man 116 B1
Walnut Cres. Lgwk 138 B4
Walnut Dr. M Keyn 58 C4
Walnut Dr. M Mor 41 F2
Walnut Tree Cl. Bou E 185 D1
Walnut Tree Cl. H Wyc 172 B4
Walnut Tree Ct. S Man 116 B2
Walnut Tree La. Lgwk 138 B3
Walnut Way. Bou E 185 D1
Walnut Way. H Hea 153 E2
Walpole Rd. Slough 204 B4
Walsh's Manor. M Keyn 34 B4
Walsingham Gate. H Wyc 173 D2
Walton Cl. H Wyc 162 C1
Walton Dene. Ayl 115 F4
Walton Dr. H Wyc 162 C1
Walton End. Walt 48 B3
Walton Gr. Ayl 115 F4
Walton Green. Ayl 115 F4
Walton Heath. M Keyn 57 E4
Walton La. Burn 197 F2
Walton Pl. W Tur 116 C2
Walton Rd. Ayl 115 F4
Walton Rd. B Bkhl 48 A2
Walton Rd. Walt 48 A3
Walton Rd. Walt 48 B4
Walton Rd. Wave 48 B4
Walton St. Ayl 115 F4
Walton Way. Ayl 116 A4
Wandlebury. M Keyn 35 D4
Wandsworth Pl. M Keyn 34 B2
Wannions Cl. Bot 145 D1
Wantage Cl. Wing 79 F2
Wantage Cres. Wing 79 F2
Wappenham Rd. Syr 27 D4
Wapping. L Cre 125 E3
Wapseys La. Hedg 187 F2
Ward Cl. Iver 207 F4
Ward Gdns. Slough 204 C3
Ward Pl. Ame 165 D4
Ward Rd. Brac 38 A3
Ward Rd. M Keyn 47 F2
Ward Royal. Wind 210 B3
Wardes Cl. Pres 151 E3
Wardrobes La. Lac G 149 E4
Wargrave Rd. Rem H 191 F1
Warmstone Cl. Wadd 99 D3
Warmstone La. Wadd 99 D3
Warneford Ave. Wen 131 E3
Warner Cl. Slough 204 C3
Warners Cl. G Bkhl 59 E1
Warners Hill. Cook 195 E4
Warners Rd. Nwtn L 57 E2
Warren Bank. M Keyn 47 F3
Warren Cl. Buck 52 C4
Warren Cl. Slough 206 C2
Warren Field. Iver H 200 B2
Warren Rd. Ick 201 F4
Warren Rd. Yard G 18 C3
Warren The. Char 143 F2
Warren The. Hol G 163 D3
Warren Wood Dr. H Wyc 173 E3
Warrendene Rd. Hgh V 162 A4
Warrender Rd. Ches 144 C1
Warrington Ave. Slough 205 E4
Warrington Rd. Oln 7 D4
Warrington Rd. Warr 7 D4
Warwick Ave. H Wyc 172 A3
Warwick Ave. Slough 198 B1
Warwick Cl. Ast C 117 F3
Warwick Cl. Maid 202 A2
Warwick Dr. Wing 79 F1
Warwick Pl. M Keyn 57 F4
Warwick Pl. Uxb 201 E3
Warwick Rd. Beac 175 E2
Warwick Rd. Hans 11 D2
Warwick Rd. M Keyn 57 F4
Warwick Rd. W Dra 208 C3
Wash Hill Lea. Bou E 185 F2
Wash Hill. Bou E 185 F2
Washfield. M Keyn 46 B2
Washingleys. Cran 25 E1
Washington Ct. Mar 184 A2
Washington Dr. Slough 204 B3
Washington Dr. Wind 209 F2
Wastel. M Keyn 47 D3
Watchet Ct. M Keyn 46 B2
Watchet La. Hol G 152 A2
Watchet La. L Kin 152 A2
Water Eaton Rd. M Keyn 58 B4
Water End Rd. Bled R 159 E2
Water La. Berk 135 E2
Water La. Bov 146 A1
Water La. Brac 38 A4
Water La. Ches 154 A4
Water La. Dint 128 A4
Water La. L Buzz 80 C4
Water La. Lac G 150 B2
Water La. Sher 13 F1
Water Meadow. Ayl 101 F2
Water Meadow. Ches 154 A4
Water Tower Cl. Uxb 201 F4
Waterbeach Rd. Slough 205 E4
Waterlily. Ayl 101 F2
Waterloo Ct. M Keyn 46 C1
Waterloo Rd. L Buzz 80 C3
Waterloo Rd. Uxb 201 E2
Waterlow Cl. N Pag 22 B1
Watermill Way. W Tur 116 C1
Waterperry Rd. Worm 123 E3
Waterside Ct. Ches 154 B4
Waterside Dr. Slough 207 D2
Waterside. Berk 135 E2
Waterside. Ches 154 B3
Waterside. M Keyn 47 E4
Waterside. Uxb 208 B4
Waterside. Woo G 185 F4
Waterslade Pens. Hadd 126 C3
Watery La. Beac 44 A3
Watery La. Brac 38 A4
Watery La. Frie 170 A1
Watery La. Mars 104 C1
Watery La. Woo G 185 F4
Watling St. M Keyn 33 E1
Watling St. Pott 18 B2
Watling Terr. M Keyn 47 F1
Watlington Rd. Lewk 157 D4
Wattleton Rd. Beac 175 F1
Watts Cl. Hans 11 D2
Wavell Ct. M Keyn 35 D4
Wavell Gdns. Slough 197 F1
Wavell Rd. Beac 176 A1
Wavenden Gate. Walt 48 B3
Wavendon House Dr. Wave 49 D4
Wavendon Rd. Sal 37 E1
Waveney Cl. N Pag 22 C2
Waverley Rd. Slough 205 E4
Waxwing Cl. Ayl 101 F2
Wayside Gdns. Ger C 188 B2
Wayside Mews. Maid 202 C4
Wayside. H Wyc 173 E4
Wealdstone Pl. M Keyn 35 D1
Weasel La. Nwtn L 57 E3
Weatherby. Dun 93 F4
Weathercock Cl. Asp G 49 D3
Weathercock Gdns. Hol G 163 E4
Weathercock La. Asp G 49 E2
Weathercock La. Wbn S 49 E2
Weavers End. Hans 11 D1
Weavers Hill. M Keyn 33 D2
Weavers Rd. Tri 118 C2
Webb Cl. Slough 206 B1
Webber Heath. Walt 48 B2
Webster Cl. Maid 202 A3
Webster Cl. Tha 125 F1
Webster Rd. Ayl 116 A3
Wedgewood Ave. M Keyn 22 A1
Wedgewood Dr. Hgh V 162 A3
Weedon Cl. Ger C 177 D1
Weedon Hill. Char 153 E3
Weedon La. Ame 154 A2
Weedon Rd. Ayl 101 E1
Weekes Dr. Slough 205 D2
Weill Rd. Ayl 116 A2
Weir La. Bktn 81 D2
Weir La. E Clay 74 C3
Weir La. Whit 86 C3
Welbeck Ave. Ayl 116 B3
Welbeck Rd. Maid 202 B3
Welby Cl. Maid 202 A2
Welden. Slough 206 B4
Welders La. C St G 177 D2
Welders La. Ger C 177 D2
Welders La. Se Gr 177 D2
Welford Way. Cudd 112 C2
Well Head Rd. Tott 93 E3
Well La. Wing 79 F1
Well St. Buck 52 B4
Welland Cl. Slough 212 A4
Welland Dr. N Pag 22 C2
Welland Rd. Ayl 115 E3
Wellbank. Tapl 196 C1
Wellbrook Mews. Tri 119 D2
Wellcroft Rd. Slough 205 D3
Wellcroft. Ivin 105 F3
Weller Cl. Ame 154 C1
Welles Rd. H Wyc 173 F4
Wellesbourne Gdns. H Wyc 162 B1
Wellesley Ave. Iver 207 F2
Wellesley Rd. Slough 206 A2
Welley Ave. Wray 211 F2
Welley Rd. Hort 211 F1
Welley Rd. Wray 211 F1
Wellfield Ct. M Keyn 35 E4
Wellfield Rd. La En 171 D4
Wellfield. Ty Gr 163 D2
Wellhouse Rd. Maid 195 F1
Wellhouse Way. Wal A 161 F3
Wellingborough Rd. Oln 6 C3
Wellington Ave. P Ris 139 D2

Wellington Pl. Ayl 115 F2
Wellington Pl. M Keyn 58 A4
Wellington Rd. Ayl 115 F2
Wellington Rd. H Wyc 172 C3
Wellington Rd. Maid 202 B4
Wellington Rd. Uxb 201 E2
Wellington St. Slough 206 A2
Wells Cl. Wind 210 A4
Welsh La. Chac 40 B3
Welton Rd. Ayl 116 A4
Wendover Rd. Ayl 116 B2
Wendover Rd. Bou E 185 D3
Wendover Rd. Burn 204 A4
Wendover Rd. S Man 116 B2
Wendover Rd. Wen 116 B2
Wendover St. H Wyc 172 C4
Wendover Way. Ayl 115 F3
Wendover Way. H Wyc 173 D3
Wenlack Cl. Den 190 A1
Wenning La. She B E 46 A1
Wentworth Ave. Slough 198 A1
Wentworth Cl. H Wyc 173 E4
Wentworth Cres. Maid 202 B3
Wentworth Way. M Keyn 57 E4
Wenwell Cl. Dra B 118 A2
Werner Ct. Ayl 115 F2
Werner Ct. Ayl 115 F2
Werth Dr. Asp H 49 D1
Wescott Way. Uxb 201 E2
Wesley Hill. Ches 144 A1
Wessex Rd. Bou E 185 D1
Wessex Rd. Harm 213 E2
Wessex Way. Maid 202 A2
Wessons Hill. Cook 195 E4
West Acres. Ame 165 E4
West Ave. Ty Gr 163 E1
West Cl. Medm 193 E4
West Comm. Ger C 188 B3
West Common Cl. Ger C 188 C3
West Common Rd. Uxb 201 E3
West Cres. Wind 209 F3
West Dales. M Keyn 34 B3
West Dean. Maid 202 C4
West Dr. H Wyc 173 E4
West Drayton Pk A. W Dra 208 C2
West Drayton Rd. Uxb 208 C4
West Edge. M Gib 71 F1
West End Ct. Sto P 198 C2
West End La. Sto P 198 C2
West End Rd. Ched 104 C4
West End Rd. H Wyc 172 C4
West End St. H Wyc 172 C4
West End. W Tur 116 C1
West Farm Way. Emb 13 F4
West Furlong. Pad 53 D1
West Hill. Asp G 49 E2
West Hyde La. C St P 178 A2
West La. Bled 138 A1
West La. Emb 13 F4
West Leith. Has 118 C1
West Point. Slough 204 B3
West Rd. Berk 135 D3
West Rd. Cran 24 B1
West Rd. Maid 202 C4
West Rd. W Dra 208 C2
West Rd. Wbn S 49 D3
West Ridge. Bou E 185 D2
West Side Rise. Oln 6 C2
West Sq. Iver 207 F4
West St. Adsk 53 F1
West St. Ayl 101 E1
West St. Buck 41 E1
West St. Dun 93 F4
West St. Hen-O-T 191 E1
West St. L Buzz 80 C4
West St. Maid 202 C4
West St. Mar 183 E1
West St. Oln 6 C2
West St. Stp Cl 63 E1
West View. Ches 144 B1
West Way. Beac 174 C1
West Waye. H Wyc 162 B1
West Well Cl. Ting 51 D3
West Well La. Ting 51 D3
West Wycmb Hl R. H Wyc 160 C1
West Wycombe Rd. H Wyc 161 E1
Westanley Ave. Ame 165 E4
Westborne Ct. M Keyn 34 A3
Westborough Ct. Maid 202 B3
Westborough Rd. Maid 202 B3
Westbourne St. H Wyc 172 C4
Westbrook End. Nwtn L 57 E2
Westbrook. Holy 203 F1
Westbury Cl. N Pag 22 A2
Westbury La. N Pag 22 A3
Westcliffe. M Keyn 33 E1
Westcroft. Slough 198 A1
Westdean La. Char 143 E2
Western Ave. Buck 41 E1
Western Ave. N Den 201 E4
Western Ave. Uxb 201 E4
Western Dene. Hol G 163 D3
Western Dr. Bou E 185 F3
Western Dr. Hans 11 D2
Western La. Wins 65 F2
Western Perimeter Rd. Harm 213 D2
Western Perimeter Rd. Stan 213 D2
Western Rd. G Hrwd 55 D2
Western Rd. M Keyn 33 E3
Western Rd. M Keyn 47 E1
Western Rd. Tri 118 C2
Westfield Ave. Dean 31 E3
Westfield Cotts. Medm 192 C3
Westfield Rd. Beac 175 E1
Westfield Rd. Berk 134 C3
Westfield Rd. Dun 93 F4
Westfield Rd. M Keyn 58 B4
Westfield Rd. Maid 202 A4
Westfield Wlk. H Wyc 172 B3
Westfield. H Hea 153 E2
Westfield. S Man 115 F2
Westfield. Slough 198 A1
Westfields. Buck 52 A4
Westfields. P Ris 139 E2
Westgate Cres. Slough 204 C3
Westgate Ct. H Wyc 174 A2
Westhill. M Keyn 34 B4
Westhope Rd. Mar 183 F2
Westland Cl. Stan 213 F1
Westlands Ave. Slough 204 B4
Westlands Cl. Slough 204 B4
Westlands Rd. Lac G 149 F3
Westmead. P Ris 139 D3
Westmead. Wind 210 A2
Westminster Cl. Brac 38 A4
Westminster Cl. H Wyc 173 D2
Westminster Cres. Brac 38 A4
Westminster Dr. Ayl 115 F3
Westminster Dr. M Keyn 47 D1
Westmorland Ave. Ayl 116 A3
Westmorland Rd. Maid 202 B3
Westmount Ave. Ame 165 E4
Weston Ct. Ast C 117 E3
Weston La. G Has 136 C4
Weston Rd. Ast C 117 E3
Weston Rd. Lewk 157 D4
Weston Rd. Oln 6 C2
Weston Rd. Rav 5 C1
Weston Rd. Rav 5 F1
Weston Rd. Slough 204 C4
Weston Rd. W Und 6 C2
Westover Ct. H Wyc 161 E1
Westover Rd. H Wyc 161 E1
Westpits. Emb 13 F4
Westrick Walk. Pres 151 E3
Westwood Cl. L Chal 166 B4
Westwood Cl. M Keyn 45 F4
Westwood Dr. L Chal 166 B4
Westwood Rd. Mar 183 E1
Westwood. H Wyc 172 A2
Wetherby Gdns. M Keyn 57 E3
Wethered Dr. Burn 204 A4
Wethered Rd. Mar 183 E1
Wexham Park La. Iver H 199 E1
Wexham Park La. Sto P 199 E1
Wexham Rd. Slough 206 A3
Wexham St. Sto P 199 D2
Wexham Woods. Slough 206 B4
Wey La. Ches 154 A4
Whadden Rd. She B E 45 F1
Whaddon Chase. Ayl 101 E1
Whaddon Rd. Mur 67 E4
Whaddon Rd. N Pag 22 A2
Whaddon Rd. Nash 44 A1
Whaddon Rd. Nwtn L 57 E2
Whaddon Rd. She B E 46 A2
Whaddon Way. M Keyn 46 C1
Whales La. M Gib 71 F1
Whalley Dr. M Keyn 47 D1
Wharf Cl. Wen 131 D3
Wharf La. Berk 134 B4
Wharf La. Bou E 185 D2
Wharf La. Hen-O-T 191 F1
Wharf La. Old S 32 B4
Wharf Rd. Wen 131 D3
Wharf View. Buck 41 F1
Wharfside. M Keyn 47 F1
Whatmore Cl. Stan 213 D1
Wheat Cl. S Man 115 F2
Wheatbutts Meadow. Eton 204 C1
Wheatcroft Cl. M Keyn 47 D3
Wheatfield Cl. Maid 202 A2
Wheatlands Rd. Slough 206 B2
Wheatley Cl. She B E 46 B1
Wheatley Way. C St P 177 F2
Wheeler Ave. Ty Gr 174 B4
Wheeler Cl. Ayl 116 A4
Wheeler Rd. Chin 147 E3
Wheelers La. M Keyn 34 A3
Wheelers Orchard. C St P 177 F2
Wheelwright Mews. M Keyn 34 C3
Wheelwright Rd. Lgwk 138 B4
Wheelwrights. W Tur 116 C1
Whetstone Cl. M Keyn 34 A2
Whichcote Gdns. Ches 154 B3
Whichert Cl. Beac 175 E3
Whichford. M Keyn 22 A1
Whielden Cl. Ame 165 D4
Whielden Green. Ame 165 D4
Whielden La. Ame 165 D3
Whielden La. Cole 164 C3
Whielden St. Ame 165 D4
Whinchat. Ayl 101 F2
Whincup Cl. H Wyc 172 C2
Whinneys Rd. Loud 174 B2
Whipass Hill. Beac 176 A3
Whipsnade Rd. Dun 93 F3
Whitby Cl. M Keyn 47 D1
Whitby Rd. Slough 205 E3
Whitchurch Cl. Maid 195 F2
Whitchurch Cl. Wcot 98 A4
Whitchurch La. Oving 86 C4
Whitchurch Rd. Cub 78 A1
White Alder. M Keyn 33 F3
White Cl. H Wyc 161 E1
White Cl. Slough 205 E3
White Cres. Hal 131 E4
White Hart Close. C St G 177 D4
White Hart La. Hadd 127 D3
White Hart Meadow. Beac 175 F1
White Hart Rd. Maid 202 C4
White Hart Rd. Slough 205 E2
White Hart. Lud 96 A4
White Hill Cl. Ches 144 B1
White Hill. Ash Gr 145 E4
White Hill. Beac 185 F4
White Hill. Ches 144 B1
White Hill. H Wyc 162 A1
White Hill. Rem H 192 A1
White Hill. Woo G 185 F4
White Horse Dr. M Keyn 46 B1
White Horse La. Whit 87 D3
White Horse Rd. Wind 209 E3
White House Cl. C St P 177 F2
White Lilies Island. Wind 210 A4
White Lion Cl. Ame 166 A4
White Lion Rd. Ame 166 A4
White Lion Rd. L Chal 166 A4
White Lodge Cl. Mar B 183 E3
White Paddock. Maid 202 A1
White Rock. Maid 196 A1
Whitebaker Ct. M Keyn 34 C3
Whitecross Rd. Hadd 126 C3
Whitefield La. G Mis 152 A3
Whiteford Rd. Slough 205 F4
Whitegate Cross. M Keyn 47 D3
Whitehall Ave. M K Vil 36 B1
Whitehall Cl. Uxb 201 E2
Whitehall La. Wray 212 A1
Whitehall Rd. Uxb 201 E2
Whitehall St. Ayl 101 E1
Whitehill Ct. Berk 135 E3
Whitehill. Berk 135 E3
Whitehill. Oln 6 C3
Whitehills Cl. Mar B 183 E3
Whitehorns. N Pag 22 A2
Whitehouse Cl. Woo G 174 C1
Whitehouse La. Woo G 174 C1
Whitehouse Way. Iver H 200 B1
Whitelands Ave. Chor 167 D3
Whitelands Rd. H Wyc 172 B4
Whitelands Way. H Wyc 172 B4
Whiteleaf Way. P Ris 139 E3
Whiteley Cres. M Keyn 57 F3
Whiteley. Wind 209 F4
Whitepit La. Fla H 185 E4
Whites La. Datch 211 D4
Whitethorn Ave. W Dra 208 C3
Whitethorn Pl. W Dra 208 C3
Whitewood Rd. Berk 135 D2
Whitfield Rd. Hgh V 162 A3
Whitfield Way. Chor 167 F1
Whitley Cl. Stan 213 F1
Whitley Ct. Ayl 115 F2
Whitmees Cl. Oln 6 C2
Whitsun Pasture. M Keyn 35 D4
Whittaker Rd. Slough 197 F1
Whittenham Cl. Slough 206 A3
Whittle Parkway. Slough 204 B4
Whitton Way. N Pag 22 B2
Whitworth La. M Keyn 46 A4
Whurley Way. Maid 195 F1
Whyteladyes La. Cook 195 F3
Whytingham Rd. Tri 119 E2
Wick Rd. Wigg 133 E4
Wicken Rd. Leck 30 C1
Widbrook Rd. Maid 196 A2
Widdenton View. La En 171 E3
Widecroft Rd. Iver 207 F4
Widmere Field. Pres 151 E3
Widmere La. Mar B 183 D1
Widmore Cl. Char 143 F3
Widnell La. Pidd (B) 95 E4
Wigan's La. Bled R 148 B3
Wigmore Ct. Ayl 101 D1
Wigmore Rd. Ayl 101 D1
Wildacre Rd. She B E 46 A2
Wilderness The. Berk 135 E2
Wildgreen N. Slough 207 D1
Wildgreen S. Slough 207 D1
Wilford Cl. M Keyn 35 E1
Wilford Rd. Slough 206 C1
Wilfrids Wood Cl. Bou E 185 D3
Willen La. M Keyn 34 C4
Willen Park Ave. M Keyn 35 D4
Willen Rd. M Keyn 35 F2
Willen Rd. N Pag 22 B2
Willetts La. Den 200 C4
Willey Ct. M Keyn 32 C2
William Bandy Cl. Wing 79 F2
William Burt Cl. W Tur 116 C1
William Ellis Cl. Old W 211 D1
William Hill Dr. Bier 102 B2
William Moulder Ct. Ches 144 A2
William St. Berk 135 E2
William St. Slough 205 F3
William St. Wind 210 B3
Williams Circ. Walt 48 A2
Williams Cl. Ayl 101 E1
Williams Cl. Hans 10 C2
Williams Way. Lgwk 138 B3
Williiam Smith Cl. M Keyn 35 E2
Willis Rd. Hadd 127 D3
Willoners. Slough 205 D4
Willoughby Rd. Slough 207 D2
Willoughby's Wlk. H Wyc 161 E1
Willow Ave. H Wyc 172 A2
Willow Ave. N Den 201 E3
Willow Ave. W Dra 208 C3
Willow Chase. Ty Gr 162 C2
Willow Cl. Fla H 185 E3
Willow Cl. Iver 212 B4
Willow Cres E. N Den 201 E4
Willow Cres W. N Den 201 E4
Willow Ct. H Wyc 173 F2
Willow Ct. Wal A 161 E4
Willow Dr. Buck 52 C4
Willow Dr. Maid 203 D1
Willow Gr. Old S 32 A3
Willow Herb. Ayl 101 F2
Willow La. Ame 165 F3
Willow Park. Sto P 199 D3
Willow Pl. Eton 210 B4
Willow Rd. Ayl 101 E1
Willow Rd. Brac 38 A3
Willow Rd. Chin 147 E3
Willow Rd. G Hrwd 55 D2
Willow Rd. Stan 212 C3
Willow Rd. Tha 125 F1
Willow Rise. Hadd 127 D4
Willow Way. Loud 174 A1
Willow Way. M Keyn 58 B4
Willow Way. P Ris 139 D2
Willow Way. Wing 79 F2
Willow Wlk. Ty Gr 163 D2
Willowbank. Wen 131 D4
Willowbrook. Slough 205 E1
Willowford. M Keyn 33 F3
Willowmead Sq. Mar 183 C2
Willowmead Cl. Mar 183 F2
Willowmead Gdns. Mar 183 C2
Willowmead. Sto 114 C3
Willows Rd. Bou E 185 D2
Willows The. Ame 154 A2
Willows The. Lgwk 138 C3
Wilmar Cl. Uxb 201 E3
Wilmin Gr. M Keyn 46 A4
Wilmot Rd. Burn 197 D1
Wilsley Pound. M K Vil 48 A4
Wilson Ct. She C E 45 F4
Wilton Ave. M Keyn 58 A4
Wilton Cl. Harm 213 E4
Wilton Cres. Beac 175 F2
Wilton Cres. Wind 209 E2
Wilton La. Se Gr 176 C2
Wilton Rd. Beac 175 F2
Wiltshire Ave. Slough 198 B1
Wiltshire Rd. Mar 183 F2
Wimbledon Pl. M Keyn 34 B2
Wimpole Rd. W Dra 208 B3
Winbury Ct. Maid 202 C4
Wincanton Hill. M Keyn 57 E3
Winchbottom La. Lit M 184 A3
Winchendon Rd. Chea 112 A1
Winchester Circ. M K Vil 36 A1
Winchester Cl. Stan 212 C3
Winchester Ct. Loud 174 A2
Winchester Dr. Maid 202 A2
Windemere Dr. M Keyn 58 B3
Windermere Cl. Ayl 116 A3
Windermere Cl. Chor 167 E2
Windermere Gdns. L Buzz 80 B4
Windermere Way. Slough 204 B4
Windermere Way. W Dra 208 C3
Windmill Cl. Buck 41 F1
Windmill Cl. Ivin 105 F3
Windmill Cl. Wind 210 A3
Windmill Dr. Hol G 162 C3
Windmill Hill Dr. M Keyn 57 E4
Windmill Hill. Chipf 156 C4
Windmill Hill. Cole 164 C1
Windmill Hill. P Ris 139 D1
Windmill La. Hol G 162 C4
Windmill Rd. Cook 195 F3
Windmill Rd. Fulm 199 E4
Windmill Rd. Ger C 177 E2
Windmill Rd. Hadd 126 C3
Windmill Rd. Slough 205 E3
Windmill Rd. Tha 126 C1
Windmill St. Bri 96 A1
Windmill Way. Cran 25 E2
Windmill Way. Tri 118 C2
Windmill Wood. Ame 154 A1
Windrush Ave. Slough 207 D2
Windrush Cl. Ick 201 F4
Windrush Ct. H Wyc 173 F4
Windrush Dr. H Wyc 173 F3
Windrush Way. Maid 202 C4
Windsor Ave. L Buzz 80 C4
Windsor Ave. N Pag 22 B2
Windsor Cl. Bov 146 A2
Windsor Cres. Loud 174 B1
Windsor Dr. H Wyc 162 B1
Windsor End. Beac 186 C4
Windsor Hill. Bou E 185 F3
Windsor Hill. P Ris 139 E3
Windsor La. Burn 197 E1
Windsor La. L Kin 152 B2
Windsor Rd. Ayl 116 A4
Windsor Rd. Ches 144 A2
Windsor Rd. Datch 211 D4
Windsor Rd. Ger C 188 B2
Windsor Rd. Holy 203 E1
Windsor Rd. Maid 203 E1
Windsor Rd. Oak G 203 E1
Windsor Rd. Slough 205 F2
Windsor Rd. Wray 211 F1
Windsor St. M Keyn 33 E3
Windsor St. M Keyn 58 B4
Windsor St. Uxb 201 E3
Winemar Cl. Hans 11 D2
Wing Cl. Mar 183 B1
Wing Rd. Cub 78 B1
Wing Rd. L Buzz 80 B3
Wing Rd. Stew 78 C3
Wingate Ave. H Wyc 173 F4
Wingate Circ. Walt 48 A2
Wingate Cl. H Wyc 173 F4
Wingate Walk. Ayl 116 A4
Wingrave Rd. A Abb 88 C2
Wingrave Rd. Lon M 104 B1
Wingrave Rd. Tri 119 D3
Winkers Cl. C St P 177 F1
Winkers La. C St P 177 F2
Winkfield La. Oak G 209 D1
Winkfield Rd. Oak G 209 F1
Winnock Rd. W Dra 208 B3
Winsford Hill. M Keyn 46 C2
Winslow Field. G Mis 151 F4
Winslow Gdns. H Wyc 174 A4
Winslow Rd. G Hrwd 54 C1
Winslow Rd. Gran 75 F4
Winslow Rd. L Hrwd 55 E1
Winslow Rd. Mur 67 D2
Winslow Rd. Nash 55 E4
Winslow Rd. Swan 66 C2
Winslow Rd. Win 89 D2
Winstane Cl. Ame 154 A3
Winstanley La. She B E 46 B2
Winston Gdns. Berk 134 C2
Winter Hill Rd. Cook 195 D2
Winter Hill Rd. Maid 195 D2
Winter Hill. Cook 184 B1
Winterburn. M Keyn 34 A3
Winters Way. Hol G 163 E4
Winterton Dr. Ayl 115 F2
Wintoun Path. Slough 197 F1
Winvale. Slough 205 F2
Winwood Dr. Qntn 85 D3
Winwood. Slough 206 B4
Wise La. W Dra 208 B1
Wisley Ave. M Keyn 34 B2
Wistmans. M Keyn 46 B2
Witan Gate. M Keyn 34 B1
Witchell. Wen 131 D2
Witham Way. Ayl 115 E2
Witheridge La. Ty Gr 175 D4
Withey Cl. Wind 209 F3
Withington. M Keyn 34 A3
Withy Croft. Slough 206 C4
Withycombe. M Keyn 46 C2
Witney Cl. Ick 201 F4
Wittmills Oak. Buck 41 F1
Wivelsfield. Eat B 92 C3
Woad La. M Keyn 34 C4
Woburn Ave. M Keyn 33 E3
Woburn La. Asp G 49 F2
Woburn Rd. Asp H 49 E1
Woburn Rd. Hth 60 B1
Woburn Sands Rd. B Bkhl 48 B2
Wodehouse Wlk. N Pag 22 A3
Wolf La. Wind 209 C2
Wolfcotes La. She B E 46 A2
Wolsey Gdns. M Keyn 34 A2
Wolstan Cl. Den 190 A1
Wolverton Rd. Have 20 B1
Wooburn Common La. Tapl 186 A2
Wooburn Green La. Beac 186 A4
Wooburn Mews. Bou E 185 F3
Wooburn Mnr Pk. Bou E 185 F3
Wood Cl. Wind 210 B2
Wood End Cl. Far C 187 E1
Wood End La. Moul 23 F1
Wood End. L Hrwd 55 F1
Wood End. Nash 55 E4
Wood La. Asp G 49 E2
Wood La. Iver 207 E4
Wood La. M Keyn 34 C4
Wood La. Pott 18 C2
Wood La. S Hea 152 C4
Wood La. Slough 205 D2

Wood La. W Und 6 A1
Wood Lane Cl. Iver H 200 A1
Wood Pond Cl. Se Gr 176 B2
Wood Rd. Harr 3 F4
Wood St. M Keyn 33 F4
Wood St. Wadd 99 D4
Wood St. Wbn S 49 D2
Wood Way. Beac 174 C1
Woodbank Ave. Ger C 188 B3
Woodbank Dr. C St P 177 E4
Woodchester Park. Beac 175 E3
Woodcock. Wal A 161 D4
Woodcote Green. H Wyc 161 E1
Woodcote Lawns. Ches 144 A2
Woodcote. Maid 202 B3
Woodcroft Rd. Ches 144 B2
Woodfield Rd. P Ris 139 E2
Woodfield Dr. Maid 202 A3
Woodfield Park. Ame 154 A2
Woodfield. Lac G 149 E3
Woodford Way. Slough 198 A1
Woodhall Cl. Uxb 201 E4
Woodhill Ave. Ger C 189 D3
Woodhouse Ct. M Keyn 34 B3
Woodhurst Dr. Den G 189 F3
Woodhurst Rd. Maid 196 A1
Woodland Ave. L Buzz 70 C1
Woodland Ave. Slough 205 E3
Woodland Ave. Wind 209 F2
Woodland Cl. H Wyc 172 B3
Woodland Cl. Mar 183 F2
Woodland Cl. Tri 118 C1
Woodland La. Chor 167 E3
Woodland Rd. Map Cr 178 B3
Woodland View. Ches 154 B3
Woodland View. M Keyn 33 E3
Woodland Way. Mar 183 F2
Woodland Way. Wbn S 49 D2
Woodlands Ave. Berk 135 E2
Woodlands Cl. Ger C 189 D3
Woodlands Cl. Hol G 163 E3
Woodlands Cres. Buck 41 E1
Woodlands Dr. Beac 175 E2
Woodlands Dr. Wal A 161 E4
Woodlands Glade. Beac 175 E2
Woodlands Glade. Far C 187 E1
Woodlands Hill. Beac 186 C3
Woodlands Park Ave. Maid 202 A1
Woodlands Park Rd. Maid 202 A2
Woodlands Pk R. Whi Wa 202 A2
Woodlands The. Ame 154 B2
Woodlands The. Ty Gr 162 C2
Woodlands. Ger C 188 C3
Woodlands. Hedg 187 E1
Woodlane Cl. Fla H 173 E1
Woodley Headland. M Keyn 47 E4
Woodley Hill. Ches 154 B3
Woodman Cl. Wing 79 F2
Woodmoor End. Cook 196 A4
Woodpiece Rd. U Arn 94 C4
Woodruff Ave. M Keyn 34 C2
Woodrush Cl. M Keyn 47 D2
Woods Pl. Wen 131 D2
Woodside Ave. Ame 154 B2
Woodside Ave. Beac 175 E2
Woodside Ave. Fla H 185 E4
Woodside Cl. Beac 175 E2
Woodside Cl. Ger C 177 F1
Woodside Cl. Loud 174 A1
Woodside Hill. C St P 177 F1
Woodside Rd. Ame 154 B1
Woodside Rd. Beac 175 E2
Woodside Rd. H Wyc 174 A4
Woodside Way. L Buzz 80 B3
Woodside Way. Ty Gr 174 B4
Woodside. Asp G 49 E2
Woodside. Eat B 92 C3
Woodside. Fla H 185 E3
Woodside. M Keyn 32 C3
Woodstock Ave. Slough 206 B1
Woodstock Cl. Ayl 116 A3
Woodstock Cl. Maid 195 F1
Woodstock Ct. M Keyn 34 A4
Woodstock Dr. Ick 201 F4
Woodview Dr. Lac G 150 B3
Woodville Cres. Yard G 18 C3
Woodville. Chin 147 E3
Woodway. Lac G 149 E3
Woodways. Hadd 127 D3
Woollerton Cres. Wen 131 E3
Woolmans. M Keyn 33 D2
Wooton. Ash 97 F1
Wootton Way. Maid 202 B3
Worcester Cl. Maid 202 B2
Worcester Cl. N Pag 22 A2
Worcester Rd. Uxb 208 B4
Wordsworth Ave. N Pag 22 A2
Wordsworth Dr. M Keyn 58 A4
Wordsworth Rd. H Wyc 173 D3
Wordsworth Rd. Slough 197 E1
Wordsworth Way. W Dra 208 C1
Worlds End La. Wen 130 C4
Worminghall Rd. Ick 123 F2
Worminghall Rd. Oak 109 E2
Wormsley Cres. Skch 158 B2
Worple The. Wray 211 F1
Worster Rd. Cook 195 F3
Worthies The. Ame 165 D4
Worthington Rd. Dun 93 F4
Wotton End. Lud 96 B4
Wotton Path. Ayl 115 F2
Wotton Rd. Ash 97 F1
Wren Cl. Buck 52 C4
Wren Cl. H Wyc 173 D4
Wren Ct. Slough 207 D2
Wren Dr. W Dra 208 B2
Wren Rd. Pres 151 E3
Wren Wlk. Edle 92 C2
Wrensfield. Mar 183 B1
Wright's La. Pres 151 E3
Wright. Oak G 209 E3
Wrights Cl. La En 171 D3
Wyatt Cl. H Wyc 172 C4
Wyatt Rd. Wind 209 E2
Wyatt's Rd. Chor 167 F3
Wychwood Gdns. H Wyc 172 B3
Wychwood Rise. L Kin 152 A2
Wychwood. L Kin 152 A2
Wycombe End. Beac 175 F1
Wycombe Industrial Mall. H Wyc 172 C4
Wycombe La. Woo G 185 F4
Wycombe Rd. B Bot 159 E2
Wycombe Rd. Bled R 149 D2
Wycombe Rd. Hol G 163 D3
Wycombe Rd. La En 159 F1
Wycombe Rd. Lac G 149 D2
Wycombe Rd. Mar 183 F2
Wycombe Rd. Mar B 183 F3
Wycombe Rd. P Ris 149 D2
Wycombe Rd. Pres 151 E3
Wycombe Rd. Skch 159 D2
Wycombe View. Fla H 174 A1
Wye Cl. Ayl 115 E3
Wye Cl. M Keyn 46 C1
Wye Estate. H Wyc 173 F3
Wye Rd. Woo G 185 E4
Wykeham Gate. Hadd 126 C3
Wykeham Rise. Chin 147 E3
Wykeham Way. Hadd 126 C3
Wykeridge Cl. Ches 144 A2
Wylands Rd. Slough 207 D1
Wymblington Dr. M Keyn 47 D2
Wymering Rd. Ayl 116 B3
Wymers Cl. Burn 197 D2
Wymers Wood Rd. Tapl 197 D2
Wynbury Dr. H Wyc 162 C1
Wyndale Cl. Hen-O-T 191 F1
Wyndham Ave. H Wyc 161 F1
Wyndham Cres. Burn 197 D2
Wyness Ave. L Bkhl 59 F3
Wynford Green. Ayl 115 F3
Wyngates. L Buzz 80 C3
Wyngrave Pl. Beac 175 E3
Wynn Gr. Ty Gr 163 D2
Wynnstay Gdns. Mar B 183 F3
Wynnswick Rd. Se Gr 176 B3
Wyre Cl. Hadd 127 D3
Wyvern Way. Uxb 201 D3

Yardley Ave. Pit 105 E2
Yardley Green. Ayl 101 F1
Yardley Rd. Cast 19 E1
Yardley Rd. Oln 6 C3
Yardley Rd. Pott 18 C2
Yarrow Pl. M Keyn 34 C2
Yarrowside. L Chal 166 A4
Ye Meads. Tapl 203 F3
Yeates Cl. N Pag 21 F3
Yeates Cl. Tha 125 F1
Yeomans Dr. M Keyn 22 A1
Yeovil Rd. Slough 204 C4
Yew Ave. W Dra 208 C3
Yew Tree Cl. Beac 175 F1
Yew Tree Cl. Bot 145 D1
Yew Tree Cl. Eat B 92 C3
Yew Tree Cl. Ivin 105 F2
Yew Tree Cl. Maid 202 C4
Yew Tree Cl. Nwtn L 57 E2
Yew Tree Cl. S Man 116 A1
Yew Tree Ct. Bov 146 A2
Yew Tree Dr. Hol G 162 C3
Yew Tree Rd. Slough 206 A2
Yew Wlk. Ty Gr 163 D2
Yolsum Cl. Hadd 126 C3
York Ave. Slough 205 E4
York Ave. Wind 210 A3
York Cl. Ame 165 F4
York Pl. Ayl 115 F4
York Rd. H Wyc 172 C2
York Rd. Hen-O-T 191 E1
York Rd. M Keyn 32 B3
York Rd. Maid 203 D4
York Rd. Mar 183 B1
York Rd. Uxb 201 E3
York Rd. Wind 210 A3
Yorke Cl. Ast C 117 F3
Youens Rd. H Wyc 172 B3
Young Cl. Ayl 116 A3

Zealand Ave. Harm 213 F4

Ordnance Survey

STREET ATLASES

The Ordnance Survey Street Atlases provide unique and definitive mapping of entire counties

Street Atlases available

- Berkshire
- Bristol and Avon
- Buckinghamshire
- Cardiff, Swansea and Glamorgan
- Cheshire
- Derbyshire
- Durham
- Edinburgh
- East Essex
- West Essex
- Glasgow
- Greater Manchester
- North Hampshire
- South Hampshire
- Hertfordshire
- East Kent
- West Kent
- Lancashire
- Merseyside
- Nottinghamshire
- Oxfordshire
- Staffordshire
- Surrey
- East Sussex
- West Sussex
- Tyne and Wear
- Warwickshire
- South Yorkshire
- West Yorkshire

The Street Atlases are revised and updated on a regular basis and new titles are added to the series. Each title is available in three formats and as from 1996 the atlases are being produced in colour. All the atlases contain Ordnance Survey mapping.

The series is available from all good bookshops or by mail order direct from the publisher. However, the order form on the following pages may not reflect the complete range of titles available so it is advisable to check by telephone before placing your order. Payment can be made in the following ways:

By phone *Phone your order through on our special Credit Card Hotline on 01733 371999 (Fax: 01733 370585). Speak to our customer service team during office hours (9am to 5pm) or leave a message on the answering machine, quoting your full credit card number plus expiry date and your full name and address.*

By post *Simply fill out the order form (you may photocopy it) and send it to: Reed Books Direct, 43 Stapledon Road, Orton Southgate, Peterborough PE2 6TD.*

Ordnance Survey **STREET ATLASES ORDER FORM**

NEW COLOUR EDITIONS

	HARDBACK	SPIRAL	POCKET	£ Total
	Quantity @ £10.99 each	Quantity @ £8.99 each	Quantity @ £4.99 each	£ Total
BERKSHIRE	0 540 06170 0	0 540 06172 7	0 540 06173 5	
MERSEYSIDE	0 540 06480 7	0 540 06481 5	0 540 06482 3	
	Quantity @ £12.99 each	Quantity @ £8.99 each	Quantity @ £4.99 each	£ Total
SURREY	0 540 06435 1	0 540 06436 X	0 540 06438 6	
	Quantity @ £12.99 each	Quantity @ £9.99 each	Quantity @ £4.99 each	£ Total
DURHAM	0 540 06365 7	0 540 06366 5	0 540 06367 3	
GREATER MANCHESTER	0 540 06485 8	0 540 06486 6	0 540 06487 4	
HERTFORDSHIRE	0 540 06174 3	0 540 06175 1	0 540 06176 X	
TYNE AND WEAR	0 540 06370 3	0 540 06371 1	0 540 06372 X	
SOUTH YORKSHIRE	0 540 06330 4	0 540 06331 2	0 540 06332 0	
WEST YORKSHIRE	0 540 06329 0	0 540 06327 4	0 540 06328 2	
	Quantity @ £14.99 each	Quantity @ £9.99 each	Quantity @ £4.99 each	£ Total
LANCASHIRE	0 540 06440 8	0 540 06441 6	0 540 06443 2	

BLACK AND WHITE EDITIONS

	HARDBACK	SOFTBACK	POCKET	£ Total
	Quantity @ £12.99 each	Quantity @ £9.99 each	Quantity @ £4.99 each	£ Total
BRISTOL AND AVON	0 540 06140 9	0 540 06141 7	0 540 06142 5	
CARDIFF	0 540 06186 7	0 540 06187 5	0 540 06207 3	
CHESHIRE	0 540 06143 3	0 540 06144 1	0 540 06145 X	
DERBYSHIRE	0 540 06137 9	0 540 06138 7	0 540 06139 5	
EDINBURGH	0 540 06180 8	0 540 06181 6	0 540 06182 4	
GLASGOW	0 540 06183 2	0 540 06184 0	0 540 06185 9	
STAFFORDSHIRE	0 540 06134 4	0 540 06135 2	0 540 06136 0	

See more titles overleaf

Ordnance Survey STREET ATLASES ORDER FORM

BLACK AND WHITE EDITIONS

	HARDBACK Quantity @ £12.99 each		SOFTBACK Quantity @ £8.99 each		POCKET Quantity @ £4.99 each		£ Total
EAST ESSEX	☐	0 540 05848 3	☐	0 540 05866 1	☐	0 540 05850 5	➤ ☐
WEST ESSEX	☐	0 540 05849 1	☐	0 540 05867 X	☐	0 540 05851 3	➤ ☐
NORTH HAMPSHIRE	☐	0 540 05852 1	☐	0 540 05853 X	☐	0 540 05854 8	➤ ☐
SOUTH HAMPSHIRE	☐	0 540 05855 6	☐	0 540 05856 4	☐	0 540 05857 2	➤ ☐
EAST KENT	☐	0 540 06026 7	☐	0 540 06027 5	☐	0 540 06028 3	➤ ☐
NOTTINGHAMSHIRE	☐	0 540 05858 0	☐	0 540 05859 9	☐	0 540 05860 2	➤ ☐
OXFORDSHIRE	☐	0 540 05986 2	☐	0 540 05987 0	☐	0 540 05988 9	➤ ☐
EAST SUSSEX	☐	0 540 05875 0	☐	0 540 05874 2	☐	0 540 05873 4	➤ ☐
	Quantity @ £12.99 each		Quantity @ £9.99 each		Quantity @ £4.99 each		£ Total
BUCKINGHAMSHIRE	☐	0 540 05989 7	☐	0 540 05990 0	☐	0 540 05991 9	➤ ☐
WEST KENT	☐	0 540 06029 1	☐	0 540 06031 3	☐	0 540 06030 5	➤ ☐
WEST SUSSEX	☐	0 540 05876 9	☐	0 540 05877 7	☐	0 540 05878 5	➤ ☐

BLACK AND WHITE EDITIONS

	HARDBACK Quantity @ £10.99 each		SOFTBACK Quantity @ £8.99 each	POCKET Quantity @ £4.99 each	£ Total
WARWICKSHIRE	☐	0 540 05642 1	—	—	➤ ☐

Name..

Address...

....

....Postcode

◆ Free postage and packing

◆ All available titles will normally be dispatched within 5 working days of receipt of order but please allow up to 28 days for delivery

☐ Please tick this box if you do not wish your name to be used by other carefully selected organisations that may wish to send you information about other products and services

Registered Office: Michelin House, 81 Fulham Road, London SW3 6RB.
Registered in England number: 1974080

I enclose a cheque / postal order, for a **total** of ☐
made payable to *Reed Book Services*, or please debit my

☐ Access ☐ American Express ☐ Visa

account by ☐

Account no ☐☐☐☐ ☐☐☐☐ ☐☐☐☐ ☐☐☐☐

Expiry date ☐☐ ☐☐

Signature..

Post to:
Reed Books Direct, 43 Stapledon Road, Orton Southgate, Peterborough PE2 6TD